UNIVERS

Indicators of Sustainable Development for Tourism Destinations

A Guidebook

Indicators of Sustainable Development for Tourism Destinations: A Guidebook
ISBN 92-844-0726-5

Published and printed by the World Tourism Organization, Madrid, Spain
First printing in 2004

World Tourism Organization
Calle Capitán Haya, 42
28020 Madrid, Spain
Tel.: (+34) 915 678 100
Fax: (+34) 915 713 733
Web site: www.world-tourism.org
Email: omt@world-tourism.org

Table of Contents

III

Acknowledgements

WTO would like to recognize the considerable efforts from over 60 authors from more than 20 countries who helped make this book a reality. Specific sections, boxed inserts and many of the issues sections and cases were written by experts with the specific expertise and experience on each topic. The acknowledgements for individual issues or sections written by these contributors are contained in the List of Authors (Annex A, p. 467), along with some information about each author.

In the first place, WTO would like to express its gratitude to Dr. Edward W. (Ted) Manning, the lead expert and principal author of this book. Dr. Manning has been working with WTO in the field of sustainable tourism indicators since 1992, leading an initial expert group, pilot studies, the preparation of the indicators guide published in 1996 and various workshops. He is the author of many chapters and most photos throughout this guide, and he coordinated and reviewed the contributions of other authors as well. His wide experience in sustainable tourism matters and good organization skills were fundamental in the worldwide review of indicators initiatives that lead to this publication.

The work has benefited from the guidance and input of an expert committee from the inception of the project. Several of the experts met in Madrid in the spring of 2003 to clarify the need and to seek consensus on direction and contents of the Guidebook. All helped to identify who was involved worldwide in tourism indicators, and who could be contacted for contributions.

WTO would particularly like to thank Carolyn Wild and Louise Twining Ward who both helped identify contributors to fill gaps and who provided ongoing review and critical comment on sections. Margo Manning also deserves recognition for her editing and review of all of the sections and year long service as initial content editor for this project, as well as writer of several sections.

Gabor Vereczi, Programme Officer, Sustainable Development of Tourism Department, has been the main coordinator of the indicators study at WTO. He has been involved in WTO's sustainable tourism indicators programme since the first regional workshop took place in 1999. He has been instrumental in identifying information sources and contributors for this guide, in the preparation of several sections, the overall revision and production of the publication. Henryk Handszuh, Head of WTO's Quality and Trade in Tourism Department, contributed by identifying sources, preparing and revising sections on health, leakages, safety and security.

One of the most important products of this initiative is the creation of a worldwide network of experts and practitioners; it is hoped that this will continue to act as a forum to advance work on indicators for sustainable development of tourism and to exchange information on progress and best practices.

Eugenio Yunis
Head, Sustainable Development of Tourism
World Tourism Organization

Preface

Tourism is now one of the global engines of development. Every year, more people are in motion than ever before in history. With good planning and management, tourism can be a positive force, bringing benefits to destinations around the world. If poorly planned and managed, tourism can be an engine for degradation. It is clearly in the interest of the tourism sector to maintain and sustain the basis for its prosperity, the destinations for tourism. This Guidebook, produced by the World Tourism Organization, is intended to help the managers of tourism companies and destinations, their partners and other stakeholders to make better decisions regarding tourism. It focuses on the use of indicators as a central instrument for improved planning and management, bringing managers the information they need, when it is required, and in a form which will empower better decisions.

Since the early 1990's the WTO has pioneered the development and application of sustainability indicators to tourism and to destinations. Over the past decade, studies and workshops have been held at destinations in various regions of the world, with the objective of creating an effective system to support better decision-making for tourism. This volume is built on the studies and workshops, and on the experience of some 60 experts and practitioners working on indicators in more than 20 countries. It is intended to bring information on the state of the art in development and use of indicators to those who need good information and who can influence the future of tourism and its destinations. This Guidebook is designed to bring practical assistance to tourism and destination managers, and to encourage them to use indicators as a building block for sustainable tourism in their destinations.

Readers are encouraged to use this book as a resource. It contains a range of tools and examples which can be of direct use. Most users will not need to read all sections, but, through the table of contents and index be able to find the sections which respond to their needs. Readers are recommended to begin with the section "How to Use this Guidebook" on the following page, for a quick introduction to what is available and how it may be of use.

© 2004 World Tourism Organization - ISBN 92-844-0726-5

How to Use This Guidebook

This Guidebook provides building blocks and references which can be used to develop indicators in response to the policy and management issues or challenges found in any destination. Most readers will not need to read the entire Guidebook; instead they are encouraged to use those sections which respond to their specific needs. **The TABLE OF CONTENTS and the INDEX are designed with keywords to help readers locate the specific sections of interest to them.**

The Guidebook provides:

An introduction to indicators and their use **(PART 1)** which explains **why indicators are important** and how they are used.

A participatory process for indicators development: (PART 2): a recommended 12-step procedure to develop indicators in the context of tourism planning processes. The procedure contains **a sequence of practical steps in order to identify indicators** that respond best to specific issues of destinations, and that are easy to measure and use for decision making. **The Templates in Annex C** help guide the process, including support for stakeholder consultations.

A list of the most common issues of destinations with suggested indicators: (PART 3) a comprehensive analysis of the environmental, socio-economic and managerial issues likely to be of concern to tourism destinations. For each issue and their specific components practical indicators are summarized in tables, and their applications are explained in terms of data sources, means to use or portray the indicators and possibilities of benchmarking where applicable. Concrete examples in boxes and references are provided for most issues. **This long list of issues is designed as a reference; managers are urged to select and use the sections most pertinent to their destination(s)**.

Baseline issues and baseline indicators (PART 3, 3.14): a smaller list of selected issues that can be considered as essential for most destinations, and with simple, understandable indicators recommended for each of them. Implementing this essential list of indicators can be **a good starting point for choice of indicators** and also will help destinations to make comparisons with the same indicators from other destinations.

Destination applications (PART 4): indicators and issues that are common to specific types of destinations (e.g., small islands, cultural sites, natural areas). Many destinations contain several components: **readers will wish to consult all sections that seem to fit their destination**. References are included for specific issues detailed in Part 3.

Indicators application in tourism planning and policy-making (PART 5): guidance and examples relating to the specific use of indicators for planning, management, certification, benchmarking, reporting and other purposes that aid the formation and implementation of sustainable tourism policies.

Case Studies (PART 6): 25 examples of comprehensive indicators applications at different levels (national, regional, destination, site and company levels), and through different types of tourism activities (e.g. beach tourism, community-based, or ecotourism). The cases are referenced throughout the guidebook and keywords referring to their contents are included in the index.

Conclusions and recommendations for specific stakeholder groups (PART 7): suggestions for public authorities, private companies and organizations, academic and research institutions, NGOs and international organizations on how to apply or promote the use of indicators.

References: Publications and websites are cited in the specific sections and in a comprehensive list **(Annex B)** for further information and reading.

© 2004 **World Tourism Organization** - ISBN 92-844-0726-5

Part 1

Introduction

Tourism is now a major sector of the world economy, especially as it refers to the international trade in services. The management of tourism affects the conditions of destinations and host communities, and more broadly, the futures of ecosystems, regions and nations. Informed decisions at all scales are needed so that tourism can be a positive contributor to sustainable development in keeping with its role as a significant source of both benefits and potential stresses. During the decade since the 1992 Rio conference, planners and academics in many nations and specific destinations have been working to develop indicators suitable for their management needs. These indicators have focussed both on issues of impact and sustainability for tourism, and on more traditional management indicators that respond to particular needs at many scales.

This Guidebook has been produced to help tourism managers obtain and use the best information possible in support of better decision-making regarding sustainable development for tourism. Indicators are proposed as key building blocks for sustainable tourism and as tools which respond to the issues most important to managers of tourism destinations. While the primary focus of this Guidebook is at the destination level (See Box 1.2) some attention is also given to indicators that focus on issues at a broader scale, such as at the regional or national level, particularly as they may affect destinations. Reference is also made to issues which may be site or enterprise specific, but which also tend to affect the sustainability of tourism operations and their destinations.

Box 1.1 Sustainable development of tourism:

Sustainable tourism development guidelines and management practices are applicable to **all forms of tourism in all types of destinations**, including mass tourism and the various niche tourism segments. Sustainability principles refer to the **environmental, economic and socio-cultural** aspects of tourism development, and a **suitable balance must be established** between these three dimensions to guarantee its long-term sustainability. Thus, sustainable tourism should:

1) **Make optimal use of environmental resources** that constitute a key element in tourism development, maintaining essential ecological processes and helping to conserve natural heeritage and biodiversity.

2) **Respect the socio-cultural authenticity of host communities,** conserve their built and living cultural heritage and traditional values, and contribute to inter-cultural understanding and tolerance.

3) Ensure viable, long-term economic operations, **providing socio-economic benefits to all stakeholders** that are fairly distributed, including stable employment and income-earning opportunities and social services to host communities, and contributing to poverty alleviation.

Sustainable tourism development requires the **informed participation of all relevant stakeholders, as well as strong political leadership** to ensure wide participation and consensus building. Achieving sustainable tourism is a **continuous process** and it requires **constant monitoring of impacts,** introducing the necessary preventive and/or corrective measures whenever necessary. Sustainable tourism should also maintain a **high level of tourist satisfaction** and ensure a meaningful experience to the tourists, raising their awareness about sustainability issues and promoting sustainable tourism practices amongst them.

(WTO Conceptual Definition 2004)

1.1   Indicators of Sustainable Development for Tourism

Indicators are measures of the existence or severity of current issues, signals of upcoming situations or problems, measures of risk and potential need for action, and means to identify and measure the results of our actions. Indicators are information sets which are formally selected to be used on a regular basis to measure changes that are of importance for tourism development and management. They can measure: a) changes in tourism's own structures and internal factors, b) changes in external factors which affect tourism and c) the impacts caused by tourism. Both quantitative and qualitative information can be used for sustainability indicators. An indicator is normally chosen from a range of possible data sets or information sources because it is meaningful with regard to the key issues to which tourism managers must respond. Use of that indicator can lead to actions to anticipate and prevent undesirable (or unsustainable) situations at destinations.

In the context of sustainable development for tourism, indicators are time series information which is strategic to the sustainability of a destination, its assets, and ultimately, the fortunes of the tourism sector.

In any destination, the best indicators are those which respond to the key risks and concerns regarding sustainability of tourism, and also provide information which can help clarify issues and measure responses. Indicators will normally respond to issues concerning the natural resources and environment of a destination, concerns relating to economic sustainability, issues relating to cultural assets and social values, and more broadly to organization and management issues, both within the tourism sector and the broader destination.

The criteria and procedures for the definition of a good indicator are elaborated in some detail in Part Two of this Guidebook. Relevance to the **key issues** of a destination and **practicality** of generation and use are the foremost considerations. In addition, criteria relating to scientific **credibility, clarity,** and ability **to be used as benchmarks** for comparison over time and with other destinations are used to help choose the indicators likely to have the greatest impact on decisions or actions. Indicators are considered relevant only if they effectively address the key issues associated with planning and management of a destination. They must also be feasible to collect and analyze and practical to put in place. As a consequence, the indicators development process is usually iterative: in effect a procedure of negotiation between the ideal information important to key

> **Box 1.2 What is a destination?**
>
> According to the World Tourism Organization's working group on destination management, "A local tourism destination is a physical space in which a visitor spends at least one overnight. It includes tourism products such as support services and attractions, and tourism resources within one day's return travel time. It has physical and administrative boundaries defining its management, and images and perceptions defining its market competitiveness. Local destinations incorporate various stakeholders often including a host community, and can nest and network to form larger destinations."

issues and decisions surrounding them, and the realities of what can be obtained and at what cost. The procedure is dynamic as the continuous improvement of information sources and processing, aiming at more accurate indicators, is an implicit objective. This Guidebook provides some guidance in how to manage the process to produce and use effective and meaningful indicators for the sustainable development of tourism and tourism destinations.

1.2   Why Use Indicators?

Over the past decade, a great deal of work has occurred on the clarification of the key issues in sustainability for tourism and the means by which indicators can support better decisions and actions. The development and use of indicators is increasingly viewed as a fundamental part of overall destination planning and management, and an integral element in efforts to promote sustainable development for the tourism sector at all scales. The stimulus for the tourism sector comes from the perception that many destinations have been at risk due to insufficient attention to the impacts of tourism and to the long-term sustainability of destinations. Incidences of contaminated beaches and damaged cultural and ecological assets, hostile reactions to tourists and to tourism development, and resultant problems for the tourism sector have occurred in many regions. Studies done by the WTO and many others have supported the conclusion that the planning and management of tourism in many destinations have occurred with insufficient information, particularly with regard to the impacts of tourism on destinations, the impacts of changes in the social and natural environment on tourism and the longer term maintenance of the key assets which make a destination attractive. Within this context, indicators are an early warning system for destination managers of potential risks and a signal for possible action. They serve as a key tool, providing specific measures of changes in factors most important to the sustainability of tourism in a destination.

Tourism sector decision-makers need to know the links between tourism and the natural and cultural environments, including the effects of environmental factors on tourism (possibly expressed as risks to tourism) and the impacts of tourism on the environment (which may also be expressed as risks to the product). Responsibility requires knowledge. Using existing and newly gathered data, changes in environmental, social and economic conditions can be detected. This information, in turn, enables the status of issues relevant to a destination's sustainability to be gauged on an ongoing basis. Decision making in tourism planning and management can, therefore, be improved. The objective is to reduce future risks to the tourism industry and to destinations.

Box 1.3 The World Tourism Organization (WTO) indicators initiative

Since 1992, the World Tourism Organization (WTO) has been active in the effort to develop and implement indicators which help in the sustainable development of tourism at different destinations. Begun as a means to address sustainability issues at all scales, the program has been most successful in its efforts to aid managers of tourism destinations to anticipate and prevent damage to their product - and to thereby foster sustainable tourism at a destination-specific scale. In 1995-96 a manual for indicator development was prepared based on initial pilot tests in Canada, US, Mexico, Netherlands and Argentina. Since the publication of the manual, there have been several regional workshops and case studies, including those organized by the WTO in Mexico, Argentina, Hungary, Sri Lanka, and Croatia, where participants from many nations learned about indicators application, helped to advance the methodology, focused on specific cases to ensure practical application and testing of the approach.

This Guidebook is designed to build on the experience gained in the various applications of indicators by WTO and by many other experts and jurisdictions since 1995, and to continue to support improvement in the planning and management of tourism globally, destination by destination.

Some of the benefits from good indicators include:

1.   better decision-making - lowering risks or costs;

2.   identification of emerging issues - allowing prevention;

3.   identification of impacts - allowing corrective action when needed;

4.   performance measurement of the implementation of plans and management activities – evaluating progress in the sustainable development of tourism;

5.   reduced risk of planning mistakes - identifying limits and opportunities;

6.   greater accountability - credible information for the public and other stakeholders of tourism fosters accountability for its wise use in decision-making;

7.   constant monitoring can lead to continuous improvement - building solutions into management.

Box 1.4 Information and indicators

Tourism destinations often already have some data and information available that can serve as indicators, if their relevance is understood.

Tourism professionals work regularly with some indicators; the most commonly used and understood measure economic aspects like tourism revenues and expenditures, tourism base line data and statistics like tourist arrivals, overnights spent, accommodation capacities, etc. These are reference points for business decisions and respond to ongoing management issues.

Many existing data sources can be adapted as indicators measuring sustainability. For example, the number of tourists, (a baseline figure measured in nearly all destinations) can be considered a sustainability indicator, when it is related to desired levels of tourism or to known limits of capacity. As part of a carrying capacity assessment or estimate of limits to acceptable change, tourist numbers (in particular peak use figures) can be related to the use of natural resources (e.g., average water use per tourist) and used to indicate potential levels of stress on natural or built systems. When these same tourist numbers are compared with the number of local residents, a ratio is formed that can serve as an indicator of potential social stress - one indicator of the socio-cultural sustainability of tourism. Any data can become a useful indicator – if it responds to the issues important to a destination.

Many managers operate in an environment which can be considered as data-rich but information-poor. Indicators can help to select, process, analyse and present data to better link with sustainability issues. Decision-makers are often inundated by large quantities of data, and often find it difficult to determine which data are important. Some have become generally used indicators for management, for example tourist numbers. Often the same data can be useful to support decisions which lead to more sustainable tourism development, particularly when their relevance to sustainability is understood. For example, the number of tourist arrivals is a basic indicator conventionally used to measure the success of the tourism sector. It can also be essential information to a number of sustainability issues which are related to tourist numbers and levels of stress on resources. Environmental issues, such as water supply or waste (consumption of water by tourists, amount of waste produced by tourists in peak seasons), or social issues related to host communities (ratio of tourists and host population in different periods of the year) can only be effectively understood when linked to tourist numbers.

1.2.1 Indicators at Different Levels

Indicators can support information-based decision making in all levels of tourism planning and management:

*   *National level* - to detect broad changes in tourism at the national level, compare with other nations, provide a baseline for the identification of changes at more localized levels and support broad level strategic planning; (see EEA case p. 377);

*   *Regional level* - as input into regional plans and protection processes, to serve as a basis for comparison between regions and to provide information for national level planning processes; (see Caribbean case p. 360);

*   *Specific destinations* (e.g. coastal zones, local municipalities and communities) to identify key elements of assets, state of the tourism sector, risks, and performance; (See Part 4 for examples);

- *Key tourist use sites* within destinations (e.g. protected areas, beaches, historic districts within cities, areas of special interest) where specific indicators may be key to decisions on site control, management and future development of tourist attractions (e.g., national parks, theme parks) where management level indicators can support site planning and control; (see for example the section on tourist sites in or adjacent to national parks p. 272 or the El Garraf case p. 371);

- *Tourism companies* (e.g. tour operators, hotel-, transport- and catering companies) who may access indicators to feed their strategic planning process for the destinations; (see for example the ACCOR hotels case p. 327);

- *Individual tourism establishments* (e.g. hotels, restaurants, marinas) to monitor the impact and performance of their operation. (See for example the Chiminos Island case p. 368 and the Bow Valley Convention Centre Operational Indicators p. 289).

Indicators generated at different scales are often strongly interrelated. If aggregated, many can be used to create higher-level indicators. Related to other sites or regions, they can contribute to comparative analysis or benchmarking. For example, indicators of environmental performance gathered at individual tourism establishments are normally reported to the central management of hotel and restaurant chains, transportation companies and tour operators as a part of normal business and can be important inputs to company level decision making planning processes. Sustainability indicators for a destination are often based on data collected at a more specific level from key tourist use sites, specific tourist attractions, and individual tourism establishments. Destination level indicators are essential inputs for regional level planning processes that can further accumulate information to support the development of indicators at the national level.

1.2.2 Types of Indicators

There are different types of indicators, each with different utility to decision-makers. While the most directly useful may be those that help to predict problems, several other genres exist:

- *early warning indicators* (e.g., decline in numbers of tourists who intend to return);

- indicators of *stresses on the system* (e.g., water shortages, or crime indices);

- measures of the *current state* of industry (e.g., occupancy rate, tourist satisfaction);

- measures of the *impact* of tourism development on the biophysical and socio-economic environments (e.g. indices of the level of deforestation, changes of consumption patterns and income levels in local communities);

- measures of *management effort* (e.g., cleanup cost for coastal contamination);

- measures of *management effect*, results or performance (e.g., changed pollution levels, greater number of returning tourists).

While all categories of indicators can be valuable in supporting sustainable tourism, the early warning indicators are frequently most useful to tourism managers and may provide the ability to anticipate serious negative effects on the destination, or on the overall tourist experience. Ideally, indicators can enable actions to be taken *well before* serious threats to sustainability occur. It should also be noted that the same indicator can frequently serve different purposes and its use can change over time. (E.g. an indicator of *stresses on the system* will serve later on to measure the *effects and results of management* efforts taken in response to the problems identified, becoming in effect, a performance measure for the response).

1.2.3 Measurement and Expression of Indicators

An indicator can be applied in practice only if there is a feasible mechanism to measure it. To find the adequate measures is critical in the design and use of indicators, considering that the data gathering and processing must be technically and economically feasible. A certain indicator can have different alternative and complementary methods of measurement (use of different instruments) and can be portrayed in different forms:

The different means to be used to portray indicators include the following:

Quantitative measurements: (where comparable numbers can be obtained over time)

- **Raw data** (e.g., number of tourists visiting a site/year/month, or volume of waste generated /month/week expressed in tonnes);

- **Ratios,** where one data set is related to another showing a relationship (e.g. ratio of the number of tourists to local residents in high season - showing whether tourists outnumber locals, and if so by how much);

- **Percentage,** where data is related to total, a benchmark or an earlier measure (e.g., % of waste water receiving treatment, % of local population with educational degrees of different levels, % change in tourist arrivals and expenditures over last year).

Qualitative/normative measurements:

- **Category indices** - which describe a state or level of attainment on a graded list (e.g., level of protection of natural areas according to the IUCN Index, Grades in the scales of environmental certification systems);

- **Normative indicators** - related to existence of certain elements of tourism management and operation (e.g., existence of tourism development plan, or plan with tourism components at local, regional and national levels, "Yes or No" questionnaires of evaluation in certification systems, such as existence of beach clean-up programmes, beach zoning, first aid booths, pet control etc.);

- **Nominal indicators** which are in essence labels (e.g., Blue Flag certification, which is based on an extensive independently applied checklist in beach management and safety but that appears to users as a single Nominal Yes/No indicator);

- **Opinion-based indicators** (e.g., level of tourists' satisfaction or level of satisfaction of local residents relative to tourism or specific elements). These are normally based on questionnaires and may be expressed as numbers, percentages as above - where essentially qualitative data is quantified.

Note that often, where good data is not readily obtainable at an affordable cost, an alternative indicator may be available to measure the same risk or issue indirectly, but at lower cost. (See Box 2.11 p. 45).

Field group from the WTO Indicators workshop looks at shore erosion at Beruwala, Sri Lanka. Recommended indicators from the workshop for the extent of coastal erosion were:
- metres change per annum
- % of beach area affected

1.2.4 Indicators and Planning

Indicators first became a subject for attention from the tourism sector, as a response to the global focus on sustainability stimulated by the Brundtland Commission (1986) and the Rio Earth Summit (1992). The goal of sustainable development for tourism and for the destinations of tourism has become increasingly accepted as providing the framework within which identification and evaluation of indicators is situated. Indicators should not be seen as an end in themselves; they are specific tools, part of a broader process of planning for tourism.

It has become increasingly apparent (e.g. Kukljica, Kangaroo Island, Lanzarote – see case studies in Part 6) that tourism cannot be planned or managed in isolation from the environments, economies and communities that are part of the destination. Indicators are therefore shared with other stakeholders (ministries, local authorities, private and non-governmental organizations) in destinations that may have specific mandates, for example, for environmental protection, infrastructure development or social wellbeing. As well, information and sometimes specific indicators are shared with other agencies such as the jurisdictions that are the sources of tourists for the destination, tour operators and transportation companies which bring them to the destinations or nearby destinations that may be part of a tourism experience.

Because indicators are frequently shared with other sectors or organizations, work in other domains related to indicators often provides examples or lessons useful to tourism. In the past decade, there has been considerable development of indicators to address issues such as community based regional planning, carrying capacity for natural areas, or quality of life issues in many nations, and the key elements are often the same as those which are important to tourism.

The work to develop and use indicators in other contexts sometimes explicitly addresses tourism, but more often addresses issues that are shared with tourism (e.g., costs of repair for protected areas, local crime statistics, peak use levels for transportation hubs) – and can be a ready source of information for the tourism sector.

Indicators have increasingly become a component of planning and management processes for specific ecosystems that are also destinations for tourists. Similarly, indicators have been important components of broader planning exercises, such as the TOMM initiatives for Kangaroo Island, South Australia (see case p. 391) for land use planning for a national park and island community in Haida Gwaii British Columbia (http://srmwww.gov.bc.ca/cr/qci/docs/Haida_Gwaii_QCI_Framework.pdf) or the development of carrying capacity estimates for Malta (Mangion, 2001). In each of these cases, selected indicators have been developed within the context of the goals and objectives set for the destinations – and act both as signals of what is important to the destination and also as potential performance measures for progress towards planned goals.

Tourism occurs in a spectrum of destinations ranging from those which are well established to those which may be new and even outside any planning process. Indicators can be of use both where there is a plan in place and where none exists. In each case, the process of establishing and using indicators can be a catalyst for improvement of the decision process, and create greater participation in solutions and accountability for the results. Where there is already a plan, good indicators can help strengthen it. Where no plan is in place, indicators development can be the catalyst to initiate the process, or a key component in an iterative planning process. (See Box 2.1.for links and relations between indicators and planning procedures p. 23). Ideally indicators play a part in the entire project cycle as part of a process of continuous improvement. In any case, indicators need to relate directly to the goals and targets of tourism development. (See also Part 5 of this Guidebook p. 302).

Where plans and management systems are already in place, indicators can respond to the key issues identified and ideally to the goals and objectives of the plan or strategy. Indicators can help clarify goals, providing precision (e.g. not just "better water supply" but "provision of reticulated potable water to 90% residents and hotels within the municipality by 2007"). The act of considering indicators tends to promote precision, and even cause reconsideration of the goal or target where clarity reveals inconsistencies.

Where clear goals (with specific targets associated) are in place, indicators become key both to monitor implementation towards them and as a means to claim successes where they occur. At a broader level, indicators may assist in drawing attention to whether a plan or strategy responds to the overall goal of sustainability. A focus on indicators promotes dialogue on the specific definition of what is most important to be sustained, and whether these have changed.

Where a planning process is already in place, some information has usually been collected and plans developed at least in part in response to that information. A more systematic development and application of indicators can reinforce and improve the process by stimulating better use of existing data sources, identification of new ones, improvement of data collection and analysis processes, and improvement of reporting and communication for the stakeholders involved. Clarification of key indicators can frequently stimulate re-examination of plans and clarification of performance measures. In a recent WTO application in Cyprus an indicators program was implemented to complement an ongoing planning and policy process and to act as a catalyst for greater participation by stakeholders in both defining issues and providing data.

Box 1.5 Providing clarity to policy and program goals: Canadian rural indicators

Policy goals are often defined very broadly. In 2000, Canada defined a broad set of policy goals for rural development through an extensive public consultation process. The goals defined were very broad, including such goals as "improved rural leadership" and "improved quality of life for rural residents"... Through a subsequent series of indicators development workshops with the officials who would have to respond to these, a series of indicators was developed. The process was essentially one of clarifying what was really meant by such general goals as "leadership" and "quality of life" – not an easy task. While other goals such as "improved access to education" or "health" were amenable to some measurement, the process demonstrated the need to further examine what was really meant by the goals, and stimulated a re-examination, with the stakeholders, of what were the real issues. In this case, the attempt to develop and report on progress towards the public goals led to a re-examination of the goals and an objective assessment of whether they were realistic, and attainable.

Box 1.6 What if there is no plan? What if there is one?

The sustainable development of tourism destinations requires a sound planning process, as well as continuous management of the key elements that support tourism and its destinations. (e.g., maintenance of assets, involvement of the community, involvement of tourism in the planning process for the destination) Indicators are an intrinsic component of the planning process.

Where no plan currently exists

* Where no plan exists that includes tourism, the procedure by which indicators are developed is analogous to the first step in plan development. Both involve the identification of the key assets and key values associated with the destination. Both normally involve the assessment of the actual problems, current or potential impacts or risks associated with development, as well as documentation of the major current or expected trends or events which may affect these;

* An indicators study can be the catalyst for development of a formal plan or planning process, beginning with identification of potential issues (pollution, loss of access, impacts of development in other sectors). Response will likely require some form of plan or management procedure;

- An indicators exercise can help identify key elements that must be included in plans, such as the resource base for the industry, or risks to the assets or product;

- Performance indicators can be defined relative to the specific goals and targets of the plan. Each specific development project can integrate performance indicators in order to measure the success of management actions in the implementation phase. This information will serve to decide whether corrective actions are needed and also can provide a tool for continuous monitoring;

- Indicators defined to analyse actual environmental and socio-economic conditions at the initial phase of the planning process can became performance indicators in the implementation phase. For example, indicators determining the actual state of seawater quality at beaches or actual levels of community income from tourism will serve later on to measure achievement relative to these goals.

Where there is a plan

- An indicators study can assist in evaluation of current regional or tourism plans to determine whether all of the key risks to sustainable development of tourism are covered;

- The indicator identification exercise can be applied to already defined problems, issues and objectives to improve the provision of accurate data and information where needed;

- Where no monitoring system or performance measures are included in an existing plan, the indicators development process can assist in identifying and clarifying key areas where performance measures are needed;

- Indicators discussions can often stimulate greater precision in redefining goals and targets.

Indicators as tools for public information and education

- Within and outside of the planning process, indicators are a form of education all tool - helping to highlight key concerns for public information;

- The results of indicators use may well foster demands for action - and lead to public support for more inclusive planning procedures to protect and sustain the key values in any destination.

Source: WTO Kukljica Final Report

1.2.5 Indicators as a Catalyst

If there is no strategy or plan (or even planning authority) the process to develop indicators is an effective means to focus attention on key issues, obtain information on the state of actual conditions, set goals and identify actions to produce improvements. In other words, indicators can be the trigger for a more systematic planning or management process. The procedures delineated in this Guidebook can bring potential stakeholders together to discuss what is important, to define key assets and sensitivities, and often to realize that many of the most important issues are shared. Ideally, the indicators development process can begin a dialogue which results in some form of plan and stimulate response to key issues in a destination. It has also proven very useful in creating partnerships for solutions that can benefit many different stakeholders. In many of the regional applications using the WTO methodology, (e.g., Keszthely - Hungary, Cozumel - Mexico, Peninsula Valdes - Argentina, Beruwala -Sri Lanka) the indicators workshops held by WTO were the first time a majority of the key local stakeholders had met together, and many who had arrived with the conviction that the others were adversaries left with a changed understanding of shared goals and the potential to work together for shared solutions, even if it only meant sharing information. Participation by officials at all levels of jurisdiction reinforced the realization that there were shared interests and that indicators developed by one level could often be adapted or combined to support information needs at other levels.

Box 1.7 A hierarchy of indicators

Indicators can be defined at all scales, from local to global. Important indicators for a destination may refer to a limited local phenomenon such as reduction in a key endangered species, which is the basis for the tourism in the destination, to much more global issues involving health or security issues (Sudden Acute Respiratory Syndrome -SARS is a contemporary example), which cause risk to the sustainability of a destination.

The documents cited in the following sections are pitched at a variety of levels, from global systems to very local applications (and even to the enterprise level). Indicators at a destination level can sometimes be rolled up to be used to address national and broader issues. They may also be used at a regional or national level to identify site or destination specific anomalies (e.g., the "worst" site in the nation in terms of crowding, or the "greatest progress" in improvement of beach cleanliness or service quality).

Indicators at many different scales are potentially relevant to the management of tourism in a destination. Here is one example with reference to Prince Edward Island National Park and its peripheral community in the Atlantic region of Canada... (Indicators pilot study 1995, summarized in Manning et al, 1997).

National,	% of visitors to Canada who visit PEI National Park;
Regional,	% of visitors to the Atlantic region who visit PEI National Park;
Local destination,	% visitors to the Park region who stay over night;
Site,	Maximum number of visitors to the beach area on peak day;
Establishment	% occupancy of accommodation in Park region.

Note that specific indicators when aggregated may be of use to higher order jurisdictions to measure collective results (such as average occupancy at the regional level).

1.3 Progress in Indicators Development and Use

1.3.1 Growing Indicators Initiatives Worldwide

There is now an increasing role for indicators in support of tourism management processes, including policy development, regulation and enforcement, and the development of certification and standards. Indicators research and applications have been done in all parts of the world by governments, academic institutions, and private companies and by communities themselves.

Box 1.8 Global initiatives:

There are various international initiatives that provide the rationale for indicators of sustainable development and also suggest particular measures which may be of use at many scales. These include:

* *The Agenda 21, defined at the Rio Earth Summit,* in Chapter 40 defines the need for appropriate information that supports decision-making, and suggests the elaboration of indicators of sustainable development;

  http://www.un.org/esa/sustdev/documents/agenda21/english/agenda21chapter40.htm

* *The Agenda 21 for Tourism* (WTO, WTTC, EC, 1995), presents indicators as one of the priority action areas, and a principal tool for monitoring. http://www.world-tourism.org/sustainable;

* *The UN Commission on Sustainable Development* has developed a Theme Indicator Framework, which address overall sustainability issues, with specific subsets that may be directly applicable to tourism destinations or to key assets. It also defined guidelines for developing a national indicator programmes;

  http://www.un.org/esa/sustdev/natlinfo/indicators/isd.htm

* *The Global Reporting Initiative (GRI)* attempts to set world standards on environmental reporting for public and private organizations. http://www.globalreporting.org/;

* Based on GRI, the *Tour Operators Initiative* has elaborated guidelines for sustainability reporting through performance indicators for tour operators. http://www.toinitiative.org/.

Often indicators development has occurred in response to specific issues or risks. For example, in Canada, workshops and applications have more frequently focussed on issue-specific indicators (e.g., park management, mountain ecosystems). Indicators development has occurred at the community scale on social and ecological sustainability (South Africa), and limits to acceptable growth for impacted natural destinations, (USA, Australia). There have been several innovative applications to heavily used destinations in many parts of Europe, within the context of carrying capacity, (e.g. Malta) visitor management strategies (e.g., Britain), Local Agenda 21 processes (coastal destinations of Spain), and comparative analysis of the state of destinations (e.g., France, Spain). In many cases, indicators have been a means to attract political attention to tourism management issues and to create leverage for their solution.

1.3.2 Advances in Indicators Methodologies

There has been growing interest from a number of academic institutions, (see references section) both to help advance indicator development related to sustainability issues and to use indicators as a vehicle for teaching purposes. Research projects has begun work to solicit input from a range of academics and practitioners concerning their opinions on the characteristics of successful tourism sustainability indicators, and on whether there are standards that may be attributed to these indicators within an overall framework of sustainability.

Work on destination management and the identification of approaches to sustainability have all invoked indicators and measures that may be of use more broadly. A 2002 project on indicators in Cape Breton Island Canada (p. 355) tests the utility of indicators as a tool to help differentiate between overall destination sustainability and the specific risks to ecotourism products and assets. Several international initiatives have suggested broad sets of indicators for uses relevant to tourism. (See Box 1.8 and European Environmental Agency case study p. 377) The broad range of initiatives now provides a rich reservoir of examples and applications that can be of use to those seeking to improve

management of destinations through the development and use of indicators. The results of these studies can also be used to benchmark indicators for use in other destinations. Similarly, at the corporate level, organizations such as the International Hotel Environmental Initiative have established the means for hotels to generate and exchange information on a wide range of economic, social and environmental factors related to sustainability, permitting benchmarking between hotels.
(http://www.benchmarkhotel.com).

1.3.3 Indicators Initiatives of Other Sectors

Since the beginning of the 1990's there have been many developments in sectors other than tourism pertinent to indicators development and application. These range from broad efforts to create universal indicators lists for application to global, national or community sustainability, to efforts to create specific indicators to support a range of planning and development objectives. Examples include indicators development for integrated regional development (e.g. Chile), indicators of the state of urban systems (Spain), broad national or international reporting programs on state of the environment (e.g., OECD, European Environmental Agency, UNDP, China, Canada), indicators to be applied to sustainability of specific sectors or to cultural and natural assets (UNESCO, EEC, many national applications).

There have also been many examples of interesting local applications to e.g. national parks (USA), or small islands (Small Island States section, UN Millennium Indicators (http://millenniumindicators.un.org/unsd/). In Chile, for example, a comprehensive program of development of regional indicators has been undertaken, linked to the regional planning process. The tourism industry is a participant in this process, particularly in those regions where it is an important sector of the regional economy (CONAMA, (http://www.conama.cl/portal/1255/article-26210.html).

In addition to explicit work on indicators, there has been considerable de facto development of indicators to address issues such as regional planning, carrying capacity, and community quality of life. Such indicators have frequently been the engine for direct application in the planning and management process (e.g., US Parks Service). Similarly, the use of indicators has been a key element during broader planning exercises, such as the Tourism Optimization Management Model (TOMM) initiatives for Kangaroo Island, South Australia (p. 391), and the development of carrying capacity estimates for Malta. It should be noted that there is growing work in academic institutions in many countries to advance the concept of indicators both, from the industry perspective and from those of impacted communities and ecosystems (Several interesting cases can be found in the case studies section, Part 6).

Because tourism is clearly part of broader development processes, the tourism sector can benefit significantly from the information, data and indicators developed by other sectors. The information, data and indicators produced through global and national processes, as well as other administrations (e.g. environment, economy, trade, transportation, etc.) and economic sectors provide important information for tourism indicators, given that tourism itself is an activity incorporating many different sectors. Collaboration between ministries has also been important for the production of indicators of interest to more than one constituency. For example, in Spain an initiative of the Secretary of the Environment has, in collaboration with the tourism sector, produced Environmental Indicators for Tourism... (España, Ministerio de Medio Ambiente 2001).

In the work to develop indicators, much has been done which is potentially relevant, both in theory and in application, to efforts directed at planning and implementing measures to support sustainable tourism. For example, direct parallels to the indicators work done by WTO can be seen in the development and use of indicators and performance measures for regional planning in nations including Chile, Taiwan, Australia, Canada, and many European countries. Some of this work has been aimed at aggregating data for national decisions, while other work has focussed on smaller regions similar in scale to the destination-specific work that has been the focus of WTO applications.

1.3.4 Indicators and Performance Measurement

The fields of evaluation and results-based management are also an emerging source of information on advances in indicators development and application. This is particularly important in relation to the expansion of traditional performance evaluation methods to account for broader social outcomes. Social accountability is an increasing focus for the governments of many OECD countries, where performance measurement is increasingly aimed at the identification of indicators to assist in the assessment of whether social goals, environmental objectives and standards, and more abstract goals such as equity, quality of life, and sustainability are being achieved. Certification initiatives necessarily involve the establishment of criteria. Compliance with the criteria is measured by indicators, associated with specific performance to obtain the official recognition. (See the Performance Measurement section of Part 5 (p. 302) for specific examples).

Evaluators begin with the identification of broad goals and objectives and then seek appropriate measures or indicators to allow monitoring of their achievement. The identification of key performance measures is often done via a consultative process with key stakeholders to define those indicators that best capture the desired outcomes, and which can support decisions on policies and programs. Clear definition of which indicators are needed can then result in more strategic positioning of data gathering and better targeted analysis, so that the information is most likely to make a difference.

Initiatives aimed at the measurement of success in regional development (OECD and EEC), the achievement of rural and regional development goals (England), and the measurement of comparative quality of life (UNEP) are of interest to the tourism sector. A further source of methodology and applied examples is in the growing field of rapid assessment (e.g., rapid project assessment, RUEA - rapid urban environmental assessment, rapid assessment of health risks or environmental conditions) where international development organizations are increasingly using participatory processes to identify key issues and indicators relevant to project and program goals, and using data mining (use or manipulation of existing data) to obtain information to support the process. While rapid assessment is designed to provide an initial evaluation of state, rather than performance over time, the participatory process does identify key factors of importance and ideally leads to monitoring (and the identification of key indicators) as part of the next steps of any project or program.

1.4 Expected Use and Users

While the principal target for use of this Guidebook is the destination management organization (usually at the local authority level), this Guidebook can also be of use to others in, or associated with, the tourism industry. Destination managers or authorities are the key front line decision-makers for many of the issues and challenges related to the sustainable development of their destination; yet, the causes of the issues and the partners in their solution will necessarily include others, whose main interest may focus at local, national or even international levels.

In addition to destination managers, other potential users of the Guidebook may include:

- Tourism administrations and other public authorities at the regional and national levels, who may need to aggregate data from several sites or destinations;

- Tour operators, transportation companies and other service providers;

- On-site managers of specific attractions, natural and cultural sites or protected areas, and those who manage product development;

- Facility planners and managers for resorts, accommodation and other tourism establishments;

- Researchers and students dealing with tourism-related development issues;

*   Members of interest groups, community organizations and the host community, who wish to be informed participants in the development of destinations;

*   Informed tourists, who wish to understand and help maintain the basis for their tourism.

Users are encouraged to make use of all of the sections of this Guidebook in the development of indicators most suitable to their needs.

Moorea, French Polynesia. Even paradise has risks and can benefit from good indicators.

Part 2

Indicators Development Procedures

This section contains a recommended framework for use in indicators development processes. Indicators development will occur at several scales, but the primary focus of this Guidebook is at the destination level – with destinations being defined generally in terms of the marketable destination, which may range in size from a small nation to a region, or to a specific resort or site. This section will be used by those who are interested in creating indicators for their destination. All destinations may not need to use all of the steps (particularly if they have some planning system or monitoring program in place on which they can build). This process need not be onerous, and should be adapted to the specific needs and conditions of the destination.

The indicators development process has twelve steps:

Research and Organization

Step 1.   Definition/delineation of the destination.

Step 2.   Use of participatory processes.

Step 3.   Identification of tourism assets and risks.

Step 4.   Long-term vision for a destination.

Indicators Development

Step 5.   Selection of priority issues.

Step 6.   Identification of desired indicators.

Step 7.   Inventory of data sources.

Step 8.   Selection procedures.

Implementation

Step 9.   Evaluation of feasibility/implementation.

Step 10. Data collection and analysis.

Step 11. Accountability, communication and reporting.

Step 12. Monitoring and evaluation of indicators application.

These steps are outlined below. While they may be followed in order, at any point it may be useful to return to an earlier step for additional clarification or information.

© **2004 World Tourism Organization** - ISBN 92-844-0726-5

2.1 Key Steps to Indicators Development and Use

The recommended methodology for indicators development is a phased approach that results in operational indicators for a destination. The methodology features a participatory process which, in itself, produces benefits for the destination and for the participants, and is used as a training tool. The suggested procedure for indicators development includes various steps that form part of normal tourism planning processes (e.g. the identification of tourism assets and initial assessment of risks and opportunities). As noted in Part 1, wherever there is already an established tourism development strategy and planning process, the focus on indicators can help improve the provision of accurate information, and lead to productive monitoring processes. Where a plan already exists, it can be the point of departure for indicators development, and information may already be regularly collected, and it will be available to support some indicators. In Box 2.1 the relationship between indicators development steps and traditional approaches to planning is outlined, showing the links and uses indicators may have at any stage in the planning process. Where there is no formal tourism planning process in place, this approach stresses the importance of starting with the basic steps to be as clear as possible on what it is intended to sustain; the indicators development process can help to clarify this, and can trigger policy formation and tourism planning. Even where there is a strategy or plan in place, it is useful to review all of the steps: the focus on indicators can improve data sources and processing capacities, as well as reporting mechanisms that support monitoring and management processes. (See also Box 2.5 which shows the process applied in Kukljica, Croatia, and Part 5 which addresses means to use and portray indicators).

Box 2.1 Indicators and planning procedures – links and relations

Planning process	Steps in indicators work	Role of indicators
A. Definition/delineation of the destination /development area.	**Research and organization** 1. Definition/delineation of the destination (to identify scope of information needs for indicators).	The definition of area reflects data boundaries (management or political units for access and utility).
B. Establishment of participatory planning process.	2. Use of participatory processes for indicators development.	Indicators are part of participatory planning process and catalyst to stimulate it.
C. Formulation of vision and/or mission statement. D. Initial assessment and analysis of assets, risks, impacts (situation analysis).	3. Identification of tourism assets and risks. 4. Long-term vision for a destination – clearly defined. **Indicators development** 5. Selection of priority issues and policy questions. 6. Identification of Desired Indicators. 7. Inventory of data sources. 8. Selection of indicators. **Indicators implementation** 9. Evaluation of indicators feasibility and implementation procedures. 10.Data collection and analysis.	Key step in indicators work is to identify existing vision, and clearly define key elements. Indicators are essential to clarify key issues, assets, risks and provide accurate information on them. Indicators are used to report on the results of the initial assessment to the stakeholders involved.
E. Setting up development objectives (for the short, medium and long term according to priority needs). F. Formulation and evaluation of strategies targeting development objectives. G. Formulation of action plans and specific projects based on the optimal strategy.	*Ideally indicators are built into the action phases of planning and implementation.* *Data gathering and analysis occur on an ongoing basis.* *Policy objectives can also target development of data sources and processing capacities that supports indicators application.*	Indicators help to provide clarity to development objectives – can be used to set targets and performance measures. Essential for definition of clear targets and timeframes, and communicate them to stakeholders. Indicators can be used to define or analyze fit between issues and strategies. Indicators become performance measures for projects and activities and assist in definition of specific targets.
H. Implementation of action plans and projects. I. Monitoring and evaluation of plan and project implementation.	11.Accountability, reporting and communication *Monitoring and evaluation of implementation should be conducted on an ongoing basis, with periodic reporting of results, using indicators.* 12.Monitoring of indicators application *Priority issues, information sources and processing capacities can change, so it is also necessary to verify the appropriateness of indicators periodically.*	Indicators are what is monitored and evaluated about: - management processes, direct program and project outputs; - progress in achieving defined objectives; - changes in environmental and socio-economic conditions as a result of actions. Indicators form key part of public accountability for implementation and results.

Initial Phase: Research and Organization

The initial phase involves the collection of key information on the destination, tourism conditions, stakeholders, past concerns, and previous studies that can be used to support the development and implementation of indicators. Initial contacts are made at this stage with key local experts at the destination. The objective is to obtain clarity in the identification of the current state of the destination and its tourism, determine trends and potential risks to the industry, and make clear the roles of key stakeholders before focusing on issues and indicators.

Step 1. Definition / Delineation of the Destination

Establishment of destination boundaries

Definition of the destination is a necessary first step. For a successful indicator program, it is important to be completely clear, at the beginning, on the geographic boundaries and political jurisdictions that circumscribe the area to which the program is to apply. While there is a generally accepted definition of "destination" (See *Box 1.2: What is a destination?*), in practice the delineation of boundaries can be a challenge. When indicators are to be applied to a defined destination (e.g., a national park or a resort community) the existing jurisdictional boundaries can be a point of departure. Even in these types of destinations, tourism often affects adjacent areas or communities. For example, park peripheries typically contain many of the services used by tourists visiting the park. Visitors to a resort normally will also visit nearby mountains, islands, communities or other attractions which may be outside the property or jurisdictional boundaries of the primary site of the visit. As a consequence, the

Research and Organization
1. Definition/delineation of the destination
2. Use of participatory processes.
3. Identification of tourism assets and risks.
4. Long-term vision for a destination.

Indicators Development
5. Selection of priority issues.
6. Identification of desired indicators.
7. Inventory of data sources.
8. Selection procedures.

Implementation
9. Evaluation of feasibility/implementation.
10. Data collection and analysis.
11. Accountability, communication and reporting.
12. Monitoring and evaluation of indicators application.

selection of boundaries is usually a compromise – an attempt to encompass the main assets and activities and to reflect the political, ecological or other boundaries to the maximum extent possible. Adjustments (and selection or delineation of sub-destinations, critical sites or hot spots) may occur during subsequent phases of indicators development as key data are found, based on other boundaries, or as new information is acquired regarding relationships with adjacent areas.

Even in island destinations, which may appear initially to be the easiest to demarcate, it has proven necessary to respond to the fact that many visitors use the adjacent sea for much of their vacation activities, and typically visit adjacent mainland sites or other nearby islands as part of their vacation, drawing as well upon services from the areas outside the island. (e.g., in the case of the WTO study of Cozumel, Mexico, it was found that most visitors also spent some time in Cancun or the Costa Maya. In the case of the islands of Ugljan and Pasman, Croatia, most visited the city of Zadar, which was easily accessible by ferry). In these two destinations, the political organization was such that for many planning decisions and programs the islands were combined with mainland areas, with some potentially useful data currently available only for the combined areas.

The following rules of thumb may assist in the choice of destination boundaries:

a) *Include key sites and assets.* The boundaries should wherever possible surround all of the key assets of the destination. Does the defined destination contain all the areas affected by tourism activity? (e.g., where the tourist sector workers live);

b) *Try to match existing boundaries.* Where feasible, political boundaries should be followed. Can the destination boundaries be matched to the boundaries of existing data units such as census areas, municipal boundaries, or management districts for which data is likely to exist? Where different agencies have different boundaries, the boundaries used by the principal potential user of the indicators (likely the planning authority) should be favoured;

c) *Reflect natural or ecological areas.* Wherever possible, boundaries should be selected reflecting physical or ecological boundaries. The ideal is sometimes attainable by selecting political boundaries which best emulate biophysical ones. (e.g., combining political sub-areas to best match the limits of the valley, the island, or the mountain range);

d) *Consider subdividing the destination.* In some cases it may be useful to subdivide the destination into parts for separate analysis, particularly where there are significant differences between parts of the destination such as a core area where most of the activity occurs and a peripheral area which is also clearly impacted or involved. (e.g., the study of Prince Edward Island National Park in Canada divided the "destination" into the Park itself and the peripheral resort municipality and, where necessary, defined indicators for each separately);

e) *Consider specific sub-areas for special consideration.* Within each destination there may be areas of concentrated activity or "hot spots" (e.g., the beach, a specific ecological asset), which will not be adequately addressed by indicators that refer to the overall destination. Such areas should receive special treatment as a subset of the overall destination (where measurements, for example, of density of use are calculated just for that area and will be much different than density measures for the entire destination). The WTO studies of Keszthely on Lake Balaton, Hungary and Villa Gesell, Argentina found it useful to establish a small separate set of indicators for the intensively used managed beach areas, focusing on localized impacts. The Cozumel study recommended specific indicators to be developed for the reef area and the Chankanaab ecological park.

Documentation of tourism and broader sustainable development issues at the destination

One of the initial steps is to obtain information on the current state of the destination and its tourism. This is done in order to help understand the scope of the initiative, and to recognize that much information may already exist, which can help in better understanding the destination, its tourism, and where potential issues may exist or emerge. Basic information that can be collected early in the process includes identification of who comes to the destination, when, where and for what purposes? What is the typical experience? What are the trends in tourism for the destination? Have there been any tourism planning or regulation processes put in place and are results evident? Are there existing problems which are likely to drive any planning or management process, and are there proposals currently on the table (from the tourism sector or from others) which may affect the future of the destination? This is basic background information for any indicators initiative. For example, in a case application to the tiny island of Mexcaltitan (Mexico), the fact that the destination had virtually no tourism now, but had just been "discovered" by Conde Nast and could anticipate a rapid massive growth in day tourism (mainly by bus from Puerto Vallarta and Mazatlan) became both the impetus for the project and a key factor in the identification of potential issues and indicators. It is important at this stage to also obtain information about the other development issues affecting the destination; often the plans and actions of other sectors can be very important factors in any approach to overall sustainability. How does tourism relate to the overall situation in the destination?

How is tourism managed?

Who has the mandate to deal with tourism issues and with the planning and management of the destination? It is important to identify the key client(s) for the use of indicators and to understand their needs to the extent possible. In the 1996 publication from WTO on this subject the sub-title was "What Tourism Managers Need to Know". A key initial step is to identify the current and potential managers and to obtain from them information on their current and predicted needs. Ideally, any indicators initiative (whether driven by government, academics, community, or the industry itself) will need to serve the key destination managers – and ideally have them as full partners from the outset. This is also true of the other stakeholders whose participation and agreement will be critical to the implementation and use of the information created.

Step 2. Use of Participatory Processes

The development of indicators is necessarily a participatory process. While the impetus may come from a local authority, from the community itself, the tourism operators or as a response to a specific proposal, early involvement of other government departments, the industry, its key allies, local stakeholders and community organizations, those who plan the assets and infrastructure critical to tourism, and those who will help define issues and sources of information for indicators is considered essential. The complexity of stakeholder groups, their interests and relationships, at the local level cannot be underestimated. Box 2.2 identifies some of the key participants who should be considered for any consultative process.

Research and Organization
1. Definition/delineation of the destination.
2. Use of participatory processes
3. Identification of tourism assets and risks.
4. Long-term vision for a destination.

Indicators Development
5. Selection of priority issues.
6. Identification of desired indicators.
7. Inventory of data sources.
8. Selection procedures.

Implementation
9. Evaluation of feasibility/implementation.
10. Data collection and analysis.
11. Accountability, communication and reporting.
12. Monitoring and evaluation of indicators application.

Gaining local participation

Those who know the destination most intimately tend to be those who live within or in close proximity to it. Local knowledge can be a key source of unique information on such factors as local use of resources, key traditions, and the values they hold most important regarding the destination. Local residents often will have clear ideas regarding the current situation and strong opinions on what is likely to be acceptable in the future. Their support and participation in providing information to assist in key issues identification and indicators selection is invaluable.

Key factors in obtaining constructive local participation include:

* Early contact with local groups, active individuals and those most likely to be affected by any changes;

* Provision of forums, meetings, discussion opportunities where all interested stakeholders can identify their interests and concerns;

* Provision of feedback in a clear form – showing participants that their input has been taken into consideration;

* Ongoing involvement of key players throughout the process (openness and transparency are essential).

Box 2.2 Potential stakeholders in tourism at local destinations

This is an indicative list – each destination will have its own unique groups or individuals with an interest in tourism or related aspects of the destination.

Communities

* Local community groups;
* Native and cultural groups;
* Traditional leaders;
* Private sector employees;
* Property and building owners (might live in the community or might be outsiders);
* Tenants.

Public sector

* Municipal authorities;
* Regional authorities (e.g., planning areas, conservation authorities, coastal zone, regional parks, authorities);
* National (and State, Province, County, Departments or equivalent) ministries responsible for tourism and its key assets;
* Other ministries and agencies in areas affecting tourism (e.g. transport, natural resources, environment, culture, infrastructure, planning, heath, etc);
* Agencies with an interest in the planning or maintenance of specific attractions (e.g., parks, protected areas, museums, marketplaces, cultural sites and events).

Private sector

* Tour operators and travel agents;
* Accommodation, restaurants and attractions, and their associations;
* Transportation and other service providers;
* Guides, interpreters and outfitters;
* Suppliers to the industry;
* Tourism and trade organizations;
* Business development organizations.

NGOs

* Environmental groups (in the destination and outside but with an interest);
* Conservation groups (e.g., wetlands, native species, parks, cultural heritage);
* Other interest groups (e.g., hunters, fishers, sports and adventure associations).

Tourists

* Organizations representing tourists' interests at the point(s) of origin;
* International tourism bodies.

Note: local knowledge is necessary to identify all stakeholders; anyone or any group who believe that they are involved or affected should be considered a stakeholder.

An important point to keep in mind in any participatory process is that expectations may exceed the capacity of any organization to respond, and care needs to be taken to help participants understand that it may not be possible to completely satisfy everyone all the time. For instance, after all has been considered, your favourite indicator reflecting your concern for a specific environmental or social issue may not necessarily be included in the short list. A further caution is that indicators themselves do not solve problems, only help in greater understanding and provision of accurate information, which may lead to more effective solutions.

In seasonal destinations, like Norway's Lofoten islands, it may be difficult to get all the stakeholders together for a consultation process, particularly off season, yet in season local operators may be too busy to participate.

Institutional mechanisms for participatory processes

In most tourism destinations there are many different governmental, semi-governmental and private bodies involved in the planning and management of the resources and programs affecting tourism and conditions at the destination. A challenge lies in bringing these agencies, organizations and firms together to participate in indicators development and use. In particular, local authorities, planners, and the tourism industry are key players.

In most destinations there are utilities, economic planning groups, hotel associations, transport organizations, unions or labour boards and organizations charged with the development or maintenance of key assets such as parks, beaches, or cultural sites. Any participatory process should recognize both the interest of such bodies, and also the constraints associated with their participation in public processes.

Logistics

In the past decade, much work has occurred using participatory processes in the development of tourism indicators and indicators for related environmental and social purposes. Experience has shown that there is probably an optimal level of consultation and participation, and that this is often difficult to predict in any one community or destination. Key factors are:

* *Timing:* Consultation processes that begin too early, before at least some direction or proposal is on the table, can cause participants to ask why they are there and why they are not told what is proposed; in contrast, timing that brings in participants late in the process risks the accusation that all has already been decided and that the opportunity to really influence what takes place has been missed. Optimal timing may also vary from culture to culture, or from community to community based on their varying interests and past history of interaction with authorities. A key consideration is the positioning of the indicators initiative relative to other initiatives, such as new developments, creation or review of regional, local or destination plans. Coordination with such events can be of direct benefit, showing both relevance and links to direct users.

Box 2.3 Managing participatory processes

It is often presumed that tourism stakeholders are eager to become involved in destination monitoring. In reality, convincing people to participate, attend meetings or join committees is not always easy, nor is gaining their confidence and maintaining their interest. Key areas to consider include stakeholder analysis, stakeholder planning and stakeholder management.

The aim of *stakeholder analysis* is to establish the extent to which a particular group needs or wants to become involved in the project. This will depend on the degree to which tourism affects their professional and personal lives, their interests or those of their organisation, their understanding of monitoring and their available time to participate. A much broader group of stakeholders tends to be involved at the start of the indicator development process, to identify key issues, and a smaller, more specialised group is required for the collection of data, analysis of results and decisions regarding appropriate action. It may also be useful to establish an indicator committee or working group, made up of representatives from all the key stakeholder groups, to oversee the entire indicator development process and monitoring (see Samoa case p. 413). This gives the project greater continuity, cross-sectoral expertise and adds significant value to the work.

In *stakeholder planning* it is important to recognise that not all forms of participation are of equal worth. Collecting information from various sources is not the same as seeking advice; informing people is not the same as giving them decision-making powers. Individual responses given in privacy provide different information from those collected in a group setting. The appropriate level and type of participation will depend on factors such as scope of the project, phase of the work, cultural norms, experience of stakeholders, existing institutional frameworks and consultation processes, and logistical factors such as geography and communication technology. Decisions on these areas will need to be taken by the user-group or the advisory committee early on in the planning stages.

Different tools exist for *managing stakeholders* such as participatory rural appraisal, participatory action research, adaptive management and co-management. These processes encourage activities such as participant observation, workshops, seminars, focus groups, structured and semi-structured interviews, committees, advisory panels, community surveys and questionnaires. Because indicator development involves a number of different stages, it is likely that the whole suite of tools, rather than just one will be used during the process.

Participatory processes are complex, time-consuming and inherently unpredictable. They depend on good communication, transparency and patience, and some would argue that the technical nature of monitoring is better suited to a top down management style. However, importing indicators unconditionally will never result in the same awareness and understanding of the issues or the commitment required for long-term monitoring to be successful. The bottom line is that people are much more likely to value, use and react to indicators if they can relate to and have had a part in developing them.

* *Frequency:* Meetings or events are best tied to key decision points. If meetings are too seldom, participants may feel left out of the process. Too frequent meetings may cause participants to drop out due to excessive demands on their time or lack of visible progress between meetings or events;

* *Duration:* The participation process ideally has a long time span, from the first steps in defining the project or the need for planning through the plan development, and into implementation. Some of the most successful destination planning and management processes have incorporated consultation or participation into an ongoing process – where there is a form of advisory body or even co-management;

* *Size considerations:* Large groups can be very inclusive but the larger the group the less the capacity to involve all who wish to participate or to achieve consensus or even good discussion. One method can be to have large information meetings but smaller breakout groups, working groups or task groups to split off and work on specific issues. (*See Box 2.3*);

* *Consultation techniques:* The most traditional approach that has been used for indicators development has been through organized meetings with selected stakeholders. This is the most direct approach but also can be very time consuming and a significant user of resources, and may not be sufficiently inclusive and accessible to all stakeholders. Use the approach most likely to generate acceptance and engender a sense of ownership and/or group loyalty if at all possible.

Broad consultation processes like those cited above can also be very expensive and time consuming both for officials and participants. As a result, a number of new models for consultation have been developed, including increased use of mail consultation to complement meetings and open access to the process.

The use of modern technology, such as Internet and email, gives opportunity for a broader consultation, an easier process of inputs, enhanced dissemination and visibility of contributions and results. (*See Box 2.4*) As part of the preparatory conferences for the International Year of Ecotourism 2002, WTO organized an international web-conference,

> ### Box 2.4 On-line consultation in Australia
>
> In Australia, through on-line consultation, a large number of stakeholders provided comments and position papers for the medium to long term strategy for the Tourism Industry in 2003 (Tourism White Paper). The list of organizations that participated in the consultation and their inputs are also made public in the website of the Department of Industry, Tourism and Resources, together with the advanced strategy draft incorporating the different views. www.tourism.gov.au/

conducted through emails in order to facilitate access to stakeholders that could not attend the regional meetings. At the destination level, the WTO has been experimenting with an abbreviated workshop approach (*See Box 2.5*), which can be of considerable use to destinations and as a training tool – to help achieve significant progress towards indicators in a short time.

In contrast to nationwide consultation procedures, consultation can be simpler at the destination level, as the identity of most stakeholders may be well known, and access by the stakeholders to a small number of public or face-to face meetings may be easier than for wider policy exercises. Even so, some use of mail or electronic input may make contact easier for those who are unable or unwilling to participate in public meetings or more formal procedures.

> ### Box 2.5 A participatory workshop approach for indicators development and training
>
> The WTO has adopted a participatory approach to indicators development and for the training workshops it organized between 1999 and 2001 for officials of its Member States. Access to local knowledge and the consideration by experts of the full range of values and risks to them, has become a cornerstone of the WTO approach to creating indicators of sustainable tourism. In this approach, a study is done employing a workshop approach to both assist in the consideration of indicators, and as a vehicle to expose participants to the indicators development process; encountering all of the issues, obstacles, and different opinions which make the development of indicators both interesting and at times difficult. This is a quick means to catalyze the identification of key issues and potential indicators, and to mobilize stakeholders. It also serves as a training ground for experts in indicators development.
>
> **Workshop logistics**
>
> A) *Site visits and presentations* by local officials and experts in order to familiarize participants with the study area. At the WTO workshops the participants (including both local and foreign

experts) were presented by facilitators and experts with key materials on the destination, its issues, and on the indicators development process. A field trip took the participants to the key areas of concern in the destination and showed them both the assets and potential changes envisioned. In most cases, presentations by local experts and some key stakeholders were made to workshop participants;

B) *Participation in the definition of key risks and opportunities.* After an initial introduction to the process, the attendees were divided into small working groups, each having both local and foreign representatives. Each group was first set the task of creating a long-list of issues risks of opportunities) for the destination (e.g., loss of jobs, crowding of villages, impact on sensitive sites, short season, lack of funding for infrastructure, foreign control of industry etc.);

C) *Participatory identification of priority issues.* In small groups the long list of issues was deliberated and priorities established where information was useful and needed to respond to the risks and opportunities. The prior analytical work of the workshop consultants was added, where useful, to assist in these deliberations. A form of nominal group technique was used to select the key issue areas of concern for the active development of indicators by the working groups;

D) *Indicator development.* Each group was given a set of priority issue areas as a focus for the selection of potential indicators. The updated WTO criteria for indicator selection were used (see Step 8 Selection Procedures p.40). Each small group was tasked with assessing and fleshing out a set of potential indicators responding to the key issue areas - and doing an initial ranking using the evaluation worksheets. The presence of a wide range of knowledgeable local and other specialists assisted in the identification of potential information sources to power the indicators. The results from each group were then presented to the plenary for discussion;

E) *Participation in the development of recommendations for next steps.* The workshops use open participatory sessions to develop recommendations for follow up activities and the application of sustainability indicators at the study area, as well as at other similar destinations where appropriate. (For example the Kukljica sessions also suggested use of the process for other Croatian islands besides Ugljan and Pasman). Each of the participants was guided through the actual process of identification of indicators, faced with the problems of prioritization, and able to work through the practical process of choosing which indicators are most important to implement for the improved planning and management of the destination.

The process is as important as the result, both as a procedure for identifying concerns, and as a means to develop responses. Participants discuss the logistics of indicators for a specific destination, including the problems associated with data, participation, leadership, analysis etc – helping in the understanding of the compromises needed to make an indicators program work.. While the relatively brief workshops are not intended as a substitute for the more thorough analysis of risks and areas of decision which the indicators are designed to serve, the workshops are an essential part of the indicators development process, and both a learning and decision-support tool. The broad range of participants in the case applications has provided a rich source of information and stimulated lively debate on both the issues and the indicators to be used. In several cases, it has been a catalyst for the partnerships necessary to carry the indicators process further in the destination, as well as for other building blocks towards sustainability for the destination. It has also stimulated interest in indicators use in other destinations in the host nation and the region.

(Based on WTO Workshop Report, Kukljica, Croatia 2001)

Participatory processes will vary in form and procedures from culture to culture. Use of open public participatory processes may not be appropriate in some cultures where there is a strong history of centralization of control or a tradition of decisions taken by elder groups or similar. Even so, some appropriate means to access the local and/or traditional knowledge in the identification of important issues and indicators and in other elements of the destination planning process is necessary.

The process of indicators development, from obtaining the information through to indicators development and agreement on implementation, can normally take several weeks to months, especially if it is integrated into a broader tourism planning and policy-making process. A focussed project, such as the destination workshops conducted by WTO, can concentrate much of the core work on issue identification, and identification of candidate indicators into a shorter period (typically from ten days to two weeks) involving several days of participatory workshops. The result of such short concentrated work can serve to accelerate the indicators development process, get enthusiastic local support, and provide a sound basis for subsequent work on implementation.

It can be very helpful to the process to create an ongoing indicator advisory group or working group that meets on a regular basis. This means that additional institutional memory is created, opportunities for exchange of information and learning are maintained throughout the project or program, and the group can act as a continuing impetus once the indicators have been developed.

Step 3. Identification of Tourism Assets and Risks

Where a formal planning process or strategy exists, the work already in place can be the point of departure for an issue scan regarding the destination. Where no plan or strategy exists, or where a strategy is partial or does not involve all key players, the early involvement of stakeholders is essential to help identify what is important. This step is central to the identification of the assets on which tourism is based, and the values which are associated with them by different stakeholders. The objective of this step is to have as clear an understanding as possible of what the key assets are in a destination, and which elements of them are valued by both the residents and the current or potential tourists.

Identifying the destination's assets

What are the priority tourist use areas and current/potential attractions, such as beaches, historical sites, marketplaces, waterfalls, viewpoints, areas of natural interest, landscapes, wildlife, festivals, food, cultural

Research and Organization

1. Definition/delineation of the destination.
2. Use of participatory processes.
3. **Identification of tourism assets and risks**
4. Long-term vision for a destination.

Indicators Development

5. Selection of priority issues.
6. Identification of desired indicators.
7. Inventory of data sources.
8. Selection procedures.

Implementation

9. Evaluation of feasibility/implementation.
10. Data collection and analysis.
11. Accountability, communication and reporting.
12. Monitoring and evaluation of indicators application.

experiences? This is a baseline inventory of the assets upon which tourism in the area is currently or potentially based. This can be an initial step: experience has shown that the participatory process can frequently reveal other assets or potentials for the destination. It should also cover the key assets that support the local community (e.g., forests, fish, game) whether or not these are currently seen as assets by the tourism industry. It should be noted that the definition of assets can differ among stakeholders and therefore the review should include all perspectives to the greatest extent possible.

Identification of key values

Exploration of the key values of all stakeholders is essential to determine which tourism assets are critical to the needs and expectations of both tourists and local residents. How sensitive are these to changing demands by the tourism industry and to the impacts of other changes that may alter their attractiveness to tourists or utility to the community? As well, how sensitive are the values of local residents to the changes which tourism can bring? This step can be accomplished through interviews as well as by reference to past studies or planning documents. It should be noted that the research in this phase may involve contacting a number of different agencies or non-governmental bodies, both local and in regional or national administrative centres, who may have published or unpublished material relevant to the site, plans relating to the destination or to particular assets, or new regulations, policies etc., which will address certain values. For example, a transportation agency may be planning to open a new route or restrict traffic on an existing route; a forestry department may be contemplating limits on use of the forest in peak season, etc. Such plans and actions show the values of the sector associated with use of the shared resources. They also help to identify plans that impinge upon current uses by others and upon their values.

Obtaining information on thresholds and system sensitivity

Integral to sustaining the economic, social and environmental assets of a destination is a recognition of the potential limits to use (or carrying capacity) of the destination. Past or current studies are often a good source. Hence, any information that can be obtained which documents the biophysical and social dimensions of sustainability for the destination is useful. Work done in these areas can assist in identifying the nature and extent of potential impacts of new developments or changes and can assist in identifying thresholds beyond which tourism may no longer be sustainable at that particular destination. Where there is no plan that has considered such stresses and possible responses, the indicators development process may itself be a form of initial survey which can help to identify these sensitivities. The objective of this step is to look at the potential impacts of changes or trends on the key assets and their associated values.

Fishermen's nets in Kerala, India: Traditional activities provide tourists with an experience, but values of small communities can be very sensitive to impacts of tourism.

Box 2.6 SWOT analysis

Before starting to select indicators, it is useful to assess a destination's Strengths, Weaknesses, Opportunities and Threats (SWOT). A SWOT analysis assesses tourism potential and helps managers to decide what type of indicators will be useful in monitoring trends and progress towards achieving the tourism goals of the destination. In other words, "What have we got, what do we want to do with it and how do we measure success?" A SWOT analysis should give a succinct picture of the destination's assets and shortcomings and reveal the opportunities and challenges it faces. It will help clarify issues (see detailed discussion of issues in Part 3), and the types of indicators that will be valuable. It is important information which may help to generate consensus on which issues and risks are of greatest importance and to whom.

Guidelines for a SWOT analysis

Strengths	*Destination assets:* local, complementary attractions, natural and cultural assets, infrastructure and support services;
	Community support: active participation, common objectives;
	Workforce: availability, skill levels;
	Management capacity: skill levels, funding available.
Opportunities	*Economic opportunities:* for businesses, employment;
	Product and market opportunities: unique, authentic products, product-market match, niche markets;
	Community enhancement: socio-cultural benefits;
	Conservation: tourism's contribution to natural and cultural heritage.
Weaknesses	*Lack of tourist appeal:* few significant or unique tourism attractions, poor accessibility, lack of infrastructure;
	No vision: uncertainties in direction, lack of understanding or cohesion in the destination community;
	Preparedness: lack of plans, training needs, funds, alternative priorities.
Threats (and constraints)	*Environmental impacts:* disturbance of loss of habitat, increased use of resources, waste;
	Cultural degradation: daily lives, customs and practices disrupted;
	Poor quality: tourist dissatisfaction, lack of standards;
	External threats: regulations, travel security, environmental impacts.

A SWOT analysis helps to clarify the risks and opportunities and can assist in discussion of which indicators are most likely to be of use to address the sustainability of the destination and its desired tourism.

Step 4. Long-Term Vision for a Destination

In workshops dealing with indicators development, it has become increasingly clear that knowing what the stakeholders wish to accomplish with respect to the tourism sector helps greatly in determining what is most important for a destination. This is central to determining which issues are considered most critical and therefore may require indicators. While a focus on indicators can contribute to discussions on destination futures, where a vision has already been developed, indicators ideally respond to key elements of the vision. These indicators may also be used as performance measures on the path to achieving this vision. Where there is no current agreed vision, plan or consensus on a desired future, the process of defining indicators can become the catalyst for a visioning process. The indicators development process, through its emphasis on broad participation, and definition of key issues, can lead to better definition of a long term vision, or at least to the clarification of stakeholders' shared objectives. In practice, participatory sessions which focus on future

Research and Organization

1. Definition/delineation of the destination.
2. Use of participatory processes.
3. Identification of tourism assets and risks.
4. **Long-term vision for a destination**

Indicators Development

5. Selection of priority issues.
6. Identification of desired indicators.
7. Inventory of data sources.
8. Selection procedures.

Implementation

9. Evaluation of feasibility/implementation.
10. Data collection and analysis.
11. Accountability, communication and reporting.
12. Monitoring and evaluation of indicators application.

visions for a destination can be helped by reference to key indicators. The pragmatic need to quantify and clarify, which is central to indicators definition, can be a significant aid to consensus on long and shorter term goals – forcing clarity on what is really desired (e.g., not just "more tourism", but how much, when, of what type, and at what cost to other values important to the stakeholders?) This is very similar to and complementary to the setting of objectives, using the indicators to define target values. (See case of La Ronge *Box 2.8*).

Indicator Development Phase

This phase focuses on the definition of which indicators are important and can respond to the issues of greatest importance to the destination.

Step 5. Selection of Priority Issues and Policy Questions

The selection of indicators is directly related to the issues that are important in a destination. Therefore, a key step is the identification of the most important issues from the perspective of all stakeholders. The work done in Phase 1 provides the background needed for an informed selection of issues currently or potentially of importance to a destination and to its tourism. Using a participatory group approach if possible (or alternatively through a series of interviews with key players) priority issues and policy questions can be identified. The objective is to obtain consensus on a list of issues which are likely to be of greatest importance. This list of important issues becomes the checklist against which candidate indicators can be developed. (What is needed to respond to these issues?) If stakeholders are able to agree on the priority issues, they are likely to be more willing to use the indicators that address them and to assist in supporting the indicators implementation. The issues addressed later in this Guidebook (See Part 3) can be used as a reference point for the types of issues typically encountered; over 50 issues ranging from health to seasonality, water use, climate change, tourist satisfaction and competitiveness are examined and indicators suggested for each. While this menu can suggest issues each destination has its own unique mix of issues related to its own environmental, economic, social and administrative conditions. Reference to issues and indicators from other destinations with similar characteristics (For example the Coastal destinations, Mountains, and Small and Traditional Communities sections in Part 4) can also be of assistance as a catalyst for discussion.

Achieving consensus on key issues

A valuable tool to help destinations obtain agreement on which issues are important can be a participatory workshop, with a broad range of participants. In WTO workshops on indicator development, agreement is initially sought concerning the principal social, economic, cultural and ecological risks to the destination and to the tourism which it supports. It has been found in many cases that an initial focus on risks (and opportunities) is a good icebreaker, and helps get most issues and concerns on the

Research and Organization

1. Definition/delineation of the destination.
2. Use of participatory processes.
3. Identification of tourism assets and risks.
4. Long-term vision for a destination.

Indicators Development

5. Selection of priority issues
6. Identification of desired indicators.
7. Inventory of data sources.
8. Selection procedures.

Implementation

9. Evaluation of feasibility/implementation.
10. Data collection and analysis.
11. Accountability, communication and reporting.
12. Monitoring and evaluation of indicators application.

table quickly. Where there is already an agreed vision (for example, where there has been a planning exercise that has defined desired future scenarios and a set of objectives for the destination) risks may be defined in terms of achievement of that vision. In practice, discussion focuses on the values and expectations that both tourists and local residents hold concerning the destination, and may reaffirm the vision, or add dimensions that may have been missed. Where there is no such plan or vision in place, the discussion becomes a de facto visioning exercise, identifying risks or opportunities related to the futures which all stakeholders (or some stakeholders) desire.

Issues may be both within the management purview of the tourism industry (e.g., control of waste from the industry), or beyond its ability to affect (e.g., climate change). The desired result of this step is an agreed list of key issues for which indicators would be useful for tourism managers to respond effectively to the most important risks. In practice, where there is no agreement on whether an issue should be on the list, it is recommended to keep it there for the next step, as discussion on how it can be measured often aids in clarification and may create understanding of why it should be considered a key issue, or not.

Box 2.7 Prioritization of issues

Nearly every attempt to create lists of indicators begins with a very long list. Often dozens of potential indicators will be suggested for each issue, and the process typically at some point may reach a list including hundreds of potentially interesting indicators. The challenge to organizers is to shorten the list. In the Samoa case, 270 possible indicators were identified in initial brainstorming, 57 made the cut for further investigation, and only 20 were eventually selected for initial monitoring. In the Beruwala workshops (WTO 2000), over 200 were suggested to respond to the key issues, and more than 50 were identified for further work, aimed at selection of about a dozen for initial monitoring. Similar experiences are reported from many other case applications. Most jurisdictions, despite creating long initial lists, end up with from 10 to 25 for practical implementation. (See also *Box 2.10 How Many Indicators?*)

One challenge in identifying key issues is to maintain a focus on the tourism sector and its interests. Consultations regarding indicators development show that sometimes issues or specific indicators of interest to a single stakeholder may be raised, and may be of great importance to the proponent but outside the realm of influence of the tourism sector or to the destination. (e.g., opposing tax policies, keeping a school open in the destination, preventing urban sprawl, opposing genetically altered species etc.) While such issues may be raised, and could in some cases result in cooperation to address them, few will make the priority list for tourism indicators. The focus for indicators exercises is on what is important overall to the tourism sector and what it is likely to be able to manage or influence; and this is important to which issues (and indicators) are chosen for implementation. At the same time, a too narrow interpretation will also be insufficient because the future of the tourism industry is so closely linked to what else is happening in and to the destination.

Box 2.8 Clarifying issues through indicators

The definition of indicators demands precision. This precision can often help clarify issues, or even show that they are not real. In a workshop in northern Saskatchewan (Canada), hunting guides and ecotourism operators appeared to be in conflict over access to lakes in the region, each fearing that new rules would remove rights of access for them. The issue was access to desired lakes. Discussion on what they really wanted showed that neither wanted exclusive rights, that each would be satisfied with shared access as long as they were not on the same lakes at the same time, as those who want to view live animals and those who wish to shoot them do not share the same images. The discussion resulted in an accommodation where each has some access and both are accommodated. The discussion on issues and specific indicators (not just access, but how much, when, where, under what conditions?) helped not only to clarify but also to identify workable community level solutions.

(Tourism Conference: La Ronge Saskatchewan. 1999)

Step 6. Identification of Desired Indicators

This procedure normally involves the generation of a wish list of possible or candidate indicators developed to address each of the main issues and policy questions. Based on the risks and issues identified, a consultative procedure, or a designated group of experts can be used to define a list of possible indicators that might be of use in understanding the issues/risks, and in helping to manage or influence them. What are the sets of information that will allow managers at the destination and at the site specific level to understand the changes that may affect the key assets and the industry as a whole? Some of the suggested indicators may not be practical, but at this stage all potential indicators are noted. In practice, this list can initially be quite long, but provides a menu from which the best indicators can be selected. Subsequent steps are designed to help the indicators developers and the stakeholders sort or prioritize from this list through discussion.

Research and Organization

1. Definition/delineation of the destination.
2. Use of participatory processes.
3. Identification of tourism assets and risks.
4. Long-term vision for a destination.

Indicators Development

5. Selection of priority issues.
6. Identification of desired indicators
7. Inventory of data sources.
8. Selection procedures.

Implementation

9. Evaluation of feasibility/implementation.
10. Data collection and analysis.
11. Accountability, communication and reporting.
12. Monitoring and evaluation of indicators application.

Some of the most potentially useful indicators may be found not to be feasible due to technical, financial, staff or other constraints that impede the gathering or processing of data. Such indicators can be set aside for future development, as the indicators process is not fixed in time and constant improvement is always desirable. This step is one for which it is most important to use some form of consultative procedure.

In the workshops run by WTO, (see Box 2.5 on the WTO workshop approach) a small group process has been used, ideally with from 8 to 10 participants in each working group, led by a facilitator. It has been found most productive to have a mix of expertise in each discussion group, ranging from local officials and politicians, industry participants, academics, consultants with studies in the region, national-level officials, and experts from other countries.

In applied workshops, at least half a day has been needed for this step, with small groups reporting back to a larger plenary where the results are shared. Where there is an opportunity for a number of meetings, an alternative approach can be to have small working groups focusing on different issues, bringing their suggestions for indicators back to a larger more open group for deliberation.

There can be a range of processes employed in indicators identification. In some cases, a technical group is needed to deal with highly technical issues and to recommend appropriate measures which may support key indicators. In the case of Calvia, Spain for example (Calvia Local Agenda 21 see www.calvia.com) the issues and objectives were developed through wide consultation with the local population, but for the indicators definition and evaluation steps a technical committee of experts was designated to come up with the specifications for each indicator. Processes that involve specialized working groups or technical subcommittees who will take issues away from the table and advance them can be very rewarding, and avoid burdening the non-technical stakeholders with excessive detail. The results of such work should, however, be brought back to the broader consultative process for their review and response.

Step 7. Inventory of Data Sources

Information is necessary to produce and maintain indicators. Indicator selection requires information on current and potential data sources. Two distinct but related basic approaches are in widespread use:

a) *A data-driven approach* which asks the question - what can we do with the data we have, or for what issues do we have data? (E.g. the France Aggregated Reporting case p. 382 can be characterized as largely data driven, building on a strong existing data presence and working to enlist destinations to follow a data template);

b) *An issue (and /or policy-driven) approach,* which asks the question - what issue or policy questions are most important, and can we obtain the data to address them? (The Kangaroo Island case, p. 391, Kukljica case p. 412 and Samoa case, p. 413 can be characterized as policy-driven).

Research and Organization

1. Definition/delineation of the destination.
2. Use of participatory processes.
3. Identification of tourism assets and risks.
4. Long-term vision for a destination.

Indicators Development

5. Selection of priority issues.
6. Identification of desired indicators.
7. Inventory of data sources
8. Selection procedures.

Implementation

9. Evaluation of feasibility/implementation.
10. Data collection and analysis.
11. Accountability, communication and reporting.
12. Monitoring and evaluation of indicators application.

In practice, the process of indicator development addresses both questions, and is at best a pragmatic process – form of negotiation between what information is needed and what can be created or obtained now, and how can information sources be improved in the future. The table in Box 2.9 provides a comparison of these two approaches. In this Guidebook, examples of both types of procedures are shown.

Box 2.9 Comparison of data-driven and issue/policy-driven indicators approaches

	Data driven approach	**Policy or issue driven approach**
Departure point	Begin with data inventory.	Begin with needs analysis, identification of key goals and issues.
Key question	What can we do with the information we have?	What information do we need to respond to the issues?
Indicators selection	Based first on availability, then on application to needs and policy questions.	Based first on needs, then on what can be done to satisfy the needs.
Strengths	Uses existing information, can yield quick responses based on data in stock.	Focuses on what policy issues are most important. Can identify needs for new data or means to extract what is needed.
Weaknesses	May miss key issues because data is not available.	May identify needs which cannot realistically be served at the present.
How to make it work	Make sure that perspective is not limited by what is now available. Identify new needs for future data.	Make sure that a prioritization process is done – with practical considerations regarding data. Identify long term needs for data, set objectives and plans for developing data sources and capacity for processing them.

Practical indicator development will involve trade-offs regarding both needs and capabilities; ideally an indicators exercise will contain elements of both approaches. The indicators development procedure suggested in this guidebook applies a combined approach, considering both policy priorities (issues) and feasibility of indicators (practical considerations of data collection and analysis). It therefore recommends:

* Departure point: Identification of priority policy issues;
* When defining indicators, analyses data sources in order to:
    - Build strongly on available data sources;
    - Identify data gaps;
    - Using alternative measurement methodologies for immediate needs, when data gathering exceeds current capacities. (e.g. approximate measures, see Box 2.11);
    - Set objectives for improving or developing data sources and processing capacities.
* Monitor the application of indicators and develop new indicators with improved measurement techniques if needed.

The identification of potential data sources, at least initially, can occur early in the procedure and act as a building block for the discussions. This is particularly useful where there is already an extensive data source – such as mature destinations that already have an extensive tourism data base and operating planning process. The discussion can then be framed in terms of how the existing data can best be used to address key issues.

For destinations where there may not be an existing data and monitoring program it may be most effective to defer identification of data sources until the identification of key issues is in place and a wish list of potential indicators has been created. Then the search for data can be focused on that which is needed to support the desired indicators. This stage is designed to create an initial list of potential sources of data which may be suitable to support indicators. This information is then brought to the table to help in the next step – the reduction of the long list to a shorter set of indicators for the destination. A further elaboration of the data occurs for those priority indicators selected in the next step.

Step 8. Selection Procedures

Which indicators are the ones that the destination will actually try to implement? The following selection procedure is suggested:

Indicators rating criteria

Five criteria are used in the evaluation of each indicator. It is recommended that this initial screening be done wherever possible in a participatory forum (or at least in small groups) to both obtain a range of knowledge to be applied to the selection, and to maintain transparency. This initial review can assist in reducing the wish list to a manageable scale, using the collective knowledge of participants. The subsequent process focuses on further refinement and elaboration of the indicators that initially appear to meet these criteria.

The criteria to be used are:

Research and Organization
1. Definition/delineation of the destination.
2. Use of participatory processes.
3. Identification of tourism assets and risks.
4. Long-term vision for a destination.

Indicators Development
5. Selection of priority issues.
6. Identification of desired indicators.
7. Inventory of data sources.
8. Selection procedures

Implementation
9. Evaluation of feasibility/implementation.
10. Data collection and analysis.
11. Accountability, communication and reporting.
12. Monitoring and evaluation of indicators application.

1. *Relevance* of the indicator to the selected issue. Does the indicator respond to the specific issue and provide information that will aid in its management? The ideal indicator will provide useful information when needed, which will make a difference to a decision affecting the sustainability of tourism and of the destination. It should also be noted that there can be many issues directly related to tourism that are not managed by the tourism sector directly: (e.g. issues of the management of energy, water, waste, communication and other infrastructure, which are responsibilities of other government departments and private companies). These may be very relevant to the tourism sector and require cooperation between the different sectors for resolution. Indicators may be needed to help guide joint response;

2. *Feasibility* of obtaining and analysing the needed information. How can the information be obtained? Is there an organization identified as data source? Is it already available or will it require special collection or extraction? To what extent is the data processed, how systematically and in what form is the data collected (e.g. is there an electronic database)? What are the staff and cost implications of data collecting and processing. What level of effort is likely to be needed to create

and maintain the indicator? This criterion may be used in concert with relevance to address the question – is it worth the cost to obtain the benefit? At this stage, the assessment is in the form of a pre-scan (although as noted above, compilation of some knowledge of key sources and providers prior to this assessment is recommended as one of the initial steps in preparation). For more details see Evaluation of feasibility/implementation procedures under Phase 3, where the feasibility of practical implementation of those indicators chosen for potential implementation is done in detail;

3. *Credibility* of the information and reliability for users of the data. Is the information from a reputable and scientifically sound source? Is it considered objective? Will it be believed by users? Data, for example, on seawater cleanliness will have greater credibility if it is collected and analyzed by an independent institute than if it is collected and presented by the beach hotel association;

4. *Clarity* and understandability to users. If users receive the information, will they be able to understand it/act on it? Some good technical information may be very difficult to understand (e.g., parts per million of a toxic substance) unless the user has specialized knowledge. A more understandable indicator addressing this same issue may be percentage of days when the toxicity exceeds the legal limit. Note that it is frequently useful to portray information differently for different users. The same information may be needed in a technical form for a manager of a response program (when to close the beach) but may be better portrayed publicly in a more simple form (e.g., pollution exceeds tolerable standards);

5. *Comparability* over time and across jurisdictions or regions. Can the indicator be used reliably to show changes over time, relative to standards or benchmarks at the same destination, or relative to other destinations? This Guidebook provides examples of indicators in use in other destinations and addressing specific issues that may assist in applying this criterion. In some cases the data that supports the indicator has been never produced before, and the information generation might start with the newly defined indicator. In this case the continuity of the data generation should be ensured (e.g., if tourists' satisfaction survey is gathered for the first time, it is important to allocate resources for periodic surveys in the future that would generate trends over time). In many cases, because all destinations are unique, the best benchmarks are changes over time in the same locality.

A template is provided for use at this stage in the indicators evaluation. See the Indicators Selection Worksheet (Annex D); this will be useful in the initial evaluation process.

Box 2.10 How many indicators?

There is clearly no ideal number of indicators. While any attempt to cover all aspects of sustainable tourism with only a few indicators would be unrealistic, a list of more than 100 indicators would both be impractical and mean that individual indicators could be buried. The challenge is to respond to all significant issues facing the destination with the minimum number of indicators possible. If only economic indicators are chosen, social or environmental issues may be missed. If indicators are predominantly environmental, social or economic considerations may receive scant attention.

Too many indicators can overwhelm users with too much information and can also overextend resources to support them. In initial working lists, the potential numbers of indicators which have been put forward by stakeholders can be in the hundreds (e.g., See case studies of Samoa, p. 413 and the Balearics p. 345). Most practitioners agree that it is essential to prioritize issues and the indicators that correspond to them to help create a shorter list. A central challenge is to get to an agreed shorter list without important gaps.

The number of indicators will depend on the size of the destination, the number of critical issues, the interests of the user group, the information and the resources available to track and report on the indicators. In the UK, the Department of Culture, Media Sport were commissioned to produce the smallest set of indicators possible to measure sustainable tourism, and ended up with 21. The British Resorts Association suggests 12 to be about the right number of indicators for measuring tourism's impacts and good management practice amongst local authorities. In the case of Samoa, 20 indicators were developed for destination monitoring from an initial list of 270, in Kangaroo Island, South Australia 17 indicators were selected to monitor and manage tourism on the island. In short, most practitioners agree 12-24 indicators are optimal, and a central challenge in the indicators development process is to end up with consensus on a short list without important gaps. Following this approach, in this book ➤ **Baseline issues** and the responding ➤ **Baseline indicators** (p. 244) were selected from the complete list of over 50 issues and some several hundred possible indicators which are a menu of potential measures.

The baseline list of issues and indicators provided in Part 3 of this book is one point of departure. It suggests a range of indicators that cover social, economic and environmental issues likely to be found in most destinations. The addition of a few others central to the characteristics of a particular destination is also important. For example, in Peninsula Valdes, Argentina, it was critical to measure the numbers of whales in the bay – the main tourism asset, along with the water supply and usage – a critical resource issue facing tourism in this semi-desert environment.

It should also be noted that different user groups will have different needs with regards to the number of indicators they require. Those who manage a destination, or who are responsible for its planning for example, may need a more extensive or detailed set than potential visitors making holiday plans. Individual stakeholders may use their own specific indicators for their own purposes (e.g., management of a particular property or resource). The more detailed indicators which they use may not be adopted for a destination level tourism indicators list, but are nonetheless useful. During discussions of 'how many indicators' it is therefore important that decision-makers do not sacrifice key issues for the sake of the target number of indicators.

The answer to how many indicators are required is therefore "enough" to respond to the agreed priority issues.

In a significant percentage of cases the desired indicators will not be easy to produce. This can occur because the sources of information are widely dispersed (e.g., every guide or outfitter providing services in a region), because there is no jurisdiction with authority to gather the information, or where the cost of data collection may be prohibitive. This selection procedure forces active and participatory comparison of what is desired with what is practical, often causing discussion of substitutes that may be easier to support, given the current availability of information. (See *Box 2.11* on approximate data p. 45) This process also has the benefit of stimulating a discussion of what is not practical (at least right now) with the potential to stimulate future implementation. The use of a participatory process for this stage can be productive, particularly with participation from the key stakeholders and potential data providers.

It is suggested that the identification of priority indicators be done in discussion groups charged with assessing each candidate indicator relative to the five criteria. A template for this step, Indicator Selection and Development Worksheet are provided in Annex C, (p. 485), which are useful to focus discussion at this point; the same template, will act as worksheet for elaboration of those indicators that are chosen for implementation. Evaluators working in discussion groups are also advised to raise the question of the long and short term utility of the indicators. *"Who will use it and for what purpose?"* In addition, as it is unlikely that all indicators recommended will be amenable to immediate implementation, indicators can also be screened relative to urgency of need. *"Is it needed now, or can it wait until the next census or season?"* This can assist in the establishment of priorities for action on implementation. In some of the WTO workshop applications, a "five star" rating system has been used to identify those indicators that are most urgently needed to address important issues. While this approach is necessarily subjective, it has served as a means to highlight which of the issues and related indicators are seen by the evaluators (or public consultation procedures) as having the highest priority for immediate implementation. This approach can be of use where choices need to be made of which indicators to implement first.

How many pilot whales are there? How likely is a tourist to see a whale on a tour? Who will count them and how will the information be reported? For Pleasant Bay Nova Scotia Canada, these may be the most important indicators of sustainability for its most important tourist product.

Implementation Phase

The goal of this phase is to take the indicators defined in the first two phases and put them into operation in the destination. Ideally this occurs as part of a continuing monitoring program supporting sustainable development for the destination and its tourism.

Step 9. Evaluation of Feasibility / Implementation procedures

In this step, each of the selected indicators is further elaborated and re-evaluated using a procedure that will clearly identify:

* Specific source(s) of the data to be used to construct the indicator;

* Specific characteristics of the data – level of detail (data fields, number of integers, means of provision (paper, digital etc), tabular formats;

* Frequency of collection of the data, (will it be needed/ available every five years, annually, quarterly, monthly, weekly, on line in real time?);

* Time lags between gathering and availability. Data is sometimes held for some time until an official publication is released containing those data and other data sets which may have different periodicity of production. (e.g. while energy data may be collected in real time by metering, the output of that data may only be done monthly and may be produced for individual sectors or regions annually);

*   *Considerations of access and confidentiality.* Will the data be made directly available in raw form so that any analysis can be done by the indicators group, or is it protected so that only aggregated outputs can be obtained? Will early access be given to the indicators production group to data which is new, or will any analysis have to wait until data is officially published?;

*   *Reporting units, validity and accuracy concerns* at different scales. Is data available for the desired scale (e.g., each hotel, or specific communities) or is it available only for fixed reporting units (e.g., counties, towns, districts)? If so, are these suitable for use? What would it cost to have data gathered or output on different criteria? Is data complete or done on a sampling basis? If so, is the data sufficiently representative to allow valid use at a local scale? (e.g., a 10% sample of all hotel workers);   •

Research and Organization
1. Definition/delineation of the destination.
2. Use of participatory processes.
3. Identification of tourism assets and risks.
4. Long-term vision for a destination.

Indicators Development
5. Selection of priority issues.
6. Identification of desired indicators.
7. Inventory of data sources.
8. Selection procedures.

Implementation
9. Evaluation of feasibility/implementation
10. Data collection and analysis.
11. Accountability, communication and reporting.
12. Monitoring and evaluation of indicators application.

*   *Responsibility for provision of data,* data analysis, and any additional manipulation. Who will extract the data, who will create tables, and who will validate or verify the data?;

*   *Costs and technical requirements* of data gathering and analysis. Are the needed data readily available, can data be derived from existing measuring processes, or does it have to be collected specifically? Is there technology, trained staff to compile and process existing data or to gather new data, or new techniques and technology which needs to be introduced, staff needing training, or experts who need to be hired for it?

Completion of the above review procedure should result in agreement on the process for creation and support for each selected indicator. A worksheet template is provided to assist in this process (See Annex C 2, p. 485).

Data availability

Both primary data sources (direct collection of data through measurement, surveys) and secondary sources (data derived from existing information) need to be considered. See the following data collection section for greater detail on collection procedures. Direct data collection tends to be costly, so existing sources should normally be considered first. Data assessment can be done through a data mapping process, which matches needs to available sources, followed by an assessment of gaps. (See for example the process used in the EEA case p. 377).

Box 2.11 Approximate measures

In some cases a measurement that does not provide precise data but indicates approximately the seriousness of an issue can be useful, especially if there are no other viable options. These are sometimes also called proxy measures.

For example, the most precise method to monitor seawater quality at beaches is through periodic laboratory tests that cover such elements as heavy metal content, coliforms, turbidity, biological oxygen demand (BOD) or chemical oxygen demand (COD), etc. However, if at certain destinations lab analysis is impossible due to lack or high cost of skilled personnel or equipment, or long distances to the nearest laboratory, there are alternative indicators that can be used as surrogates to give an idea of the existence and level of problems:

* Number and type of skin irritations or other cases caused by seawater, reported or treated;
* Complaints about seawater quality registered at local authorities or beach facilities;
* Incidents of algae growth or excessive turbidity reported to local officials;
* Depletion of fish stocks, or changes in success rates for fishermen.

These measures are approximate because not all cases are reported or registered; furthermore tourists' reactions are individual and subjective. Nevertheless significant changes in these measures can be signals of emerging problems with water quality - and may be the stimulus for the initiation of the scientific tests noted above.

Experience with the development of indicators for the tourism sector has shown that the data needed to calculate many indicators may be obtained from existing data sources; this information is often collected by agencies such as utilities, resource or sectoral departments of government for their own purposes. Frequently data can be used directly, because the agency (e.g., an energy utility measuring electricity use by sector for its own reporting or billing purposes) has already done some simple analysis that can be used to separate out parts of the tourism industry. In other cases, discussions may be needed with the potential data provider to obtain data which breaks out the factors of interest to the tourism sector (how many of the park users are local and how many are tourists?) or to provide data re-aggregated for the desired use (e.g., water use calculated for the peak tourist season). It may also be necessary to make arrangements with the data provider to collect new variables that may allow analysis relative to tourist sector needs (e.g., can we have the information collected on amount of seashore developed collected in a way which separates residential properties from those built for tourist use ?) It should be noted that this is done essentially as a negotiation or coordination process with the potential data provider. In practice, it may be strategic to try to create a data alliance, where the supplier obtains some advantage from their provision of data (such as access to other data, use of analyzed results, and integration of their data with other data) as compensation.

Refinement of key indicators

Based on the detailed evaluation of each candidate indicator and the findings regarding actual acquisition of the needed data, it can prove necessary to revisit the indicator and make changes to facilitate implementation. This may entail compromise, to accommodate the logistics of data collection and availability. The questions asked at this step address the

Saturn Resort, Romania. How many are on the beach? Where there is no access control, the calculation of numbers can be a challenge.

possibility of working with existing data (e.g., data available on a three year cycle can be sufficient to create a useful indicator) as a substitute for more expensive data gathering (e.g., the desired annual collection and reporting). Can we work with the existing data grouped by sector, or is it necessary to undertake re-aggregation of the original data to break out specific places or types of enterprise?

This is the point of decision regarding the actual form and delivery of the indicator and indicators program and will necessarily involve those who will lead implementation of the program.

Step 10. Data Collection and Analysis

Data collection procedures

This section provides advice and considerations to be addressed in the actual data collection and management associated with production of indicators. The form in which the indicator will be used and how it will be calculated can greatly affect the collection procedure. This step builds on the initial assessment process, where some consideration of the potential form of the indicator has occurred. It may already have been decided that the most suitable indicator is not wholly quantitative, but rather a data-based classification. (e.g., not arithmetic mean of average price of room sales but % of rooms sold at within 10% of rack rate). In some cases, it will be clear that new data must be collected and that this may have to involve some form of sampling process as it would not be feasible to cover all tourists or all restaurants to collect comprehensive data. It should be noted as well, that not all indicators will necessarily be quantitative - and that qualitative (e.g., rates four on a 1-5 scale) semi-quantitative information (e.g., % of beaches meeting the Blue Flag standard), ordinal data (e.g., rank of destination on exit survey relative to other destinations) or even simple yes/no information (does the destination have a formal plan?) can be of use in some circumstances.

For each indicator it is essential to clearly document the specific means to be used to obtain information. Typical procedures include:

* Use of existing data being collected by the tourism sector or by others (e.g., direct use of data from the census, industry statistics, traffic counts or utility records);

* Extraction and manipulation of data from existing sources (often similar sources to above but which require additional effort to extract, integrate or re-assemble);

Box 2.12   What do decision-makers really need?

While it may be desirable to have good, detailed scientific data, it may not always be necessary. A recent indicators study of a beach, which was apparently eroding rapidly away and imperilling hotel foundations as well as transport infrastructure, found that traditional air photo, satellite or even historical survey data was not available for reasons of national security. While an independent survey might provide detailed data on beach erosion at considerable cost, the practical solution was simply to set up measuring posts at a dozen key coastal points, and have the distance to the sea measured each month by a local college science class. For the purposes (and detail) needed to support decisions on remedial action, these data were sufficient, and nearly without cost.

Research and Organization

1. Definition/delineation of the destination.
2. Use of participatory processes.
3. Identification of tourism assets and risks.
4. Long-term vision for a destination.

Indicators Development

5. Selection of priority issues.
6. Identification of desired indicators.
7. Inventory of data sources.
8. Selection procedures.

Implementation

9. Evaluation of feasibility/implementation.
10. Data collection and analysis
11. Accountability, communication and reporting.
12. Monitoring and evaluation of indicators application.

- Creation of new comprehensive data (e.g., beginning a new process to monitor tourist stays and expenditures by tourist enterprises on a monthly basis by direct contact with each enterprise in the destination);

- Creation of sample data (e.g., establishing an exit survey of a percentage of tourists from the region to query their behaviours or attitudes). This may include methods such as sampling, use of questionnaire instruments, and extraction of data from existing statistical sources. Note: model questionnaires appropriate for exit surveys and resident surveys are provided to assist – see Annex C.

For an applied example of new data collection on physical impacts of tourism see the Yacutinga, Argentina case (p. 453).

It is often useful to consider the involvement of other administrations or organizations in the collection or provision of data, particularly where there are shared or complementary goals (e.g., the transportation ministry may also want data on tourist travel behaviour or use of access roads). The limits and cautions associated with the use of such data sets (e.g. comprehensiveness, validity, definition of survey frame, confidence limits, and representativeness) should be formally evaluated at this point, in conjunction with the potential data providers. (A template is provided to assist in these evaluations Annex C p. 485)   Indicators developers using survey data are encouraged to use a good statistical or sampling manual to help identify the limits of data and its use.

A good practical website on this subject is that from Statistics Canada (http://www.statcan.ca/english/edu/power/ch13/first13.htm) which provides support and examples of use of various data sets including that obtained through sampling procedures.

Box 2.13 Iguazu Forest Natural Reserve: Participation in data collection

The active participation of stakeholders in data collection is an effective way to obtain information, particularly where financial resources are an issue. The participation of tourism guides who operate on the routes inside the Iguazú Natural Forest Reserve, situated in the international tourist destination of Iguazú Falls, is an example of participation in data collection. Iguazú Forest is a private reserve, created in 1999, inside the Port Peninsula forest reserve in the northeast of Misiones province. It is administered by the Argentine Government, where 16,000 hectares of paranaense forest adjacent to Iguazú National Park are protected.

The opening of the forest reserve to different economic activities, in addition to traditional sustainable forest extraction, favoured the creation of an ecotourism project, based on sustainability. It started as a result of growing awareness of sustainable tourism in the local private sector (see Yacutinga Lodge case p. 453) Among the routes and products that were organized, the interpretive circuits through the forest have been the most important. Supporting the main attraction of the reserve: the observation of wild fauna and flora. Identifying the best places for observation of fauna in the reserve was the first step. To satisfy this need, and with the complementary objective of obtaining information that provided data of interest for the Ecological Center for Subtropical Research(CIES), a registration system for the fauna observed was established, to be supported by all those using the reserve. A registration form was provided for any single observation of wild fauna designed to be simple and easy to complete.

The data collection procedure was organized in the following way:

- All tourism vehicles circulating inside the reserve would have to complete a registration form;

- Training was provided to all those involved in filling in the forms;

- As a way to expand participation and to generate added value for the tour, tourists were encouraged to participate in completing the forms;

* Everyday, at the end of a tour, all completed forms would be delivered to the operations head office that entered the data in data files;

* Monthly calculation of fauna observation results;

* Location of these results on a map of the reserve, and identification of sites with better conditions for fauna observation.

The information contained in the registration form was the following:

* Popular name and scientific name (this was completed in office) of the sighted animal;

* Day and hour of observation;

* Place of observation by path/trail (points of reference had been established by circuit);

* Number of individuals observed, by sex and by approximate age (where easily identifiable);

* Number of the persons that carried out the observation (visitors, employees and tour guides of the reserve);

* Type of animal activity at the moment of observation;

* Climatic conditions at the moment of observation: intensity of the sun, (sun exposure) general temperature (observed without use of thermometer) etc.

This way of data collection helped identify places of greater concentration of attractive or interesting fauna for the visits. The information collected on the activity, information on the sex and the possible age of the animal observed, contributed useful information for subsequent management of the species observed in each habitat. Also the number of observations per day, per single circuit or as a whole, according to seasonality and climatic conditions (season of the year and time of day) and trends could be calculated with the data collected. Though the system is not necessarily fully scientific in application, the simple fact of its implementation generated indicators with multiple benefits.

Besides being a constant source of information supporting sustainable management providing monitoring of key indicators on every circuit (attractiveness of the sites/circuits for photographic safaris; number of observations by species; number of babies or young individuals observed; number of individuals in the group etc), the collecting activity caused an increase of awareness in the local community involved in the project, on the value and the importance of fauna both from economic and ecological perspectives.

In spite of the obvious benefits, there was a problem with regularity of the data collection, and this affected the utility of the indicators. Despite this, the program is considered a success.

Further information: Charles Irala, Director Aguas Grandes, Iguazú Forest Natural Reserve. www.aguasgrandes.com

Where data from other organizations is used, the same questions regarding data quality and applicability should be asked. (e.g., Is this data on all hotels, or just a sample? If it is a sample, how many were sampled, and how many of these were located in the defined destination? How were respondents selected? Did all reply? If any respondents did not reply, was substitution done, and on what basis?)

The methodology to be used to calculate each indicator should be specified. This becomes the formula to be used consistently to calculate the indicator and to allow changes to be measured over time. As noted in the introductory section of this report, there are many forms of indicators, and not all indicators will be numeric, although each will be designed in a way to show when changes have occurred.

Remember that indicators will not all be fully quantitative; they can be any of:

* *Quantitative:* (e.g., litres of water consumed per tourist – allowing actual calculation of changes in volume consumed – 2litres per tourist more this year than last);

* *Qualitative:* (e.g.: percentage of tourists who agree that the destination is clean – but which can also yield the ability to show change numerically – six percent increase in the percentage who consider the destination clean relative to five years ago);

* *Normative:* (e.g.: Number of beaches meeting Blue Flag Standard – allowing measurement of change in % which meet the standard);

* *Descriptive:* (e.g.: Site has environmental plan – Yes/No. (This answer can change over time and can also allow aggregation to show % of sites with such plans).

Calculation (quantification or qualification) of indicators

Users are urged to refer to the indicators in Part three of this Guidebook for model procedures and for references to indicators in use that may serve for comparison or benchmarking if the same methodologies are adopted. Documentation of the methods used is important; both to serve as a guide for subsequent calculations and as information potentially of use to others who may wish to use the data or replicate the method for the purposes of benchmarking. See *Box 2.14* on calculation of tourist density which illustrates the challenges and benefits of clarity in definition. It is also useful to consider alternatives again at this point, given the additional information that will be at hand regarding the data characteristics and the limits which may be revealed.

Expression and portrayal of indicators.

If indicators are to be used effectively, it is essential to find the most effective means to portray results. Clarity is one criterion for

Box 2.14 Calculation of tourist density

The density of tourist activity has been used as an indicator applied to intensively used sites from Thailand to the Balearics to Argentina. Density has been described per square metre, per linear metre of coastline, relative to actual use numbers and to potential numbers who could use the site. The most frequently used indicator when applied to beaches has been number of actual tourists per square metre of beach at peak use.

Use of this definition requires:

* Calculation of the site (beach) area – considering how much is open to use as in many littorals significant parts may be privately managed. (solution: calculate both, including and excluding this area – resulting in two different indicators - overall density and density in public areas);

* Measuring number of tourists on the beach. (Note: this is easiest for beaches with controlled entry. Otherwise do counts from photos to calculate density – for large beaches, a sampling process may be sufficient);

* For controlled sites, dividing numbers by beach area. For non-controlled sites extrapolating counts to entire area.

Issues to be considered: do we include the adjacent service area, the water out to a defined depth? All these need to be clearly stated.

(Note: most applications have not included the water but consider the services which are on the beach to be part of the beach area for calculation).

indicator selection. Which forms of analysis are chosen is influenced by the way in which the results are to be used. While in most instances, the analysis of data will be relatively simple, involving for example analysis of simple trends (e.g., change in tourist arrivals over last year, calculation of ratios (expenditures per tourist day), or use of simple contingency tables to separate cohorts (e.g., % of youth

Box 2.15 Visual Portrayal of Indicators

Indicators may be more accessible and have greater impact if shown in graphic form, for example:

Number of tourists per area of beach:	▲▲▲▲▲ high density
	▲▲▲ medium
	▲ low

Tourist revenues:

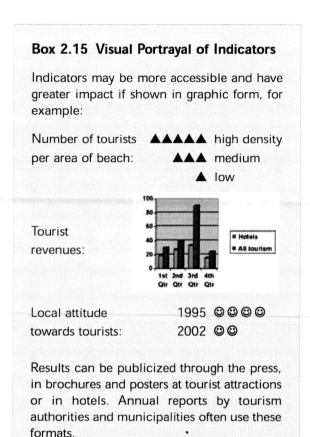

Local attitude towards tourists:	1995 ☺☺☺☺
	2002 ☺☺

Results can be publicized through the press, in brochures and posters at tourist attractions or in hotels. Annual reports by tourism authorities and municipalities often use these formats.   .

visitors going to the beach relative to % of all other groups), it can sometimes be useful to employ more sophisticated analytical techniques such as derived indicators or composite indices to address issues. Nevertheless, it is usually better to portray the results as simply as possible. For example, the formula used to determine whether a beach deserves a Blue Flag is relatively complex, involving several different tests which must be passed. (See Box 4.2 p. 253) But the key indicator for most users is whether or not a beach has a Blue Flag, or what percentage of the beaches in the destination has Blue Flags.

Wherever possible, developers of indicators should consider the needs of the potential user (in this case potential tourists or operators) and portray the indicator in terms most accessible to them. Similarly, use of a simple indicator such as percentage of seacoast which is protected as parkland is in itself a meaningful indicator to potential visitors, but the percentage change in this in the last decade may be a more useful indicator to the planning or environmentalist community. It is also useful to consider graphic presentation of indicators (trend lines, pie charts etc.) for some uses. The industry is very familiar with the use of such symbolic indicators as "five stars", "three knives and forks" or "first class" to portray to the public the results of complex classification procedures.

Step 11. Accountability, and Communication and Reporting

Because the purpose of indicators is to be of use in decision making and communication, attention is needed regarding the specific means to be used for regular reporting to stakeholders, the public, and to specific decision-makers whom the indicators are designed to influence. Ideally, the intended use, user, format(s) and presentation have been discussed in the decision on which indicators are likely to be most useful.

Note: if the actual use of the indicator is still questionable at this point, the deliberations may result in returning to the earlier analytical procedures or may even cause reconsideration of whether this is still a useful indicator.

The key to implementation is commitment. Ideally the indicators become part of a planning process for the destination - helping to define

Research and Organization
1. Definition/delineation of the destination.
2. Use of participatory processes.
3. Identification of tourism assets and risks.
4. Long-term vision for a destination.

Indicators Development
5. Selection of priority issues.
6. Identification of desired indicators.
7. Inventory of data sources.
8. Selection procedures.

Implementation
9. Evaluation of feasibility/implementation.
10. Data collection and analysis.
11. Accountability, communication and reporting
12. Monitoring and evaluation of indicators application.

what is important and ultimately used to develop performance measures for the planning and management of the destination. They also enter the public domain, and become a source of knowledge for the residents, tourists and managers regarding what is being done to sustain what is most important to the future of the destination. See the section 5.5 on Reporting and Accountability (p. 312).

Examples exist of effective communication of indicators in ways which reinforce the public accountability of authorities for the sustainability of communities and regions. To date, most of these have come from other social, economic, and environmental constituencies and authorities who have begun to report regularly on such varied issues as air quality, health sector performance, employment, crime, or state of the currency (these are all critical to the sustainability of tourism).

Box 2.16: Indicators make a difference – When actually used

Indicators can make a real difference to the decision process particularly when the results of indicators are used publicly; they become part of the understanding of what is important, and can be a catalyst for action. When environmental data was first publicized in North America and Europe, it became the impetus for environmental movements, political action, and much of the legislation and regulation now in place. Now, countries from China to Mexico, from India to South Africa have regular data on key indicators which are important to tourism – such as air quality, noise, crimes against tourists, and tourist arrivals frequently in the press. China publishes air quality regularly for most major cities. These data both show concern, and ultimately portray progress on such issues.

Indicators can make a difference in three main ways: through the *information* they generate; the *partnerships* they create; and the action they produce. Indicators start to make a difference even before they are fully developed as new concepts are explored and lessons learned. During the indicator development process, information is generated through discussion, consultation and appropriate use of publicity, web sites, regular progress reports, and press releases. By participating in indicator development, stakeholders have the opportunity to consider what is important to them and to re-evaluate the impact of tourism on their lives and their community. This often results in issues such as the need for greater composting of biodegradable wastes and the need to provide tourists with information about village protocol, being brought to the closer attention of hoteliers, tour operators, NGOs, tourists and the general public.

During the monitoring process *partnerships* are developed and many non-tourism bodies will necessarily become involved and learn about how tourism impacts on their area of work. Involving a wide spectrum of government, non-government and private sector groups will improve linkages and cooperation between agencies, allowing partnerships to develop and generating greater cross-sectoral understanding of sustainable tourism. The partnerships can then assist tourism authorities to implement cross-sectoral projects such as the upgrading of airport or waterfront facilities or to control impacts through planning legislation.

Action taken as a result of monitoring is perhaps the most obvious difference indicators can make. What has changed or occurred as a result of the indicator monitoring? What actions have been taken in pursuit of more sustainable tourism? Projects might include new planning legislation, training workshops for hoteliers, the preparation of a new visitor survey, a green award for sustainable tourism operations or a manual for tour guides.

In short, indicators make a difference not only through the information they provide but also through the partnerships and actions that result from their development. The question then becomes not so much 'do indicators make a difference' but how can the information, partnerships and action that indicators generate be used most effectively to guide destinations towards a more sustainable future.

Despite the growing work on indicators at all levels, there are few examples of indicators developed by or pertaining expressly to the sustainability of the tourism industry that have received similar public acceptance and use as those in use by other sectors. The publicity given to the negative effects of some world events (e.g., SARS effects on tourism in Beijing, Hong Kong or Toronto, the impact of terrorism on global tourism or 9/11 on behaviour of outbound US tourists) has begun to change this, and to highlight the importance and linkage of tourism to what occurs elsewhere and to other sectors.

The WTO issues statistics on international tourist arrivals and revenues globally and regionally, which are widely used as an indicator of both importance of tourism as an economic sector and a monitor of changes related to tourism at a global scale.

It is important to clearly identify who is responsible for the management of an indicators program and accountable for its completion and continuation. While the local planning authority is the most frequent responsible agency, the role can also be carried out by stakeholders of the tourism industry, by a non-governmental organization or academic institute, although the cooperation and support of the local authority is critical, and participation by all of these organizations is desirable.

It should be noted that indicators that are collected for specific destinations can be aggregated for regional and national reports (See the France Aggregated Reporting case p. 382) and the EU case (p. 377) for examples). Often tabular reports are used to show the relative values of different destinations, urban centres or districts relative to certain indicators. Another effective means of reporting and portrayal is by maps, showing in different colours the value of selected indicators (e.g., total tourist numbers, or ratio of tourists to residents in the geographic unit) for all of the different jurisdictions or tourist areas. For this to be most useful, the same approach must be followed in collection and interpretation of the data for each of the mapped areas. It should be noted that for some jurisdictions this can be difficult as spatial data units may vary greatly in size, providing a challenge in interpreting the information. Despite these issues, colourful mapped data can be a real aid in displaying important trends, regional anomalies and hot spots. Users will normally refer immediately to the status of their own destination relative to others, to competitors, or to the national mean. (See Box 6.26 Tourist Density in French Municipalities (p. 385) for an example that visually portrays tourism data for all of France).

Box 2.17 Aggregate national reports

Indicators can be used at many scales. Some indicators are used primarily at the national scale (e.g. contribution of tourism to GNP, total arrivals, total jobs in tourism). Other indicators are gathered at specific destinations or for local jurisdictions. When aggregated, such indicators can be very revealing of national trends, anomalies (area where the most is spent by tourists, area where the least is spent), highlighting the location of specific issues (the data unit where the average occupancy of hotel rooms is the lowest, or the wages received by tourism sector employees is lower than the national average). The example of how regional indicators have been developed and used by France is elaborated in the case study: Aggregated national reports: the case of France which delineates how regional indicators are used to show issues and to measure sustainability at the national level. (See France case p. 382).

Step 12. Monitoring and Evaluation of Indicators Application

Indicators are not meant to be a one-time exercise. Regular review is required both to see whether the information is indeed making a difference to users and helping solve key problems and also to determine whether the issues have changed. Periodic review of indicator applications can lead to re-design and redirection of elements of an indicators program. As was noted in Part 1, indicators are intended to be a central component of a planning and management process. As the issues which destination managers must address change, so do their needs for indicators. With use, it will become clear which indicators are serving the purpose well, and which will need to be updated or even replaced. While there is certainly a strong reason to retain indicators, as they are likely to become more useful over time as the record becomes longer, it is still worthwhile to revisit indicators every few years seeking improvement.

The indicators development process is the first step in providing ongoing information that will improve decisions, and build collaboration to deal with the principal issues of the destination. Once identified and implemented, a monitoring regime must be kept in place to gauge success or failure in managing tourism at a destination in ways that continue to be sustainable. In particular, it is useful to set defined targets as part of a planning process. Indicators can then be the vehicle by which changes can be compared to the targets.

Research and Organization

1. Definition/delineation of the destination.
2. Use of participatory processes.
3. Identification of tourism assets and risks.
4. Long-term vision for a destination.

Indicators Development

5. Selection of priority issues.
6. Identification of desired indicators.
7. Inventory of data sources.
8. Selection procedures.

Implementation

9. Evaluation of feasibility/implementation.
10. Data collection and analysis.
11. Accountability, communication and reporting.
12. Monitoring and evaluation of indicators application

WTO consultative group visit castle site as part of field trip in Ugljan Island, Croatia. The field visits to key assets and problem areas and on-site meetings with local stakeholders are part of the participatory approach to workshops on indicators.

> **Box 2.18 Indicators re-evaluation checklist**
>
> 1. Are the indicators being used – by whom and how?
> 2. Which indicators are not being used?
> 3. Do the users find the current set useful?
> 4. Do users now have other needs?
> 5. Are there new potential users?
> 6. Are the indicators in the right form, or are other output forms now needed?
> 7. Are there new means to collect or analyze data for the indicators which might make production easier or more efficient?
> 8. Are there new issues which have arisen and which require indicators?
> 9. Is information now available which could permit indicators which were too difficult to produce, but which were seen as important, to be added?
> 10. Is there evidence of outcomes which have been influenced by indicators use?
> 11. What are the barriers, if any, which have prevented optimal use of the indicators?
>
> This is a simple checklist – a more formal evaluation framework can be used, likely in conjunction with a broader plan or policy review exercise. (See template for re-evaluation Annex C 4 p. 490).

This process is critical to sustainable tourism management, but because it requires an ongoing commitment of resources, it can be difficult to maintain over the long-term. Establishment of the ongoing commitment and operational process needs to be both acknowledged and ideally clearly addressed during the indicators development process. Monitoring systems need to be put in place to repeatedly gather and disseminate the priority indicators to those who need to know the information. Similarly, it is useful to monitor the overall process itself, to ascertain whether the right information is getting to the right people, and ultimately whether tourism at the destination is more sustainable as a result. Ultimately, indicators become performance measures of progress towards the sustainable development of the destination. The review of indicators is ideally done as part of the periodic review of plans and strategies as a key building block for continuous improvement of the overall destination planning and management process.

2.2 Use of Other Sections of the Guidebook within this Process

This part of the Guidebook has provided a twelve step process that can guide destinations towards definition of their own issues, and identification of which indicators are likely to be of greatest use in addressing these issues. The other sections of this book supplement this process, and are designed to provide examples of how indicators have been used to address a number of issues most likely to be encountered by destination managers. The issues and indicators in these sections should not dictate which are to be chosen for any single destination, but should serve as a menu for destinations and with ideas to create their own indicators. In Part 4 a selection of destinations is examined in detail to illustrate how specific indicators can be applied. The several case studies Part 6 help clarify which issues have proven important in different types of tourism destinations and what procedures and techniques have been used in indicators applications. This may help a destination to choose which issues to consider and provide examples of which indicators have proven useful to others. Ultimately, the indicators chosen by each destination will be its own, and will be the most useful to respond to the real issues it faces on the path to sustainability.

Part 3

Sustainability Issues and Indicators in Tourism

This chapter provides guidance to indicators that respond to issues common to many destinations. **This extensive chapter and the wide range of issues covered DO NOT suggest that managers have to deal with all of these issues and their indicators.** It is a MENU, allowing planners and managers to select the issues most pertinent to their destinations and gain ideas for application from the suggested indicators and case examples. It has not been developed to present a prescription for indicators, rather to generate ideas to develop indicators to respond to the specific conditions and stakeholders' needs of each destination, covering a range of social, economic, environmental and management issues related to sustainability of tourism. It is important that destination managers set their own priority for issues and develop indicators that adequately respond to them and which are feasible to implement. For a suggested procedure of indicators development please consult Part 2.

Issues are grouped so that users of the Guidebook can find closely related topics in each section, such as impacts on host communities, management of natural and cultural resources, controlling tourism activities and destination planning, among others. A total of some 50 common issues or sets of issues are examined, with their specific components identified and a set of indicators suggested.

At the end of Part 3, a short list of selected **Baseline issues** and related **Baseline indicators** is identified as a suggested minimal set to be considered by destinations and which can allow comparisons with other destinations. In the body of this chapter, issues featured on the baseline list are noted by the addition of the term: ➢ **Baseline issue**.

The indicators recommended for each ➢ **Baseline issue** have been selected considering their direct relevance to the issue and their relative simplicity to measure and understand. **These are marked with the term ➢ Baseline Indicator**.

The Presentation of the Issues and Their Indicators

Each issue section starts with an introduction detailing key trends, problems and considerations of the given topic. Wherever possible, a range of indicators is discussed in the context of each issue and examples are provided of cases where indicators have been used. Boxed inserts provide further examples or methods which may be of use. For most issues, a table is provided showing subcomponents issues and their related indicators. **Reference to related ➢ Baseline indicators are distinguished in the issue/indicator tables in boldface**. For those indicators considered to be central to each issue, information is provided regarding:

* *Reason for use of this indicator* - how the indicator responds to the issue;

* *Source(s) of data* – where data can normally be found for this indicator, or how it can be collected;

* *Means to use the indicator* - providing suggestions on how the indicator can support decision making and reporting processes;

* *Benchmarking* – where possible, where similar indicators have been used or standards exist for comparison purposes.

Some other indicators which may be useful in addressing the issue are also listed without the same level of detail.

Where indicators are common to several issues, cross references are provided to the other issues. In most cases, the detailed description of indicators is not duplicated, although in some cases, where the indicator is focused differently or used in a different way, it will be treated separately in each section. The issues and indicators applications are further detailed and cross-referenced in Part 4 on Destination Applications.

3.1 Wellbeing of Host Communities

3.1.1 Local Satisfaction With Tourism ≻ **Baseline Issue**

Attitudes, Dissatisfaction, Community Reaction

Small communities worldwide are hosts for tourists. Some visit communities to see monuments, interesting local practices and customs or experience the ambience. Other communities serve nearby natural attractions, or are the hosts for visitors to beaches, mountains, events, etc. The community can be impacted both positively from tourism through jobs, economic activity and improved social services and negatively due to stress or damage on local resources and cultural values. Local satisfaction with tourism is critical for sustainability. In extreme cases, community hostility has driven tourists away. Actions by the industry to maintain a positive relationship between hosts and tourists can anticipate and prevent incidents and negative effects. The components of satisfaction cover a range of real and perceived issues – including crowding, access to jobs, sharing in benefits, reaction to tourist behaviour, etc. This issue addresses overall satisfaction. Individual substantive issues related to satisfaction (and which may be identified through complaints or use of surveys) are treated separately.

Components of the Issue	Indicators
Level of community satisfaction	• Local satisfaction level with tourism (and with specific components of tourism) based on questionnaire (see Annex C 6 Local questionnaire) ≻ **Baseline Indicator**
Problems or dissatisfaction	• Number of complaints by local residents

Indicator of community satisfaction:

* **Local satisfaction level with tourism (and with specific components of tourism)** ≻ **Baseline Indicator**

   Reason for use of this indicator: Changes in level of satisfaction can be an early warning indicator of potential incidents or hostility, and a means to obtain information about emerging problems or irritants before they become serious. This is a direct measure of actual opinion, and is the most straightforward way to measure local opinion of tourism and its effects.

   Source(s) of data: While it is possible to obtain some information through interviews with officials or the use of focus groups (and these help considerably when it comes to understanding more quantitative data) the most effective means is through a community questionnaire (see model questionnaire in Annex C 6 p. 494). A general questionnaire, repeated each year, with customized questions on specific issues of local concern (e.g., tourist sports fishing impact on the community fishery) should be used.

Means to use the indicator: Both overall level of satisfaction (e.g., over two thirds of the community agree that tourism benefits the community) and changes over previous years (e.g., the percentage of residents who believe they benefit directly from tourism has fallen 20% in the past two years) are useful measures.

Benchmarking: The best comparative use of these data is at a local level – comparing two or more similar communities in the same destination or measuring trends over time in overall satisfaction levels, and importance of specific irritants.

Indicator which signals areas of dissatisfaction:

* **Number of complaints by local residents**

    Reason for use of this indicator: In terms of local reaction, perception may be more important than any objective measure. The monitoring of complaints is less representative of all opinion but can be an early warning system for emerging discontent and can help in the design of any questionnaire used to measure the issue more objectively.

    Source(s) of data: Local authorities may be the best source for complaints, providing the authority has a known place to register complaints and this remains constant over time. A specific question can be added to focus on a particular issue (such as access, violation of norms, impact on cultural events, etc); some of these are addressed in greater detail under specific issue sections.

    Means to use the indicator: Simple counts of number of complaints are useful – particularly if a log of complaints is kept and classified. Where there is a surge in numbers complaining about a specific issue (e.g. complaints to the local council about tourists throwing garbage in the streets) this may be a warning of an emerging problem. See Annex C 6 (p. 494).

    Benchmarking: Because the issues are likely site specific and unique, compare with previous years to show changes. Design issue-specific questions for the residents' questionnaire to obtain objective information.

Nilgiri Hills, India.
Local residents, doing their normal daily activities are
part of tourism, whether or not they agree to be.

3.1.2 Effects of Tourism on Communities ➤ **Baseline Issue**

Community Attitudes, Social Benefits, Changes in Lifestyles, Housing, Demographics

Many communities perceive that with tourism comes a range of negative impacts on their community and culture. Some report specific negative effects on community resources or cultural assets. At the same time, tourism may be an important source of benefits for a community. How can a community measure the effects of tourism, both positive and negative?

The social, cultural and economic impacts on a host community are inextricably linked. There may be beneficial synergies or inverse relationships amongst the three impact areas and differing opinions amongst several community groups and individuals as to what constitutes a benefit and what is negative for the community. The extent to which local culture is incorporated into tourists' experiences may be a contentious issue. Some traditional or Indigenous communities may not want to share their culture with tourists at all, while a rural, agricultural community may not even recognize the interest tourists might have in their way of life. Yet it is virtually impossible for communities to isolate themselves from visitors and impacts from other cultures in this ever-globalizing world.

Accepting economic development often means accepting the cultural changes that accompany tourism development. This may happen without the opportunity for communities to decide whether they actually want change. If community-based tourism is to be sustainable, there need to be common goals, possibly developed by some type of committee, and with community support. Developing indicators and monitoring changes and trends can empower the community to make choices that suit it. The community, its culture and its tourism goals may change over time and may be affected by changing demographics and workforce immigration. For example, recent school graduates may be more interested in offering mountain biking tours than the lower key activities of their parents, or successful growth in tourism may bring new workers to the community with different backgrounds and values. This may challenge the community, and will certainly involve change.

Socio-cultural benefits to communities can be very difficult to measure. It may be simpler to measure economic benefits as an indicator of community socio-cultural benefits. (See related section which focuses on ➢ **Economic Benefits of Tourism** p. 128) Besides economic benefits, communities can also benefit from improved infrastructure (roads, sanitation, water, energy) and social services (health, schools, etc.) that tourism can bring. These are very important parts of local community wellbeing, but this approach does not capture some of the subtleties of community satisfaction with tourism. Questionnaires can elicit attitudes and perceptions of community members (see ➢ **Satisfaction with Tourism** p. 56).

Components of the issue	Indicators
Community attitudes to tourism (including community agreement and coherence on tourism, perceptions and acceptance of tourism)	• See ➢ **Local satisfaction with tourism** p. 56; • Existence of a community tourism plan; • Frequency of community meetings and attendance rates (% of eligible who participate); • Frequency of tourism plan updates (see section on planning and management issues); • Level of awareness of local values (% aware, %supporting); • % who are proud of their community and culture.
Social benefits associated with tourism	• Number of social services available to the community (% which are attributable to tourism) ➢ **Baseline Indicator**; • % who believes that tourism has helped bring new services or infrastructure. ➢ **Baseline Indicator**; • Number (%) participating in community traditional crafts, skills, customs; • % of vernacular architecture preserved.
General impacts on community life	• Number of tourists per day, per week etc; number per sq km (see ➢ **Controlling Use Intensity**) See also the specific issue of Access p. 65); • Ratio of tourists to locals (average and peak day) ➢ **Baseline Indicator**. • % locals participating in community events;

	• Ratio of tourists to locals at events or ceremonies; • Perception of impact on the community using the resident questionnaire – with reference to specific events or ceremonies (see Questionnaire, Annex C 6); • % of local community who agree that their local culture, its integrity and authenticity are being retained.
Changes to resident lifestyles, (cultural impact, cultural change, community lifestyle, values and customs, traditional occupations)	• % of residents changing from traditional occupation to tourism over previous year(s); men and women; • Number or % of residents continuing with local dress, customs, language, music, cuisine, religion and cultural practices. (e.g. change in number of local residents participating in traditional events); • Increase/decrease in cultural activities or traditional events (e.g. % of locals attending ceremonies).
	• Number of tourists attending events and % of total; • Value of tourist contribution to local culture (amount obtained from gate, amount of donations); • % of locals who find new recreational opportunities associated with tourism (local questionnaire See Annex C 6).
Housing issues	• % of housing affordable for residents; • Mode and average distance of travel to work or school; • Number of new housing starts and % for local residents Note: prices of other goods can also rise or fall (see also the ➢ **Economic Benefits** p. 128); • Note: Availability and access to some other services (e.g. health, water, sanitation) can also change, positively or negatively with social effects –see specific sections.
Community demographics	• Number of residents who have left the community in the past year; • Number of immigrants (temporary or new residents) taking tourism jobs in the past year; • Net migration into/out of community (sort by age of immigrants and out-migrants).

Indicators relating to community attitudes:

* **See indicators for ➢ Local Satisfaction with Tourism (p. 56);**
* **Existence of a community tourism plan;**
* **Frequency of community meetings and attendance rates (% of eligible who participate);**
* **Frequency of tourism plan updates (see section on planning and management issues);**
* **Level of awareness of local values (% aware, %supporting);**
* **% who are proud of their community and culture.**

Reason for use of these indicators: Helps to measure key local concerns and helps to identify current and emerging issues.

Source(s) of data: Questionnaire. Local authorities may conduct regular surveys or consultations. Local students may interview residents as part of a geography or tourism course.

Means to use the indicators: Average level of satisfaction/dissatisfaction on a scale; list of concerns for residents to check; open-ended questions; correlation of key concerns and level of satisfaction/dissatisfaction, e.g. The noise, pollution and number of tourists from large buses have the greatest correlation with overall dissatisfaction.

Benchmarking: A qualitative measure only. Benchmarks or specific goals can be set with respect to key concerns. (E.g. 65% of respondents are dissatisfied or very dissatisfied with the number of tourists in the town square on Sundays and this is considered to be excessive... we wish to take measures in order to reduce the % of dissatisfied residents to less than 30%).

Indicators of social benefits for the community:

* **Number and capacity of social services available to the community (% which are attributable to tourism) ≻ Baseline Indicator;**

* **% who believes that tourism has helped bring new services or infrastructure. (Part of a questionnaire or survey on satisfaction of locals) ≻ Baseline Indicator;**

* **Number (%) participating in community traditional crafts, skills, customs;**

* **% of vernacular architecture preserved.**

  (See Built Heritage, p. 76)

  Reason for use of these indicators: To identify the degree to which tourism contributes to what are seen as social benefits or disbenefits for a community.

  Source(s) of data: Local authorities should have data on the types and capacities of social services (e.g. medical services, schools). There are examples where these services are clearly attributable to tourism development (e.g. general infrastructure development due to tourism investment or a hotel or tour operator donates to the construction of clinics and schools). Besides the facts on social services, it is also important to evaluate the opinion of locals about these social services; and this will require a community questionnaire to obtain the perception of benefits, (See Annex C).

  Means to use the indicators: The community may use these indicators to inform discussion of whether it is benefiting suitably from tourism.

  Benchmarking: This is best compared over time for the community.

Indicators regarding general impacts on the community:

* **Number of tourists per day, per week etc; number per sq km (see ≻ Controlling Use Intensity** p. 192);

* **≻ Ratio of tourists to locals (average and peak day);**

* **Average length of stay;**

* **% participating in community events;**

* **Ratio of tourists to locals at events or ceremonies;**

* **Perception of negative impacts on the community using the resident questionnaire – with reference to specific events or ceremonies (see Questionnaire, Annex C 6);**

* **% of local community who agree that their local culture, its integrity and authenticity are being retained;**

* **See also Security (p. 104), Public Safety Health (p. 94) and Community Benefits (p. 128) and ≻ Local Community Satisfaction with Tourism** p. 56).

  Reason for use of these indicators: To set targets or limits for the number of tourists a community believes it can sustain while gaining optimal benefits.

Source(s) of data: Often difficult to measure unless there is only one entry point, such as an airport for an island destination. Very small communities with low numbers of tourists may be able to do a simple count of number of cars, buses, and total number of tourists. Others can conduct surveys to estimate totals and number of days tourists stay in a community. Hotel and accommodation occupancy rates are useful, but not always reliably reported. Surveys of locals help to determine whether the levels are considered acceptable.

Means to use the indicators: The community may use these indicators to provide hard data to help them decide how many tourists are too many or too few. A comfort level may be established on the ratio of tourists to local residents. This is a form of social carrying capacity – see the section on Controlling Use Intensity (p. 192) for additional indicators and means of calculation. See also Carrying Capacity and Limits (p. 309).

Benchmarking: Communities can monitor the number of tourists during specific time periods or in certain geographic areas for comparison over time to note changes in visitation patterns.

Box 3.1 Sustainable tourism indicators for mediterranean destinations

The indicators proposed aim at offering a tool for evaluating the tourism development and the practices used so far in existing destinations linking tourism industry to the economic, environmental and socio-cultural context of a resort or a region. The following indicators relate to socio-cultural issues:

Socio-cultural
* Ratio of local population to tourists in peak season;
* Ratio of local population to annual number of tourists;
* Marriages between tourists and locals as a percentage of all marriages;
* Number of bars/discos per local population;
* Divorces as a percentage of marriages;
* Females employed as a percentage of the labour force;
* Rate of growth of population;
* Unemployment rates in the off-season periods.

Local Participation
* Existence of educational/informational programs for the public;
* Number of local meetings to discuss issues before policies are implemented;
* Availability of procedures for public and stakeholders involved to suggest changes in policies;
* Public-private partnerships/investments.

Source: http://www.iacm.forth.gr/regional/papers/tourism-today.pdf

See also the Issue section on Economic Benefits for economic indicators proposed for Mediterranean destinations. A pilot application was done to test the indicators in Hersonissos Greece (http://www.iacm.forth.gr/regional/papers/XIOS-englishversion.pdf) with one of the key issues being availability of data – particularly to estimate multipliers and leakage.

Indicators regarding cultural changes:

* **% of residents changing from traditional occupation to tourism over previous year(s);**

* **Change in number of residents continuing with local dress, language, customs, foodstuffs and cultural practices;**

* **Increase/decrease in cultural activities or traditional events.**

Reason for use of these indicators: To allow community to monitor the impacts tourism is having on the socio-cultural fabric of the community. Likely to be of importance to residents concerned with youth continuing with traditions.

Source(s) of data: Number of local residents working in tourism: a simple count in very small communities; survey/business statistics for larger communities and towns. Community leaders may report declines in attendance and participation at ceremonies and events. Religious or spiritual leaders may note changes in dress and customs.

Means to use the indicators: Change in attendance at traditional events is relatively easy to measure, but should be used in conjunction with indicators on change (increase/decrease) in attendance by residents versus tourists. Declines in cultural practices may also signal a potential decline in interest of tourists in visiting the community. Surveys on tourist satisfaction might show changes they consider in the authenticity and cultural attraction of the destination (see Exit questionnaire Annex C).

In some communities, where the language of tourists is different than the local language, or where local residents are being replaced by newcomers who may have different cultural origins, language capability can be an important measure.

Benchmarking: Communities need to set their own benchmarks for what is acceptable to them - the limits of acceptable change or social carrying capacity. Some may be comfortable with a faster rate of change if it brings improved housing, employment and opportunities for their children. Others may wish to maintain traditions and see tourism interest in their lifestyle as an opportunity for their children to continue to practice traditional skills.

Other indicators of interest to capture socio-cultural impacts from tourism for host communities:

* **% of housing affordable for residents;**
* **Distance to travel to work or school;**
* **% of new housing starts for locals/tourists.**

These indicators are important for communities in destinations with high tourism values, such as scenic location, good climate, beaches etc. The small community may risk being taken over and being turned into a tourism town in which the original residents are marginalized and can afford accommodation only on the outskirts of their former village; e.g. in a former fishing community whose beachside location becomes a resort, local residents who still fish are dislocated from their huts and boats while others now service the tourism industry.

* **Damage to cultural artefacts and built structures – where graffiti, theft or vandalism, and cumulative damage from large numbers are evident;**

* **Costs of repair and mitigation – where the hosts can document real costs of cleanup or repair associated with tourist activities;**

* **Number of instances of damage to cultural assets (see Built Heritage p. 76).**

Indicators on community demographics:

⚬   **Number of residents who have left the community in the past year;**

⚬   **Number of immigrants (temporary or new residents) taking up tourism jobs in the past year;**

⚬   **Net migration into/out of community (sort by age of immigrants and out-migrants).**

Growth in tourism can lead to a significant change in the composition of local residents, with long-time residents leaving because their community or town has changed too much for them, and with new residents arriving to take up jobs and opportunities due to tourism. A community is rarely sustained by tourism alone and tourism needs to be considered in conjunction with other economic and social factors. Indicators that track the inflow and outflow of residents give a measure of the stability of the community and acceptable or manageable rates of growth and change.

Cinque Terre, Italy. Tiny cliffside villages receive thousands of visitors during the July- August peak season.

Box 3.2 A survey on the socio-cultural impacts of tourism in the Keszthely-Hévíz Region, Lake Balaton, Hungary

Residents' mean response to tourism's effect on the region

Variable	Mean	Std. dev.
General prices for goods and services	4.71	0.67
Cost of land and real estate	4.57	0.77
Residents' concern for material gain	4.46	0.69
Congestion	4.40	0.82
Settlement's overall tax revenue	4.36	0.89
Noise	4.22	0.75
Organised crime	4.21	0.90
Individual crime	4.15	0.92
Hospitality and courtesy toward strangers	4.12	0.76
Residents' pride in their settlement	3.97	0.91
Prostitution	3.95	1.03
Gambling	3.83	1.04
Littering	3.83	1.01
Vandalism	3.77	0.82
Politeness and good manners	3.66	0.85
Residents' pride in their settlement	3.97	0.91
Drug abuse	3.56	1.28
Alcoholism	3.53	0.89
Sexual permissiveness	3.51	1.07
Honesty	2.73	1.01
Mutual confidence among people	2.73	1.09
Unemployment	1.73	0.82

* - Response range was 1-5. 1 = Significantly decrease   2 = Decrease somewhat 3 = Not make any difference 4 = Increase somewhat   5 = Significantly increase

According to the Table, the following impacts of tourism were perceived by local residents:

Positive impacts: Perceived **increase** of a settlement's overall tax revenue, residents' pride in their settlement, hospitality and courtesy toward strangers;

Perceived **decrease** of unemployment.

Negative impacts: Perceived **increase** of costs of living, costs of land and housing, general prices for goods and services, residents' concern for material gain, prostitution, gambling, organised crime, individual crime, noise and congestion;

Perceived **decrease** of mutual confidence among people.

Box 3.2 (cont.)

For the rest of the variables, their mean (not above 4.0 and not below 2.0) may indicate that the current level of tourism has had relatively less impact on them, though in certain cases (where standard deviation is relatively high) the neutral average resulted from a co-effect of both positive and negative impacts. For example, in the case of housing conditions, respondents perceived an improvement in interior design in order to meet the requirements of the tourists, and in the quality of new buildings due to increased financial resources, but they also considered that during the main season many families move out (even from their house to garages or cellars) in order to accommodate tourists.

The survey also investigated residents' opinion on a wide range of other factors, including employment opportunities, income and standard of living, general infrastructure, quality of life, cultural and leisure facilities, cultural identity, housing conditions, public security, availability of real estate, among others.

Source: Ratz, T. (2000): Residents' perceptions of the socio-cultural impacts of tourism at Lake Balaton, Hungary. In: Richards, G. and Hall, D. (eds). Tourism and Sustainable Tourism Development. London: Routledge, pp. 36-47. **http://www.ratztamara.com/balimp.html**

3.1.3   Access by Local Residents to Key Assets

Access to Important Sites, Economic Barriers, Satisfaction with Access Levels

In some destinations, the development of tourism can come at the expense of real or perceived access to key valued assets by the local residents. The local community which has traditionally used beaches, trails, roads, or natural resources may find its access changed. In some cases, formerly public shorelines or forests may become private, or restrictions placed on the permissible uses (e.g., hunting or fishing prohibited, fees charged per day use). This issue is a specific subset of community impact of tourism and may be closely related to overall satisfaction. It is a frequent issue in new destinations, where traditional access may be affected by new development and new rules.

Components of the issue	Indicators
Retaining access to important sites for local residents	• Access by locals to key sites (% of site freely accessible to public); • Frequency of visits by locals to key site(s); (see also accessibility issue with regard to access for persons with disabilities p. 90).
Economic barriers to access	• Cost of access expressed in hours of local wages.
Maintaining satisfaction with access levels	• Perception of change in accessibility due to tourism growth (see Local questionnaire annex C 6); • Number of complaints by local residents regarding access.

Local users may be displaced by visitors (no room at the tavern) or priced out of regular use (trail access fees, launching charges). Where protection of cultural or ecological resources is involved (see also the issue on Protecting Critical Ecosystems p. 147) limits may be placed on those allowed access.

Indicators regarding site access and use:

* **Access by locals to key sites (% of site freely accessible to public);**

* **Frequency of visits by locals to key site(s).**

Reason for use of these indicators: These indicators measure potential access or limits to access and also measure actual behaviour of locals relative to site use.

Source(s) of data: Site or destination managers, entry control or ticket booths.

Means to use the indicators: At the planning stage, the % of the site left open to the public is a good measure of access potential. Significant changes may cause concern. How much access is sufficient? Real or perceived problems with access can lead to reduced use of the site by locals. (e.g., in many jurisdictions access below the high water mark is legally public, yet a resort may take effective control of the beach by fencing access points, or providing guarding or policing which can deter local users or deflect them to other areas for their beach activities).

Benchmarking: These indicators tend to be very site specific. Therefore the best comparative use of the data is relative to the same sites in previous years. Some data for beaches may be available through the Blue Flag program (see Box 4.2 p. 253).

Indicator regarding financial barriers to access:

* **Cost of access expressed in hours of local wages.**

Reason for use of this indicator: Where site access becomes subject to entry fees, the fees themselves can become significant barriers (see Tourism and Poverty Alleviation p. 135). Often fees are set to accommodate the purses of the visitors. In some destinations high fees may effectively exclude local residents. While dual fees are sometimes employed (e.g. where a year long pass to the park costs the same as two or three day entries), or locals purchase passes at a lower price, any dual fee system can lead to the creation of a grey market where locals sell their lower cost passes to visitors for a profit.

Source(s) of data: Site management normally can provide a fee schedule. Local mean hourly wage is normally available from local or regional/national published data. Many nations can

> **Box 3.3 Access to protected areas in Cape Breton, Canada**
>
> The establishment of a National Park and adjacent Provincial protected areas over the past decades has had a direct impact on the use patterns of the traditional residents of the northern peninsula of Cape Breton Island. Back roads originally established by loggers were always used as access to the interior of the peninsula for hunting, snowmobiling and use of off-road motorized vehicles. The establishment of the protected areas has been accompanied by efforts to close many of the roads to reduce impacts on fauna and flora. This has resulted in a degree of antipathy between local communities and the managers of the protected areas. The recent indicators study has recommended the use of a local questionnaire to both clarify the nature and extent of concern relative to the access issues and to monitor changes. The key indicators would include those related to extent and frequency of use and to perceptions of accessibility. The same access routes are key points of entry for tourists to the interior of the region, and any measures designed to facilitate tourist use (coast trails, links between villages and along the park periphery) have also complicated the mix of values and objectives. Indicators both of physical impacts and local and tourist attitudes are now part of the planning process for the Park and protected areas, and a vehicle for greater local and industry involvement in a broader planning process. (See indicators list from workshops in Cape Breton case p. 355)

provide wage data at local levels. Where no specific local data is available, it is reasonable to use national or provincial data in most cases as a measure of mean hourly wage.

Means to use the indicator: Express the result in the form of "it takes three hours work for the average resident to purchase entry to the attraction – up (or down) nearly an hour from last year".

Benchmarking: While the best comparisons will be time series for the same site, the indicator can be also benchmarked against the mean wage of visitors (where the greatest group of tourists is from a particular nation, the access fee can also be expressed in terms of the hourly wage of that country). For comparisons with fees at other sites, many sites have their own websites with posted fees.

Indicators of satisfaction regarding access:

* **Perception of change in accessibility due to tourism growth (See Questionnaire Annex C 6);**

* **Number of complaints by local residents regarding access.**

Reason for use of these indicators: In terms of local reaction, perception may be more important than any objective measure of accessibility or use. These indicators measure changes in the perception of access. The questionnaire asks the residents directly for their perception of access. The monitoring of complaints is less representative but can be an early warning system for emerging discontent. An appropriate questionnaire may help to precisely locate sites or areas where there are problems – and permit a wide range of solutions which may include zoning, timing of use, co-management, etc.

Source(s) of data: The indicator on perception requires use of a residents' questionnaire (see Annex C 6). Local authorities may be the best source for complaints, providing the authority has a known place to register complaints and this remains constant over time. A specific question can be added to focus on a particular issue or location where access is thought to be an issue.

Means to use the indicators: Simple counts of number of complaints are useful – particularly if a log of particular complaints is kept and classified. Where there is a surge in numbers complaining about a specific issue (e.g. local fishermen complaining that they no longer have room at the dock for their boats due to mooring by tourist craft) this may be a warning of an emerging problem. See Annex C for means to portray results of local survey information.

Benchmarking: Because the specific issues of access are likely site specific and unique, compare with previous years to show changes. Design issue-specific questions for the residents' questionnaire.

Note: the indicators suggested above are related with *local opinion on tourism. See the questionnaire in Annex C 6, Controlling Use Intensity (p. 192) and the destination section on Small and Traditional Communities p. 281) which are also likely to be of interest relative to the access issue. If there is a specific site where access is considered to be a problem, it may be useful to frame a question which asks specifically about access to that site (the hotel beach, the park etc)*

Meech Lake, Quebec, Canada: visitors unwelcome

3.1.4 Gender Equity

Family Wellbeing, Equal Opportunities in Employment, Traditional Gender Roles, Access to Land and Credit

Gender equity is unlikely to appear on a list of top ten stakeholder concerns, but it is nevertheless of significance to the movement towards socio-cultural sustainability. Gender equity is not just about whether women are getting tourism jobs, their relative seniority, training opportunities and possibilities for advancement, but also how the impacts of tourism differ on the lives of men and women in the destination. Women often suffer from loss of natural resources first, but at the same time may be the first to benefit from infrastructural improvements that often accompany tourism development such as piped water and electricity. In traditional societies, the issues of whether women and men have equal access to land and credit can be a key constraint on the ability of women to become tourism entrepreneurs.

In accordance with the CEDAW principles (http://www.un.org/womenwatch/daw/cedaw/), the South Pacific Tourism Organisation (SPTO), in collaboration with UNIFEM, has recently conducted a pilot study of the social and gender implications of tourism in Samoa, Vanuatu and Fiji (SPTO 2003). They identified four main areas of concern in terms of tourism gender equity: family well-being (as a result of the long hours and demands of shift work), equal opportunities in formal employment (for the advancement of disadvantaged groups), traditional gender roles in the community, and access to land and credit which defines who can play the lead role in tourism development. These issues are used to structure the discussion on possible indicators.

Components of the issue	Indicators
Family wellbeing	
Stress	· % tourism employees (male/female) suffering increased fatigue and stress as a result of work.
Childcare	· % of tourism operators who provide day care and other benefits for employees with children.
Health and safety	· % of tourism operators who have regulations/made commitments regarding equal gender opportunities; · % of operators who promote staff awareness of occupational health, safety and issues affecting female employees.
Transport	· % of tourism operators who provide transport for women returning from night shifts.
Discrimination against women/men	· % employees who believe their gender has affected their job advancement, pay or benefits.

Equal opportunities in formal employment	
Opportunities for Women	• Women/men as a % of all tourism employment; • Women/men as a % of all formal tourism employment; • Women/men as a % of all tourism informal occupations; • % women/men in part-time employment.
Seniority	• % of women/men in different tourism income earning categories; • % of women/men in unskilled, semi-skilled and professional positions in the industry.

Components of the issue	Indicators
Entrepreneurs	• % of owner-operator tourism businesses run by women/men; • % of tourism businesses registered under women/men.
Training	• % women/men tourism employees with formal training; • % women/men employees sent on training programmes.

Traditional gender roles	
Community tourism	• % women/men involved directly (providing services) in village-based tourism projects; • % women/men involved indirectly (supplying goods) in village-based tourism projects.
Ownership	• % women/men owning/controlling village tourism businesses.
Rewards	• Average income for women/men working in village-based tourism business; • % women/men involved in village-base tourism satisfied with their work and rewards.

Access to land and credit	
Land ownership	• % women/men with rights to land in tourism development areas; • % women/men holding rights to tourism leases.
Loans	• % bank loans issues to women/men for tourism ventures; • % women/men defaulting on bank loans; • % donor grants issued to women/men for tourism ventures.

Indicators of family well-being:

* **% tourism employees (male/female) suffering increased fatigue and stress as a result of work;**

* **% of tourism operators who provide day care and other benefits for employees with children;**

* **% of tourism operators who have regulations/made commitments regarding equal gender opportunities;**

* **% of tourism operators who promote awareness amongst staff regarding occupational health, safety and issues effecting female employees;**

* **% of tourism operators who provide transport for women returning from night shifts;**

* **% employees who believe their gender has effected their job advancement, pay or benefits.**

Reason for use of these indicators: Tourism can affect the family. The demands of tourism can require odd hours, and normally bring contact with other cultures or values. Like other sectors, employment in tourism may have impacts on family cohesion, women's roles, workload, stress and reproductive health. More than many other sectors, tourism can be seasonal, expose women to potential for harassment and require journeys to and from work for late shifts. While benefits may be derived from the employment, in many cases jobs may be entry level, low paying, and with little opportunity for advancement.

Source(s) of data: The data for these indicators can be collected by employee surveys and employer surveys. Some destinations may already collect these data through ministries of employment, tourism, or similar.

Means to use these indicators: It should be noted that many of these indicators are the same as recommended for a range of social and economic issues (see for example, the issues on Economic benefits of tourism (p. 128) and Effects of Tourism on Communities (p. 57). The difference is that efforts are made to identify gender differences in the data, to permit action where necessary to respond to gender issues.

Benchmarking: Benchmarking can be done relative to overall statistics or to highlight differences between males and females (likely in different age cohorts or employment categories) and to show changes over time. These indicators can also serve to highlight differences between employment of women in tourism and in other sectors.

Indicators of equal opportunities in formal employment:

* **Women/men as a % of all tourism employment;**
* **Women/men as a % of all formal tourism employment;**
* **Women/men as a % of all tourism informal occupations;**
* **% women/men in part-time employment;**
* **% of women/men in different tourism income earning categories;**
* **% of women/men in unskilled, semi-skilled and professional positions in the industry;**
* **% of owner-operator tourism businesses run by women/men;**
* **% of tourism businesses registered under women/men;**
* **% women/men tourism employees with formal training;**
* **% women/men employees sent on training programmes.**

Reason for use of these indicators: Depending on the destination, women may fare differently from males in the tourism industry, both in terms of roles and benefits. Seniority of women employees relative to their male counterparts and their relative pay and benefit packages may be less. Women often are underrepresented as entrepreneurs and owner-operators and training opportunities for female/male staff may not be the same. Discrimination against female or male employees may affect the workplace and overall welfare.

Source(s) of data: Labour statistics where available. If not, use employee surveys.

Means to use these indicators: For these indicators, it is most effective to show data relative to overall statistics or to highlight differences between males and females (likely in different age cohorts or employment categories).

Benchmarking: Compare with other sectors and between men and women over time. For most of these indicators, national or regional data can serve as a benchmark – likely published by national employment authorities. An employee questionnaire may be necessary for some of the information on attitudes of employees.

Indicators of traditional gender roles:

* **% women/men involved directly (providing services) in village-based tourism projects;**
* **% women/men involved indirectly (supplying goods) in village-based tourism projects;**
* **% women/men owning/controlling village tourism businesses;**
* **Average income for women/men working in village-based tourism business;**
* **% women/men involved in village-base tourism satisfied with their work and rewards.**

Reason for use of these indicators: The respective roles of men and women in traditional communities providing tourism services can be a concern, as can proportion of women participating in tourism decision-making and the relative rewards/pay structure for men/women working in community-based tourism venture.

Source(s) of data: May be difficult to obtain except via direct survey.

Means to use these indicators: Show relative percentages to demonstrate level of involvement and influence of women.

Benchmarking: Compare genders over time.

Indicators of access to land and credit:

* **% women/men with rights to land in tourism development areas;**
* **% women/men holding rights to tourism leases;**
* **% bank loans issues to women/men for tourism ventures;**
* **% women/men defaulting on bank loans;**
* **% donor grants issued to women/men for tourism ventures.**

Reason for use of these indicators: There may be a difference between who has access and control of land in areas desirable for tourism development. In many communities there are barriers to credit for tourism development for both men and women.

Source(s) of data: May be available from credit institutions.

Means to use these indicators: Data will highlight changes in the relative position of males and females over time.

Benchmarking: Compare over time with the same destination.

Note: As well as those indicators suggest above, acknowledging the need for gender equity in tourism monitoring can be as simple as making indicator data collection gender sensitive, disaggregating male and female responses. For example when monitoring local satisfaction from tourism, note responses from male and female participants. This can help alert the monitoring team to gender equity issues they had not recognized.

3.1.5 Sex Tourism

Child Sex Tourism, Education, Prevention Strategies, Control Strategies

Sex tourism exists in every region of the world, but is most prevalent in developing countries where tourism has flourished but where it has provided few economic opportunities for local people, especially women. Issues such as HIV/AIDs, child abuse and human trafficking have given rise to outrage and global concern for the exploitation of women and children in tourism destinations. The international travel and tourism industry can no longer turn a blind eye to the negative effects of sex tourism or the 'unclean' image and sullied reputation of a destination when sex tourism is allowed to exist freely. Sex tourism feeds an extraordinary illegal economy of pimps, bar and brothel owners, traffickers, protection rackets and the corruption of officials and others. However, regardless of the vast sums of money exchanged in sex tourism, only a small percentage ever gets into the hands of sex workers.

Child sex tourism

Unlike the differing views of adult sex tourism, child sex tourism is a clear and unambiguous violation of human rights. There is global condemnation of child sex tourism and the international travel and tourism industry has given their support to NGOs and governments who are working to eradicate the exploitation of children in tourism destinations. Child sex tourism involves the prostitution of children or paedophilia-related child abuse and now often involves the use of children in the production of pornography. The commercial sexual exploitation of children, including child sex tourism, is considered to be a manifestation of labour exploitation and included in the International Labour Organisation's (ILO) efforts to eliminate the worst forms of child labour. (ILO Convention 182).

Children who are victims of child sex tourism are not always poor or illiterate. However the vast majority of children who are abused are vulnerable because of poverty, physical or mental abuse or social exclusion. They include local, foreign and ethnic minority children who live and work on the streets or on the fringes of the tourist areas, those who have been trafficked, lured or sold into the sex industry, those who have been abused at home, those without access to education and those forced or made responsible to support the family. Both girls and boys are victims of child sex tourism but international research indicates that it is mostly girl children who are abused.

Where does child sex tourism happen?

Offenders go to places where they think they will not get caught. Child sex tourism is most likely to happen in and around tourist destinations where there is ignorance, corruption, apathy, lack of law enforcement, and the existence of adult sex tourism. Children are abused in hotels and guest-houses, in private houses, in beach huts, in brothels and in public areas. It is nearly impossible to estimate the numbers of offenders and children involved in or affected by child sex tourism. Tourism is not the cause of child exploitation but the nature of the tourism environment can create an unsafe environment for vulnerable children. Some of these factors include:

1.   The erosion of traditional values and socio-cultural norms in tourist destinations related to dress, nudity, relationships between adults and children; men and women;

2.   The absence of police and social welfare professionals in tourism destinations;

3.   The increased demand for sex services from domestic and foreign tourists;

4.   Lack of responsibility of tourists - the 'it's not my home' mentality;

5.   No integration of human rights and children's rights in tourism industry training or policy making;

6.   Loss of traditional livelihood in and around tourism destinations.

Who are the offenders?

Sex offenders can be any age, nationality or social status. Some travel on their own and others travel with friends. Organised 'child sex tours' purchased through travel agents or tour operators are a thing of the past; however, a third party is often involved to set up the contacts or procure the children. Most research identifies two specific types of offender:

i)   The client of a brothel or 'go-go' bar - this person goes looking for an adult sexual encounter but doesn't care too much if they are offered a child. They may only do it once in their search for an 'exotic' holiday experience. However, there are numerous research reports that show this type of offender can re-offend by justifying that they are 'helping' the local community.

ii)   The paedophile - this person has a specific sexual desire for children. They travel to places where they can target vulnerable children. They are motivated by their sexual desire and can spend long periods of time 'grooming' children and their families. Paedophiles network around the world, share pornography via the internet and communicate with each other about the best places to travel where there is access to children. There are also reports of a different type of offender - the person who seeks out violent or deviant sexual behaviour with either women or children. They are neither paedophiles nor traditional sex tourists.

The travel and tourism industry can play an active role in preventing child sex tourism by developing policies and programmes that support local and international actions. It is possible, by using a variety of indicators, to identify trends and issues relating to children in tourism destinations. By using these indicators travel and tourism stakeholders can develop strategies to protect children and minimise the risk of abuse. These indicators can be adapted to a range of government and private sector operations such as hotels, tour operators, airlines, ground operations, travel agencies and at the national level.

Components of the issue	Indicators
Vulnerable children are at risk of abuse	• Numbers of children in vulnerable groups working in the destination, especially in the vicinity of the hotel or other premises.; • Number of NGOs or government services located in the destination, especially within the vicinity of the hotel or other premises, to look after the welfare of children.
Lack of knowledge about children's rights and how to protect children	• % of staff trained on children's rights and how to protect children from abuse; • Number and frequency of training sessions for staff/managers on how to protect children; • Number of contacts made with specialised NGOs; • Locations of police and relevant authorities' telephone contact numbers within hotel/premises; • Number of times reports made by company to NGOs, police or other authorities about suspected abuse on the premises; • Existence of a person in the company nominated as focal point and responsible for issues about children and community.
Children recruited through adult sex tourism establishments	• Number of places where adult prostitution occurs in close proximity to the hotel/premises; • Mechanisms for checking ID of adult sex workers accompanying guests into rooms; • Methods for registering 'Joiners' ("Joiner" is a term used for the 'guest' of a hotel guest who wasn't registered at check-in. It often - but not always - refers to a sex worker); • Existence of policy on adult prostitution that reflects national laws.
Children have no access to income and education	• % of revenue given to support children's charities; • Number of suppliers that create jobs for local people; • Number of staff volunteering to help local communities in skills transfer programmes; • Number of reports available to provide information on the economic and social development of local communities.

Components of the issue	Indicators
Sex offenders go to places where they think they will not get caught	• Number of information points showing relevant policy of hotel/premises to protect children. E.g. -posters, information packs, registration forms, in-flight videos, staff rooms, staff bulletin boards; • Number of police stations in the vicinity of the hotel/premises that have trained child protection officers.
The international travel and tourism industry guidelines and declarations to prevent child sex tourism do not often get implemented at the local level	• Preparedness of travel and tourism business to openly condemn child sex tourism; • Preparedness of travel and tourism business to develop and implement policies and programmes to protect children; • Evidence that travel and tourism business has advocated for children's rights in tourism industry meetings and conferences; • Evidence that travel and tourism business has participated in multi-stakeholder meetings on child protection and children's rights issues.
The risk to children in tourism destinations is documented and shared	• Research on child sex tourism is encouraged throughout the business and information provided to government agencies and NGOs for analysis; • Regular reporting of actions through company reports and websites.

Discussion of selected indicators: There has been no previous history of indicators for the protection of children specifically related to child sex tourism. However, inspiration can be drawn from UNICEF on indicators related to the UN Convention on the Rights of the Child (articles 32, 34, 35 and 36) related to the exploitation of children (www.unicef.org).

A large number of potentially useful indicators have been suggested in the table above, which respond to the range of issues which could be of importance to a destination; a selection of those likely to be most important to managers is elaborated below.

Box 3.4 Accor hotels Asia program: An integrated program of policy and action

In 2002 ACCOR Hotels Asia started working with the international NGO ECPAT (www.ecpat.net) and Australian NGO Child Wise in order to develop awareness and training programmes on the protection of children. The ACCOR programme now covers three key actions: awareness and staff training, displaying consumer information (posters), and developing partnership with ECPAT and WTO to promote international efforts and good practices. The Child Wise training focussed on a child rights based approach and encouraged ACCOR to develop actions that work to protect children rather than focus on the offender. ACCOR has subsequently been able to use some of the indicators listed above to measure their success. 77% of ACCOR's 3863 staff in Thailand and Laos has received training through their Child Wise training programme. The integration of training as an in-house training product and adapted to Thai language and context has meant that ACCOR trainers in Thailand have also been in contact with local NGO and police experts to help strengthen their local knowledge on the issues. ACCOR participates in local, regional and international events to advocate for travel and tourism support for the campaign to end child sex tourism and continues to distribute information to staff and clients through their website, posters in hotels, staff bulleting boards, and meetings. Other ACCOR activities include a fundraising event in Bangkok to raise funds to support child protection activities in northern Thailand. ACCOR acknowledges that the positive response from their staff and clients has encouraged the company to continue developing new initiatives. (See also the Accor Environmental Sustainability Indicators case p. 326)

Indicators regarding training of staff in these issues:

* **% of staff trained on children's rights and how to protect children from abuse;**

* **Number and frequency of training sessions for staff/managers on how to protect children.**

   Reason for the use of these indicators: Ignorance, fear and lack of knowledge of local laws create a culture of indifference. Policies and programmes must be built on current and accurate information.

   Source(s) of data: Staff development plans, trainers, training manuals.

   Means to use the indicators: Raw data will be the beginning of a training needs analysis. Periodic review of indicators will show progress toward 100% staff and management exposure to relevant issues.

   Benchmarking: Benchmarks could be developed together with NGOs and government services that can provide training expertise and training tools. The goal is to have 100% staff trained.

Box 3.5 Child prostitution and tourism watch - (World Tourism Organization and partners). Showing leadership in the international campaign against sexual exploitation of children in tourism

In recognition of the need to engage both governments and the private sector in the international campaign against child sex tourism the WTO (**www.world-tourism.org**) child prostitution and tourism watch and partners (ECPAT, International Federation of Journalists and Terre des Hommes Germany) have implemented a series of interrelated projects funded · by the European Commission over the period 2000 - 2003. (see **www.thecode.org**) Their objective is to raise and maintain awareness of sexual exploitation of children in tourism (SECT) and improve co-operation among governments, the tourism industry, NGOs, child rights campaigners, the media and the tourists themselves. The main activities include the implementation of guidelines for focal points at national tourism administrations and local tourism destinations, the application of the Code of Conduct for the Protection of Children from Sexual Exploitation in Travel and Tourism and its six criteria for tour operators, the incorporation of training modules on SECT in curricula of tourism education centres, the improvement of knowledge about SECT among journalists and young people in Europe. The project also acknowledges the diversity of tourism stakeholders and encourages all sectors to participate including tour operators, hotels, airlines and government tourism ministries. The project succeeded in bringing the international tourism spotlight onto the exploitation of children and increasing the capacity of the travel and tourism industry to respond by providing training and information resources. Condemnation of child exploitation is also included in the WTO Global Code of Ethics for Tourism.

Indicators of overall tourism sector response:

* **Preparedness of travel and tourism business to openly condemn child sex tourism. (Number and percentage participating);**

* **Preparedness of travel and tourism business to develop and implement policies and programmes to protect children;**

* **Evidence that travel and tourism business has participated in multi-stakeholder meetings on child protection and children's rights issues.**

   Reason for the use of these indicators: Leadership is required amongst the world's travel and tourism industry to condemn child sex tourism and to encourage action at the international, regional, national and local level. Collaboration and coordination between government, private sector and NGOs is the most effective form of partnership to protect children.

Source(s) of data: Internal and external reports, NGOs, World Tourism Organisation (WTO) Focal Point reports, National Action Plans, media and public affairs reporting.

Means to use the indicators: Indicators can identify leadership in corporate responsibility and social accountability. Indicators can identify effectiveness of awareness raising activities.

Benchmarking: Benchmarks are the principles and guidelines on the protection of children by travel and tourism organizations such as International Air Transport Association (IATA), International Hotel and Restaurant Association (IH&RA), International Federation of Tour Operators (IFTO), Pacific Asia Travel Association (PATA), Universal Federation of Travel Agents Association (UFTAA) and World Tourism Organisation (WTO).

3.2 Sustaining Cultural Assets

3.2.1 Conserving Built Heritage

Cultural Sites, Monuments, Damage, Maintenance, Designation, Preservation

The first Article of the Venice Charter for the Conservation and Restoration of Monuments and Sites (1964) acknowledges that an historic monument *embraces not only the single architectural work but also the urban or rural setting in which is found the evidence of a particular civilization, a significant development or an historic event.* This applies not only to great works of art but also to more modest works of the past having acquired cultural significance with the passage of time.

The factors that individually and/or collectively determine the shape of change involving cultural assets include:

Government development policies: particularly in developing countries that are often subject to external pressures such as structural adjustment and aid disbursement;

Local politics: balancing the desire of local constituencies to create jobs and economic development versus the retention of significant built and natural resources;

Tourism: a major income generator and image-maker often dependent on cultural assets in urban areas to draw visitors;

Private initiatives: the determination of developers or individuals driven by the possibility of substantial profits to replace existing assets, with those promoting higher value and use on a site; and

Economic change: the commensurate reordering of national and international priorities during a recession, or increased building and redevelopment in "boom" times.

One of the key tools in signifying the inherent historic value of a built structure, monument or district, and as a means of garnering assistance for maintenance and financial support, is through its designation as a heritage asset worthy of conservation or preservation (designation at the local, provincial/state, national and international levels).

From a tourism standpoint, the official designation of structures or districts as sites of interest or for protection often proves invaluable in terms of establishing touchstones or themes by which an area can be marketed. Designation can attract tourists, and can also be a catalyst for development of tourist services. From an international standpoint, designation by international organizations such as UNESCO for a place to be deemed as a World Heritage Site (see *Box 3.6*), while having no actual legal standing with the conservation laws of individual countries, provides a high profile listing and marketing role for tourism development around a duly-recognized monument or historic district. Hence, governments are often eager to provide financial support (if available) and assistance to maintain these assets and ensure that tourists have iconic images (e.g., Eiffel Tower, Taj Mahal) to be drawn to their respective countries.

Components of the issue	Indicators
Legislative basis for protection	• Number and type of new legislation or amendments introduced to preserve structures at local, provincial/state/canton or national levels.
Designation	• Number and type of designation under which historic structures, monuments and districts are recognized; • Percentage of eligible sites and or structures receiving designation.
Funding for protection	• %/Amount of funds allocated to the restoration, preservation and maintenance of cultural assets on a yearly basis, (differentiated according to different sources of funding, such as visitor/entrance fees, tour operator fees, donations, government funds, private foundations, international financial and development institutions, NGOs, etc.); • Voluntary contributions (number and duration of programmes, number of volunteers, estimated value of contributions); • Tourism contribution to preservation (amount from each source).
Profile of the issue	• % change/number of electronic and print articles generated on historic structures, monuments and districts by local, regional, national and international media.
Condition of setting and environment	• %/change in the development of the surrounding area to a cultural asset, and whether maintenance or improvements have taken place; • Condition of the building or site (cost of restoration per annum).
Threats to the integrity and authenticity of the property	• Increase/Decrease in threats and their type to the original purpose and use of a site. (subjective classification); • See also ➢ **Controlling Use Intensity** (p. 192).

UNESCO's partner, the International Committee on Monuments and Sites (ICOMOS) performs an important advisory and monitoring role of global cultural sites. Programs such as the yearly *Heritage at Risk* reports are intended to identify threatened heritage places, monuments and sites, present typical case studies and trends, and share suggestions for solving individual or global threats to the cultural heritage.

World Heritage Site Visit Reports examine the elements of cultural asset presentation, interpretation, management and marketing and can be a source of information on each site.

Indicator of legal basis for protection:

* **Number and type of new legislation or amendments introduced to preserve structures at local, provincial/state/canton or national levels.**

   Reason for use of this indicator: Legislation is important as a means for governments, preservation professionals and organizations, and tourism officials to ensure that there is legal standing whenever a structure(s) is under threat. Amendments to existing instruments and new legislation (and supporting programs) will help determine to what degree maintenance and support can be requested or is required for existing structures.

Source(s) of data: An inventory of existing legislation at the local, provincial/state/canton or national levels is necessary to determine the baseline, with follow-up monitoring on a yearly basis to determine if there are any changes or additions. The level of effort can be determined by the funds and human resources available, and the level of government undertaking the inventory and monitoring.

Means to use the indicator: A listing at each level: local, provincial/state/canton or national of amendments and new legislation (or none) undertaken on a yearly basis, to demonstrate what legal efforts are being made to preserve and maintain historic structures, monument and districts.

Benchmarking: Published government data is available at appropriate scales from many destinations – particularly mature destinations in Europe.

Indicators of designation:

* **Number and type of designation under which historic structures, monuments and districts are recognized;**

* **Percentage of eligible sites and or structures receiving designation.**

Reason for use of these indicators: The number of structures that are designated officially recognizes the value of individual cultural assets within a city, province/state/canton or country and where financial and technical support can be directed.

Source(s) of data: An inventory of designated structures, monuments and districts at the local, provincial/state/canton or national levels is necessary to determine the baseline, with follow-up monitoring on a yearly basis to determine if there are any changes or additions. The level of effort can be determined by the funds and human resources available, and the level of government undertaking the inventory and monitoring.

Means to use the indicators: A listing at each level: local, provincial/state/canton or national of amendments and new designation (or none) undertaken on a yearly basis, to demonstrate what legal efforts are being made to preserve and maintain historic structures, monument and districts.

Brimstone Hill World Heritage Site, St. Kitts

Benchmarking: Published government data is available at appropriate scales from many destinations, or on a comparative basis, e.g. neighbouring countries, provinces/states/cantons, or cities.

Indicators of level of funding support for protection:

* **Amount of funds allocated to the restoration, preservation and maintenance of cultural assets on a yearly basis (differentiated according to different sources of funding, such as visitor/entrance fees, tour operator fees, donations, government funds, private foundations, international financial and development institutions, NGOs, etc.);**

* **Voluntary contributions (number and duration of programmes, number of volunteers, estimated value of contributions);**

* **Tourism contribution to preservation (amount from each source).**

Reason for use of these indicators: Funding is necessary for the maintenance and ongoing support of cultural assets. Decreases or increases in the allocation of funds may determine if a structure or monument can be restored or preserved, or conversely, eventually erodes or becomes structurally unstable. It is important to define how are funds, generated and received from different sources, used for the maintenance of the sites and monuments. Academic and research institution and their students often donate their expertise and time for restoration, preservation and maintenance work, which are important contribution to many sites where there are staff and financial limitations to deliver such tasks.

Source(s) of data: There are published sources of data from governments, finance, private and non-governmental organizations, academic and research and institutions that are involved with cultural assets. An inventory of funding at the local, provincial/state/canton or national levels is necessary to determine the baseline, with follow-up monitoring on a yearly basis to determine if there are any changes or additions. The level of effort can be determined by the funds and human resources available, and the level of government or the authority/organization managing the site in order to undertake the inventory and monitoring.

Means to use the indicators: A listing at each level: local, provincial/state/canton or national of in terms of funding and how it has been allocated can demonstrate trends, sources, and areas of concentration by funding bodies. This indicator can also be used to compare available funding to estimates of needs for restoration, maintenance etc.

Benchmarking: Published government data is available at appropriate scales from many destinations – particularly mature destinations in e.g., Europe.

Indicator of profile of the heritage preservation issue:

* **Number of electronic and print articles generated on historic structures, monuments and districts by local, regional, national and international media.**

Reason for use of this indicator: Media profiling is one of the most important ways under which NGOs, NGIs and preservation professionals can lobby governments to retain and support cultural assets. Depending upon its assessed level of significance, the issue pertaining to the historic structure, monument or district can be raised to the international level, impacting global opinion and tourism impressions.

Source(s) of data: There are several online resources whith inventory on individual topics, tourism and public information administrations, or media clipping services. Sources include the Tourism Information and Documentation Resource Centers Database (INFODOCTOUR), an online access system to libraries, documentation services, information brokers and databases related to tourism worldwide:
www.world-tourism.org/doc/E/infodoctour.htm
and CARL - the Colorado Alliance of Research Libraries: www.loc.gov/z3950/carl.html.

An inventory of media coverage at the local, provincial/state/canton or national levels is necessary to determine the baseline, with follow-up monitoring on a yearly basis to determine if there are any changes or additions. The level of effort can be determined by the funds and human resources available, and the level of government undertaking the inventory and monitoring.

Means to use the indicator: An electronic and print clipping inventory at each level: local, provincial/state/canton or national of in terms of coverage, what it was specifically targeting, and whether it could be deemed as positive or negative in its intent. This can even be used to monitor a specific issue, such as public opinion on the potential refurbishment or loss of a historic structure, monument or district.

Benchmarking: It is difficult to obtain published data of this type, but a research project could be taken over a period of time on a comparative basis, e.g. similar types of media coverage and profile in neighbouring countries or cities.

Indicators of condition of the site:

* **%/change in the development of the surrounding area to a cultural asset, and whether maintenance or improvements have taken place;**

* **Condition of the building or site (estimated cost of repair).**

Reason for use of these indicators: The senses of arrival and place are often key elements in setting the tone for visitor experience and expectations. Given the fact that sites can operate in evolving urban environments, or see development creep up to their edges, change in the surrounding environment is inevitable.

Source(s) of data: Historic maps and photos can provide a visual representation of how a cultural asset and its environs may have originally appeared. These can be supported by cadastral maps and aerial surveys. On a qualitative basis, accounts and reports over time can provide a historical perspective on the change that has taken place. Site managers will often have studies which estimate costs of restoration or repair.

Means to use the indicators: A baseline map or model can be employed, demonstrating the original condition of a site and its surroundings, with mapping layers or different coloured buildings demonstrating over time what has been added or lost in terms of structures, urban infrastructure, and interpretive elements and embellishments. There are a number of excellent Geographic Information System (GIS) and visual modeling software packages which could be helpful in this regard.

Benchmarking: It can be difficult to obtain published data of this type, but a research project could be taken over a period of time to identify past state and stresses from published sources (maps, reports) and re-create measures of change.

Indicator of level of threat to the cultural assets of a site or property:

* **Increase/decrease in threats to the original purpose and use of a site.**

Reason for use of this indicator: Processes such as adaptive reuse may assist with the retention of a historic structure, but the choice of colours, additions, "improvements" and use can compromise the heritage value of the site. Simultaneously, in developing countries, where land can be scarce, cultural assets can be carved into to subdivide a building lot, be overpopulated and overused, or be steadily weakened due the removal of structural materials to be used for building purposes elsewhere. This is a subjective indicator and may require establishment of a site specific scale.

Source(s) of data: Historic maps and photos can provide a visual representation of how a cultural asset may have originally appeared. These can be supported by internal site plans, available from archives at the national, provincial/state/canton, or municipal level, identifying the original external appearance and internal layout of individual structures. The process would be both quantitative and qualitative: tallying the amount of changes that have taken place applying the former, and determining on a subjective basis how these changes have affected the buildings use and heritage character with the latter.

Means to use the indicator: Photographic morphing over time can demonstrate the change of use and condition of a cultural asset and can demonstrate how far a site or collection of structures has evolved or distanced itself from its original purpose and use.

Benchmarking: Where available, archives, local history departments and public libraries or museums can prove useful in providing the necessary photographic records to compare the past with the present and show the evolution in between. Where this is not available this process will be more difficult. There is no common international standard against which a given site can be benchmarked.

Note: See also the Destinations section on Built Heritage Sites (p. 278)

Rila Monastery World Heritage Site, Bulgaria

Box 3.6 UNESCO: Indicators on protecting the world's heritage

Angkor. Timbuktu. Everglades National Park. These names represent unique, high profile destinations whose valued cultural and natural status has caused them to be nominated and then named as World Heritage Sites by UNESCO. They are also unfortunately marked with the status of "World Heritage in Danger", acknowledging the fact that they are threatened by man-made or natural hazards. Countries often depend on their iconic World Heritage sites to anchor their national tourism marketing efforts; any indication of these significant cultural and natural destinations not being well maintained or managed can tarnish those efforts.

As of July 2003, there are 754 properties that the World Heritage Committee has inscribed on the World Heritage List (582 cultural, 149 natural and 23 mixed properties in 129 States Parties). Sites are either nominated or selected applying the natural criteria: sites which are of outstanding universal value from point of view of science, conservation or natural beauty, or the cultural criteria: sites which are of outstanding universal value from the point of view of history, art or science. The key indicators are:

* Uniqueness;

* Outstanding example of a genre or style (i.e. cultural value represented by architecture or traditional human settlement, and natural examples of unique biodiversity or significant on-going biological and ecological evolution); and

* Representative of a specific era in human or natural history.

Once a site has been named as a place of international value, it is assumed that World Heritage status will act as some kind of protective armour against predation or degradation. The reality is that conflict, political and economic decisions, neglect, natural disasters and the eroding effects of time are hindering the ongoing existence of a site's cultural or natural resource base. Recognizing this reality, the World Heritage Convention included a significant clause on "World Heritage in Danger" to characterize this designation and recommend steps for action. Consequently, there are currently 35 sites around the globe that have this designation (17 cultural, 18 natural).

UNESCO's main indicators which are monitored and can lead to inclusion on the "World Heritage in Danger" list include threats to sites from:

* Disappearance caused by accelerated deterioration, large- scale public or private projects or rapid urban or tourist development projects;

* Destruction caused by changes in the use or ownership of the land;

* Major alterations due to unknown causes;

* Abandonment for any reason whatsoever;

* The outbreak or the threat of an armed conflict; or

* Calamities and cataclysms such as serious fires, earthquakes, landslides; volcanic eruptions; changes in water level, floods and tidal waves.

The World Heritage Committee can make nominations for this endangered status at any time, in case of urgent need. The nominated site is then included as a new entry in the List of "World Heritage in Danger" and publicized immediately, to focus global awareness and support on the threat. The World Heritage Committee can then develop and adopt, in consultation with the State Party concerned, a programme for corrective measures, and the subsequent monitoring of the site's situation. Countries which do not improve the situation of these sites can then potentially have them delisted as a World Heritage site.

Box 3.6 (cont.)

Removal from the "World Heritage in Danger" list has occurred in the past when State Parties have carried out remedial actions. Indicators on these actions include:

- Outside assistance and funding obtained to repair sites;

- Concessions made to divert threats such as pollution prevention or the creation of buffer zones;

- Mechanisms installed, such as dehumidifiers or light shielding, to slow or remove degradation factors of monuments;

- Protective legislation enacted and enforced;

- Conflict ceased.

Source: UNESCO World Heritage Centre http://www.unesco.org/whc

3.3 Community Participation in Tourism

3.3.1 Community Involvement and Awareness

Information, Empowerment, Participation, Community action

The development of a sense of ownership and responsibility regarding sustainable tourism in host communities is a key issue for managers and planners. Neither of these elements is easily achieved in the short term without a strong focus on awareness building, engagement of community and ultimately, empowerment of the individual so he or she can recognise and understand the direct and indirect benefits of a sustainable approach to tourism and how to become involved. The key is a participatory approach which empowers the local community and the tourism industry so they can develop an appreciation and knowledge regarding local and individual issues and costs associated with developing tourism. That way the awareness and responsibility can be an outcome of the planning process.

Box 3.7 Building ownership: Kangaroo Island TOMM, Australia

The creation of a Tourism Optimisation Management Model (TOMM) for Kangaroo Island provided a focal point for the issue of sustainable tourism development. The Island has long been a major tourist attraction due to its abundance of wildlife and spectacular scenery.

The TOMM process provided a platform on which to begin an awareness raising campaign regarding the issues associated with sustainable tourism development and specifically, promote the TOMM and the availability of information it generated on tourism impacts on Kangaroo Island. The long term aim of this process was to generate a sense of ownership of the future of tourism on the Island.

Through the TOMM resident survey, (see Kangaroo Island TOMM case p. 391) indicator data has been collected on the local community knowledge of TOMM and what it is aiming to achieve. This has steadily increased since the inception of the project. Similarly, through success in tourism awards and ongoing promotion of the Model through the tourism industry, its application elsewhere is now generating a sense of pride amongst community members.

There is a need for a continuous engagement of local community stakeholders, through a series of actions, in order to develop responsibility in sustainable tourism development. Besides local stakeholders (See Box 2.2 regarding indicators development procedures) there are a number of other agencies that can have an influence on local decision making, e.g. national government authorities and educational institutions, tour operators (outgoing and incoming), transportation and other tourism-related companies serving the destination, the media, the tourist market and the tourists themselves.

Building awareness regarding sustainable tourism practice requires a strategic approach if long term attitudinal change and engagement is to be achieved. The challenge is how to quantify such change given its intangible nature. Information is the key for effective community involvement in tourism planning processes. The following aspects are considered essential for informed decision-making:

1. *Availability of information:* If people are aware of information relating to sustainable tourism practice or a specific management model, they will be more likely to try to gain access to it;

2. *Access to information:* Making it as easy as possible for people to gain access to generic information will ensure a greater sense of interest in the process;

3. *Analysis of information:* The information available has to be presented in a variety of forms depending upon the audience and in languages that are easily understood and relevant;

4. *Application of information:* Understanding how the information on sustainable tourism is used by communities and agencies ensures it can be relevant. This element also identifies the potential for ongoing education and training so understanding is improved;

5. *Advocacy of information:* The aim of any ownership is the advocacy that is generated amongst stakeholders. Having passionate people within the community that can pro-actively sustain the management process is essential; as they have the potential to not only inspire others, but feed back into the awareness building process due to their contact with the broader stakeholder groups;

6. *Action on the information:* The awareness of and desire to make a difference – requires action if any results are to be achieved. Those promoting sustainable tourism practice intend ultimately to have an impact upon the actual behaviour of both visitors and stakeholders in sustaining the tourism asset and community / environmental resource. Through building awareness, a sense of responsibility leading to greater understanding and ultimately action, individuals can begin to make a difference in the development of sustainable tourism practice. These lead to a number of indicators to measure the level of access, impact and engagement:

Components of the issue	Indicators
Availability of information	• Number and types of avenues/channels used to promote sustainable tourism (e.g. audiovisual and printed media, events, Internet); • Number of places in the destination where information is available.
Access to information (per type of information)	• Number /% of people accessing information; • Frequency of access (per person).
Analysis of information	• % of people that have a clear understanding of the role of sustainable tourism planning (e.g. a Model such as TOMM or what sustainable tourism means).

Components of the issue	Indicators
Application of information	• Number of times information on sustainable tourism is used within the broader community context; • Number of agencies applying information on sustainability aspects to their strategic planning processes; • Degree to which the community is satisfied with the quality and quantity of information it receives re tourism issues and sustainability (% who approve); • Percentage of partners and key stakeholders who are satisfied with access to appropriate information; • Percentage who agree that the right information on sustainable tourism is available to me when I need it. (local questionnaire).
Advocacy of information	• Number of promotional opportunities relating to sustainable tourism practice; • Number of tourism operators offering information on sustainable tourism practice (both general and for a specific planning process like TOMM where it is in place); • % of visitors receiving information on sustainable tourism practices provided prior to their visit to the destination and at the destination.
Action/impact of the information	**Accessibility of information** • Number (%) of tourism operators providing interpretation on sustainable tourism practice; • Number (%) of tour companies in destination offering tours/guides with trained knowledge of sustainable tourism practice / information on local management plan; • Number of educational programmes / institutions incorporating sustainable tourism learning into curriculum; • Number (%) of self guided opportunities that educate regarding sustainable tourism practice. **Level of demonstration of good practice** • % of agencies incorporating sustainable tourism principles in to their strategic planning processes; • Number (%) of tourism industry operators applying sustainable tourism concepts within their business; • Number of operators certified by an environmental or sustainability scheme (and % of all eligible). **Impact of tourism information** • % of residents with an understanding of what constitutes sustainable tourism practice; • Number (%) of residents who support sustainable tourism for their destination (see also questions on specific elements in questionnaire Annex C 6); • Number of registered/reported incidents in respect to accepted codes of good practice (where in place); • % of residents who believe tourism is good for their community. (see Questionnaire Annex C 6); • % who believe that they or their family benefit from tourism.; • % actively participating in outreach/advocacy; • % who believe that they understand tourism and its impacts.

Because the sources and uses for most of these indicators are similar, to avoid duplication all of the components of the issue are treated together below.

Indicators of community involvement and awareness: (See table above)

Reason for use of these indicators: The degree of involvement of the community, and their attitude towards tourism, the planning and management of tourism in their destination and the impact on the community itself is a central part of sustainability – particularly in the eyes of the residents. These indicators help community leaders understand the level to which the community is engaged, whether the information they receive is appropriate, and whether it is affecting their attitudes and behaviour.

Sources of these data: Data would be available from resident surveys, through ongoing media monitoring, access to educational institutions, particularly local schools which can use the sustainable tourism information and materials provided in curriculum programmes and local authorities using information within the strategic planning process. Local authorities which produce information will normally have some record of numbers of brochures, leaflets, other outreach materials printed, distributed, sold, etc, although use levels (by tourists or locals) may be harder to obtain. (See also Image and Branding p. 236).

Means to use the indicators: Indicators showing successes are an important element in enthusing and motivating local communities regarding the benefits of sustainable tourism practice. They are used to determine the level of engagement and understanding of sustainable tourism practices by operators as well as the implementation of these in their operations. These indicators can be used as a performance measure for efforts to increase confidence in the process of sustainable tourism management. Results can feed back into the awareness building process and inform on opportunities to improve communication systems. Improvements in levels of involvement of the community may be leading indicators of either growing levels of concern, or the opposite, growing interest in participating in something seen as positive. These indicators are particularly useful for community leaders and agencies involved in sustainable tourism management, as they can be used as indicators for funding applications, strategic planning and communication and demonstrate community involvement or commitment. See also the section on ➤ **Local Satisfaction with Tourism** (p. 56).

Benchmarking: Due to the specific nature of each community and awareness building process, comparisons with previous year's data visitor and resident surveys will most effectively demonstrate changes. (See Local questionnaire, Annex C).

3.4 Tourist Satisfaction

3.4.1 Sustaining Tourist Satisfaction ➤ Baseline Issue

Expectations, Complaints, Problems, Perceptions

Tourist satisfaction is central to whether tourists return, recommend the destination to others or conversely advise others to stay away. It is therefore a leading indicator of the longer-term sustainability of a destination. Tourist satisfaction is based on many different factors, including the range of attractions of a destination, its market positioning, the quality of services, the expectations of tourists, and the experiences of each tourist during his/her stay. Many of the elements which affect tourist satisfaction (e.g., cleanliness of accommodation, water and food safety, friendliness of hospitality) are at least in part within the management purview of the industry and destination managers. Others (e.g., weather, crime, acts of hostility) are less so.

Satisfaction is the product of a number of factors:

1.   Meeting tourists' expectations;

2.   Providing a sense of good value for money;

3.   Ensuring a clean, safe and secure environment;

4.   Hospitality;

5.   Quality of sites, events, attractions and services related to them;

6.   Expectations and interests. Many individual responses depend on personal interests (did the birdwatcher see birds, did the skier have good snow conditions, was the local festival interesting to the visitor, was the food to the taste of the tourist?).

Many of these can be explicitly addressed in an exit questionnaire, tailored to the needs of the destination (for model Exit questionnaire see Annex C 5).

Components of the issue	Indicators
Determining whether tourists were satisfied upon leaving	<ul><li>Level of satisfaction by visitors on exit (Q) (including specific question re key activities and attractions) ≫ **Baseline Indicator**;</li><li>Perception of value for money ≫ **Baseline Indicator**;</li><li>Complaints received.</li></ul>
Measuring the impact of satisfaction levels on the industry and destination	<ul><li>% of return visitors ≫ **Baseline Indicator**;</li><li>Changes in average price paid per room;</li><li>Complaints registered;</li><li>Ratings by guidebooks/travel sites;</li><li>(See also – Image and Branding p. 236).</li></ul>

Indicators of tourist satisfaction ≫ Baseline issue

*   **Level of satisfaction expressed on exit questionnaire;** ≫ Baseline Indicator

*   **Perception of value for money**. ≫ Baseline Indicator

Because satisfaction is so individual, the core indicators suggested for measurement of satisfaction are based on direct sampling of exiting tourists. (See: Sample exit questionnaire Annex C 5).

The central queries which address this issue are: (respondents are asked if they strongly agree, agree, are neutral, disagree or strongly disagree to these statements).

1.   *I enjoyed my experience in "this destination";*

2.   *"This destination" provided a good variety of experiences;*

3.   *I feel I received good value for money;*

4.   *I would recommend "this destination" to my friends.*

In case of negative answers, the reasons for the opinion can be asked. This could point to specific causes of dissatisfaction, in order to take specific corrective action. In addition, the questionnaire provides a number of examples of questions regarding specific attractions/sites within the destination or experiences which can be used to determine why the respondent answered as they did. This approach is used to attempt not only to measure satisfaction or dissatisfaction (those who would recommend it to their friends was down 15% this year from last year... I wonder why?), but also to act as an early warning of emerging problems or issues which have caused changes in satisfaction levels.

Questionnaires can be conducted at exit points of transport (e.g. airports, ferries), upon leaving at specific sites and attractions, in hotels. This work can be done by local tourism authorities, transportation companies, hotel management and tour operators. Help can be sought from schools and researchers (e.g. tourism students doing practical course work, summer students).Often the best sites are at places where and when tourists are gathered, particularly if they are waiting in an airport or ferry lounge or in line for ferries. (On longer ferry rides, it may be useful to do the sampling on board). Some logistical advice on approach, sampling, timing etc is provided in Annex C 5 Exit Questionnaire. If a questionnaire is too long, many will be reluctant to respond, so questionnaire structuring has to be done carefully, according to the survey conditions and targeted tourists.

The following indicators are also of use in addressing satisfaction, but tend to provide less direct measurement than the questionnaire.

Indicator regarding impact of satisfaction:

*   **% of return visitors** ➤ **Baseline indicator**

Reason for use of this indicator: The percentage of tourists who return is a strong indicator that they were happy with their experience in previous visits. The indicator is unique to any particular destination because of the differing mix of attractions, the distance visitors must travel from their homes to the destination, and the nature of competing or intervening opportunities. Change in percentage who return signals changes which may be important, particularly if paralleled with more or diminished tourism overall. Other questionnaire data may be useful to help interpret the meaning of such changes.

Source(s) of data: Some tourism authorities collect this information – usually through existing exit surveys or via providers of accommodation. These data can also be collected via a specific questionnaire.   .

Means to use the indicator: This indicator is best portrayed as a percentage – and monitored for changes from year to year. It is also useful to sub-divide figures by different tourist segments (e.g. domestic visitors, international visitors from different countries and regions, independent travellers, package tourists etc.)

Benchmarking: While some comparison with other destinations is possible, the most significant information is likely to be obtained by comparison with other years for the same destination.   At the level of the individual hotel or resort, examples exist where over 80% of guests are returnees, especially if the hotel caters for tourists travelling shorter distances or from the same region or country, whereas some more remote, exclusive, or long haul destinations (e.g. some islands of the South-Pacific or Antarctic) can be a predominantly one-time visit for many tourists.

Indicator measuring levels of dissatisfaction:

*   **Complaints received.**

Many tourism authorities and establishments keep lists or books of complaints or document numbers and specific complaints received. Where it is not possible to collect information directly from tourists, using a complete survey or random sample, this can be an alternative. Complaints are likely to identify a strong negative response to some facet of the experience or the destination. Rising numbers of complaints may highlight potential issues, but are often not representative of the majority of tourists who may not share these concerns.

Reason for use of this indicator: Complaints are a source of information about negative experiences and lack of satisfaction.

Source(s) of data: Complaint books in tourist offices, accommodation, restaurants, at sites and attractions or other service providers (e.g. transportation, guides). Note that the data may be influenced by the accessibility of the complaint book, hours of operation, level of knowledge that there is a place to register complaints, and also cultural factors relating to relationship to authorities and therefore willingness to complain. Another factor is company policy or willingness of tourism establishment to share information on complaints.

Complaints registered with outbound and inbound tour operators (travellers may wait until they return home to complain) can be also a useful source. This may be difficult to obtain in situations where there is not a group of operators with continuing linkage to the destination and destination authorities.

Means to use the indicator: This can be an early warning that there may be emerging issues but is not in itself a strong indicator of importance or representativeness. Complaints can be classified and weighted according to topics, especially if there are repeated complaints on the same feature.

Benchmarking: Because of the unique conditions of each destination and its clientele, this indicator is best compared with the same information over time for the same destination or for nearby destinations where the same complaint process is followed.

Other potentially useful indicators related to satisfaction levels or perception of the levels of satisfaction of others who have visited the destination:

*   **Changes in average price paid per room** (may show that the destination has had to cut prices to retain visitors, or raise prices to take advantage of growing demand and high satisfaction levels. Use along with occupancy figures);

*   **Ratings by guidebooks/travel sites** (particularly where there is ranking relative to competitors on quality or popularity (e.g., National Geographic Traveller, Conde Nast, Michelin, lists of "ten best", "ten worst" etc.);

*   **See also – Image and Branding** (p. 236).

Kootenay Lake, Canada. Ferry ride offers a 30 minute opportunity to survey visitors and in season to query those waiting in line.

3.4.2 Accessibility

Mobility, Older Tourists, Persons with Disabilities

The issue of access to destinations and attractions for those with impaired mobility is a rapidly growing concern, as older persons and those with disabilities become a larger part of global tourism. One of the most rapidly growing demographics is the sixty and over group, many having more time and discretionary income than other groups. Thus demands for access, even to places which have not been easy to climb or traverse, are growing. An international effort to remove barriers to those with disabilities is reinforcing this demand.

Many countries have specific programs designed to ease access to public sites and to encourage the modification of access points, washrooms, stairs, transportation vehicles, rough paths etc to facilitate access for those who are less able to cope with barriers. There is an emerging subset of tourism providers who cater directly to those who need additional services (some custom delivered) – such as door to door pickup, special vehicles, and trained attendants, or tours designed to not include inappropriate sites or accommodation for those with mobility impairments (e.g., stop at the viewpoint where the scenery is visible from the vehicle rather than one which requires a hike up a path).

The WTO defined guidelines to facilitate tourism for peoples with disabilities as early as 1991 (see WTO General Assembly resolution "Creating opportunities for handicapped people in the Nineties": This document is available on line at http://www.world-tourism.org/quality/E/docs/std%2Bhlh/ handiang.pdf). Indicators can be established relative to access itself, and relative to measures taken to include provisions for disabled tourists in tourism information and publicity, preparation of staff, facilities and infrastructure.

Porters carry elderly tourist along ice covered stairs en route to his hotel at the top of Huang Shan, one of China's most famous tourist sites.

Components of the issue	Indicators
Access throughout the destination	• Existence of disabled friendly policy; • Existence of disabled access program including e.g., airports, piers, bus stations, sidewalks, public washroom facilities (% meeting standards); • Existence of public transport suitable for mobility of persons with disabilities (#//% transport vehicles); • Number of tour companies in destination offering tours/guides trained for persons with disabilities.
Access to public buildings, hotels and tourist services	• Number/% of hotels with rooms accessible to persons with disabilities (easy access, bathrooms that accommodate wheelchairs, safety bars etc.); • Number(%)of access doors to buildings which have automated openers or attendants on the door; • % restaurants, hotels and public buildings with wheelchair accessible restrooms (level entry, larger stalls, lower sinks, safety bars etc.)
Access to tourist attractions, including natural and cultural sites, viewpoints, (including some which have traditionally been accessible only to the fit)	• % of attractions with wheelchair access; • % of attractions offering alternative access for those with mobility concerns (e.g. drop off points, elevators, ramps or walkways accessible to mobility assist devices).
Access to tourist experiences, including adventure travel Access to suitable tours, which match the capabilities of the traveller	• Number of tours to destination with specific program to accommodate persons with disabilities; • Number of persons with disabilities visiting destination and key sites; • % of key sites considered accessible or inaccessible for those with differing levels of mobility or fitness.
Assistance when needed (including specialized assistance for those with disabilities such as blindness, deafness, mobility restrictions, or with need for nursing and other care)	• Distance to nearest hospital (Km) or medical facility (Estimated time to nearest medical assistance – whether ambulance, paramedic, hospital, heli-evacuation); • (for longer tours/cruises) Presence of medical personnel; • (for tours catering to persons with disabilities) percentage of staff with medical or paramedical training suitable to the range of needs of clients.
Satisfaction by those with disabilities with the destination or attraction	• See exit questionnaire (the same questionnaire can be provided explicitly to groups of travellers with disabilities to identify their concerns).

Indicators of general accessibility:

⊛ **Existence of disabled-friendly policy;**

⊛ **Existence of disabled access program including e.g. airports, piers, bus stations, sidewalks, restaurants, public washroom facilities (% meeting or exceeding standards);**

* **Existence of public transport suitable for mobility impaired (number of or % transport vehicles);**

* **Number of tour companies in destination offering tours/guides trained for persons with disabilities.**

   Reason for use of these indicators: Some destinations can be considered friendly to those who have mobility constraints while others can have significant barriers.

   Source(s) of data: These data are normally available from local authorities, particularly where there is a program in place to enhance access. Where there is no program, it may be necessary to do an on–site survey, to collect from public offices, individual companies and establishments.

   Means to use the indicators: These indicators can be used as a performance measure for efforts to increase accessibility for the destination as a whole. Positive results can feed marketing of the destination or tour as friendly to those with disabilities.

   Benchmarking: For examples of destinations with accessibility programs for persons with disabilities search for "travel, persons with disabilities" or "travel, handicapped access" on the internet. Destinations such as the US states of Minnesota and Virginia, Vancouver, Canada, and Venice, Italy have websites explicitly designed to showcase their ease of access, some with specific indicators. The website of The Society for Accessible Travel and Hospitality links to standards and some indicators on this topic is http://www.sath.org/ . See also ➤ **Tourist Satisfaction** p. 86.

Indicators of access to tourist accommodation and public buildings:

* **Number and % of hotels with rooms accessible to persons with disabilities (easy access, bathrooms which will accommodate wheelchairs, safety bars);**

* **% of access doors to buildings which have automated openers;**

* **% restaurants, hotels and public buildings with wheelchair accessible restrooms (level entry, larger stalls, lower sinks, safety bars etc.)**

   Reason for use of these indicators: Access to restroom facilities, accommodation and food services is a key factor in every vacation and may be a prime concern for travellers with disabilities.

   Source(s) of data: Where an accessibility program exists, these data will normally be collected. Building authorities may also have the information. Where no program exists, data may have to be obtained through a survey of establishments or through hotel or restaurant associations.

   Means to use the indicators: These data can be used to show progress in accessibility and to advertise the range of accessible properties.

   Benchmarking: Many destinations have set a target of 100% accessibility for persons with disabilities to public facilities, hotels and restaurants.

Indicators of access to tourist attractions, including natural and cultural sites and viewpoints:

* **% of attractions with wheelchair access;**

* **% of attractions offering alternative access for those with mobility concerns (e.g. drop off points, elevators, ramps or walkways able to accommodate mobility assist devices, sedan chairs, carts or wagons pulled by animals, motorized carts etc.)**

   Reason for use of these indicators: The attractions are the reason for visits. Older and other less mobile tourists desire access. This demand may extend to visits to some sites that have traditionally been accessible only to the very fit.

   Source(s) of data: These data are likely to be kept by tourism or planning authorities and at a site level by attraction or park managers.

Means to use the indicators: These data can be used to show progress in accessibility and to advertise the range of accessible attractions.

Benchmarking: Many national park authorities and attraction managers have set goals of 100% accessibility to popular sites. Standards for access to less popular and more remote sites are not generally available.

Indicators of access to travel experiences:

* **Number of tours to the destination with specific programs to accommodate persons with disabilities;**
* **Number of persons with disabilities visiting destination and key sites;**
* **% of key sites considered accessible/inaccessible for those with different levels of mobility or fitness.**

Reason for use of these indicators: Persons with disabilities are a growing segment of the tourism market, including demands for soft adventure travel and access to suitable tours that match the capabilities of the traveller. Some destinations are now targeting persons with disabilities as potential visitors and investing in the facilities and products to serve their needs.

Source(s) of data: Data may be kept by local tourism authorities, particularly where there is an accessibility program in the destination.

Means to use the indicators: These data can be used to show progress in accessibility and to advertise the range of accessible attractions and the success in serving persons with disabilities.

Benchmarking: There is no specific Source(s) of data to benchmark these indicators. Use of the indicators may produce benchmarks for future use or comparison.

Indicators of availability of assistance when needed:

* **Distance to nearest hospital or medical facility(Km)** (or estimated time to nearest medical assistance –ambulance, paramedic, hospital, helicopter evacuation);
* **Presence of trained medical personnel** (number per 100 tourists) (particularly for longer tours or cruises);
* **% staff with medical or paramedical training suitable to the range of needs of clients** (particularly tours or establishments catering to persons with disabilities).

Reason for use of these indicators: Persons may require assistance to deal with disabilities such as blindness, deafness, and mobility restrictions. Some may have specific medical requirements or needs for nursing and other care. Some tourism destinations are remote, tours may travel to sites many hours or even days from medical facilities. As with other tourists, illness or accidents can occur while travelling.

Source(s) of data: Tourism authority or tour company.

Means to use the indicators: Used to assure tourists that suitable assistance is available. Use of the indicators may also reveal gaps which need to be filled.

Benchmarking: Most jurisdictions have their own standards for health care access. These vary greatly among countries and even regions within countries. See WHO website for further information (also see Health issue p. 94).

A local community project provides wheelchair accessible walkways through Purdon Orchid Reserve, Lanark County Ontario, Canada.

3.5 Health and Safety

3.5.1 Health

Public Health, Community Health, Food Safety, Worker Health and Safety

This section deals specifically with health aspects of safety at the destination (not including air travel). Health issues have always been crucial to international travel and are clearly among the most important determining factors of a sense of safety. Managing health issues in tourism is an important consideration with several dimensions: the traveller, the industry and the local community. It can be approached from preventive and curative perspectives dealing with illness, accidents and other health related problems. From the perspective of the tourist there are a range of health and safety factors involved in travel. This section deals specifically with health and safety at the destination. Many physical and environmental changes are encountered during travel, especially international travel, which upset the equilibrium of our 'normal' environment – seasonal and climatic changes; changes to air and water quality; exposure to changes in altitude, humidity, micro flora, temperature and time zones all create stress on our bodies than can result in illness, particularly in combination with the fatigue often associated with travel itself or with chronic health problems.

Additional risks associated with travel are determined by key factors which include: the destination; length of stay; nature of activities undertaken; standards of accommodation and food hygiene; behaviour of the traveller (relating to sex, alcohol, drugs, crime and modes of transport at the destination such as hitchhiking), together with the health status, gender, age and experience of the traveller. The most common problems are accidents, heart problems, food poisoning and diarrhoea, and malaria. Additional to the well known problems are serious emerging health threats. In the past year SARS (Severe Acute Respiratory Syndrome Box 3.10) and now the Avian 'bird' influenza are causing high levels of concern amongst travellers, the industry and health authorities. (See: Epidemics and International Transmission of Diseases p. 101).

In destinations where accommodation, hygiene, sanitation, medical care and water quality are of a high standard, risks are reduced considerably. However, common health and safety problems still frequently occur in relation to excess exposure to sun; insect bites; excess alcohol consumption; swimming, especially in the surf; and accidents related to cars and motor bikes and adventure activities. Visitors have a clear responsibility for their own safety, including taking precautions such as immunization, carrying their own health supplies (including condoms, insect repellent, sun block, anti-malarial drugs, etc.) and comprehensive travel insurance.

Many problems relate to collecting data for illness, accidents and crime. Most cases go unreported, often because they are minor in nature and treatment is not required, or self treatment is adequate. Additionally, illness may occur after the visitor has returned home, or, they may prefer to visit their own general physician on their return. With the increase in telemedicine, some more serious cases may be dealt with using non local services. Therefore even the best reporting mechanisms will give only a hint at the issues. Equally, the success of health promotion and preventive measures are even more difficult to assess; the absence or reduction of problems being the main indicator. The World Health Organization and the Center for Disease Control in Atlanta USA collate notifiable data globally. Equally important is the impact of tourism on the health, safety, well being and quality of life of local people. Visitors and the tourist industry can negatively affect local populations (e.g. transmit diseases, modify traditional cuisine and habits such as less healthy food, fast food, contribute to reduction of arable land which may elevate-risk of malnutrition, increased discharge of sewage waste resulting contamination of water). On the other hand, if well planned and managed, tourism can make a useful contribution to health and wellbeing of those working in the industry (e.g., teach food hygiene and help improve health standards) and of local people (e.g. introduce and contribute to construction of sanitation infrastructure, hospitals, medical treatment, safe drinking water, etc.)

The WTO policy on health in tourism is defined in the instrument Health Information and Formalities in International Travel (Tourist health information, Health insurance and assistance in International Travel, Health Formalities and Vaccinations), adopted by a General Assembly resolution (A/RES/310(X), Bali, Indonesia, 4-8 October 1993), modified in 1996 in consultation with the World Health Organization, and currently (2004) under revision to provide for consistency with the new International Health Regulations (IHR, 2005).

From the industry perspective there are a range of issues relating to regulatory responsibility; insurance and indemnity; and loss of business and reputation. Health issues involve tourism industry personnel from various sectors before visitors leave home, during their travel and at their destination, which are at the focus of this section.

Indicators related to visitor death and illnesses

Components of the issue	Indicators
Visitor health and safety	• Number of illnes and death cases of tourists and the cause; • Number of visits by tourists to local doctors; • Reports of food poisoning; • Types of tourism operations involved in cases/outbreaks of food poisoning (number); • Reports of communicable diseases.
Visitor health and safety: Prevention, regulations	• % of food handlers receiving food hygiene training (including hotels, restaurants, take away and street vendors); • % of commercial food outlets (as above) with adequate temperature control for commercial food storage; • Food hygiene standards and regulations in place and monitored (% of establishments monitored, number per month and adequate reporting of findings); • Incidence of breaches of regulations; • Provision of awareness campaigns for food regulations and support to owners of food service operations (extent, measurement of effectiveness through increased compliance); • Adequate cleaning procedures (% of enterprises - accommodation and food outlets with staff training and detailed procedures that meet public health requirements); • % of commercial food outlets including street vendors with provision of adequate hand washing facilities for food handlers (number of violations); • Routine pest control (% of food and accommodation businesses with a pest management plan); • Water quality (See Baseline issue ≫ **Drinking Water Quality** p. 169); • % of tourism businesses included in local tourist guide information complying with all relevant indicators above.

Reason for use of these indicators: According to the World Health Organisation, the most common illness associated with travel is food poisoning, accounting for 30 – 80% of morbidity. As many as 75% of short-term travellers to tropical and sub tropical areas report some kind of problem; less than 5% need medical attention. Malaria and sexually transmitted infections (including HIV) are an increasing problem. Promiscuous behaviour with fellow travellers and locals is increasing, often unprotected/unsafe sex. Infectious diseases account for very few deaths (<1%). Cardio vascular disease in the elderly accounts for some 50% of deaths.

While many health risks are the responsibility of the individual, the level of sanitation, food hygiene, water quality are often defined by central authorities and control over these are the responsibility of the destination. Regular auditing, staff training and development, the production of publications, health warnings and the promotion of tourist health resources are all essential to protect the visitor and the industry.

Source(s) of data: Records from hospitals, doctors, health clinics, accommodation providers with health services; trauma and emergency units; epidemiology reports (including WHO's Weekly Epidemiological Record). Illnesses could be self reported through exit visitor surveys at airports.

Means to use the indicators: Trends over time; percentages of deaths and illnesses compared to total numbers of visitors; age group and gender with highest rates of illness; types of businesses and activities with which highest incidence occurs; seasonal variations. Use to inform level of training required and to develop strategies including visitor safety information; implement better reporting procedures amongst local health professionals; greater collaboration between tourism industry, health departments and local government health and building inspectors.

Benchmarking: Given the unreliable nature of data on traveller illness benchmarks are not available. Look for changes over time. The World Health Organisation and the Centre for Disease Control in Atlanta, USA collate notifiable data globally.

Indicators related to visitor accidents

Components of the issue	Indicators
Accidents	• Number of reported accidents involving tourists and their causes; • Number of publications for visitors with health and safety warnings (% of businesses who actively distribute these and number distributed); • % of facilities with adequate safety signage; • % Staff in tourism businesses with first aid training; • % establishments with Occupational Health and Safety (OHS) programs standards and regulations in place and monitored; • % of tourism businesses with a risk management plan; • Frequency of monitoring or regular checking of OH&S measures and risk management plans; • Number of licenses and permits for tourism businesses requiring a risk management plan; • Frequency of staff training on safety procedures; • % of establishments with training programs; • % with formal monitoring of safety procedures/equipment; • % of businesses in government endorsed/produced tourist brochures with good safety procedures, training and equipment.

Reason for use of these indicators: Accidents and trauma account for around 25% of mortality in overseas travellers, and at a rate of 2 – 3 times higher for 15 – 44 year olds compared to rates at home. Fatalities are most commonly due to traffic or swimming accidents, with alcohol frequently a contributing factor. Accidents are the most common form of health problem for travellers. The industry and individual operators need to ensure appropriate training, standards, facilities, monitoring are routinely maintained.

Source(s) of data: Records from hospitals, doctors, health clinics, accommodation providers with health services, trauma and emergency units, car and bike hire businesses, insurance companies, beach patrol/life saving reports.

Accidents could be self reported through exit visitor surveys at airports.

Means to use the indicators: Trends over time; percentages of accidents compared to total numbers of visitors; age group and gender with highest rates of trauma; activities with which highest incidence occurs.

Benchmarking: Given the unreliable nature of statistics, benchmarks are not available.

Look for changes in the indicator over time. Use to inform level of training required, frequency of monitoring of safety procedures, emergency response and to develop strategies including visitor safety information; implement better reporting procedures amongst local tourism and health professionals.

Indicators related to community health and safety

Components of the issue	Indicators
General community health and safety	<ul><li>% of tourism businesses with effective effluent treatment (see ➢ **Sewage** p. 171);</li><li>Frequency of monitoring and compliance of effluent treatment with public health legislation;</li><li>Volume of waste disposal and run off from tourism businesses (% of businesses decreasing the volume of waste per customer);</li><li>% arriving international visitors reviewed for health issues – with appropriate quarantine procedures if needed;</li><li>% of local staff working in the tourism industry receiving development and training programs on personal hygiene;</li><li>Evidence of tourism training outcomes on hygiene being taken to the home or village setting;</li><li>Existence of collaboration with public health/ promotion units to reinforce health messages (level of effort and successes).</li></ul>
Access to health care	<ul><li>% of local tourism sector employees receiving free/subsidised health checkups and clinics for staff and family members;</li><li>% of employees with employer sponsored comprehensive health insurance.</li></ul>
Malnutrition	<ul><li>Level of protection of water for irrigation of food crops and food processing;</li><li>% of tourism businesses supporting local agriculture and aquaculture to maintain fresh supply of accessible local foods, especially protein foods (% buying locally; % using local foods in menus and souvenir stores);</li><li>Number /% of employees in hospitality and food service sectors provided with nutrition education;</li><li>% of employees in tourism establishments with access to healthy in house food services (canteens, cafeterias);</li><li>Level of malnutrition in hotel employees (relationship to overall level in community) (health survey based).</li></ul>
Quiet and safe neighbourhoods	<ul><li>% of community protected by regulations eg. of noise, congestion, alcohol consumption and loitering, controlling tourist behaviour in proximity to residential and children's play areas.</li></ul>
Substance abuse	<ul><li>Number of education programs and policies on responsible service and use of alcohol (% of employees trained and any measures of effectiveness on local quality of life indicators and incidence of domestic violence);</li><li>Number and coverage of health programs on drug abuse.</li></ul>
Smoking	<ul><li>% of workplaces which are smoke free;</li><li>% of workplaces with 'Quit' incentive programs.</li></ul>
Family support	<ul><li>% of workplaces providing child care facilities;</li><li>% of workplaces with family-friendly rostering (work shifts and rotation).</li></ul>

Components of the issue	Indicators
Education and training (see also ➢ **Employment section** p. 119)	• Percentage of employees who are from the local community; • Number of scholarship and training opportunities for local youth (% of total); • Extent of work programs for at-risk youth (number, %).
Access to safe drinking water, power and sanitation	• % of large tourism developments which include infrastructure in development to benefit local community (e.g., including provision of potable water, sewage and waste disposal) level of investment.

Reason for use of these indicators: Tourism is often responsible for the over-consumption of scarce natural resources of water and energy; displacement of agriculture and aquaculture; production of excess solid waste and waste water with high levels of chemical, pathogen and nutrient load; environmental degradation leading to loss of biodiversity, ground cover and soil, amenity and open space. In such cases, tourism is not only destroying the asset on which it is built; it is also directly affecting the health and well being of local people. Ironically 'spa' or 'health' tourism which may contribute significantly to the relaxation and wellbeing of the tourist in many cases is responsible for much a higher ecological load and excessive use of water. Tourism can also contribute to the introduction or incidence of non-communicable diseases caused by changes in diet and lifestyle. The introduction of high cost, high fat, fast foods into developing countries, for example, can have devastating impact on health and draw heavily on low incomes away from essentials for children's health and education. However, if well planned and managed, tourism can make a useful contribution to health and wellbeing.

Source(s) of data: An approach that integrates community wellbeing into tourism planning requires collaboration across various community, non government, government bodies and the industry. The indicators chosen need to be specific to the local context and therefore sources of appropriate data will flow from these groups and the issues identified. It might involve formal survey work or be part of other processes such as social planning at the community level.

Means to use the indicators: As a part of tourism planning process at the local government, to identify and highlight issues relating to non economic benefits of tourism and to foster improved resident satisfaction with tourism and hence support.

Benchmarking: No benchmarks yet exist. This is an aspect of tourism that has been generally neglected. It is an area that each community needs to develop over time, a sense of comfort that tourism is beneficial to their needs and future, and measure the goals of tourism planning and outcomes against the goals for community development as a whole.

Sources: World Health Organisation 2003 International Travel & Health. WHO, Geneva http://www.who.int/health_topics/travel/en/

Adventure travel brings additional challenges regarding health, safety and provision of services. Alpine climbers, Le Palud Italy

Box 3.8 Turtle Island, Fiji: Tourism and community health

Turtle Island is a 14 room five star luxury resort located on a 500 acre privately owned island (Nanuya Levu) in the Yasawas group of islands, Fiji. Purchased in 1972 by Richard Evanson, who remains as owner manager, the island was uninhabited and degraded after decades of neglect, overgrazing and clearing. Flora and fauna were depleted, soils eroded and the ecosystem including mangroves, coral reefs and beaches were damaged. Mr Evanson made a commitment to restore the island. Eventually the resort opened in 1980 with a vision to *provide a genuine and loving Fijian experience for caring people, and to be a vital resource to our community*. The vision also made a commitment to be one of the leading ecotourism resorts in the world.

Turtle Island has implemented a range of innovative environmental and community based programs and activities to achieve these objectives. This includes planting over 1 million trees established from a nursery set up on the island. Vegetation cover has grown from around 10% to over 82% across the island. These include many native fruits. This has halted erosion and provided habitat for birds and wildlife that are now rich in diversity and number. Key indicators: number of trees planted, % cover in natural vegetation.

All biodegradable solid waste is composted on the island. With no natural streams, several dams have been built to ensure abundant supply. Some 90% of fresh fruit, vegetables and herbs are grown in the resort garden Reforestation has provided sufficient timber for building works. Local staff have been retrained in environmental management and rehabilitation, market gardening; complex carpentry and building; as well as work within the resort operations. Key indicators: % produce grown locally, % staff trained in key skills.

Due to the vision of the resort and the special visitor experience, philanthropic gestures are quite common. In 1992 the Yasawas Community Foundation was established to receive guest donations for special projects in the Turtle Island communities. The focus has been on secondary education. Key indicators: value of donations, number of students supported.

Turtle Island has been augmenting the quality of health care available through the provision of health care resources including responding to the endemic problem of blindness due to cataracts and diabetes. In this time more than 11,000 Fijians have had their eyes tested, more than 9,000 pairs of glasses have been issued free of charge, over 1,000 operations have been performed (mostly cataracts), and 20 corneal implants. Turtle Island runs other health clinics including dermatology, women's health and dental clinics, providing specialist health services that would otherwise not be available. Key indicators: numbers treated, level of funding.

This example shows how a single tourism business is able to make a significant contribution to the health and wellbeing of its local community as well as significant ecological restoration and conservation work. Turtle Island has provided funding under a social entrepreneurial program, expending over $1 million in the construction of three budget resorts. Turtle Island plays an active role in the governance, marketing and management of the resorts and a proactive role in skills transfer. The resorts have directly and indirectly, created over 100 new sustainable jobs in the community. The interest free loan to establish these businesses will be recovered from the profits of the resorts built. Key indicators: number of new jobs created, number of businesses funded.

Sources: Andrew Fairley, Turtle Island and Berno, T 2002, Turtle Island: to be a vital resource to their community. University of South Pacific.

3.5.2 Coping with Epidemics and International Transmission of Disease

Facilitation, Contingency Planning, Impacts on Tourism

Changing social and environmental conditions around the world have fostered the spread of infectious disease, including new emerging communicable diseases such as pneumonic fever, Severe Acute Respiratory Syndrome (SARS) and recently, avian influenza, together with the increasing prominence of strains of pathogens highly resistant to current antimicrobial drugs. The resurgence of infectious diseases around the world has been attributed in large part to the massive increase in rapid international travel, and travel to increasingly remote and undeveloped locations.

Global infectious disease trends include increasing mortality in developed countries, with death rates from infectious disease in the USA increased by more than 50% between 1980 and 1992. The World Health Organisation established a new division of Emerging Viral and Bacterial Diseases Surveillance and Control (now known as the Communicable Diseases Surveillance and Response unit). New human pathogens such as HIV/AIDS and more recently SARS, have focussed both medical professionals' and others' concerns on the impacts of these diseases.

Given the role of travel in the spread of these diseases and the impact epidemics have on the industry, it is vital that the tourism industry take responsibility for full co-operation and proactively work toward public health strategies to assist in halting these alarming trends. The WTO's *Recommended Measures for Tourism Safety* (1991) urged to *"develop reporting systems on health problems of tourists"*.

While the issue occurs at a global level, it is important as well for particular destinations. The indicators suggested below will be of use to managers who wish to keep abreast of the global trends, and for those who are concerned with the impacts on their particular destination.   An important issue for the health industry is the problem of collection of data on preventative medicine and health promotion. It is not often feasible to collect statistics on % of incoming visitors who have had any one of a number of vaccinations or to determine how many have been exposed to potential disease.   As with many tourism and travel related issues, many jurisdictions are involved and the systems are not in place for coordinated gathering and exchange of information. A major challenge for the World Health Organization (see website www.who.int/en/) is to help establish an effective program involving all nations in the form of global compliance with the International Health Regulations (IHR, 2005) providing for the notification of all events constituting a public health emergency of international concern as part of the legal framework for WHO's global health security epidemic alert and response strategy. The planned facilities include putting in place a "situation room" to provide for instant and round-the-clock information on health emergencies worldwide.

Components of the issue	Indicators
Facilitation, warning and information	• Issue of travel advisories (number of destinations affected, duration of travel warnings); • Travel industry information disseminated on 'safe' and 'at risk' countries (% of travellers who have access to this information; number of travellers accessing information pre travel; visitation patterns to designated 'at risk' destinations); • Warnings about precautions and vaccinations (% of travellers receiving vaccinations before arriving at destination); • Degree of collaboration between industry and health officials in affected destinations (number of tourism businesses distributing health warning information to customers; collating and reporting the number of visitors requiring medical assistance or medication through in-house services; number of businesses involved in other aspects of disease surveillance; number of businesses undertaking voluntary quarantine procedures such as sending any ill staff to medical centre); • Public health education to alert travellers and industry staff to effective personal protection and socially responsible behaviour to avoid further transmission (% of staff, % travellers provided with information; number of public health training programs run for the tourism industry).
Contingency planning mitigation and response	• Quarantine precautions for air travellers to and from affected regions (number and nature of quarantine measures eg.; checking temperature of all arriving passengers); • Effectiveness of surveillance and reporting of cases (number of air travellers arriving/departing identified as infected; number of reported cases at the destination); • In addition to all above; public health education campaigns to be disseminated through consumer channels about symptoms, essential precautions and treatment (Expenditure per annum on campaigns; number and type of tourism businesses involved in the dissemination process); • Strategies to support affected nations (Level of foreign aid given/received for this purpose; level of travel industry support to encourage return business after the outbreak); • Strategies to build consumer confidence (level of effort/expenditure by destination, number of international companies such as airlines or hotel chains actively promoting affected destination).
Impacts on tourism	• % drop in visitor numbers; • Number of staff stood down; • % drop in room occupancies; • Length of time taken to recover back to pre outbreak levels of visitation and room nights; • Number of tourists reporting infection/incidents; • % of tourists who fear travel to the destination (survey); • % of travellers who say they changed travel plans because of the epidemic.

See also the section on Health (p. 94) for a number of indicators relating to illness in visitors and preventative measures. An elaboration of the difficulties in collection of data on social and health issues can be found in the Sex Tourism section (see p. 71).

Reason for use of these indicators: Coping with epidemics requires the highest level of diplomatic co-operation between international agencies such as WHO, IOM (International Organization for Migration), and ICRC (International Committee of the Red Cross) national governments and the world tourism industry bodies, in particular the WTO and others such as WTTC and IATA, all of whom play a role in briefing the industry, undertaking rapid analysis of the situation and the costs, assisting with travel advisories, and then rebuilding consumer and industry confidence. There is an important role in assisting with reporting and surveillance so that effective public health measures are not sacrificed for economic benefit. In the past the industry has sometimes ignored or minimized such issues for fear of the economic implications. This is very short term thinking and an unsustainable approach. The economic implications arise anyway, to build consumer faith requires that the general public can trust the industry leaders.

Source(s) of data: Information should be available through national tourism authorities who have access to information from WHO; national health departments, and directly from WHO and WTO.

Means to use the indicators: As these are global issues, it is essential that the leading international tourism bodies take a prominent role in viewing commercial concerns against the background of public health priorities and using this opportunity to provide both ethical and logistic leadership. The indicators are core to facilitation of responses – level of effort to prepare, react, mitigate and respond, and can be used to both clarify risk and to measure performance in prevention and mitigation. The indicators which measure tourism impact are" following` indicators which serve to demonstrate the impact which has occurred , and are likely to be useful to show the importance of contingency planning and preventative measures.

Benchmarking: WHO web site http://www.who.int/csr/sars/en/index.html provides data on infectious outbreaks, spread of the disease, number of cases reported. The World Travel and Tourism Council web site http://www.wttc.org assessments the economic impacts of outbreaks such as SARS and comparisons are made of the impact on different destinations.

Box 3.9 The impact of SARS outbreak in international tourist arrivals 2003 (WTO)

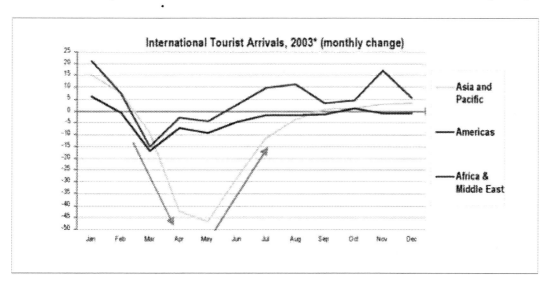

> **Box 3.10 Severe Acute Respiratory Syndrome (SARS) outbreak**
>
> July 5th 2003 WHO announced the last known case of human to human transmission of SARS coronavirus, bringing to an end the initial outbreak of a severe new respiratory disease that began in mid November, 2002 in Southern China. It had huge implications for the tourism industry.
>
> The most severely affected countries were China (including Hong Kong Special Administrative Region and Taiwan), Canada, Singapore and Viet Nam. According to WHO data, there were a total of 8422 cases in 29 countries. In the countries already mentioned there were 908 deaths. Early reports and continued epidemiological data suggest an animal reservoir in southern China, but the species are yet to be confirmed.
>
> In Hong Kong the outbreak began in a single housing estate, linked to contaminated sewage. A single infected guest in a Hong Kong hotel resulted in at least 16 cases and seeded the international spread. The rate of person to person transfer of the virus is unusually high. Its containment within 4 months of the first global alert was due to high level political commitment and co-operation, driven by concerns over the economic impact of its spread, and expert public health measures put quickly in place. The latter included early detection through temperature surveillance, including travellers passing through airports in the affected countries. This measure became essential after the identification of a number of cases of in-flight transmission cases (27 cases linked to five flights). Travellers were recommended to postpone all but essential travel to areas of high risk.
>
> The SARS outbreak therefore had a serious effect on tourism, and dominated results of tourism in the Asia-Pacific region in 2003, especially in destinations in North- East and South-East Asia, causing around 50% decrease in international tourist arrivals during March-May of that year (WTO) (see graph Box 3.9).
>
> http://www.who.int/csr/sars/en/index.html

3.5.3 Tourist Security

Risk, Safety, Civil Strife, Terrorism, Natural Disasters, Impacts, Management Response, Contingency Planning, Facilitation

Sustainability is threatened by man-made incidents and natural disasters which harm tourists, destinations and their populations. A single event can cause immediate cancellations, redirection of tours to alternative destinations or closing of tourist facilities. The impact of events may cause the repositioning of cruise ships, changing of air routes, and loss of access. The impact may last for months or years, as the perception of the travelling public towards the destination, while very quick to perceive risk, may take a long time to respond when conditions change and order is restored. Terrorist attacks, rebellions, civil strife, natural disasters tend to affect not just the places where they occur; entire regions may see reductions in tourist arrivals due to incidents even two or three countries away. The decision of where to go depends greatly on the perception of safety or danger. Widespread perception of risk (real or not) can cause downturns in particular forms of travel, and may affect the willingness to travel at a global scale, not just to specific destinations which may have been directly affected.

Box 3.11 Characteristics of a safe destination in terms of facilitation (preparation, planning, information, emergency services)

Indicators can be developed to measure each of the following principal characteristics of a safe tourism destination (existence and extent of these arrangements and services):

1. General and specific commitment by the government to aid visitors who fall victim to safety and security problems;

2. Adequate protection of tourism facilities and sites;

3. Staff at tourism enterprises, facilities and sites trained to deal with safety and security issues affecting customers and visitors;

4. Responsibilities defined and assumed by the public sector by area of competence and the private sector, by activity;

5. Adoption of and compliance with safety and security standards and practices at tourism facilities and sites regarding: fire prevention, food safety, other health requirements specific to the destination, environmental standards, prevention of illegal interference and violence (terrorism), other relevant standards specific to the destination;

6. Adoption of an information and education policy aimed at ensuring transparency and dealing with crises including:

   - effective communication to the parties concerned of existing safety and security standards and practices;

   - identification of possible risks and dangers of tourism for visitors;

   - requirement of risk management according to area of activity (for example, in adventure tourism, sports activities, etc.);

   - effective communication of possible risks and dangers to the parties concerned;

   - effective communication to the parties concerned of the services, facilities and measures available to assist visitors in case of emergency.

7. System for the collection, analysis, and communication of tourism safety and security information including health information (outbreaks of disease, suspected exotic pathogens, etc.), data on the geographic distribution and number of victims, and specific information according to the characteristics of the destination;

8. Existence and effective access to emergency services: institutional, public and private measures, facilities and services available to assist visitors in case of emergency or difficulty: including immediate assistance (telephone help lines, first aid, emergency services, police services),reliable health services (facilities, personnel, materials),expatriate services (access to consular and diplomatic representatives and collaboration with them), travel assistance, insurance services, consumer protection, measures for compensation by the state, particularly in cases of terrorism, repatriation services.

Source: WTO

WTO has initiated work to clarify how destinations can respond to these issues. The focus of response lies in facilitation of sufficient information and services to officials, tourism companies and tourists, so that they can take appropriate measures to avoid risks. The focus is on establishing the conditions, procedures, formalities and information requirements at point of entry into a national destination (country), and for departure from the national destination, as well as for travel within the national territory to reach the destination. Key elements of response can include:

1   Information; made available on websites, at embassies and/or consulates, at tourism information offices, and at the point of entry into the national destination (transport at airports or stations, security);

2   Entry measures including strengthened procedures for entry visas, training of immigration officers, health formalities upon entry, security measures, baggage controls, customs and currency importation formalities and exchange services, and coordination among entry services;

3   Departure formalities including all the corresponding services and measures mentioned under entry formalities, and protection of species and objects of historical or cultural value;

4   Conditions of travel within the national territory: management of links with local destinations via public or private transport, enhanced safety of national transport , management of processes for obtaining transport tickets, access to banks/use of payment cards, and establishment of requirements for notifying the police of whereabouts during national travel.

Work by the WTO has begun to identify the key attributes of a safe destination in terms of facilitation (See Box 3.11), and some of the steps destinations can take to establish and maintain improved levels of safety and security.

Components of the issue	Indicators
Incidents	• Number of incidents (per month, per annum and per types of incidents); • Number of tourists harmed.
Impacts of incidents on tourism sector	• Number of % change in tourist arrivals; • Number of % change in numbers employed in tourism; • Number of % change in tourism revenues; • Number of % change in occupancy rates; • Number of % hotels closed; • % change in number of direct flights.
Perceptual effects	• Number of incidents reported in international press; • Frequency of mention of destination (or region) in international news of incidents (per media type); • Opinion of travellers of safety of destination (% believing it to be dangerous) - surveys (e.g. in travel magazines, others); • Rating of destination in magazines, guidebooks and other media dealing with places considered to be dangerous and risky; • Rating (listing) of site on travel warnings, as part of travel advisories, in principal countries of origin, government websites (Number of countries posting warnings); • Rating (listing) of site on travellers advisory in principal countries of origin, government websites (Number of countries posting advisories).

Components of the Issue	Indicators
Management or response to risks (level of facilitation of information and services)	• Level of expenditure on security (nation, region, enterprise); • Level of security at borders (guards or officials per visitor); • Existence of a contingency plan for tourists and visitors to the region in the event of incidents; • Existence of emergency services; • Number of tourists helped by tourist aid programs; • Number of % tourists informed of security levels (various methods); • Number/% of tourism establishments complying with safety and security standards (e.g. fire prevention, food safety and other health requirements, environmental standards); • Existence of safety and security standards for attractions and establishments.

(See Box 3.11 on Safe Destinations)

Indicators of direct impact on tourists and facilities (global and for specific destinations or regions):

* **Number of incidents (per month, per annum);**
* **Number of tourists harmed.**

Indicators of indirect effects (impacts):

* **Number of /% change in tourist arrivals;**
* **Number of /% change in numbers employed in tourism;**
* **Number of /% change in tourism revenues;**
* **Number of % change in occupancy rates;**
* **% change in number of direct flights;**
* **Number of /% hotels closed.**

Reason for use of these indicators: These indicators measure the results of security issues and tend to be indicators showing the impacts of incidents which have occurred or of actions taken by tourists in response to real or perceived risks. These indicators can help to judge the severity of impacts, and to measure recovery and the effects of actions to reduce impact or change security levels.

Source(s) of data: Data on incidents and damage are normally available from national and other security agencies. Data regarding impacts can normally be obtained from tourism authorities at local regional or national levels (as well as international compilations from WTO, ICAO and regional tourism organizations).

Means to use the indicators: Normally these will be used to explain levels of change related or correlated with security incidents, or to illustrate the need for emergency measures, preparedness or contingency planning.

Benchmarking: Long term trends are normally available at national and more local levels – and can show impacts of past occurrences (incidents or regional crises).

Indicators of perceptual effects:

* **Number of incidents reported in international press;**

* **Frequency of mention of destination (or region) in international news of incidents (per media type);**

- **Opinion of travellers of safety of destination (% believing it to be dangerous) - surveys (e.g. in travel magazines, others);**

- **Rating of destination in magazines, guidebooks and other media dealing with places considered to be dangerous and risky;**

- **Rating (listing) of site on travel warnings, as part of travel advisories, in principal countries of origin, government websites (Number of countries posting warnings).**

Reason for use of these indicators: The decision to travel, and where to travel is often based more on perception than on any objective measure of risk, safety or destination conditions. These indicators can be a warning of perception of risk, and may lead to changed levels of tourism. The public has access to these sites and publications and widespread use of them leads to perception of risk… real or not.

Source(s) of data: Scanning of key public sites – at international level, particularly in the principal origin countries for tourists for the destination. It is also possible to commission a survey in origin countries and to sample on a repetitive basis.

Means to use these indicators: These indicators can signal emerging perceptions of risk – which may help direct responses to reduce the risks and/or to reassure tourists.

Benchmarking: Compare over time in same markets relative to the destination and relative to competitors if multi-destination surveys are done.

Indicators of facilitation (level of management or response to risks):

- **Level of expenditure on security (nation, region, enterprise);**

- **Level of security at borders (guards or officials per visitor);**

- **Existence of a contingency plan for tourists and visitors to the region in the event of incidents;**

- **Existence of emergency services;**

- **Number of tourists helped by tourist aid programs;**

- **Number of /% tourists informed of security levels (various methods);**

- **Number/% of tourism establishments complying with safety and security standards (e.g. fire prevention, food safety and other health requirements, environmental standards);**

- **Existence of safety and security standards for attractions and establishments.**
  (see also Box 3.11 on Safe Destinations)

Reason for use of these indicators: These indicators essentially measure level of effort or preparedness of a destination to deal with incidents – both to try to prevent them and to demonstrate that action is being taken to respond to risks and be able to cope if incidents occur.

Source(s) of data: Direct information from national and local authorities re level of programs.

Means to portray or use these indicators: Show preparedness to public and to partners. Keep the public informed to the extent possible about risks and what to do if problems occur.

Benchmarking: Compare over time for the same destination. It is difficult to obtain comparative data from other destinations for security reasons.

3.5.4 Local Public Safety

Crime, Risk, Harassment, Public Security, Tourist Anxiety

Public safety at destinations is particularly important for tourism. Tourists who are victims of crimes, harassment, sickness (see Health issue p. 94) or any acts which they perceive to be hostile or dangerous can ruin a trip. Tourists returning after unfortunate incidents will frequently inform others of their problems, often in public fora such as online chat rooms, newspaper complaint columns, letters to the media, or TV shows. Poor public security in destinations or particular sites can both directly harm visitors and locals, affect the decisions by others on whether to visit a destination, and hamper the transfer of economic benefits of tourism to the local economy. Maintenance of good public security is a key factor in a good image or brand for a destination (see Marketing for Sustainable Tourism p. 228 and Protecting Image p. 236), ➢ **Tourist satisfaction** (p. 86) and ultimately in the overall sustainability of a destination. This issue is closely related to national and international security and as a result is dealt with in greater detail in the section on Tourist Security (p. 104).

The prevention of crime and facilitating adequate warnings to visitors of risks associated with particular places and activities are a responsibility of destination authorities and individual businesses. They require that government departments of police, health, environment, and tourism work closely with each other and with the industry to provide appropriate legislation and enforcement, resources, assistance, training, monitoring and visitor information. Clear visitor advice should be in place appropriate to local conditions and events. Visitors themselves can also be the perpetrators of crime, most frequently associated with alcohol and drug abuse. Licensed operators need to be responsible and observe safe service and sales of alcohol to avoid problems for other guests and the community.

Public safety is not measured only in crime, health or accident statistics. Perception of safety and security is also very much in the eye of the beholder. Some tourists who live in a small quiet safe village in their own country may feel very uneasy in a milieu where they are besieged by vendors and touts, surrounded by large numbers of people in a crowd or shouted at by local youth. Others may consider these types of experiences to just be part of local colour and perceive no threats. Similarly, tourists from densely populated areas may feel ill at ease on a mountainside out of sight of any other people or services – fears of getting lost, attacked by fauna, etc, whereas others may relish the experience. For this reason, it is important not only to document the objective incidence of safety problems (number of tourists robbed, number of hikers lost, and number of reports of harassment by locals) but also to try to understand the level of unease perceived by tourists, which will affect their experience, and also constitute a risk to tourism in the destination. Perception of local safety is also affected by broader issues related to international security (see p. 104).

Components of the issue	Indicators
Crime	• Total number of crimes reported involving visitors (by type) (Number per thousand of visitor/tourist arrivals); • Number of visitors charged with crimes (by type); • Cost of destination security per annum, per visitor/tourist (Where possible, cost of local policing specifically aimed at tourism); • Perception of severity of crime problem by visitors (Exit questionnaire Annex C 5 p. 491).
Harassment of tourists	• Number of incidents reported (and per tourist day); • Perception of level of harassment or anxiety (Exit questionnaire p. 491).

Components of the issue	Indicators
Health	◦ Number (%)of tourists reporting health problems (see additional indicators in Health section p. 94).
Crime prevention and control	◦ Level of policing (police per tourist); ◦ Cost of destination security per annum, per tourist; (Where possible, cost of local policing specifically aimed at tourists/ tourism); ◦ Level of information for tourists regarding crime and prevention.

Indicators of crime:

*   **Total number of crimes reported involving visitors (by type). (Number per thousand of visitor/tourist arrivals);**
*   **Number of visitors charged with crimes (by type);**
*   **Cost of destination security per annum, per visitor/tourist**

    (Where possible, cost of security specifically aimed at tourism);

*   **Perception of severity of crime problem by visitors** (Exit questionnaire p. 491).

Reason for use of these indicators: Crime levels affect the visitor experience and are a high risk to reputation of the destination.

Source(s) of data: Police records. Exit questionnaire for visitor perceptions.

Means to use the indicators: Trends over time and seasons, association with specific events; percentages of assault and crime compared to total numbers of visitors; age group and gender with highest rates of involvement; areas where highest incidence occurs and at what times of the day and night; percentage in which assault is against a visitor; perpetrated by a visitor; or visitor against visitor. Can be used in marketing where crime rates are low.

Benchmarking: Look for changes over time. Use to inform level of law enforcement required and to develop strategies such as alcohol free zones and other regulatory controls; to provide visitor safety information.

Indicators of harassment of visitors:

*   **Number of incidents reported (and per visitor/tourist or tourist day);**
*   **Perception of level of harassment or anxiety** (Exit questionnaire p. 491).

Reason for use of these indicators: Local harassment can be an early warning of community problems which affect tourism. It can also warn of emerging problems which may affect the industry. Both reported incidents and perception are important.

Source(s) of data: Local hotels and tourist boards for complaints. Use Exit questionnaire (p. 491) with specific questions regarding level of agreement/disagreement with statements including:

> *"I felt safe and secure during my visit"*
>
> *"Tourists were well protected in the destination"*
>
> *"I received good information regarding safety and security at the destination"*
>
> *"I was (or was not) harassed by the locals during my vacation"*

(Note these can be asked in the positive or negative ... but need consistency over time)

Means to use these indicators: Use as early warning system for issues both for tourists and community.

Benchmarking: Measure over time for the same destination.

3.6   Capturing Economic Benefits from Tourism

3.6.1   Tourism Seasonality ➣ **Baseline Issue**

Occupancy, Peak Season, Shoulder Season, Infrastructure, Product Diversity, Employment

Very few destinations have consistent tourism throughout the year. Some destinations experience extreme seasonality. Even resorts which seek all-season status through a diversity of offers can have low seasons where it is difficult to justify operation. Tourism seasons, especially in beach tourism, are largely dependent on climate and weather patterns both at the destinations and at the source markets ("push-pull factors"). Low seasons reflect unfavourable weather conditions at destinations (cold, rain, excessive heat and humidity, storms). High seasons with optimal weather at destinations can be affected by warmer and more favourable weather conditions in source countries. For example, warmer summers in Northern Europe can result in tourists choosing destinations closer to home and fewer of them leaving for the Mediterranean region.

A growing trend is the establishment of four season resorts, (e.g., Whistler British Columbia, Cortina d'Ampezzo Italy) which attempt to diversify the tourism product and serve a range of different niche markets in different seasons (skiing, golf, swimming, bicycling, conferences, and festivals) to fill the calendar. During the summer, many of the winter trail facilities are able to convert to mountain bike trails with converted ski lifts to carry bikers and their bicycles up the mountain. Where there are larger population centres nearby, smaller towns or venues will bolster their income by advertising mainly to locals, sometimes offering discounts to attract domestic tourists in shoulder or off seasons. During the shoulder seasons for skiing at many Rocky mountain resorts, operators market directly to nearby residents with advertisements for low cost packages, 50% off lift tickets or free lessons, since few tour operators will take the chance that the snow will be there early or late in the season. Such discounts can also help to keep local residents content, particularly if high prices (sometimes eliminating locals, students etc) are charged in peak season.

Anse Aux Meadows World Heritage site where Vikings landed in Northern Newfoundland is a destination which gets nearly all of its visits in a ten week period in June to August each year.

Box 3.12 The local impacts of seasonality- examples from WTO indicators study sites

Villa Gesell (Argentina) is a beach destination with a local population of about 25,000. During the January and February peak season, the small town among the dunes hosts over 100,000 visitors at a time, with the peak day reaching 200,000, most of whom stay at least one night. In summer, streets are crowded; there are lines for seats in restaurants, auto services, and entry to parking areas. While the summer peak has brought Villa Gesell a wide range of tourist-related services, only a small percentage are open year round. In the winter, many key services are closed, and residents of Villa Gesell may have to drive long distances to obtain them.

Lake Balaton (Hungary), and the north coast of Prince Edward Island (Canada) show the same pattern, and locals complain that the services are there mostly for the tourists, with serious gaps outside the peak season. Jobs in these regions are also seasonal, and many leave the area for any upward mobility. Often jobs in the brief peak season are filled by students, or migrants from other areas who stay only for the season – themselves stressing the available accommodation during the time when it is most heavily used. In communities like these, the year-round economic base is often insufficient to support the infrastructure needed to handle the peak periods, even to pay those who are needed to maintain it if it is built.

The key components of the seasonality issue and corresponding indicators are the following:

Components of the issue	Indicators
Measuring degree of seasonality (And the results of management actions to respond this issue)	* **Tourist arrivals by month or quarter (distribution throughout the year) ➢ Baseline Indicator;** * % of annual tourist arrivals occurring in peak month, in peak quarter; * Ratio of number of tourists in peak month to lowest month; * **Occupancy rates for licensed (official) accommodation by month (distribution throughout the year) ➢ Baseline Indicator;** * **% of all occupancy in peak quarter (or month); ➢ Baseline Indicator;** * Inquiries at tourism information centres by month (ratio peak month to lowest month).
Strengthening shoulder season and low season tourism (measuring the level of effort designed to reduce seasonality)	* % tourism authority budget spent promoting off-peak and shoulder seasons; * Number of facilities offering alternative activities during shoulder and low season (capacity and use levels per activity type); * % of main attractions open in shoulder/off seasons; * Special events (e.g. festivals, conferences) held during shoulder and low season (number of events, participants). *See also the exit questionnaire (Annex C 5) which can be used to ask what would cause the respondent to visit outside peak season.*
Provision of sufficient infrastructure year-round (especially services for tourists in high seasons and for local communities in low seasons)	* % of business establishments open all year; * % accommodation and services open all year (can be further subdivided into e.g., hotels, attractions, restaurants etc.); * % of water, electricity, sewage and garbage system capacity used for tourism and for locals. Seasonality of use; * Funding allocated for the operation and maintenance of infrastructure, especially in high seasons. *(See also ➢* **Community and Destination Economic Benefits** p. 128*).*

Components of the Issue	Indicators
Short term and seasonal employment, with related issues of lack of training, retention of good employees, provision of career paths	* Number and % of tourist industry jobs which are permanent or full-year; * % tourist industry jobs which are for less than 6 months; * Local unemployment rate in off-season.

Indicators measuring degree of seasonality (and the results of management actions to respond this issue):

* **Tourist arrivals by month or quarter (distribution throughout the year) – see also Use intensity ➢ Baseline Indicator;**

* **% of annual tourist arrivals occurring in peak month, in peak quarter;**

* **Ratio of number of tourists in peak month to mean and to lowest month (and % of all occupancy in peak quarter, or month (can be subdivided by type) ➢ Baseline Indicator;**

* **Occupancy rates for licensed (official) accommodation by month (distribution throughout the year);**

* **Inquiries at tourism information centres by month (ratio peak month to lowest month).**

Reason for use of these indicators: These indicators are direct measures of seasonality and can show the economic impact of seasonality on the key sectors of tourism. Accommodation is the easiest to measure in most jurisdictions. Data for the opening dates of tourist establishments may be available from local governments, or tourism associations. Also the indicators show changes in services available to local residents over the season.

Source(s) of data: Tourist counts where arrivals/departures are directly measured (easiest for sovereign states, islands, attractions, controlled access points). Indirect measures may be done through sample counts. An alternative source can be providers of officially recognized accommodation based on records of occupancy (below). Users of this source will need to recognize the existence in many destinations of unofficial accommodation and also day-visitors that stay outside the destination, and subjective adjustments may be needed to make the information useful.

Means to use the indicators: Monthly distribution of tourist arrivals throughout the year helps identify peak, low and high periods; it is easy to portray in graphs. Peak absolute numbers (peak day), percentage of visits concentrated in peak season show stress on the destination; ratio of peak to average may be better measure regarding decisions on infrastructure, services. These indicators can show both stress on accommodation in season and potential economic problems in low seasons and can show progress in programs aimed at lengthening the season.

Benchmarking: This can be compared to other destinations as many collect these data. A useful form of benchmarking is against similar destinations or similar accommodation classes. Tourism authority websites are a useful source for published data on occupancy rates.

Note: Peak day may be associated with particular events, as in Box 3.13 below. In Sturgis, a quiet town in the Black Hills of South Dakota, the population expands immensely during the annual cyclists rally, making provision of basic services an issue. For example, portable toilets are brought in from hundreds of miles away to serve the event, and planning for the event is a major year-round activity.

Box 3.13 Sturgis South Dakota Motor Cycle Rally - An example of extreme seasonality

"They came by train, RV, plane and motorcycle. They sweltered in the 108 heat early in the week, then covered themselves with leather and rain gear for the 70 temperatures at the end of the week. They watched concerts racing, rode in the Black Hills and met new and old friends. It was the 2001 Sturgis Rally. The numbers were down from the 400,000 to 600,000 in 2000 but the 200,000 to 300,000 was a comfortable rally."

Source: www.Sturgis.com

Indicators regarding strengthening shoulder season and low season tourism (and measuring the level of effort designed to reduce seasonality):

* **% of tourism authority budget spent promoting off-peak and shoulder seasons;**

* **Number of facilities offering alternative activities during shoulder and low season (capacity and use levels per activity type);**

* **% of main attractions open in shoulder/off seasons;**

* **Special events (e.g. festivals, conferences) held during shoulder and low season (number of events, participants);**

* **See also the exit questionnaire (Annex C) which can be used to ask what would cause the respondent to visit outside peak season.**

Reason for use of these indicators: Many factors can affect the seasonality of a destination. These show level of effort to address the issue and identify many of the factors which may enable or impede efforts to lengthen seasons.

Source(s) of data: Local tourist authorities.

Means to use these indicators: Can be a public measure of efforts to attract tourists in off season. This can also show some reasons why tourists do not arrive outside peaks.

Benchmarking: Compare over time for the same destination. Tourist guidebooks often show dates of opening for attractions and hotels and can be a source of comparative information about competing destinations.

Indicators relating to provision of sufficient infrastructure year-round (especially services for tourists in high seasons and for local communities in low seasons).

* **% of business establishments open all year;**

* **% of accommodation and services open all year (can be further subdivided into e.g., hotels, attractions, restaurants etc.;**

* **% of water, electricity, sewage and garbage system capacity used for tourism and for locals. Seasonality of use (see ➢ Energy p. 152, ➢ Water Availability p. 165, ➢ Sewage p. 171, ➢ Solid Waste p. 173);**

* **Funding allocated for the operation and maintenance of infrastructure, especially in high seasons.**

See also ➢ Effects of Tourism on Communities (p. 57).

Reason for use of these indicators: Tourism can place stresses on facilities ranging from private businesses to infrastructure. If capacity is built to serve peak levels, it may be unused off season. If insufficient is built, it will be overstressed in peak season.

Source(s) of data: Local business associations, municipal authorities.

Means to use the indicators: These indicators show a form of carrying capacity (See p. 309) and what is being done to suit capacity to tourism and community needs. They also relate to seasonality of demands for labour and services.

Indicators regarding the effects of seasonality on employment:

* **Number and % of tourist industry jobs which are permanent or full-year;**
* **% tourist industry jobs which are for less than 6 months;**
* **Local unemployment rate in off-season.**

Reason for use of these indicators: Tourism seasonality is a factor in unemployment, seasonal employment and turnover of staff, as well as having social and economic impacts on the destination. In extreme cases, tourist communities may virtually shut down in the off season, and even those residents who choose to stay may have to leave the community to obtain basic services.

Old Orchard Beach Maine, USA in May 2004. Most accommodation services and attractions are closed except for the June to August summer season when the beach is crowded.

Source(s) of data: Governments normally collect employment data on a monthly basis, but may not be able to separate jobs by sector. For destinations without formal employment records, hotel records can be used, but many establishments may not collect these variables, or be persuaded to provide the data for use. In many destinations the employment of undocumented workers may make data collection difficult. In the absence of a government data program, an industry association may be able to collect and aggregate data from members.

Means to use the indicators: Both raw data and percentages/ratios are useful to show changes in the nature and seasonality of the workforce.

Benchmarking: Published government data is available at appropriate scales from many destinations.

(See the Balearic example of labour seasonality indicators Box 3.14)

Box 3.14 Index of labour seasonality: Balearic Islands, Spain

Socio-economic Indicator

Status: Indicator

Scope: Balearic Islands

Period: 1989-2000

- Although labour occupation has increased over the last years, seasonality is still the same: employment increases in summer and decreases in autumn and winter.

Observed trend : The labour occupation is higher in the summer months than in autumn and winter.

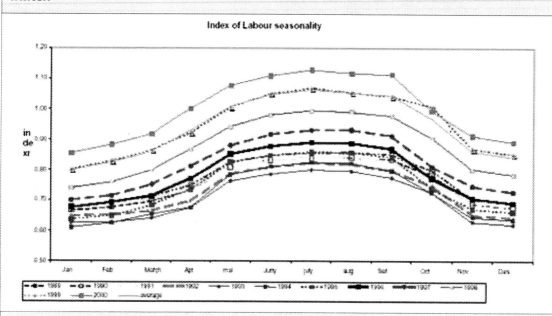

Index of Labour seasonality

Desirable trend : Stabilise the values along the year.

Description: this index measures the labour seasonality using monthly occupation data and monthly averages.	Data sources for the indicator:
	· Evolució Econòmica de Sa Nostra. Caixa de Balears.
Methodology: the index of labour seasonality results from dividing the monthly occupation by the annual average occupation. It is desirable that the occupation remains stable throughout the year.	· Institut Nacional d'Estadística. INE.
	· Institut Balear d'Estadística. IBAE.
	· Instituto Nacional de Empleo. INEM.

Labour stability = Average monthly occupation "x" year "n"
                    ———————————————————————————————
                    Average year occupation year "n"

Source: Centre d'Investigacions i Tecnologies Turístiques de les Illes Balears (CITTIB)

3.6.2 Leakages

Imported Goods, Foreign Exchange, Internal Leakage, External Leakage, Invisible Leakage

Leakages are broadly defined as the loss of foreign exchange and other hidden costs deriving from tourism related activities (Perez-Ducy de Cuello 2001). The term "leakage" suggests the existence of a weak economy or the lack of control over the tourism sector performance, each making it possible that a significant, excessive or simply unnecessary portion of the revenues obtained through tourism "leak" away from the economy in a visible or "invisible" manner or that obtaining such revenues is taking place in detriment to its tourism resources and potential or at a high domestic and social cost which can be measured in economic terms. Some studies (UNEP) have revealed leakages as high as 85 percent for the African Least Developed Countries (LDCs), 80 percent in the Caribbean, 70 percent in Thailand, and 40 percent in India. According to Ralf Corsten, former Chairman of the Board of TUI, "at the beginning of development... 80% of the revenue do not reach the destination in the first place, or flow back to the source markets via imports" (see www.world-tourism-org, under "Quality and Trade").

In an open economy it is normal that certain factors of production (goods, services, commodities, labour, capital, ideas) are imported and that such factors, including those used in tourism activities, are entitled to fair remuneration or payment abroad. Some of these imports may be fundamental for the appropriate use of tourism destination resources or for determined tourism activities.

While certain inputs from abroad and imports cannot be avoided, and others may become welcome and encouraged, reducing leakages.is essential for maintaining vital local economies, and for the overall sustainability of destinations, which requires building a reliable domestic supply chain for goods and services that otherwise would be purchased externally.

Tourism leakages are difficult to measure and there is no single, universally accepted methodology to do so, but using the Tourism Satellite Account methodological framework (See Box 3.19, p. 134) in combination with the indicators in the leakage categories explained below can significantly help in comprehensive measurement. Approximation to measuring leakages in tourism is possible in various ways. In package travel a simple method often used is comparing the price paid to the tour operator with the payment for destination-generated resources and services. A serious indication of leakage can be seen in decreasing foreign exchange receipts per visitor arrival or tourist overnight irrespective of increasing numbers of arrivals and the total volume of receipts.

For a comprehensive account, three leakage categories (from Gollub et. al 2003): should be considered:

External Leakages: Represented by earnings which accrue to foreign investors financing tourism infrastructure and facilities, through repatriated profits and amortization of external debt. Monies which flow to external intermediaries for bookings; foreign airlines, cruise ships, and other forms of foreign-owned transportation; insurance and travel assistance companies; and to source-market tour operators. For example, in 1992 in South America, tour operators were reported to have received between 45 and 50 percent of prearranged tourism booking prices (Economist Intelligence Unit 1992). Key indicators will therefore focus on measurement of these flows.

Internal Leakages: Internal leakages primarily arise from tourism through imports that are paid and accounted for domestically. These leakages can be tracked with reasonable reliability through Tourism Satellite Accounts (TSA). Where in place, TSAs measure foreign exchange payments along the entire tourism value chain for imported goods and services. The extent of internal leakages in any destination is largely a function of tourist demand for level and quality of leisure services and entertainment-related and retail goods. The particular tourist segment catered to may require, for example, wine and name brand alcoholic beverages that are produced elsewhere, organic produce, scuba equipment produced to international safety standards, hotel quality linens and mattresses, modern heating and air-conditioning systems, sophisticated security equipment, and satellite television access, etc. Particularly in small or less developed tourist destinations, each of these goods and services will likely need to be imported.

Invisible leakages are those losses or opportunity costs that are not documented reliably, but which can exert cumulative and significant effects. One major source of invisible leakage is financial, associated with tax avoidance, informal currency exchange transactions, and off-shore savings and investments. Another source of invisible leakage arises from the non-sustainability of environmental, cultural, historic, and other tourism assets over time in ill-planned and ill-managed tourism development. Resource depletion and damage (for example, to coral reefs, beaches, wildlife, forests, water availability and quality, historic structures or districts) may negatively impact tourism arrivals and expenditures over the short term, and also lead to depreciation of a destination's value as an attraction over the longer term as well as to the deterioration of the quality of life for local residents. Leakage can also occur due to the social costs caused by visitor consumption of scarce resources (e.g. water, energy), subsidized and financed by public authorities or external aid.

Leakage indicators can be developed to address the various aspects of leakages that are relevant to tourism activities at a destination. The table given below contains a comprehensive set of such indicators. Depending on the activity concerned, destination management organizations will note that some indicators will be more or less relevant or may be more or less important than others in the particular case of their destination.

In a comprehensive approach, indicators should address:

* all relevant tourism characteristic activities (largely external and internal leakages);
* relevant tourism-connected activities (largely external leakages);
* relevant tourism-non specific activities (largely external leakages, also "invisible leakages").

Components of leakage	Indicators
Import content of services (external and internal leakages)	
a. Facility/activity creation	* Value of imported goods (construction materials, equipment, sundry); * Value of imported services (systems, software, consultants, experts, architects, etc.).
b. Facility operation and carrying out of activities	* Value of imported goods for visitor use and consumption including of agricultural products, restitution, spare parts, etc.; * Value of imported services, including insurance; * Foreign exchange costs of marketing and distribution abroad; * Remittances abroad by expatriate staff; * Remittances of profits and dividends; * Remittances due to foreign debt servicing (originating from general tourism development loans and related to specific facilities/activities).
Invisible leakages (estimates)	* Foreign exchange value of deteriorated resources (repair/rehabilitation/recycling costs); * Quantification of lost market/lost business value; * Foreign exchange loss due to differences between official and market exchange rates; * Foreign exchange loss due to sales of non-licensed and un-taxed services; * Foreign exchange loss equivalent of social costs caused by international visitor consumption of scarce, subsidized and imported resources financed by international aid.

The value, costs and losses thus calculated should be compared to:

* The overall or specific activity-related foreign exchange revenue from the supply of tourism services concerned;

* The evidence of foreign exchange investment, including total value of foreign investment to create facility/activity (direct foreign investment (FDI), portfolio investments) and international non-refundable aid.

Comparison to other productive sectors (other services sectors, goods, agriculture, commodities) in terms of both manufacturing and trade is also necessary as it may well happen that other sectors' activities may have higher or lower leakage incidence compared to tourism. This may indicate whether tourism is a better or worse development option.

It cannot a priori be established in general which level of leakage is sustainable or justified with respect to tourism activities, as answers will vary from destination to destination, but the objective measure will remain to be rewarding fairly, in financial terms, the destination resources, in particular labour and natural resources. Cost opportunity studies can help establish a "leakage break-even point" as a function of the destination's economic capacity to serve different types of tourism and eventually choose the type most suitable for a project or country. Leakage analysis will also help identify and enhance options for developing linkages or activities leading to the reduction of leakage.

The WTO deals with these issues under its Quality and Trade in Tourism programme (http://www.world-tourism.org/quality/E/main.htm).

As well, futher information on this topic can be found at:

Tourism in the Least Developed Countries (WTO/UNCTAD, 2001)

http://www.world-tourism.org/cgi-bin/infoshop.storefront/EN/product/1170-1

Leakages and Linkages in the Tourism Sector: Using Cluster-Based Economic Strategy To Minimize Tourism Leakages (WTO, 2003).

http://www.world-tourism.org/quality/E/trade2.htm

3.6.3 Employment

Training, Quality, Skills, Turnover, Seasonality, Pay Levels

A tourist destination can have many of the ingredients for success: interesting attractions, good weather, five-star accommodations, and superb amenities. However, if there are no qualified employees to provide the services and to operate the facilities, tourism at the destination will not be sustainable. There are many issues that contribute to the quality of employment in tourism, which in turn affect the economic sustainability of tourism. The key components of the employment issue and corresponding indicators are the following:

Components of the issue	Indicators
Number and quality of employment in the tourism sector (turnover, seasonality, pay levels)	• Total number employed in the tourism sector, by industry (e.g. traveller accommodation, restaurants, air transportation etc.) occupation and level; • Retention levels of employees; • Percentage of jobs that are full time, full year; • Local unemployment rate in off-season; • Income analysis.
Professional and personal development	• Number (%) of employees qualified/certified; • Training funds spent per employee, frequency of training programmes and level of participation; • Possibility of on-the-job training.
Contentment from work including, type of work, environment, safety, development, etc.	• Employee satisfaction; • Promotion; • Income levels (absolute and compared to other sectors); • Ability to influence change/improvements in business processes; • Number of workplace accidents (and cost of compensation);
Lack of skilled labour	• Measures of errors, or resulting waste (with value calculated where possible); • Tourist dissatisfaction (See ≻ **Tourist Satisfaction** p. 86); • Complaints (by employers, by tourists); • % labour imported (from outside region, from other countries).

Indicators of employment numbers and quality of employment in tourism (turnover, seasonality, pay levels):

* **Total number employed in the tourism sector by industries (e.g. traveller accommodation , restaurants, air transportation etc.), occupation and location (See ≻ Community and destination economic benefits p. 128);**

* **Number (and %) of employees qualified/certified;**

* **Total number employed in the tourism sector;**

* **Retention levels of employees;**

* **Percentage of jobs which are full time, full year;**

* **Local unemployment rate in off-season;**

   (See also ≻ Seasonality (p. 111)

* **Income analysis.**

   Reason for use of these indicators: To determine whether tourism sector employees are earning an adequate income in comparison to other sectors; and to assess whether tourism sector employees are earning an adequate income in relation to the cost of living and maintenance of an adequate quality of life. To measure sector changes relative to other industries and to other competitive destinations re factors affecting the quality of employment.

   Source(s) of data: Salary surveys; Cost of living surveys (Note: most jurisdictions do salary surveys, although many do not disaggregate data so the tourism industry is not easy to identify, but many do isolate service sectors, or specific parts such as hotels or food services.) The authorities who collect basic employment statistics will often be able to disaggregate subsets, such as length of employment, seasonality, and pay level or job type. If these are not available, surveys may be required, of tourism companies and establishments.

Means to use the indicators: In some countries the labour market is very competitive, and the tourism sector may be at a disadvantage relative to other competitors for trained staff. In others, tourism may be seen as a good sector, relative to more traditional employment in e.g. resource industries. The income made, in comparison with other sectors, is very important. Moreover, the ability to make an income that allows the employee to live within the local cost of living is vital. It is useful to differentiate seasonal or part time employment from full-time jobs in this analysis, particularly in very seasonal destinations.

Benchmarking: Benchmarks will likely be national or regional, reflecting the nature of the job market. Any analysis should take into consideration the raise of inflation and increased cost of living per year in the destination, and the relative rates of other sectors.

Indicators of professional and personal development:

* **Number (%) of employees qualified/certified;**
* **Training funds spent per employee, frequency of training programmes;**
* **Possibility of on-the-job training.**

Reason for use of these indicators: A key measure of the economic importance of the sector, its contribution to destination and national economies, and direct measure of the opportunities and employment levels/types in the tourism sector.

Source(s) of data: Where possible, national or local authorities, industry databank of qualified (certified, licensed, trained) individuals, or union/industry associations. If unavailable, a sample of employees in the industry may have to be surveyed.

Means to use these indicators: Tracking the number of employees trained and qualified can be used as a numeric illustration of the professional and personal development in which employees have been involved and the general level of training of the workforce.

Benchmarking: Benchmarks can be obtained from national industry statistics where collected. Targets can be set for the adequate number of employees qualified in occupations for which there is an official qualification or certification program. For example, the goal may be that 80% of employees in an organization be qualified officially via courses or on-the job training, or that 70% of all guides or hotel clerks receive appropriate qualifications by 2005.

Indicators of employee contentment or satisfaction regarding work including type of work, environment, safety, development, etc.:

* **Employee satisfaction;**
* **Promotion (rates, % per annum);**
* **Income levels (absolute and compared to other sectors);**
* **Ability to influence change/improvements in business processes (use employee survey);**
* **Number of workplace accidents (and cost of compensation).**

Reason for use of these indicators: In order to understand the quality of tourism employment it is important to consider the opinions of the employees working in the sector as well as to assess their opportunities and risks.

Source(s) of data: Employee surveys, employer records.

Means to use the indicators: Speaking directly to the employees is a key method of understanding what they believe to be the quality of tourism employment. There are various methods for structured surveys and questionnaires that can be used, especially in larger companies and establishments. Implementation of changes to business processes suggested by employees can have positive effect on profit. It also relates to the ability to recruit and retain good employees.

Benchmarking: Employee surveys can be conducted at regular intervals (e.g., one time per year). Cumulative results can be compared to chart improvements and declines. Benchmarks in each category can be set in order to identify standards for employee satisfaction and comparison with other enterprises, sectors or destinations.

Box 3.15 Assessing tourism employment in Canada

In 1998, tourism accounted for 2.3% of overall Gross Domestic Product for Canada, generating $22 billion in taxes for all three levels of government.

Similar to many other economically prosperous nations, Canada is facing an overall labour shortage as the retirement of the baby boomer generation is met with a smaller population to follow in their footsteps. Attracting labour is an issue for most Canadian sectors, including tourism. In 2001, the tourism-related industries in Canada employed 1.6 million people with 563,500 people employed as a direct result of tourism spending. Total tourism sector employment growth outpaced the employment growth rate for all industries.

As competition increases for labour and tourism continues to grow in Canada, supplying the tourism sector with adequate labour (and in particular skilled labour) will become more and more challenging. Tourism already faces many challenges attracting labour to the sector, including: low wages, seasonal work, perception in society, sporadic hours, and limited career advancement opportunities. In order to ensure sustainable tourism in Canada, the quality of employment offered in the tourism sector must be improved.

Indicators are maintained to measure the above attributes/challenges and to support analyses of tourism labour force trends relative to other sectors. The results of the analysis of tourism labour force data feed policy decisions related to human resource training nationally. The existence of regular indicators gives the tourism sector the ability to influence programs of governments in the field of tourism human resources at many scales. Indicators regarding labour force, training, etc are provided regularly to government ministries and are a visible part of the policy and program management process.

2001 Tourism Performance, Canadian Tourism Commission. http://www.canadatourism.com Canadian Tourism Facts and Figures 2001, Canadian Tourism Commission. http://ftp.canadatourism.com/ctxUploads/en_publications/Tourism2001.pdf

Source: Canadian Tourism Human Resources Council

Other indicators of interest to level of contentment from tourism sector employment:

* **Retention levels of employees (% turnover per year);**

* **Training funds spent per employee;**

* **Number of workplace accidents (and where applicable, cost of insurance claims or compensation).**

These indicators are important to illustrate the quality of tourism employment because they demonstrate the type of work environment. If there is a large turnover rate, then employees may not be content in their jobs or they are able to find more appealing employment in other sectors. If the employees are not content then the quality of employment may be poor. Moreover, if employers are not investing in their employee-base to continue to develop their skills, not only will employees become dissatisfied but the quality of the skills will deteriorate. If there are a number of accidents in the workplace, demonstrating an unsafe work environment, then it could be surmised that the quality of employment is sub-par.

Note: See the section on ≫ **Seasonality** (p. 111) for an indicator on % of seasonal jobs and also on unemployment off season. See also ≫ **Community and Destination Economic Benefits** (p. 128).

Famous fish head soup, Tian Mu Hu, China. Well trained workers can be the key to the tourism experience.

3.6.4   Tourism as a Contributor to Nature Conservation

Financing for Conservation, Local Economic Alternatives, Constituency Building, Tourist Participation in Conservation

The Convention on Biological Diversity (CBD) defines biodiversity as "the variability among living organisms from all sources including, inter alia, terrestrial, marine and other aquatic ecosystems and the ecological complexes of which they are part; this includes diversity within species, between species and of ecosystems" (Convention on Biological Diversity 2002). Biodiversity is a mayor asset for nature-based tourism, which has been experiencing a rapid growth. It is clear that tourism has significant potential for contributing to biodiversity conservation, because biodiversity is a critical component of the natural environment that tourists enjoy. The mutual benefits between   sustainably managed tourism and nature conservation have been also recognized throughout the International Year of Ecotourism 2002, and at its main event, the World Ecotourism Summit:
http://www.world-tourism.org/sustainable/IYE-Main-Menu.htm.

Tourism can be a threat to conservation; how and where it develops is of importance to biodiversity conservation. But in a growing number of cases, tourism delivers benefits for conservation and provides those in the industry, especially local people, with an economic incentive to protect biodiversity. Because it is based on an enjoyment of the natural and cultural environment, tourism can be motivated to protect them, can play a positive role in awareness raising and consumer education through its vast distribution channels, and provide an economic incentive to protect habitat that might otherwise be converted to less environmentally friendly land uses.

The relationship between tourism and biodiversity may not always be positive, particularly when tourism development occurs without management standards and hence the importance for monitoring the industry and indicators to help track the industries impact. Monitoring is an essential element of any planning or management of tourism business. All stakeholders need to learn and measure biophysical and social conditions of the industry, (i.e., the impact of the industry on nature and quality of the experience). Indicators should be identified early and should be related to tourism impacts at natural sites, and issues or conditions that influence tourism activities. The suitability and relevance of indicators should be reviewed from time to time, according to the changing conditions. The guide on sustainable tourism in protected areas, published by IUCN, WTO and UNEP (2002) includes the following suggestions about the use of indicators to monitor tourism in protected areas:

1.   Indicators should try to identify conditions or outputs of tourism development or protected area management e.g., the proportion of the park impacted by human activity or annual labor income from tourism, or income from tourism invested in conservation programs, rather than just inputs e.g., the money spent on a program. (see also Indicators Selection Procedures, Step 8 pXXX);

2.   They should be descriptive rather than evaluative;

3.   They should be relatively easy to measure; and

4.   Initially only a few key variables be selected for monitoring.

Indicators, though sometimes difficult to document, include: donations to local conservation projects; continued correspondence between locals and visitors; increased support for conservation/development projects and an increased level of commitment and activism. An indirect indicator would measure the levels of educational and interpretative experiences for visitors, including quantity and quality of interpretative programs, and tourists satisfaction with them, especially those that permit interaction with local people and their issues and that reveal how ecosystems function. In the following table, indicators are suggested which document both the positive contributions made by tourists and the industry, and the level of effort and results associated with controlling negative effects. (Note that the latter are covered in greater detail in the sections on Protecting Critical Ecosystems, p. 147, ≫ **Development Control** p. 207, and ≫ **Controlling Use Intensity** p. 192).

Components of the issue	Indicators
Measuring potential impact of tourism on the natural environment	• Reports on a scientific understanding of potential environmental (number, depth); • % of projects where tourism impact is evaluated; • % of conservation projects where tourism financial contribution is a component.
Source of financing for biodiversity conservation and maintenance of protected areas (Note need for benchmarking for funds or value of contribution to conservation.)	• % of the protected area, conservation site budget originated from tourism activities (cash, value of in-kind contributions); • Value generated through visitor fees (e.g. at parks); • Value of contribution from operators (concession fees, donations, services provided); • Value of donations received from tourists; • % of businesses in the destination or near the site contributing to conservation; • % of tourism products (tours etc) with specific contributions built into the price or surcharges; • Number and % involvement in support clubs (e.g. "friends of the park") both locally and in foreign lands.

Components of the issue	Indicators
Economic alternatives for local people to reduce exploitation of wildlife and resources	• Value of receipts or invoices of funding for local groups; • % of the local community employed in tourism; • % of the local community employed in conservation activities; • Number (membership) in local programs (lists of supported programs or lists of membership); • Level of effort to engage locals in protection activities (number of meetings, programs, expenditure) – See also Community Involvement and Awareness p. 83; • Number and percentage of locals actively involved in conservation programs; • % of goods and services purchased locally; • Value of infrastructure investment by tourism enterprises; • Value and % discounts or incentives for locals.
Constituency building which helps promote biodiversity conservation by tourists	• % of tourists participating in protection activities; • % of tourists contributing to conservation (by type of contribution: fees, donations, in-kind, volunteer time); • Level of activity designed to engage tourists in protective activities (measure each appropriate type: information, interpretive efforts, and educational programs); • % of tourists aware of importance of conservation site; • % of tourists who receive conservation materials, % who read, respond; • % increase/decline in after visit correspondence from former visitors. (Could be in form of "thank you letters", "how can we help letters", notes in suggestion box, citings on internet websites posted by former tourist visitors, etc.); • % of locals who receive conservation materials , % who receive, respond; • % of stakeholders for whom materials are in their native language.
Site-specific regulations (See also Protecting Critical Ecosystems p. 147)	• Applied codes of conduct (group size, mode of transport, equipment, waste disposal, noise pollution, staff, energy efficiency, construction methods and materials, etc) designed to minimize negative impacts; • Percentage compliance (Refer to specific issue sections on each of these impacts).
Provision of opportunities for participation by tourists in conservation (these provide a means of participation in support for conservation)	• Number of conservation organizations coordinating for tourism activities at conservation sites; • Number of conservation programs/activities open for tourist participation (level of participation) (e.g. clean up days, guided learning events); • Number of tour operators offering conservation activities as part of tourist programs (and level of participation); • Survey questionnaire re satisfaction (% filling out questionnaire, % noting contribution if asked); • % of tourists receiving marketing materials which provide contribution opportunities; • Existence of customer code of practice and guidelines (% receiving, % compliance); • Vehicle and other powered equipment user codes (% receiving, % complying); • Level of cultural sensitivity of educational materials (will require focus groups or textual analysis).

Key indicators directly measuring contribution are:

* **Value of contribution from operators (concession fees, donations);**

* **Value received from tourists (fees, donations, etc);**

* **% of tourists participating in protection activities;**

* **% of tourists contributing to conservation (by type of contribution: fees, donations, in-kind, volunteer time);**

* **% of businesses in the destination or near the site contributing to conservation;**

* **% of the protected area, conservation site budget originated from tourism activities (cash, value of in-kind contributions).**

Reason for use of these indicators: As tourism grows, the opportunities to mobilize both tourists and the industry as a whole to support conservation objectives will also grow. The indicators in this section are designed to document the level of opportunities available to the tourists and the industry to be part of conservation solutions and participate in related activities, the degree to which they take up the opportunities and the results that are obtained. The list is long, and managers will wish to select those most suitable to their destination and their programs.

Source(s) of information: The information will normally be found in the records of the protected area or in information produced by conservation organizations and local authorities. For information on the reaction by tourists or locals, a questionnaire method will be necessary,(see the suggested Exit questionnaire and Local questionnaire in Annex C). One challenge is to identify the broad range of indirect and related contributions made by tourists and the tourism industry. For greater detail on the benefits that can be associated with tourism, funding mechanisms and sources of revenue, see Sustainable Tourism in Protected Areas 2002 (IUCN,WTO,UNEP), Chapter 9. Financial Aspects of Tourism in Protected Areas.

Means to use the indicators: These indicators help both measure the level of engagement of tourists and their contributions. The results can help direct programs to better engage them in conservation and measure the level of response.

Benchmarking: Benchmarking will generally occur on a site-specific basis over time showing changes in level of engagement or support. While many destinations and sites have specific programs to obtain tourism support, there is no single source for information.

Park entry Lao Shan, Shandong, China – park fees help pay for protection.

Box 3.16 Monitoring the Gudigwa Camp Project, Botswana

Conservation International has been supporting the development of Gudigwa Camp, a community-based ecolodge development owned by the Bukakhwe Cultural Conservation Trust (BCCT). Gudigwa Camp opened in March of 2003 and caters to upper end tourists on safari in Botswana. The camp itself is located 5 kms outside of Gudigwa Village and is one of the first community-owned and operated businesses of its size in the area. The aim of the BCCT is "to achieve a long term and sustainable means of generating income for the Gudigwa community so that traditional culture and nature is conserved, local people are educated and trained, and our standard of living is raised." In order to measure the success of the Gudigwa Camp enterprise in achieving these goals, Conservation International established a monitoring program, which tracks a number of critical issues related to both CI and BCCT's objectives.

These include:

1. Changes in local land-use patterns and how they maybe impacting on biodiversity;

2. Socio-economic benefits to the community; and,

3. Behavioural, attitudinal, and socio-cultural impacts from the newly present tourism in the area.

These issues are monitored using three main instruments: land-use mapping; biological surveys; and socio-economic and cultural surveys. Land-use mapping of the areas surrounding the camp and village record changes in local usage patterns for cattle grazing, agricultural, firewood collection, and tourism activities. Biological surveys of pre-determined transects are conducted during each of the Okavango Delta's distinct seasons in order to monitor the diversity and number of wildlife, birds, and plant species in the area. With guidance from CI-Botswana's Senior Biodiversity Officer, camp guides and community members chart the following indicators when completing a biological survey:

1. Wildlife (type, number, sex, behaviour at sighting);
2. Fresh spoor (both domestic and wildlife);
3. Nests, burrows, etc;
4. Fire scars (when did the fire occur, what was the level of damage, etc.);
5. Wildlife carcasses (what animal, how long has it been there);
6. Evidence of poaching (traps).

Together with the University of Botswana, CI-Botswana's Community Development Officer, Molefe Rantsudu completed its first annual socio-economic and cultural impacts survey of community members in Gudigwa shortly after the opening of Gudigwa Camp. Methodologies used include secondary research, structured and unstructured interviews with community members and camp staff, and key focus group discussions with representative community members and the BCCT board.

The report will provide the baseline for annual monitoring of the following key indicators:

1. General demographic data of BCCT members and Gudigwa Village;
2. Development of organizational and business structures in the Gudigwa Village;
3. Health and diseases developments;
4. Socio-cultural and economic roles of community members;
5. Decision-making in households;
6. Cultural knowledge.

> **Box 3.16 (cont.)**
>
> 7. Socio-cultural impacts i.e migration;
> 8. Impacts of tourism on employment and household economic activities;
> 9. Perceived benefits from the camp; and,
> 10. Changes in perceptions towards wildlife, hunting, and tourism.

3.6.5 Community and Destination Economic Benefits ➢ Baseline Issue

Capturing Benefits, Tourism Revenues, Tourism Contribution to the Local Economy, Business Investment, Community Investment, Taxes, Satellite Account

Tourism can bring investment and employment opportunities to a destination. It can also bring investment in public sector infrastructure and services. A community needs to evaluate the return on its own investment in tourism, in direct and indirect jobs created, on revenue earned from tourist spending, on taxes earned from tourism businesses, and any increase in asset value (land and infrastructure prices). These economic considerations also have a socio-cultural element. Questions to consider include, for example;

1. Is the community as a whole making economic gains?;

2. Are just a few people profiting, or are the benefits widely spread?;

3. To what extent do outsiders (not-resident at the destination) control tourism businesses and profits? For example, outsiders may own the major hotels, tour bus operations, or attractions;

4. What are the economic multipliers? Communities can estimate their economic inputs and outputs to demonstrate spin-offs in other business generation beyond tourism;

5. What is the economic leakage? How much tourism revenue is leaving the community? Smaller and less developed communities may show greater economic leakage if many goods and services have to be brought in from the outside. (See Leakage p. 177);

6. How is tax money from tourism spent?.

Communities need to consider how much tourism (and how many tourists) they want and what assets they have to make the community a destination. Tourism may also bring indirect economic benefits through the development of support services and increased opportunities in other industries ranging from food and agriculture to hardware, crafts and construction, creating diversified local economies. On the negative side, economic leakage may result in much of the economic benefit being siphoned off to outside tour operators, accommodation owners and other suppliers. The potential economic gains for the community through tourism employment, business development and revenue must be weighed against community expenditures that support tourism and the possible increase in the cost of living or change of lifestyle for residents. A balance must be found between the overall welfare of the community and that of the tourism industry.

Ideally the measurement of economic benefits would be integrated with socio-cultural benefits with a full social benefit/cost analysis (see related section on ➢ **Effects of Tourism on Communities** p. 57). Such an analysis may yield indicators such as the net benefit of each additional tourist to a destination, but in practice it often tends to be complex and costly. Work on satellite accounts for tourism (See Box 3.19 and http://www.world-tourism.org/cgi-bin/infoshop.storefront/EN/product/1194-1 for details and methodology) will help to clarify the economic contribution of tourism, and efforts to implement such procedures are under way in many countries.

Components of the issue	Indicators
Employment (see also issue section on Employment p. 119)	• Number of local people (and ratio of men to women) employed in tourism ➣ **Baseline Indicator;** • Ratio of tourism employment to total employment; • % of tourism jobs held by local residents; • Average tourism wage/average wage in community; • Ratio of part time to full time employment in tourism; • Average tourism employee income (and ratio to community average).
Business investment in tourism	• Number of tourism businesses in the community, and % owned locally; • Number and type of business permits and licences issued; • Ratio of the number of local to external businesses involved in tourism; • Asset value of tourism businesses and % owned locally; • Longevity of tourism businesses (rate of turnover).
Tourism revenue	• Tourist numbers; • Tourist spending/spending per tourist; • Occupancy rates in accommodation establishments; • Revenues generated by tourism as % of total revenues generated in the community ➣ **Baseline Indicator;** • Local GDP and % due to tourism (see Box 3.19 on Tourism Satellite Accounts); • Total fees collected by community for access/use of community attractions; • Revenue from business permits, licenses or concessions and taxation.
Community expenditures	• Existence of tourism budget/plan; • Annual expenditures on tourism (% of total tourism revenue); • Amount and % of infrastructure expenditures for tourism; • Amount and % of total annual operating expenditures for tourism ; • Cost of tourism advertising and promotion per number of tourists; • Amount and % contribution of tourism revenues to the cost of water, sewage, roads, food production, energy, waste management, air quality, human resources development, etc.
Net economic benefits	• Net tourism revenues accruing to the community; • Economic Multipliers: Amount of additional revenue in other businesses for every dollar of tourism revenue (based on satellite accounts where available).
Changes in cost of living	• % increase/decrease in land and housing prices over time; • % increase/decrease in average family weekly income; • % increase/decrease in expenditures (groceries, transportation, leisure etc.).

Indicators regarding employment:

*   **Number of local people (men and women) employed in tourism** ➢ Baseline Indicator;
*   **Ratio of tourism employment to total employment;**
*   **% of tourism jobs held by local residents;**
*   **Average tourism wage/average wage in community;**
*   **Ratio of part time to full time employment in tourism;**
*   **Average tourism employee income (and ratio to community average).**

Reason for use of these indicators: Employment is a key factor in many decisions to support and invest in tourism. Leaders and politicians are often heard to quote the number of jobs tourism development will bring.

Source(s) of data: Employment/unemployment statistics from local, municipal or industry sources.

Means to use the indicators: Employment numbers and ratios, wage rates and income levels are key indicators in the assessment of the benefits of tourism to a community or destination. The indicators suggested here help put tourism employment in perspective with other industries.

Benchmarking: Tourism employment indicators can be used as benchmarks for comparison with other sectors and as a guide to the community's dependence on tourism. Compare over time for the same destination.

(See also the Issue section on Employment, (p. 119) for additional indicators related to human resources for the tourism industry).

Box 3.17 Sustainable tourism indicators for Mediterranean destinations: Economic measures

Destinations and communities in a geographic area often have much in common. By working together to monitor tourism, communities can compare their achievements and make decisions to improve tourism throughout the region. The following economic indicators have been proposed by a research team at the Foundation for Research and Technology Hellas, Heraklion Greece for use at the local scale for Mediterranean destinations:

Economic Indicators

*   Employment in tourism as a percentage of total employment;
*   Number of "locals" employed in tourism as a percentage of total employment in tourism;
*   Revenues generated by tourism as a percentage of total revenues generated in the area;
*   Business establishments offering tourist services and owned by locals as a percentage of all business establishments;
*   Income multiplier for the tourism sector as estimated in an input-output table;
*   Revenues exported as a percentage of total revenues in the business establishments owned by foreigners.

A pilot application was done to test the indicators in Hersonissos Greece (http://www.iacm.forth.gr/regional/papers/XIOS-englishversion.pdf) with one of the key issues being availability of data – particularly to estimate multipliers and leakage.

Source: http://www.iacm.forth.gr/regional/papers/tourism-today.pdf See also the issue section on ➢ **Effects of Tourism on Communities** (p. 57) for the related socio-cultural indicators proposed for Mediterranean destinations.

Indicators regarding business investment in tourism:

* **Number of tourism businesses in the community, and % owned locally;**
* **Number and type of business permits and licences issued at the local level;**
* **Ratio of the number of local to external businesses involved in tourism;**
* **Asset value of tourism businesses and % owned locally;**
* **Longevity of tourism businesses (rate of turnover) (% over one year, five years in business);**
* ➢ **Tourist numbers.**

  Reason for use of these indicators: Knowing the extent to which community members have invested in their own region is important to determine how and if a community should encourage local or outside tourism development or if they should slow down development. The number of opening and closing ventures can give information on the stability of tourism-related businesses (rate of turnover), and the dynamism of the industry.

  Source(s) of data: Local, municipal or regional business directories. Business registration data, licensing and quality control authorities, e.g. for tour operator licences, commercial accommodation, or concessions under community control.

  Means to use the indicators: Show the commercial investment in tourism. Positive changes can become a further stimulus to assist communities to attract new business investment or to encourage new local entrepreneurs.

  Benchmarking: Communities can set benchmarks to monitor the successful establishment of tourism businesses and to measure the extent to which the tourism industry is broadly or locally held. Comparisons can be made with investment in other sectors.

Indicators regarding tourism revenues:

* **Tourist spending/spending per tourist;**
* **Revenues generated by tourism as % of total revenues generated in the community** ➢ **Baseline Indicator;**
* **Local gross domestic product (GDP) and % due to tourism (according to satellite accounts if possible (See Box 3.19 p. 134);**
* **Total fees collected by community for access/use of community attractions;**
* **Revenue from business permits and taxation;**
* **Revenue retention (% exported, retained from total expenditures) See WTO website re leakage and multipliers.**

  (See http://www.world-tourism.org/sustainable/doc/CSD7-99-WTOcontribution.pdf) for some guidance on how to approach this indicator.

  Reason for use of these indicators: As a basis to monitor the increase/decrease in tourist spending, contribution to GDP, and to community revenue.

  Source(s) of data: Business income filing records, community financial statements, tax records. Actual calculation of contribution (net gain, net benefit/cost, multipliers and leakage is very complex and may require satellite accounts and detailed economic studies).

  For information on visitor spending survey techniques see both the material on exit questionnaires in Annex C and the WTO document "Measuring visitor expenditure on inbound tourism" at: http://www.world-tourism.org/isroot/wto/pdf/1301-1.pdf

Means to use the indicators: Help inform decisions on types of tourism and tourists that are likely to give the best economic return to the community. This information can also serve as a reference for the setting of fees or tax rates.

Benchmarking: Best done in conjunction with information on net economic benefits (tourism revenues less expenditures or use of satellite accounting for tourism).

Indicators relating to community expenditures:

* **Annual expenditures on tourism;**
* **Amount and % of infrastructure expenditures for tourism;**
* **Amount and % of total annual operating expenditures for tourism;**
* **Amount and % contribution of tourism sector to costs of infrastructure;**
* **Cost of community advertising and promotion per number of tourists.**

Reason for use of these indicators: A community needs to know how much is being spent on the provision of tourism services and infrastructure and who pays for what. The indicators can help answer whether it would be better to spend money on something else like alternative employment or welfare programs for example, or if more spending for provision of tourism infrastructure would be needed.

Source(s) of data: Community records, local authorities or tourism organizations.

Means to use the indicators: Expenditures need to be used in conjunction with current and forecast revenue projections as a way to establish the level of investment or the sense or viability of continuing to invest in tourism.

Benchmarking: A basic budget should be set as a benchmark for operating. It is advisable to set capital expenditure and public investment plans for mid-term periods (at least a five year time frame).

Indicators of net economic benefits:

* **Net tourism revenues accruing to the community (see Box 3.18 and Box 3.19);**
* **Economic multipliers (attributable to tourism) – from tourism satellite accounts where available.**

Reason for use of these indicators: To help determine if it makes economic sense to invest in tourism infrastructure and services. These indicators are often raised by destinations to help understand whether the net benefit of existing or new tourism is positive. Note that these indicators are very complex and may require a tourism satellite account to be created, or a detailed social benefit cost analysis to be done to obtain the information. Where the destination is not a discrete spatial unit with the ability to measure border costs and benefits (or inflows and outflows of investment and goods and services) it may not be possible to create these indicators.

Source(s) of data: Often difficult to obtain meaningful data on net tourism revenue. Access to commercial revenue data may be limited due to lack of collection or confidentiality. Economic leakage may be similarly difficult to establish. Economic multipliers may be available as industry standards or national level estimates but need care in use due to variability between places.

Means to use the indicators: Use as broad measures of economic benefits. These indicators should be used in conjunction with other indicators on non-economic and socio-economic benefits.

Benchmarking: Economic experts may be contracted for input-output analysis to establish net economic benefits, leakage and multipliers.

Other potential indicators:

* **% increase/decrease in land and housing prices over time;**

* **% increase/decrease in price of tourism and other business real estate;**

* **% increase/decrease in average family weekly income and expenditures (groceries, transportation, leisure etc);**

* **changes in costs of living and their components (e.g., accommodation).**

See also the issue on "Tourism and Poverty Alleviation" (p.135) for other indicators related to lifestyles and economic benefits.

Box 3.18 Estimating direct revenues and direct costs from tourism.

(From Julie Leones and Douglas Dun: Strategies for Monitoring Tourism in Your Community's Economy (1999) , page 14. See website for more examples from this source.: http://cals.arizona.edu/pubs/marketing/az1113.pdf).

Promotion and Operation Costs: Let's say the annual costs for tourism promotion and operation of the visitor center plus other local public service costs are **$250,000.**

Bed Tax: This community has a 2 percent bed tax and collected **$80,000** in bed tax revenues. This means that there was $4,000,000 in lodging expenditures in the community.

Estimate of Visitor Spending: Let's say that a recent survey tells us that 22 percent of visitor expenditures are on lodging. So the estimated total expenditures of visitors is $4,000,000/.22 = **$18,200,000**. Note: for information on visitor spending survey techniques see both the material on exit questionnaires in Annex C and the methodological website at: www.world-tourism.org/isroot/wto/pdf/1301-1.pdf.

City Retail Tax: The same survey shows that 61 percent of all visitor expenditures are on taxable retail items (i.e., groceries are not included). Visitors spent a total of $18,200,000 x .61 = $11,100,000 on taxable retail items. If the city retail tax is also 2 percent, then retail tax revenues from tourists would be $11,100,000 x .02 = **$222,000**.

Total direct revenues from tourists are **$222,000 + $80,000 = $302,000**. In this case, direct revenues more than cover the direct promotion costs of $250,000. **The ratio of revenues to costs** is then **$302,000/$250,000 = 1.2**.

Box 3.19 Tourism Satellite Accounts (TSA)

Satellite accounts are a procedure to measure the size of economic sectors which, like tourism, that are not defined as industries in national accounts. Tourism, for example, is an amalgam of industries such as transportation, accommodation, food and beverage services, recreation and entertainment and travel agencies, among others. A Tourism Satellite Account (TSA) is a means to calculate tourist consumption of these goods and services supplied within a country, using a common method which will permit comparisons over time and with other countries.

Tourism Satellite Accounts are designed to provide:

1. credible data on the impact of tourism and the associated employment;
2. a standard framework for organizing statistical data on tourism;
3   a powerful tool to help design economic policies related to tourism development;
4. data on tourism related to a nation's balance of payments;
5. information on the characteristics of human resources in tourism.

Many of the most important economic indicators have proven difficult to extract from traditional sources of data. Indicators important to tourism include leakage (See Leakage p. 117) employment in tourism (See Employment p. 119), and total value of tourism to an economy.

As increasing numbers of countries establish TSAs, it becomes more practical to calculate and use complex indicators such as the following:

* **Tourism's contribution to Gross Domestic Product (GDP);**
* **Tourism's ranking relative to other economic sectors;**
* **The number of jobs created by tourism in an economy;**
* **The amount of tourism investment;**
* **Tax revenues generated by tourism;**
* **Tourism consumption;**
* **Tourism's impact on a nation's balance of payments;**
* **Characteristics of tourism's human resources**.

Work on TSAs has focused on the national level, and countries such as Australia, Canada, Chile, France, New Zealand and the United States now are able to report such results as tourism counted for 4.5% of GDP in Australia in 1997-98, or 624,200 were employed in tourism-related industries in France in 2000. Initiatives are now under way to try to develop regional and destination level tourism satellite accounts, allowing similar measures at a more local level.

The Tourism Satellite Account represents a principal field of activity of the World Tourism Organization. WTO was instrumental in developing a conceptual framework and a standardized methodology for TSA that was approved by United Nations Statistical Commission (UNSC) in 2000. Based on this framework, the Organization has been actively promoting the development of National Systems of Tourism Statistics through training programmes and technical assistance.

Source: WTO Basic Concepts of the Tourism Satellite Account.

See also the WTO website at: http://www.world-tourism.org/frameset/frame_statistics.html

3.6.6 Tourism and Poverty Alleviation

Equity, Micro Enterprises, Employment and Income Opportunities, SMEs

Tourism is an important economic base for many of the world's poorest nations, generating foreign exchange earnings, employment and funds for development. Many developed and less developed countries have a comparative advantage in tourism resources, considering their rich natural and cultural heritage that provides a good potential for tourism development and operations.

Box 3.20 The World Tourism Organization's programme for poverty reduction through tourism

WTO has been assisting developing countries to strengthen their national and local economies through tourism development since its foundation in 1975. Reduction of poverty through the sustainable development of tourism has become a central issue in the work of the Organization since the Summit on World Summit on Sustainable Development (WSSD - Johannesburg 2002), in pursuit of the UN Millennium Development Goals. The main activities of this programme include:

* The Sustainable Development – Eliminating Poverty (ST-EP) Initiative, launched at WSSD;

* Country missions to identify tourism projects that can specifically target poverty reduction;

* Capacity building and training seminars on poverty reduction through tourism development and related issues (e.g. ecotourism, tourism management in protected areas, indicators, etc.).

More information: http://www.world-tourism.org/step/menu.html

http://www.world-tourism.org/sustainable

Sustainable tourism strives to contribute to the ecological, economic and social well-being of all destinations; however, the positive value of tourism is perhaps best observed at the local level in Least Developed Countries (LDDs) where the real contribution of tourism can be measured directly in terms of poverty alleviation. It can also be an important revenue generator for less developed areas within developing and developed countries. Marginalised and indigenous communities are often located in isolated rural areas that have not benefited from traditional forms of development. Similarly, poorer parts of urban communities may not be in a position to benefit from tourism which occurs in their urban centre.

Providing paid employment in the community may not be the only (or the best) way to improve livelihood standards. Assets, (% home ownership, business ownership, possession of tools) rather than an income, are often a better indicator of poverty reduction, as a growing asset base provides greater stability and more opportunity to diversify income-generating activities. Tourism development may be able to not just increase cash income but also support the community's livelihood priorities.

Box 3.21 How can spending associated with tourism reach the poor?

The WTO publication "Tourism and Poverty Alleviation: Recommendations for Action" identifies seven ways in which the poor can benefit directly or indirectly from tourism.

1. Employment of the poor in tourism enterprises;

2. Supply of goods and services to tourism enterprises by the poor or by enterprises employing the poor;

3. Direct sales of goods and services to visitors by the poor (informal economy);

4. Establishment and running of tourism enterprises by the poor - e.g. micro, small and medium sized enterprises (MSMEs), or community based enterprises (formal economy);

5. Tax or levy on tourism income or profits with proceeds benefiting the poor;

6. Voluntary giving/support by tourism enterprises and tourists;

7. Investment in infrastructure stimulated by tourism also benefiting the poor in the locality, directly or through support to other sectors.

Indicators can be established to monitor activities related to these practical approaches.

More information:

http://www.world-tourism.org/cgi-bin/infoshop.storefront/EN/product/1349-1

Components of the issue	Indicators
Stabilising and improving the community's income	• Annual total income generated by the community; • Ratio of income attributable to tourism versus traditional income generating activities; • Ratio of time dedicated to tourism versus traditional income generating activities; • Ratio of time dedicated to tourism versus tourism income (i.e. income per hour worked).
Improving local employment opportunities	• Total number of workers in the community (% workers in the community directly employed by tourism, % full time, % part time); • Ratio of local to "outsiders" directly employed by tourism; • % local workers employed at different skill levels (unskilled, technical, administrative, middle/senior management, contract); • Ratio of men to women employed directly by tourism; • % indigenous people employed directly by tourism (if appropriate).
Operation and support of micro, small and medium sized enterprises (MSMEs), or community based enterprises	• Number of tourism-related MSMEs operating in the community (subdivided by types, e.g. accommodation and catering, guiding, transportation, tour operation, etc.); • Incentives for MSMEs (e.g. special credits, tax advantage, grants, legal conditions, etc.): availability, level provided/used; • Capacity building for establishment and improvement of MSMEs: number of programmes/events, level of participation.

Components of the issue	Indicators
Achieving equitable distribution of tourism funds / benefits across the community	• % workers in the community directly employed by ratio of the top to the lowest paid local tourism worker (cohort distribution of income from tourism – e.g, top 5%, bottom 5%); • Annual financial contribution by tourism to community projects (common fund, tourism taxes or net value of programs); • Infrastructure development stimulated by tourism also benefiting the poor in the locality (directly or through support to other sectors): amount of investment, extension of new infrastructure; • Number and type of development programs in place (education, training, health, natural resource management, conservation etc.); • Community survey assessment of the usefulness and success of the various development programs.
Evaluating less tangible, non-economic, livelihood priorities	• Annual audit of the contribution of different activities to household needs; • Survey of household capacity to fulfil livelihood priorities for the year (rating level of food security, ability to meet cash needs, local empowerment, decreased vulnerability to external policy, decreased vulnerability to external conditions, cultural values and physical security).
Other related issues	• See also issue sections on Access by Local Residents to Key Assets(p. 65), Employment (p. 119), ➢ **Effects of Tourism on Communities** (p. 57) and ➢ **Economic Benefits** (p. 128).

Indicators re stabilizing and improving the community's income:

• **Annual total income generated by the community;**
• **Ratio of income attributable to tourism versus traditional income generating activities;**
• **Ratio of time dedicated to tourism versus traditional income generating activities;**
• **Ratio of time dedicated to tourism versus tourism income.**

Reason for use of these indicators: To directly measure tourism's contribution to community earnings, the inter-relationship with traditional income earning activities and time versus tourism earnings to measure if effort results in profit.

Source(s) of data: Survey with community members (particularly leaders) to determine how much income was generated over the last year, how much was attributable to tourism and the percentage of time that was dedicated to each income generating activity. Government employment statistics may be available- it may be a challenge to extract statistics for poor cohorts or poor districts.

Box 3.22 The challenge of monitoring household earnings

Monitoring of household earnings in rural communities can have constraints, as surveying on direct indicators can be intrusive. Community members, especially women, are often reluctant to report their earnings. If women are required to reveal their earnings from tourism they often lose their control over these family resources. Other, indirect indicators can be more suitable, in that they are in the public domain: for example the number of bicycles, better housing, ability to send children to school etc.

Another possible approach is to measure household income and other community indicators from the demand side. Surveys of tourist expenditure can reveal a great deal about community benefits without having to investigate household earnings in rural communities. It is possible to discover from tourists what they have been spending and where, and from this information to make good estimates of the amount of money flowing into local communities from tourism. Similarly it is a relatively easy matter to identify from the tourism industry the amount of money that is being spent in the local community.

Source: Final Report of the Seminar on Planning, Development and Management of Ecotourism in Africa. Regional Preparatory Meeting for the International Year of Ecotourism, 2002. Maputo, Mozambique, 5-6 March 2001. http://www.world-tourism.org/sustainable/IYE-Main-Menu.htm (see section on "Events" and "WTO Regional Ecotourism Conferences and Seminars")

Means to use the indicators: The total income is an indicator of the economic well-being of the community that can be assessed year to year. The proportion of income derived from tourism directly outlines the real net economic benefit of tourism in the community. The ratio of time dedicated to tourism versus other traditional income earning activities is important in assessing the reliance of the community on tourism. Diversification of income generating activities creates a buffer from external threats whereby shortfalls in one area (i.e. agriculture due to drought) can be compensated by other activities (such as tourism). For this strategy to work, it is important that locals continue to invest time in each income generating area. Time invested in tourism versus tourism earnings will determine how effective (and efficient) local efforts are in producing tourism-derived profit.

Benchmarking: Over time the community will obtain baseline data that enables a year's earnings to be benchmarked against that of previous years. Further analysis could help the community to identify longer-term patterns, set goals and strategies to maximise income generation.

Indicators re improving local employment opportunities: (see also the section on Employment p. 119)

* **Total number of workers in the community;**
* **% workers in the community directly employed by tourism ➢ Baseline Indicator (see ➢ Economic Benefits p. 128);**
* **Ratio of local to "outsiders" directly employed by tourism;**
* **% local workers employed at different skill levels ranging from unskilled, technical, administrative, middle management, senior management to self - employed;**
* **Ratio of locals working full to part time or casual;**
* **Ratio of men to women employed directly by tourism;**
* **% indigenous people employed directly by tourism (if appropriate).**

Reason for use of these indicators: It is often assumed that tourism will generate employment opportunities for local people but this is not necessarily the case, as tourism companies may bring in their pre-trained staff to run operations rather than invest in training locals. These indicators help the community to measure tourism employment in terms of new jobs, types of jobs, who is getting these positions and how many people are leaving their traditional activities to participate in tourism. The community can see if tourism measures up to its promises but also target employment towards specific sectors of their community, those most vulnerable to poverty. The first three indicators measure the direct contribution of tourism to employment generation in the community. The fourth indicator aims to measure the employment options tourism is creating for the local people (also infers income levels available to local people). The fifth identifies whether the opportunities are full time or must be complemented by other income generating activities. The final two indicators address the equitable distribution of employment opportunities within the community by specifically targeting information on traditionally marginalised groups, women and indigenous people.

Source(s) of data: Local government records, census data or community leaders should be able to provide the total number of workers in their community. Data corresponding to the other indicators may be available from tourism business employee records.

Means to use the indicators: These indicators can show need for action to address employment access issues, and to measure progress towards resolution.

The community can measure itself over time to see, for example, if education and training programs are enabling local people to move into more senior roles and to see if programs for women or indigenous peoples result in their greater integration into the industry.

Benchmarking: Best done as comparison over time for the same destination.

Indicators on operation and support of micro, small and medium sized enterprises (MSMEs), or community based enterprises:

* **Number of tourism-related MSMEs operating in the community (subdivided by types, e.g. accommodation and catering, guiding, transportation, tour operation, etc.);**

* **Incentives for MSMEs (e.g. special credits, tax advantage, grants, etc.): availability, amount provided;**

* **Capacity building for establishment and improvement of MSMEs: number of programmes/events, level of participation.**

  Reason for use of these indicators: Poor communities can benefit through direct sales of goods and services to tourists in the informal economy, but the formation of small enterprises is vital for more stable economic activities, enhanced quality standard of services and access to support programmes and incentives.

  Source(s) of data: Development and support programmes/projects, local authorities, industry registers, community groups and leaders.

  Means to use the indicators: Indicators on the development and operation of enterprises in poor communities provide baseline information on local economic development and they can serve as performance measure of support programmes.

  Benchmarking: Between destinations, development and support programmes, showing trends over time at destinations and project sites.

Indicators re achieving equitable distribution of tourism funds / benefits across the community:

* **% workers in the community directly employed by tourism (as above);**

* **Ratio of the top to the lowest paid local tourism worker;**

* **% total tourism income received by the most highly paid cohort in local tourism. Also calculate relationship between poorest cohorts (e.g bottom 10%) and overall data;**

* **Annual financial contribution by tourism to community projects (common fund, tourism taxes or net value of individual programs);**

* **Infrastructure development stimulated by tourism also benefiting the poor in the locality (directly or through support to other sectors): amount of investment, extension of new infrastructure;**

* **Number and type of development programs in place (education, training, health, natural resource management, conservation etc.);**

* **Community survey assessment of the usefulness and success of the various development programs (community Questionnaire Annex C).**

Reason for use of these indicators: To measure the distribution of tourism-derived income from direct employment, and to then audit the amount of money tourism contributes to common funds and community-level development objectives. Also to evaluate indirect benefits, accruing through infrastructure development stimulated by tourism investment.

Source(s) of data: Tourism businesses should be able to outline employment details and the different levels of income within their organization. They may provide information on their community projects or this may be available from local community groups and leaders. Managers of community funds, for the purposes of responsible management, should have data on their operations. Details of the different programs may be obtained from the project coordinators. Surveys and interviews would be required to assess the broader community opinion on the successes and downfalls of the development programs.

Means to use the indicators: In most cases, the community benefits when tourism income is shared across the community. The greater the % of the community working in tourism, the greater number of people will share in tourism income. The closer the ratio between the incomes of the top paid worker(s) to the lowest paid worker (i.e., 2:1 instead of 8:1), the more evenly financial benefits are shared. The % total tourism income gained by the highest paid individual is another indicator of whether tourism reaps benefits for all or a select few.

Common funds and community programs enable the positive influence of tourism to extend beyond those directly involved in the industry, in order to fulfil broader community development objectives. These indicators address economic and social accountability; the total annual financial contribution by tourism to the fund (transparency) and assessment of the utility / success of programs. It is effectively an audit of development programs enabling the community to review, and then assess, the economic and non-economic value of these programs.

Benchmarking: The community can compare the data over time or use it to establish goals to improve the distribution of tourism income within their community. Ideally tourism should be challenged to increase its contribution to shared funds and this can be measured year to year. Discussions around the allocation of community funds will be easier when the community knows how many of each type of program exists and can choose to support the most successful (as determined by community surveys).

Indicators re evaluating less tangible, non-economic, livelihood priorities:

* **Annual audit of the contribution of different activities to household needs;**

* **Survey of household capacity to fulfil livelihood priorities for the year (rating level of food security, ability to meet cash needs, local empowerment, vulnerability to external policy, vulnerability to external conditions, cultural value and physical security).**

Reason for use of these indicators: Provides a non-economic assessment of development achievements within the community.

Source(s) of data: Community surveys, focus groups, community meetings and discussions with community leaders. Note: some of the indices can be complex and may not be easily obtained without explicit surveys. Note that the ratings may require professional analysis and community level research to obtain data. If poverty is an important issue, these data may be obtainable from government or NGO sources who undertake such surveys.

Means to use the indicators: An annual audit of the contribution of different activities to household needs firstly identifies the basic needs of each household and then ranks the contribution of tourism compared to other activities but it is a "level of importance" rather than an "economic" ranking. It is a guide to the social acceptability of tourism among workers. The household survey, by evaluating where households fell short of achieving their goals, indicates in which areas development programs should target their poverty alleviation strategies and how tourism can contribute to them.

Benchmarking: The community can review how different needs have been addressed over-time and determine where weaknesses still lie in their development programs, useful for strategic planning.

Sustainable development of tourism, as it relates to poverty alleviation, relies heavily on positive economic and social outcomes.

Bongani South Africa. Local performers benefit from tourist interest in culture.

Therefore several of the indicators used to address other issues will also be of interest, particularly those related to Employment (p. 119), ➢ **Effects of Tourism on Communities** (p. 57) ➢ **Economic Benefits** (p. 128), Land tenure issues can also be important relating to community control over their lands; amount of land that tourism is subsuming each year, ownership of local land (is it being sold to outsiders?) and, importantly, access of locals to their community spaces. (See Access by Local Residents p. 65).

Box 3.23 Tourism and poverty alleviation in Namibia

In Namibia, the main livelihood priorities were: to increase food security, meet cash needs, increase local empowerment, decrease vulnerability to external policy and conditions (including drought), foster cultural values and maintain the physical security of residents. Local tourism decision-making did not place emphasis on cash income but, instead, carefully considered each livelihood factor.

In the Torra Conservancy, for example, residents negotiated with two tourism companies but selected only one project (even though the projects were not mutually exclusive). According to livelihood priorities, a 16-bed tented camp was determined to be more appropriate than a small, exclusive lodge. Decisions were based on the details provided in each proposal, summarised in the table below.

Comparison of the tented camp and lodge proposals

Proposal 1: Tented Camp	Proposal 2: Lodge
Likely community income of N$ 50-70,000 per year.	Possible community income of N$100-200,000 per year.
Exclusive use of a small tourism-only area. Access to a larger mixed-use area. No other lodges/camps in large area.	Exclusive use of large area: no livestock or people, nor other tourism developments. Area included a spring useful for droughts.
Low risk – well established company.	High risk – no tourism track record.
Clear on what was wanted.	Plans changed, goal posts moved.
10 year contract with 5 year renewal.	Wanted 30 year contract.
Community free to develop trophy hunting if area agreed with the company.	Wanted rights to both tourism and trophy hunting, but plans for the latter remained unclear.
Community gains ownership in years 11 – 15.	Unclear ownership at end of contract.
Contract negotiated, signed and implemented.	Draft contracts negotiated but did not proceed.

The community decided to go ahead with the tented camp because there was less risk to the potential cash income (as the company was well established) and also because this proposal did not jeopardise current income generating activities (as grazing rights were secured, as was full access to important drought water resources). The contract period was less for the tented camp and long term ownership was retained by the community, in contrast the lodge required a 30 year contract and post-contract ownership of the facility was unclear. These examples show that a number of factors are involved in the selection of alternatives, and also define some of the values which it will be useful to monitor over time with indicators.

Source: Ashley, C. 2000, The impacts of tourism on rural livelihoods: Namibia's experience, Overseas Development Institute, London, UK.

3.6.7 Competitiveness of Tourism Businesses

Price and Value, Quality, Differentiation, Specialization, Vitality, Business Cooperation, Long-term Profitability

Unlike most of the other issues discussed in this section, the competitiveness of a destination is a relative measure. Any indicators of competitiveness relate to how well a destination is doing compared to others. For example, how a destination's tourism profile compares to others, how it competes on price or quality, or the extent to which it is carving out its own niche to differentiate itself from other destinations.

Competitive strategy economic theory suggests that at the core, competitive advantage is achieved because of cost advantages (and hence price), differentiation (a unique product or bundle of products and services or perceived uniqueness), or a focus strategy to serve a particular target better than more broad-based competitors (e.g. niche tourism products and markets).

If tourism at a destination is to be sustainable, not only must it be economically profitable over the long run and compete successfully with other destinations on a local, national or international basis, but it must also consider socio-cultural, environmental, and other factors. The natural and cultural assets and advantages of a destination need to be protected in the long term and not exploited in the short term.

Box 3.24 The dimensions of tourism competitiveness

A recent publication suggests that the nature of tourism competitiveness and sustainability is evolving. Contributing factors in this evolution include the travel experience demanded by tourists, demographics, and external crises forced upon destinations. The dimensions of tourism competitiveness considered include:

1.   economic competitiveness;
2.   political competitiveness;
3.   the renaissance of the city-state;
4.   socio-cultural competitiveness;
5.   technological competitiveness, and
6.   environmental competitiveness.

Source: The Competitive Destination: A Sustainable Tourism Perspective
J.R. Brent Ritchie & Geoffrey L. Crouch, CABI Publishing, Oxford, 2003

A successful competitive tourism strategy will yield above average returns for a destination when compared to others. Measuring success can be difficult. Indicators must be collected and valid over many years to show long-term profitability and stability at a destination, even though there may be many changes, some gradual and planned, some significant and unexpected. The key components of the competitiveness issue and corresponding indicators are the following:

Components of the issue	Indicators
Cost advantages, price and value Input costs: employment, taxes, overheads & premiums, costs of services and supplies, human resources costs (hiring, training, retaining) transportation costs	• Cost/Price ratios (including gross margin) of accommodation, attractions, tours or packages compared to industry norms or ratios for similar products at other destinations.
Differentiation Unique products and experiences, Inherent attractions, positioning the destination, branding, quality, standards perceived or psycho-logical advantages (e.g. a perception of exclusivity may allow higher prices to be charged)	• % of tourists attracted to destination because of unique features (questionnaire); • Rating of destination by tourists; • Attractiveness compared to similar destinations; • Expectations met or exceeded; • Value/price rating by tourists; See also Image and Branding (p. 236).

Specialty niches/focus strategy
 Narrowing the focus for tourism products and target markets, Intangibles; tourist "experiences", destination "appeal".
 Business clusters around a theme e.g. a "food and wine cluster" involving accommodation, restaurants, chefs, vineyards, cycle tours, cuisine, specialty book stores, wine merchants
	• Measure of uniqueness; e.g.;
	   - destination is the only location for.........(a specific type of activity, attraction);
	   - destination is one of only 2 (or 3,4,5) in the country (in the world) offering.......(specify);
	 • Number (or %) of tourism businesses and support services within a "cluster";
	 • % of tourism revenue due to niche products or clusters.

Cooperation/overcoming fragmentation Cooperation amongst businesses; common marketing, image, branding of the destination. Research, training, support for small businesses	• % of tourism businesses that have integrated their goals and objectives with the destination tourism strategy; • % of tourism business participating in cooperative marketing; • % of marketing expenditures in cooperative initiatives (e.g. through private associations and joint public-private initiatives); • Amount and % of public authority budget designated for supporting business development, level of participation in support schemes.
Vitality of the industry	• The longevity of tourism businesses (rate of turnover); • Re-sale value of tourism businesses (average for type of business); • Level of participation by business in tourism strategy development, and marketing initiatives; • Strength of membership in tourism industry associations (number, %); • Tourism revenues (growth rates); • Annual profit of tourism businesses. • ≫ **Occupancy rates for Accommodation** (See ≫ **Seasonality** p. 111)

In a nutshell, a successful competitive strategy yields better profits – over time. As a consequence, most of the social, environmental and political factors (and issues) addressed in other parts of this book are important, as they will affect the bottom line. Sustainability is in some ways a synonym for competitiveness – in that those enterprises which are competitive over the long term are more likely to be sustainable, and vice-versa. **Benchmarking is critical** for competitiveness, because competitiveness is inherently a comparative measure demonstrating that the destination or enterprise is better (or not) than the average, the others, key competitors, etc. Note that some authors (e.g., Ritchie and Crouch 2003) suggest a compound competitiveness indicator that combines yearly profitability with environmental and socio-cultural indicators of significance to the destination – such complex measures can be done but may be very difficult to support for most destinations).

Indicators of price and value:

* **Cost/price ratios;**
* **Gross margin (direct cost of sales as % of revenue).**

    Reason for use of these indicators: To determine cost as a percent of sales as an indication of cost advantages or the need to trim costs to compete. Ratios may be an aggregate for a company's total sales or based on prices charged and costs for the specific tourism products sold.

    Source(s) of data: Tourism business financial data

    Ways to use the indicators: Ratios can be compared to industry norms. Some tourism industry associations may share information amongst members, but these ratios tend to be business confidential.

    Benchmarking: Various input costs such as labour and transportation provide benchmarks against which to measure success in minimizing cost/price ratios.

Indicators related to attractiveness:

* **% of tourists attracted by unique features;**
* **Uniqueness ratings (from questionnaire);**
* **Value/Price measures (from questionnaire).**

    Reason for use of indicators: To assess the extent to which a destination's unique features are core to attracting tourists and delivering a satisfying experience for the price paid.

    Source(s) of data: Questionnaire to tourists on location or after their visit.

    Ways to use the indicators: To determine if the attractiveness of the destination is enduring over time, and what the critical elements of features of the destination are from a tourist's point of view. Some features may be of minor importance or lose their appeal over time; others may be more important or gain in importance. It may be useful to ask tourists to compare to other destinations relative to their perception of uniqueness or value for price.

    Benchmarking: A destination wishing to stay highly differentiated (e.g. a specialty niche) will refer to higher measures of uniqueness, and higher percentages of tourists attracted by uniqueness as benchmarks. Benchmarks provide comparisons to other similar destinations. Benchmarks may be used across a range of features at a destination or within a tourism cluster – these will likely have to be collected directly from the tourists.

Other indicators of factors related to competitiveness:

* **Number (or %) of tourism businesses and support services within a "cluster";**
* **% of tourism revenue due to niche products or clusters.**

These indicators give a measure of the effectiveness of competing with niche products for specific target markets. If a destination is successful in a given niche, there may be a tendency for more generic tourism to develop, perhaps changing the nature of the destination. For example a rainforest area may increase the number of general interest nature tourists, but perhaps negatively impact the opportunities for wildlife watching or birding enthusiasts.

* **% of tourism businesses that have integrated their goals and objectives with the destination tourism strategy;**

* **% of tourism business participating in cooperative marketing;**

* **% of marketing expenditures in cooperative initiative.**

These indicators are a good measure of the extent to which tourism businesses are cooperating to maximize the competitive differentiation of the destination, rather than competing against each other.

* **Annual profit of tourism businesses;**

* **A compound competitiveness indicator (economic, social, environmental)** (see Ritchie and Crouch 2003 for an example).

Both these indicators tracked over the long term give a destination a measure of its competitive success. The second is a complex composite indicator which tries to model overall competitiveness and will likely be difficult to use for most destinations due to data requirements and analysis. Unfortunately business profits tend to be confidential, so destinations may have to rely on other indicators such as the following to provide some information on strength of the tourism sector:

* **The longevity of tourism businesses (rate of turnover);**

* **Re-sale value of tourism businesses (average for type of business);**

* **Level of participation by business in tourism strategy development, and marketing initiatives;**

* **Strength of membership in tourism industry associations (number, %);**

* **Tourism revenues (growth rates);**

* ➤ **Occupancy rates for Accommodation** (See ➤ **Seasonality** p. 111)

Because competitiveness is a relatively complex concept, it may take the use of several of these indicators to support dialogue on the issue in a given destination.

Box 3.25 Caribbean Program for Economic Competitiveness: Organization of Eastern Caribbean States (OECS)

Key Competitiveness Issues A study of the OECS tourism sector identified five key competitiveness issues. These relate to:

* **Competitive Positioning:** the need to develop and implement regional marketing programs, positioning the Caribbean region in the context of other major world destinations;

* **Product Quality:** shortfalls in the tourism sector (particularly small hotels, attractions and services);

* **Environment:** environmental and resource management concerns at both destination and tourism facility levels;

* **Commitment:** shortfalls in commitment to the importance of tourism and the absence of strong tourism awareness programs;

* **Cooperation:** the need to foster increased local participation in the tourism sector.

The study notes that it is generally acknowledged that larger hotel properties are making headway in the competitiveness environment they face world-wide. However, of particular concern to most countries is the difficulty local entrepreneurs face in achieving viable participation in the tourism sector.

Source: http://www.cpechrd.org/oecstourism.htm

3.7 Protection of Valuable Natural Assets

3.7.1 Protecting Critical Ecosystems

Fragile Sites, Endangered Species

Rare flora and fauna and unique ecosystems are significant attractions for tourists. The growth of niche tourism which focuses on experiences and visiting fragile sites to observe or study these species and ecosystems both enhances learning about environments and brings the risk of damage to them. Ecotourism as well, while intending to tread lightly, also can focus stresses on the most fragile sites. (See Ecotourism p. 268) Worldwide efforts are being made to provide protection for the world's ecological treasures even as the demand to visit and experience them grows. Governments are making increasing efforts to protect natural areas and there have been numerous reserves established by NGOs, community organizations and private companies, often for ecotourism purposes. The number and extension of protected areas has been constantly increasing through the past decades. In 2002, there were around 44,000 sites registered as protected areas, according to IUCN definition, that cover around 10% of the land surface of the Earth (data by UNEP and WCMC cited in IUCN/WTO/UNEP 2002).

Components of the issue	Indicators
Area protected, and to what degree	• Existence of protected area(s) at the destination; • Extent of protected area(s) – square km (classified by level of protection, according to IUCN categories).
Intensity of use	• (See ≫ **Controlling use intensity** p. 192).
Disturbance to species and fragile systems particularly specific impacts on rare and endangered species	• Health of population of key indicator species (counts, sightings); • Breeding success rates for selected species.
Costs of maintenance of protection	• Cost of protection/restoration; • Tourism contribution to protection and restoration.

For more detailed information on indicators see the Natural and Sensitive Ecological Sites, p. 263 Parks and Protected Areas sections p. 269. in Part 4.

Indicators for protection:

* **Existence of protected area(s) at the destination;**

* **Extent of protected area(s) – square km (classified by level of protection, according to IUCN categories).**

  Reason for use of these indicators: For known areas of fragility or important habitats, the area protected (existence, number, level of protection/status, spatial extent) can be an important measure of potential protection of the key species (assets for tourism). There are several different levels of protection used, depending on local, national or international regulations, ranging from complete prohibition of use to various forms of controlled access. Zoning of protected areas defines specific uses and protection levels, often with core conservation zones, zones with limited tourist access and buffer zones with more intensive use for visitor facilities. If impacts are very severe, access may be limited or denied to the tourism industry. Tourism can be a partner in protection through sensitive products, trained guides, and effective controls as well as a contributor to programs which support conservation (see Tourism as a Contributor to Nature Conservation p. 123). These indicators are often most effectively used at a very local or site level.

Source(s) of data: Local authorities, parks and protected area managers.

Means to use these indicators: Percentage of the critical site or habitat which is protected to different levels is probably the most useful categorization. Another may be % of site open to tourist use, or %/area under restricted access.

Benchmarking: The IUCN designation for protection is an international standard for levels of protection. See their website for publications on this guideline and on certain applications: http://www.iucn.org/themes/wcpa/pubs/guidelines.htm . These basic indicators on protected areas can be easily compared between different sites within national and regional jurisdictions. It is also important to track changes over time regarding the extension of protected areas and their designated use zones.

Indicators regarding ecosystem health:

* **Health of population of key indicator species;**

    (One or more species to be selected based on status in destination, with reference to species status in global Red Book.)

* **Breeding success rates for selected species.**

    Reason for use of these indicators: In many destinations, certain species are the reason why tourists visit. Species such as whales (Gulf of California, Cape Breton, Lofoten Islands, Peninsula Valdes) Red Crested Cranes (coastal China), rhinoceros in many African nations, wildflowers, rare orchids or unique ferns, etc., are the principal draw, also called "flagship species". Harm to the species can derive from impacts of tourism or other sectors. Knowledge of the health of the species is therefore invaluable from both the point of view of the ecology and the tourism industry.

    Source(s) of data: Data are often collected by environmental agencies or through studies from institutes or universities. In some sites, there may be only a one-time study which may serve as a baseline for repetition. In some sites, there may never have been studies, and the tourism industry may have to be the catalyst for such research to be done. Species counts of many birds, mega-fauna, as well as other species can be done by protected area personnel, tour guides, and tourists can be involved in monitoring activities as well (e.g. bird-watching groups, conservation volunteers). (See Uganda Heritage Trails p. 440, Yacutinga p. 453). If animal sighting is difficult, especially in the case of low population density for certain species (e.g. predators, such as jaguars), monitoring of tracks can be used, and there exist sophisticated remote sensing techniques as well. In some countries frequency of road kill of animals (e.g., marsupial possums in New Zealand, deer in Canada, turtles and vipers in the Mediterranean) can be a crude surrogate for population health where no other measure exists. Ironically, the higher the road kill toll, the greater the numbers of members of the species.

    Means to use the indicators: Species counts for the same area showing increases or declines. Note that it may be difficult to relate any changes to tourism.

    Benchmarking: This is a unique indicator related to specific species populations and best used in time series against past years in the same site or destination.

Indicators regarding protection costs and expenditures:

●   **Cost of protection/restoration;**

●   **Tourism contribution to protection/restoration** (see p. 123).

Reason for use of these indicators: The impacts of tourists (and sometimes other sectors' activities- such as acid rain, noise from transportation, leachate from mines etc) may harm species and their habitats. Where sites are managed, budgets are established for protection and restoration where necessary. The trend line in this budget (or where there is insufficient funding, the desired budget) can reveal important changes in the ability to sustain the systems and may be a signal of need for new programs or fundraising. Rising needs may be a sign of increased damage to assets that may point to need for a range of preventive or restorative actions.

Source(s) of data: Financial records, budget documents, or annual plans/submissions of protection agencies, regional authorities.

Means to use the indicators: Trend lines in expenditures may reveal increased costs of repair or protective activities (e.g. ten new wardens hired to stop poaching, two tourist rangers hired full time to prevent damage to the bamboo grove by visitors).

Benchmarking: While some data on levels of expenditure are available from e.g. IUCN or UNESCO for selected heritage sites, the conditions are very different from destination to destination and the most useful benchmark is likely to be the data for the same site over time.

Unique limestone formations, Viñales, Cuba

3.7.2 Sea Water Quality

Contamination, Perception of Water Quality

A majority of the world's tourism is located in coastal areas. Beaches are the target for a majority of those who visit coasts, but other activities such as fishing, diving, boating or nature viewing are also affected if water quality is compromised. For many destinations the quality of the beach and in particular the water itself is a significant factor in choice of destination.

Components of the issue	Indicators

Contamination events which may harm the health of bathers or damage coastal ecosystems (particularly marine fauna, fragile reef and coastal wetland systems, shellfish and fish habitat). Gradual degradation of water quality from cumulative effects of industrial, urban or agricultural effluents.	* Level of contamination of seawater (faecal coliforms, campylobacter);
	* Level of contamination of seawater (heavy metals);
	* # days beach/shore closed due to contamination events;
	* Turbidity of water (simple tests);
	* Alternative proxy indicators where laboratory testing is difficult:
	  - frequency of algae blooms;
	  - counts of dead fish or birds on shore;
	  - frequency counts of indicator species which are particularly vulnerable (sponges, corals, sea-urchin).

Loss of tourism custom associated with contamination or changes in seawater quality (including changes in such factors as water temperature, algae, turbidity or salinity)	* Tourist perception of quality of seawater.
Note the related issues which may be of interest, particularly in coastal zone destinations: beach cleanliness, erosion of coastal areas, perception of beach quality, and density of use of coastal zones.	See additional indicators in the issue section on ➤ **Sewage Treatment** (p. 171), Impacts on reefs, (p. 250) and Cruise Ships (p. 297) where these are relevant. See also the indicators in the Health issue (p. 94) where health effects quality are a concern.

The destinations sections on Coastal Zones (p. 247), Beach Destinations (p. 251), reefs (p. 250), and Small Islands (p. 253) provide more on how this issue can impact on a destination. See also the sections on Cruise Ships (p. 297) and the issue section on ➤ **Sewage Treatment** (p. 171).

Indicators of water contamination:

* **Level of contamination of seawater (faecal coliforms, campylobacter);**
* **Level of contamination of seawater (heavy metals);**
* **Turbidity of water (simple tests).**

Note alternative proxy indicators which can be used where laboratory testing is difficult or too expensive:

* Frequency of algae blooms;
* Counts of dead fish or birds on shore;
* Frequency counts of indicator species which are particularly vulnerable (sponges, corals).

   Reason for use of these indicators: Among all potential pollutants, these are the most frequently used as indicators of contamination levels. They are also relatively easy to measure. Most health authorities use e-coli, and many are now also collecting data on campylobacter.

   Source(s) of data: In many jurisdictions these are systematically collected by environmental authorities or health departments. Local institutes also can readily collect samples where there is no broader program.

Means to use these indicators: The indicator is usually used by authorities to open, close or limit use of shore zones. (See also the Blue Flag program which uses E.Coli as one of the criteria for attaining the Flag (www.blueflag.org). Results are normally used to determine/announce which activities are safe to do in the water. The results can also be portrayed at regional/national level as % samples exceeding safe limits/standards (e.g. Mediterranean Tourism).

Benchmarking: This is a very common indicator, providing many sources of benchmarking. For detail ed water standards from the World Health Organization, see http://www.who.int/docstore/water_sanitation_health/Documents/IWA/iwabookchap18.htm#18.3 A coastal indicators website is also available for some benchmarking and additional indicators - http://ioc.unesco.org/ (then type "indicators" in the search box). Another which may be of use is "A Reference Guide on the Use of Indicators for Integrated Coastal Management" from the same source.

Indicator of contamination impact on tourist use:

⊛ **Number days beach/shore closed due to contamination events.**

Reason for use of this indicator: This is a simple measure reflecting the need for action to close beaches or limit shore use due to contamination events, regardless of source (sewage releases, algae blooms, oil spills, jellyfish invasion, etc.) This is a very public indicator – measuring direct effects on the public, including tourists.

Source(s) of data: Local beach managers, health authorities, environmental agencies. If no-one is collecting it, a tourism authority or industry association can easily document incidents itself.

Means to use the indicator: Simple information on number of days each year (overall, and in swimming season) the beach was closed to swimming, or other shore activities. (Note that the US Environmental Protection Agency has a very simple standard for portraying the quality of water under the terms: "drinkable", "swimmable", "fishable" and "boatable" with the worst - "not boatable" -being too contaminated even for boating activities. This is a very graphic portrayal of levels of contamination/quality in terms accessible to and meaningful to the public).

Benchmarking: Benchmark against other destinations (Data for many beaches can be obtained on line from many US, Australian, Canadian and Hong Kong beaches. US national summaries are available from http://www.americanoceans.org/beach/link.htm which provides access to other beach monitoring sites). Perhaps the best measure is changes over time against other years for the destination. (Note that results from other beach monitoring sites provide a rough benchmark as standards may not be applied in the same way in all destinations, even in the same jurisdiction).

Indicator of how tourists view the seawater quality:

⊛ **Tourist perception of quality of seawater.**

Reason for use of this indicator: The perception of seawater quality may have a greater impact on tourist decisions than more scientifically obtained information. Tourist perceptions of seawater quality may be affected by such factors as water clarity, temperature, turbulence, smell, colour etc., even more than the presence or absence of specific contaminants. The actions taken by tourists are affected by these perceptions.

Beach crowd, Costinesti youth resort,
Black Sea coast of Romania

Source(s) of data: Exit questionnaire – (see Exit questionnaire Annex C), number of complaints registered at local authorities, hotels, beach management.

Means to use the indicator: The % of tourists who agree that the quality of the seawater is good or very good can be a signal to authorities that action is needed, or a positive factor to tell tourists.

Benchmarking: There is some potential to benchmark against other similar destinations which use the same questionnaire. The most useful benchmark is likely to be changes over time in the specific destination.

Other indicators of interest relating to seawater quality:

- See issue section on ➢ **Sewage Treatment** (p. 171);
- Impacts on reefs, (Box 4.1 p. 250);
- Cruise Ships (p. 297) in Destinations;
- Health (p. 94).

3.8 Managing Scarce Natural Resources

3.8.1 Energy Management ➢ **Baseline Issue**

Energy Saving, Efficiency, Renewables

Significant levels of energy are consumed by the tourism sector both through fixed assets (buildings etc.) and mobile assets (motor vehicles, trains, ferries etc.). A reduction in energy consumed will have a positive impact on operational costs of enterprises (and can reduce pressure on utilities) and have major environmental benefits, primarily through reducing consumption of natural resources and lowering associated greenhouse gas emissions. Energy is produced from a variety of sources, including non-renewable (e.g. natural gas, gasoline, diesel, coal) and renewable (e.g. wind, biomass, solar heat, hydroelectric, etc.)

In tourism destinations, the industry itself can be a major component of consumption. Efforts to reduce its consumption can be beneficial not only to the industry, through cost savings to individual enterprises, but can also bring benefits to the destination as a whole, in the form of reduced demand for energy (a particular issue where sources are fully utilized, or where the main source of energy is imported fuels.) Indicators regarding energy therefore focus on consumption, the use of alternative (renewable) sources, and on the introduction of energy efficiency and saving programs.

Box 3.26 Energy consumption – Douglas Shire, Queensland, Australia

Douglas Shire Council has attempted to minimize the overall consumption of energy for the Shire whilst promoting greater use of renewable energy resources through the highlighting the following initiatives:

- A Domestic Remote Area Power Scheme (DRAPS) subsidy for residents unable to access mains electricity. These systems consist of Photovoltaic panels, batteries and a back up diesel generator;

- Residents are being given incentives to introduce solar hot water systems through rebate grants. These systems contribute around 40% of the average domestic energy consumption;

- It is estimated that 367,350 kWh of electricity used North of the Daintree River within Douglas Shire is created from renewable sources of energy. (Source: Daintree Futures Study, 2000 cited in Report on Douglas Shire Baseline Data, August 2001);

- Further incentives for energy efficient buildings are due to be introduced into the new planning scheme being prepared for the Shire;

- The Mossman Central Sugar Mill produces renewable energy as a by-product of the cane crushing process, and 326 mWh was exported to the national grid during the 2000 crushing season.

This project was undertaken in collaboration with Douglas Shire Council as part of a wider research project by the Cooperative Research Centre for Sustainable Tourism.

Components of the issue	Indicators
Measuring energy use and conservation	• **Per capita consumption of energy from all sources (overall, and by tourist sector – per person day)** ≫ **Baseline indicator** Note: can also be used as derived indicator of energy use per resident relative to energy use per tourist.
Energy management programs	• **Percentage of businesses participating in energy conservation programs, or applying energy saving policy and techniques** ≫ **Baseline indicator**
Use of renewable energy sources	• **% of energy consumption from renewable resources (at destinations, establishments)** ≫ **Baseline indicator**; • Number, of % of establishments (e.g. hotels) using renewable sources, generating own energy (see Box 3.27 re energy sources).

Indicators of consumption/conservation:

- **Per capita consumption (Total energy consumption (MJ) per annum / Person years per annum) This can often be isolated for the tourist sector through utility records, permitting derived indicators such as ratio of per capita use tourists/locals** ≫ **Baseline Indicator;**

- **Consumption by source;**

- **Savings in energy expenses, Use of Renewable Energy sources** ≫ **Baseline Indicator;**

* **Percentage of businesses participating in energy conservation programs, or applying energy saving policy and techniques ≫ Baseline Indicator.**

Indicators relating to consumption of resources and production of wastes, which are calculated on a per person per annum basis, need to take into account both residents and visitors - international and domestic ones (overnight visitors and same-day visitors).

Reason for use of these indicators: Minimize overall energy consumption and encourage greater use from renewable energy sources. Measure success relative to any conservation initiatives.

Source(s) of data: All energy sources used within the destination should be used to calculate the total energy usage. Electricity consumption is often quoted in kilowatt hours (kWh) and other sources, such as diesel, petroleum, liquefied petroleum gas (LPG) and natural gas, by volume. All should be converted to megajoules (or a common unit for comparison purposes). There are a number of energy calculators available which will readily do this e.g., the Green Globe energy calculator (www.greenglobe21.com) which was developed by the CRC for Sustainable Tourism.

Box 3.27 Energy Sources

Energy Sources	Renewable or Non-renewable	Suggested Data Sources
1. Electricity(this should include domestic, commercial and industrial figures)	(may be produced from either renewable or non-renewable sources – SEE BELOW)	These data should be available through the local energy supply authority (note that electricity has different sources – ranging from oil, natural gas, hydroelectricity, wind, geothermal, nuclear) If it is possible to document the source, it may be feasible to measure changes in the source mix.
2. Aviation turbine	NR	
3. Bagasse (cane waste) or other local fibres (corn, reeds etc)	R	
4. Coal	NR	
5. Diesel	NR	Data should be available either from the top down via the major fuel suppliers or from wholesale fuel suppliers. Other appropriate sources would include the bureau of statistics, any energy program or environmental protection agency (government data).
6. Gasoline(automotive)	NR	
7. Gasoline(aviation)	NR	
8. Geothermal	R	
9. Hydro	R	
10. Kerosene (lighting)	NR	
11. Liquefied Petroleum Gas	NR	
12. Methane (animal sources)	R	
13. Naphtha	NR	
14. Natural gas	NR	
15. Nuclear	-	
16. Oil(fuel)	NR	Note that where independent sources of electrical power are used, (e.g generators, local hydro, solar power) the user may have their own purchase and operational records.
17. Oil(heating)	NR	
18. Solar	R	
19. Town gas (or coal oil)	NR	
20. Wind	R	
21. Wood	R	

Box 3.27 outlines a common list of energy sources used in destinations. For more detailed calculations regarding energy sources, percentage deriving from renewable or less contaminating sources, etc, a source table can be compiled for the destination. Ideally this has already been done by the utility serving the destination or by a regulating authority. Note it may be difficult to ascribe specific energy sources to particular uses, as once energy is in an electrical grid, it is essentially interchangeable and therefore substitution (obtaining more from wind power and less from coal) will usually occur at a utility-wide or destination level. However, conservation will occur at an establishment level. Normally overall electricity consumption can be calculated at tourist establishments and businesses, as they have

meters and pay for consumption. Measurement of consumption is not just important at destination (municipality) level but at operations and establishments as well. Tourism-specific data at a destination might be accumulated from companies.

There are many cases of good practices on energy efficiency, reduction and use of renewables at companies and establishments. Where tourist properties (e.g. resorts, hotels) have their own independent generation sources, or rely on fossil fuels for e.g., heating, it may be possible to calculate separate budgets for each energy type used.

Hotels may use solar sources for pool heating, laundry, or space heating. Many guidebooks exist which show a wide range of approaches to energy use reduction (timed lighting, systems which turn off utilities when visitors are not in their rooms, means to reduce energy use in laundries etc.)

> *Means to use the indicators:* These indicators are useful to display trends in energy consumption and allow the destination to monitor performance and measure any changes in mix and use levels. Where data can be isolated for tourism, its use trends can be compared with other sectors.

> *Benchmarking:* This indicator can be benchmarked in two ways: over time for the individual destination and its tourism establishments or by using comparative data from certification systems that verify energy use at destinations and tourism facilities.

Note that individual establishments may produce their own energy and may undertake direct substitutions. The use of energy (and conservation) can therefore be calculated for an individual establishment (hotel, resort, ski operation etc) or for a larger unit such as a destination or a community. Users are directed to a range of hotel and other initiatives aimed at more environmentally sound practice for examples of how to obtain energy savings. (See Accor Case p. 327)

Traditional water mills in Slunj, Croatia: Energy and water are themselves a tourist attraction

3.8.2 Climate Change and Tourism

Mitigation, Adaptation, Extreme Climatic Events, Risks, Impacts on Destinations, Greenhouse Gas Emissions, Transport, Energy Use

The weight of evidence supports concern that the global climate is changing. Most of the change is attributable to the impacts of human activity; both in causing an increase in greenhouse gas emissions and in changing the buffering capacity of the natural environment to absorb (sequester) carbon. Tourism activity is a significant contributor to global production of greenhouse gases – through transportation, heating, and cooling and other forms of energy use. The industry is also likely to be affected significantly by changes in climate both globally and locally.

Both the adaptation to potential changes and the reduction of tourism's contribution to climate change are concerns for the tourism industry worldwide. Through their initial communications on climate change, most nations have begun to identify the potential to reduce emissions by each sector, or mitigate potential negative impacts, and to adapt through changes in planning and construction so as to reduce potential damage from weather related events.

The First International Conference on Climate Change and Tourism (Djerba, Tunisia, April 2003), convened by WTO, offered a unique opportunity for tourism interests and scientists to exchange views on the consequences, opportunities and risks presented to the tourism sector as a result of changes in the world's climate. The main outcome of the Conference, the *Djerba Declaration on Climate Change and Tourism,* recognizes the complex two-way relationship between climate change and tourism. On the one hand, tourism is impacted by climate change, especially considering tourism destinations in coastal, mountain, drought- and flood-prone areas; on the other, tourism is also contributing to the causes of climate change, especially through emissions resulting from transportation and the use of energy.

The Conference Final Report, including the Djerba Declaration text is available at:

http://www.world-tourism.org/sustainable/climate/brochure.htm

The potential impacts of climate change on tourism

Climate change can impact tourism in many ways:

* Changing and more erratic weather patterns are making tourism planning and operations more difficult;

* Climate-related natural disasters harm infrastructure, natural and cultural heritage and host communities; much tourism infrastructure is located in vulnerable areas;

* Climate changes can affect tourist comfort levels and the range of activities;

* Climate-induced changes in general health conditions can affect visitors and insurance practices;

* Rising sea levels and temperatures are threatening coastal and island destinations and marine sites;

* Climate change affects natural habitats and the biodiversity of species, which are attractions for nature-based and ecotourism;

* Alterations in precipitation patterns and the hydrological cycle can affect the availability of freshwater resources at destinations, which is a basic asset for tourists;

* Diminishing snow conditions are directly affecting mountain and winter-sport tourism.

Kurumba, Maldives. The entire nation is considered vulnerable to climate change as nearly all of the country is within two metres of sea level and already affected by storm surges

Climate impacts can bring both problems and opportunities for tourism destinations, significantly altering tourism demand flows. For example, due to global warming, Northern European territories and coasts can be increasingly attractive for summer vacations, causing a possible decline for Mediterranean destinations, which in turn could be more frequented during pre- and post high season periods or wintertime. The changes in demand patterns can cause major effects in socio-economic conditions of destinations (e.g. employment and social services), producing knock-off effects in related economic activities (e.g. agriculture, transportation). As well, tourism is a significant consumer of water, often in destinations which, even without climate change, have supply problems. Changes in precipitation patterns may alter water supply, limiting the numbers who can be supported. (See ➤ **Water availability and conservation** p. 165).

Many tourist activities (e.g. skiing, swimming, beach activities, wildlife and nature based tourism generally) require specific sets of weather conditions. Small rises in winter temperature for example, will eliminate the lower slopes from most of the ski resorts in the Alps, and remove the possibility of skiing in many other resorts which at best have short or marginal seasons. Temperature changes may also alter biodiversity, change migration paths and the location of habitats where wildlife may be found. The response of tourists to the impacts of climate change may produce adverse impressions of a destination's attractiveness (i.e. dead coral, habitat loss, scarcity of species). In consequence; there is a need to develop adaptation measures to reduce the vulnerability of tourism destinations.

Components of the climate change issue: adaptation	Indicators
Level of damage related to extreme climatic events	• Frequency of extreme climatic events; • Value of damage to tourism sector.
Level of exposure to risk	• Percentage of tourist infrastructure (hotels, other) located in vulnerable zones.
Degree of planning for climate change impacts	• Degree to which key tourist zones are covered by contingency or emergency planning (existence of plan, % area included).
Impact on seashores	• Value of tourism infrastructure in coastal zone below estimated maximum storm surge levels or equivalent; • Value of damage annually due to storm events or flooding; • % of tourist area and infrastructure with sea defences (could be classed by level of protection).
Impact on mountains	• % ski areas or ski-able terrain with snowmaking equipment; • % of developed ski area which would lack access to ski-able conditions with warming. (use IPCC warming scenarios for the destination).
Impact on wildlife and biodiversity	• % of tourism dependent on viewing species (% of key species considered vulnerable to changes in climate).

Indicators of climate related damage:

* **Frequency of extreme events;**
* **Value of damage to tourism sector.**

Reasons for use of these indicators: Extreme events (hurricanes, cyclones, typhoons, tornados, flooding, blizzards, drought events, temperature extremes) can all affect individual tourists, the infrastructure of tourism and the perception of a destination. Both the frequency of such events and the damage caused are measures of impact, and may show trends important to the industry and the destination.

Source(s) of data: Normally these data are kept by environment departments or weather services and emergency measures organizations and where they exist. If there is no government program, some data can be kept locally by the industry itself, particularly for remote destinations where the weather may not be similar to that at government weather stations. (e.g., the weather at the top of the mountain).

Means to use these indicators: The value of actual or potential damage can be expressed in monetary terms, which is easily understood by tourism stakeholders.

Benchmarking: While it is possible to compare with weather data worldwide, the most meaningful information is that of changes over time in the destination.

Indicator of level of exposure to risk:

∗   **Percentage of tourist infrastructure (hotels, other) located in vulnerable zones (as defined in each country's climate change program or equivalent).**

Reason for use of this indicator: Shows the degree of exposure of the industry to significant storm events (hurricanes, storm surges, major flood events etc) which may increase in frequency and/or severity.

Source(s) of data: For most nations these data are available from the country's initial Communication on Climate Change. Tourism authorities normally have an inventory of hotels and resorts by location, although data on related infrastructure or services such as restaurants and entertainment facilities etc may be less readily available.

Means to use the indicator: Use as % of beds, % of hotels (and if available, value of infrastructure or number of tourism sector jobs) which are considered vulnerable.

Benchmarking: See the UN site http://unfccc.int/resource/natcom/nctable.html which contains National Communications from most nations, whether or not they are signatories to the Framework Convention on Climate Change. Many identify vulnerability by sector (and many nations where tourism is important provide data for tourism).

Indicator of level of planning for potential impacts:

∗   **Degree to which key tourist zones are covered by contingency or emergency planning (existence of plan, % area included).**

Reason for use of this indicator: As much of the tourism industry and its assets are located in areas vulnerable to storms, flooding, erosion etc., and many of the attractions (reefs, ski slopes) are climate/weather dependent it is useful to have in place some form of contingency planning to cope with possible impacts. The tourism contingency plan will likely be related to overall emergency planning and response that may be in place to deal with all emergencies, (major storms, earthquakes, fires etc) whether or not they are related to climate change.

Source(s) of data: Local authorities (or emergency measures organizations where these exist). Often land use or ownership maps, coastal zone maps, flood zone maps exist which will define zones at risk (e.g. Within 100 year flood line, area subject to inundation in storm surges, area considered to be unstable for earthquake or land slips).

Means to use the indicator: The existence of a plan is in itself an indicator of some degree of planning or preparation. It may also be possible to relate this to the existence of structural controls, design requirements which are designed to mitigate extreme events or to reduce potential for damage.

Benchmarking: Because of the unique nature of risks to each site or destination, there is no single benchmark. Comparison with extent of coverage, degree of preparation over time is likely to be most useful.

In addition to the more general indicators, several more specific indicators are suggested for particularly vulnerable destinations including:

Impact on seashores which have the majority of tourism infrastructure:

* **Value of tourism infrastructure in coastal zone below estimated maximum storm surge levels or equivalent;**

* **Value of damage annually due to storm events or flooding;**

* **% of tourist area and infrastructure with sea defences (could be classed by level of protection).**

The information can be obtained from planning authorities and from the national communications, and may affect planning and protection policies. (See also Coastal Zone destinations p. 247)

Impact on mountains where many activities are climate dependent and where access and infrastructure can be vulnerable:

* **% ski areas or ski-able terrain with snowmaking equipment;**

* **% of developed ski area which would lack access to ski-able conditions with warming.** (Use IPCC warming scenarios for the destination).

   (See also the Mountain destinations section p. 259)

Impact on native wildlife and biodiversity, a major draw for tourism:

* **% of tourism dependent on viewing species;**

* **% of key species considered vulnerable to changes in climate.**

   (See also the section on Natural and Sensitive Ecological Sites p. 263)

Note that the indicator **Number of rooms with climate control - AC or heating**, outlined in the following mitigation section is also a useful indicator of adaptation – as a measure of level of preparedness should the temperature become warmer or cooler.

See also the section on ➤ **Seasonality** (p. 111). One of the potential impacts of climate change can be the alterations in tourist season so the indicator % visitation in peak season/shoulder season may be useful to measure changes due to climate change.

While the top of mountains will still have snow, many lower ski stations in the Alps will be below the snow line under many of the climate change scenarios.

Box 3.28 Snowmaking as an adaptation to climate variability and change

The winter tourism industry, in particular alpine skiing, is highly weather-sensitive and experiences considerable inter-annual variability in operating conditions. For example, between 1982-83 and 2001-02 the length of the ski season in the major ski regions of the United States has varied as follows: Pacific 109-151 days, Rocky Mountains 121-145 days, Midwest 78-105 days, Northeast 101-136 days and Southeast 78-110 days. The ski industry in North America has used a range of adaptation strategies that reduce their vulnerability to climate variability (and consequently any climate change in the future), including the implementation of snowmaking systems, business diversification and the limited use of weather insurance.

Snowmaking is the most wide spread climate adaptation and has become an integral component of the ski industry in eastern North America during the past 30 years. Ski areas in eastern Canada and the Midwest, Northeast and Southeast regions of the US have invested million of dollars in snowmaking technology and operations. In eastern Canada, all ski areas in the Province of Ontario have snowmaking systems that cover 100% of the skiable terrain, while in Quebec snowmaking coverage varies in the 50-90% range of skiable terrain. In 2001-02, all of the ski areas in the Northeast, Southeast and Midwest ski regions of the United States had snowmaking systems. The average skiable terrain covered by snowmaking varied in these regions, from 62% in the Northeast region, to 95% and 98% in the Southeast and Midwest regions, respectively. In addition to infrastructure costs, the average operational cost of snowmaking at ski areas in the Northeast US ski region was US$728,000 in 2001/02 (for an average of 252 acres).

In addition to its current importance, research has documented the importance of snowmaking as a climate change adaptation strategy. In their analysis of one ski area in central Ontario, Scott et al. (2003) estimated that snowmaking had extended the period with a skiable 30cm snow base by 33% to 830% during the 1980s and 1990s. A study that examined the potential impact of climate change at six ski areas in Eastern Canada and the US found that ski season losses were drastically reduced by snowmaking technology (Scott et al. 2004).

Key indicators: *length of season, area of ski-able terrain, % covered by snowmaking, cost of snowmaking, benefit/cost ratio of snowmaking, cost of weather insurance.*

Mitigation of the Impacts of Tourism

Tourism's impacts that contribute to the causes of climate change:

While concerns about tourism's polluting effects can influence many aspects of a tourist's activities, the primary issue relates to travellers' consumption of transport services, notably road and air transport. In the wider area of the sustainability of tourism, the impacts of tourism contributing to climate change can be related to tourism's high per capita consumption of water and energy, and the effects that tourism can have on flora and fauna. To reduce tourism's negative impacts, there is a need to implement measures by applying advanced environmental management techniques and technologies.

Tourism contributes to greenhouse gases (GHG) primarily through transportation and heating and cooling of accommodation, both of which may use fossil fuels. GHG emissions through the use of transportation, accommodation and other tourism services occur from the beginning of a tourist's trip until she/he returns home. Therefore, mitigation actions should address tourism activities through the complete supply chain, involving international, national and regional transportation systems, outgoing and incoming tour operators, as well as local accommodation, transportation and other service providers at destinations.

Destinations can respond to the climate change issue through a variety of mitigation strategies, including:

1.   Greater energy efficiency;
2.   The use of less carbon intensive fuels;
3.   Carbon sequestration and trading.

One important strategy to reduce greenhouse gas production is to introduce more efficient equipment and procedures. However, application of this "cleaner production" or "ecoefficiency" approach takes time. Additionally, many operations within the community (the tourism industry or the local community that tourism is situated in) may already be energy efficient and/or further significant reductions in energy from non-renewable sources may not, for operational and commercial reasons, be feasible.

A second strategy is using fuels that produce less greenhouse gases such as liquid propane gas (LPG) or ideally moving towards greater use of energy from renewable sources (e.g. wind, solar or hydro).

A third strategy includes involvement in carbon sequestration projects (a process where plants as they grow capture and store the carbon in the gas carbon dioxide (CO_2) in biomass) as an immediate move towards offsetting greenhouse gas production. The tourism industry can contribute in partnership with e.g., forestry firms, conservation organizations to the preservation of natural areas as one means to offset its greenhouse gas contribution- while enhancing the tourism resource base.

Many communities are making significant efforts to utilize energy from renewable sources (e.g. wind, solar), thereby conserving resources and minimizing greenhouse gas emissions.

Components of the climate change issue: mitigation	Indicators
Greenhouse gas emissions by the destination and by the tourism component	◦ Total CO_2 produced due to the community's energy consumption; ◦ Consumption of fossil fuels by the tourism sector (see also ≻ **Energy** p. 152).
Transportation fuel use	◦ Total consumption per capita of fossil fuels for transportation; ◦ Total consumption of fossil fuels in the destination for tourist transportation (note also issue section on Transportation p. 210).
Energy consumption related to temperature control	◦ Number and % rooms with air conditioning and/or heating.
Coverage of natural areas	◦ % of natural area coverage in the territory of the destination (change over time).

Indicators of Greenhouse gas emissions:

◦   **Total CO₂ produced due to the community's energy consumption** (tonnes);

◦   **Consumption of fossil fuels by the tourism sector** (tonnes).

Note that energy consumption itself will not be expressed in tonnes ... you will need to calculate energy consumption in kWh or M3 and then convert to CO₂ tonne equivalents to reflect the local energy mix. (Tonnes per person per year)

> Indicators relating to consumption of resources and production of wastes, which are calculated on a per person per annum basis, need to take into account both the resident and the transient (tourist) populations. These figures should be available from the bureau of statistics in your country or your local tourism authority.

Reason for use of these indicators: To support efforts to minimize the net production of the greenhouse gas, carbon dioxide (CO_2) from energy consumption, particularly by the tourism industry. Tourism is a significant consumer of fossil fuels for transportation, heating and cooling (see also ≫ **Energy** p. 152). Reduction of fossil fuel use is a mainstay of plans by most nations to respond to climate change. Both overall use and use per capita are relevant.

Source(s) of data: In some nations, energy use is monitored by sector. Surveys of use by sector were done by many nations in the preparation of their Initial National Communications. All energy sources used within the destination should be used to calculate the total energy usage. By using the same energy balance produced to assess the destination's energy consumption, the destination can also estimate the amount of CO_2 produced per person (and per tourist). There are a number of energy calculators available which are capable of estimating the amount of CO_2 produced per person using the energy balance figures e.g. the Green Globe energy calculator (See: www.greenglobe21.com) The table provided with the ≫ **Energy** issue (p. 152) outlines a common list of energy sources used in destinations which can be used to estimate total use and to identify the percentage that is based on fossil fuel consumption.

Means to use the indicators: Overall use trends, tourism as a percentage of national and destination energy use, and fossil fuel use per capita are all useful. This indicator is useful to display trends in greenhouse gas emissions and allows the destination to monitor and act on their performance. Identification of the contribution of the tourism sector may lead to actions by that sector.

Benchmarking: This indicator can be benchmarked in two ways: over time for the individual destination or by using comparative data from companies such as Green Globe (www.greenglobe21.com) or the International Hotels Environmental Initiative (www.benchmarkhotel.com).

See also the UN website http://unfccc.int/resource/natcom/nctable.html, as well as the UNEP publication "Transport and the global Environment: Accounting for GHG reduction on Policy Analysis (UNEP 2001), http://uneprisoe.org/OverlaysTransport/TransportGlobalOverlays.pdf

Note: see also the Keep Winter Cool case in Part 6 (p. 400) which identifies approaches to greenhouse gas reduction by North American ski resorts.

Indicators of transportation fuel use:

* **Total consumption per capita of fossil fuels for transportation;**
* **Total consumption of fossil fuels in the destination for tourist transportation.**

(Note also Transportation p. 210)

Reason for use of these indicators: Destinations have their own programs to respond to the need to reduce fuel consumption. Tourism use of transport (both to get to the destination and within the destination) can be a major component.

Source(s) of data: These data will likely be available from transportation authorities, and where there is an initial communication on climate change from the country, they may be aggregated for easy use. It may not be easy to isolate the component of transportation associated with tourism, particularly where facilities are used widely by both locals and tourists, although often tour buses are licensed or regulated separately from local transport. Transport mix data may also be available

Means to use these indicators: Both raw data and per capita consumption.

Benchmarking: The best use of this will be comparison over time, particularly if used in relation to programs designed to reduce energy consumption for transportation.

Indicator of energy consumption related to temperature control:

⁕   **Number and % rooms with air conditioning and/or heating.**

Reason for use of this indicator: Use of energy for air conditioning and heating is an important area of energy consumption. In many destinations, climate control is more likely to be found in tourist accommodation than in the homes and businesses of locals. The tourism sector has a comparative advantage in efforts to reduce consumption of energy for these purposes, both through energy efficient design, and conservation initiatives (such as efforts to turn off air conditioning when rooms are not in use).

Source(s) of data: These data are likely available from the local tourism authority, ministry in charge of building, or from hotel associations.

Means to use the indicator: As noted above, this indicator cuts two ways. Lower numbers of heating/cooling units will contribute to reduction of energy use (and in most cases fossil fuels). At the same time, the existence of units with climate controls can act as a form of adaptation to potential effects of climate change (e.g., cold spells, heat waves) and may also help lengthen shoulder seasons.

Benchmarking: These data are not normally collected and reported systematically but may become so with growing emphasis on climate change. At the same time, there seems to be an emerging de facto standard that has all 4 and 5 star (and a growing percentage of 3 star) accommodation with room climate control.

Additional potentially useful indicators:

⁕   **The percentage uptake of renewable energy systems** (see ➢ **Energy** p. 152)

⁕   **Percentage of accommodation with Environmental Management Systems or certifications** (p. 318)

Box 3.29 Tourism and climate change: Adapting indicators to targeted French stakeholders

Indicators are a way to make environmental information more easily understandable and accessible to the users. Depending on the targeted stakeholders, the same information can be presented in different ways. For example, in the French experience (see France case study p. 382) the contribution of tourism transportation to greenhouse gas emissions was first evaluated for the whole tourism sector at the national level. It was also calculated for a specific Paris/ Nice trip, according to the mode of transport, to promote individual responsibility by tourists. This same indicator could also be calculated for a selected destination (as the Municipality of Calvia, Majorca, Spain did for a tour operator, to point out the fact that actions from all stakeholders are required to cope with climate change. In all cases where indicators are used publicly, it is important to provide sources of data used, as well as a short methodological note, to ensure a transparency of the process and avoid challenges to the results.

Box 3.29 (cont.)

An indicator for national decision-makers:

* **The contribution of French tourism road transport to CO_2 emissions.**

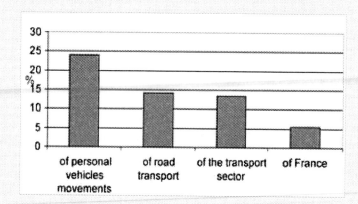

Domestic tourism road transport is responsible for 5,5% of French CO_2 emissions. The total contribution of tourism transport to French CO_2 emissions is roughly about twice as large.

Source: Tourism Environment Consultants, based on SNCF, European Environment Agency (Copert III and MEET programmes), IPCC, Airbus Industries, EDF.

An indicator for tourists and business operators :

* **Contribution to climate change of a family Paris-Nice trip, according to the mode of transportation.**

In this example for a Paris/ Nice trip, a family will have contributed three times more to global warming with an airplane than with a car, five times more than with a train.

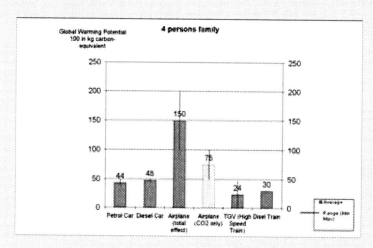

Source : Tourism Environment Consultants, based on SNCF, European Environment Agency (Copert III and MEET programmes), IPCC, Airbus Industries, EDF.

Remarks. Range: from the most to the least polluting vehicle in each category.

Cars. Variables: age, horsepower, type of journey (motorway or main road).

Planes. variables: type of airplane. Two estimations are given: one for the effects of carbon dioxide (CO_2), which are well known, and the other for the impact on the greenhouse effect of all pollutants emitted during the flight ; In this case, the effects of nitrogen oxides, water vapour, sulphur oxides and jet trails are all taken into account .

Trains. Variables: type of energy used to produce electricity for a TGV , from hydraulic power (0 or near 0) to coal (47)

3.8.3 Water Availability and Conservation ➤ *Baseline Issue*

Water Supply, Water Pricing, Recycling, Shortages

Water is a critical resource for tourism. The provision of services to tourists is heavily water dependent: studies have shown that consumption of water per capita by tourists is typically double to triple that of residents of destinations. Particularly for areas where water is in short supply, water can become a constraint to development, a limit on tourist activities, and a contentious issue with local residents over allocation and pricing. New (additional) water supplies can be difficult to obtain and costly (e.g. import, or desalinization). Conservation is one means to reduce or mitigate demand.

Components of the issue	Indicators
Overall water use relative to supply	• Water use: (total volume consumed and litres per tourist per day) ➤ **Baseline indicator.**
Conservation initiatives and results	• Water saving (% reduced, recaptured or recycled) ➤ **Baseline indicator**; • % waste water or grey water recycled; • Number of establishments participating in water conservation programmes, applying water conservation policies and techniques, recycling treated wastewater (e.g. for irrigation purposes, hotels using water saving shower heads, flush systems, advising guests on water saving, water issues, reusing of towels).
Seasonal shortages Water shortages	• # shortage incidents per year or number of days per year where there are supply shortages; • % loss from reticulated system; • % water supply imported to region.
Allocation of water among users – such as agriculture, local residents, tourist accommodation, and often specific large users such as water parks or golf courses	• Total use as percentage of installed capacity; • Total use by each sector (Tourism as a % of all users); • (note consumption by key users – derived from consumption data).
Cost and pricing of water	• Water price per litre or cubic metre.
Quality of water	(see following Water Quality issue where this is treated separately).

(See also the related issues of ➤ **Drinking Water Quality** p. 169 and ➤ **Sewage** p. 171)

Indicator of water use:

* **Water use: (total volume consumed and litres per tourist per day)** ➤ **Baseline indicator.**

    Reason for use of this indicator: Responds to the need to manage supply and demand of water. This indicator can be a key measure of physical carrying capacity for water-poor destinations and also can provide warning of potential limits or stresses on the supply system.

    Source(s) of data: Data to support this indicator is normally available from the utility which provides the water (where there is a reticulated system). In many destinations, the records of utilities are sufficiently detailed to separate tourist use (at least for official hotels and apartments or specific major tourist uses such as water parks or sports and cultural facilities) from other domestic, agricultural or industrial uses. Note that for some destinations that are without a formal water utility (e.g., many rural and remote sites obtain their water from independent sources) data may be available only from selected accommodation. While this is a possible source of information, the indicator may not be representative of all users or meaningful for the destination. Where data is not collected in a way that segregates different types of users, an alternative can be to measure differences in overall water consumption by season or month – attributing the difference in the tourist season to additional consumption by the tourism industry and tourists. (Note: for many destinations peak tourism season coincides with the low rainfall months – potentially amplifying shortages) It is recommended that data be expressed in litres consumed per day for comparison with other sites.

Means to use the indicator: Water use (litres per capita per day) can be shown for tourists relative to locals. This can become a performance measure for water conservation activities of the tourism industry. Total savings of water and also savings expressed in monetary terms (cost of production of additional water or savings from reduction in consumption) can be a meaningful number both for local use and portrayal of tourist sector efforts to other stakeholders. Total use statistics (percentage of capacity of system being used) can be a useful indicator of levels of stress on system capacity and a signal for attention to infrastructure or conservation issues.

Benchmarking: This figure is available from many destinations and comparisons can be made of consumption per tourist, per tourist day, as well as seasonal differences. Benchmark as well against overall consumption averages for the destination and, where possible, domestic consumption rates.

Indicators of water conservation:

* **Water saving (% reduced, recaptured or recycled) ➢ Baseline indicator;**

* **% waste water or grey water recycled;**

* **Number of establishments participating in water conservation programmes, applying water conservation policies and techniques, recycling treated wastewater** (e.g. for irrigation purposes, hotels using water saving shower heads, flush systems, advising guests on water saving, water issues, reusing of towels).

Reason for use of these indicators: Conservation is an important opportunity to relieve pressures on water supply and water systems and an opportunity for the tourism sector to show leadership. Because of the amount of discretionary use, tourism often has greater opportunity to show water savings than other sectors.

Source(s) of data: Water utility data. The first indicator is a means to express savings (total or %) over time. It is built on the same base data as water use per tourist – (above) but may require greater detail in data to differentiate between those participating in programs and those outside such programs if attribution is sought. An alternative data source can be records of participating establishments – and provision of such data could be a requisite of participation in such programs. The second indicator can be obtained from the same records.

Means to use these indicators: Can be used to demonstrate savings in water or water costs (see below) and could be a performance measure for the tourism industry and/or the water utility for its conservation initiatives. Conservation of water is likely to both save money through water charges (see following indicator) and promote a "green" image in the marketplace. This indicator will often be used in concert with the use per capita indicator to show performance which may be attributable to conservation programs.

Benchmarking: The International Hotels Environmental Initiative is one potential source of comparative data for large properties. Green Globe also publishes some data for member destinations and properties.

Indicator of cost of water:

* **Water price per litre** is a potential supplementary measure for water supply.

   Reason for use of the indicator: New water sources are frequently more expensive than current supplies. Where readily available sources such as shallow wells, surface streams or lakes are exhausted, water can still be obtained through methods such as desalinization, deep wells, and import by pipeline or tanker. Where water is priced, competition can cause price changes and reallocation of supplies. It is potentially useful to monitor both the actual cost of provision of water, and its sale price. It should also be noted that water price and water quality will in many cases be linked – as supplies of good water are depleted, the price for new water reflects the difficulty to obtain it, and the cost is affected by distance to new sources, depth to tap alternative underground sources, and/or the cost of taking poor water and making it clean enough to be used for the desired purpose. Note that where grey water may be available for some uses (such as watering gardens and golf courses or recycling to flush toilets) there can be dual pricing – with the real price of grey water being significantly lower than potable water.

   Source(s) of data: Water utility records, water bills for specific properties.

   Means to use the indicator: Show trend lines in price per litre. This can be a good leading indicator for water shortage as supplies become more difficult to access.

   Benchmarking; Data on rates is published by many water utilities. See for example World Bank web source – which has regional water supply pricing data for municipalities in different regions: http://www.worldbank.org/watsan/ and many municipal sites which feature current pricing. The WTO workshops and case studies in Cozumel, Beruwala, Villa Gesell, Peninsula Valdes and Cyprus all identified water supply as an important issue and suggested indicators to respond. Other possible benchmarks for these indicators are the Mediterranean Tourism Indicators program (several measures of consumption and conservation per capita) and the Balearic program which also measured water recycling. (See Balearic Case p. 345).

Box 3.30 Water supply for Cozumel

Cozumel is a small island off the coast of Mexico's Yucatan peninsula. The 51 sq km island had 57,000 permanent residents in 2000 and was host to nearly 400,000 tourists, not counting the over 1 million cruise ship visitors who landed from up to a dozen ships at a time. Nearly all of the tourist impact is concentrated in and around the town of San Miguel.

The sole water supply for Cozumel, like that of many small islands, is annual precipitation captured in the underground aquifer. The island is quite dry receiving 1,500 mm of rain annually, mostly from May to October in the rainy season with little falling in the peak tourist season of December to March. The freshwater aquifer floats on salt water from the surrounding sea. Fresh water frequently runs out at the end of the dry season, which coincides with the peak tourism season. The WTO study of Cozumel revealed that the island's sole water source, the aquifer underlying the island, effectively ran out of water nearly every May as pumping resulted in salinization from sea water influx to replace the fresh water drawn out of the aquifer. The water authority was forced to shut off water periodically to residential areas. Because of the sensitivity of the tourist industry to water, normally the hotels were not cut off. This is considered unfair by many locals, who see the hotels (and tourists) as a cause of the problem.

There appear to be opportunities for water conservation as water is not priced by volume used and there is little incentive to conserve or even turn off running taps. As well, the water infrastructure is aging with much leakage, although some does find its way back into the aquifer. The Cozumel study recommended that the tourism industry cooperate with officials to measure and report water use, losses due to leakage from the system, and potential (and hopefully actual)

Box 3.30 (cont.)

gains through conservation or use reduction. Water availability (and recycling) also became important in discussions regarding creation of a golf course on the island which was being planned to use recycled grey water, some of which could be returned to the aquifer when sprayed on fairways possibly helping to replenish it, instead of being lost to the sea through outfalls.

Reference: WTO 1999

Other indicators which have been identified to address water supply issues include:

* **% loss from reticulated system**, (particularly old systems with significant leakage);

* **Number shortage incidents per year or number of days per year where there are supply shortages** (See Cozumel Box 3.30);

* **Water supply imported to region as percentage of installed capacity** (Importation by tanker ship or truck is often done in water-short destinations, particularly in desert regions or areas with significant dry seasons, especially where these coincide with peak use/tourist seasons);

* **waste water or grey water recycled** (use along with total water use to calculate net use of new water, use with water cost to examine the benefits of recycling) (See also the indicators on Drinking Water Quality (p. 169); these are often linked to quantity, particularly where high use causes destinations to rely on lower quality sources or depleted aquifers);

* **Total use as percentage of installed capacity**. This is an indicator of short to medium term stress on the water system, as well as an indicator that expansion or conservation programs may be required.

Saguenay Falls, Quebec, Canada. Water and energy supply is also a tourist attraction

3.8.4 Drinking Water Quality ≫ **Baseline Issue**

Purity of Supply, Contamination Impact on Tourist Health and Destination Image

Most tourists are very risk averse. Illness will spoil a vacation. Drinking water quality is one of the most important factors in tourist wellbeing and poor drinking water quality is implicated in intestinal diseases afflicting many tourists. The image of a destination where visitors are likely to get sick can deter tourists.

Components of the issue	Indicators
Purity of the drinking water supply	• Percentage of tourism establishments with water treated to international potable standards. ≫ **Baseline indicator;** • % of local population with access to treated water (UN Sustainable development indicators); • Number of incidents of violation of water standards.
Impact of contamination on tourist health	• Frequency of water-borne diseases: percentage of visitors reporting water-borne illnesses during their stay. ≫ **Baseline indicator.**
Impact of water related contamination on image of destination	• Perception of cleanliness of food and water (Exit questionnaire – see Annex C).

Indicators of drinking water purity:

* **Percentage of tourism establishments with water treated to international potable standards.** ≫ **Baseline Indicator;**

* **% of local population with access to treated water (UN Sustainable development indicators);**

* **Number of incidents of violation of water standards.**

Reason for use of these indicators: To measure progress in potable water service in a destination. The key use is to show safety of water supply. (Note that this indicator may be less relevant as secure supplies of potable water become available through bottled water, although it still may be relevant where food services have limited access to clean water supplies for food preparation, ice cubes, or tourists need to be wary of water while brushing teeth washing hands, cutlery etc) .

Source(s) of data: Local water utility. (This is difficult when there is no agency or utility in control of the water supply). Where there is no utility, an alternative indicator of water safety may be used. (e.g., frequency of waterborne diseases – locals and tourists)

Means to use the indicators: Useful to advise tourists of risks, and to show safety where good water systems are in place.

(Note: where entire system is on reticulated clean water systems this indicator can be redundant – and simply advertising that the destination system meets these standards may be the best use of a simple public fact (or indicator) See alternative indicator at end of this section on number of violations/incidents.

Benchmarking: Many mature destinations have 100% of properties on systems which meet international standards. International benchmarks can be found for many water authorities on the Internet, including the World Health Organization website. National or regional agencies responsible for water supply and/or water quality will likely have data which can be used as a benchmark. (Typically part of a ministry of infrastructure, public works, environment or health although in many jurisdictions delegated or carried out by more local authorities or private suppliers).

Other useful indicators regarding access to clean drinking water are:

* **% of local population with access to treated water (UN Sustainable development indicators)** - a general measure of the destination's quality of water in a range of areas, some of which may be visited by tourists, this also relates to community wellbeing in destination;

* **# of incidents of violation of water standards** - a risk measure, signalling the degree to which water may be safe (where destination has a normally potable reticulated water system this may become a key indicator).

Indicator regarding tourist health:

* **Percentage of visitors reporting water-borne illnesses during their stay**. ➢ Baseline indicator.

   Reason for use of this indicator: This is an indicator of impact due to problems with water supply (or food contamination from sources including water). It identifies a risk to both health and the image of a destination.

   Source(s) of data: Normally national or regional health authorities will collect this data, although there is inconsistency in reporting and even definition of which diseases are monitored. This limits the ability to benchmark between destinations. (Refer to World Health Organization publications and websites for standards). Not all those experiencing illness (particularly mild forms) will necessarily report it.

   Means to use the indicator: This indicator can be used to market safety for destinations meeting all standards and with low risk (benchmark against WHO). This is also a key risk indicator for many destinations.

   Benchmarking: World Health Organization website on drinking water quality at: http://www.who.int/water_sanitation_health/dwq/en/

Indicator of perception of risk:

* **Perception of cleanliness of food and water** (% who "strongly agree" or "agree" that food and water quality was good, - conversely the percentage who disagree can also be used to illustrate perception of problems).

   Reason for use of the indicator: Often perception of conditions or of risks is a stronger predictor of tourist behaviour than actual statistics on such risks.

   Source(s) of data: Questionnaire-based – from exit survey. (See the questionnaire in Annex C, which suggests a means of obtaining visitor perception of quality of their experience, with specific reference to perception of cleanliness, health etc).

   Means to use the indicator: This can be an early warning indicator of changes in perceived quality – related to food and drink. Where a very high percentage agrees that cleanliness is good, this can also be used in marketing.

   Benchmarking: Use over time for the same destination.

Box 3.31 Monitoring scarce water resources: Byron Bay, Australia

 The town of Byron Bay is a very popular tourist coastal resort on the north coast of New South Wales, Australia which is featured in many tourist guides around the world. With a permanent population of around 30,000 Byron regularly receives influxes of tens of thousands of visitors. Over the Easter long weekend alone, more than 20,000 visitors attend a local music festival. In relation to the impacts of tourism, Byron Bay Council has a number of issues relating to landscape, biodiversity, water, waste, noise, air pollution, community ambience and local economics. In particular water is a scarce resource given the region is prone to drought. As well, disposal of waste water is expensive.

While the destination does not have a formal indicators program, it is monitoring some important trends. According to the local authority, in January 2002 flows into two treatment works servicing the town were up 24% on the main-holiday month in the previous year. Water consumption was up 44%. A $24M upgrade of the sewage treatment plant is due to be completed in early 2004, but if tourism numbers continue to rise sharply, the plant will still be unable to cope with peak tourist periods. This example shows how important water is to a community, and how indicators relating to use, costs and pressures are important signals which can lead to action relative to key elements of destination sustainability.

3.9 Limiting Environmental Impacts of Tourism Activity

3.9.1 Sewage Treatment ➢ **Baseline issue**

Wastewater Management, Extent of System, Effectiveness, Reducing Contamination

The management of liquid waste (sewage) is a key concern for tourism. The industry has frequently been harmed by contamination of its key resources – beaches, lakes, rivers. Pollution both from resorts themselves and from local communities and industries can degrade the destination, and may also contribute to disease and damage to wildlife and natural resources. Widely publicized incidents (e.g. oil spills, cholera) and beach closures on all continents due to e-coli or other contaminants can virtually close down destinations and harm the image and tourism arrivals for years. In extreme cases, contamination has resulted in virtual closure of resorts (e.g., breakdown of sewage infrastructure was a key contributor to the closure of several Iberian beach hotels in the 1970s and abandonment of Black Sea resorts in the 1990s.)

Components of the Issue	Indicators
Sewage receiving treatment	* Percentage of sewage from the destination/site receiving treatment (also break out sewage from tourism sector if possible) ; ➣ **Baseline indicator;** * % of treated sewage recycled (e.g. for irrigation).
Extent of sewage treatment systems	* Percentage of tourism establishments (or accommodation) on (suitable) treatment systems ➣ **Baseline indicator;** * Percentage of the destination served by storm water systems (separating sewage from runoff and surface drainage).
Effect of sewage treatment	* Number of reported pollution or contamination events per annum (by month) in watercourses receiving effluents; See also indicators in section on Seawater quality (p. 149)

Indicator of treatment levels:

* **Percentage of sewage from the destination receiving treatment** (Measure each of primary, secondary, tertiary treatment levels and calculate separately for tourism sector if possible) ➣ **Baseline indicator;**

* **% of treated sewage recycled (e.g. for irrigation).**

Reason for use of these indicators: The key assets of tourism can be damaged by sewage releases – either from the tourism sector or from others. Impacts on the environment and implications for the communities, the tourism industry and the overall economy can be significant.

Source(s) of data: These data are normally available from environmental or health authorities or from the utilities themselves for most destinations. Where there is no reticulated system, data can often be obtained from individual properties which have their own treatment systems.

Means to use these indicators: This is related to destination quality and also to standards like Blue Flag. From the point of view of the tourism industry it is essentially an early warning indicator of potential risk to their product and a stimulus to action to improve their own or community systems.

Benchmarking: Benchmarking is essentially done over time for the same destination although national, regional and international standards exist which can be used (e.g. Blue Flag, national standards for treatment for many nations).

Indicator of extent of sewage treatment systems:

* **Percentage of tourism establishments (or accommodation) connected to (suitable) treatment systems ➣ Baseline indicator.**

Reason for use of the indicator: Because of the dispersed nature of many tourism properties, community wastewater systems may not be available for many. This indicator identifies the overall percentage of establishments which have approved treatment systems (community systems, their own treatment facilities, approved septic and cesspool systems)

Source(s) of data: Data is likely available from local planning, building or environmental authorities.

Means to use the indicator: (same as above).

Benchmarking: Over time for the same destination.

Other indicators which may be of use relative to wastewater (sewage) management include:

• **Number of reported pollution or contamination events per annum** (by month) in watercourses receiving effluents;

• **Percentage of the destination served by storm water systems**
(See also Sea Water Quality for destinations where the sea is the recipient of effluents p. 149).

Box 3.32 Beruwala Sri Lanka Waste: The Beach Boys know where the effluents flow

During the field work for the WTO indicators study in the beach resort of Beruwala, the visiting experts became aware of an issue regarding sewage. Beach boys contended that black sewage flowed across the beach from one hotel. The hotel manager showed the group the treatment plant, and the environmental manager showed the group the report done daily of outflow clarity. No such black water event was noted.

A live demonstration was done of the regular flushing of the holding tank. The experts and some beach boys were at the outlet when the release commenced. Those at the outlet saw thirty seconds of foul black water run across the beach, followed by clear water. By the time the environmental manager made it to the outlet from the valve he had turned on, the water was flowing clear.

The WTO group further examined the holding tank, and found that it had been poorly installed with the outlet at the bottom. Thus sludge was flushed in the initial water release each time. A cheap fix, adding a length of pipe to raise the outlet was all that was needed to remedy the problem and bring the system more into compliance.

3.9.2 Solid Waste Management ➤ **Baseline Issue**

Garbage, Reduction, Reuse, Recycling, Deposit, Collection, Hazardous Substances

Solid waste is a major source of pollution for the planet. Waste is generated in nearly all activities that humans undertake. To date, the main solution to managing this waste has been to throw it away – most frequently where there is a waste collection system to bury it under the ground in a landfill. Used or waste materials sent to landfill represent a loss of resources, and their replacement will increase greenhouse gases during both their production and transport. In places where there is no system, waste material is frequently just abandoned where it is created, or someone is paid to take it "away".

Due to problems of contamination and negative impacts on both the environment and often the image of the destination, it is increasingly necessary for destinations to measure waste production and to manage its treatment. The 'out of sight, out of mind' solution has not been very effective and has created a new set of problems that need to be dealt with. Problems with old-style rubbish heaps and landfills include the:

1. Production of offensive odours;
2. Generation of leachate, which can contaminate nearby waterways;
3. Emission of greenhouse gases;
4. Attraction of vermin and concomitant disease.

All of these can damage tourism and the destination.

There is a widely recognised hierarchy for minimising waste: reduce, reuse, recycle, residual treatment, residual disposal. Destinations need to quantify waste volumes, and identify sources and destinations, so effectiveness of future management strategies can be monitored. That is, you need to measure your waste in order to manage it. This can be done at many scales (See results of one audit in the destination section on Convention Centres p. 286)

A **waste audit** is simply an assessment of waste. It is valuable as it tells you:

1.   How much waste there is in total;
2.   What the waste actually consists of and the quantities of each type of material;
3.   Where the waste was generated;
4.   Where it ends up (e.g. landfill, composting plants, incineration, etc.).

Using this information it is possible to target activities and industries (such as tourism) producing significant amounts of waste going to landfill. It also helps to identify where reducing waste at the source is going to be most practicable and effective. Waste assessments also identify environmentally viable alternatives to landfill for the waste that cannot be eliminated. The first step for the destination should be to look to reduce quantities of materials consumed (including packaging), to then consider reuse, or if not possible, recycle. Consideration should be given to the options that have the best local environmental impact. While on vacation, people tend to use more disposable products than at home; food bought may be heavily packaged. Recycling may not always be the best option (e.g. no local facility) and waste used for energy generation systems may be a better route for some destinations, obtaining both energy and a reduction in the weight of waste disposed. Tourism establishments can also seek means to substitute less wasteful procedures (e.g. serving in edible containers, recyclable bottles etc.).

Components of the issue	Indicators
Managing total waste collected in a destination	• Total amount of waste collected; • Waste volume produced by the destination (tonnes) pa / Person years pa (by month) ➢ **Baseline Indicator;** • Waste disposed by different methods (specify, e.g. incinerated, deposited in landfill, etc.); • Waste attributable (by month or season) to tourism.
Reducing waste produced	• Volume of waste recycled (m³) / Total volume of waste (m³) (specify by different types) ➢ **Baseline Indicator;** • Number of tourism establishments collecting waste separately, capacity of collecting separated waste from local residents; • Number of tourism establishments recycling their own waste (e.g. composting).
Providing waste collection services	• % of destination area (especially in urban sites) covered by solid waste collection services; • Percentage of tourism establishments covered by waste collection programs.

Components of the issue	Indicators
Hazardous substances (reduction, handling)	• Number and volume of hazardous substances in use (for key substances, volume of use over time); • % of these substances for which appropriate management and disposal policies and programs are in place; • % of employees informed and trained in the use and disposal of the substances they use (e.g., cleaners knowledgeable of how to deal with waste cleaning fluids, engineers trained in emergency spill handling).
Maintaining clean image for the destination	• Quantity of waste collected from public areas and streets; • **Quantity of waste strewn in public areas (garbage counts)** ➤ **Baseline Indicator;** • Image of cleanliness of destination (questionnaire based).

Municipal services of waste collection and processing have to be coordinated well with accommodation, catering and other tourism establishments to reduce, reuse and recycle waste. Recycling and reuse should start at the source of waste (establishments), by collecting different types of waste separately. Tourism establishments can also have their own waste processing facilities (e.g. composting organic waste). Without adequate municipal infrastructure, however, efforts of tourism facilities are diminished. There are examples of hotels with excellent environmental management systems, where the carefully separated waste ends up in the same landfill, due to lack of processing capacity at the local destination. There are also examples where the hotel maintains a good relationship with the local community, and residents reuse specific waste items (e.g. bins, bottles) in their households. For the above reasons, it is also important to collect information on waste generation and processing from tourism establishments as well, and inform them adequately on municipal activities.

Indicators of waste production:

* **Total amount of waste collected;**

* **Waste volume produced by the destination (tonnes) pa / Person years pa (by month)**
  ➤ **Baseline Indicator;**

* **Waste disposed by different methods (specify, e.g. incinerated, deposited in landfill, etc.);**

* **Waste volume attributable (by month or season) to tourism.**

Indicators relating to consumption of resources and production of waste, which are calculated on a per person per annum basis, need to take into account both the resident and the transient (tourist) populations.

Box 3.33 Solid waste reduction - Douglas Shire, Queensland, Australia

Douglas Shire is a local authority on the Queensland coast where tourism is a major part of the economy. Douglas Shire Council actively encourages a reduction in the quantity of solid wastes being generated through approaches such as avoiding excess packaging, reuse of packaging where possible, recycling waste where possible and committing waste to landfill only as a last resort. Recycling includes old tires and grease trap waste. Results are monitored.

An integrated waste management project was put into operation in 2002 to provide best practice waste management and aims to reduce landfill by up to 65%. As well, effluent from the sewage facility is used for golf course irrigation The program is targeted at all sectors, with tourism as a major participant.

Reason for use of these indicators: Used or waste materials sent to landfill represent a loss of resources, and their replacement will increase greenhouse gases during both their production and transport. The first step for the destination should be to look to reduce quantities of materials consumed (including packaging), to then consider reuse, or if not possible, recycle.

Source(s) of data: The information which the destination needs to collect is the weight of solid waste being sent to landfill. This can be done in a number of ways depending on what facilities are available in the area. If the local refuse transfer station has a weigh bridge the weight of waste can be sourced from here. If there is no weighbridge, other methods of calculation include calculating the volume of waste being sent to the landfill; this can then be converted to a weight using weight to volume conversion factors depending on the amount of compaction. Where there is no official collection, it may be necessary to survey properties to obtain estimates of volumes, or access private waste audits.

Means to use these indicators: These indicators are useful to display trends in solid waste production and allow the destination to monitor and act on their performance. They can sometimes be used as a proxy measure for other stressors, such as total pressures on a particular site, although the relationship is not always easy to show.

Benchmarking: This indicator can be benchmarked in two ways: over time for the individual destination or by using comparative data from other destinations.

Indicators of waste reduction:

* **Volume of waste recycled (m³) / Total volume of waste (m³) ➢ Baseline Indicator;**
* **Number of tourism establishments collecting waste separately, capacity of collecting separated waste from local residents;**
* **Number of tourism establishments recycling their own waste (e.g. composting).**

Reason for use of these indicators: The first step for the community should be to look to reduce quantities of materials consumed (including packaging), to then consider reuse, or if not possible, recycle. The basis of recycling is separating different types of waste, which is best to start at the source. Therefore, it is important to monitor, whether separate waste collection is conducted at tourism establishments, or if there are facilities (bins) that allow local residents to deposit their waste separately, and subsequently to collect waste separately.

Source(s) of data: The information can be sourced from the data collected during a waste audit. If an audit has not been carried out it will need to be collected from records from recycle operators, disposal firms and also from the local disposal sites. Tourism establishments can be also, good sources of information, especially where waste collection and recycling is not organized centrally at the destination.

Means to use these indicators: This indicator is useful for displaying trends in recycling allowing the destination to monitor and control their performance.

Benchmarking: This indicator can be benchmarked over time for the individual destination or by using comparative data from other sources such as regional or national authorities. Note that waste volumes can also be used as rough indicators to measure levels of activity if there is no direct indicator (in some WTO case applications, the change in number of trucks collected for the destination or for a particular site have been suggested as a potential indicator of tourist volumes in season).

Indicators of adequacy of waste collection services:

* **% of destination area (especially in urban sites) covered by solid waste collection services;**
* **Percentage of tourism establishments covered by waste collection programs.**

Reason for use of these indicators: Some destinations do not have waste collection services. Particularly in new destinations or destinations where attractions and accommodation are widely scattered, there may be no local authorities, and therefore little regulation or service provision.

Source(s) of data: Local authorities where they exist, or poll of establishments.

Means to use the indicator: Shows development of waste services, or demons-trates need.

Benchmarking: Ideal is 100%. This may be provided through local authorities or private collection services.

Indicators relating to handling and disposal of hazardous substances:

*   **Number and volume of hazardous substances in use (for key substances, volume of use over time);**

*   **% of these substances for which appropriate management and disposal policies and programs are in place;**

*   **% of employees informed and trained in the use and disposal of the substances they use (e.g., cleaners knowledgeable of how to deal with waste cleaning fluids, engineers trained in emergency spill handling).**

Other potential indicators:

*   **Whether or not the enterprise or attraction has an environmental management system (see p. 241) or a hazardous waste program;**

*   **For destinations, percentage of enterprises with toxic waste management programs;**

*   **% of hazardous waste generated in the community which is collected in a special waste program.**

Reason for use of these indicators: Compared to other industries, tourism generates little hazardous waste, although some toxic substances are in use, mainly as cleaners, ingredients in fire control devices, pesticides used on lawns, gardens (and some attractions such as golf courses) and in some cases, lubricants, fuels, paint, and occasional biologically hazardous materials (for example waste from clinics in hotels or cruise ships) . It can also include ash from boilers and heating systems and sewage sludge from cesspools and septic systems.

Source(s) of data: The key to waste management of hazardous substances is a thorough inventory of the substances in use or produced. (See for example the box in the section on Convention Centres p. 286 where such an inventory is included in their environmental management system). Once a thorough inventory is done, it is possible to monitor (and hopefully reduce through substitution and efficiency) the use of such substances.

Besides the contamination effects, inappropriately and illegally deposited waste has severe visual impact at tourism destinations, contributing to poor image.

Means to use these indicators: These indicators can be used to show compliance with laws and regulations and as a signal of risks.

Benchmarking: Guidelines for hazardous waste management are available from on-line sources. Specific chemical safety fact sheets for most commonly used toxics are available in many languages on line at http://www.cdc.gov/niosh/ipcs/icstart.html.

Indicators of impact of waste on the destination:

* **Quantity of waste collected from public areas and streets;**
* **Quantity of waste strewn in public areas (Garbage counts on key sites) ➢ Baseline indicator;**
* **Image of cleanliness of the destination (questionnaire based).**

Reason for use of these indicators: Waste that is not managed can accumulate, creating environmental and health issues and also disturbing tourists and affecting the image of the destination.

Source(s) of data: Debris counts in public areas. Measure collection volumes from collectors. (loads of waste from streets and public areas).

Means to use these indicators: Can measure both effects of programs to reduce litter and dumping and results of cleanup programs.

Benchmarking: Measure changes over time for one destination or for different sites within a destination. Compare to other sites: - note that some destinations have effectively achieved near zero waste in public areas. (e.g., Northern Europe, Canada) through a combination of public education and cleanup programs.

Few tourists are prepared to enter or leave the water via the sewage outlet

Box 3.34 Waste management through multi-stakeholder partnership in Side, Turkey

The Tour Operators Initiative (TOI), comprising over 20 inbound and outbound tour operators, organized a workshop in the Municipality of Side in Turkey's Antalya region, where TOI members and their local partners bring approximately 300,000 tourists each year. The meeting was attended by the Mayor of Side, representatives of WWF Turkey, and representatives of the private sector, individual hoteliers, excursion providers and local travel agencies as well as UNEP, UNESCO and WTO. The meeting gave the participants the opportunity to share their views on the main threats to sustainability in the Side region and ways to address these. Among the three priority actions waste management (with a focus on waste separation and recycling), was identified as an urgent matter. During follow up meetings with local stakeholders, a detailed plan of action was developed, and a locally based coordinator was appointed, financed by the Side administration and the Side Tourism Association (TUDER).

Activities implemented in the two-year program include:

* A waste separation scheme for the municipality of Side. It is in operation, recycling companies have been identified and pick-up times set for participating hotels;

* The local recycling company posts signs on its vehicles to promote the Side initiative, and hotels and restaurants post signs at their entrances;

* The Side Tourism Association has placed containers for collecting used batteries in every Side hotel, in the Ali Ihsan Barut elementary school and in the Tourism Hotel Vocational High School;

* Waste separation bins for organic and recyclable waste have been placed in Side for use by residents and tourists;

* Training sessions on solid waste management and waste separation techniques, organized with technical input and background material from UNEP, were held for managers and staff at hotels, apartment hotels and pensions, Side Municipality sanitation workers, sanitation managers and association presidents; members of the Garment Association and of the Bar and Restaurant Association.

Indicators demonstrate the significant progress achieved in waste management:

* Over 100 hotels and all local shops and restaurants participate in the waste separation scheme;

* Waste collected during the last seven months of 2003:

  - 276 tons of inorganic waste;

  - 11,978 batteries collected from hotel desks, hotel technical services and primary school;

  - 102 storage batteries collected from hotels.

Moreover, the new land fill area has been identified and approved and it will be in operation in Fall 2004. For more information on TOI and its indicators program see Box 3.47 p. 243.

Twenty waste bins were placed in the town of Side to separate organic and inorganic waste

Source: UNEP, www.toinitiative.org

Indicator of perception of destination cleanliness

- **Image of cleanliness of destination (questionnaire based).**

    Reason for use of this indicator: If a destination has a poor reputation for cleanliness, some travellers may avoid it. Reaction to garbage can be very individual, and is related to conditions in the tourists' place of origin. Perception of cleanliness may figure more strongly in the decision regarding whether to return to a destination or recommend it to others than actual conditions.

    Source(s) of data: Exit questionnaire (Annex C).

    Means to use the indicator: This is an indicator of risk to the destination deriving from tourist reactions to garbage.

    Benchmarking: This should be compared over time to exit survey results for the same destination. If there is a strong negative response, further questions should be used to pinpoint problem areas, or specific reasons for negative reactions.

3.9.3 Air Pollution

Air Quality, Health, Pollution from Tourism, Perception by Tourists

Air pollution has become an issue for many destinations, related primarily to the levels of industrial contamination in the outdoors. Travellers' advisories have been posted for some popular tourist destinations, including Mexico City, Seoul, Tokyo, Sao Paulo, Athens and Beijing. The latter two are summer Olympic sites, and concern has been raised that the levels of contamination may exceed safe

standards and affect athletic performances. Those most affected by air pollution warnings are the elderly and those with respiratory ailments and allergies. Air pollution is also considered a major contributor to degradation of cultural heritage (acid rain effects on limestone monuments) and natural heritage (harming species and altering ecosystems). At a more localized level, the centres of many major cities have raised levels of contaminants, particularly in the still summer months, when pollution from industry and traffic are concentrated near their sources.

Tourism itself can be a contributor to air pollution. Buses left running while tourists visit monuments can be significant factors in urban centre pollution and in damage to buildings.

Santiago de Chile from the Andes through the smog

Many governments have established air quality standards related to concentrations of key contaminants such as particulates, ground level ozone, sulphur dioxide and volatile organics. The World Health Organization publishes standards for air pollutants at http://www.euro.who.int/document/aiq/3summary.pdf which provides detailed standards for different airborne substances. Many jurisdictions provide public warnings when readings reach levels considered to be harmful to health (e.g. a reading of 50 parts per million in a North American city draws a public health warning to avoid strenuous exercise and for those with respiratory conditions to remain inside.) Readings exceeding 1000 parts per million have been recorded in some urban tourist destinations.   Many jurisdictions now publish air quality data on a regular basis – for example, China provides graphs showing urban air quality for major cities on a weekly basis in major newspapers, including those for foreign visitors. Some destinations are acting to shift polluting industries outside the most affected cities, replace old factories and vehicles to reduce pollution loading, change fuel sources for heating and power generation to less polluting ones, and limiting trucks and other traffic in cities, particularly when there is a pollution emergency. Some cities have moved to reduce car use: for example cars are banned from city centres, limited to access on certain days, or permitted access days related to the numbers on licence plates but overall growth in car numbers in cities like Mexico City, Santiago or Beijing have thwarted many of these initiatives.

Components of issue	Indicators
Quality of air	◦ Number of days exceeding standards.
Impact of air quality on tourists and residents	◦ Incidence of respiratory problems (local and tourist); ◦ Number of health problems reported by tourists.
Reaction of tourists to air quality	◦ Perception of air quality by tourists; ◦ Number of warnings regarding the air pollution of the destination in major publications and guidebooks (would be done by a survey of these print sources).
Impact of air pollution on tourist assets	◦ Cost of repair to buildings and cultural sites.
Impact of tourism sector on air quality	◦ Contribution of the tourism industry to greenhouse gases.

Indicator of air quality:

◦ **Number of days exceeding standards.**

Reason for use of this indicator: Uses existing standards in destination to show levels of concern and changes over time. This can also help pinpoint which seasons are of greatest concern (e.g., the heating season in a city which uses coal fires, the hot summer season with photochemical fogs).

Source(s) of data: Existing monitoring programs (often health or environment departments).

Means to use the indicator: Use to show risk; also use to demonstrate improvements or show potential visitors that there is little risk in certain seasons.

Benchmarking: Compare over time with jurisdictions using the same standards and monitoring systems. International standards for most chemicals are published by WHO. Many nations have their own criteria for when warnings are issued.

Indicators regarding impact of air quality on tourists and residents:

◦ **Incidence of respiratory problems (local and tourist);**
◦ **Number of health problems reported by tourists (See Health p. 94)**.

Reason for use of these indicators: This is an indicator of risks. Use with the above indicator. Local conditions – such as length of time a pollution event lasts, and altitude of the destination can affect the impact on tourist and local health.

Source(s) of data: Health department statistics (See Health p. 94) An alternative may be WHO data (aggregated from nations) or insurance firm data related to numbers of health problems among travellers.

Means to use these indicators: Measures progress in overall health in the destination with emphasis on diseases known to relate to air quality.

Benchmarking: Use WHO data, national data among destinations within a country.

Indicators of reaction of tourists to air quality:

*   **Perception of air quality by tourists;**

*   **Number of warnings regarding the air pollution of the destination in major publications and guidebooks (would be done by a survey of these print sources).**

    Reason for use of these indicators: Perception of air quality may be as important to tourism as the actual physical data on contamination. Perception can be very individual; some tourists are much more sensitive to poorer air than others. Tourists from very clean cities may react more to bus fumes and strong smells than those who are used to them at home. The message delivered to other potential tourists may reflect the reaction rather than any specific air quality measure. (e.g., the hotel was just downwind from the sewage lagoon or near to the fish market). The broader response of tourists can affect the decision of whether or not to visit the destination.

    Source(s) of data: Exit questionnaire. For general perception of pollution of a destination, it may be necessary to conduct a broader survey, not just of those who have visited. As a very rough surrogate, a web survey of frequency of mentions of the destination along with the terms "air pollution" could also be instructive. A search by the authors found Paris, Los Angeles and Mexico City each with more than 100,000 entries, Beijing and Sydney with about 30,000 each and, Auckland with 8000 entries. This is a rough measure with some difficulties of comparison due to linguistic issues, but will be a reasonable indicator of changes in visibility of the issue over time.

    Means to use these indicators: This is an early warning indicator that tourists may find the air a problem. It is primarily of use to stimulate work to remedy the issue, and ultimately to measure progress.

    Benchmarking: Compare over time for the same destination.

Additional indicators which may be of use relative to air pollution issues:

*   **Cost of repair to buildings and cultural sites** (see p. 76) which can help measure some of the costs associated with air pollution damage;

*   **Contribution of the tourism industry to greenhouse gases** (see p. 160) which can help the industry understand its own role in air pollution and other related issues. See also – Issue sections on Tourism and Climate Change p. 155, **Energy** p. 152, and Environmental Management Systems p. 241, for indicators relative to tourism sector contribution to air pollution.

Sometimes noise and air pollution go together in a destination

Box 3.35 Indoor air pollution

Indoor air pollution is an emerging issue, related to the use of toxic substances in construction of or cleaning of buildings, including hotels, restaurants, the use of scents in shops and enclosed spaces, and to issues related to smoking. Concern for indoor air quality is an issue for some tourists, and may influence their choice of establishment or destination related to their perception of health issues. Some may not visit cities where smoking is permitted in restaurants; others may avoid cities where they are not allowed to smoke in bars and restaurants. Some travellers may seek "safe" environments with filtered air, hotel rooms which meet high standards of air quality, or hotels with posted standards regarding use of organic or green cleaning supplies.

Indoor air quality is fundamentally an issue for workers, who spend many hours daily in the same environments – where toxic fumes, cooking smoke, etc. can be a health hazard. Tourists will likely be less directly affected unless they spend long periods under the same conditions.

For further information on this issue, informative sources are:

An American medical site: http://www.nlm.nih.gov/medlineplus/indoorairpollution.html

A Swiss hotel school site: http://www.ehlite.ch/jan03/10e.asp

A commercial site: http://www.hotelair.com/report.html

World Health Organization indoor air quality site: http://www.who.int/indoorair/en/

3.9.4 Controling Noise Levels

Measuring Noise Levels, Perception of Noise

Noise has arisen as an issue in studies of many urban destinations and heavily used seasonal sites, particularly beach resorts. Some cities like Bangkok, Rome and Tokyo have identified noise as one of the key issues harming the tourist experience. While there are well established standards for noise levels in workplaces, related to hearing loss and health impacts, noise standards for outdoor areas tend to be more subjective. The noise tolerated and even expected at a rock concert or amusement park would be intolerable elsewhere (or to those within hearing range who do not enjoy that form of music). What is acceptable during the day will be much less welcome at night. Loud radios, noisy motor vehicles, and raucous tourists are the main sources of unwanted noise in many destinations.

There is a well established measure, the decibel, used to monitor noise levels. Some urban centres have real-time decibel monitors at key intersections (e.g. many Chinese cities) which show the actual decibel level, and you can watch it rise from e.g., 78dB to 94 dB as traffic accelerates.

Particularly in beach destinations noise levels draw complaints: this is often an indicator of cultural conflict between e.g., the young and older tourists or the tourists who wish to party until dawn and the longer term or local residents who wish to sleep at night. Where a destination is shared among different market niches, noise conflicts may occur. Both actual noise level and perception of noise are relevant. Noise levels will tend to be quite site specific. For example loud on one street where there are late night clubs, outdoor attractions, outdoor restaurants or a major intersection and much quieter two blocks away. For example, the City of Honolulu has set a standard of 68dB (no more than 10% of the time can noise exceed this limit) for noise produced from the Waikiki band shell, as audible from nearby hotels and apartments. Noise level limits may need to be as precise as this due to the fact that noise levels decline with distance from the source.

Components of the issue	Indicators
Actual noise levels	· Noise levels at site in decibels (also can be reported by time of day).
Impact of noise on tourists and locals	· Perception of noise; · Complaints received.

Indicator of physical noise levels:

·   **Noise levels at site (day, night) in decibels.**

Reason for use of this indicator: Actual noise levels can be monitored or sampled using a decibelometer. Typical levels are shown in the box above.

Source(s) of data: Fixed decibel meters on key sites, and/or sampling using mobile decibel meters. Note that for mobile measurement, time of day or day of week, as well as season will be important.

Means to use the indicator: Graph of monitoring data can be very useful. Raw data may reveal specific sites at specific times exceeding desired levels. To reveal whether sites are becoming noisier over time, compare the same sites for both average and maximum levels from year to year.

Benchmarking: Many jurisdictions have established maximum levels allowed (for example no more than 70dB between midnight and 6AM). These are very specific – often with different levels permitted in residential areas or near parks etc. (For typical bylaws search on the web using the combination of keywords: "noise, bylaws, limits" and look for a site or community similar to your own).

Box 3.36 Typical decibel levels (dB)

Rustling leaves	20dB
Quiet room at night	32dB
Quiet street	50dB
Ringing alarm clock (1metre)	80dB
Loud orchestra in large room	82dB
Beginning of hearing damage due to prolonged exposure	**85dB**
Heavy city traffic	85-92dB
Gas lawn mower	98dB
Jet airliner (150m overhead)	115dB
Thunder (close by)	120dB
Ambulance siren	120dB
Pain threshold	**135dB**
Rock concert	110-140dB

More information and examples:
www.lhh.org/noise/decibel.htm

Indicator of noise impact on tourists:

·   **Perception of noise.**

Reason for use of this indicator: Different groups will perceive noise differently. If large numbers or cohorts find the noise objectionable, this may have more direct impact on their opinion of the site (and of the whole destination) than any objective assessment of decibel levels. Note that this indicator will probably relate as well to number of complaints received, but because noise tolerance is very site specific, activity specific, and culture specific, complaints may not be a good indicator, but can demonstrate the need for monitoring or a more specific questionnaire approach.

Source(s) of data: Exit questionnaire (and resident survey) (See Annex C). Calculate the percentage who agrees that: "I was bothered by noise". Where high agreement levels are received, probe for where and why.

Means to use the indicator: Can show whether noise is a serious irritant and may affect return or opinion of the destination. If noise has been a problem, it can be used to measure success of mitigation and reduction activities.

Benchmarking: The strongest benchmark will be changes over time for the destination.

3.9.5 Managing Visual Impacts of Tourism Facilities and Infrastructure

Siting, Construction, Design, Landscaping

Tourism facilities and their related infrastructure too often violate or intrude upon the environment with visual pollution. Architectural design of facilities must demonstrate unique responses to the local environment, climate and culture. Therefore, the architectural and the related infrastructure of the facility should not compete with the natural landscape and the surrounding vegetation, but should be harmoniously integrated with the environment. The presence of the facility should not disturb or intrude upon its natural setting. It is also important to take into account any existing architectural forms in the region, whether they are synchronised with the landscape or not. These local building forms have evolved over hundreds of years and normally make the most efficient use of local materials, orientation and space and are a response to the relative climatic environments.

Infrastructure such as roads, power lines, mobile telephone towers, satellite dishes etc can cause serious visual impacts in nature areas and at historic monuments, and therefore should be integrated into the landscape and architecture. Two of the fundamental considerations in designing a facility are physical and cultural context; sensitivity to the local environment and culture are essential to a sustainable facility that has low visual impact on its surroundings.

Physical context:

A facility should be designed within the natural physical context of the area in which it is situated. It should be designed in keeping with its natural surroundings and should not violate or intrude upon the physical landscape as a foreign structure. The facility should interact with the natural ecological/geological features, aiming to blend into them as much as possible. This, in turn, would render the design visually sustainable, as it would act as a timeless piece of architecture and an organic feature of the natural landscape.

The following principles should be given particular attention in addressing such issues as physical context.

1.   Form;
2.   Colour;
3.   Integration with the surrounding landscape.

Cultural context:

A facility should demonstrate the same level of sensitivity to the cultural context as it does to the physical context. The design of the facility should be congruous with the cultural environment in which it operates, incorporating cultural motifs and traditional styles of vernacular architecture wherever possible. The use of vernacular architectural principles in the design will allow the facility to reflect the local cultural history and be visually and culturally sustainable over time.

The use of an area's vernacular architecture helps assimilate buildings into the local cultural context, and here the facility can serve two additional roles: First, it can help reduce any feelings of cultural intrusion that may be felt toward the facility by local traditional peoples. Secondly, if it is done well, it can enhance the tourists' experience and appreciation of the local cultural forms and styles.

Box 3.37 Lobo Lodge- Design for reducing visual impacts

An outstanding example of physically sensitive uses of form in lodge design comes from the Serengeti plains of Tanzania. Lobo Lodge reflects sensitivity to the site and the natural surroundings. The built structures harmonize with the physical environment, and are so well situated in the kopje (rock outcrop) that it is difficult to determine where the natural landscape ends and where the buildings begin, or vice versa. Some of the techniques and approaches used in the design of Lobo Lodge include the use of existing natural rocks for structural purposes; glass detailing to create inside-outside relationships; natural rocks to define internal space; and existing rock contours to create a swimming pool.

Components of the issue	Indicators
Design and construction of infrastructure	• Total length of roads; • Total run of overhead electrical cables; • Presence of satellite dishes; • Presence of communications tower; • Height of water tank; • Sewage ponds (size, siting); • Erosion on the side of roads (% eroded); • No. and size of signposts.
Night lighting	• Number of light fixtures that throw direct light; • Quality in viewing the night sky (in natural areas).
Physical form	• Height of buildings (average and maximum); • Number of buildings (area covered) exceeding height of natural vegetation (like treetops); • Shapes of buildings (% matching vernacular); • Shapes of signs (% matching vernacular style or natural environment); • Density of buildings per hectare (footprint and floor space per unit area).
Planning / Building permits	• Existence of aesthetic considerations in planning approval process; • See ➢ **Development Control** (p. 207).
Material selection	• Color (% matching or coordinating with vernacular); • Texture (% matching vernacular).
Siting and orientation	• Ridgeline or coastline continuity (% intrusion on ridge and coastline); • Slopes (% built on slopes); • Against the natural light – reflections; • Soil Erosion (% and total area eroded).
Integration with the landscape	• % of site cleared for development; • Number. of indigenous plants removed for development; • % of landscaping done with native species; • % of site covered by indigenous plants.

Indicators regarding infrastructure:

* **Total Length of roads (Km);**
* **Total run of overhead electrical cables (Km);**
* **Presence of satellite dishes (number);**
* **Presence of communications tower (also height and visibility);**
* **Height (and visibility) of water tank;**
* **Sewage ponds – area and visibility;**
* **Erosion on the side of roads (% eroded);**
* **No. and size of signposts.**

Reason for use of these indicators: In several parks around the world, vehicular routes are being closed and reclaimed and shuttle systems have been introduced i.e. Denali National Park, Grand Canyon National Park some very popular sites i.e., Yosemite, visitor impacts have reached critical levels. Provision of transport hubs and public transport systems will be necessary to limit these impacts by reducing traffic and thus the necessity of extending the infrastructure and increasing its visual impacts.

Box 3.38 Selected guidelines for infrastructure design

1. Prior to construction of the roads, inventory and move plants and topsoil that could be disturbed by construction activities. After road gradation has been completed, they should be returned as closely as possible to their original sites.

2. Appropriately signpost all roads, endeavouring to stimulate appreciation of the natural and cultural environment, providing interesting and pertinent information, and also encouraging suitable behaviour. Avoid excessive signposting, which mars the natural landscape.

3. On hilly areas, avoid locating roads on ridgelines since this scars the landscape. They should be a minimum of 5-8m (16-26 ft) distance below the ridgeline.

4. Design roads using the topography to minimise visual impacts and create dynamic variation in views and orientation.

5. Ensure that water runoff from the road does not create erosion channels. Consult an engineer if there is doubt about building gravel sinks or other drainage tool.

6. Clearly mark vehicle access and parking areas and limit it to those locations.

Source(s) of data: Site review or assessment, review of plans. See International Ecolodge Guidelines. (www.eco-mon.com)

Means to use the indicators: Some of these can be used as simple checklists. Measures of impact (e.g. erosion) or of management (adequate signage) can be seen a performance measures which can change over time.

Benchmarking: The box above implies standards against which a design or a constructed facility can be compared.

An asphalt road (hidden by trees in the foreground) designed through a steep slope in the Nyungwe Forest National Park, Rwanda has caused erosion and the resultant visual impact spoils the visitor experience.

Indicators regarding lighting:

*   **Number of light fixtures that throw direct light (and % of site lit) at natural sites;**

*   **Quality of viewing of the night sky (number of stars or constellations visible – use astronomical standard).**
    See for example www.epa.gov/oar/visibility/report/CHAP01.pdf for light indexes which can be used for both day and night measurement).

Reason for use of these indicators: Site lighting should be limited and controlled to avoid visual disruption to the nocturnal cycles of wildlife, and so light the minimum area for the minimum time at the lowest wattage. All-night illumination to areas with all-night use or extreme security concerns should be limited and simple timers or photocells can be used to turn lights on and off at seasonally appropriate times.

Source(s) of data: direct measure of lighting levels and visual impacts at night.

Means to use these indicators: Some jurisdictions have established standards.

Benchmarking: Compare to published standards or to other sites nearby.

Box 3.39 Means to limit light pollution

1. Review outdoor lighting to assure that neighbouring properties are protected from the view of bright light sources and plant screening shrubs to protect the facility from off-site light pollution;

2. Eliminate all upward radiation of light through use of full cut-off luminaires. Avoid disturbance on the horizon so stars are clearly visible at night;

3. Shield all landscape fixtures through plantings;

4. Consider essential driveway lighting attached to low bollards, directed downwards only and spaced along the edges.

Indicators of structure:

*   **Height of buildings (average and maximum height);**
*   **Shapes of buildings (% matching vernacular, number of distinct shapes);**
*   **Number of buildings (area covered) exceeding height of natural vegetation (like treetops);**
*   **Shapes of buildings (% matching vernacular);**
*   **Shapes of signs (% matching vernacular style or natural environment);**
*   **Density of buildings per hectare (footprint and floor space per unit area).**

Reason for use of these indicators: Architects should draw on the beauty of the existing landscape as a vital theme for the facility's form. The facility should be planned and designed such that it follows the contours and forms of the natural landscape features, and therefore, enhances itself by such interplay. Buildings and other structures should not dominate the landscape and/or surrounding vegetation, which constitute the main attraction, together with the local wildlife (and, this being the case, the local cultural environment). Designers should conceive the shape of the buildings and roof to be a function of activities inside the buildings. The degree of overhang or extension of the roof beyond the building line can provide better integration with the landscape. Avoid building high structures, so that the architectural form does not stand out above the vegetation or surrounding rock formations. There are not only aesthetic benefits, but such designs can also gain protection against intense weather conditions. Some sites may be ideally adapted to tree house type tall structures and this may reduce ground footprint.

Source(s) of data: Design drawings for proposed developments, inventory of structures for existing sites. Planning agencies may hold these data.

Means to use these indicators: For sites where a large percentage of architecture matches traditional, these indicators can be used to market authenticity. (e.g., no structures in the Maldives are permitted to exceed the height of palm trees).

Benchmarking: These indicators should be compared over time to the same site.

Indicators of external materials:

*   **Colour (% matching or coordinating with vernacular);**
*   **Texture (% matching vernacular).**

Reason for use of these indicators: The colour and texture of exterior finishes are particularly important design elements for any facility, and can enhance the feeling of harmony and unity between the final built form and the natural environment. On the other hand, colour can diminish the feeling of the physical context if used incorrectly. The wrong colours can sharply contrast the shades of colour found in the natural landscape, and can create a feeling of intrusion upon that environment.

At natural sites, the colours used for a facility should be drawn from shades found in the surrounding elements - such as the leaves, barks, rocks, soil, etc., (commonly referred to as earth tones) which soften the presence of the built form. Use colours that blend with their surroundings and be inspired by the rocks, the sea, desert sand, plants and distant mountains. Remember that white reflects solar radiation, and though it may cause comfort inside the facility it may provoke annoying glare outside and may clash with the surroundings and detract from the effects and appreciation of site.

Source(s) of data: Plans and design drawings.

Means to use these indicators: Often used to draw tourists, for example to the "white cities" of southern Spain, or the colourful buildings in the Caribbean and Latin-America. This can also be used as a performance measure for efforts to encourage preservation of character of communities.

Benchmarking: Compare over time to the same destination.

Indicators of siting and orientation:

*   **Ridgeline continuity (% intrusion on ridgeline);**
*   **Slopes (% built on slopes);**
*   **Against the light – reflections;**
*   **Soil erosion (% and total area eroded).**

Reason for use of these indicators: From the lessons learned through the site analysis process, a site plan should be designed whereby the buildings are in harmony with the landscape. Draw upon local precedents for determining the relationship between structure and environment. To achieve this, one of the primary techniques would be to protect sensitive habitats from development. The facility should be planned around natural features rather than imposing typical resort design solutions. Buildings should not try to compete with the surrounding plant and landforms, which, after all, are the main attractions. In colder climates, wind directions are a major factor when siting facility units.

Source(s) of data: Plans for new developments, inventory of existing structures.

Means to use these indicators: Use these as a performance measure for efforts to promote good siting and orientation.

Benchmarking: Compare with the same destination over time.

Indicators of integration with landscape:

* **% of site cleared for development;**
* **% of site that is landscaped;**
* **% of landscaping done with native species.**

Reasons for use of these indicators: The built structure of any facility can be made to blend in with and appear as an extension of the natural environment through carefully designed minimal landscape plantings. Landscape designs that emphasise native trees, vines, shrubs, and perennials help to preserve the character of regional landscapes.

Source(s) of data: Plans for new developments, site inventory.

Means to use these indicators: This is a performance measure for efforts to conserve or enhance natural environments.

Benchmarking: These are key performance measures for results and mitigation of visual impacts of construction.

Box 3.40 Guidelines for sustainable and sensitive landscaping

1. Integrate the facility into the surrounding landscape through the planting of various indigenous trees and shrubs whenever and wherever possible. The landscaping should be guided by the patterns of the existing natural landscape as much as possible and native vegetation (e.g., shrubs and trees) and rocks should be laid out in an informal, natural manner.

2. Use plants which are native to the area (endemic) since they will be in greater harmony with the existing surroundings, require less maintenance, be well adapted to the local climate and soil conditions, and in some cases, attract native bird and butterfly species.

3. Avoid superfluous landscaping and the use of exotic plants. Preserving the existing landscape should be a priority.

4. Use a natural landscape approach and concentrate your planting efforts adjacent to the facility, especially near the entry. Groundcovers should begin this transition, which should progress to larger shrubs closer to the building walls.

5. Design a simple massing concept, as this is generally more successful than a complicated planting scheme. Remember that simplicity is the desired result.

6. Avoid using plants with forms and colour from outside the area.

   Note that the recommended indicators can help measure the degree to which these guidelines are followed.

   For further information on design see:" International Ecolodge Guidelines" (TIES, 2002) www.eco-mon.com, www.edsaplan.com

Prizewinning Kandalama Lodge (Sri Lanka) is a big facility with around 300 rooms. It is set into the cliff, is almost invisible from the air and harmonizes well with its surrounding thanks to the vegetation cover using local plants.

3.10 Controlling Tourist Activities

3.10.1 Controling Use Intensity ≫ **Baseline Issue**

Stress on Sites and Systems, Tourist Numbers, Crowding

How many tourists are too many? The issue which has probably received the greatest attention by destination managers is that of tourist numbers and intensity of use. Nearly all sites monitor tourist numbers. In the research to develop this Guidebook, over 50 examples were encountered of indicators used to measure or calculate tourist density, and intensity of use of sites and destinations. Often, the indicators have been used to compare use levels to specific goals, estimates of maximum carrying capacity (ecological limits, space standards, infrastructure capacity etc). The objective of most applications is to measure tourist numbers relative to desired levels of use, however calculated, and to determine when standards or thresholds are likely to be reached. The numbers and density of tourists are understood to be a driving factor in many of the other issues related to site or destination management, and therefore indicators relative to this issue will be one of the key management tools for destination managers.

The measure of stress on sites and systems can be both an indicator of potential damage, and one of damage already done. Ideally, something is known about the capacity of a site in ecological or cultural terms, or at least the maximum capacity of key infrastructure (such as toilets, or seating space) or management (e.g. lifeguards, policing or guiding capacity) to establish some points of reference. Often this occurs through a process of trial and error as site managers discover that damage has occurred, or the system has been stressed through what is considered excessive use.

In part 5 there is a detailed description on the application of the concept of carrying capacity with some practical approaches (See section 5.4 p. 309).

Components of the Issue	Indicators
Total numbers of tourists visiting the destination or key sites, peak numbers of tourists stressing the limits of capacity	* Total tourist numbers (mean, monthly, peak) (categorized by their type of activity) ≫ **Baseline Indicator.**
Measuring and managing the intensity of use of the destination	* Number of tourists per square metre of the site (per square kilometre of the destination) - mean number/peak month average/peak day ≫ **Baseline Indicator.**
Measuring and managing use density for specific heavily used sites within the destination	* Density counts for vehicle use of site (cars per minute on park roads; boats per minute on canals, mangrove tours; boats per square Km on watercourses, jeeps per hour in a wildlife park); * Ratio of number of vehicles per parking space.
Levels of use relative to design capacity/other capacity measures	* % of total capacity used (average and peak).
Perception of use levels and crowding (same as for above issue of density)	* Percentage of tourists who believe that the destination is too crowded (exit questionnaire) and local residents who believe it is too crowded (local questionnaire).

Note: many other issues are subsets of the use intensity and crowding issue, and the indicators proposed for them address specific symptoms of stress. Destination managers may wish to use a participatory process or focus groups to assist in discovering which limits are most important, and therefore which of these may require a specific indicator. Note also that limits may not remain the same over time, particularly those which are built; new roads, services can alter the capacity of a site or a destination, as can changes in levels of control or management.

Fundamental to the understanding of stress on a site is the simple monitoring of numbers of users, although the relationship is much more complex (see for example Carrying Capacity (p. 309). The impact of each tourist or day visitor is cumulative. Each tourist is not equal; a tourist riding on an off road vehicle has many times the potential impact on a site than a birdwatcher, and the behaviour of each can also alter the impact.

Indicator of level of tourism:

* **Total tourist numbers (mean, monthly, peak) (categorized by their type of activity) ≫ Baseline Indicator.**

    Reason for use of this indicator: This is a basic information requirement for nearly all forms of tourism planning and management. Nevertheless, it is not as simple as it may seem. While the usual definition of tourist for a destination implies an overnight stay (and the WTO encourages destinations to use this definition at the destination level to measure tourism) it can often be complicated by other factors. For example, some discrete destinations may also accommodate a great deal of day use, and these day visitors can significantly augment the pressures on destination facilities. (E.g., day bus and car visitors outnumber overnighters in most of the major North American national parks; day visitors from cruise ships outnumber significantly the tourists who stay overnight in destinations such as Cozumel Mexico and some Greek islands). It is therefore recommended that both overnight visitors and day visitors be monitored where the impact on sites is significantly affected by day visitors.

Total number of tourists (and tourists plus day visitors) is a key piece of data to address potential stress on a destination and on specific sites within the destination. It is also a vital component for many other indicators measuring per capita impacts, densities etc. The overall numbers indicate average stress on the destination, the peak day will show maximum potential stress.

Source(s) of data: While some destinations (and managed sites within destinations) have managed entry points where those who enter are routinely counted (and in some cases classified as to local or foreign, student or elder etc) many destinations do not have this easy means of documentation. Island states, or small states which can be considered to be a single destination can monitor arrivals at borders (but even this can be difficult for small states which are part of a larger customs union or which have open borders (e.g. Monaco). While specific sites (e.g., the Acropolis, Disneyland, many national parks and historic sites) have access control or sell tickets, others are open or have limited controls. For controlled sites, daily records are likely the best source. For others, sample data (at entry points), transport data (ferry passengers to an island), or counts on site (use of photography is very helpful for crowded sites) may be necessary. A further alternative may be occupancy records of accommodation, with some study done to try to document how this relates to total numbers. (i.e., adjusting for % who stay outside the destination, % who stay in unofficial accommodation).

Means to use the indicator: This indicator is used to measure % changes in visitation – and is useful as raw data, or as the basis for calculation of per capita derived indicators (e.g. water use per tourist, garbage produced per tourist).

Benchmarking: Benchmark against other years for the same destination using the same data source. Compare as well to the growth rates in other destinations of the nation or region as a whole. (e.g., Pirate Beach doubled its tourism numbers in only five years whereas the other destinations in the region took more than ten years for the same growth).

Indicator of density and use intensity:

*   **Number of tourists per square metre of the site (per square kilometre of the destination) - mean number/peak month average/peak day ➤ Baseline Indicator.**

Reason for use of this indicator: This is a baseline indicator for management of any destination or site. Total numbers are fundamental to the calculation of the density data as well as the derivation of many other indicators. Density of use is understood to relate to and in some cases help predict stresses on ecological and cultural assets, infrastructure, levels of management and mitigation needed, and several aspects of longer term sustainability.

Source(s) of data: Data are readily available for sites or destinations where access is controlled or entry is sold. One concern is the definition of the boundaries of the destination (see Part 2 of this book for recommended procedures p. 21). For controlled access parks, cultural sites, beaches, etc, this can be easily done and is likely known by managers. For other destinations, both extent/boundaries and the calculation of tourist numbers may be more difficult. Readers are reminded that accommodation occupancy counts or vehicle counts may not capture all visitors (particularly day visitors whose impact on a site is added to that of tourists, and may in some cases because of numbers be much greater than that of tourists who stay overnight). For some sites without access control it may be necessary to do sampling and/or photo counts of densities (e.g., open access beaches, public squares).

Means to use the indicator: Both potential density (number of persons on the island who could be at the beach or plaza), and actual (density of actual beach use, actual level of crowding in the plaza) are meaningful.

Benchmarking: Use intensity has been calculated in many studies, nearly all of which use the persons per square metre or Km indicator. See for example, the WTO study on Villa Gesell an Argentina, the Mediterranean Tourism Indicators study, or the UEC standards for community tourism (Thailand) as reference examples. (see Annex B References p. 475) Some studies have reported beach densities on peak use days of less than one square metre of beach per bather.

Indicators of use density for specific sites:

⁕   **Density counts for vehicle use of site (cars per minute on park roads; boats per minute on canals, mangrove tours; boats per square Km on watercourses, jeeps per hour in a wildlife park);**

⁕   **Ratio of number of vehicles per parking space.**

Reason for use of these indicators: Many sites are visited primarily through use of vehicles. While it may be possible to also measure vehicle occupancy, the density of vehicles may be more important in terms of crowding. In Bentota Sri Lanka, boats may collide due to congestion in the narrow mangrove channels. Buses may have to line up waiting to park in national parks in North America and Europe. Hundreds of paddle boats may crowd Bei Hai park in Beijing on a sunny weekend, kilometre long waiting lines occur as cars try to access Cinque Terre in Italy in August, when bicycles and motorcycles are hung from trees to make their own parking space.

Source(s) of data: For most controlled sites, receipts from vehicle operators and/or parking/access control points will be a useful source. For other sites a specific count may be needed.

Means to use the indicators: Simple portrayal of data as vehicles per minute, vehicles per space, % use of total capacity, or boats per square Km is sufficient, as well as changes in these densities over time can provide useful information.

Benchmarking: Use time series for the same site.

Indicator of stress on site and facilities capacity:

⁕   **% of total capacity used (average and peak)** Note that site capacity measures will be specific, and may be controlled by one specific factor such as water supply, number of parking spaces, or a known ecological or culturally based limit which has been established for the site. (See Carrying Capacity p. 309).

Reason for use of this indicator: Many sites have known or defined capacity limits, related to e.g., the number of seats, the capacity of infrastructure, fire regulations, or policy based standards. Average use can be used to show the need for new infrastructure, issues of low use relative to built capacity etc. Where peak use reaches or exceeds regulations or design limits, this information can be used to support a range of responses – from means to spread use, control numbers, or change built capacity.

Source(s) of data: Tourist numbers are noted in the above indicator, capacity data will likely be available from local authorities. Often a single limit (spaces, toilets, fire regulations) will be the key capacity constraint.

Means to use the indicator: Use to show percentage of capacity used, trends data relative to capacity, or number of instances where capacity limits are reached or exceeded.

Benchmarking: Because capacity is unique, this is best compared over time to the same site or destination. See also the section on ➣ **Controlling use Intensity** (p. 192)

Indicators of reaction to crowding:

⁕   **Perception of crowding by tourists (exit questionnaire);**
⁕   **Perception of crowding by locals (community questionnaire).**

Reason for use of these indicators: All tourists do not perceive the same densities as problems. Those used to the densities of a Shanghai street market will likely be much more tolerant of crowds than those from places where crowding is rare. As a result, perception of crowding may be at least as important an indicator as actual density of use. The locals may have significantly different perceptions of what is crowded than the visitors.

Changes in perceived crowding may be a leading indicator of concern relative to either local or visitor satisfaction with the destination, (See also ➤ **Tourist Satisfaction** p. 86 and the Arches case study which demonstrates another method to measure visitor response to crowding p. 342). It is interesting to note that some tourists may perceive a destination to be too empty while others at the same time perceive it to be too crowded relative to their expectations and/or comfort levels.

Nanjing Road, Shanghai - Crowds are considered normal by local residents, interesting to many tourists and frightening to others.

Source(s) of data: Exit and local questionnaires (Annex C) Note that specific questions can be added on key sites which may have crowding issues.

Means to use the indicators: Show as a percentage, those who feel the site is too crowded/un-crowded/empty. It may be possible in some cases to identify subsets of tourists or locals who feel most strongly. If a significant identifiable cohort is dissatisfied, this may be a signal for actions ranging from site design, crowd control, behavioural modification etc. (For a more extensive examination of these tools, see Manning and Prieur 1998)

Benchmarking: Compare with time series data for the destination.

3.10.2 Managing Events

Sport Events, Fairs, Festivities, Crowd Control

Events are both significant for tourism and also bring challenges to event organizers. Events vary from pilgrimages to cultural festivities, concerts, fairs, conferences and sports, with a large variety of organizers and participants. The competitors and spectators who attend sports events are all visitors from a tourism point of view. The box in this section shows an approach to managing major sports events (see Box 3.41) but the impacts they have on a destination parallel many of the impacts of tourism events in general. For example common issues include; benefits to the community, waste management, and protecting ecosystems and built sites, and managing. There are also very specific issues related to the sustainability particular kinds of events, especially major ones like the Olympics, the World Cup, or Formula One racing, as well as for large concerts, and other outdoor events. Indicators are being developed to monitor these impacts. The following box addresses issues of particular interest to managing sustainable sports events. The lessons will also pertain to other forms of events like parades, fairs, and music presentations.

Box 3.41 Excerpts from: Sustainable sport management: Running an environmentally, socially and economically responsible organization by David Chernushenko with Anna van der Kamp and David Stubbs, published by UNEP

Sport events of any size can be planned and managed sustainably. While the "green games" initiatives of major events like the Olympics may have garnered most of the publicity, there is no reason why a smaller local event or a medium-sized regional event, whether single-sport or multiple sport, cannot implement an environmental program and capture the benefits.

A basic action plan

* Develop and approve an environmental policy;
* Define specific objectives and targets (measurable where possible) to deal with each priority issue;
* Adopt "green office" practices in all stages of planning and organizing: reduce the use of materials, re-use wherever possible and, finally, recycle;
* Develop a waste reduction strategy for all venues;
* Involve suppliers, donors and sponsors in the "sustainable event" initiative;
* Reduce the amount of private car use by participants and spectators by emphasizing and facilitating the use of public and active transport means;
* Promote healthy conditions for sport (i.e. air and water quality) at venues and in the community;
* Promote conservation of energy and water in facilities and during operations;
* Protect sensitive green spaces and water bodies from development and excessive or inappropriate use;
* Publicize environmental efforts and achievements in the community and to a broader audience through the media.

Some common ways in which sport events affect the environment

* Impacts from facility construction/ operation;
* Consumption of non-renewable resources (fuel, metals, etc.);
* Consumption of natural resources (water, wood, etc.);
* Creation of greenhouse gases (electrical, transportation);
* Air and noise pollution from movement of people/goods;
* Soil erosion and compaction by spectators;
* Spectator waste sent to landfill, incinerator and sewage plant;
* Paper consumption by media;
* Waste generated from signs, banners, temporary booths, etc.

Waste

The most common types of materials that are brought into a sport organization pass through and ultimately emerge as materials/wastes to dispose of might include:

* Construction and demolition materials of all types;
* Packaging materials, containers and pallets;
* Food and beverage containers;
* Organic materials (food and beverage, grass clippings, etc.);
* Office supplies and equipment;
* Appliances, machinery and vehicles;
* Merchandise for sale or distribution;
* Hazardous and medical wastes.

Partnerships

Greater sustainability can rarely be achieved without working closely with other interested parties. Partnerships involving all stakeholders with a vested interest in improving the sustainability of a sport organization or operation will attempt to make the maximum use of the resources (physical and intellectual) brought by all parties. Examples of powerful partnerships include:

* Involving host communities, seeking input that will lead to events/facilities that are better for the community and the environment;

* Leaving behind a positive legacy for the community;

* Inviting respected environmental groups to play a positive role in all aspects of running an event or facility, whether as members of a committee or as designated "watchdogs"; and

* Working with sponsors/donors/suppliers to ensure that issues such as packaging waste and recyclability are considered from the earliest stage.

Trends

Sports that rely heavily on the natural environment for their appeal are becoming active in multistakeholder initiatives to protect and even restore that environment. Examples include golf clubs promoting biodiversity, mountain biking clubs actively organizing trail maintenance and user education programs and ski resorts tackling the range of challenges associated with fragile alpine environments and working to reduce their ecological footprint. More and more sports governing bodies are and should be developing their own sustainability charters and associated guidelines, practices, partnership programs and restoration projects.

Sources: David Chernushenko www.greengold.on.ca
United Nations Environment Programme www.unep.org

For specific issues related to convention centres and urban events, see also Conventions and Convention Centres in the Destinations section. (p. 286).

Components of the issue	Indicators
Site environmental sensitivity: - Features of the site including ecological fragility, animal habitat, sensitive periods for flora and fauna	• Total area of site used by those at the event (artists, competitors, organizers, spectators, participants, vehicles, infrastructure and service); • % of site changed; (soil compaction, erosion/soil loss, loss of ground cover, damaged vegetation, permanent facilities, site improvements, km new trails, habitats protected for event and beyond).
Social sensitivities – Impact on local communities - degree of involvement of local citizens and businesses - use of site by area residents (before and after the event) - impact on community during the event (access to usual facilities and services; noise; vehicle and pedestrian congestion)	• Existence of a participatory planning process for events; • % local population who support the event (questionnaire); • Ratio of numbers of spectators to population; • % of site permanently changed by the event; e.g. trails or structures added/changed affecting local use; • % increase/decrease in use of the site after the event.
Impact caused by participants in the event - intensity of use of site and specific areas	• Number of participants in/at the event; • Number of circuits/repetitions per area or length of track (sports).
Impact caused by spectators - distribution and movements of spectators - damage to natural habitats; disturbance of wildlife - damage to built environment (e.g. graffiti, vandalism) - litter - human waste	• Existence of a spectators management plan (Y/N); • Number of spectators; • Ratio of expected number of spectators to actual; • Density of spectators: over total; at peak viewing areas; at fragile sites; • Area cordoned off for/from spectators; • Number of waste bins (bins/spectators); • Number of recycle bins for plastic, aluminum, paper products, organic waste; • Number of WCs (or portable toilets) (spectators/WC).
Safety and security (see also Public safety p. 109 and Security p. 104)	• Number of security personnel (as % of spectators); • Number of incidents (arrests, complaints); • Number of medical/first aid posts; • Level of facilitation of information related to safety issues (e.g. clear information on event scheduling, place, access, safety issues of buildings and spaces, availability of services, etc.)
Impact caused by vehicles - types of transportation - traffic jams - air pollution; noise, smell - parking; soil compression - gasoline and oil spills/leaks	• Number of vehicles; • % spectators using public transport; • % increase in number of vehicles; • Area for parking.
Catering - production of waste - increased use of water and power - waste water	• % of catering waste which is recyclable and recycled; • Weight/volume of waste produced; • Energy and water demand (absolute amount and % increase).
Impact due to infrastructure: - temporary, permanent (related to physical impact on the site and social benefits)	• Area impacted/loss of natural habitat/landscape; • Increased use of site after the event.

Several of the general indicators of site stress are the same ones recommended for any situation where large numbers converge. See the sections on ➤ **Controlling use intensity** (p. 192) and on specific types of sites impacted for additional information on appropriate indicators. The following are specific to events:

Indicators of site sensitivity:

* **Total area of site used;**
* **% of site changed.**

   Reason for use of these indicators: An aggregate measure of the total physical impact the event has on the competition site. The indicators respond to the need for event organizers to plan and manage physical stress to the site. The changes to the site may be planned and considered positive, while others may be unforeseen and damaging. For example, parking areas and trails may be hardened off to minimize impacts, yet crowds may surge onto fragile areas for a better view or to take a shortcut. Temporary structures may leave permanent damage while planned permanent buildings may be a benefit to the community and may be sited in areas where impact is minimized.

   Source(s) of data: Local or regional maps for the total area of the site.

   Management plans for the event. These would usually indicate the areas for vehicles, parking, competitors, spectators, facilities and services, and protected areas.

   Site inspections before and after the event may note the percentage of areas that have been impacted by the event. Note this is an indicator of the area impacted rather than the degree of positive or negative impact, though types of impacts are ideally assessed by event planners.

   Means to use the indicators: Total area used by the event, % protected and % with competitor and spectator access are measures to demonstrate intent to protect important habitats. % of total area restored to its former (or better) state after the event and % of total area damaged by the event support organizers in their bid for future events and as a guide to mitigating damage.

   Benchmarking: The state of the site before the event is the base for measuring change. A benchmark may be set as the % of change that is tolerable and/or repairable given the resilience of the site and financial budget for repairs and restoration. For example, it may be acceptable to harden off 5% of the site for vehicular and pedestrian access, while another 5% damaged by trampling or parking can be readily repaired by soil aeration or laying new turf if crowds significantly exceed the number expected.

Indicators of social sensitivity:

* **Existence of a participatory planning process for events;**
* **% local population who support the event (questionnaire);**
* **Ratio of numbers of spectators to population;**
* **% of site permanently changed by the event; e.g. trails or structures added/changed affecting local use;**
* **% increase/decrease in use of the site after the event.**

   Reason for use of these indicators: A small local sports or cultural event may go largely unnoticed by local people with no direct connection to the competitors or participants, but a major sports event or festival can be a divisive issue with political and legal ramifications. Organizers and community representatives need to know the extent to which the population supports the event and what will be affected. Residents nearby a proposed Grand Prix race track for example may be pleased to have a free track-side view; others may be severely perturbed by the noise and pollution, while others may take the economic opportunity to rent their houses to competitors or spectators. Some within hearing of a loud concert may appreciate the experience while others resent the intrusion. The wider population may think such an event is in conflict with their city's "green" image while politicians may think it a superb opportunity to put their city "on the map" with international television exposure.

Source(s) of data: A questionnaire to determine support for a major event may be done by local governments. (If not, the next elections may give the population's opinion by proxy). If there is no questionnaire conducted, the amount and type of coverage in the local media can be a guide as to whether the majority supports the event of not.

Means to use the indicators: The percentage of population who support the event may be given as a simple percentage of those in favour or against. A more complex questionnaire could elicit the percentage on a scale from definitely against, to neutral to very strongly in favour. A content analysis of local media may reveal prevailing attitudes of the population. Similarly radio or television "talk-back" shows can act as straw polls; and internet-based voting sites can give an indication of support for an event.

Benchmarking: An initial benchmark, say 60% of the population in favour of the event, may serve as the level of support organizers require to go ahead with planning. For a recurring event, organizers may seek to increase the percentage by 5% per year, or set a target to be reached pre and/or post event.

Indicators regarding impact of attendees:

- **Number of participants and spectators (see ➤ Use Intensity p. 192);**

- **Number of waste bins (bins/spectators or attendees);**

- **Volume of waste produced (see ➤ Solid Waste p. 173);**

- **Number of recycle bins;**

- **Number of WCs (or portable toilets) (see ➤ Sewage p. 171);**

- **Number of spectators/WC;**

- **Area cordoned off for/from spectators;**

- **Number of vehicles (and per parking space).**

Issue/reason for use of these indicators: Unlike tourism which brings tourists year round or seasonally, event participants descend on the destination in big numbers over a short period of time. For sports events the absolute numbers of competitors, their support teams and spectators are an important measure as a guide to the destinations ability to host them, supply their needs and manage their waste. Similarly, fairs and festivals may concentrate very large numbers in small destinations stressing the infrastructure. (See the example of Sturgis Box.3.13).

Source(s) of data: The number of expected participants and spectators should be available from the event organizers. The number of tickets sold or receipts at the entry gates plus free passes gives the total number of spectators. For free events an estimate of the crowd can be made. Event plans should list the number of waste bins and toilets available or brought into the site.

Ways to use the indicators: The absolute number of visitors to the event gives a plain statement of number of people that need accommodation, food and beverage services, toilet facilities, etc. It also gives a basis for decisions on security and crowd control. The percentage of these visitors relative to the population has relevance as well. Consider for example the case of any local resident within a two kilometre radius of an event who is likely to be out-numbered 5:1 by spectators from out of town.

Benchmarking: A destination needs to set a benchmark for the number of visitors it has the capability to manage to ensure the sustainability of the destination. This benchmark can also be the basis on which alternative or emergency plans are developed should numbers exceed expectations. Alternatively, the benchmark may simply be a measure of the success in achieving the expected number of visitors. A more graphic or dramatic benchmark can be related to the number of toilets required, (e.g. "one thousand people per portable toilet " or "a 100 porta-pottie event"!).

Indicators regarding safety and security:

* **Number of security personnel (as % of spectators);**
* **Number of incidents (arrests, complaints);**
* **Number of medical/first aid posts;**
* **Level of facilitation of information related to safety issues (e.g. clear information on event scheduling, place, access, safety issues of buildings and spaces, availability of services, etc.);**

(see also Local public safety p.109 and Tourist Security p. 104).

Issue/reason for use of these indicators: Events have become a focus for safety and security issues ranging from vandalism and crime to threats of civil disorder or terrorism. Safety and security is a central preoccupation for those holding major sports or cultural events.

Source(s) of data: The number of expected participants and spectators should be available from the event organizers, as should numbers of personnel involved in provision of safety and security. Organizers should have clear documentation of level of preparedness and contingency planning as well as records of level of effort expended to provide information.

Means to use the indicators: These indicators help to demonstrate preparedness for all forms of emergencies.

Benchmarking: A destination needs to set a benchmark for the number of visitors it has the capability to manage to ensure the sustainability of the destination. Ministries charged with security, and records from other events can be used as benchmarks.

Thousands of tourists visit Ottawa, Canada from all over North America for national day celebrations. Provision must be made for more than 100,000 including access and facilities.

Box 3.42 Indicators for mountain bike competitions

Selected examples excerpted from UCI Guidelines, guidelines of the International Cycling Union, Switzerland, where indicators are used to respond to specific guidelines or recommendations. www.uci.ch

Recommendation	Indicators
Select or create courses with respect for the environment	• Meters of course affecting environmentally sensitive sites; • % existing, % new, % open country etc; • % accessible to the public after the competition.
Define, apply, audit and review protective measures for important environmental aspects	• Number of measures adopted; • Area of protected zones, km of tape, route markings and barriers; • Number of audits carried out.
Establish and implement a traffic plan	• Number of parking spaces, dry weather; • Number of parking spaces, wet weather (hard surface); • % spectators using public transport; • Average distance between parking areas/station and competition sites; • Number/frequency of shuttle buses.
Establish and implement a spectator management plan which respects the environment	• Number of spectators expected; • Size of security service.
Catering: favour suppliers who reclaim and recycle their products and waste	• Number and type of substances over which agreement is reached with suppliers in the specifications (e.g. glass, PET, cardboard, aluminum, wood, plastics etc.).
Establish and implement a waste management plan	• Number of collection points and their position on site; • Amount and type of waste being reclaimed, recycled or re-used; main types: glass, PET, aluminum, wood, plastics etc.; • Amount and type of waste with guaranteed reclaiming, recycling or re-use; • Number of fixed/mobile toilet factlities; • % waste water (sewage) treated before disposal.
Restore sites to their original condition	• Availability and amount of human and financial resources for restoring the sites.

Other indicators of interest to managing large events:

*   **Number of vehicles:** this indicator may be even more important in terms of highlighting potential environmental damage and pollution as well as social dissatisfaction due to traffic congestion. (See Transportation p. 210 for more details).

*   **% of spectators using public transport:** a measure to show success in minimizing vehicular impact (See Transportation p. 210).

*   **% of catering waste which is recyclable and recycled:** this indicator is a good measure of ability to manage waste produced at the event. Good data should be available if organizers require

caterers and concession holders to provide agreements in advance and if recycling bins are provided.

* (See indicators on ➢ **Solid Waste Management** (p. 173) for more detailed discussions of waste management issues. See also the destination section on Conventon centres for similar use of indicators for major events).

Major events have similar impacts to those related to tourism impact at destinations in general, keeping in mind the intense use of the site over a short time. An unruly event for example with pollution, waste, noise or crime can cause local and tourist distress, and negatively impact the image of a destination.

The following issues are likely to be of particular importance:

* ➢ **Sewage treatment (p. 171);**

* ➢ **Solid waste management (p. 173);**

* **Air pollution (e.g. motor sports and tourist vehicles)(p. 180);**

* **Noise (p. 183);**

* **Security (p. 104);**

* **Protection of Image (p. 236);**

* ➢ **Effects of tourism on communities p. 57).**

3.11 Destination Planning and Control

3.11.1 Integration of Tourism Into Local/Regional Planning

Information for Planners, Plan Evaluation, Results of Plan Implementation

From its very beginnings sustainable tourism has been associated with the need for tourism planning; the idea being that with careful destination planning, many of the adverse impacts of tourism could be avoided. The Charter for Sustainable Tourism adopted by the Lanzarote World Conference in 1995 identifies the need for 'integrated planning' as a key principle of sustainable tourism, and similar principles are stressed by Agenda 21 for the Travel and Tourism Industry, the UN Commission on Sustainable Development, and many other recent WTO documents. Over the years, approaches to tourism planning have evolved from rigid master plans, to more flexible, strategic plans with a strong component of local participation, regular review and monitoring using performance indicators. For the sake of greater sustainability, this more adaptive approach to planning needs to be supported by up-to-date information about environmental, social, cultural and economic issues and priorities affecting the destination.

Monitoring can assist tourism planning in three main ways.

1. An indicators program and monitoring process allows for the *information generated by indicators* to feed directly into the planning process. This saves time for planners, and can also increase the depth of analysis. Indicators can help highlight priority considerations in terms of environmental planning, provide important economic data, inform the impact assessment section of the plan, and act as a filter for development projections and product development possibilities.

2. Indicators can be used to *evaluate tourism plans* in terms of their sustainability. This is especially useful mid-way through the planning cycle, giving planners a chance to reassess goals and objectives in the light of developments that have taken place in the intervening period.

3.   Indicators can be used to assess the sustainability aspects of the *planning and policy environment/framework* in the destination.

The principal areas of interest to the planning process include:

●   *Information for planners on the issues and areas of concern:* Performance of the tourism industry, impacts of tourism on the destination, quality of the tourism product, threats to tourism from other areas;

●   *Evaluating elements of a tourism plan:* Existence and implementation of an up-to-date tourism plan, completion/plan for of mid-term review of the plan, assessment of environmental and socio-economic components of a plan, measuring level of public participation in the planning process, evaluating level of monitoring of the plan;

●   *Assessing the planning and policy environment/framework:* Existence of environmental and planning legislation, existence of indicators and monitoring framework, involvement of stakeholders in tourism authority activities, understanding of sustainable tourism objectives in government departments and in the private sector.

While many of these overlap on the subject matter of other issues covered in this book, particularly the first category which is basic information relating to the industry, the indicators here relate primarily to the degree to which the planning process is responsive to the issues and inclusive of all key elements. See the specific issue sections for information on individual indicators.

Components of the issue	Indicators
Basic information for planners	
Performance of the tourism industry	● ➣ **Tourist Numbers** over time/purpose of visit; ● Average length of stay; ● Visitor expenditure per day; ● Revenue generated from tourism (p. 128); ● Leakages from the economy (p. 117).
Impacts of tourism on the destination	● Traffic generated from tourism (p. 210); ● ➣ **Ratio tourists to locals**; ● ➣ **Local satisfaction** with tourism (p. 56); ● ➣ **Visitor/local water usage** (p. 165); ● Economic dependency on tourism -Contribution to GDP.
Quality of the tourism product	● Attractiveness of sites and facilities; ● ➣ **Satisfaction of tourists** (p. 86); ● % returning visitors.
Threats to tourism from other areas	● Number of sites damaged by other development; ● Environmental threats (logging, industrial pollution, reduction of fish populations); ● Environmental vulnerability (storm events, flooding); ● Crime rate per capita; (Other risks unique to any specific site – use procedure detailed in Part 2 to identify risks and suitable indicators).

Components of the issue	Indicators
Evaluating a tourism plan	
Existence of tourism plan or strategy	∘ Up to date plan exists; ∘ Plan review completed or scheduled.
Costs of plan	∘ Plan budget; ∘ Budget designated/spent for research and formulation; ∘ Budget designated/spent for plan implementation; ∘ Budget designated/spent for consultation and public participation; ∘ Level of staff resources assigned to planning.
Impact assessment and balance of actions	∘ Impact assessment of environmental, social and cultural aspects of tourism completed (yes/no or measure re standard); ∘ Number of environmental, social, cultural and economic actions recommended in plan (% in each sector).
Public participation	∘ Degree of stakeholder participation in the planning process (e.g. number of meetings, dissemination channels and other consultation mechanisms used, level of participation); ∘ Degree of stakeholder participation in the process of implementing plans (numbers/% involved in review, advisory panels etc).
Monitoring of plan implementation	∘ Existence of performance indicators designated for evaluating the plan developed and used; ∘ % of plan objectives which have been met; ∘ % environmental, social, cultural actions recommended in plan which have been implemented.
Assessing the Planning and Policy Environment for Sustainable Tourism	
Legislation	∘ % of accommodation units using primarily local architecture; ∘ % that have completed an Environmental Impact Assessment (EIA); ∘ % tourism facilities and service providers regularly inspected for environmental health and safety; ∘ Number of incidents of non-compliance with regulations.
Monitoring sustainable tourism	∘ Sustainable tourism indicators developed and monitored (Y/N) (see Reporting and Accountability in Part 5 p. 312).
Public participation	∘ Involvement of stakeholders in tourism development activities of tourism office (% of activities, number involved).
Government understanding of sustainable tourism	∘ % public sector employees with tourism training; ∘ Level of tourism sector involvement in public policy (advisory bodies, review panels etc).
Private sector cooperation for sustainable tourism	∘ % tourism managers with environmental training; ∘ % Tour operators and hotels with environmental strategy or policy.

Reason for use of these indicators: Ideas on linking indicators to planning have therefore progressed in recent years from "does a tourism plan for the destination exist", to supplying information to planners, evaluating the planning process and content, and monitoring the policy environment in which it is to be implemented. Most of the information to use these specific indicators will be collected during the planning process, and this can be used as an internal checklist by the destination planners. See also Box 2.1 Indicators and Planning Procedures p. 23)

Sources of information for indicators regarding the planning process: The indicators regarding the planning process itself, and the policy environment can in most cases be based on the operating records of the planning authority, and the way in which they are used will frequently be internal – to help direct the planning process.

Means to use the indicators: The specific indicators shown in the above table are in many cases the same ones as defined relative to the other issues described in this section, but may be used in different ways – to help planners respond, or to signal that new plans or activities are required. Publishing the results of planning process evaluation is important information for tourism stakeholders and the general public at tourism destinations in order to justify government efforts and expenditures and demonstrate results. See the appropriate section on the specific issues important to the destination for detail on each of the substantive indicators.

Benchmarking: The most pertinent benchmarking for the operational indicators will be the internal records for the destination and its process, or the first year's data collection. If several destinations are planned under the same legislative framework, some cross-comparison between them may be possible.

Male, Maldives: The Maldives have one of the most comprehensive tourism development planning processes of any nation. (See Box 3.43)

3.11.2 Development Control ➤ **Baseline Issue**

Control Procedures, Land Use, Property Management, Enforcement

If there is no control process for development, the community and the tourism industry may have little ability to influence the outcomes they desire for their destination. Many examples of unfortunate development exist, from building too close to shorelines, creating densities incompatible with ecological limits or infrastructure capacity, or juxtaposition of uses where each adversely affects the other. Where planning systems are in place, there is a capability to guide development towards desired futures, and to influence the location, type and density of development. The model can range widely, from simple indicative zones with little formal control to, at the other end of the spectrum, systems which prescribe specific uses, densities, site planning, design control, and even permitted and banned behaviours.

Two related elements are important: the planning process, and the degree and means of enforcement. A range of tools can be used including prescriptive zoning which designates specific uses and densities for each site, indicative zoning which defines the desired character of a destination and uses some form of review procedure, or establishment of density limits (e.g. no more than 40% of the coast to be built to more than one storey, footprint of buildings to occupy no more than half the property) as a regulated limit.

Land use plans and development controls can vary greatly in extent, form and content, but it is important to clearly identify the implications for tourism activities. Most destinations which use indicators relative to this issue have settled for a simple yes/no indicator of whether a comprehensive development or land use plan exists for the destination, with some also

> **Box 3.43 Planning and control in the Maldives**
>
> The Maldive Islands have in place one of the most comprehensive planning and control systems used for tourism development. All resort property belongs to the state, and is leased to tourism developers. No new development is permitted until existing occupancy is at 80%. Each development is placed on an unoccupied island. No building is allowed to be higher than the palm trees (in effect 2 storeys) and trees must be left between the buildings and the shore. No tree can be cut without permission; no changes can be made to shores or reefs. No more than 20% of the surface area of any island can be built. Construction and operations are closely monitored; failure to comply can result in loss of the lease. The nation uses indicators such as occupancy levels to decide when to allow new resorts, and monitors many site specific indicators on a regular basis.

identifying whether it has explicit application to tourism. There are some destinations which have also used indicators on area protected and to what extent or level of control, and there are many different specific control criteria (growth rates, densities, occupancy quotas, height controls, buffer areas, % of site built, etc.) used in different combinations and enforced with different levels of rigour (see Tunisia case p. 435). There is no commonly used indicator which will allow quality of the planning process to be easily assessed. Local reaction to the impacts of tourism (using questionnaire in Annex C) may help assess whether the current plan or lack of it may be causing stresses in the local community or is responding to key plan goals or expectations of locals or tourists.

Components of the Issue	Indicators
Whether any land use or development planning process exists explicitly incorporating tourism.	× ➣ **Existence of a land use or development planning process, including tourism** (can be categorized by degree to which it expressly covers tourism, e.g. land use planning that includes zones for tourism development, specific criteria for tourism properties); × ➣ **% of area subject to control (density, design, etc).** × % of area designated for tourism purposes, for buildings.
Extent and effectiveness of monitoring and control processes	× Existence of specific criteria for tourism development control in plans, such as maximum numbers of hotels/beds, density standards, design controls, environmental and social, etc. ; × % building proposals receiving environmental review, or undergo environmental impact assessment (EIA); × % denied or sent for revision.
Whether or not there is systematic enforcement of the plan and its criteria	× Existence of review procedures (e.g. site visits, evaluations); × Number of charges for plan, zoning or site plan violations.

Note that the indicators used to measure e.g., ➣ **Use intensity - tourists per square Km** (p. 192), and protection (area protected, level of protection p. 147) may also be of use relative to the impacts of such plans and controls.

Indicator relative to the planning process:

* **Existence of a land use planning process [involving tourism](yes/no)** ➣ **Baseline Indicator.**

    Reason for use of this indicator: Many destinations, even in developed nations, are outside the formal land use planning zoning and control process which in many countries (e.g., US, Canada, Argentina) has been primarily urban in focus. This is a very simple indicator. Over time as planning is put in place, greater differentiation can be sought using other indicators.

    Source(s) of data: Information on planning status is normally available from the national provincial or local planning authority. Standard of plans may vary greatly.

    Means to use the indicator: This indicator is of greatest use as a means to show authorities that, if no plan exists, it is considered desirable to have one. Once a regional, site or land use plan is in place, the other indicators below may become more important. At the national or provincial level, this can be used to identify what percentage of destinations or sites have plans or development controls in place.

    Benchmarking: This is likely to be most useful over time to show the progress towards establishment of planning for all destinations in a country or region, rather than for any specific destination.

Indicator of extent of application of planning:

* **% of area subject to control (density, design, etc)** ➣ **Baseline Indicator.**

    Reason for use of this indicator: Often the limits of a destination exceed that of an authority, or the planning process has been applied only to selected areas. For example, urban, land use plans may be in place only for parks or designated areas, or for built communities rather than for all of a destination. Density or design controls may apply to only some zones or to areas where access is controlled.

    Source(s) of data: Local planning authority.

    Means to use the indicator: % of destination subject to each form of control.

    Benchmarking: Compare over time for same destination. Aggregate the data for several destinations or sites in a nation or province to show percentage or area which is collectively under control or protection of different levels.

Indicators regarding extent and effectiveness of monitoring and control processes:

* **% building proposals receiving environmental review;**

* **% denied or sent for revision;**

* **Number of charges for plan, zoning or site plan violations.**

    Reason for use of these indicators: Often land use plans are easier to write than implement. Many jurisdictions have review procedures which are strong on paper but seldom enforced – due to lack of political will, lack of trained monitors and inspectors, or systemic failure.

    Source(s) of data: Local authority – enforcement data is often kept.

    Means to use the indicators: These indicators are, in effect, performance measures for local planning.

Benchmarking: Measure local changes over time.

Note: a questionnaire approach could be used to document level of concern with the planning process and with certain effects of its implementation. An item could be added to a local questionnaire (Annex C) addressing the level of satisfaction with local planning and control and with certain of the effects of planning or lack of planning.

3.11.3 Tourism-Related Transport

Mobility Patterns, Safety, Transport Systems, Efficiency, In-Destination Transport, Transport to/from Destination

The success of a tourist destination is critically linked to the issue of accessibility and mobility and also linked to the preservation of the very 'environment' to which visitors require transport and access. While tourism is the main driver behind the increase in demand for passenger transport, cars and airplanes remain the most used forms of transport for tourism. This situation results in growing pressures on the environment: greenhouse gas and air pollutants emissions, infrastructure development, intensified consumption of land, energy use, noise pollution, and deterioration in the quality of landscapes, to name a few of the most obvious negative effects. The development of sustainable tourism therefore has at its core the need for environmentally sound transport planning, both at the local level within the tourist destination itself and at the regional, national, and even international level.

In order to achieve this objective of shifting the balance between the modes of transport from road and airplanes to more sustainable modes, there must be a significant improvement in the quality of service of public transport. An important step towards the implementation of improved quality in the public passenger transport sector has been the creation of a European standard on service quality (EN 13816), (see website at: http://www.eionet.eu.int/ - search for "transport service quality") which provides a framework for establishing quality agreements and covers eight fundamental aspects of service quality for all modes of public passenger transport, namely availability, accessibility, information, time, customer care, comfort, security, and environmental impact. This standard is an important tool to assist authorities and operators in the definition of quality criteria for service contracts as well as in the formulation of key performance indicators.

This section has been divided into two sub parts; the first deals with transport to and from destinations and the other focuses on transportation impacts within the destinations, each with its own set of suitable indicators. Approximately 90% of energy used in tourism is spent on access and return travel. Mobility within the destination on the other hand has a different action radius and different effects, the latter being primarily regional and local.

Historic trams in Valparaiso, Chile have become a form of tourist transport to viewpoints in the hills above the harbour.

Transport to / from destination

Components of the issue	Indicators
Knowledge of tourism related mobility patterns	• ➣ **Tourist numbers visiting site** (including one-day visits) ; • ➣ **Seasonality** of tourism and length of stay; • Annual number of same-day visitors (see ➣ **Use Intensity** p. 192); • Total of km traveled per tourist per trip; • Modes of transport used by tourists to reach destination (airplane, car, coach, rail, bicycle, walking, other).
Access to the holiday destination (Availability / enhancement of road network, railway's, port, and airport infrastructures. State of accessibility to the area in terms of public transport)	• Density of roads (highways / motorways, roads) (route kms per km ^{2}); • Density of public transport (route kms per km ^{2}); • Annual levels of investment in public transport compared with road infrastructure; • Frequency, capacity of services and use levels (land, sea and air transport); • Number of direct flights, , number of cities served by direct flights (and % passengers arriving without stops); • Time of travel by passenger to destination (hours). Number of modes required.
Journey time and reliability (Road / air / water traffic congestion with related issues of long journey times for tourists, unpredictable traffic conditions, as well as air, noise and water pollution traffic congestion and emission	• Ratio of public passenger transport versus private transport speed to reach destination in peak holiday periods to lowest periods (per modes of transport per main markets); • Ratio of travel expenses by public versus private transport to reach destination; • Level of air and ground emissions for passenger transport during peak holiday periods to lowest (per passenger-km); • Level of noise pollution (see Noise, p. 183).
Safety (Traffic congestion, stress, fatigue, unfamiliar weather conditions and unfamiliar road layout result in more traffic accidents. Airport saturation results in less traffic security. Human health effects associated with outdoor air pollution)	• Number of transport accidents and fatalities (land, air and maritime) during peak holiday periods to lowest periods; • Trends in the number of days per year on which fixed air pollution thresholds are reached; • Impact on local health (see Health p. 94); • Level of facilitation of information and services (e.g. provision of information on road and traffic conditions – e.g. on website ; aid and emergency services, etc.)- level of resourcing, % passengers contacted (see Tourist Security p. 104).

Indicators of mobility patterns:

* ➣ **Tourist numbers visiting site (including one-day visits);**

* ➣ **Seasonality of tourism and length of stay**;

* **Annual number of same-day visitors** (see ➣ **Use Intensity** p. 192);

* **Total of km traveled per tourist per trip;**

* **Modes of transport used by tourists to reach destination (airplane, car, coach, rail, bicycle, walking, other).**

Reason for the use of these indicators: The nature of the tourist mobility demand for transport choice needs to be fully understood. For successful planning, a clear diagnosis and understanding of the level of accessibility as well as the current situation and forecasts of future tourist mobility patterns are needed. Also important is the assessment of the increase of transport pressure caused by tourism: modes of transport, peak periods, length of stay, etc.

Source(s) of data: National statistics agencies, public authorities responsible for public passenger transport systems and tourism, existing national and international mobility, tourism and sustainable transport databases (e.g EcoNETT, ARTIST, Dobris Assessment, Eurostat, WTO, OECD, etc.); tour operators (e.g. coach trips, charter flights, groups).

Means to use the indicators: Use total figures per year if available, percentage in case of guest surveys or estimates. If possible, list % share of each mode: car, rail, air, sea. Indicators should lead to establishing a forecasting mechanism of future tourism mobility trends, and indicating seasonal variations.

Benchmarking: While many countries and destinations collect these data, the definitions and sources are often so different that it is very difficult to compare the trends in different countries in a consistent manner. This requires comprehensive, relevant data, supported by a set of common definitions. Compare instead over time for the same destination.

Indicators of access to the holiday destination:

* **Density of roads (highways / motorways, roads) (roads kms per km^2 per types);**
* **Density of public transport (route kms per km^2);**
* **Annual levels of investment in public transport compared with road infrastructure;**
* **Frequency, capacity of services and use levels (land, sea and air transport);**
* **Frequency of direct and indirect flights to the destination, (and % passengers arriving without stops);**
* **Time of travel by passenger to destination (hours). Number of modes required.**

Reason for the use of these indicators: Reducing pollution and congestion by means of increasing road capacity is now proven not to be the best option. The cost of construction of road (and parking) capacities in densely populated areas continues to increase even though studies indicate that improving and extending road infrastructure results in more journeys overall as road users make use of the new or improved facilities. It is useful to monitor the extension of roads against the extension and improvement of passenger public transport.

Source(s) of data: Public authorities responsible for public passenger transport systems and/or land planning, research groups. Data published at national level and by many international research groups. See for instance the Commission for Integrated Transport - Research Reports - European Best Practice in the Delivery of Integrated Transport (http://www.cfit.gov.uk).

Means to use the indicators: The proposed indicators should contribute to assess the general state of accessibility and highlight the efforts done on reinforcing public passenger transport services as an alternative to the use of private cars.

Benchmarking: Difficult due to the problem of determining the relevant geographic area, and of compound budgets and variety of public bodies responsible for roads.

Indicators of journey time and reliability:

* **Ratio of public passenger transport versus private transport speed to reach destination in peak holiday periods to lowest periods (per modes of transport per main markets);**
* **Average passenger journey time and length per mode;**

- **Average speed per mode per km;**

- **Vehicle kilometres or passenger journeys per incident (accident, injury);**

- **% adherence to timetable.**

  Reason for the use of these indicators: When the priority for tourists is to minimize journey time between home and the holiday destination, travel by private car may be seen as the fastest option, providing a perceived sense of greater reliability and predictability of journey and arrival time than public transport (i.e. less vulnerable to delays, time lost at interchanges and technical problems). Road traffic congestion on Western countries' main holiday routes greatly reduces speed of travel by private car causing environmental damages. (See quality standards: European Standard on Transportation Services – Public Passenger Transport – Services Quality, Definition, Targeting and Measurement ref pr EN 13816:2000; CEN/European Committee for Standardization.

  Source(s) of data: Public authorities responsible for public passenger transport systems, national statistics agencies, national and supra national environment agencies i.e. European Environment Information and Observation Network (EIONET) http://www.eionet.eu.int/

  Means to use the indicators: It is necessary to have good reference data in order to devise methods for accurate assessment of pollution levels directly linked with tourism and to identify potential efficiencies.

  Benchmarking: Measure over time and compare to results in same destination.

Indicators of traffic congestion and emission:

- **Level of air and ground emissions for passenger transport (per passenger-km and by mode);**

- **Noise pollution (see Noise p. 183).**

  Reason for the use of these indicators: Road transport contributes to about a half of NOx and SO_2 emissions and is strongly associated with CO_2 and volatile organics in the urban environment. Aircraft emissions have also a significant effect at ground level. Aircraft cause about 3.5% of global warming from all human activities. Aircraft greenhouse emissions will continue to rise and could contribute up to 15% of global warming from all human activities within 50 years (Intergovernmental panel on climate change – 2001). Air and ground traffic at major airports can lead to pollution levels as high as city centres. For a typical journey under 500km (i.e. London to Amsterdam), the amount of CO_2 produced per passenger is 0.17 kg/km for air travel, 0.14 kg/km for travel by car, 0.052 kg/km for rail and 0.047 kg/km by boat (i.e., ferry). (Note: see issue section on Climate Change p. 155 for additional information on indicators of contribution to greenhouse gases).

  Source(s) of data: Public authorities responsible for public passenger transport systems and / or environment, environmental Impact Assessment studies, national or regional environment agencies, UNEP (Transport and the global Environment: Accounting for GHG reduction on Policy Analysis, UNEP 2001, http://uneprisoe.org/OverlaysTransport/TransportGlobalOverlays.pdf

  Means to use the indicators: For NOx, sulphur dioxide (SO_2), volatile hydrocarbons (VHC) and carbon dioxide (CO_2) emissions for passenger transport (per passenger-km and by mode). Use Decibels for noise (See Noise p. 183). It is important that adequate air and noise quality monitoring is carried out at major destinations and airports to ensure that national standards are achieved (Kyoto protocol), to better appreciate the real cost (internal) of these modes of transport on society, to develop initiatives that move towards fairer and more efficient pricing (polluter pays principle), thereby giving positive pricing signals to more environmentally modes of transport, and again, to widely communicate to tourists and holidaymakers (awareness campaigns).

  Benchmarking: Can be benchmarked as many countries / regions / airports collect these data.

Indicators of transport safety:

⦾   **Number of transport accidents and fatalities (land, air and maritime) during peak holiday periods to lowest periods;**

⦾   **Trends in the number of days per year on which fixed air pollution thresholds are reached. (See also Air Pollution p.180).**

Reason for the use of these indicators: Promoting healthy and sustainable transport alternatives lessens negative effects of transport on human health. Health issues should therefore be assessed and considered when formulating transport policies. The proposed indicators can become performance measures for developing methods and tools for health impact assessment (HIA) and to support authorities at appropriate levels in the definition and management of mobility policies beneficial to health (promotion of healthy transport modes, promotion of integrated approach to road safety).

Source(s) of data: Public authorities responsible for public passenger transport systems and / or health, World Health Organization, OECD, Transport, health and environment pan-European program (THE PEP). http://www.thepep.org/en/welcome.htm

Means to use the indicators: Fatalities refers to deaths occurring at the site of an accident or within 30 days following an accident. The figure covers the total fatalities of pedestrians, cyclists, motorcyclists, public transport passengers and car drivers/passengers during peak holiday periods against low season. It is also a good measure of local communities' quality of life.

Benchmarking: Can be benchmarked as many countries / regions collect these data.

Transportation within the destination	
Components of the Issue	**Indicators**
Spatial and transport planning, management of tourism related transport demand, and improvement of modal split.	⦾ Implementation of an integrated environmentally sound transport planning strategy (yes / no); ⦾ Strategy translated into an action plan (yes / no); ⦾ Number and extent of issues covered by the action plan (transport, tourism, land use and biodiversity, energy, water, waste, social issues, economic issues, etc.); ⦾ Action taken to formulate interregional transport plans(Y/N).
Tourists' demand management regarding mobility within destination	⦾ Tourists' and visitors' perceptions and demands of local or regional transport supply and services (by transport mode); ⦾ Number of passengers transported by local public transport for tourism / leisure purposes (also compared to number of tourists using individual transport).
Access to the amenities within the holiday destination (Public transport, traffic management issues. Development of less environmental damaging transport system for tourism travel)	⦾ % of accommodations, tourism facilities and other tourist attractions accessible by public transport (less than 10 minutes walking distance to nearest station/stop); ⦾ Extra means of transport especially set up for tourists: type of transport and number of passenger places available during peak times.

Components of the issue	Indicators
Safety and security • Traffic congestion, stress, fatigue, unfamiliar weather conditions and unfamiliar road layout result in more traffic accidents	• % of death, or serious injuries due to road accidents during peak holiday periods; • Total expenditure on building / maintaining dedicated cycle and walking routes; • Level of pedestrian infrastructure (area or %); • Parking capacities and use levels; • Ratio of number of incidents including visitors and tourists in peak holiday periods to lowest periods; • Existing safety standards (yes / no); • Number of staff on duty/surveillance system; • Level of facilitation of access to information on emergency measures and contingency plans (see issues on Local public safety p. 109 and Tourism security p. 104).
Intermodality / Integration of services • Links between long-haul and local transport networks • Seamless journey for the tourists • Use of new technologies to maximise co-ordination between transport modes • Integration of public transport services/fares	• Existence of multi-modal platforms (yes / no); • Existence of integrated public transport services (yes / no); • Existence of integrated public transport fares (yes / no); • Provision of park-and-ride and bike-and-ride facilities: number of parking spaces (public and private) for cars or bicycles at public transport stops/stations serving tourist amenities.
Ease of access • Clear, accessible, reliable information about services/ timetables/ ticketing before and during the stay • Door –to-door services	• Ratio of annual public expenditure on information services for public transport users to specific information services for holidaymakers, visitors and tourists; • Existence of public transport service information on the Internet or mobility centres (yes / no); • Use of electronic booking for public transport (yes / no); • Number of door-to-door services for visitors and tourists.
Promotion of environmentally friendly transport modes as part of the holiday and measures to give public transport priority	• Length of cycle and walking paths, availability of bicycle rental services; • Extent and capacity of public transport; • % of travellers using alternative transport (bicycles, walking, other low energy use options); • Level of support for low energy alternatives to vehicle transport; • % of the tourism related vehicle fleet meeting specified air and noise emissions standards by mode of transport; • Energy consumption and emissions per passenger; • Existence, capacity of environmental-friendly vehicles and transport modes (e.g. metro, trams, electric vehicles, etc.); • Availability and % of reserved public transport lanes and parking spaces • Existing measures of restricting car access or parking spaces (yes / no).

Indicators of transportation planning:

• **Implementation of an integrated environmentally sound transport planning strategy (yes / no);**

• **Strategy translated into an action plan (yes / no);**

- **Number and extent of issues covered by the action plan (transport, tourism, land use and biodiversity, energy, water, waste, social issues, economic issues, etc.);**
- **Action taken to formulate interregional transport plans(yes/no);**
- **Initiatives taken to formulate interregional transport plans (yes / no).**

Reason for the use of these indicators: Importance of establishing a coherent, integrated strategy, clearly linked with wider transport policy objectives that includes clear statements about the environmental and socio economic impacts of actions to be taken, in which consideration is taken of partnership and cooperation between all stakeholders (public and private). The effectiveness of sustainable tourist related transport planning depends on good coordination with other policy areas: tourism and environment. An appropriate coordination with land-use planning and information and communication technologies are particularly important tools.

Source(s) of data: Ministries responsible for tourism, transport, mobility and environment, public authorities responsible for public passenger transport systems. Often it is difficult to measure extent and quality of plans or cooperation, and yes/no measurement may be all that is available.

Means to the use the indicators: Existing dedicated sustainable transport policies in addition to general transport policy actions. Monitoring of the success of the strategy as part of an iterative process in which performance is continually improved.

Benchmarking: Many destinations collect such data and can provide information for comparison. Use "destination transport planning" in a search engine for a range of websites. There are also regional initiatives to foster more sustainable transport policies and practices. A good example is the ALPS MOBILITY initiative, promoting trans-national pilot projects (Germany, Austria and Italy) for environmentally sound travel logistics linked with electronic booking and information systems in alpine tourism regions (http://www.alpsmobility.org).

Indicators of tourist demand management regarding mobility within destination:

- **Tourist and visitor perceptions and demands for local or regional transport supply and services;**
- **Number of passengers transported by local public transport for tourism and leisure purposes.**

Reason for the use of these indicators: There is an obvious need to understand the issues: the nature of the tourist mobility demand and reasons for transport choice need to be fully understood, and integrated with the concept of the tourist (and local community) as clients of transport services.

Source(s) of data: Ministries responsible for tourism, transportation and environment, public authorities responsible for public passenger transport systems.

Means to use the indicators: Measure performance against strategies and targets. An assessment of the tourists' and visitors' perceptions and demands of transport supply and services within the destination linked with the value of the economy of these visits is a basic, yet significant, piece of information required for an area. It is an essential part of the understanding process.

Benchmarking: This information is not widely collected. Moreover, this indicator is difficult to benchmark to other destinations due to the local factors (elements taken into account in the visitors' perception questionnaire). This indicator is therefore best measured over time for the same destination.

Indicators of access to the amenities within the holiday destination:

- **% of accommodations, tourism facilities and other tourist attractions accessible by public transport (less than 10 minutes walking distance to next station/stop);**
- **Extra means of transport especially set up for tourists (type of transport and number of passenger places available during peak time).**

Reason for the use of these indicators: Acknowledging and improving the concentration of leisure / tourism services and amenities at stations along public transport corridors will ensure a high density of trip-attracting activities in central areas well served by public transport, reducing the need for private car use both for local communities and tourists. Also important is the linkage of central areas or mass tourism infrastructures (i.e. historical sites, theme parks, etc.) located in peripheral areas to inter-modal stations or central zones.

Source(s) of data: Public authorities responsible for tourism, public passenger transport systems and / or land planning.

Means to use the indicators: Performance measure of efficiency of tourism, land planning and transport strategies within destinations (synchronization between the system and tourist demands). % of tourist attractions accessible by public transport and linkages of peripheral areas with central zones through public transport can be a useful indicator of quality of life of local communities.

Benchmarking: Data available in many destinations for comparison.

Indicators of safety:

* **Number and % of deaths due to road accidents during peak holiday periods (road deaths relative to all deaths);**

* **Total expenditure on building / maintaining dedicated cycle and walking routes;**

* **Level of pedestrian infrastructure.**

Note: Indicators are similar to those for transport to / from destinations - Well-designed, dedicated cycle and walking routes can also provide a safer environment for tourists. The total expenditure on building / maintaining dedicated cycle and walking routes and paths will highlight the efforts done on reinforcing soft mobility services as an alternative to the use of private car. Monitoring pedestrian areas in city centres give a good measure of level of vitality, ambience and quality of life for local communities.)

Indicators of security:

* **Ratio of number of security incidents on public transport including visitors and tourists in peak holiday periods to lowest periods (type, place, modes);**

* **Existing safety standards (yes / no);**

* **Number of staff on duty/surveillance system on transport vehicles or system.**

Reason for the use of these indicators: The key challenge in promoting more sustainable forms of transport is how to build trust in alternatives to the private car, and thereby reduce some of the risk associated with non-car travel. Objective and subjective safety is a key element to achieve such a shift in behaviour. It is important to consider both safety on public transport facilities and vehicles as well as for other modes of mobility.

Source(s) of data: Public authorities responsible for public passenger transport systems and land planning, transport operators, and local police.

Means to use the indicators: Assessment of statistics on crime and other incidents concerning customer and staff safety and security. Ratio of number of incidents including visitors and tourists in peak holiday periods to lowest may be a good measure regarding decisions on amenities, initiatives and services required to enhance safety (objective and subjective). (See also Local Public Safety p. 109).

Benchmarking: While data on crimes and incidents are collected in all destinations, it will not necessarily be broken down by type of passenger. Data on cycle and walking paths is widely available from destination tourism authorities and policing bodies.

Indicators of inter-modal capacity:

* **Existence of multi-modal platforms (yes / no);**
* **Existence of integrated public transport services (yes / no);**
* **Existence of integrated public transport fares (yes / no);**
* **Provision of park-and-ride and bike-and-ride facilities (yes/no, or number of park-and ride spaces);**
* **Number of parking spaces (public and private) for cars or bikes at public transport stops/stations serving tourist amenities.**

Reason for the use of these indicators: The effective integration of individual modes (including walking and cycling) and public transport services is crucial to reduce traffic flows in destinations. The simplest form of a multimodal platform is the park-and-ride, which allows for the interchange between the private car and public transport. Ideally such facilities should offer secure, covered parking for bicycles, thus enabling cyclists to fully utilise public transport. While multimodal platforms allow for the speedy and easy change between these different modes, integrated ticketing systems make travelling easier for passengers as they are able to purchase a ticket at the start of their journey which is valid throughout. Note that most of these are yes/no. It may also be possible to measure the percentage of the network served in one integrated system.

Source(s) of data: Public authorities responsible for public passenger transport systems and land planning, transport operators.

Means to use the indicators: Assess level of coordination between central zone and peripheral areas. These indicators will also give a good measure on expected higher modal share of means of transport.

Benchmarking: Data is available for many destinations; however, the definitions and sources are often so different that it is difficult to compare the trends in different countries in a consistent manner. This requires comprehensive, relevant data, supported by a set of common definitions. The best comparison may be over time for the destination.

Indicators of accessibility of public transport services:

* **Ratio of annual public expenditure on information services for public transport users to specific information services for holidaymakers, visitors and tourists;**
* **Existence of public transport service information on the Internet or mobility centres (yes / no) (number of users, % using);**
* **Use of electronic booking for public transport (yes / no, number using);**
* **Number of door-to-door services for visitors and tourists (number using the service).**

Reason for the use of these indicators: Fundamental to achieving a shift in perception and subsequent behaviour towards sustainable modes of transports is the provision of high quality user-friendly services that match the mobility demands and needs of tourists and holidaymakers. Door-to-door services (i.e. bus stop on demand, luggage logistics, etc.) are a great incentive to use public transport. It is essential that tourists, visitors and holidaymakers are kept informed before and during the stay about what is available in terms of transport choices, timetables and mobility related transport services within the destination of their choice.

Source(s) of data: Public authorities responsible for public passenger transport systems and tourism, public passenger transport operators.

Means to use the indicators: Report on the efforts done to promote sustainable modes of transport among visitors and tourists within the destination and measure of the delivered quality.

Benchmarking: Data are available in many destinations although conditions and criteria may be different.

Indicators of promotion of sustainable transport modes as part of the holiday and measures to give public transport priority:

* **Length of cycle and walking paths;**

* **% of the tourism related vehicle fleet meeting certain air and noise emissions standards (alternative fuels-especially bio-fuels, natural gas and hydrogen) by mode of transport;**

* **Energy consumption and emissions per passenger kilometre;**

* **% of travellers using alternative transport (bicycles, walking, other low energy use options);**

* **Level of support for low energy alternatives to vehicle transport;**

* **% of reserved public transport lanes, existing measures of restricting car access or parking spaces (yes / no).**

Reason for the use of these indicators: Environmentally-friendly modes of transport can be encouraged. To reduce impacts, there needs to be a shift away from the use of the private car to the increased use of cycling, public transport, rail transport, short-distance sea-shipping and inland waterways. Public passenger transport is more sustainable in environmental terms. Data on air pollution show that emissions of the main urban air pollutants per passenger km are between four and eight times less for public transport and use five times less energy per passenger than cars as well as causing less noise and pollution. In terms of land use, public transport again demonstrates advantages. Per passenger, buses require only 5% of the road space required for cars. Bus lanes or reserved tramways allow public transport to avoid the congestion caused by other traffic, which has important effects for promoting public transport. Some measures giving priority to public transport also have the effect of restricting access for cars or restricted available car parking spaces in central zones, freeing the space for public transport. Ideally this should be linked to the provision of park-and-ride facilities in the outer zone.

Source(s) of data: Public authorities responsible for public passenger transport systems, transport passenger operator.

Means to use the indicators: Assessment of policies designed to reduce the negative impacts of passenger transport on the environment as well as the dominance of cars in tourist destinations and improvement of conditions for pedestrians and cyclists. Measure the quality of life of local communities (air pollution and noise).

Benchmarking: Data is available in many destinations, particularly those with programs aimed at alternative transport.

3.11.4 Air Transport - Responding to Changes in Patterns and Access

Environmental Impacts, Planning and Security

Thirty-nine percent of international tourists arrived by air in 2002 (WTO). At a global or national scale, the air transport industry has a number of characteristics which can have implications for sustainability. As well, there are specific considerations related to the effects on individual destinations, related to levels of service and access, demands on infrastructure, and effects on the destination itself. The airline industry is a major consumer of fossil fuels, and it has environmental impacts ranging from atmospheric pollution to noise and conversion of land from other purposes to airports. In some small island destinations, the airport which provides access is a significant user of land and can occupy a significant percentage of the total area of the destination. Air transport and routings can also be very volatile, and change rapidly in the face of changing circumstances at the origin or destination, or with the fortunes of the air carrier. Where a destination has direct flights, it can have a pronounced marketing advantage over destinations where transfers are required. In Ottawa Canada, for example, direct charter flights to Cuba or Cancun have diverted much of the traffic from other destinations in the Caribbean where travellers must change planes to go there. Loss of direct scheduled flights from key markets can make marketing to these cities much more difficult. See also the section on Transportation (p. 220)

Indicators related to environmental impacts:

⁕ **Energy consumption (total consumption and consumption per passenger Km);**

⁕ **Atmospheric pollution (total contribution by airline/flight to greenhouse gases).**

Reasons for use of these indicators: Energy consumption and efficiency is one of the most important air transport indicators relative to sustainability. The indicator has to be linked with distance and type of aircraft. New aircraft used for the same routes generally consume less fuel than older aircraft with less efficient engines. Noise from aircraft is one of the most disruptive noise sources (See also Noise p.183) Aircraft contribute to pollution in populated areas as well as to overall global greenhouse gases.

Source(s) of data: These data are generally available from airlines – often from annual reports, or from regulatory bodies. .

Means to use these indicators: These indicators can serve to show progress in reducing impacts of air travel at an international level – likely in support of efforts to reduce greenhouse gas emissions (See Climate change p. 155)

Benchmarking: Airline websites can provide benchmarks related to their environmental programs.

Components of the Issue	Indicators
Environmental impacts of air travel	• Energy consumption (total consumption and consumption per passenger Km) (see ➣ **Energy management** p. 152); • Atmospheric pollution (total emission of greenhouse gases by airline/flight, emission per passenger km).
Impacts of airports and related infrastructure	• Land occupation (% of destination territory within airport boundary, % of territory altered); • % or number of access roads with severe traffic congestion (beyond design capacity or in state of failure); • Noise (area affected by noise around airports and runways); • Congestion: Number of hours spent by average tourist using airport .
Socio-economic concerns related to air travel	• Total public expenditure on airport infrastructure (as % of total destination budget, an per passenger); • Cost of safety and security measures (total and per passenger); • Number of employees to be trained in the air transport system per tourist; • Cost of skills and training for airport personnel; • % of annual costs (operations and capital) covered by revenues at airport from different sources.

Components of the Issue	Indicators
Access	• Number of cities served with direct flights to/from the destination (scheduled, charter); • Number of flights per day and number of passengers; • %/number tourists who arrive on charter flights; • Number of airlines serving the destination (number of flights per day, per month); • Seasonality of service (ratio of peak month flights to low month) See ≫ **Seasonality** p. 111).
Security	• Cost of screening of passengers and luggage for issues related to health, crime, terrorism; • Number of incidents at the airport; • Level of expenditure on security; • Guards or officials per traveller; • Existence of a contingency plan for the airport in the event of incidents; • Level of emergency services; • #/% tourists informed of security levels at airport.

Indicators related to land and urban planning:

- **Land occupation (% of destination within airport boundary, % hardened);**

- **Noise (area affected by noise cone of airport runways);**

- **Congestion: Number of hours spent by average tourist using airport**   (Also, where serious, monitor number of complaints from tourists and local residents and opinion using questionnaire).

  Reason for use of these indicators: There are direct impacts on tourists and locals associated with the impact of air travel and how it is planned and managed. Some have direct monetary costs while others indirectly affect lifestyles.

  Source(s) of data: These data are generally available from the local authorities and airport management.

  Means to use these indicators: These indicators address the level of impact of air travel on communities – and should be used with other indicators relating to the local reaction to tourism. (See questionnaire Annex C)

  Benchmarking: See the issue on Noise (p. 183) to benchmark that concern. The other indicators can be used to measure change over time related to changed plans or development in the airport area.

Issues related to socio-economic impacts on the destination:

- **Total public expenditure on airport infrastructure (as % of total destination budget, and per passenger);**
- **Total public expenditure on road access to airport;**
- **Cost of safety and security measures (total and per passenger);**
- **Number of employees to be trained in the air transport system per tourist;**
- **Cost of skills and training for airport personnel;**
- **% of annual costs (operations and capital) covered by revenues at airport from all sources.**

Reasons for use of these indicators: For many destinations the provision of airports and the infrastructure to support them can be a major public investment. As well, operating an airport can involve continuing costs related to maintaining the capital assets, training and overall management.

Source(s) of data: Local airport authority

Means to use these indicators: Use for annual planning purposes.

Benchmarking: Websites   of   IATA   –   International   Air   Transport   Association, http://www.iata.org/index.htm and. ICAO - International Civil Aviation Organization http://www.icao.int/ can provide some comparative data.

Indicators relating to access to the destination:

* **Number of cities served with direct flights to/from the destination (scheduled, charter);**
* **Flights per day (and total passengers);**
* **% of tourists who arrive by air;**
* **% tourists who arrive on charter flights;**
* **Number of airlines serving the destination (number of flights per day, per month);**
* **Seasonality of service (ratio of peak month flights to low month).**

Reasons for use of these indicators: For many destinations, air transport is the key means of access for tourists. Changes in the ease of access for tourists can affect the number and type of tourists, the focus of marketing, and the sustainability of the destination. Charters may change the pattern of access – some destinations are easily accessible in season with direct flights from major cities but relatively inaccessible outside peak season. (e.g., Caribbean and Indian Ocean islands from European capitals) Loss of direct access may mean loss of the market.

Source(s) of data: Local tourism authority, ICAO and IATA websites which can provide early warning of some air route changes and international agreements, national air transport authorities

Means to use these indicators: This is a key indicator for those who seek to establish stable relationships with origins for tourists. It also can help to target marketing programs

Benchmarking: Comparisons can also be done using on-line reservation sites such as Orbitz, DER or Expedia, or from travel agent's destination reference books.

Indicators related to security:

* **Cost of screening of passengers and luggage for issues related to health, crime, terrorism;**
* **Number of incidents at the airport;**
* **Level of expenditure on security;**
* **Guards or officials per 1000 travellers (or travellers per guard);**
* **Existence of a contingency plan for the airport in the event of incidents;**
* **Level of emergency services;**
* **#/% tourists informed of security levels at airport.**

Reasons for use of these indicators: Security is a rising concern and cost, related primarily to air transport, but which can also affect other transport means.

Source(s) of data: Local air transport authorities

Means to use the indicators: These indicators can be used to show level of effort and may also become performance measures for effectiveness of screening programs.

Benchmarking: See IATA website for several sources (http://www.iata.org/index.htm).

3.12 Designing Products and Services

3.12.1 Creating Trip Circuits and Routes

Corridors, Links, Cooperation

Tourists often follow a route that links different attractions and tourism services, travelling by car, as part of a group in a bus, on a boat or train or even on foot or by bicycle or canoe or other means. The route may be linear taking them from a beginning destination to an end, or a circular route linking several destinations. Tourists may plan their own unique itinerary or follow a historic trail such as the Silk Road or a branded route promoted by participating destinations.

Circuits and routes can be thought of as being at the top of the tourism planning process. They pull together attractions, transportation, accommodation, food, activities etc. The choices for tourists are still varied but fall within a geographic region often with a theme. For example, the Ruta Maya is a tourism brand that links five countries in Central America. Tourists can follow ancient Mayan routes, exploring Mayan heritage. Other typical themes include food and wine, arts, local culture, history, agriculture, and scenic routes. Routes and circuits may be deliberately branded and promoted for tourism, or they may be natural features, man-made routes or historic paths.

Box 3.44 Biodiversity and tourism corridors in Swaziland: The Swaziland Biodiversity Conservation and Participatory Development Project (BCPD)

The Swaziland project's development objective is to promote environmentally, economically and socially sustainable development in the rural areas of Swaziland, based on conservation, wise use of its rich biodiversity resources and local participation in resource management, with a particular emphasis on enhancing the country's participation in regional tourism markets. This will be achieved through a participatory, integrated spatial development planning (ISPP) process, leading to the development and implementation of an Integrated Corridor Management Plan (ICMP) plan for each of two "Biodiversity and Tourism Corridors" (B-T Corridors) on a geographic scale that captures essential ecological and economic linkages. Note B-T Corridors will include four main categories of land use:

1. core conservation/protected areas;

2. core tourism development zones;

3. linkage zones to provide connectivity for biological and/or tourism purposes, and

4. support zones in which investment in improved natural resource management will support the conservation and tourism objectives and areas.)

Excerpt from: http://www.ecs.co.sz/bcpd/

For trip circuits and routes to contribute to sustainable tourism, the focus for indicators needs to be on overall organization, marketing, cooperation and integration. Individual tourism elements (attractions and services) are promoted together as a destination and communities benefit by working together. One of the key challenges is raising and sustaining funds for product development and marketing. The creation of routes often requires some infrastructure development (e.g. road improvements, signs and visitor centres) and the development of new product packages (bundling the different attractions and places to stay along the route). Creating and maintaining markets requires ongoing operational funds for promotion and organizational support. Many communities turn to the public sector or development agencies for support. The key components of the Managing Tourism Circuits and Routes issue and corresponding indicators are the following:

Components of the Issue	Indicators
Integrity of the Route Destination and Product Coherence - support and funds for organization - travel on circuits should harmonize with tourism at destinations along the route - common quality standards - complementary not competing attractions - common branding, signage	• Existence of a multi-stakeholder tourism plan; • Amount of infrastructure and operational funds • Money spent on marketing the route or circuit (and % contribution of each community); • % of towns and communities along the route participating; • ➢ **Tourist satisfaction** (p. 86)(questionnaires, on-route interviews); • % tourists stopping at interim sites along the route versus passing through.
Community Conflicts or Cooperation - amongst communities - different modes of transportation Conflicts on route/circuit - different types of users, e.g. hikers versus mountain-bikers; cyclists on country roads at risk from tour buses	• % representation from each community in organizing team/ssociationM • Number and participation level of coordination meetings and use of other mechanisms; • % of funds/investment allocated to each community; • Number of reports/complaints from tourists and tour operators; • Number of accidents on route (per year, per season).
Intensity of Use Environmental issues and impacts; carrying capacity, limits of acceptable change; land-based and water-based circuits	• Average and peak seasonal number of users and types of users (people, cars, buses, 4WDs, boats, bicycles, snowmobiles, all-terrain vehicles etc.)(measured against planned or acceptable figures). See ➢ **Use Intensity** p. 192)
Economic Impacts - on towns and communities along the routes - how is tourist spending distributed along the route	• % of tourists in the region attracted because of the circuit or route (questionnaire, information inquiries, website visits, etc.); • Number of stops per tourist on route; • Average stay per tourist at stops on route; • Revenue earned attributable to the existence of the route; • % of local business supplying services to tourists along route. (See also Protection of Image, p. 236)
Local Support	• % of local populations supporting tourism on the route (questionnaire); • Number, % of tourism and related businesses participating in/ contributing to product development, marketing and other joint activities; • Number of community members actively participating; e.g. volunteers in visitor centres; members of route tourism association.

Indicators regarding integrity of the route:

* **Existence of a multi-stakeholder tourism plan;**
* **Amount of infrastructure and operational funds;**
* **Money spent on marketing the route or circuit (and % contribution of each community);**
* **% of towns and communities along the route participating.**

Reason for use of these indicators: Participating communities need to know how much support there is for the tourist route, and how much funding is available (and from what sources) to develop and promote the route.

Source(s) of data: The route tourism association, local government agencies or chamber of commerce.

Means to use the indicators: To show the financial and community support for the route and for annual comparisons of funding gains/losses and requirements

Benchmarking: A benchmark might be considered for the minimum number of participating communities or funds required for the route to be considered a viable tourist attraction.

Indicators regarding conflict and cooperation:

* **% representation from each community in organizing team/association;**
* **Number and participation level of coordination meetings and use of other mechanisms (see Community Involvement p. 83);**
* **% of funds/investment allocated to each community;**
* **Number of reports/complaints from tourists and tour operators;**
* **Number of accidents on route (per year, per season).**

Reason for use of these indicators: These indicators can be both measures of cooperation or the potential for conflict amongst communities.

Source(s) of data: The route tourism association

Means to use the indicators: Tourism associations can use these indicators to gauge the level of support for the route, the need to raise more funds or involve more local people.

Benchmarking: Comparisons can be made with other destinations successfully promoting routes

Indicator of intensity of use:

* **Average and peak seasonal number of users and types of users.**

Reason for use of this indicator: Primarily an environmental indicator to monitor impacts from intensity or volume of use by different types of tourists and modes of transportation. Socio-cultural impacts from tourist volumes are also important (See ≫ **Effects of tourism on Communities** p. 57).

Source(s) of data: Traffic counts for vehicles. Tourist visitation numbers from managing authority. See ≫ **Use Intensity** (p. 192).

Means to use the indicators: Show changes over time for the destination.

Benchmarking: Comparisons can be made with other destinations with trail systems. Best comparisons will likely be time series data for the route to gauge annual increases or decreases.

Indicators of economic benefit:

* **% of tourists in the region attracted because of the circuit or route;**
* **Number of stops per tourist on route;**
* **Average stay per tourist at stops on route;**
* **Revenue earned attributable to the existence of the route;**
* **% of local business supplying services to tourists along route;**

* These indicators are similar to those in the section on ≫ **Economic Benefits** (p. 128) and Transportation p. 210. (Might need complex economic analysis, Tourism Satellite Accounts, p. 134);

  Many will require a questionnaire (Annex C) to extract information on the behaviour of the tourists while en route.

Other useful indicators:

* **Tourist satisfaction (questionnaires, on-route interviews):** Questionnaires can be designed to give feedback on tourist perceptions of the route overall, its importance in attracting them to the region, and the level of quality or consistency of products and experiences along the route;

* **% tourists stopping at interim sites along the route versus passing through:** This indicator shows whether the benefits of tourism are being spread across communities. Some routes are designed to slow tourists down, to get them to stop and explore (and spend money), rather than just rushing non-stop through a region to the next big attraction.

Indicators of local support: Local support is important for cohesion amongst communities. As well as support in principle, communities may contribute funds and in-kind support. Relevant indicators include the following:

* **% of local populations supporting tourism on the route (questionnaire);**

* **Number of businesses involved in promotion of route (and money spent);**

* **Number of community members actively participating; e.g. volunteers in visitor centres; members of route tourism association.**

3.12.2 Providing Variety of Experiences

Product Diversification, Range of Services

An issue for some destinations is creating or maintaining a variety of experiences. Often, greater variety will result in tourists staying longer to experience more. Tourists who take advantage of a variety of experiences in a destination (walking, horseback riding, local theatre, fishing, boat tours, wildlife watching, scuba diving etc.) may find the overall experience more rewarding. Destinations with little variety may find that tourists are disappointed, particularly if rainy days, storms or unsuitable temperatures prevent the tourists from enjoying the other experiences (e.g. swimming, skiing, nature viewing, sunbathing etc). Small destinations have often worked together to provide variety (e.g. tourist routes – see Trip Circuits p. 223). Often national or regional authorities have published guidebooks to help tourists find variety en route – showing the location of crafts, interesting vistas, local history, regional cuisine, potential walks and other attractions. (See Cape Breton Case p. 355). This issue also relates to the issues of seasonality (where out of season the variety is much less) and to ≫ **Tourist Satisfaction** (p. 86), the issue of limited variety has proven particularly important to small, rural or remote destinations (e.g., see Kukljica case p. 402). See also Protection of Image. (p. 236)

Components of the Issue	Indicators
Maintaining a variety of experiences	* Number of different attractions in or near destination (classified by type of attractions, e.g. cultural and natural heritage sites, events and festivities, leisure activities and sites, etc.).
Provision of the full range of needed tourism services	* Range of tourist services available in the destination (classified by type, e.g. accommodation and catering, transportation, information and guiding, conferences and meetings, etc.); * Range of tourist services available year round (in high and low seasons) See issue section on ➢ **Seasonality** (p. 111).
Determining whether the tourists are satisfied with the variety of the destination	* Perception of variety by tourists (questionnaire).

Indicator of variety:

* **Number of different attractions in or near destination.**

    Reason for use of this indicator: This is a simple count of attractions to show degree of variety.

    Source(s) of data: These data can be subjective – dependent on the definition of "attraction". A consistent definition should be used (i.e., decide at the outset whether to count services such as boat rental, go-cart tracks, horseback riding, game arcades, craft markets etc and be consistent over time in their use.) There is no standard in general use and one major "attraction" (e.g., a theme park) with many components may easily overshadow several others. It is suggested that each instance of an "attraction" should not be counted separately – that is ten different wax museums should be counted as one attraction type, as should six skydiving firms, two aquariums or three local museums etc. The key is consistency over time for the destination.

    Means to use the indicator: This can be used to show both total numbers of attractions and variety (e.g., 20 different types of attractions).

    Benchmarking: Because of lack of a standard classification and methodology to identity what qualifies as an attraction, the best benchmarking will likely be relative to other years in the same destination using a custom definition which incorporates all of the types of attractions found there. Note, however, that sometimes a concentration of several similar attractions can also be a draw (e.g., "We get to visit ten art galleries or craft shops in the same village").

Indicator of extent of services:

* **Range of tourist services available in the destination.**

    Reason for use of this indicator: This indicator can be used to show changes in the number of key services available. The services covered include accommodation, food, sports equipment and supplies, rental of equipment, repair for equipment (e.g., bicycles, boats, and automobiles), policing, hospital or clinic. Note that variety may change according to season (see ➢ **Seasonality** p. 111).

    Source(s) of data: Local business associations, local authority.

    Means to use the indicator: This is a performance measure for efforts to provide services. It is likely to be of interest to those managing or marketing the destination.

Benchmarking: See for example, the UK local indicators on services (English Tourism Council 2001). Because of the unique mix in each destination, the most useful point of comparison will likely be other years for the destination.

Indicator of tourist satisfaction with destination variety:

- **Perception of variety by tourists.**

Reason for use of this indicator: As noted above, because of the unique nature of destinations it is not easy to find standard definitions for what should be counted when assessing variety. As a result, it is suggested that the perception by tourists of variety may be a stronger indicator – and may directly influence their decisions.

Source) of data: Exit questionnaire (See Annex C). Respondents are asked whether or not they agree that "the destination provided a good variety of experiences".

Means to use the indicator: The percentage who agree (and strongly agree) that the destination provided good variety can be monitored from year to year.

Benchmarking: The strongest comparison will be for the same destination over time, but because this question is being recommended for widespread use, there may be an opportunity to compare to other destinations.

3.12.3 Marketing for Sustainable Tourism

Green" Marketing, Products and Experiences Emphasizing Sustainability, Market Penetration, Tourist Response, Marketing Effectiveness

The creation and maintenance of markets for destinations, tours, accommodation and attractions that contribute to sustainability is a concern for many enterprises and destinations which wish to take advantage of a perceived growing interest in this area. Environmental and social factors are increasingly important elements of enhanced quality of experience and visitor satisfaction. Managers seek information regarding the nature and extent of the marketplace, the degree to which there is a market niche or premium for environmentally sound and socially responsible products and practices, and the response to any marketing done to portray the destination or enterprise as "green", to showcase environmental or cultural achievements, to obtain results from resources invested in marketing and to judge the effectiveness of any marketing activities. While it may be easy to measure level of effort (using internal records of an enterprise) results (requiring measurement of factors and outcomes external to the organization) may be more difficult to assess.

Components of the Issue	Indicators
Identifying the market for more sustainable (environmentally friendly or culturally sensitive) products	• % of visitors who seek environmentally friendly and culturally sensitive experiences, (exit Questionnaire); • % of visitors willing to pay extra for these experiences of enhanced value (exit Questionnaire); • Number of requests to local tourism authorities related to environmentally or culturally sensitive products (hotels, restaurants, tours, ecotourism and cultural tourism sites), phone and mail inquiries, hits in websites.
Measuring the image of the destination or products considering sustainability aspects	• % of establishments and operators marketing sustainable, sensitive or green products or experiences; • % of businesses that include information on environmental and social aspects of their operation (destination conditions, company policies), and the extent (quality) of this information (e.g. in websites, brochures, guides and interpretation programmes, etc.); • % of certified businesses that include reference (e.g. logo) of the certification system in their promotional material; • % visitors who arrive seeking "green" experiences (same as above on exit questionnaire).
Meeting client expectations re authenticity of products	• Number (%) tourists who are satisfied with the environmental and cultural experiences (exit Questionnaire); • Number of complaints (re specific issues about how sensitive or sustainable the product or experience was).
Measuring level of marketing effort	• Volume of marketing products divided by type (brochures, advertisements in different media, posters, websites, etc); • Level of representation/contact (number of fairs, exhibits, journalists' trips, familiarization trips for tour operators); • Cost of marketing (by type, where possible by cost per contact).
Targeting the right clientele. Measuring degree of contact and reach of marketing	• % of clients who self-identify as "green" or eco tourists (interested in environmentally and culturally sensitive experiences), using entry and/or exit Questionnaire; • Numbers of potential tourists contacted (by interest, location).
Measuring response to any marketing	• Market penetration, response surveys, or conversion studies (See Box 3.45 , Box 3.46); • % clients who arrive in response to specific ads or initiatives (reservations, return of promotional coupons, poll source of information on arrival); • % of clients who participate in activities while at the destination, in response to specific ads or initiatives (e.g. reservations, return of promotional coupons, or questioned at the beginning of the programme); • Note: indicators on e.g. arrivals, occupancy, length of stay by source and type are all related to results but difficult to attribute to specific marketing initiatives (See Box 3.46 p. 235).

Components of the Issue	Indicators
Evaluating client response and satisfaction	• Occupancy rates in establishments promoting sustainable products (and ratio to rates for all tourism); • Price per room night (and ratio to industry average); • Market share (compare to other destinations) – will require survey in tourist home locations; • % clients who are satisfied with their experience (exit questionnaire – ask specifically about green products); • % tourists who agree that the reality matched what was advertised (See Protection of Image p. 236); • Rank re other competing destinations – re quality, environment, image, satisfaction; • % tourists who perceive barriers to visiting the destination.
Responding to external demands	• Number (%) of operators who request "green" products, % of establishments with green programs (certifications, EMS); • Numbers of requests (numbers seeking "green" products); • Number of complaints received (annual changes); • Speed of response to complaints (average, maximum days); • % satisfaction with how complaints were handled.

Indicators relative to identifying the market for sustainable, sensitive or greener products:

* **% of visitors who seek environmentally friendly and culturally sensitive experiences, (exit Questionnaire);**

* **% of visitors willing to pay extra for these experiences of enhanced value (exit Questionnaire;)**

* **Number of requests to local tourism authorities related to environmentally or culturally sensitive products (hotels, restaurants, tours, ecotourism and cultural tourism sites), phone and mail inquiries, hits in websites.**

    Reason for use of these indicators: Managers of destinations properties or attractions can obtain information on the nature and extent of demand for more sustainable products.

    Source(s) of data: Tabulation of requests.

    Means to use the indicators: Use to determine trends in interest in sustainable or "green" products or experiences at the destination.

    Benchmarking: Best used to measure trends over time in the same destination, or relative to other competing destinations who may be promoting sustainable forms of tourism.

Indicators related to the image of the destination or products:

* **% of establishments and operators in the destinations marketing sustainable, sensitive or green products or experiences;**

* **% of businesses that include information on environmental and social aspects of their operation (destination conditions, company policies), and the extent (quality) of this information (e.g. in websites, brochures, guides and interpretation programmes, etc.);**

* **% of certified businesses that include information, reference (e.g. logo) of the certification system in their promotional material;**

* **% visitors who arrive seeking "green" experiences (same as above on exit questionnaire);**

Reason for use of these indicators: If a destination has a green or culturally and environmentally sensitive image, it may be the basis for marketing or the result of past marketing. If the numbers change, it can be a signal of risk to the image (see Issue section on Protection of Image p. 236).

Source(s) of data: Local tourism authority or tourism association.

Means to use the indicators: Can be used to show trends in demand for sustainable experiences and products. Use with the exit questionnaire to determine if tourists seeking these experiences or products do indeed find them.

Benchmarking: Use over time for the same destination.

Indicators of authenticity of sustainable or green products and services:

* **Number (%) tourists who are satisfied with the environmental and cultural experiences (exit Questionnaire);**

* **Number of complaints (re specific issues about how sustainable the product or experience was).**

Reason for use of these indicators: Many tourists are dissatisfied with the level of environmental or cultural sensitivity of products advertised as being environmentally or culturally sensitive or "green". There is a risk to the product and to the destination if many are dissatisfied.

Source(s) of data: Exit surveys (see Annex C) and complaints registered at tourism authorities and establishments

Means to use the indicators: Show as dissatisfaction (or satisfaction) levels. High levels of positive response can be used in future marketing.

Benchmarking: Compare over time for the destination or where available compare with competitors.

Indicators of level of marketing effort:

* **Volume of marketing products divided by type (brochures, advertisements in different media, posters, etc);**

* **Level of representation/contact (number of fairs, exhibits, journalists' trips;**

* **Cost of marketing (by type, where possible by cost per contact).**

Reason for use of these indicators: Overall marketing effort is expected to yield results, in the form of greater stability, more sustainable tourism activity, and to promote particular types of tourism – such as low impact, "green" or cultural tourism.

Source(s) of data: Records of marketing agency/tourism authority.

Means to use the indicator: Best used in relation to results – as a performance measure for marketing. (See Box 3.46 for issues regarding how to deal with attribution of results to marketing activities)

Benchmarking: Compare over time for the destination or where available compare with competitors level of effort.

Indicator regarding targeting the right clientele:

* **% of clients who self-identify as green or eco tourists, or alternative/sensitive (entry or exit questionnaire);**

* **Numbers of potential tourists contacted (by interest, location).**

Reason for use of these indicators: Growing or diminishing numbers who self-identify as green tourists or ecotourists can be a leading indicator which may require response in changes to the product or changed levels of environmental sensitivity in management of the destination. Mix of requests for information can show growth or diminished interest in specific sites or niches.

Source(s) of data: Entry or exit questionnaires, mix of requests for information.

Means to use the indicators: Use as an early warning of changing nature of tourist demands. This can also be used as a performance measure if a destination or enterprise seeks to expand green niche marketing.

Benchmarking: Compare over time for the destination or where available compare with competitors.

Indicators for measuring response to marketing:

* **Market penetration, response surveys or conversion studies;**
* **% clients who arrive in response to specific ads or initiatives (poll source of information on arrival);**
* **Note: indicators on e.g. arrivals, occupancy, length of stay by source and type are all related to results but difficult to attribute to specific marketing initiatives.**

Reason for use of these indicators: These indicators can help gauge effectiveness of marketing (and can also be used as performance measures to measure response per dollar spent; See Box 3.46 regarding problems of attribution to marketing efforts).

Source(s) of data: Records of tourism authorities and individual enterprises – re both levels of expenditure and response numbers.

Means to use the indicators: These indicators show both numbers reached and numbers who respond. Both can help guide new marketing.

Benchmarking: Compare with past marketing initiatives. Where part of a larger marketing program with other destinations, internal comparisons can be done.

Indicators of client response and satisfaction:

* **Occupancy rates (and ratio to rates for all tourism);**
* **Price per room night (and ratio to industry average);**
* **Rank re other competing destinations – re quality, environment, image, satisfactio;**
* **% tourists who perceive barriers to visiting the destination.**

Reason for use of these indicators: The ultimate intent of marketing is usually to obtain more custom at higher prices. These indicators can show strength and weakness of the market. Higher occupancy may occur only through reduced pricing, so both should be used together.

Source(s) of data: These data are normally available through tourism authorities, although price per room night may be more difficult to obtain. Satisfaction can be obtained through exit surveys. Market surveys (in key source countries) may help clarify perception of barriers and of comparative destination quality.

Means to use the indicators: Each indicator can be used alone, but in tandem can show strength (higher occupancy at higher prices, higher occupancy than similarly priced non-green products, better image of quality) or weakness (maintain occupancy only by reducing prices, potential tourists see transport or administrative barriers to going to the destination)

Benchmarking: Compare over time with the same destination. Where national or regional data is available it can also be used to benchmark performance.

Box 3.45 Conversion studies

Conversion studies are the most widespread methodology in use internationally for the evaluation of promotional activity and attributing cause to these activities. The method is designed to monitor the success of a specific promotional input through measured tourism impacts: to identify how many inquiries were generated by a single or multiple range of promotional inputs (adverts, trade events, website, etc.), how many were converted to visitors, and what the monetary value of those conversions was.

Conversion studies can be used to compare the relative performance of different advertisements and campaigns; the impact of different promotional events and media; and to measure the cumulative effectiveness of a destination agency's marketing and promotional efforts.

A Conversion Study depends upon a destination agency keeping a database of people who have responded by requesting further information to a specific promotional input (a coupon, a TV or radio advertisement etc), in order to find out how the information affected their behaviour. The marketing organization or tourism administration then keeps the names and addresses of respondents and calls back on them after a specified time to find out if they have taken action (booked or planned to take a holiday) as a result of the promotional event and often this communication is used to provide further information on the tourism products. A representative sample is usually done in order to specify causality from a conversion study. There must be questions in the call-back questionnaire that elicit to what extent the campaign being evaluated was the sole or main reason for the respondent taking a holiday. Conversion studies also include questions that enable the organization to know how many people have actually taken a holiday, or how many plan to do so at some point in the future.

When questioning people about past behaviour it is important that questions about amount of expenditure on a trip should be asked as close after the trip as possible to avoid both under and over estimates of expenditure. Questions on travel intentions to the destination should attempt to discriminate how far in the future the respondent's holiday intention stretches to (e.g. "planning to take holiday at destination in the next year", "in the next two years" etc).

Once questionnaires have been analysed, return on investment (ROI) calculations may be made by extrapolating the results obtained from the survey sample to the total number of people who originally requested information. The ROI analysis may involve calculations designed to arrive at estimates of: total revenue generated; average revenue per inquiry; estimated average cost per inquiry (see further details on ROI in box 3.46).

This box is based on information from the WTO publication "Evaluating NTO Marketing Activities" (http://www.world-tourism.org/cgi-bin/infoshop.storefront/EN/product/1331-1). This report contains details on the issues associated with processing questionnaire results and suggests a range of methods and questions which may be of use to destination managers who wish to undertake conversion studies and other investigations to evaluate marketing activities.

Indicators of external demand:

•   **Number (%) of operators who request "green" products and services;**

•   **% of establishments with green programs (certifications, EMS).**

Reason for use of these indicators: Some inbound operators may seek properties meeting green standards, or entire destinations which can demonstrate some form of environmental certification. (see Certification p. 318).

Source(s) of data: These data are frequently available through tourism authorities, particularly in cases where the authorities are promoting certification.

Means to use the indicators: The indicators both measure demand and industry response. Where a high percentage of establishments (or in some cases entire destinations) has certification, this can be used in marketing – both to operators and to tourists themselves.

Benchmarking: Some ability to benchmark can be obtained through certification programs. (See Certification p. 318).

Wildlife is the focus of tourism marketing and product development in many destinations.

Danube Delta, Romania

Bongani South, Africa

Box 3.46 Measuring the real return on investments in marketing activities

Marketing is a key element in the success of destinations and can support destination sustainability. Return on Investment (ROI) calculations are made in order to appraise the efficiency with which promotional investment is made. The return may be estimated in monetary terms (the most common measure), visitor numbers, or in some other kind of measured output (e.g. increase in employment in tourism; increase in number of out-of-season visitors) depending on the objectives of the promotional investment (WTO, 2003). But measurement is not simple, and causal relationships are difficult to document.

Data collection is a challenge. For monitoring the internal operations of a marketing agency, its own records will be the principal source. Most other data will require direct collection, both from the tourism industry and from individuals such as current or potential tourists. The main problem is that there exists a time lag between the marketing activities and the actual visit, as well as the fact that tourists are exposed to many other stimuli. The only way to measure impact of marketing is through surveys. Visitor surveys are not always successful; as practice has shown that it is extremely difficult for tourists to give an answer on the influence marketing has had on their decision making. "I just wanted to come" and "Information by friends or relatives" are most mentioned. Even when marketing would have been an influence, or even the main source for decision making, its influence is often not easily remembered and, in the western world at least, tourists may be reluctant to admit that they were influenced.

One solution is to query a representative sample of the persons with whom marketing contact was established around 4 to 6 months later to ask if they came to the destination and if so, what influence the marketing had on the decision. Internet and the use of websites for promotion and information can be approached in the same way as other activities. Pop-ups with some basic questions and the request to give an email address to send a questionnaire after some months is just as valid for use as direct or mail contact. The key disadvantage is that one cannot guarantee a representative sample and this limits how the information can be used.

What do answers really mean? The question of what influence marketing has had on tourist decisions is difficult to analyze; some tourists may not always be objective and may simply give the answer they expect is wanted. Often the added value of marketing activities is considered to be real when respondents say that the contact they had with the marketing material or office was "fully" or "to a very great extent" the reason for their visit. The question "would you have come if no contact had been made" may be more productive in eliciting replies regarding marketing success, but this too is subject to question. Some of the negative replies and part of the demand that "resulted from no contact" was likely influenced by marketing activities but not noticed or remembered by the respondent. This is virtually impossible to prove or disprove. Objective data on actual behaviour can be of use. Additional demand, and related measures such as the numbers per tourist group, the length of stay and the amount spent per day can be used to estimate economic results and related to the actual costs spent on marketing (sometimes by specific market sector) This can yield information on the Return on Investments (ROI) in tourism marketing.

To measure marketing costs it can be useful to create a system in which all the recognisable costs are included, however difficult it may be. The Netherlands Board of Tourism and VisitBritain both have applied such a system. It is remarkable that VisitBritain calculates an ROI of around 1 to 30, so 1 currency equivalent spent on tourism marketing brings 30 into the (national) economy and that in Holland the ROI comes to 1 to 42. Despite the caveats discussed above, changes in key indicators can show important factors which will help direct marketing efforts, and some measurement of performance can be done. Monitoring marketing activities, in particular by measuring their effectiveness, is essential for destination marketers. It is the main way to prove that there are results from these activities and that they can benefit the destination.

3.12.4 Protection of the Image of a Destination

Branding, Vision, Strategic Marketing

The decision to visit a destination is frequently based on the image a potential visitor has of that place. The image held by the tourists may be based on their own experience, what they have read, the opinions of others, or on the image or brand displayed or portrayed in materials marketing the destination. Sustaining tourism in a destination involves ensuring that appropriate images of that place are established, are refined as market and circumstances change and are protected. The image of a destination can be affected by many factors, in the destination itself and by association. Events in other sectors or other destinations can change the image of a destination in the minds of prospective travelers – civil strife, reports of environmental degradation or disease can affect the image of entire regions, whether or not the destination is specifically affected. Recovery from damage to a positive image can take a very long time, even if the destination is quick to respond to actual or perceived problems.

Driven by increasing global competition for travel markets, tourism managers are becoming more sophisticated and targeted in their approaches to marketing their tourism destinations. In many of the more competitive destinations, a critical component of strategic marketing activities centers on developing and conveying a distinctive brand and image. This is intended to not only capture the central values and attributes of the place, but also to create a clear affinity and position in the minds of preferred travel markets. The intent of these branding activities is to build strong consumer loyalty for the destination based on the values and attributes portrayed by the brand. Measuring the success of such branding initiatives remains a challenge for many tourism destination managers. Appropriate indicators can then act as early warning signs regarding how a destination image is perceived, and can also help in addressing the establishment and maintenance of a distinctive brand for the destination.

A destination brand is a "name, symbol, logo, trademark or other graphic that both identifies and differentiates the destination; furthermore, it conveys the promise of a memorable travel experience that is uniquely associated with the destination" (Ritchie & Crouch 2003, 196). Indicators relating to protection of image can help to understand the image (if any) which tourists hold of a destination, and can measure changes in that image which may affect visitation. The effectiveness of actions to establish and maintain a brand can be measured. Four areas can be monitored: brand development; brand refinement; brand effectiveness and brand protection. Of course, a brand can be only established and promoted if there are corresponding and quality tourism products supporting it. Many of the following indicators can be used also more broadly on marketing activities, as branding is one of the specific marketing tools.

Petra, Jordan - Tourists are attracted by a unique image – in a protected site.

Components of the Issue	Indicators
Destination Image	
Image held by current tourists	• % of tourists who have a positive image of the destination (exit survey based); • % of tourists who would recommend the destination to their peers (exit questionnaire); • specific responses to key questions re key attractions and activities (see Exit Questionnaire Annex C); See also the issue section on ➣ **Tourists satisfaction** (p. 86).
Image held by those who have not visited the destination	• % of potential market(s) who have a positive image of the destination; • Rank of destination on list of destinations (key competitors) on broad surveys in key market(s); (see also issues on Public Safety p. 104 and Tourist Security p. 209).
Image in marketplace	• % of operators (inbound, outbound) who perceive the destination as a safe, attractive, interesting, good value etc destination (survey based).
Branding	
Brand development (resourcing, strategies, response to market)	• Level of funding allocated to brand development and other branding activities (amount and % allocated); • Degree of match with the preferred values of the destination's targeted markets and partner organizations (surveys or repeat focus groups on a regular basis); • % of key actors (hotels, attractions, partner organizations) whose marketing carries the brand features (logo, slogan, etc.), or uses complementary images.
Brand refinement (advertising - Promotion - Research - Macro-environment - Local perceptions - Organizational - Awareness	• Annual percentage of the tourism-marketing budget allocated to advertisement and promotion; • Reach of advertising - Number of tourists receiving/recognizing, responding. Number reached for the dollar spent (conversion study -See Box 3.45 p. 233); • Percentage of market, operators, local representatives, employees and stakeholders perceiving brand to positively reflect their preferred attributes and values (focus groups or surveys).

Brand effectiveness (visitor satisfaction, brand positioning, expectations, brand awareness, loyalty)	• Annual value/percentage of the tourism-marketing budget allocated to
	• monitoring satisfaction. (and Number of tourists reached per dollar spent (See Box 3.46);
	• Percentage of visitors who :
	  - believe the brand values, attributes and benefits communicated were met during their trips;
	  - think the brand attributes, values and benefits rank more favourably than other similar destinations (the competition);
	  - recall the brand name (% recall on same day, % recall in longer term)
	  - are repeat visitors and/or expect to return to the destination. (by tourism sectors/categories. See exit questionnaire Annex C);
	  - who intend to return specifically to experience key brand values, benefits and attributes (identify key values, benefits and attributes explicitly in exit questionnaire).

Components of the Issue	Indicators
Indicators of brand protection (Level of effort, trademark, use guidelines control)	• Level of protection for key branding tools (i.e. logo, word mark). Percentage which are patented/copyrighted; • Perceived value of the branding programs to stakeholders (survey). Percentage of stakeholders surveyed who believe the branding programs help improve the value and performance of their tourism operations (survey after approximately six months to one year); • Level of effort to monitor public image (print, web, other media (money spent annually, personnel level); • Percentage of stakeholders, consumers and competitors who attribute the brand features (name, logo, etc.) solely to the destination (survey, brand recall, focus groups).

For the purposes of this document, a few of the more important indicators are elaborated below to illustrate their potential utility in assessing destination brand management performance. A case study, Super Natural British Columbia (p. 422) shows how image branding can work in practice to establish and sustain the image of a destination.

Indicators of destination image:

* **% of tourists who have a positive image of the destination (exit survey);**

* **% of tourists who would recommend the destination to their peers (exit questionnaire);**

* **Specific responses to key questions re key attractions and activities (see Exit Questionnaire Annex C);**

* **% of potential market(s) who have a positive image of the destination;**

* **Rank of destination on list of destinations (key competitors) on broad surveys in key market(s);**

* **% of operators (inbound, outbound) who perceive the destination as a safe, beautiful, interesting, good value etc destination (survey based);**
  See also the issue section on Tourist satisfaction (p. 86).

Reason for the use of these indicators: The response to the image of a destination may be an early warning indicator of tourist (or potential tourist) reaction to problems or issues of many kinds in a destination which can harm its sustainability.

Source(s) of data: Perception of image is held by individuals and the only effective means to obtain information is via a survey or questionnaire process. Surveys of tourists on image will be best done as part of an exit questionnaire (See Annex C 5, p. 491). Other surveys or focus groups may be done to obtain information from the marketplace and from potential tourists.

Means to use the indicators: Changes in perception of the destination, its image can be used to warn of future perceived risks, or as performance measures for efforts to market or brand the destination.

Indicators of brand development:

* **Degree of match with the preferred values of the destination's targeted markets** (repeat focus groups on regular basis);

* **Comparison of the brand's vision to those of other potentially supportive regional and national tourism organizations** (degree of match or complementarity -use focus groups).

Reason for the use of these indicators:

Target market: Development indicators examine the extent to which the brand adequately communicates the attributes, benefits, values, personality, culture and user it was intended to portray (Kotler and Turner, 1998). Branding efforts should reflect values, attributes and benefits sought by travel markets the destination is trying to attract.

Brand vision: The brand vision provides a long-term guide for focusing the destination marketing organizations' goals and objectives. It should complement the visions of other supportive national and regional tourism organizations in order to garner resources and synergistic support.

Source(s) of data: Market surveys in target market can clarify key values and reaction. Where it is not already in place, a participatory approach is recommended to develop vision/goals for the destination (note that a large percentage of destinations will not have any developed vision or brand). Brand vision: focus group research with key stakeholders will help to identify level of compatibility

Means to use the indicators: This can be in vision statements and goals of the organization and those of the destination. Clear links between the destination's target market and brand vision should be expressed in written and graphic form. Changes in level of compatibility may signal need to reassess market strategy.

Benchmarking: Selected benchmarks are dependent upon the goals and objectives of the company or destination evaluating their brand. Possible benchmark comparisons could be with other competing destinations ·or with supportive complementary organization performance indicators. (See Performance Measurement p. 322)

Indicators of brand refinement:

* **Annual percentage of the tourism-marketing budget allocated to advertisement and promotion;**

* **Reach of advertising - Number receiving/recognizing, responding. Number reached for the dollar spent (conversion study);**

* **Percentage of the audience which perceives the advertisement/promotional campaigns to positively reflect their preferred attributes and values (focus groups or surveys);**

* **Percentage of tourism operators who feel their product's values and attributes are reflected in the brand (survey quarterly, annually, etc);**

* **Percentage of local representatives, employees, and stakeholders who believe the brand reflects their community values (survey quarterly, annually).**

Reason for the use of these indicators: Advertisement/promotion: Identifies how the target audiences perceive the brand and provides guidance on how it matches with preferred travel market expectations. Refinement indicators examine the extent to which shifting levels of awareness and preference for the brand's values, identity etc., have been used to periodically strengthen the position of the brand in the minds of targeted travel markets. These indicators also help determine possible threats and opportunities (political, social, environmental, and economic) that can strengthen or constrain the brand's performance.

Source(s) of data: Advertisement/promotion: focus groups and surveys. Macro-environment: travel promotion research studies and travel trade media publications (repeat monitoring of same sources for measurable changes)

Means to use the indicators: Advertisement/promotion: presence of a well-received brand perception in the market place that matches with the destination's ability to meet expectations translates into strong brand value. This can be used to enhance destination competitiveness and brand equity over time. Knowledge of forthcoming changes in the macro-environment will help destination managers to capitalize on opportunities or mitigate threats related to its branding activities. Awareness of these changes can enable the marketing team to allocate effort where it will be best utilized.

Benchmarking: Advertisement/promotion: Selected benchmarks are dependent upon the goals and objectives of the company managing their brand. Possible benchmark comparisons could be with other competing destinations or with supportive complementary organizations.

Indicators for brand effectiveness:

* **Annual value/percentage of the tourism-marketing budget allocated to monitoring satisfaction and number of tourists reached per dollar spent (see also Box 3.46);**

* **Percentage of visitors who:**

    - **believe the brand values, attributes and benefits communicated were met during their trips;**

    - **think the brand attributes, values and benefits rank more favourably than other similar destinations (the competition);**

    - **recall the brand name. (% recall on same day, % recall in longer term);**

    - **are repeat visitors and/or expect to return to the destination (by tourism sectors/categories. See exit questionnaire Annex C);**

    - **who intend to return specifically to experience key brand values, benefits and attributes (identify key values, benefits and attributes explicitly in exit questionnaire).**

Reason for the use of these indicators: Visitor Satisfaction: Effectiveness indicators gauge the degree to which the brand lives up to the expectations of its consumers (Upshaw, 1995).High overall ratings of destination trip satisfaction can translate into potentially greater brand loyalty (i.e. return visits).

Source(s) of data: Local tourism authorities or a tourism association may gather exit and market origin survey information. Data may be gathered through local tourism authorities or tourism association, or a website review of stakeholder promotional material. Data may also be gathered through exit or intercept surveys of visitors (e.g. key questions would relate to what other brands were considered when choosing a holiday) % brand recall, % brand loyalty, perceived value of the brand for destination selection purposes). For a valuable source see European Travel Commission and WTO 2003, Evaluating NTO Marketing Activities.

Means to use the indicators: A measure of visitor satisfaction: This indicator can be used to demonstrate how brand satisfaction/dissatisfaction levels relate to the product delivered. Low levels of satisfaction would indicate the need for a review of brand advertisements/ promotions communicated and an assessment of the degree to which those tourism operators using the brand can meet its standards.

Benchmarking: Visitor Satisfaction, Competitiveness: Selected benchmarks are dependent upon the goals and objectives of the company evaluating their brand. Possible benchmark comparisons could be externally with other competing destinations when data is available (rarely), or internally through changes in indicator scores over a select period of time.

Indicators of brand protection:

* **Level of protection for key branding tools (i.e. logo, word mark). Percentage which are patented or copyrighted;**

* **Perceived value of the branding programs to stakeholders (survey) Percentage of stakeholders surveyed who believe the branding programs help improve the value and performance of their tourism operations (survey after approximately six months to one year);**

* **Level of effort to monitor public image (print, web, other media (money spent annually, personnel level);**

* **Percentage of stakeholders, consumers and competitors who attribute the brand features (name, logo, etc.) solely to the destination (survey, brand recall, focus groups).**

Reason for the use of these indicators: Protect the brand trademark. Protection indicators measure the extent to which managers can protect their brand and its uniqueness. Brand trademark and or copyright ensures the unique image and or brand (logo, wordmark etc).

Source(s) of data: Brand trademarks and copyrights can be obtained from legally approved organizations, records of the number of tourism operations who have been approved to use the brand, the number of countries where trademarks have been acquired. Activities to reinforce brand identity can be extracted from: tourism organization records of the number of programs/activities and the number of stakeholders who participate in approved branding programs, and operator surveys monitor number and percentage of participants who feel the program is beneficial.

Means to use the indicators: These indicators can be used to support a review of the effectiveness of brand management and investment strategies.

Benchmarking: Possible benchmark comparisons could be external with other competing destinations or internally with time series.

3.13 Sustainability of Tourism Operations and Services

3.13.1 Sustainability and Environmental Management Policies and Practices at Tourism Businesses

Environmental Management, Social Responsibility

With the emergence of a number of formal management certification standards, most notable those related to ISO 9000 for management, 14000 for environment and the new ISO 18000 series for workplace health and safety, there is strong global support for better management systems to create better outcomes for enterprises and the environments they affect. These systems also help to enhance the degree of control managers have over their operations and impacts. Related programs for risk reduction on, for example, the food chain (Hazard Analysis and Critical Control Points), as well as formal third party certification for tourism companies and destinations also aim at improving sustainability aspects of tourism operations (see Certification p. 318).

Tourism companies (both larger international companies and smaller local ones) are increasingly aware of the social impacts tourism can bring to any destination community; therefore company policies increasingly reflect social responsibility towards employees and host communities. Certification can also bring recognition from the marketplace by showing responsibility.

Components of the Issue	Indicators
Environmental management systems and environmental initiatives	• % of establishments in the destination with formal certification (In each or all of EMS, ISO 14000, HACCP etc. or national equivalents); • Existence of company policy on environmental and sustainability issues (including revision and reporting mechanisms), % companies with policies; • Existence of designated personnel for environmental and sustainability management issues at the company; • Training of staff on environmental issues (% trained); • Application of environmentally friendly technologies and techniques (e.g. water, energy saving devices, waste recycling, green purchasing, local sourcing) - % using.
Social responsibility	• Existence of company policies aiming at social issues of employment and relation with host communities (e.g. sourcing of employment and supply of goods from local community, staff training, support to community development, etc.) % of companies with policies/programs). See also socio-cultural issues and indicators, such as Employment (p. 119), and ➢ **Economic Benefits** (p. 128) and Poverty reduction (p. 135).

Indicators of environmental management:

• **% of establishments in the destination with formal certification (In each or all of EMS, ISO 14000, HACCP etc. or national equivalents)** (Note, can also be subdivided by class or type of accommodation or type of tourist service).

Reason for use of this indicator: The percentage of establishments (of each type or classification) is a good indicator of management effort to take charge of environmental factors and reduce risks. It is inclusive of the other indicators suggested here – as EMS, and ISO 14,000 require these other initiatives as part of certification. Where no formal certification is obtained, (or other certification programs like HACCP – (Hazard Analysis and Critical Control Point programs for the food system) or other specific certifications are obtained, these also require risk analysis, monitoring and consistent management action (including training and reporting) .

Source(s) of data: Logs of certification may be kept by national or regional governments, particularly where the promotion of certification is part of the policy of tourism authorities. If this source is not available, hotel associations may maintain such records, or it may be necessary to poll establishments. Local tourism authorities will normally have a reasonable appreciation of who has received certification.

Means to use the indicator: Individual hotels or other organizations may use certification as a part of their marketing – demonstrating quality assurance. At the destination level, the percentage of establishments certified can also be used to show environmental sensitivity and progress. Where a government or industry association policy is to promote certification, this indicator becomes an important measure of performance for that policy or associated programs.

Benchmarking: Where internationally recognized certifications are attained, direct benchmarking with other destinations is possible. See the websites for e.g. ISO, HACCP and also see Certification section (p. 318).

Note: only one direct indicator is recommended for this issue, It should be recognized that the results of effective environmental management and risk management will become evident in many other substantive areas – and reflected in other indicators which measure environmental results at the destination level (e.g., water quality, health, visitor satisfaction etc.) Users of this

Guidebook are urged to also refer to the appropriate sections which address the key environmental issues of their destination.

If there is no formal certification program, the following indicators are components of environmental management and can be individually monitored :

- **Existence of company policy on environmental and sustainability issues (including revision and reporting mechanisms) (% with policy);**

- **Existence of designated personnel for environmental management issues at the company (% companies environmental manager);**

- **Training of staff on environmental issues (% trained by category and level);**

- **Application of environmentally friendly technologies and techniques (e.g. water, energy saving devices, waste recycling, green purchasing, local sourcing).**

This hotel on Egypt's Red Sea coast is part of the Accor Hotels group that applies environmental management system at all of its properties. Accor is a member of the Tour Operators Initiative. See case study p. 327

Box 3.47 Tour Operators Initiative

The Tour Operators Initiative (TOI) was established by a group of 15 major tour operators with support from WTO, UNEP and UNESCO in1999. At present, 25 tour operators from 17 different countries, catering for over 30 million tourists, are members of the TOI, committed to promote corporate social responsibility and sustainability at the destinations they operate in. One of the key tools being developed through an international working group is indicators for sustainability reporting. The working set of performance indicators covers several areas, including product management and development, internal management, supply chain management, customer relations and cooperation with destinations. Details on the program and its progress can be found at http://www.toinitiative.org/

The 47 tour operator's performance indicators are divided into categories that reflect the life cycle of the holiday product: from the planning stage, to the development and delivery of the product. The indicators have been grouped under five categories:

1. Product management and development (PMD) includes actions related to the choice of the destination as well as the type of services to be included (e.g., the use of train vs. plane).

2. Internal management (IM) reflects all the operations and activities that take place in the headquarters or country offices (e.g., use of office supplies, production of brochures, direct employment).

3. Supply chain management (SCM) addresses actions related to the selection and contracting of service providers.

4. Customer relations (CR) summarizes the actions taken to deal with customers, not only with regards to the responsibility to serve them and reply to their comments, but also the opportunity to provide information and raise consumer awareness regarding sustainability.

5. Cooperation with destination (D) includes all activities and decisions related to destinations that tour operators make beyond the production and delivery of their holiday package. This mainly includes efforts made by tour operators to engage in dialogues with destination operators about the impacts of tour packages, and philanthropic activities.

During the process of developing the supplement, the participants began to develop 'guidance notes' listing recommended best practices, as well as more specific instructions on the sustainability issues to be taken into account for three specific indicators (PMD3, SCM9 and D1). The guidance notes have not been officially reviewed and approved as part of the Global Reporting Initiative framework and represent the experience and recommendations of the TOI and the members of the Multi Stakeholders Working Group.

The program addresses both the key areas for attention by operators, and the kinds of monitoring or measurement which may be appropriate.

For complete details see the website. http://www.toinitiative.org/

For a concrete case application by a TOI member see Accor Hotels Case study, p. 327.

3.14 ➤ Baseline Issues and ➤ Baseline Indicators of Sustainable Tourism

The following table is a collection of the ➤ **Baseline issues** and the ➤ **Baseline indicators** covered in this part of the Guidebook. While this list is put forward as a short list of useful indicators extracted from the issues and indicators discussed above, users are urged not to stop at this list, but to follow through the procedures outlined in **Part Two** to create a custom list which is most likely to encompass all issues important to stakeholders in their destination. Some would argue that other issues and indicators should also be on the short list – issues such as health, security, environmental protection, employment with their corresponding indicators. As a consequence, users are urged to consider the importance of all the issues in the list, as well as those which are perhaps unique to their destination before settling on a final list for implementation in their destination.

➤ Baseline Issue	Suggested ➤ Baseline Indicator(s) See section on each issue for additional details and a longer list of potential indicators and examples
Local satisfaction with tourism	➤ Local satisfaction level with tourism (Questionnaire)
Effects of tourism on communities	➤ Ratio of tourists to locals (average and peak period/days) ➤ % who believes that tourism has helped bring new services or infrastructure. (questionnaire-based) ➤ Number and capacity of social services available to the community (% which are attributable to tourism)

➤ Baseline Issue	Suggested ➤ Baseline Indicator(s)
Sustaining tourist satisfaction	➤ Level of satisfaction by visitors (questionnaire-based) ➤ Perception of value for money (questionnaire-based) ➤ Percentage of return visitors
Tourism seasonality	➤ Tourist arrivals by month or quarter (distribution throughout the year) ➤ Occupancy rates for licensed (official) accommodation by month (peak periods relative to low season) and % of all occupancy in peak quarter or month) ➤ % of business establishments open all year ➤ Number and % of tourist industry jobs which are permanent or full-year (compared to temporary jobs)
Economic benefits of tourism	➤ Number of local people (and ratio of men to women) employed in tourism (also ratio of tourism employment to total employment) ➤ Revenues generated by tourism as % of total revenues generated in the community
Energy management	➤ Per capita consumption of energy from all sources (overall, and by tourist sector – per person day) ➤ Percentage of businesses participating in energy conservation programs, or applying energy saving policy and techniques ➤ % of energy consumption from renewable resources (at destinations, establishments)
Water availability and conservation	➤ Water use: (total volume consumed and litres per tourist per day) ➤ Water saving (% reduced, recaptured or recycled)
Drinking water quality	➤ Percentage of tourism establishments with water treated to international potable standards ➤ Frequency of water-borne diseases: number/percentage of visitors reporting water-borne illnesses during their stay
Sewage treatment (wastewater management)	➤ Percentage of sewage from site receiving treatment (to primary, secondary, tertiary levels) ➤ Percentage of tourism establishments (or accommodation) on treatment system(s)
Solid waste management (Garbage)	➤ Waste volume produced by the destination (tonnes) (by month) ➤ Volume of waste recycled (m3) / Total volume of waste (m3) (specify by different types) ➤ Quantity of waste strewn in public areas (garbage counts)
Development control	➤ Existence of a land use or development planning process, including tourism ➤ % of area subject to control (density, design, etc.)
Controlling use intensity	➤ Total number of tourist arrivals (mean, monthly, peak periods) ➤ Number of tourists per square metre of the site (e.g., at beaches, attractions), per square kilometre of the destination, - mean number/peak period average

Part 4

Destination Applications

Each destination has its own mix of assets and issues. This section is designed to enable destination managers to approach the development and use of indicators from the point of view of the characteristics of their destination, with reference to the issues which have been found to be important to them. **More detailed descriptions of the issues and indicators referenced here can be found in part** 3. Where ➢ **Baseline Issues** and ➢ **Baseline indicators** are referenced, they are shown in red. In some cases, variants on the baseline issues/indicators are used modified to reflect the specific application to destination conditions. Links are provided to the baseline issues and indicators. The other issues and indicators can be found in Part 3: use the index.

In addition to physical destination types, this chapter also contains examples of selected types of attractions which have a mix of issues similar to the other destinations (e.g., cruise ships and their ports, convention centres, theme parks, trail systems and built cultural sites.) Most local destinations will have a range of assets, activities and issues; for example, a mountainous island destination will likely have issues which occur in small islands, coastal zones and mountains; some examples of how indicators have been applied to issues in each of these three destination types may be of interest. Examples are also provided of how destinations of these types have applied indicators to their mix of issues. See also the Case Studies section (p. 327) which concrete additional examples. In each destination section, cross references to the relevant issues which are treated in greater detail in Part 3 are also provided.

4.1 Coastal Zones

Coastal Zones are the target of over three quarters of the world's tourism. Coastal tourism in the Mediterranean region alone is calculated by WTO at around 100 million tourist arrivals a year (WTO, 2001). Tourists seek coastal zones for several types of activities including:

1.   Beach activities - swimming, sunbathing, sports;

2.   Viewing and photography of landscapes, wildlife or coastal flora;

3.   Fishing;

4.   Boating;

5.   Touring - by motor vehicle, bicycle, riding animals, or on foot;

6.   Temperature (moderation).

Coastal Resort, Lianyungang, China

© 2004 World Tourism Organization - ISBN 92-844-0726-5

Coasts contain a variety of ecosystems which may be affected by tourist use, including fragile dune and beach systems, coastal wetlands and areas subject to erosion and adjacent marine ecosystems. Coastal zones which provide the point of contact between land and sea and between cultures also contain historic communities, ports, and coastal defences, all of which may be attractions.

The range of issues found in coastal destinations is broad, and may encompass nearly all of the issues noted in the previous section. Coastal zones have received a great amount of attention in the development of indicators for local municipalities and the tourism industry. The studies and workshops using the WTO methodology in Lake Balaton (Hungary), Villa Gesell (Argentina), Cozumel (Mexico), Prince Edward Island (Canada), Beruwala (Sri Lanka), Kukljica (Croatia) and Cyprus all provide examples of issues common to coastal zones, and have resulted in the development of indicators to respond to these issues. (See Kukljica case study p. 402).

Otway Sound Penguin Colony is a fragile ecosystem which is a popular destination for cruise ship visitors to Punta Arenas, Chile

Nearly all coastal destinations share the issue of control of shore use and building, issues of sea (or lake) water quality, issues of crowding of some specific localities in peak (beach) season, provision of docks and jetties, erosion, removal of solid waste from beachfront areas, identification and protection of fragile habitats or species, and seasonality of use. In addition, due to these issues - notably high use and limited seasons, shore destinations also tend to have issues related to employment, training, retention of services out of season, and provision of funding for infrastructure which is heavily used only for parts of the year. Beach areas as a specific subset of coastal zones are treated separately in the following pages.

While each destination will have its own unique set of issues, the following issues (and indicators) are worthy of consideration by managers of coastal destinations.

Issues	Suggested Indicator(s)
Damage to the natural environment of the shore zone	• % of coastal area in degraded condition; • Annual cost of repairs (or value of repairs needed).
Sustainability of key species (whales, seals, sea birds, fish, aquatic and coastal flora)	• Annual species counts for key species; • Level of effort for fish catch; • Number of incidents involving harassment of viewed species (e.g., whales, large mammals, etc).
Erosion of the shoreline	• Annual change in measured shore/beach area; • % shoreline considered to be in eroded state; • % shoreline subject to erosion; • Cost of erosion prevention and repair measures.
➤ **Use Intensity** (crowding) (see p. 192)	• ➤ **Tourist Numbers** Persons per hectare (or square metre) on key sites; • Visitors per linear Km of coastline (use where use of area is linear - such as coastal trail use or number of fishermen who line a shoreline.) (note: for annual averages, and peak day, peak month).
➤ **Seasonality** (even most tropical destinations have a hot, wet, stormy/monsoon or hurricane season when there is much lower use or when the comparative advantage relative to tourist origins is low) (see p. 111)	• ➤ **% of total tourists visiting in peak month, in peak quarter;** • Ratio of number of tourists in peak month to lowest month; • % of business establishments open all year; • ➤ **Occupancy levels (accommodation) around the year;** • % tourist industry jobs which are permanent or full-year; • % tourist industry jobs which are for less than 6 months.
Beach management (see following section for greater detail on beach destinations)	• Cost of beach cleaning/maintenance; • Level of revenue from users (managed beaches); • Blue Flag status, or other certification systems; • (see following section on further specifics for beaches).
Seawater (freshwater lake, river) contamination	• Number of days per year (month) when beach or shoreline is closed due to contamination (based on measurement of key contaminants such as faecal coliforms, heavy metals, pesticides, etc); • Number of shore contamination events per annum (e.g., oil spills, sewage pollution events); • Complaints by tourists.
Reef systems	• Species counts (number, populations); • ➤ **Number of visitors to the reef (Divers/snorkellers)\ per square metre of reef)** (or per square Km for large reef systems); • % of reef area in degraded condition (See Box 4.1 Reef Systems).
Perception of cleanliness/quality	• % of tourists who believe that the area is polluted, dirty or contaminated (exit questionnaires).
Safety and security (see p. 104, 109)	• Number of tourists affected by crime; • % of tourists who perceived threats to their safety or security while in the destination.

Box 4.1 Reef Systems

Coral reefs are a special case; fragile ecosystems with immense biodiversity which are a magnet for tourists. Reefs are vulnerable to changes in the water temperature and turbidity - major die offs of the coral and of resident species occur in response to fairly minor changes. As well, fishing and boating activity can destroy reef systems, particularly if there is dynamiting of fish, spills of fuels and bilge water or dragging of anchors.

Tourists themselves can cause damage, either directly by touching reefs, causing turbidity, and disturbing reef species, or indirectly through purchase of corals and other species taken from the reefs. Reef systems in many destination countries of the Caribbean, Red Sea coast or Asia-Pacific are impacted by tourism activity, yet are the principal tourism asset for the destinations. Strict control systems are now in place for some reefs but in all cases enforcement remains a challenge, particularly for users of the reef who are not part of guided tours.

Key issues for reef systems include: maintenance of biodiversity, reef health, mining of coral, fishing, management of tourism and other human activities on the reef, provision of protection and control services.

Indicators: Some of the indicators which have proven important to the managers of reef systems considering tourism are the following:

* **% of reef system considered to be degraded (biological surveys)**;

* ➤ **% of reef area under protection**;

* **Biological diversity of the reef (species counts)**;

* ➤ **Number of visitors to the reef per square metre of reef** (or per square Km for large reef systems) maximum and average, per type of users: snorkel, diving, boating, sport fishing, etc);

* **% of visitors to the reef who are guided**;

* **Number of boats per day on/near the reef**;

* **Number of dive operators adapting environmental policies, promoting codes of conduct for divers**;

* **Number of incidents of anchor damage, spills, etc per month**;

* **Number of control/enforcement officers patrolling reef area**;

* **Funds generated for reef protection from user fees (tourists, operator licences)**;

Reef Snorkelling, Bonaire.The entire coast of Bonaire in the Netherlands Antilles is a marine protected area

* **Funds allocated for reef protection from public sources, donor and development   agencies, private funds, etc.**

Reefs are the main aquatic focus for sports and ecotourism, experiencing growing numbers of tourists worldwide. Indicators on the health of reef ecosystems are very important for sustainability of these tourist destinations and the global environment as well.

Further references:

* Reef Check Guide to Coral Reef Monitoring at www.ReefCheck.org (click- methods, indicators - indicator species)

* The International Coral Reef Initiative (ICRI) http://www.icriforum.org

4.2 Beach Destinations and Sites

With growing numbers of beach users, many destination managers are faced with a broad range of issues which, along with many of the other issues affecting heavily used sites, have particular implications for beaches. The focus of this section is on managed beaches at a more site-specific scale than the coastal zone section above, where a single destination may contain several distinct beaches under different levels of development and control. Thus these indicators can often be used for comparative benchmarking for different beaches within a single destination, as well as for comparison with other, often competing destinations.

Issues of concern in beach destinations include:

Issues	Suggested Indicator(s)
Sustaining the beach area (limiting loss of sand, erosion)	• Annual gain/loss of beach area; • Volume of sand imported per month/year for those beaches where sand importation is done; • Costs of erosion-protection measures (e.g. sea walls.).
➤ **Use Intensity** (density of visitors/intensity of use of the beach area) (see p. 192).	• ➤ **Number of persons per hectare (or square metre) on the beach** (for annual averages, and peak day, peak month); • ➤ **Number of persons per hectare (or square metre)** of publicly accessible beach, and for concession areas, private areas.
Access	• Number of local residents using beach; • % of beach area open to and accessible by local residents; • Cost (in local hours wages) of admission to beaches where there is a charge.
➤ **Seasonality** (even tropical beach destinations have a peak season and lower seasons with less use due to heat, storms etc.)	• ➤ **% of total tourists visiting in peak month;** • ➤ **Number of tourists on peak day);** (See also the ➤ **Seasonality** issues for Coastal Zones p. 249 and Climate Change p. 155).
Beach contamination	• Cost of beach cleaning/maintenance; • ➤ **Volume of garbage collected (by month, week, peak day)** (p. 173); • ➤ **Garbage levels on beach** (counts); • % tourists who found the beach dirty (questionnaire).
Seawater contamination	• Number of days per year (month) when beach is closed due to contamination; • Number of shore contamination events per annum (e.g., oil spills, sewage pollution events).
➤ **Tourist satisfaction** (Sustaining the image/quality of the beach)	• % of tourists who believe that the area is polluted, dirty or contaminated (exit questionnaires); • % tourists who believe the beach is clean; • % tourists who consider the beach to be good quality; • % tourists who are bothered by noise.
Provision of services	• Number of toilets and showers per beach user (peak day, average day in peak month); • Number of restaurants/food concessions per tourist.

Issues	Suggested Indicator(s)
Costs and benefits	× Level of revenue from users (managed beaches); × Ratio of costs of management and maintenance to revenues; × Number employed (on site, adjacent).
Control (behaviour, animals, access)	× Number of incidents reported to beach managers classified by type (e.g. glass cuts, harassment, drownings, rescues); × Number of dogs (and other animals where applicable) on the beach; × For controlled access beaches, % users who have entered without paying.
Certification and Standards	× Blue Flag status of beach (see box 4.2 p. 253) % beaches in destination with Blue Flag or equivalent independent certification.

Publicly visible indicators (like the Blue Flag flown on beaches achieving the standard) can have an immediate and significant impact on the choices made by tourists. Destinations which fail to obtain the certification, or lose the certification, often experience direct repercussions which may be reflected in changes measured by many of the other indicators suggested for beach destinations (e.g., tourist numbers, jobs).

Blue flag at Sunny Day Beach Black Sea Coast, Bulgaria. Co-ordination Foundation for Environmental Education (FEE)

Box 4.2 Blue Flag Beaches

The Blue Flag appearing on European and some Caribbean beaches is a visible signal that the beach meets an internationally agreed, and independent standard for:

* Water Quality;
* Environmental Education and Information;
* Environmental Management;
* Safety and Services.

The flag is renewed each season. Inspections are done without prior notification by independent certifiers.

For each of the above standards there is a defined set of criteria to be met. These include such elements as providing regular checks on sea water quality, regular cleaning of the beach, control of prohibited or restricted activities, beach guards, access for the disabled, and sanitary facilities (see the Blue Flag Website for a complete list of criteria and of beaches meeting the standard in each member country. http://www.blueflag.org) The application of the criteria is slightly different in Europe and the Caribbean to reflect different regulatory regimes and environmental conditions. The system is currently being extended to countries in other regions as well (e.g. in South Africa, Chile).

4.3 Small Islands

Many of the issues facing tourism on small islands are similar to those found in coastal zones and in small communities, but these are often amplified on small islands. Islands are often isolated - ecologically, culturally, and economically. As a result, the natural and cultural resources may be unique, limited in extent, and vulnerable. The image of islands draws many tourists to take advantage of these characteristics which are important assets for tourism. Because of small size, and often small indigenous populations, small islands can be particularly vulnerable to the impacts of tourism, particularly if it is large in scale. For most small island nations, tourism is their principal source of foreign exchange and a main source of GDP and employment. While an island may provide a visible unit for planning and management, its boundaries also can be barriers, limiting access to tourism flows and basic resources such as water, food or fuel.

Key issues which tend to be of particular importance to small island destinations include the following:

1.   Intensity of tourism: This is particularly important for smaller islands and specific sites such as beaches or cultural sites on islands where tourists concentrate.

2.   Seasonality: Particularly for sun-sea-and-sand destinations or for islands which have cold winter temperatures, or storm seasons such as typhoons, cyclones or hurricanes. Some island communities have only seasonal access or much reduced access in low season.

3.   Access: Conditions of access influence movements of tourists and locals and supply of goods and resources. Some destinations have reduced air or boat service outside peak season.

4.   Water supply: Many islands have constrained water supply. Dry islands rely on a freshwater lens which can be easily depleted or contaminated. There are cases when import of water is needed, especially when the dry season coincides with the high tourism season and water demand. This may be a serious constraint on tourism activities.

5. Sewage treatment and solid waste (garbage) management: Like all coastal destinations, small islands and surrounding marine ecosystems can be adversely affected by contamination from sewage or waste. The smallest islands may be so small that on-site treatment is not feasible. In some island destinations, solid waste is regularly shipped away for disposal.

6. Energy. Most small islands must rely on fossil fuel import for electricity generation and for any other fuel requirements. Transfer of fuels from tankers is nearly impossible to do without some spillage, affecting shores, reefs etc.

7. Access to natural resources (fish, agricultural land, wood). Small islands tend to have limited natural resources which may already be near capacity of use.

8. Retention of benefits on the island (See Leakage p. 117): Many small islands must import nearly everything that tourists consume. Currency leakage can be nearly 100%, and ownership and control of resources by non-residents can be an important issue.

9. Out-migration to places with greater economic opportunity (particularly by youth) is a frequent issue, similar to that found in many small communities.

10. Preservation of unique cultural traditions.

11. Climate change is of particular concern to small islands, affecting the resource base, infrastructure and access. In many low islands, the entire island is within the storm surge zone for extreme storm events, and vulnerable to even small rises in sea level.

Note that the destination issues found in the sections on Coastal Zones (p. 247) and on Small and Traditional Communities (p. 281) will also be of interest to island destinations. Please consult the corresponding issue sections on the above points.

Aerial view of Mexcaltitan, Mexico. This tiny island in a coastal wetland not far from Puerto Vallarta Mexico has begun to experience increasing visits as it finds itself featured in tourist guides and tour itineraries.

Issues	Suggested indicator(s)
➤ **Controlling use intensity on the island** (see p. 192)	⁙ ➤ **Ratio of tourists to locals (average, peak day or month);** ⁙ ➤ **Tourists per square metre or (Km2) (see also coastal zones);** ⁙ ➤ **Persons per hectare (or square metre) on key sites;** (note for annual averages, and peak day, peak month); ⁙ % total jobs which are in tourism sector.
➤ **Seasonality** (see p. 111)	⁙ ➤ **% total tourism which occurs in peak month (or season);** ⁙ % employment in tourism which is full-time/full year; ⁙ % accommodation and services open all year; ⁙ ➤ **Accommodation occupancy rate throughout the year.**
Access	⁙ Ratio of transport volume peak month vs. lowest month; ⁙ Price of transport on/off island(as % hourly local wage for locals to get to island); ⁙ Price of travel to island from main tourist source; ⁙ Duration of travel to island from main tourist source (hours).
➤ **Water availability** (see p. 165)	⁙ % total developed water supply consumed; ⁙ % total known potential natural supply consumed; ⁙ ➤ **Volume of water consumed by tourists as % of total consumption (also use per person per day for tourists and for locals) ;** ⁙ Number of months/days each year with water shortages; ⁙ Cost of water per cubic metre (also consider cost of new supply for each additional cubic metre).
➤ **Sewage treatment** (p. 171) ➤ **Solid waste management** (p. 173)	⁙ Percentage of sewage receiving treatment (primary, secondary, tertiary); ⁙ Number of contamination events per annum; ⁙ ➤ **Volume of garbage collected** (pXXX); ⁙ Percentage of solid waste recycled; ⁙ % put in suitable landfills; ⁙ % shipped away (outside destination).
➤ **Energy** (see p. 152)	⁙ Percentage of energy supply which is imported to the island; ⁙ Number of supply shortages (brown outs) per month/annum; ⁙ Cost per KwH of electricity; ⁙ ➤ **Energy use by tourism industry as % of total ;** ⁙ ➤ **Energy use per day by tourists relative to locals.**
Access to natural resources (fish, agricultural land, wood)	⁙ Percentage of island territory (and of shoreline) in tourism use, extension of agricultural and protected areas; ⁙ Percentage of wood, food consumed on the island which is produced locally (if possible separate local/tourist use).
Retention of benefits on the island (import substitution, currency leakage, ownership and control of resources)	⁙ Percentage of wood, food consumed on the island which is produced locally (if possible separate local/tourist use); ⁙ % of land/shoreline which is owned by non-residents; ⁙ % tourist infrastructure owned by/managed by island residents; ⁙ ➤ **Number and % of employees from the local community.**

Issues	Suggested indicator(s)
Out-migration	• %migration (in, out) annually. (also calculate for youth); • Total population resident year round.
Retention of unique cultural traditions	• % speaking language(s) of tourists (See Small and Traditional Communities p. 281) (See ➢ **Effects of Tourism on Communities** p.. 57).
Climate change (see p. 155) (Note: the country's Initial Communication on Climate Change may identify specific issues for the island, and some indicators)	• % of island which is outside the storm surge zone; • % of tourist infrastructure (number or value) which is located within the storm surge zone; • Level of beach erosion (% of coastline eroded); • Reef health (e.g. coral bleaching) (See Box 4.1 on reef systems).
See also coastal zone destination in this section. Also see beach issue in part 3.	For expanded discussion of many of these indicators, see the corresponding issues section in Part 3.

Visitors to Panama's San Blas Islands use local dugouts to reach the tiny islands, carrying their supplies with them.

4.4 Destinations in Desert and Arid Areas

Deserts and semi-desert ecosystems cover about 20% of the surface area of the planet. Tourists are drawn to deserts for their physical beauty (the Namib), specific geological formations (Ayers Rock, Devils Tower) remoteness (the Gobi, the Empty Quarter) and the chance to visit physical extremes (parts of the Atacama have never recorded rainfall). Tourists are also drawn to deserts because of the cultural history and archaeological sites found there (Petra, Mohenjo Daro, Abu Simbel, Hopi Cliff dwellings of Arizona), as well as experiencing living cultures (like nomad communities). Many of the most attractive sites for tourists are remote; in fact the preservation of many of the relics of past civilizations may have depended on this remoteness and the fact that decomposition of organic material is very slow in the dry climate. Modern transportation and air conditioning has meant that remote desert destinations are more accessible to large numbers of tourists. As well, many seek desert conditions for reasons associated with health (allergies, respiratory problems). Increasingly, tourism developments in water-short environments include such water consuming features as golf courses, lawns and gardens and swimming pools. Major desert resorts such as Hurghada Egypt or Las Vegas must import water long distances to satisfy consumption. Desert regions are also particularly vulnerable to climate change which may affect water supply and contribute to greater desertification. (See Climate change p. 155).

Issues likely to be of importance to tourism in desert environments include the following:

* Water supply (water tends to be the pre-eminent limiting factor);
* Impact of tourism activities on desert flora and fauna;
* Soil erosion and compaction (See photo of Giza sandstorm below);
* Energy for heating and cooling (as desert environments tend to have both extremes);
* Design suited to the desert environment;
* Health issues for tourists associated with heat and dehydration.

While the baseline indicators will be of interest to managers of tourism in desert environments, those indicators relating specifically to the climatic conditions will be more important than in most other destinations (For a similar situation see Box 4.3 on tourism in Arctic and alpine environments).

Sandstorm at Giza, Egypt

Issues	Suggested Indicator(s)
➤ **Water supply**	▫ % of local natural supply capacity used; ▫ ➤ **Water use per capita per day (tourists, locals);** ▫ Distance to nearest practical source of new water; ▫ Cost per cubic metre for current and for new supply; ▫ ➤ **% of water supply used by tourism industry;** ▫ Number of days in year/season with water supply shortage; ▫ See ➤ **Water supply** issue section (p. 165) for additional useful indicators and the Climate Change issue (p. 155).
Impact on flora and fauna soil erosion and compaction	▫ Total area considered degraded due to tourist/visitor use (may include area trampled, eroded, affected by off-road vehicles).
➤ **Energy supply**	▫ ➤ **Per capita consumption of energy;** ▫ Energy use per capita for heating or cooling; ▫ Cost per tourist day for energy; ▫ See ➤ **Energy** (p. 152) re energy use from different sources.
Design of buildings and facilities	▫ % buildings incorporating desert design elements (e.g., ventilation, high ceilings, thick walls, etc); ▫ % landscaping using xerophytes (desert plants). ▫ See managing visual impacts of tourism facilities and infrastructure (p. 185).
Health issues in desert climate	▫ Number of incidences of dehydration, sun or heat stroke, hypo or hyperthermia reported.
Impact (positive and negative) on isolated communities	▫ ➤ **% of local residents in desert community who believe they benefit from tourism ;** ▫ ➤ **Number of local people employed in tourism** (p. 119); ▫ ➤ **See Effects of Tourism on Communities** (p. 57) and ➤ **Economic Benefits of Tourism** (p. 128).

Luxury hotel near Petra Jordan blends into the village and uses vernacular architecture, thick walls, high ceilings, cool water flowing under floors. There are no powered forms of air conditioning or heating - the hotel takes advantage of the natural temperature flux to keep each dwelling comfortable. Note: The lower half of the photo is the 200 room hotel.

4.5 Mountain Destinations

Mountains have always been a target for tourism. On all continents, mountains are a draw for those who seek vistas, adventure, cooler climates in summer, sport and the many cultural assets of mountains - built to take advantage of the height and often isolation.

The world's mountains contain immense variety - both vertically and horizontally. Ecological conditions can vary within a few metres of altitude. Cultures in adjacent valleys may be very different. In the past, mountains were often considered to be the periphery, where natural ecosystems were near the edge of the conditions which would support them and cultural communities at the margins of the resources needed for sustainability. Tourism has significantly altered the economics of many mountain regions, as this very variety and unique relationship to resources and ecosystems has become an asset.

Issues of particular concern to mountain environments include the following:

1. Loss or degradation of flora and fauna due to tourism activity;

2. Physical erosion caused by infrastructure construction and impact of tourist use including cutting and use of trails, off road vehicle activities;

3. Visual pollution/aesthetics due to construction, extractive activity, deforestation;

4. Access, particularly to fragile sites, protected areas;

5. Management of solid waste (garbage);

6. Impacts of activities on water quality/watershed management;

7. Impact on small, and/or culturally distinctive communities (see the section specifically about this type of destination p. 281);

8. Ecotourism and adventure tourism activity - much of which focuses on mountainous areas;

9. Seasonality - particularly for seasonal sports/adventure/winter tourism dependent destinations.

Meteora, Greece. Historic monasteries
top the peaks

Issues	Suggested indicators
Loss of flora and fauna due to tourism activity	• Counts for key species (e.g. raptors, mammals, native trees, flowers); • Road kill counts by species (particularly where tourist traffic is the main user of roads); • Frequency of sightings of key species (from outfitters, guides, or exit surveys); • ➤ **Area protected (to different levels of protection)** (p. 147).
Erosion	• % of surface in eroded state (can be categorized as site disturbance due to tourist activity - compaction, denuding and erosion from other uses such as clear cutting, road construction); • % of surface without tree or shrub cover (differentiate natural and human/tourist sources if possible); • Turbidity readings from streams.
Visual pollution (may affect decisions to visit or return - see the Arches case p. 342)	• % of visible slopes without tree or shrub cover; • Tourist opinion of state of vistas (see exit Q. (p. 491) and see indicators sections on visual pollution, perception of destination quality). Image may be more important to decisions than actual physical state. See also ➤ **Sustaining Tourist Satisfaction** (p. 86) and exit questionnaire questions on overall image of destination.
Access	• Cost of entry(for controlled access areas such as parks or protected areas) or transport access expressed in hours work at local wage; • Perception of ease of access to key sites (both visitors and locals) using questionnaire methodology; • % nationals (or regional residents for larger nations) who have visited the destination in the past year; • Traffic levels (see Transportation p. 210); • Price of real estate in destination (many mountain communities lack living space and have elevated pricing).
➤ **Solid waste management**	• ➤ **Waste volume produced by the destination (tonnes)by month** (p. 175); • Visitor perception of level of litter; • Local perception of level of litter (subset:- litter attributable to tourists).
Impacts of activities on water quality	• % local streams, lakes which are contaminated by sewage; • ➤ **% sewage from key sites which receives treatment to meet standards** (note standards referenced in section on ➤ **Sewage Treatment issue.**) (p. 171); • % area reserved as protected watersheds (see also erosion above).
➤ **Effects of tourism on communities**	• ➤ For small and traditional communities, ratio of tourists to locals (by month, season, peak day) See also Small Communities (p. 281); • % hunting or fishing in destination by locals, tourists; • ➤ **Local satisfaction with tourism** . (p. 56) (questionnaire)
➤ **Economic benefits**	• ➤ **Local employment in tourism and protection** (guiding, accommodation, park management, rehabilitation); • Employment in tourism and protection as % of all employment, (or as % of resource extraction sector); • See ➤ **Economic benefits** (p. 128).
➤ **Seasonality**	• ➤ **% total tourism which occurs in peak month (or season);** • ➤ **% employment in tourism which is full-time/full year;** • ➤ **% business establishments open all year** (accommodation and services). • See ➤ **Seasonality** (p. 111).

The use of these indicators will normally require measurement over time. Where tourism is not the only user of a mountain system, one challenge will be to determine what role tourism plays in degradation or impacts on ecosystems. Where tourism is the main activity, studies may be used to identify control areas for comparison - where tourism activity is limited or where it is prohibited. The use of the indicators will assist in the identification of trends - whether considered positive or negative which may be of concern to communities. For example, rising real estate prices may be viewed as positive by current recreational owners but negative by a destination that wishes to keep young families or retain a rural character.

As with other ecosystems, measures of levels of protection and management will also be of use. (See the issue sections on these in Part 3) With regard to ski areas, a good point of reference is the Sustainable Slopes Charter which identifies key issues and environmental initiatives for the US ski industry. http://www.nsaa.org/nsaa2002/_environmental_charter.asp?mode=ss.

Kangaroo crossing sign in Thredbo, Australia. Mountain wildlife is one of the key attractions for tours to this destination.

Box 4.3 Arctic and Alpine environments

Arctic and Alpine environments share many of the same issues of fragility found in deserts and mountain ecosystems. As tourists reach mountain tops in increasing numbers (on foot or lifted by an increasing range of mechanical methods) and as adventure tourism companies expand their offers in the Arctic and Antarctic, their effects on these remote ecosystems also expand. At the same time, visitors are also exposed to risks beyond those found in less hostile areas. The ability to provide rescue in such areas may also be limited. Some jurisdictions require a cash bond from adventure travellers which can be recovered only if they return intact without any rescue (in some cases with all their equipment and garbage).

The key issues for arctic and alpine tourism relate to reduction of the impact of tourism on these fragile systems, like those of Huang Shan (China's Yellow Mountains)

Arctic and alpine ecosystems are very fragile, easily disturbed, and take a very long time to rehabilitate. Plants may take decades to recover from a simple trampling. Tire tracks made a century ago can still be seen in the permafrost. The re-establishment of vegetation may take a century if it is disturbed or removed. Some alpine systems house unique and relic populations of flora and fauna found nowhere else. Where there are human settlements, these too are usually small and widely separated, and often, associated with their remoteness, are culturally unique.

The same indicators identified for mountain systems, desert systems, and fragile ecosystems will likely be useful. In addition, the following indicators should also be considered:

* Average size of tourism group or party (in the case of cruises, the number allowed ashore at one time);

* % of visitors accompanied by trained guides;

* Number of tourists lost or injured each season;

* Number of rescues, annual cost of rescues;

* % of rescue cost recovered from those rescued;

* Area of degraded vegetation attributable to tourist use (e.g., alpine meadows, disturbed permafrost areas) (% of surface area of key ecosystems disturbed);

* % of material taken in which is brought back out;

* Distance to nearest source of fuels/supplies;

* Value of contribution by the tourists or operators to the maintenance and protection of the destination (possibly through user fees, landing fees, access charges or other contributions).

See also the Antarctic case study (p. 338).

4.6 Natural and Sensitive Ecological Sites

Natural sites are often prime tourist attractions, which receive varying levels of visitation depending on the conditions of the broader tourist region where they are located. Tourists are drawn to large waterfalls such as Niagara Falls, Victoria Falls or Iguazú Falls; or to much smaller natural systems with unique ecological conditions or which serve as habitat for a specific species (e.g. the Proboscis Monkey in Sukau River in Borneo, Malaysia or the unique ecosystems of the wetland estuaries of the Iberá (Argentina). Many such sites are sensitive to tourist use. Being identified as an ecologically unique space represents a challenge for the development of the tourism around it, since tourism has significant potential to negatively impact upon the site or to contribute positively to its sustainability; this depends greatly on the type of management and enforcement in place.

The unique features of a special ecosystem are the environmental conditions and flora and fauna found there. From the point of view of tourism, the industry has its own needs often involving development that will enhance its capacity to offer tourism activities at the site. These may be required in order to convert a resource of great ecological value into something attractive and accessible to visitors. (Viñals et al., 2002). This double component (ecological value - tourist value) will need to be negotiated at the outset of the planning process of a tourist site, to ensure sustainable tourism development without harming sensitive ecosystems.

The indicators for monitoring and control of a sensitive ecological site should include, as a first priority, measurements of changes in the ecosystem (natural processes, and man-made impacts). With respect to the key ecological assets it is very important to compile an inventory of natural resources in the area to help understand the key elements, to define their ecological value and to be able to establish warning systems.

If there are no present activities or plans for tourism use or recreational purposes, the existence of a good indicators and monitoring program on ecological assets will be of potential future use to tourism, should the site become an attraction for tourists in future.

Most organizations concerned with the designation of sites as protected areas require that a basic management system and baseline information regarding assets and potential attractions of any site be done before the declaration of protected status- whether for ecological reasons or for tourist use. Examples of this are national parks, monuments and natural reserves, among others.

Some criteria for appraisal of ecological resources relative to recreational value can be measured through indicators that are tied to perceived impacts (Viñals et al., 2002). Using these measurements, if the value of the indicators varies positively or negatively, the attractiveness to tourists as well as the ecological value can be seen to have been altered. Therefore, it can be emphasized that it is important to develop indicators for the sustainability of tourism in unique ecological places: including indicators related to ecological values, measures of tourist values (attraction) and indicators relating to levels of tourist management. The following list is based in part on an example from Spain

The Tatras, an alpine mountain range rising directly from the plains on the Slovakia, Poland border is protected by national park status in both countries. It is one of the most important regional destinations for tourism.

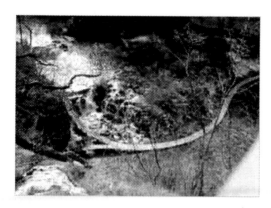

Plitivice National Park in Croatia protects a unique ecosystem of linked lakes and waterfalls, with walkways for tourist access.

(See Albufera de Valencia case p. 330) and identifies a comprehensive list of indicators which address the key values associated with natural sites. (Viñals et al. 2002)

Issues	Suggested indicators
Ecological Value	
Representativeness: (whether the resource has characteristics typical of the ecosystem)	• Nº of species typical of the area present at the site (and numbers of individuals); • Nº of unique or rare species present at the site (and numbers of individuals).
Uniqueness (rarity of the site relative to group (e.g., wetland, desert)	• % of site area occupied by rare or unique species; • Nº of individuals in the population of rare and unique species; • % of endemic species at the site.
Level of site protection	• ➤ **% of area subject to control** (IUCN categories); • Recognition by international programmes (e.g. UNESCO World Heritage Site or Biosphere Reserve, RAMSAR Convention) (Note: international recognitions can be also important indicators of tourism value, as signs of uniqueness and ecological value); • See Parks and Protected Areas (p. 269).
Tourism Value	
Fragility: degree of susceptibility to impacts related to tourism and recreational activity.	• Nº of species and endemic species; • Nº of species and endemic endangered species; • Populations of every species; • Temporal rate of variation of species.
Tourism feasibility: (access, easements, traditional uses, management capacity (to ensure its protection and/or enhancement), economic viability restoration costs, operation and maintenance costs.	• ➤ **Level of acceptance of the tourism activity by the local community** (% positive) (p.56); • Inventory of attractions (distinguished natural features, including flora and fauna, landscapes); • Nº of observations of fauna or flora per circuit and per season; • Nº of days of observation of the natural features per season (e.g., Aurora Borealis, wildflowers in bloom, whale mating, migratory birds); • Profitability of tourism activity at the site (% return on investment, net incomes - visitor fees, concession fees, fees for guiding and other services, sales of handicrafts and other items, etc.)

Tourism Value

	• Management capacity: presence of a management body; plan; site restoration and regeneration programmes. (% of site covered); • Cost of acquisition/protecting/restoration of the site; • Estimated time to full restoration of the site (for degraded sites).
Educational-interpretive value: (value of the site for educating and awareness raising - natural sciences, history and local traditions.)	• N° of opportunities for interpretation and education at the site (existence of guided visits, printed self-explanatory materials, interpretive and informative panels, trails, interpretation centres, farm schools, nature schools, educational itineraries, etc.); • Natural and educational value given to the site by educators (local, provincial, national, international organizations), by NGOs, by Tour Operators. (Subjective ratings - use questionnaire).
Accessibility: refers to the ease with which the place can be visited.	• N° of access routes in good condition for tourism use, (paths, motorized, airstrips, boat access, etc); • % of site accessible to those with disabilities (see Accessibility (p. 90).
Attractiveness: includes parameters of an aesthetic, emotional, or perceptual nature.	• Aesthetic/perceptual evaluation by the visitor (See Exit questionnaire Annex C5 p. 491); • Presence of key ecological features of the site in media and tourism promotional materials.
Tourism carrying capacity of the site: the site's capability to serve as the venue of tourism/ recreational activity.	• N° of visitors acceptable, according to the perception of the visitors themselves. (see Annex C 5 and Arches case p. 342.); • N° of visitors acceptable, according to the capacity of the equipment and facilities of the site. (depends on capacity studies establishing limits); • N° of visitors acceptable, re capacity estimates; • N° of visitors / n° of individuals per species.

Site management

Tourism management plan for the site	• ➢ **Existence of a tourism management plan for the site (also % of site covered by plan,)** (p. 204).
Regulation of the site	• Existence of rules to regulate construction, hunting and fishing, extraction of natural resources (e.g. logging) at the site (and % of key resources included); • % of site with regulated zoning /controls, extent of tourism use zones.
➢ **Use Intensity**	• ➢ **N° and origin of visitors to the site per season (day, month)** (p. 192); • Average length of stay; • N° of tour operators with permit to operate at site.
Tourism management capacity of the site	• Annual expenditure on management and control; • % of resources actually assigned / resources requested by the administration for the management of the site.
Tourism's contribution to site conservation	• Visitor fees; • Concession fees; • Donations from visitors and tour operators; • Fees from guiding and other services; • In-kind contributions (e.g. equipments, volunteers); • Sale of goods (e.g. informative materials, handicrafts, equipment).

Management of spaces for tourism use

Trails and paths (see destination section on trails and routes p. 274)	• % soil loss on trails (Example: depth and/or width of trails does not increase more than 5% per year at the most fragile sectors); • N° of soil erosion points along trails and vehicle paths; • % of protected area in eroded or degraded state; • Vehicular congestion (average travel times on main access routes during high season / during low season).
Camping areas and accommodation	• Area or campsites per tent; • N° of campfires allowed for camping areas; • N° of erosion points in camping areas; • Total density of camping use (persons per m2 in peak season; • Number of campers per toilet; • Number of beds (other accommodation); • % occupancy of camping sites and accommodation.

Community participation

Local community participation	• % of local products and services consumed by tourism (at least 70% of goods and services acquired for tourism operation of the site from local enterprises or individuals); • Employment of local residents in site management and tourism operations (numbers, income levels); • Level of satisfaction of residents regarding tourism development in the area - particularly regarding that targeting natural systems; • Level of assistance to local environmental awareness: n° of local awareness-raising actions (courses, meetings, promotion of content in the curriculum of the local educational system, etc.).

Ecosystem management

Water quality	• Water quality: contaminants in surface and ground water (See ➤ Drinking Water Quality p. 169); • Turbidity of streams.
Air, noise pollution	• Noise pollution due to motors: visitors perceiving annoying motor noises (cars, launches, motorcycles, planes, generators, etc.) in natural areas (see Noise p. 183).
Impacts on flora and fauna	• Biodiversity index of flora and fauna; • Population sizes of key species; • N° of introduced species (exotic fauna and/or flora) (% of total); • Level of illegal hunting and fishing at the site during high season (loss of animals, number of incidents); • Loss of species due to use as tourism souvenirs (% of native species used as tourism souvenirs); • Numbers of fauna run over by traffic (road kills) during high season (ratio to low season rates); • % increase in infectious diseases (local and introduced) to flora and fauna of the site; • Frequency of species census; • % variation of species; • See also Parks and Protected Areas (p. 269).

Ecosystem management	
Aesthetics	◦ Amount of litter in natural areas (seasonality of waste can relate to tourist numbers) (See ➢ **Solid waste management** (p. 173); ◦ Presence of visual barriers, visual pollution (use questionnaire to determine impact if visual barriers are considered important); ◦ Existence of viewpoints· ◦ Scenic valuation by tourists (perception, questionnaire).

Visitor satisfaction	
Visitors	◦ ➢ **Level of satisfaction of visitors** (see questionnaire Annex C 5 p. 491).
Intermediaries	◦ Opinion of local Tour Operators (% of operators with favourable opinion) Use operator questionnaire; ◦ Opinion of foreign Tour Operators (% with favourable opinion).

Note that many of these indicators will be useful in all types of destinations where ecological sites are part of the assets of the destination. See also the issues related to Protecting critical ecosystems (p. 147), and Management of tourism adjacent to protected areas. (p. 272).

For further information see Viñals et al, 2002, Rivas, 2000, and the websites of the Fundacion Vida Silvestre Argentina refugios@vidasilvestre.org.ar, www.vidasilvestre.org.ar

Kaieteur Falls, Guyana: A sensitive site visited by tourists seeking ecotourism experiences

4.7 Ecotourism Destinations

Ecotourism embraces the principles of sustainable tourism, concerning the economic, social and environmental impacts of tourism. It also embraces the following specific principles which distinguish it from the wider concept of sustainable tourism:

*   Contributes actively to the conservation of natural and cultural heritage;

*   Includes local and indigenous communities in its planning, development and operation, and contributing to their well-being;

*   Interprets the natural and cultural heritage of the destination to visitors;

*   Lends itself better to independent travellers, as well as to organized tours for small size groups. (Quebec Declaration on Ecotourism).

The main output of the World Summit of Ecotourism (2002, Quebec City, Canada) was the Quebec Declaration on Ecotourism, containing a set of recommendations to international, private, public and academic institutions, NGOs and community organizations in relation to development of ecotourism. In these recommendations the monitoring of ecotourism activities is inherent and the importance of indicators development is expressly emphasized at governmental levels of management and in the design of certification systems.

See website at: http://www.world-tourism.org/sustainable/IYE/quebec/index.htm

From the perspective of indicators, the focus needs to be on the following elements of ecotourism:

1. **Conservation of the natural environment at ecotourism destinations and areas:** The fact that ecotourism normally takes place mainly in relatively un-disturbed natural areas, which are sensitive to possible impacts by tourism activity, implies that precautions need to be taken to manage tourism. The indicators therefore are important as management tools. (See particularly the sections on Protecting Critical Ecosystems (p. 147), Tourism's Contribution to Nature Conservation (p. 123)Natural and Sensitive Ecological Sites (p. 263), and Carrying capacity, (p. 309);

2. **Relations with the local community, preservation of cultural assets:** An important part of ecotourism activities is experiencing the traditional lifestyles of communities that inhabit the natural areas. These small, traditional, often indigenous, communities are highly sensitive to the socio-cultural impacts of tourism. As is mentioned in other sections of this book, the active participation and agreement of local communities in the management of ecotourism on a continuing basis is fundamental. The participation of communities in the definition of indicators and monitoring processes is essential as tourism affects their daily life and they are those who can best evaluate impacts and decide the level of ecotourism activities that meets their expectations. (see also the issue sections on Community Involvement (p. 83) and Effects of Tourism on Communities (p. 57), as well as the Uganda Heritage Trails (p. 440) and India Corbett National Park (p. 386) case studies on participatory monitoring and planning;

3. **Operations:** Ecotourism operations are usually expected to minimise negative impacts upon the natural and socio-cultural environment, and contribute to the conservation of natural areas. For this reason activities are normally, but not exclusively, being organised by specialist tour operators for small groups. The level of sustainability depends on the operating practices and on the quality of the offered service. Indicators can help measure achievement of an operator's own standards of operation, or benchmarked standards (like in a certification system), and can assist in achieving control of impacts. (see also the Cape Breton case (p. 355) and on ➤ **Controlling Use Intensity** p. 192);

4. **Information and interpretation:** One of the basic elements of ecotourism is knowledge of nature or culture that the visitor obtains through the interpretive experience. Professional interpretation services (e.g. guides, interpretation centers and trails) are essential parts of a quality ecotourism

experience and contribute to nature conservation through awareness-raising. Poor information can lead to negative impacts on destinations, and poor interpretation can cause client dissatisfaction. Measurement of quality of information is therefore an important step. (See Community Involvement and Awareness p. 83);

5. **Marketing and management of ecotourism:** Ecotourism, to provide the expected benefits to conservation and community development, has to be an economically viable activity, therefore indicators and a good knowledge of the ecotourism market (demand and offer) are also contributing factors to sustainability. (See also Marketing p. 228, and Protection of Image p. 236);

6. **Safety for ecotourism activities:** Ecotourism activities are often organized in remote areas with specific conditions (e.g. rainforests, deserts, mountains) and involve physical activities (such as trekking, canoeing, etc.). According to a study on factors central to sustainable ecotourism (Bassotti, 2003), safety of the activity is placed second in importance to clients, after the protection of the environment. Indicators that respond to safety and security of ecotourism destinations and operations are therefore important. (see also the issue sections on Local Public Safety p. 109 and Tourist Security p. 104).

In many ways, ecotourism is a microcosm of all the issues of sustainable tourism, but focussed in a more concentrated way on specific ecosystems and traditional cultures. As a consequence, all of the issues and indicators contained in this Guidebook may be of use, particularly those covered in the section on Natural and Sensitive Ecological Sites (p. 263) and on Small and Traditional Communities (p. 281).

For more information on ecotourism - see the website of the International Year of Ecotourism 2002: http://www.world-tourism.org/sustainable/IYE-Main-Menu.htm

4.8 Parks and Protected Areas

The managers of parks and protected areas must increasingly deal with a dual mission - that of protection of the key natural and cultural assets which have led to the designation of the area and that of accommodating those who visit and take advantage of those assets. In the section on Natural and Sensitive Ecological sites (p. 263) and Conserving Built Heritage (p. 76) many of the reasons why these assets are important are addressed, along with the indicators which may be of greatest use in protecting them.

In this section, the range of indicators likely to be of most direct use to the planners and managers of areas that have official status are reviewed. National parks and other such areas are increasingly parts of the marketing for destinations, and tourists have received differing levels of welcome, sometimes seen as a source of potential revenue, and at other times as an unwanted stress on the systems the protected areas were designed to protect. See also Destinations Within or Adjacent to Protected Areas. (p. 272)

While some protected areas have controlled access points - such as a single park entrance where fees may be collected and numbers of entrants may be restricted, many protected areas have limited control on who enters and how long they stay. This is particularly an issue where there are many places of entry. Some parks and protected areas are shared with residents or other uses or users (e.g. many European protected areas encompass farmed fields and inhabited villages). This brings further challenges in protection.

Indicators directly related to protected species have long been gathered by protected area managers, often in great detail. Realization of the need to monitor visitor use and visitor impacts is more recent. A common focus has been the development of measures which could support estimates of sustainable use or sensitivity of the park or protected area's key assets to different levels of use (See Carrying Capacity p. 309). See, for example, the cases on Arches (p. 342), Albufera de Valencia (p. 330) and Cape Breton p. 355) (See also Natural and Sensitive Ecological Sites p. 263 and Built Heritage Sites p. 278).

Users may find it valuable to consult the other destination types which are encompassed in the protected area for additional indicators which may be of use.

Most protected areas have in place many specific indicators relating to the health of the specific assets, ecosystems and species which are the reason for which they were established, and to their own levels of management. These will be unique to each protected area, and are certainly of great value to park management. In some cases, dozens of indicators are maintained by managers, (for example for key indicator species - relating to such factors as range, breeding success, disease, impact of predators, strength of the food supply etc. or to state of the built asset, covering state of each building, ruin, level of damage, cost of rehabilitation etc) In this section, the indicators suggested relate primarily to the management of tourism in the protected areas, and not to the management of the park ecology or of specific assets. A good reference on tourism and protected area management is Eagles et. al (2002)., Sustainable Tourism in Protected Areas - Guidelines for Planning and Management, published by IUCN/WTO/UNEP which includes a section on indicators.

Tongariro National Park, New Zealand National parks are normally areas receiving the greatest degree of protection. They are also a magnet for tourists.

Issues	Indicators
➤ **Visitor numbers**	➤ **Total number of visitors to park and to key sites;** ➤ **Peak numbers (peak day, month);** Length of stay; ➤ **Use intensity on key sites (persons per Km2)** p.192); Revenue from paid visitors; Number of guides/operators permitted to use park/protected area; % of all visitors who are in controlled/guided visits.
Integrity of key protected systems	Number of sites/ecosystems/assets considered to be damaged or threatened (% of all defined systems/assets in protected area); Indicators of health related to key plant and animal species (see details in ➤ **Natural and sensitive sites** p. 263 and ➤ **Ecoturism** p. 268); % of park hardened for visitor or other use; ➤ **% of protected area subject to different levels of control** (for example IUCN categories of protection and access).
Damage attributable to visitor activity	% of protected system in degraded condition -(where possible classified due to cause); % trails and routes (length) in damaged condition; Cost of repair to damaged systems (annually); % of park area affected by unauthorized activities (hunting, tree cutting, trapping, poaching etc); Number of incidents of poaching identified(see Ecotourism p. 268) and Natural and Sensitive Sites p. 263).
Level of visitor control and monitoring	Number of human/animal contacts reported involving injury or risk of injury; Number of crimes against tourists; Number of incidents of vandalism; % of visitors who do not pay for entry (where entry fee is charged); Number of wardens or control staff (and number per tourist).
Marketing	Amount spent on marketing the protected area; (See Marketing p. 228).
Management	Number of park officials (wardens, managers, maintenance etc); Number of enforcement personnel per visitor; Cost of protection; Number of public/community meetings held with stakeholders including local periphery communities; Ratio of revenues to costs for Park operations (See also Tourism Contribution to Conservation p. 123).

Box 4.4 Skyline Trail, hardening for use

On the Skyline Trail in Cape Breton National Park, Canada, construction of a completely
hardened trail has permitted much
greater use without disturbance of the
fragile meadows. Hikers are able to
walk several kilometres across
wetlands and upland terrain to reach
viewpoints overlooking the rugged
coast. Protected area managers and
tourism managers had to balance the
opposition from conservationists who
wanted to keep the area "natural" with
the realities of tourism growth, impact
on the trail, and habitat protection. The
opinion of the hardened access is
therefore varied, with some welcoming
the easier access and degree of
protection, while others avoid the trail
because it is not "natural" and is
considered overcrowded.

4.9 Communities Within or Adjacent to Protected Areas

Communities built within parks and protected areas or within periphery area have unique issues,
related to the communities themselves and to the relationship which they, and their visitors may have
with the protected areas. Frequently, the authorities managing protected areas have no jurisdiction to
plan or manage how land is used or how tourism is developed on the periphery of the designated area.
Periphery communities become the sites for services, and often have a symbiotic relationship with the
protected areas. Often, activities which are prohibited or limited in the protected area become
concentrated on the periphery, and under the jurisdiction of the community. Such activities may
include a wide range of services to those who wish to visit the protected area (food, accommodation,
equipment rental, basic tourist services). Because the peripheral areas may not be organized, there may
be little ability to plan or manage the impacts, and such areas may house activities whose compatibility
with the objectives of the protected area may be questionable (e.g. paintball, off road racing, hang
gliding, and a wide range of fun farms and entertainment). Where the community acts as a gateway to
a protected area, or is located within the boundaries of the protected area the welfare of the community
may be inextricably tied to the planning and management of the protected area.

In many occasions, the park is a main attraction, and alternative programmes in adjacent communities
(e.g. cultural performances, local cuisine, visiting crafts people) can be linked with the park visit.
Linking the visitor flow to parks (main attractions) to community visits can help spread the socio-
economic benefits of tourism, and reduce stresses and visitor concentration in parks by spreading
tourism spatially. Typical issues which arise involve restrictions on the activities of locals (see Protecting
Critical Ecosystems, p. 247, ➢ **Controlling Use Intensity** p. 192 **and** ➢ **Local Satisfaction** p. 56). As
well, local issues arise with regard to the impact of the park and its management on communities,
including access to resources and key sites, employment opportunities, business opportunities related
to the protected area, and who gets to benefit from tourism - through concessions, small businesses,
guiding etc. See as well the issue sections relating to these areas.

Often there is little formal liaison between park managers and residents of nearby villages and towns which can anticipate and hopefully prevent conflict or devise joint solutions to shared problems. Can the park accommodate an increasing number of visitors - attracted by new hotels and tourism activities (e.g. events) at nearby communities? Will the park allow increased access by the local community to water supply from the park area? Will the new town sewage treatment plant be built to also accommodate waste from visitors to the park? Will the new restrictions on trucks on park roads in summer cut off the only route to the mill in town for logging trucks? Are there mechanisms in place to address these kinds of issues on shared resources and joint tourism management?

Components of the issue	Indicators
Impacts of the community activity on the park - its management and protection	• Number of incidents regarding violation of park rules by local residents.
Impacts of the park on the residents of the community	• Opinion of the value/relationship of the protected area to the community (Questionnaire based); • Number of complaints to park management.
Degree to which co-planning and management is done	• Existence of a participatory process for community and protected area collaboration in planning and management; • Degree of/frequency of participation in participatory processes;
Level of cooperation between the protected area and the gateway or park community	• Alternative tourism programmes in adjacent communities promoted or organized at the park (number and capacity, participation, tourist satisfaction with programmes).

Indicators relate to the impact of the community and visitors on the park, the effects of the protected area (restrictions, programs, employment, rules of access etc., on the community, and on the relationship between the two. Local opinion may be a leading indicator of potential conflict between the community and the protected area. Measure the % who agrees that the relationship is good and that the community benefits from the park or protected area (two potential questions on a community questionnaire). These questions can most efficiently be done with others in a community questionnaire. Complaints by locals can be a signal of arising issues, but are less useful to measure actual extent of concern. These indicators can be used as a stimulus to foster dialogue and ongoing participation between the community and protected area officials. (Note see also Community involvement and awareness p. 83).

Reason for use of these indicators: It is increasingly accepted that a participatory process can reduce conflict, assist in awareness and create partnerships to benefit both communities and protected areas. Often the community will take the lead in development of indicators, particularly for those which deal with the effects of tourism and park policies and programs on its interests. Case studies such as the Cape Breton (p. 355) and Lanzarote (p. 406) cases illustrate how the indicators process can be used to bring communities and protected area managers together to seek common issues and solutions.

Peyto Lake, Banff National Park, Canada.
Visitors stay in the town of Banff which is surrounded by the park.

4.10 Trails and Routes

Walking trails are transportation corridors often imbued with the history, stories, shrines and artefacts of those that have tread them before us, providing basic ingredients to make them interesting to tourists. Tourism developers, entrepreneurs and guides have built tourism packages and experiences on many of the world's great trails and routes such as the West Coast Trail in British Columbia (a rugged trail built to give access to shipwreck survivors), the Milford Track (New Zealand) and la Ruta Maya (historic trading and transportation paths of the Mayan Civilization in Central America). Trails and walking routes are important part of tourism activities in both natural environments (e.g. national parks) and urban and rural settings (e.g. historic city centers, traditional villages).

Linking tourism with walking trails may have begun with the early pilgrimages (e.g. Camino de Santiago, Spain (See Box 4.6). The pilgrims were a ready market for local suppliers of food, accommodation and souvenirs along the way. Today, many destinations are discovering that the natural and cultural heritage of their trails can form the basis on which to develop tourism and draw new "pilgrims". Trails are increasingly seen as multipurpose recreational corridors or links (e.g., the Trans Canada Trail http://www.tctrail.ca/ - which is used by cyclists, snowmobilers, cross country skiers, runners etc as well as by hikers who may use sections of its 18,078 Km length linking the Atlantic, Pacific and Arctic oceans).

Indicators related to this issue are centred on helping tourism and trail managers and local communities balance priorities and make decisions. Tourism values and policies must be balanced against natural and cultural heritage values and policies. Local communities and other stakeholders may have very different priorities and may be directly involved in management, maintenance and tourism. The economic benefits from tourism must be weighed against the costs and resources required to maintain the trail.

For a specific application of indicators to a nature trail, including the exact field methods used to measure degradation, see the Yacutinga Argentina Case (p. 453).

The particular issues related to the use of existing trails and the design of new walking trails are discussed here (also see Creating Trip Circuits p. 223). Although walking is considered a low-impact non-motorized activity (at least at the level of individuals or small groups), developing tourism based on walking trails requires consideration of environmental and cultural impacts, logistics, and the needs and interests of tourists to ensure long term success of tourism to the destination. This is particularly true when a trail becomes host to thousands, sometimes all concentrated in a short season when the weather is most amenable to travel or when travel is associated with cultural or religious events. Management responses may include limiting entry, permit systems, and waiting lists to limit the number of tourists and protect heritage values on the trail. Alternatively some disturbance or loss of protected area may permit expanding, re-routing or hardening-off trails to increase the capacity.

Methods exist to measure physical impacts of trail use (e.g. Yacutinga case p. 453), and to assess the beneficial and negative impacts of tourist on communities along a trail. (See Box 4.5: Heritage Trails Uganda).

New Zealand's Milford Track is booked
many months in advance by trekkers

The indicators suggested focus on the trail system itself and the integrity of the ecological and cultural assets. The physical integrity of the trail and the integrity of the ecosystem it traverses are fundamental indicators of the state of the trail and its suitability for walkers and its success as a tourism attraction. The cultural heritage of the trail needs to be maintained and interpreted to tourists. Built heritage and artefacts, wayside markers, evidence of earlier use etc. need to be protected against wear or abuse. Community support and involvement can be crucial for the success of tourism and protection of a trail. As well, managers require a range of information to make decisions on maintenance of the trail and the amount of tourism that can be supported and to keep all partners informed.

(See also ➤ **Economic Benefits** (p. 128) for other indicators of economic benefits which may derive from routes and trails).

Issues	Indicators
Environmental values/policies - the extent to which tourism use of the trail impacts its physical integrity, and flora and fauna - "take only photos, leave only footprints" - extent of damage to the trail and trail margins - ecological limits in terms of number of tourists or permits	• ➤ **Density of use** (p. 192)Number of tourists on trail: at one time: in a given time period or season; per year; • ➤ **Tourist numbers** per season, year; • % of trail hardened; • % of trail (and margins) degraded (from desired or benchmark level); • % use relative to ecological carrying capacity (maximum permitted number of tourists).
Protecting cultural heritage values - protection of built heritage and artefacts - interpretation of history and cultural heritage - renovated or restored cultural structures, e.g. shrines, resting sites	• Number of artefacts and built sites on trail and % maintained; • Number of guides trained in interpretation; • Use of self-guided signs or pamphlets; • Existence of a code of behaviour for tourists.
Community socio-cultural impacts - impact on local use - benefits for communities along trails; improvements in community services and infrastructure; e.g. education, health, transportation, local businesses - employment opportunities - revival of skills traditions	• % change in use by local population; • ➤ **Level of satisfaction by locals:** (p. 56) Community support for tourism on the trail (questionnaire, number of volunteers); • % of local residents who believe they benefit from the trail; • Number of training courses offered per year; number of people attending.
Economic benefits	• Number of jobs related to the trail; • Number of guides; • Number of businesses offering trail walks; • Revenue from local craft and souvenir sales/year; • Revenue from accommodation/year; • Number of partners working together; • Increase/decrease in partners, funding and in-kind support; • % of labour and materials supplied locally.

Issues	Indicators
Trail and tourism management - revenue sources; fees, grants, public funding - access to trail: guided/non-guided; entry fees; transportation; parking - pricing strategies (for locals, visitors) - maintenance; by government, industry, communities, volunteers tourism/trail associations - maintaining the character of the trail and quality of the experience	• Number of volunteers - increase/decrease; • Value of volunteers contribution; • % of partners and of users who believe that the expected quality of the trail is being maintained (nature, culture, ambience, levels of use) (Exit questionnaire, partner survey).
Tourism values/policies - natural environment; flora, fauna, vistas, landscape - cultural heritage, history services/infrastructure for tourists: guides, accommodation, signs, toilets, viewing platforms, board walks etc - image/brand in marketplace	• ➢ **Level of satisfaction by tourists** (p. 86); • Number of complaints/compliments per year from tourists; • Number and type of media exposures per year ; • Level of media exposure: a measure related to marketing, profile and image.

Box 4.5 Heritage trails Uganda (HTU): Impact assessment indicators

HTU is working in partnership with the Uganda Community Tourism Association (UCOTA) and pilot trail communities to assess the impact of tourism on local communities. Indicators to be used are specific, measurable, ambitious, realistic & time-bound (SMART) and cover both positive and negative impacts in areas including community involvement, training, enterprise development, access to essential resources and conservation of natural and cultural assets. The indicators in the local language of Buganda, Luganda, have been developed for 6 pilot community tourism associations and are being tested The community indicators will be measured & reviewed at regular intervals (e.g. quarterly) with assistance from the Project field team. (See the Uganda Heritage Trails case study and the Kibale community application (p. 440) for more details).

The Kabaka's Trail has been developed by the Heritage Trails Project in partnership with the guardian communities of the sites, along with The Kabaka Foundation, The Uganda Community Tourism Association (UCOTA) and Action for Conservation through Tourism (ACT UK). Income generated through tourism will go directly towards the conservation of the sites and to the benefit of the local community. Additional cultural Heritage Trails will be developed across Uganda.

UCOTA community meeting

http://www.visituganda.com/domestic/ucota.htm
http://www.visituganda.com/go/kabaka_trail.htm

Box 4.6 Camino Santiago

Since medieval times, millions of pilgrims have travelled the Camino trail from the French border to the northwestern Spanish city of Santiago de Compostela - the purported site of the tomb of St. James the Apostle. The motivation for walking the route today ranges from traditional religious reasons to a simple desire for adventure and experiences. Most of the many villages along the trail were originally established to serve the medieval pilgrims on their way to Santiago. With the resurgence in interest in the trail over the past two decades and thanks to the careful development of trail infrastructure and information, the numbers of pilgrims and visitors is increasing each year, reviving many of the villages that traditionally served pilgrims along the route. In an average year, more than 50,000 people undertake some portion of the Camino by foot, bicycle, horseback or car - most travelling between May and September, and in particular during July and August. (Completion of the entire trail by foot typically requires a little over a month). Indeed, during summer months, lodging at hostels - known as refugios - can be impossible to find for those who do not arrive early in the afternoon at their destination. Also, in Holy or Jubilee years, when St. James' day, July 25, falls on a Sunday, there is a special indulgence available from the Catholic Church and 10 times the usual number will travel to Santiago. The experiences of pilgrims, and of those living in the villages they pass through, can be quite different during the peak months (and often less pleasant) compared to the experiences during the off-peak months and non-Jubilee years. While the last thing most pilgrims want to see is commercialization of amenities along the trail, this risk is heightened with each passing year as more and more people use the trail - and as the opportunities for commercial gain posed by growing numbers of pilgrims become increasingly attractive. One of the key attractions offered by the Camino for most pilgrims is a relatively more rustic and threadbare experience than they would normally pursue, and one that they can imagine emulates the experiences of pilgrims of old. The following indicators reflect these values and the growing changes.

Indicators with associated sources of data that could be used to gauge changes in the quality of these experiences include:

* ➢ **Numbers of pilgrims** using the trail year-over-year and in peak months(data available through registration at refugios).Also, number of pilgrims per Km in peak periods and for specific trail sections. (➢ **Tourist numbers**);

* Level of occupancy in hostels(refugios), per month/season;

* Time of the day, when hostels are already full (in peak season tends to be earlier);

* ➢ **Satisfaction** of pilgrims and visitors with their overall experiences at different times of the year (surveys handed out at refugios and/or at Santiago upon completion of pilgrimage);

* **Level of pressure pilgrims feel on the trail to arrive early** at refugios to ensure a bed for the night (surveys handed out at refugios);

* **Availability of food** (survey handed out at refugios);

* ➢ **Level of satisfaction of villagers** with the experience of pilgrims passing through (random questionnaire of with local residents);

* Quality of the trail (➢ **garbage counts**, number of areas of evident degradation);

* **Appearance year-over-year of non-traditional commercial services** (e.g. number of fast food franchises, outfitters, vendors of non-traditional souvenirs).

While the indicators of stress used for other linear systems will also be of interest, these measures reflect particularly the cultural values associated with the Camino and its experience.

4.11 Built Heritage Sites

Historic residential districts, governmental, commercial and defence structures, archaeological and religious monuments, are prime tourist attractions worldwide. Among the most heavily visited sites on the planet are built heritage sites such as the Pyramids in Egypt, the Acropolis in Athens, Macchu Pichu in Peru, or the Taj Mahal in India.

Built heritage sites are normally linked with a variety of additional services, such as accommodation and catering, souvenirs and handicrafts, cultural performance, forming complex tourism products. These built heritage areas, however, can also be threatened by the physical impacts of over-visitation and congestion, and the insensitive developments due to commercialization of the authentic historic character and cultural context of a site.

Urban growth places pressures on built heritage, including both individual buildings and entire historic districts. (See George Town Penang Box 4.7) Tourism can be a catalyst for the rehabilitation and re-use of such buildings providing their deterioration is not too advanced. The key issues with regard to built heritage are the following, with some indicators suggested: (See also Conserving Built Heritage p. 76).

Issues	Suggested Indicators
Demolition of old buildings with heritage value	◦ Number/% heritage buildings demolished.
Deterioration of built structures	◦ Number/% buildings considered in degraded condition.
Threatened historic districts or structures	◦ Number of buildings and/or districts listed on endangered sites lists (i.e. World Heritage, World Monuments Fund).
Loss of historic character of districts	◦ % buildings in district which are historic; ◦ % buildings in district which are vernacular architecture.
Protection of historic buildings	◦ Number/% old buildings designated at local, national and/or World Heritage levels.
Protection of historic districts	◦ % of district which has protection (level of protection or designation).
Cost of protection	◦ Level of funding put towards restoration efforts (See also Conserving Built Heritage p. 76).
Re-use of historic buildings or sites	◦ Number of buildings reused for commercial or residential purposes; ◦ Number of buildings reused for tourism purposes (e.g. hotel or restaurant).
New legislation	◦ Quantily of new legislation introduced to preserve structures at local, provincial/state/canton or national levels.
Tourisms' contribution to preservation of built heritage sites (amount deriving from each source)	◦ Visitor fees; ◦ Concession fees; ◦ Donations from visitors and tour operators; ◦ Fees from guiding and other services; ◦ In-kind contributions (e.g. equipments, volunteers); ◦ Revenues from catering and accommodation services; ◦ Tourism-related tax designated to site maintenance; ◦ Sale of goods (e.g. informative materials, handicrafts, equipment to visitors).

Issues	Suggested Indicators
Tourism management	• Existence of congestion management practices (e.g. line management, timing, parking, reservation and on line purchase systems to avoid queues at ticket office); Existence of visitor/information center, interpretative materials, guided tours.
Use levels (see p. 192)	• ➢ **Total tourist arrivals** - Number and origin of visitors to the site per season (day, month, year); • Length of stay; • Number of tour operators with permit to operate at site; • Times during year when structure is most heavily visited; • Current building use (i.e. active, closed, abandoned or demolished), continuation or change of usage of historic structure.

Acropolis, Athens. Tourists line stairs to visit the site that is undergoing extensive rehabilitation work.

Box 4.7 George Town, Penang, Malaysia

George Town on the island of Penang, Malaysia has an eclectic mix of commercial/residential shophouse and British colonial architecture that is still essentially intact. The shophouses reflect an indigenous style influenced both by mainly Hokkien (Southern) Chinese tastes and construction methods and the cosmopolitan mix of Malays, Chinese, Arabs, South Indians, Armenians, Persians, Siamese, Burmese and Sumatrans that brought commercial vitality to the island. The charm of George Town's streets is found in the intimate relationship between the monuments and the structures housing its multi-ethnic citizenry.

The decline of trade in the main port due to the surging regional competition from Singapore since the 1950s has lessened the need for the collection of historic waterfront 'go-downs' (warehouses), and the decline of local Hokkien Chinese clan associations, resulting in the demolition of many clan houses. The sprawling 65-storey Komtar Communications Tower shopping complex on Jalan Penang (Penang Road) required the demolition of a large number of shophouses prior to construction. Komtar has drawn consumers and activity away from the shophouses on surrounding streets, diminishing their value and purpose.

Many shophouses remain due to the Control of Rent Act (1966) legislation that discouraged development on these sites. This legislation was phased out though in 2000, leaving 12,000 structures to be potentially demolished at will by developers. Consequently, George Town Historic Enclave was named by the World Monument Fund as one of the World's 100 Most Endangered Sites in 2000 and 2002. Since the town's inclusion on the 2000 list, Malaysia's federal government has submitted George Town to UNESCO for inclusion as a joint World Heritage Site, along with Malacca.

Chen Voon Fee, a former vice president of the Heritage of Malaysia Trust once stated that "we cannot afford to turn our cities into museums...conservation must be seen to pay for itself". This value has come in the form of tourism which provides jobs and income for the city through George Town's wealth of cafés, vibrant street life, markets, temples, and variety of small hotels.

Sustainable Penang, an indicators initiative funded by the Canadian International Development Agency's (CIDA) Canada-ASEAN Governance Innovations Network (CAGIN) program used as one of its focal areas the loss of historical structures. The report acknowledged that according to experts, putting Penang's heritage area listed as a World Heritage site can bring a 3-5 fold increase in tourism, which necessitates the safeguarding of heritage and controlling the social impacts of increased tourism.

The indicator that Sustainable Penang applied to built heritage, reflecting the status of the Rent Control Act was "The Number of Buildings Demolished". This specifically refers to monitoring the loss of any of the over 1400 prewar buildings along the 29 streets in George Town's historic centre. A matching tourism indicator was the "Hotel Occupancy Rate". While Penang has a well-developed beach resort area in Batu Ferrenghi, historic enclave hotels are also measured as a separate category. Triangulated with visitor surveys and an ongoing assessment of the regional and global tourism situation that may impact overall visitation, these indicators can be useful in understanding the tourism value attached to built heritage sites. These indicators can then serve the joint purpose of how the George Town historic enclave is being used, and to provide a lobbying tool for preservation groups to influence legislation to facilitate the retention of the area's heritage fabric and vitality.

Sources: Sustainable Penang

http://www.seri.com.my/ Penang Heritage Trust http://www.pht.org.my/

4.12 Small and Traditional Communities

Small, remote and traditional communities are increasingly beginning to experience significant attention from tourism, as an increasing number of travellers wish to experience living cultures and traditional ways of life. Both the advantages and disadvantages of tourism are arriving in small and traditional communities, often ill prepared to deal with them. Sometimes a community is suddenly "discovered" and tourists arrive in numbers which stress the capacity of the community to cope. Other destinations may have more time to prepare and to make decisions on how much of what kind of tourism they want.

Locals can become increasingly irritated by the influx of greater numbers of tourists. Initial visitors are often welcomed by a community who may find them interesting and potential buyers of a few local products. Often initial visitors are given a very strong welcome, even invited into homes or to ceremonies. As a destination's reputation grows, more tourists arrive - often beginning to change the local market, with fish boats selling tours, local restaurants adding tables and new dishes, and communities beginning to construct facilities expressly for visitors (toilets, new shops, and craft markets). If tourism continues to grow, at some point a reaction may begin, as tourists are perceived to pressure local resources, displace locals from their traditional places or activities and cause alterations in traditional lifestyle. In some cases, communities can become hostile to tourists, blaming them for all the problems. Often, tourists are the vector for changes from outside, affecting job prospects,

expectations by the local residents, and may cause disaffection by locals with their own lifestyle, particularly youth. All these issues can arise unless communities are actively engaged in the planning and management of tourism, helping to define the conditions under which they wish tourism to occur in their community, and what is negotiable and what is not (after Doxey 1975).

The traditional water village of Zhouzhuang, China can receive up to a hundred thousand visitors in a single day from the nearby cities of Shanghai and Suzhou

For example, local ceremonies may be considered sacred and not open to visitors, but at the same time the community may be comfortable with the staging of similar events for the tourists to see. It may be totally acceptable for visitors to see the interior of a religious building when it is not in use, but not during particular times or events. A community needs to understand the limits of acceptable change to its residents; this becomes the basis for negotiation of access and activities with tourists and operators. A participatory process based on the definition of key assets and sensitivities, coupled with the definition of indicators can help greatly in defining what values and assets are important to the community and who is prepared to act to sustain them.

Issues	Indicators
Impact on infrastructure and services	• **≻ % shops and services open year round** (see **≻ Seasonality** (p. 111); • Level of investment in infrastructure or services (% expressly for tourists); • % businesses locally owned and operated.
Violation of local norms	• Number of incidents reported; • **≻ Local satisfaction with level of tourism**- (p. 56); • % of community who favour tourism or want more tourism and those who oppose it. (Questionnaire - see template C 6 p. 494).
Tourism as catalyst for social or cultural change	• Ratio of average tourist income to that of local residents; • % of residents speaking non-local language; • % of change in traditional activities and customs (e.g. land use, language, ceremonies, religion, clothing, food, etc.); • % local residents concerned about loss of culture community structure and values (questionnaire); • % of new construction in vernacular architecture or viewed as compatible with traditional structures and vistas (see issue section on managing visual impacts (p. 185). (See also the issue section on **≻ Effects of tourism on communities** p.57).
Capture of the benefits from tourism for the community	• **≻ % local people employed in tourism (and ratio of tourism** ; • **≻ % of community income derived from tourism** ; • Average wage in tourism; • See issue section on **≻ Economic benefits** (p. 128); • % local youth able to obtain employment in tourism.
Maintaining participation in tourism development and management	• Degree of local participation in tourism planning (% participating or represented).
Tourist satisfaction (re community, traditions, authenticity etc)	• **≻ Level of satisfaction of visitors** (Exit survey p. 491).

Many of the specific issues and related indicators which will also be of interest to those concerned with tourism in small communities are addressed in greater detail in some of the issues sections in part 3. In particular readers are directed to the issue sections on ≻ **Economic benefits of tourism** (p. 128) ≻ **Effects of tourism on communities** (p. 57), and Controlling use intensity (p. 192). For examples see Uganda Heritage Trails (p. 440) and Corbett National Park, India (p. 386) as well as those sections which deal with the unique issues of each community.

4.13 Urban Tourism

Urban tourism is a growing tourism market although there is no worldwide data on urban tourism available. This is partly due to the fact that each country has its own definition regarding the focus of urban tourism (E.g. in Austria urban tourism is defined as tourism which takes place in the nine capitals of the federal provinces, whereas in Germany it is defined as tourism in cities with more than 100.000 inhabitants.)

Despite the lack of direct data, it is known that there are an increasing number of tourists attracted to urban areas.

Urban tourism has only recently been recognized as a topic for research and sustainability issues are not yet developed extensively in the field of urban tourism, compared to other tourism forms (like rural tourism). Those groups dealing with sustainability and cities (scientists, NGOs, participants in of Local Agenda 21 processes,   the International Council of Local Environmental Initiatives - ICLEI - www.iclei.org, national programmes, such as Sustainable Tourism Municipalities in Spain - http://www.femp.es/documentos/proma/vimat.pdf, etc.) are increasingly addressing tourism issues.

There are two main forms of urban tourism:

1.   Recreation tourism, with a clear focus on cultural attractions and educational aspects;

2.   Business tourism (trade shows, conventions, (see Conventions and Convention Centres p. 286) business meetings, etc.).

In some cities, both forms of urban tourism are occurring, while in others one of these two forms is predominant. Despite these differences, both have elements in common; that the average duration of stay is shorter than in other destinations (including a higher proportion of daily visitors) and that the average expenses per day are higher.

Some cities are destinations in themselves and do not directly depend on proximate seashore or mountain resorts, or nearby natural and cultural attractions. Their tourism performance will rely mostly on the urban centre's own attractions and capability to attract tourists.

The most burning issues in the field of sustainable urban tourism are traffic and city restoration. The importance of built cultural heritage for urban tourism is obvious, as it is often the main tourist attraction in cities. To preserve it has to be a primary goal for all those involved in tourism. Traffic issues and congestion are one of the main sources of problems for many cities, especially urban destinations with mass tourism. (e.g., Rome, London, Paris, Beijing)

Issues	Suggested Indicators
Improvements to the townscape and protection of the historic heritage	⁎ Percentage of restored historic buildings; ⁎ *Expenditures/m³* of public and private finance spent in improvement of the physical urban environment; ⁎ Increase of the percentage of pedestrian streets in the total road network; ⁎ Existence and extent of public open areas; ⁎ *Expenditures/m³* yearly spent in restoration of historic buildings.
Sustainable tourism enterprises	⁎ % of businesses that have adopted environmental management procedures; (see Sustainability and Environmental Management Policies and Practices p. 241).
Environmental management	⁎ Level of public and private finance spent in environmental-management systems (e.g. reduce wrapping, recycle waste, energy efficiency etc). (see also ➢ **Solid waste** p. 173); ⁎ Reduction of operational cost from environmental management (value, %); ⁎ Changes in return on investment (%); ⁎ Change in use of material/ resources (%).
Traffic /Public transport system	⁎ % of tourists arriving by public transport; ⁎ Accessibility of tourist attractions by public transport; ⁎ Existence of a control system for bus parking and level of control (% tour buses complying); ⁎ Prices for taxis (per Km).

Issues	Suggested Indicators
Integration of regional economy	• Value and % of goods purchased locally from the region (e.g. organically grown food from the region); • % of tourist shops promoting regional products.

Presentation of cultural knowledge	• Number and percentage of guided tours and/or publications which:
	  - give detailed information on the background of the cities history;
	  - cover actual issues of city development;
	  - show new and unconventional attractions.

Crowding / Spatial distribution	• ➢ **Total number of tourists per square Km in key sites;** • Variety of tours and visit sites (helping to spread out impacts and benefits); • Number of different sites receiving tours.
Resident attitudes toward tourism	• ➢ **Local satisfaction level with tourism in the city** (local questionnaire, see Annex C 6).

Sources: http://sut.itas.fzk.de, www.sustainable-cities.org

For related indicators see sections of Transportation (p. 220) and Preservation of Built Heritage p. 76)

Crowds of tourists and locals fill the streets of the Old City in Havana, Cuba. The area is Havana's key attraction and has World Heritage status.

Box 4.8 Ecological food programme in Heidelberg Germany's

The city of Heidelberg has a long tradition in the implementation of sustainability programmes and a strong commitment to implement Agenda 21. In 1999 a program was launched to promote the range of ecologically and/or regionally produced food in the Heidelberg catering trade. A multi-stakeholder partnership was formed to establish a programme, which brings together partners from the agricultural, processing and catering sector.

The scientific advisor of the project had the task to formulate goals and objectives for the one-year project period as well as verifiable indicators for the achievement of goals, which were used as a basis for an evaluation of goal achievement by the project team and the steering group. A list of detailed, clear and assessable goals and indicators was developed to evaluate the development of the project. The following table gives an overview.

Goals	Indicator	Goal achievement
Part of the offer consists of eco food	· At least five catering companies have included or want to include eco-offers in their product line.	Completely fulfilled
Stable supply relations to eco-suppliers are to be established	· Contractually stipulated supply relations are long-lasting.	Fulfilled to a satisfactory degree (there are only verbal agreements)
Convincing interested catering companies to participation in the project	· At least five hotels or restaurants should label and advertise eco-products.	Completely fulfilled (far more than five companies are integrated)
Reducing environmental pressures	· Reduction of transport, improvement of nutrition, encouragement of producers to a changeover.	Fulfilled to a low degree within the given period of time
Contributing to environmentally friendly tourism in Heidelberg	· Presentation of the project to a broad public.	Completely fulfilled
Customer behaviour is changing	· Customers and guests ask for ecologically produced food, noticeable economic success for suppliers.	Fulfilled in isolated cases
The internal project management is effective and transparent for all participants	· Establishment of the project group, steering group, moderated meetings and documentation, synergies with the project "Gemeinschaftsverpflegung" (Canteen Food)	Fulfilled

As the table clearly shows the program was highly successful, nearly all indicators or performance measures were fulfilled. Other goals like integration in the urban sustainability program or the formation of a multi-stakeholder partnership were formulated implicitly and were also fulfilled. The use of indicators was important to show the project progress and to formulate the goals of the next project period.

Source: Successful SUT Partnerships: Case Study Research, Expert Questionnaire Healthy Food in Heidelberg's Restaurants, report within the EU project: Sustainable Urban Tourism (SUT), Involving Local Agents and Partnerships for New Forms of Governance, 2001, (unpublished).

4.14 Conventions and Convention Centres

Meetings and conferences are part of what has become to known as the MICE (Meetings, Incentives, Conferences and Exhibition) segment also falling under the category of Business Tourism. It is estimated that around 20 % of all international tourist arrivals are for meetings and conferences (WTO, Tourism 2020 Vision, 2001). Many destinations with convention facilities are expanding them to compete for large events and conventions. In cities, convention facilities can be a significant draw, with impacts on the community and on its infrastructure (See Urban Destinations p. 282). Large events (international conferences, conventions, major trade shows) may occupy all of the hotel and convention space in a city - avoiding those destinations with insufficient space. Convention tourism can be an important means to balance seasonality as conventions can be organized in low tourism seasons when occupancy and prices are also lower.

Large convention centres (or those that are large relative to the community where they are located) need to be cognisant of the impacts they have on community facilities such as parking, restrooms and food services. Large conventions can fully occupy the accommodation in one city, and may flow over to affect communities some distance away, drawing on hotels, buses and taxis, police and service staff. A large convention may release several thousand attendees to get lunch all at the same time; and can overwhelm any restaurants within walking distance - and everyone may wish to be back at the convention centre within an hour.

The issues that relate to conventions and convention facilities occur at two scales - that of the community or destination and that of the facility. Both require management, and both are amenable to the use of indicators; those at the scale of the conference centre are similar in many ways to the management of other facilities such as hotels, attractions, etc. (See also the section on Events in this section which addresses similar issues) For related sections at the destination or community level, see the Urban Tourism (p. 282) and Small and Traditional Communities (p. 281) destinations.

Issues at the scale of the facility:	Indicators
Size of facility	× Total maximum capacity; × % utilization (% days/yr); × Average capacity use (% of maximum).
Range of services available	× Number of conference rooms and their capacity; × Number of restaurant seats available on site; × Number of restaurant seats within 10 minute walking distance; × Number of complaints regarding lack of services.
Accessibility	× Distance to nearest public transport; × Travel time to nearest airport; × Number of parking spaces within 1Km.; × % of area of convention centre which is accessible to those with limited mobility (see section on Accessibility p. 90).
Facility safety and security (particularly for events likely to attract crowds, hostility)	× Number of reported incidents per year - in facility and nearby involving customers; × Incidents (% of attendees affected).
Friendliness and ease of use for clients and visitors	× Exit questionnaire which measures perceived quality, value for money, reaction to facilities, other key issues (may be done as part on destination exit questionnaire - see questionnaire Annex C 5).
Location relative to amenities	× Number of key services in or adjacent to facility (e.g. bank, post office, taxi stand, travel assistance, pharmacy, souvenirs etc).
Impact on neighbours to the centre	× Indirect local employment associated with the events at the centre (both due to business from the facility and from those who use it); × Perceived impact (use modified local questionnaire as in Annex C 6- covering key areas of concern).
Location relative to other attractions or potential field trips	× See issue section on providing a variety of experiences (p. 226) for some means to measure response to this issue.
Pricing	× Price per person day (average) Benchmark against other published rates.
Solid waste management	× Volume of waste generated (and per person); × % waste recycled.
Environmental management of supply chain	× % use of disposable containers /reusable containers and cutlery china etc.; × Green purchasing policies (e.g. bulk purchase, preference to providers of environmentally friendly products).
Reputation as a conference venue	× Exit survey re quality, reputation - % approval rate, % who would recommend centre to their colleagues for similar events.

In addition to those issues at the scale of the facility, particularly for large conventions and large facilities, issues may occur that affect the entire destination.

Issues at the scale of the destination	Useful indicators
Size of conference facilities in destination	• Number of beds within destination or 30 min travel of main convention facility; • Ratio of conference attendees (by season) to available accommodation (also peak day ratio).
Variety of attractions /services in the destination	• See issue section on Variety (p. 226) and Protection of Image (p. 236).
Local safety and security (particularly for events likely to attract crowds, hostility)	• See issue sections on Local Public Safety (p. 109) and Tourist Security (p. 104).
Friendliness and ease of use for clients and visitors	• Exit questionnaire - Annex C 5 - opinion of friendliness.
Location relative to amenities	• Exit questionnaire - Annex C 5 - opinion of variety and convenience (see Variety p. 226).
Location relative to other attractions or potential field trips	• Number of major attractions/sites located within convenient one-day round trip for convention tours; • Exit questionnaire Annex C 5 - opinion of variety and quality of accessible attractions to destination.
Pricing	• See issue section on Competitiveness (p. 143), and ≫ **Tourism Satisfaction** (p. 86), questionnaire in Annex C; • Possible benchmarking of price per person against similar competing sites.
Waste management	• % of waste for which there is a functional capacity of selective collection and recycling in the destination (can be subdivided by type of waste) see ≫ **Solid waste** (p.173).
Reputation as a good destination for a conference	• See exit questionnaire Annex C. Use specific statement "*The destination was a good place to hold/attend a conference*".

The following table provides an example of indicators and performance measures for one medium sized conference centre in the urban centre of the city of Calgary, Alberta, Canada. It illustrates some of the measures in use and the results obtained.

Box 4.9 Bow Valley Convention Centre (Canada) operational indicators for "greening"

Original Issue	Environmental	Operational benefits of change	Bow walley example or application	Monetary or other indicator of progress
Waste food and/or beverages : All excess or waste food is disposed of as garbage.	Encouraging clients to take excess food with them. and to order for the size of their booking.	Less mess to clean up, less garbage to dispose of.	Clients are given re-used boxes or bags to carry their food/drink back to their office or home with them.	· Savings on garbage bags; · Savings in labour; · Savings by client due to reduced size of order, reduced waste.
Serving ware, flatware, utensils, cups and containers: Volume of disposable containers (plastic, paper, Styrofoam)	Collection of non-disposable /re-usable containers and serving ware after meetings for re-use. Recycle items where possible.	Less mess to clean up, less garbage to dispose of.	All glass bottles, aluminum trays, pizza boxes, paper, cardboard, pop cans, and juice boxes are recycled. Caterers are asked to pick up their trays -otherwise their serving ware is given free to other caterers who want them.	· Savings on garbage bags/disposal; · Savings by caterer/ food server on ware which can be passed along to customers (Tray costs if bought new: $3.00-$5.00 each); · Unused cups, disposable dishes etc. are kept by the centre for use by "forgetful" clients.
Cleaning products: Use of highly volatile, concentrated chemicals on all surfaces. E.g., bleach, concentrated. ammonia, multi-purpose floor cleaners, scouring compounds phosphate based cleaners.	Use of more natural products and "watering down" of products that still do the job in a less concentrated format. Sparse use of concentrated products.	Less toxic and less chance of accidental poisoning, less chance of cleaning staff or small children developing chemical sensitivity or allergies, less protective equipment needed when using products (rubber gloves etc.)	50% water and 50% general purpose citrus based cleaning solution is used to wipe down tables, counters and surfaces. It is effective in killing 99% of germs even at 25% strength. Non-ammonia based window cleaner is used on glass surfaces. Protective equipment is not used as products are not considered toxic.	· Cost savings in cleaning products (Most of the time non-denatured products cost less and some cost only pennies per bottle. E.g. vinegar solution window cleaner); · Lowered health care/ days lost costs; · Employee safety and satisfaction levels rise.
Cleaning tools: Use of disposable and non-biodegradable products (one-use cleaning cloths, mop-heads, dusters, chemical imbedded cleaning cloths etc.)	Move to washable and re-useable products.	Most re-useable products are highly durable and have to be replaced infrequently.	All cotton cleaning cloths are washed after use and re-used. Cloths are used for dusting, wiping and light scouring. Steel wool and scrubbing pads are re-used. Brooms, vacuums, and mops with washable heads are used.	· Direct equipment and materials savings (Note: -very cost efficient. A $20 broom will last you years, a throw away one-use" cloth and solution will cost $20 per month. Canadian dollars).

Original issue	Greener approach	Operational benefits of change	Bow valley example or application	Monetary or other indicator of progress
Cleaning methods and /standards: Wasteful daily/hourly cleaning, even of unused areas/items.	Cleaning as needed and of used areas/items only with weekly/monthly thorough cleanings.	Saves time. Just as sanitary - focuses effort on highest risk areas. Reduction in daily wear and tear caused by cleaning products or friction.	Tables, countertops and are cleaned after use. Rooms are vacuumed after client use. Hard to reach areas are dusted every 6 months. Other areas are cleaned as needed.	• Direct cost savings in the area of cleaning supplies; • Medium term savings in replacement costs for furniture/ surroundings due to wear and tear; • Cost savings in cleaning staff time.
Paper produced from officework: Used to be thrown out as garbage.	Recycled or re-used as scrap paper then recycled.	Environmentally friendly and shows commitment.	All paper and cardboard is recycled. Most paper in use at Bow Valley contains recycled material.	• Direct savings from paper re-use; • Savings from reduced trucking/waste charges.
Lighting: Incandescent bulbs left on from early morning to late evening	Use of natural light through windows. Lights (energy efficient) turned on only as needed and off after all meetings.	Fluorescent bulbs and energy efficient halogen bulbs are longer lasting than incandescent. Sunlight is an unlimited source of heat and energy, not subject to power outages.	Lights are turned on only in rooms in use. Fluorescent bulbs are used and replaced as needed. Two rooms, mostly commonly requested ones, have natural light access.	• Costs of electricity - % reduction in monthly charges; • Cost of replacement bulbs.(Fluorescents and halogens last longer and use less electricity, and are more cost efficient. Sunlight is free.).
Heat and air conditioning: Heat and air conditioning turned on and let run 365 days a year.	Heat/air conditioning turned on only in used areas of the building.	No need to heat/cool unused rooms. Saves wear and tear on heat/A/C equipment. Windows opened where possible for temperature regulation.	Air and heat circulation is only available in rooms in use. Thermostats control the temperature in each room and can be manually adjusted.	• % savings in heating/ cooling costs. (Natural air circulation through windows is free).
Furnishings and décor: Furnishings and decor dictated by style and cost with little other review.	Furnishing influenced by research on products used, origins and environmental impact.	Purchasing products that are local, not endangered; this shows a positive image to the public. E.g. second hand furniture, local non-endangered wood/animal products, limiting use of non-recyclable plastics, rugs with few synthetic products.	Wood panelling and décor are all pine or maple (local sylvicultured trees). Carpets are high fiber count local-made and replaceable in 1mx1m sections with few embedded chemicals. Other décor is done in glass and stainless steel; easily recyclable.	• Costs per unit, costs per unit year; • % purchased locally; • % made of recycled or recyclable material (High-mid end locally produced products are generally cheaper than imported. Sturdy and/ or recyclable materials can be later resold or rendered for profit).

4.15 Communities Seeking Tourism Development

Tourism is often promoted as a route to development for small communities, whether or not these communities have sufficient natural, cultural or other assets to generate a sustainable tourism product. Investments in tourism facilities are often done without any previous market studies or assessments for product development, with little real probability of payoff. What are the signs which may help communities decide whether tourism is likely to succeed, and whether sustainable tourism is a realistic option for their future?

All potential destinations need to undertake some form of assets inventory. What is there which could attract visitors, cause vehicles or tours to stop en route, convince tourists to see or buy something? Are visitors likely to stay a while (on-site activities or events which take time to do such as bird watching, walking routes, sports or cultural events which may last several days), to make a trip to see (art galleries, interesting scenery) or to stop on the road (wineries, cheese factories, craft shops). If they do stop, what is there to detain them, what is there to sell, and will they likely come again?

Some of the indicators which can help smaller and new destinations decide whether they have a future for tourism can be found in the issue sections which address the capture of social and economic benefits for a community. As well, the existence of routes that will themselves attract travellers can change the logistics of attracting tourists. Instead of trying to bring tourists or day visitors long distances to see the local museum or craft centre or to experience the pretty town square, the challenge becomes instead to divert them from the route, and make sure the attraction or community is seen as part of the route.

For communities without current tourism, or without notable attractions, events such as cultural festivals or sports tournaments can appear to provide opportunities. Organizers will need to carefully assess the costs and organizational needs (see Events p. 196) .For some small communities, provision of accommodation for passers-by en route elsewhere may be the main area with economic potential.

Where the community has no specific comparative advantage, this may pit communities against others to attract such events. See the issue sections on Competitiveness (p. 143), Events (p. 196) and Conventions (p. 286) for indicators that may assist in evaluating such opportunities. In some cases, the initial application of an indicator will be simple - does an attraction or opportunity exist? (yes/no). If there appear to be real opportunities, the indicators can assist in measuring how real they are, and whether either the opportunities or success of the community in responding to them have changed.

Issues	Potentially useful indicators
Does an opportunity exist?	• Total population within a 1hour and 2 hour travel distance; • Total number of tourists visiting or passing through the region (who might be a market for this destination); • Number of assets/attractions which could be classified as high, medium, low quality of attractiveness (where there is a classification system, it can be used and benchmarked against other destinations); • Number of local enterprises who advertise or sell to clients outside the local community; • Is there a specific asset or attraction around which it is possible to build tourism (e.g., waterfall, beach, factory producing unique products, castle ruins, wildlife refuge, etc). (Yes/no, or use quality ratings if they have been defined); • Access to the potential attractions.

Issues	Potentially useful indicators
Are we tourism ready?	<ul><li>% of community who support tourism/ tourism growth (use local questionnaire See Annex C 6);</li><li>% capacity remaining in water supply, sewage infrastructure;</li><li>% capacity use in access to key asset(s) (e.g, water supply to the beach, parking for the old mill);</li><li>Number of potential workers with skills to serve tourist needs (education, language, suitable training). Ratio of available skilled employees to projected short to medium term need;</li><li>Number of hours per week with available tourist assistance services in the community (e.g. visitor centre, vehicle service centre, community outreach office).</li></ul>
What is the nature of current tourism?	<ul><li>➢ **Total number of tourists** (p. 194);</li><li>% of passers-by on highway routes who stop in the community;</li><li>Variety of products and services in community (Variety p. 226);</li><li>Value of purchases in the community attributable to tourist;</li><li>% of establishments which cater expressly to tourists;</li><li>% of shops and restaurants preserving traditional features or which have been "beautified" to attract tourists.</li></ul>
What are the costs and benefits?	<ul><li>Estimated expenditure needed to expand tourism (per resident, per projected tourist day);</li><li>Cost per annum of new infrastructure or services needed to serve tourists (also per resident and per tourist);</li><li>Projected jobs in tourism (new , full time, part time) (See Employment p. 119).</li></ul>
Creating partnerships	<ul><li>Number of tour operators serving the region. % with tours to the community;</li><li>Number of linkages/ partnerships with operators, communities or organizations to jointly bring tourists to the community.</li></ul>
Keeping the community involved	<ul><li>Degree of community participation in discussions on tourism development (see Community Involvement p. 83) % involved;</li><li>% of potential establishments involved;</li><li>% of community in favour of more tourism/less tourism (see questionnaire Annex C 6).</li></ul>
Potential for holding of events?	<ul><li>Capacity of community for parking;</li><li>Availability of public space and facilities;</li><li>Capacity of the community for sewage (public washrooms);</li><li>Number of residents prepared to work on event;</li><li>% of community opposed to the event See ➢ **Seasonality** (p. 111)and Sturgis North Dakota example (Box 3.13).</li></ul>

Some communities have significant potential as destinations; others may have more limited opportunities. The participatory process outlined in Part 2 of this book can help greatly in the collective assessment of what the community wants to be, and whether tourism has a realistic role in that future. Many small communities remain at best, roadside stops, providing a few quick services to tourists such as fast food, toilets, gasoline and not much more. While some communities are able to build a more significant tourism industry due to, for example turning their heritage and traditions (cuisine, customs, handicrafts, factory outlet shops, natural areas, lifestyle) into marketable tourism products and

developing support services. A realistic assessment of potential (evaluation of community resources and potential tourism market) is essential.

Main street Perth Ontario, Canada. Most shops have undergone beautification to attract tourists to this historic mill town for shopping, dining and crafts.

4.16 Theme Parks

Theme parks are a worldwide phenomenon and a draw for large numbers of tourists, often from long distances. In 1997, it is estimated that they received around 266 million visitors, and some US$ 4.7 billion was spent in theme parks worldwide (WTO, Tourism 2020 Vision, 2001). Large theme parks like the Disneylands in Florida, California, Paris, Tokyo and the park under construction in Hong Kong are international destinations, as well as major domestic attractions.

At a smaller scale, local theme parks (e.g. the International Beer Park in Qingdao, China, see photo) can still be significant, with large areas for parking, impacts on the local transportation system, and demands on utilities. They can also be very significant employers, although many are seasonal. (e.g., many major parks like Paramount Canada's Wonderland, or some of the Six Flags parks in the USA are open only half the year). More limited attractions - permanent fairs, water parks, animal parks and mechanized rides can be found near potential markets, worldwide.

Theme parks can be built anywhere, more dependent on access and transportation than on any natural or cultural assets. The larger parks can be the largest users of water, electricity or transport systems in a destination. While the impacts can be similar to those of large events or sports (see Events p. 196) theme parks are not temporary; impacts are lasting, and there is greater opportunity for permanent solutions to the issues related to them. There are many examples of unsuccessful theme parks and water parks, underlining the need for good management and use of indicators that can respond to the issues associated with them.

Issues for theme parks	Indicators
Land use and planning	× Total land area used; × Area (%) with landscaping; × Consumption of utilities (% of destination capacity used for electricity, water, sewage) (See ➢ **Water availability** p. 265), ➢ **Sewage treatment** (p. 171).
Access	× % visitors using public transport; × Distance from nearest public transport facility.
Crowd management	× Number of parking spaces; × Length of line-ups (hours wait); × Number of washrooms per visitor (peak); × Number of restaurant seats per visitor (peak).
Noise	× Number of hours in operation per day; × Number of hours when noise exceeds local limits (see Noise p.183); × Number of complaints about noise.
➢ **Waste management**	× ➢ **Waste volume produced** (by month) (p. 173); × ➢ **Volume (%) of waste recycled.**
Groundskeeping	× Amount of pesticides and herbicides used per month/per hectare; × % landscaping using recycled grey water.
Human resources	× ➢ **Number of employees (% full time, all year)**; × % employees who are local; × % receiving training (see also Employment p. 119) See ➢ **Seasonality** (p. 111).

4.17 Water Parks

Water parks share the issues of most theme parks, but also have specific additional issues related to their use of water, particularly if they are located in areas where water resources are scarce or limited, especially during their peak seasons. In jurisdictions from the US Great Plains to Australia, Cyprus and Spain, water parks are a rapidly expanding phenomenon. In addition, large pumps consume significant energy to move water in many parks.

Water World Aya Napa,
Cyprus

The key issues for water parks therefore focus on water management, both quantity and quality, the amount of energy consumed, and public safety. Most of the issues which are important to all types of theme parks are likely to be of concern to water parks, but the issues and related indicators shown below will also be of interest.

Additional issues for water parks	Indicators
Water supply	• ➢ **Total water consumption;** • Water consumption as a percentage of total consumption of destination; • ➢ **Water saving.** Efficiency or recirculation and recycling (% recaptured and number of times recycled); • Cost of water (see also ➢ **Water Availability** p. 165).
Wastewater	• % wastewater recycled/reused; • Volume of water discharged; • ➢ **% of discharged water which is treated** (see ➢ **Sewage** p. 171).
Energy use	• ➢ **Total consumption of energy;** • ➢ **% from renewable sources** (see ➢ **Energy** p. 171).
Safety	• Volume and dilution % of chlorine, bromine, etc.; • Number of incidents/accidents (and per visitor day); • Number of water-related diseases (or complaints).

A crowded day in Tokyo Water Park, Japan.

Walt Disney World has its own environmental management system. A thorough case study can be found at http://www.rand.org/publications/MR/MR1343/MR1343.appb.pdf .

Box 4.10: Golf courses

Golf courses have their own issues, related to landscaping, use of native grass and tree species, maintenance of natural covers, water use, pesticide and herbicide use and, in some areas, the use of land where there are limited quantities available (e.g., small islands, urban areas, narrow valleys, habitats). On some small islands, there is concern that the area devoted to golf courses, or the draw on scarce water supplies, may be excessive. There are many initiatives to establish guidelines for greener golf courses. One example is the **Principles for Golf Courses in the United States** published by the Golf Course Superintendents Organization of America:

* To enhance local communities ecologically and economically;
* To develop environmentally responsible golf courses that are economically viable;
* To offer and protect habitat for wildlife and plant species;
* To recognize that every golf course must be developed and managed with consideration for the unique conditions of the ecosystem of which it is a part;
* To provide important greens space benefits;
* To use natural resources efficiently;
* To respect adjacent land use when planning, constructing, maintaining and operating golf courses;
* To create desirable playing conditions through practices that preserve environmental quality;
* To support ongoing research to scientifically establish new and better ways to develop and manage golf courses in harmony with the environment;
* To document outstanding development and management practices to promote more widespread implementation of environmentally sound golf;
* To educate golfers and potential developers about the principles of environmental responsibility and to promote the understanding that environmentally sound golf courses are quality golf courses.

Source: The Golf Course Superintendents Association of America

Principles like these lead to certain indicators that may be of utility:

Issues	Indicators
Limiting regional impacts	➢ **Level of water use** (% of total supply in destination); • Total area of golf courses (for small destinations, % of total surface area; • % of golf course area open to other uses; • % of destination population who support/oppose the construction of new courses.
Environmental design	• % of course using native species; • % area retained in natural habitat; • % of golf course property set aside for conservation, buffers, or protection.
Stewardship	• Amount of chemicals used (can be subdivided into different types of herbicides, pesticides); • % of runoff which is captured and treated (or monitored); • % of irrigation which is done through recycled grey water.
Economic sustainability	• Number of golfers using course; • Price per round (price in local hours wages); • See issue sections on Seasonality (p. 111), Employment (p. 119), and Competitiveness (p. 143) for additional indicators which may be of use.

4.18 Cruise Ships and their Destinations

The cruise ship industry is a rapidly growing tourism segment, with more and larger ships visiting increasing numbers of destinations, ranging from large cities to the most remote regions and cultures on the planet. In 2000, cruise demand reached almost 10 million trips, with North America accounting for almost 2/3 of demand, and Europe as a distant second with almost 2 million trips. Although North America is a relatively more developed and mature market, it still has substantial potential demand, which the Cruiseline International Association has estimated at some 43.5 million tourists over the next five years, showing good potential for growth and expansion (Worldwide Cruiseship Activity, WTO, 2003).

Each year cruise ships grow larger, and the list of destinations visited increases. Ships with more than 3000 passengers stop at tiny destinations such as the San Blas Islands of Panama, Pagnirtung in the Canadian north, or Stanley in the Falklands, where the numbers of disembarking passengers and crew outnumber the native residents several times over. Popular destinations such as Cozumel, Mexico (a 50 km-long island with a total population 40,000) may have over a dozen ships in port on a single day. Destinations may have limited influence over timing of arrivals - with some ports heavily used on weekends to begin tours, and other destinations receiving most visits in mid week (e.g., Cozumel, Thira Greece, Glacier Bay Alaska). At the same time, most cruise ships can be relatively self-contained for extended periods and therefore can have the flexibility to bring large numbers of tourists to small and fragile destinations without placing unacceptable levels of stress on such destinations (e.g. bringing their own water to water-short islands, taking sewage to the next port with suitable treatment facilities or providing on-board treatment, and limiting numbers of tourists allowed on shore at one time).

The impacts of cruise ships can be significant, bringing both benefits and risks. The sustainability issues associated with cruise ships can be put in two categories:

A) Issues related to the operation of the ships themselves (from: A Shifting Tide; Environmental Challenges and Cruise Industry Responses 2003)

* Air emissions;
* Ballast water (containing non-native species);
* Wastewater (sewage and grey water);
* Hazardous wastes (photo processing fluids, dry cleaning waste fluids and contaminated materials, print shop waste fluids, fluorescent and mercury vapour lamp bulbs, anti-foulant paint, hospital wastes);
* Solid waste (garbage - food, paper, cans, bottles, etc.);
* Oily bilge water;
* Effect on coral reefs (see destination effects below).

B) Effects on destinations (based on Lighthouse Foundation forum 2003)

* Provision of dockside facilities for services to cruise ships, including siting considerations;
* Water supply;
* Waste disposal and treatment (both liquid (sewage) and solid (garbage);
* Impact on destination services and infrastructure;
* Scheduling (including seasonality and multiple arrivals);
* Crowd management;
* Capture of benefits for the host community (revenues, jobs, capital support from cruise lines for facilities used, provisioning etc.).

* Security (including customs and immigration controls);
* Control of social and environmental impacts on targeted tour sites (including education of passengers);
* Coral reefs: protection and contribution to conservation.

Issues re ship operations	Suggested indicators
Aerial emissions (contributing to global climate change, local pollution)	• % reduction (by fleet, ship) of aerial emissions of NOx, sulphur dioxide based on 2001 baseline (or specific volume discharge by each ship/overall fleet average).
Ballast water (containing non-native species and which may affect biodiversity at the destination)	• Number of discharge violations (by ship, line); • number /% cruise ship visits to the destination which meet (to be agreed) standards.
Wastewater (sewage and grey water discharge which if not controlled may contaminate the destination)	• % cruise ship visits to the destination which use ICCL or equivalent standards; • % ships visiting the destination which have zero discharge systems, or use marine sewage treatment systems.
Hazardous wastes, which if discharged may contaminate the destination	• % cruise ship visits to the destination by ships with zero discharge systems for hazardous wastes.
Solid waste (garbage - food, paper, cans, bottles, etc.) which can pollute the sea and shores	• % ships visiting the destination with zero discharge systems for all ship garbage (including food waste).
Oily bilge or ballast water is a source of seawater and shore contamination, damage to species	• % cruise ships visiting the destination with bilge water separation systems.
Overall environmental performance of the ship - related to level of management and/or certification	• % of fleet (by firm) meeting ICCL or equivalent standards; • % of all ship visits by ships meeting ICCL or equivalent standards.
Economic sustainability	• Average occupancy of ship (by month); • Average sale price per day of berths.

Destinations often have little flexibility to influence when ships arrive or how long they stay. Distances from the home port or sailing times from the last port or to the next stop may dictate arrival and departure times. Where ships have very short stays, this can cause all tours to arrive at the same sites simultaneously, and also focus demands for other services (taxis, food, etc) in very short periods. When ships leave before dinner, passengers wait until they are on ship to eat, reducing their spending on shore. While some lines try to coordinate with others to share berthing capacity or to stagger arrivals, destinations may have little capacity to affect the decision. Where there are many destinations nearby (Greek islands, the Caribbean) destinations may compete with each other for custom, further reducing their ability to cause changes in scheduling.

The Norwegian Dream, with over 2000 passengers and crew on board, visits Puerto Chacabuco, Chile, population 300

Issues of destination effects	Indicators
Capture of benefits for the host community (revenues, jobs, capital support from cruise lines for facilities used, provisioning etc.)	• Average spending per cruise ship visitor (an indicator which is often difficult to obtain); • Total and average port fees and charges received per ship visit; • Total purchases of local goods (e.g., foodstuffs, beverages, souvenirs) per ship; • Total jobs directly attributable to cruise industry (port workers, provisioners, arranged tours etc.) (Note that indirect would also be desirable but very difficult to obtain unless there is a satellite tourism account in place); • Value of investment (capital, support for natural and cultural assets, training) by cruise ship companies in destination.
Security (including customs and immigration controls)	• Cost of security attributable to ships and their passengers.(by month, year); • Number of incidents (by type) involving passengers and crew.
Control of social and environmental impacts on targeted tour sites (including education of passengers)	• See section on ➢ **Controlling use intensity** of use of fragile natural and cultural sites (p. 192); • % of ships providing education to passengers regarding the sites and their behaviour as preparation or part of tours.

Issues of destination effects	Suggested indicators
Provision of dockside facilities for services to cruise ships, including siting considerations to minimize potential impacts.	• Number of ship visits per year (by month); • Maximum capacity of docking facilities (number ships docked at one time, and number anchored using lighters); • % Use of current shore docking capacity.
Water supply (see ➤ **Water availability** p. 165)	• Volume of water on-loaded at port; • Sale price of water per litre sold to ships (can be used in comparison with local price, or production cost per litre).
Waste disposal and treatment, both liquid	• Volume of waste accepted for disposal (solid, liquid); • Payment received (total, per unit volume) for disposal (see ➤ **Sewage** p. 171) and solid (see ➤ **Solid waste** p. 173).

Impact on destination services and infrastructure	• Peak day passengers discharged:
	  - total number;
	  - ratio of passengers discharged to local population;
	  - ratio of passengers discharged to number of local taxis;
	  - ratio of passengers discharged to number of restaurant seats in destination;
	  - other ratios based on key constraints (e.g. seats in tour buses or boats, trained guides, public washrooms, etc).

Scheduling (including seasonality and multiple arrivals)	• % annual ship visits arriving in peak month/ season; • Maximum simultaneous ship visits (peak day); • Number/% days with cruise ship(s) in port (peak season, all year); • Average duration of stay in port. (Longer visits may spread benefits, impacts as tourists have time to visit more widely, purchase longer tours or meals on shore).
Crowd management	• See issues section on density of use for key visited sites (➤ **Controlling Use Intensity** p. 192); • Total number of ship passengers eating at least one meal purchased on shore; • % visitors taking organized shore tours.

The variety of both home ports and destinations is growing. Quebec City is a new port for cruises leaving from north-eastern US cities.

In some destinations, cruise ships will berth near shore reefs or may anchor near reefs so that passengers may take advantage of access. Because of this, it is recommended that the following indicators be specifically considered for reef destinations.

Issues related to reefs	Indicators
Coral reefs: protection and contribution to conservation (note: many destinations are visited expressly for reef visits - Great Barrier Reef, Cozumel, Red Sea, Maldives, Fiji are examples)	• Volume of ship passengers visiting reefs on peak day; • Percentage of tourists who visit reefs who are accompanied by trained /certified guides; • Value of contribution by cruise ships/companies to protection of reefs in the destination. (see Box 4.1 on Reef Systems p. 250)

Cozumel, Mexico Cruise ships berth within a few hundred metres of Paraiso Reef and the ecological reserve of Chankanaab.

Part 5

Indicators Applications: Uses in Tourism Planning and Management

Throughout this Guidebook, the point has been emphasized that indicators are not an end in themselves. They become relevant only if used in tourism planning and management processes, and ideally they become effective in creating better and more sustainable decisions. In this part the role of indicators relative to destination planning and management is examined from several perspectives – based on field experiences in using indicators to support destinations and nations in their decisions regarding tourism. Examples are provided to show how indicators can be used to support a range of planning, operational and evaluation processes. In addition, several of the case studies in Part 6 (p. 327) provide good evidence of how indicators can make a difference to a destination – both in how the issues are viewed, and in the actions that follow. This section provides support to managers in building on indicators to achieve a range of management goals. Building good and responsive indicators is not enough; it is but the first step in making a difference. The real desired outcomes lie in the creation of sustainable destinations; indicators can be significant and strategic building blocks in this process.

In Part 2, a table clearly illustrates the relationship between tourism planning and management and the development and use of indicators in the different stages. (See Box 2.1 p. 23). The following sections explain some specific indicator applications in order to support tourism planning and management processes.

5.1 Indicators and Policy

A key factor in effective and responsible destination management is the identification by all stakeholders of the important policy issues that will guide the development process. Part 2 of this Guidebook provides guidance on how collaborative multi-stakeholder processes can lead to agreement on priority issues – which itself can assist in choosing indicators. These collaborative processes can also focus on setting sustainable tourism policy goals for the destination, taking into account how tourism development can help to:

* Increase GDP growth, investment, employment and foreign exchange earnings;

* Emphasize the role of tourism development in reducing poverty and increasing the quality of life of all residents;

* Protect and conserve the unique cultural and natural resources on which the tourism industry in most destinations is based;

* Ensure that natural and cultural resource protection are seen as collaborative activities between the public and private sectors as well as nongovernmental groups and communities;

* Establish the role of the private sector in the design, finance, implementation, ownership and operation of tourism facilities;

* Ensure that the poor are included in all decision making and are seen as important stakeholders in the tourism development process;

* Facilitate more effective coordination of essential governmental services at the national, regional and local levels;

- Develop an effective marketing and promotion program through a series of public/private sector cooperative efforts;

- Where appropriate explore mechanisms by which the control/regulator role of the public sector can be combined with that of the planner/facilitator/collaborator;

- Foster a positive awareness by the general public of the contribution of tourism to the destination's prosperity, reduction of poverty and overall improvement of the quality of life of its people.

This list is extensive, and illustrates the range of general policy issues that are integrally related to tourism development. This significant menu of policy goals is also a list of expectations – the public increasingly expects each sector (including tourism) to contribute to the resolution of these policy issues while it goes about the business of sustaining its own future.

The definition of indicators must occur within a collaborative environment and needs to support the information requirements of stakeholders. It must be recognized that in many destinations there are limited resources to collect indicator information and it is essential that stakeholders be realistic in their choice of factors that will be measured over time. This will likely occur in tandem with partners who share the same interests and may, through collaboration, support indicators development and use. An important part of the choice of indicators has to be a realistic assessment of budgets, time and political will to carry out an assessment process using strategic indicators; if indicators respond well, and can be produced in a cost effective way, they will be used. The indicators that have been identified should assist destination managers in formulating operational policies which will enable them to address a range of issues related to sustainable tourism:

- Conduct an active policy dialogue linking tourism to local, regional and national plans and priorities;

- Create a positive image, brand identity and positioning strategy to attract national and international visitors, in collaboration with regional, national tourism promotion agencies;

- Disseminate and adopt good practices (tested models, innovative programs, planning tools, lessons learned, or evaluation mechanisms) to local government agencies, businesses, and NGOs as well as development assistance agencies or donors;

- Establish facilitation procedures and financial mechanisms whereby resources from government, donors and private sector sources can be coordinated and effectively utilized to realize the aims listed above;

- Establish regulatory/legal frameworks and programs which support accommodations and tourist services;

- Create destination and site management plans which include guiding and interpretation programs, information services, visitor services and traffic control, environmental management standards, and quality standards;

- Establish and monitor safety and security standards and practices;

- Establish training policies for all levels of those involved in the planning; management and delivery of tourism products and services;

- Create the institutional basis for partnerships and joint venture arrangements;

- Provide support of Small to Medium sized Enterprises (SMEs) through capacity building, technical assistance, financial incentives, marketing activities;

- Create and implement directed policies that are targeted at developing tourism initiatives that serve social goals such as benefits for the poor, women, disadvantaged communities and regions.

All of these initiatives are building blocks towards sustainability for tourism. All benefit from better information on issues, clarity of goals, and means to measure progress.

In its simplest form, planning is about determining what you want, how you will go about getting it, and how you will know that you have got it. In determining and defining this process, planning cannot always be definitive. For example, planning must sometimes simplify complex situations so that they can be better understood, or so that unforseen opportunities and constraints can be accommodated in the future. To counter-balance this need for simplicity and flexibility, tools are required that provide a level of precision and certainty - indicators are one of these tools.

Strategic planning stresses the continuous nature of planning as a process of adapting to changing circumstances through integrating day to day planning and day to day management (Hall and McArthur 1998). Indicators are critical to strategic planning because they are central to all three parts of the continual improvement process - you cannot continually improve without knowing how close you are to your desired state. Indicators provide the means for continuously checking and refining integrated planning and management activity. (See Box 2.1 p. 23 which shows the relationship between indicators development and use and the normal sequence of planning). Here the specific use of indicators in planning and strategic planning is examined, and will demonstrate that indicators are not desirable to planning - they are essential.

Defining values

The foundations of planning are values - they are the tangible and intangible expression of what is most important to people. Individual and community values are used as a kind of touchstone to all planning activity. But most people are unfamiliar with describing their values precisely, and may need to use generalisations that mean different things to different people. Because indicators demand measurement and therefore precision, the definition of and use of indicators can greatly help clarify what values really are, and facilitate dialogue. For example, many tourists place a value on a destination being 'uncrowded'. But to what extent is a place considered "uncrowded" is perceived differently by different host communities and tourists of different origins and ages. For planners who wish to act to maintain satisfaction levels regarding crowding, an indicator measuring the actual number of people in a given area, monitoring the time it takes to be served, or calculating what percentage of the tourists or locals believe that it is "crowded" is needed; precisely how many people is too many, or what are the limits to acceptable crowding? Clarification of these values can lead to agreement on acceptable use levels and perhaps direct the actions needed to achieve them (See ➤ Use Intensity p. 192) Indicators become the vehicle for turning subjective values into objective, and therefore specific (often quantified) measures.

Defining desired outcomes

Desired outcomes are a common second level to planning which try to convert the values of society or stakeholders into a desirable situation or condition that is more accessible and which can lead to definable actions. Examples of broad social values which are important to sustainable tourism include: conserving the natural environment; satisfied tourists; viable tourism businesses; and a content host community. Indicators force greater clarity in definition of what is desired. For example, the broad goal (based on a range of stakeholder values) may be "conservation of the natural environment". An assessment could show for example that only 10% of the local environment is protected, and that over 20% has notable ecological value as habitat. With this indicator as a basis, an objective of 18% protected within 5 years could be established. This is a measurable objective with a specific time target. Over a plan or program period, the indicator (% with protection – or better, % of habitat with a specified level of protection) becomes the key measurement for progress.

Defining objectives, strategies and actions

After the desired outcomes have been established (often expressed as specific targets relative to the objectives), planning then focuses on how they may best be achieved. The result normally includes a range of objectives, of strategies to achieve them and actions which support the strategies. Constraints may also exist, which need to be monitored. This often shows the need for additional indicators in the planning process to help in the clear measurement of constraints (existence and degree). Some constraints may be difficult to describe and pinpoint and the questions used to clarify can lead to specific indicators: Will the community oppose a high density of development? (How many will oppose it and for how long?), or will labour be available to carry out the project when needed? (How many workers, what skills, when?)

Indicators can also be important to clarify risks and areas which require attention in the planning process. For example, an indicator helping to measure a dwindling wildlife population can trigger specific actions to protect, manage, or close a site as part of the plan. Part 2 details means to identify key risks, sensitivities, for planning and destination management purposes. (p. 21) For example, environmental indicators (based around water, energy and waste) were used extensively in the planning of the 2000 Olympics in Australia. The indicators were used as critical inputs in work to establish Ecologically Sustainable Development Plans for building and operating each facility across the Olympic site (Manidis Roberts 1998).

Social and economic indicators were similarly used by North Sydney Council in development of Cultural Tourism Plan for the broader local government area (Manidis Roberts 1997). Indicators measured type of visitor, level of patronage and economic return from alternative cultural tourism activities conducted by the council. The result was the first plan able to claim its initiatives were based on long term tracking of demand and supply.

Choosing between alternatives

Often there are alternative courses of strategies and actions to choose between. Choosing is not easy when there is a lack of information about the current situation, let alone the potential strengths and benefits of each alternative. Indicators can be important to gain a cost effective idea of these situations. For example, imagine a planner trying to choose between proposals permitting either a 50 bed or a 100 bed accommodation to proceed. If the planner is concerned about the respective water use, he/she could seek out the average amount of water used per room in similar establishments, and compare the alternative amounts with the known sustainable supply in the local area. The same indicators will act as performance measures regarding the degree to which plans and actions respond to the issue. Ideally, indicators are already in use which can be obtained by each proponent and used to guide proposals.

An example of this approach was used to select a preferred site for a canopy walk in Otway Forest (Victoria Australia) Economic indicators (visitation, visitor spending and length of stay) were used to determine the economic impact of alternative locations, as part of the planning process. An interesting use of indicators as key inputs into a geographical information system (GIS) is being developed to integrate tourism demand and supply scenarios in Canadian destinations and in the Cayman Islands, where a spatial approach tries to reconcile a range of demands with the known ecological sensitivities of the destination. (See http://www.fes.uwaterloo.ca/Tools/overview.html).

Otway forest viewing platform, Australia

Where strong indicators have been developed, they can become the inputs into a range of more sophisticated planning procedures, modelling and sensitivity analysis, which may lead to more robust and publicly accessible planning procedure, and to plans which are sensitive to a broad range of aspects of sustainability. Indicators can also signal needs and regulation and clarify elements to be regulated.

5.2.1 Using Indicators to measure plan progress

Checking performance

After a plan has been completed, its implementation begins. Planners need to know which actions and strategies are the most effective - so they can channel resources to successful approaches and re-work unsuccessful ones. If this is not done, opportunities could be missed, scarce resources could be wasted and support for the plan could diminish. Often the implementation can take years, but the planner needs to know, before the end of the planning period, what is working and what isn't. Indicators are extremely useful at testing the success of a plan as it is being implemented, because indicators are able to efficiently sample a situation to determine if changes have occurred. For example, a plan seeking to increase tourism might sample the number of operators or the number of jobs directly attributable to tourism. A good example is the case study of Cape Breton, (p. 355) where Parks Canada uses a range of indicators to monitor the effects of current tourism at the ecosystem level and is creating indicators to assist in developing and evaluating proposals for park development and use.

Revise desired outcomes

After checking performance, indicators will sometimes suggest that a plan may need to be changed because it got something wrong or because the key factors affecting the destination or its tourism have changed. Sometimes plans must change because the development occurred more quickly than expected, and to continue with the original planned activities might create a problem. Indicators, used over the course of planned activity, provide valuable direction for considering how to alter a strategy or action in a way that is most likely to improve the situation to become closer to the desired outcome. For example, in order to stimulate tourism business, the plan might have permitted access to a sensitive area. An indicator could have determined that instead of taking two years, the level of use or activity was achieved in six months, and that further stimulation would be unsustainable. The plan could, based on this new information, be changed from stimulation to management of the new activity and businesses.

Create a learning environment

Some people think that planning is the responsibility only of professional planners. This is an unreasonable assumption, as good planning needs a diversity of input and often also needs additional participation and partnership to be effective. Indicators provide a way to involve a wider range of participants in the strategic planning process. Indicators provide a reality check – forcing planners to be precise, to define in real terms (using indicators) what they are using as targets, what specific actions are intended, and what the desired goals or outcomes really mean. (Not just cleaner water, but how much cleaner, when, how much better than now, and at what cost; not just "more tourists" but how many, when, where, and bringing what benefits to the local economy.) Indicators stimulate discussion, and may lead to debate, or to consensus.

Indicators can be designed to be managed by non-planners - such as non-government organisations and community groups. The collection and reporting of information empowers these people with an understanding and sense of responsibility that helps to bring them into the planning process on an equal footing to the planners - information is power.

The sharing of this information from the indicators helps break down the formality of planning processes and create a continual learning environment. Trends from different indicators can be contrasted to determine relationships between indicators and between other events. People monitoring indicators and compiling their results may discover a problem or success before others. Indicators not only empower people with information and the opportunity to analyse it - they can also empower people to do something with it. Responses could include seeking changes to planning, action from organisations or individuals or media publicity.

Examples of the use of indicators to create a learning environment and empower communities into the planning process include Samoa (p. 413) Villarica Chile (p. 448). Kangaroo Island, South Australia (p. 391) and the Balearic Islands (p. 345). The Lanzarote case is a specific integration of indicators into a destination planning process framed as sustainable development (p. 406). The development of a means of monitoring the health of tourism and other key values in these destinations has involved a wide range of groups and has resulted in more coordinated and supportive approaches to sustainable tourism.

Indicators can provide a level of specificity that is often lacking in plans that must deal with complex issues. In this way, indicators provide people with the opportunity to understand every part of the planning process, and how to be involved. Indicators are also extremely valuable at monitoring the progress of a plan's implementation to check on its success and identify whether parts of the plan should be altered. These uses increase the level of participation in planning and subsequently add valuable insights and expertise and improve the use of scarce resources.

In summary, indicators are a necessary and ideally integral part of the planning process. As delineated in Box 2.1, indicators have an important role at all stages in planning. At the outset, good indicators show the need for plans – helping to clarify and make precise goals and objectives. In plan formulation they provide the required clarity. Indicators are the key to monitoring progress in implementation and in helping to determine whether and when plans may need to be revisited. Where there is debate, indicators are key information to permit informed discussion, allow full participation, and create accountability for outcomes.

5.3 Indicators and Regulation

Legislation, Monitoring Compliance

Regulators depend on indicators. Most regulations are based on the achievement of specific standards, whether or not these are specifically legislated or are implemented administratively to deal with particular issues. Regulations are usually expressed in the same way as indicators; e.g., parts per million permitted in emissions from the hotel generator, number of passengers allowed in a watercraft, speed of automobiles through the park, maximum decibels of noise permitted between midnight and dawn, etc. Often indicator development and use is the first step – helping to clarify a problem, and on the basis of accurate information developing a regulation or legislation if needed. For example, a rising number of ill tourists due to food-related diseases may create a demand for stronger regulation of restaurants or of providers of street food. Many regulations will require the regular use of specified indicators as part of monitoring programs – either done by the managers or by officials. Several of the issues identified in Part 3 are subject to regulation in many jurisdictions. Where available, benchmarks, international or commonly used standards, and examples of regulation are provided in the appropriate issue section as a point of reference.

A good system of indicators will help identify risks or problems which may require a regulatory response, will then be incorporated in regulations or legislation as part of a regulatory process, and ultimately can serve to measure the effectiveness of regulations and enforcement relative to the original problem through verifying compliance.

Indicators can also allow for more flexible adaptive management as an alternative to heavy use of regulation. Indicators can also be used to reduce the conventional regulatory approach to managing issues and risk, permitting a more flexible and responsive management. Often tourism in sensitive areas presents risks of potential impacts that create worries among some groups - planners included. The response of regulating use (anticipate and prevent damage by zoning or limits to uses) may not always be needed and may reduce the benefits that the initiative was seeking to create. If there are strong and agreed indicators which are used to monitor areas of concern, this can delay, and even replace, the need for creating such regulation. Monitoring the areas most at risk and incorporating adaptive management measures to respond to monitoring, permits timely action if a problem begins to be detected. Examples of this approach are described in the Sydney Quarantine Island case (p. 429) and in the private use of indicators for adaptive management in the Yacutinga Argentina case (p. 453).

5.4 Carrying Capacity and Limits to Tourism

Sensitivity, Limits of Acceptable Change, Thresholds

Carrying capacity is a much used phrase – usually in the context of how many tourists can be accommodated in a certain place or area without damaging the place or reducing tourists' satisfaction. The idea of carrying capacity is founded on the experience of pastoral agriculture - where it was observed that a pasture could support in perpetuity a particular number of cattle. If this threshold was exceeded, the supporting system was damaged, often to the point where it could no longer support grazing at all. Carrying capacity as a concept measures what level of use is sustainable. However, for tourism applications, the concept of carrying capacity is much more complex, given that there is a wide range of environmental and socio-economic factors that interact at tourism destinations, and that many of them depend on perception of host communities and tourists.

For tourism, the concept of carrying capacity has value - particularly because it draws attention to limits and thresholds beyond which we do not wish to tread. However, in dealing with the reality, we need to consider these factors (derived from Manning 1997):

* There are a large number of factors interacting in any destination (in all   dimensions of sustainability... environmental, social and economic) which affect the ability of the destination to support any specific type of tourism;

* The impact of human activity on a system may be gradual, and may affect different factors of the system at differing rates, with different impacts on potential tourism uses. (e.g., poorer water quality is likely to impact swimming before it affects uses such as sailing or sightseeing);

* There are different types of users, and many different forms of tourism activities, each of them with different needs, levels of impacts and limits;

* There are varying perceptions and expectations of different host societies and different tourist segments. Crowds attract some tourists, others seek solitude, or the ability to experience nature without disturbance (see Colima and Rimini illustrations: each is successful in sustaining its tourism product);

* Carrying capacity limits are not static, they can be modified dependent on the changes in the system and in management measures (e.g. due to improvement in site-infrastructure, organization of groups, conservation of the natural environment, the number of tourists permitted at a site without harming the environment can be increased). Also if conditions worsen over time, numbers can be further limited).

Because of these concerns, when applied to tourism a simple definition of carrying capacity involving the identification of a single threshold value will be inadequate in nearly all cases. This reinforces the conclusion in this regard contained in the paper prepared from the 1990 WTO/UNEP workshop on carrying capacity (World Tourism Organization, 1992). It also reflects some of the concerns contained in the 1981 WTO capacity standards - which suggest using working limits for particular types of tourism, but also warns users of the need to adapt these to the unique conditions of each site. Instead, a more sophisticated approach to the identification of impacts and of limits is needed, which better reflects the sensitivity of different attributes of the environment to different types and levels of impact or use.

Several approaches have been developed to consider the factors which may affect the ability to support tourism. These approaches range from work on the limits to acceptable change to applications such as those described in detail in the case studies in (e.g. Arches p. 342, Kangaroo Island p. 391 Albufera de Valencia p. 330). These cases show different approaches to the estimation of capacity, of limits to change and to total numbers of tourists or levels of development of the destination. All show that a number of factors are important to the concept:

1. Ecological capacity – where biological and physical factors provide constraints to the maximum numbers which can be accommodated (for useful indicators see the section on Tourism in Sensitive Ecosystems p. 263). Examples include the capacity of rivers to absorb waste, capacity of species to withstand disturbance or sensitivity of flora to trampling or harvesting by visitors;

2. Cultural capacity – where the impact on a local community, or the availability of human resources are the key limiting factors to acceptance of tourism and tourist numbers;

3. Social or Psychological capacity: The origin and background of tourists determines the number of tourists or the level of crowding they consider acceptable. Perception and psychological factors relating to both the host community and the tourists are determinants;

4. Infrastructural capacity – where current infrastructure (water supply systems, sewage systems, transport systems, numbers of rooms to accommodate tourists) are the short to medium term limiters for tourist numbers;

5. Management capacity – where the key constraints are institutional, related to the numbers of tourists who (with their impacts) can be realistically managed. (Note that most economic measures – which could be called economic capacity- are in fact aspects of management capacity – limits on the resources available to support management of tourism (control, design, etc)).

Colima Mexico where more tourists could spoil the sunset experience and cause the sea birds to locate elsewhere.

Tourists visit Rimini Italy in large numbers to experience the beach and many other shore activities.

Indicators and Carrying Capacity

While it has always been difficult to estimate or model overall carrying capacity (although some of the cases in Part 6 do provide tools which help to understand the relationships and complexity), indicators can be of considerable use to monitor how development is related to specific limits which may affect the sustainability of tourism. In some environments like the island of Cozumel (Mexico) See Box 3.30 p. 167), a single factor (water supply) is the most important factor limiting tourism growth. While in the longer term, sophisticated water supply and conservation programs may enlarge the supply and reduce the per-capita demand, one factor, water is at present the key limiting factor. Measurement of this factor (see ➤ Water Availability, p. 165) is probably the single most important to determine capacity in the case of Cozumel Island. In other destinations, cultural capacity may be the most important – and locals may decide on tourism limits in order to avoid major disruption in their way of life or erosion of some cultural values. Other destinations may have limits related to current infrastructure (e.g., number of parking places in a national park, number of seats in a stadium, capacity of a sewage treatment plant). Such infrastructural limits can be altered and removed if decision makers approve the costs. Indicators which measure the relative use of such capacity can be critical to the decision of whether or not to limit numbers of visitors, or whether and when to invest in new capacity. For some ecological factors, there is much less flexibility. If ecological thresholds can be scientifically estimated, indicators which measure key factors relative to these thresholds (e.g. levels of disturbance in ecosystems, species breeding success: (See Natural and Sensitive Ecological Sites p. 263) become important inputs into decisions of how much activity and what types to permit.

As understanding of the carrying capacity concept advances, several approaches have been developed to help understand what are essentially human/biosphere relationships, using information relating to measures of limits and measures of trends in use. These include:

a. Limits of acceptable change, where the capacity of a destination (often applied to a community or a protected area) is estimated primarily based on what the residents or managers are prepared to tolerate. The most important criteria or indicators tend to be those related to perceived impacts by those affected, although in some applications a number of different indicators can be used. This approach emphasizes uses which match the stakeholders' perception of what is tolerable;

b. Management tools such as Visitor Impact Management (VIM), Visitor Experience and Resource Protection(VERP), Visitor Activity Management Process (VAMP) and Recreation Opportunity Spectrum (ROS) which attempt to match permitted visitor uses with known sensitivities in a planning and management process which tries to limit negative effects while permitting types and levels of use compatible with environmental protection. (See Arches case p. 342);

c. System sensitivity, where the sensitivity of selected (usually ecological) assets to different use levels are analyzed. Often many indicators are used to show a variety of relationships. Frequently a single indicator or small set are determined to be the most critical, and use levels set to respect these. (e.g. the site will run out of water at 500 persons per day, or the biologists' work shows that any more than 10 persons on that site per day will cause the endangered species to abandon its breeding site). Often management actions can alter the limits (reduced water use per tourist, use of blinds for wildlife viewers) which may alter the numbers which can be accommodated. This approach is most used for small sensitive natural sites;

d. Multivariate models which attempt to estimate capacity and limits based on many different variables – and try to integrate many different measures and relationships to provide an overall capacity measure. (See Albufera case p. 330) Such models require a great deal of data (many indicators) and a good understanding of the relationships between many factors in the destination. In operation, this type of model can lead to the establishment of standards and limits which respond to many different types of stress on a site.

A more detailed examination of some of these approaches is contained in the IUCN/WTO/UNEP publication, "Sustainable Tourism in Protected Areas - Guidelines for Planning and Management", Chapter 6: Managing the Challenges of Tourism in Protected Areas, where the relative utility of several of these approaches is rated. Indicators are shown to be a critical element in the construction of any of these approaches; the choice of which indicators to include and the weighting, if any, can greatly affect the results of the exercise.

Carrying capacity is a difficult but important concept, because it implies limits and can be used to stimulate discussion on those limits. Thus the determination of "carrying capacity" – or the desired levels of tourism is often negotiated by the stakeholders... each an advocate for his or her own interests. To date, tourists themselves are rarely present to advocate their interests at destinations during the planning process. Their interests enter the debate via tourism organizations or enterprises who are advocates. Local planners may have access to indicators which reflect the needs or desires of different tourist segments, through market research, exit questionnaires and other feedback which can provide clarity. Sometimes innovative solutions result, as agreement can be found for different use levels at different times or places (e.g. the religious site is open to all except when religious services are under way, when only 20 visitors who are suitably attired are allowed in.)

There continues to be a demand for numeric estimates of carrying capacity – for a single number on the maximum number of tourists that can be allowed, or how many rooms are allowed to be built. It is suggested that managers consider more than a simple single limit, and make use of a range of indicators to provide the best information possible on the implications of different levels and types of use for the destination and for the specific sites within it.

Box 5.1 Carrying Capacity Assessment for Tourism in Malta

As part of a tourism development strategy for the Maltese islands, the question of carrying capacity was addressed through a number of scenarios, with indicators used to identify existing profiles and trends. A study was done and initial analysis of data became a foundation for different options. Public discussions resulted in the selection of a specific scenario, and indicators were used to show current status and to focus discussion on changes.

The indicators which were used included measures of tourist numbers, length of stay, and tourist density at an island-wide level. A range of indicators were used to measure tourist impact on infrastructure (energy, water, road traffic) accommodation, beaches, banking etc. Seasonal variation was a major factor and was applied to the analysis of most indicators.

Indicators, including most of those designated baseline in this Guidebook, were used as the key points of reference for the discussion of carrying capacity options.

For further information see: Mangion, Marie-Louise, 2001.Carrying Capacity Assessment for Tourism in the Maltese Islands, Malta, Ministry of Tourism.

5.5 Public Reporting and Accountability

Information is much more powerful if shared. All of the work associated with creating good indicators can be wasted if there is no effective means to make certain that the information gets to those stakeholders who need it, and that they have an incentive to use it. This section presents some of the means to assure that the indicators reach those who need the information, when they need it and in a form which is most useful to them. (See also Box 2.15. (p. 50) Visual portrayal of indicators) Matching information to the needs of stakeholders is vital from the very beginning of indicators development, and can be the key to consensus on policy issues, programs and action.

The key clients for indicators:

* Public authorities at all levels (tourism administrations and offices, as well as administrations in related fields, such as environment, transportation, economics, education, protected areas, etc.);

* Civil servants or public officials, program and project administrators;

* Managers of private companies and their associations (chambers of commerce, tourism trade associations, tourism boards, etc);

* Academic and research institutions that deal with tourism-related issues;

* NGOs and conservation organizations;

* The general public, including residents, tourists and all other stakeholders with an interest in the sustainable development of a destination;

* Specialists, who may help to develop the information that supports indicators, or who perform studies that help understand in greater detail the issues and trends of concern.

The users of indicators may operate at different levels – and therefore need different levels of detail. For specialists and managers directly involved with a specific issue or attraction, frequent, detailed indicators may help them make decisions – and many may already have developed their own measures and be using them. For the public and for most decision makers, the indicators important to them may be fewer, less detailed, and portrayed in ways of greater use to them. Thus the reporting of indicators may occur at different levels and use different media in order to match information to the specific needs of stakeholders.

5.5.1 Considerations regarding form and content of information provided include:

1. Level and form of information. What is provided should respond to the needs and level of understanding of user groups: Government officials and experts will likely require more detailed and technical information (e.g. on water quality they would need the lab-test results on different substances and contaminants), while for the general public the indicator results have to be communicated in simpler ways (e.g. a general graph indicating if water quality has improved or not over the years). Managers of tourism companies require indicator results in a format that supports their operations and links with business and facility level concerns (e.g. relating indicators on water-problems to water use in hotels, possible impacts on businesses);

2. Periodicity (e.g. daily press, periodic status and progress reports, annual, bi-annual, end of government terms, real-time measurements, seasonal reports, etc.) The key is to have information available when it is needed, and when it can influence a decision;

3. Channels and forms of communication. There are many means to provide information; printed and audiovisual media, press releases, bulletins, status and progress report publications, report on specific environmental and socio-economic issues, planning documents published for public consultations (including initial diagnosis, SWOT analysis), scientific study reports, Internet, conferences and events, election campaigns, etc. Each has a different constituency and may have a different impact.

The public and most decision-makers will use indicators as general information – seeking awareness and warning of emerging issues or concern. Some direct decisions may be made (Do I go to the beach today, or is the destination safe for my winter vacation?) However, most uses of indicators will be less direct or immediate, and the user may be able to wait for information to be analyzed, digested and presented in accessible form. Many different means are in use to provide indicators information to these users:

* *Issue scans, initial assessments and diagnosis for strategic planning:* Indicators are a first source for agencies seeking to do issue scans or SWOT analyses, as well as any form of any initial assessment that helps identifying problems and risks. These studies published serve as discussion papers, stimulating debate and dialogue;

* *Annual (or Periodic) status reports:* A common vehicle is the annual report – on the state of the destination (or state of the environment) and the key issues. Such documents are designed for the public, usually widely circulated (many are available on websites – particularly for corporations, tourist authorities, or government agencies focused on specific issues) and are generally graphic in nature – with lots of pictures, graphs and anecdotes which illustrate the main points. Often these are a public form of performance accountability, and a means for taking credit for success. Indicators can also serve as public reports on progress – such as achievement of plan goals, results

of programs to achieve tourism or destination objectives. A common tactic is to release indicators reports tied to a significant event. Status reports are normally tied to government events or planning periods. Often, elections become the forum where certain indicators (environmental damage, health problems, employment trends, loss of tourist links or tourist traffic, etc.) can become part of campaign issues. The fact that indicators are available may help in the choice of issues by those running for office, and may also be important in any public process (debates, party platforms, public meetings) where the public can show which issues they feel to be important. In this sense, the existence of indicators can result in an issue becoming politicized, and may lead to commitments to resolve it;

* *Issue bulletins:* Because of the amount of work in compiling extensive reports, many jurisdictions (national, international and local) have moved to reporting on specific issues (state of the beaches, air quality, coastal development) one issue at a time, issuing periodic fact sheets which, over a period of time, may constitute a complete report on key issues. This form of reporting has the advantage of permitting shorter lag times between information gathering and publication, eliminating the need to wait until all indicators have been analyzed and integrated, and also permitting reasonably rapid addition of new issues and indicators. A disadvantage may lie in having information seen in isolation, and not reporting how issues and indicators show the overall state at any point in time of the destination. (See example from Balearic islands accommodation Box 5.2, that was reported with other indicators as a unified volume) Note that the visual portrayal of indicators may have higher impact than just numbers. In Chinese newspapers, a graphic format is used to show air pollution levels, and it is easy to see in the bar graph whether your city is more or less contaminated than Beijing or Shanghai – as twenty cities are regularly featured;

* *Report cards:* A "report card" uses the information from an indicator or set of indicators to provide a subjective grade for performance – making a form of qualitative information accessible. A typical report card may give a destination an A for cleanliness, C for conservation, D for traffic control and B for public safety. While this may be done by the reporting agency, it is often most effective if done by others such as NGOs or even by opposition political parties. This generates interest in the indicators, may stimulate a public dialogue and often leads to remedial action for problem areas. Report cards are likely to draw attention and create debate – and, like issue bulletins, bring information directly to the public forum;

* *Press releases (and regular press monitoring):* One of the most effective uses of indicators is through the press, particularly if the press chooses to report particular indicators regularly. Daily or weekly reporting on air quality (e.g. Chinese cities), beach closures due to contamination, waiting times to get into national parks (call an information number to get up to date wait times in many North American parks and campgrounds), total tourist numbers, or cruise ship arrivals are all examples of how use of indicators related to tourism is entering the normal public domain. As well, specific press releases on problems revealed by indicators (tourism dropped 20% last year due to fear of terrorism, 50% increase in tourists who stayed more than one week) is important to public understanding of the issues and implications;

* *Conferences:* Conferences can be an excellent vehicle to gain attention for indicators and to reinforce their message. Often public release of reports or fact sheets can be timed to a conference, and delegates can participate in the discussion of results. This can lead to commitments being made to address the issues.

Box 5.2 Tourist Accommodation capacity in the Balearic Islands (Spain)

Demographic Indicator
Pressure Indicator
Scope: Balearic Islands
Period: 1991-2000

    ◦ Tourist accommodation capacity is one of the most important mechanisms to efficiently control human pressure on resources. The lack of this control produces unsustainability.

Observed tendency: The total accommodation capacity has risen up to 1,860,000 beds in year 2000, this means an increase of 4.78% in comparison to 1998. The main cause of this increase is the growth in 6.51% of residential homes because the tourist accommodation capacity has for the last 2 years. decreased by 0.90%.

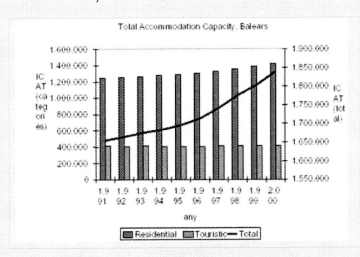

Desirable tendency: Stabilize the number of accommodation capacity. This can be achieved by disqualifying urbanizable land, as well as, promoting the restoration of houses.

Description: Total Accommodation Capacity (ICAT) has been established through residential accommodation capacity (ICAr) and tourist accommodation capacity (ICAt).

Methodology: Accommodation capacity is obtained by the sum of Residential accommodation Capacity (2.97 people per housing) and the tourist accommodation Capacity (tourist beds from legal tourist supply). Illegal tourist supply has been considered, for the purpose of this study as, residential accommodation.

Sources:

◦ Ministerio de Fomento. Housing census 1991.
◦ White book of Balearic Islands Housing 2001. Conselleria d'Obres Públiques, Habitatge i Transports, Direcció General d'Arquitectura i Habitatge.
◦ Direcció General d'Ordenació Turística, Conselleria de Turisme.

Source: Centre for Tourism Research and Technologies of the Balearic Islands (CITTIB)

◦ *Public announcements of support or commitment:* Indicators can be a signal for the need for political action. One of the most important impacts of indicators is to stimulate both demands for action, and appropriate public responses. (e.g., the article in the newspaper revealing a rise in concern by tourists about crime in the destination followed the next day by the announcement of a new tourist police program to be put in place in the next year).

* *Real time metering and reporting:* Where the intention is to alter behaviour, information provided in real time can be the most effective. (e.g., current air quality or noise levels shown on public meters at key downtown areas, or public screens showing the length of the line in hours or minutes for entry into an attraction.)   If you see directly the results of your action, you may change your behaviour – particularly if the cost to you individually is shown in real time. In some jurisdictions, it is now possible to obtain key information rapidly, designed specifically to provide key information on a most current possible basis to officials and others (such as the press) One example from a Canadian ministry is called an "information dashboard". Each morning when the manager starts his/her computer, a set of standard indicators on the issues most important to him/her is the first screen that appears, with important changes highlighted as well as key indicators on latest issues.

* *Reporting for management of tourism facilities and attractions.*

Indicators can be of use to managers in many forms, dependent on their needs.

Rapid reporting of raw data is often critical (number of complaints about food at the theme park). In other cases, the use of time series analyses of indicators – frequency distributions and contingency tables – can yield important information. (e.g., 80% of the visitors arrived after 10AM, or over half of those over 60 felt that the attraction was not accessible for them). Used as ratios (visitors per washroom) or in time series, (20% growth in disabled travellers in two years) these data can contribute significantly to knowledge needed to spot emerging issues and deal with current ones. Benchmarking (see p. 322) is likely to be very important to these managers, as they are often in a very competitive marketplace. Use of indicators to show progress or problems can be very effective (e.g." the level of satisfaction of tourists has fallen steadily each month since October" or "tourist spending up for third year in a row").

A concern for the producers of indicators is misuse or misinterpretation. Bad news may have broad impacts beyond that intended – where release of a big number (tourism down 40% this year due to health scare) may itself cause further damage, as it is used broadly and seen by prospective travellers who themselves may be deterred, even though the problem may have already been resolved. One of the most important caveats for those who produce indicators is to retain credibility – so that the indicators are seen to be objective, and can be used with assurance by all. One of the criteria for selection and use of indicators (see Annex C1, C2 p. 485) is credibility – and hyperbole can undercut the credibility of the indicator or even the entire program. In any event, proponents or opponents can be expected to put "spin" on an indicator, as can the press. "Erosion of 5% of the beach in a season" can be easily extrapolated to a bold headline of "Beach Gone in 15 Years" whether the science supports this or not.

5.5.2 Measuring Success and /or Results of Indicator Applications

Reach, Penetration, Action

Because this is about indicators, it is only natural to seek indicators regarding the success of an indicators program. In Annex C 4 of this Guidebook is a template for the re-evaluation of an indicators program and of each of the indicators it produces. The form has built into it de facto indicators to be used to measure success

The objective is continuous improvement – adapting the indicators to be the most effective possible to respond to new issues, changing data availability, and changing demands for information. Some of these are suggested in the table below.

Components of the Issue	Indicators
Success in generation of the indicators	◦ Number of indicators regularly produced on continuing basis; ◦ % of originally defined indicators set implemented; ◦ % of indicators up to date in monitoring.
Level of effort to apply the indicators	◦ Number of person days/months and amount of tourism authority or agency responsible for indicators program; ◦ Budget designated for/spent on data gathering, processing and reporting; ◦ Communication outputs frequency, number of copies of reports containing indicator results produced and distributed, participation statistics of public events, hits in websites where indicator results bare reported, etc.
Level of awareness of the indicators	◦ % of destination population aware of the indicators program (and selected indicators); ◦ % of tourism sector enterprises aware of the indicators program (and selected indicators) – by user survey.
Level of use of the indicators	◦ % of key sector stakeholders using the indicators on a regular basis – including how and where they use it, (user survey); ◦ Frequency of public reporting of the indicators (officially, and in press).
Impact of the indicators	◦ % of major decisions affecting tourism where any of the indicators were used/cited; ◦ Opinion of the utility of the indicators program (and of each indicator) by key stakeholders; ◦ % of stakeholders satisfied with selected indicators;
Continuing commitment to the program	◦ % of original partners involved in the ongoing program; ◦ Level of commitment to future indicators (user survey).

Reason for use of these indicators: To determine whether the indicators being produced are optimal, are used, and are making a difference. This is a component of an iterative planning approach which looks to continuous improvement and may result in changes to the program, addition of new indicators, or dropping of those which are not useful. They are in effect, performance measures for an indicators program.

Source of information: The authority managing the indicators program, plus regular scans of press and political use of the indicators.

Means to portray indicators: Of greatest use as an internal management tool for the indicators program. It can also be used publicly to show that indicators do make a difference.

Benchmarking: This is a relatively new field; it is expected that comparisons will increasingly be possible among destinations which adopt an indicators program. They will also be a growing source of methods to strengthen indicators and their impact.

5.6   Indicators and Certification/Standards Programs

Voluntary systems for the certification of quality in tourism have existed for many decades. Among the oldest surviving programs, with wide consumer acceptance, are the five-star rating system (generally implemented by national governments), the American Automobile Association (AAA) lodging rating system, and the Michelin Guides. Many other rating systems such as these have arisen and disappeared over the years, but a qualitative change in the types of certification used for tourism occurred in the early 1990s with two parallel developments: the introduction and popularization of process-based quality (ISO 9,000) and environmental management systems (ISO 14,000 series), along with the development of methods for evaluating environmental and social performance – what are now called "sustainability" criteria. The process-based systems, because they do not rate products and are not comparable from business to business, have not had an important impact in tourism, but performance-based and mixed systems, with predominantly environmental and safety criteria, have proliferated since the Earth Summit in 1992.

These methods include certification programs, eco-labels, ethics codes, benchmarking, best practice manuals, and prizes. The World Tourism Organization identified over 260 such programs in a study in 2001, Voluntary Initiatives for Sustainable Tourism:

Worldwide Inventory and Comparative Analysis of 104 Eco-labels, Awards and Self-Commitments, (WTO, 2001) and many more have arisen since then. More than 60 programs (two thirds in Europe) offer third-party certification – a guarantee by an independent third-party that a business or an activity complies with established criteria. Most environmental and sustainability certification systems target accommodations; others are directed for transportation and tour operator services. Other specialized guidelines and certification programs exist for adventure sports and tourism (national parks, rafting, mountaineering, canopy exploration, caving, diving, etc.)

These programs emphasize, to different degrees, the three principal aspects of sustainability: environmental, socio-cultural, and economic criteria.

The certification of tourism operations guarantees that a third party has inspected and approved the performance or processes of the business, but certification programs have additional uses: the certification process and criteria serve as a manual for exemplary practices and create a framework for improvement in business management through incentives and technical assistance on sustainability aspects. Certification basically means the measuring and verification of these improvements through indicators.

In the most credible certification programs, evaluation of compliance is done by independent third parties. Industry-based evaluation is known as second-party certification (often done by tour operators associations or by wholesalers of the products they promote) while self-evaluation without outside verification is called first-party certification (e.g. a hotel or tour operator promotes themselves as "ecological" or "environmentally-friendly", according to its own code of conduct and criteria).

5.6.1   Certification Criteria

Most reputable sustainable tourism certification programs incorporate elements of environmental, social, and business performance. Some are important at the planning stage for new businesses or products, while others relate to ongoing management.

Life cycle considerations should be brought into play at the planning stage. The social impacts of tourism should also be considered from the initial planning stage (e.g. land acquisition, use of water and public services, protection of local cultural heritage and values, contribution to the local economy, etc.)

The indicators for these certification criteria can become useful management tools in tourism businesses. Criteria for certification normally require standards to be met; standards which are often a definable point to be reached on one or more indicators or performance measures. The table below shows key components and corresponding criteria, related to issues of quality and sustainability certification. They are based on the results of the Sustainable Tourism Stewardship Council (STSC) feasibility study, (http://www.rainforest-alliance.org/programs/sv/stsc.html) which was in turn based on ISO/IEC guide 65:1996, ISO14024 standard, the Mohonk Agreement, (an agreed framework and principles for the certification of ecotourism and sustainable tourism involving many international organizations http://www.ips-dc.org/ecotourism/mohonkagreement.htm), the Tour Operators Initiative for Sustainable Development (see Box 3.47 p. 243) and the VISIT standard for Ecolabels (http://www.yourvisit.info/public/gb/gbcont_10plus.html), while they also reflect the WTO recommendations for governments on sustainability certification. (http://www.world-tourism.org/sustainable/doc/certification-gov-recomm.pdf)

The indicators or criteria cited below are divided into two sets:

1. Those that can indicate the effectiveness of a certification program;

2. Those that can be used to measure progress in sustainability at a tourism business, operation or destination.

For the process-based criteria simple yes/no indicators can be used (e.g. does the enterprise have an environmental policy, does it have a program to employ local residents?) To measure the performance-based criteria more specific qualitative and quantitative indicators are needed (e.g. liters of water or kilowatt hours of energy use per guest per night). For more detail on specific indicators and measurement methods see the corresponding issue sections in Part 3. The following list of general criteria can serve as a checklist for sustainability certification programs:

Key issues	Criteria
Criteria for effectiveness of a sustainable tourism certification program. (Based on STSC Feasibility Study, Table 7.2).	
Clarity of objectives	◦ Aims and objectives of the program are clearly stated; ◦ Criteria are in accordance with or surpass local and international standards and legislation in health, safety, consumer needs, and environmental and social performance.
Selectivity	◦ Criteria are measurable and show significant differences in environmental and social impact by certified operations; ◦ The certification label can only be used when the criteria have been met; ◦ Criteria are attainable and encourage best practice in benefiting tourist providers, tourists, local communities, and conservation; ◦ Criteria are largely performance-based.
Consultation and transparency	◦ Criteria have been developed in consultation with all interested parties; ◦ Criteria are based on sound principles of science, engineering, and social, environmental, and economic management; ◦ Criteria are publicly available; ◦ All stages of the development and operation of the program are transparent and free of conflicts of interest.

Non-discrimination	• Programs are open to all applicants who comply with the criteria; • Criteria, costs, and fees permit participation by small and medium enterprises; • Technical assistance is available to applicants and awardees, but not in such as way as to establish conflicts of interest.
Verification	• Compliance is verifiable by trained auditors; • Applicants provide credible evidence of compliance; • Certification is for a defined period and is retired at the end of that period if not renewed or in case of subsequent non-compliance.

Criteria to measure progress in sustainability at a destination. (Based on Mohonk Agreement, STSC Feasibility Study Section 7.1 and Font and Bendell, 2002).

Environmental:

Overall environmental protection	• Environmental management commitment by tourism business; • Environmental planning and impact assessment, considering social, cultural, ecological and economic impacts (including cumulative impacts and mitigation strategies); • Habitat/eco-system/wildlife maintenance and enhancement. Biodiversity conservation and integrity of ecosystem processes; • Mechanisms for monitoring and reporting environmental performance; • Specific standards for impacts specific to diving, golf, beaches, and other sub-sectors.
Energy and water consumption	• Energy (consumption-reduction-efficiency- sustainability of energy supply); • Water (consumption-reduction-quality).
Waste management (solid and water)	• Reduction through purchasing and consumption procedures; • Recycling and reuse; • Final disposal.
Site alteration and life cycle considerations	• Appropriate building materials; • Appropriate protection of habitat and land forms (site disturbance, landscaping, rehabilitation, drainage, soils, and stormwater); • Appropriate scale of activities and infrastructure and sensitivity towards sense of place.
Purchasing	• Sustainability of materials and supplies (recyclable and recycled materials, locally produced, certified timber products etc.); • Use of nature-friendly cleaning products; • Hazardous substances (reduction-appropriate handling).
Contamination	• Air quality and emissions; • Noise reduction; • Transport (public transport- green alternatives provided).
Environmental information.	• Interpretation/education for customers; • Staff training, education, responsibility, knowledge and awareness in environmental aspects.

Sociocultural:

Community (relations-welfare)	· Mechanisms to ensure rights and aspirations of local and/or indigenous people are recognized; · Emphasis and conservation of local/regional culture, heritage and authenticity; · Measures to protect the integrity of local community's social structure; · Minimize impacts upon social structures, culture, and economy (on both local and national levels); · Appropriateness of land acquisition/access / land tenure.
Community (participation-organization-involvement)	· Mechanisms to ensure that negative economic impacts on local communities are minimized and preferably there are substantial economic benefits to local communities; · Contributions to the development/ maintenance of local community infrastructure.
Employee training and promotion	· Local residents are employed, including in management positions; · Training for local employees.
Sociocultural information	· Interpretation/education for customers; · Staff training, education, responsibility, knowledge and awareness in social and cultural aspects.

Economic and quality:

Creation of local employment	· Creation of networks of "green businesses" within a given destination; · Use of locally sourced and produced materials and food; · Use of organic food; · Supply chain management through green and sustainable purchasing policies.
Ethical business practice	· Personnel: fair treatment; · Mechanisms to ensure labor arrangements are not exploitative, and conform to local laws or international labor standards; · Accurate, responsible marketing leading to realistic expectations.
Overall business competence	· Mechanisms for reservations, accounting, marketing, and administration.
Customer satisfaction	· Requirement for consumer feedback regarding quality of the tourism experience.
Health and safety	· Business meets or exceeds applicable health and safety regulations.
Employee capacity building/ qualifications	· Programs for training employees in both aspects of sustainability and core business practices.

5.6.2   Validation of Indicators for Certification Programmes

There remains considerable variety in the standards, criteria and indicators in use for certification by various bodies, nationally and internationally. The sustainability certification of tourism enterprises, activities and products is still relatively new, lacking broad acceptance and use among tourism businesses and consumers. Unfortunately, there has not yet been adequate field verification of the validity and effectiveness of all of the indicators and criteria in use when applied as part of a certification program.

Quality of services and products, safety, and hygiene are increasingly treated as essential aspects of sustainability. There are programs based on food safety and handling, such as HACCP (*Hazard Analysis and Critical Control Point*), with wide acceptance. Others, such as Service Best (Canada and Central America), focus on quality of service, but do not consider environmental parameters. Those programs with quality components have tended to receive much faster consumer and travel wholesaler (tour operator) acceptance, than those systems focusing only on environmental or social aspects. For more information on quality standards in tourism visit the following WTO webpage: http://www.world-tourism.org/quality/E/standards2.htm

Environmental indicators in certification programs tend to be much more circumscribed in developed countries than elsewhere. In Europe, for example, many programs concentrate on energy and water consumption, along with solid waste reduction and recycling, and enter into great technical detail. Programs from other countries tend to have a broader, but less technical, view of environmental impacts of tourism, taking into account additional factors such as sewage, gray water, and runoff management; conservation of adjacent natural areas; display, use of, and trade in endangered species; etc. Examples of these programs include CST (*Costa Rica, Central America*), NEAP (*Australia*), and NEAP's international offspring, IES (*Green Globe 21 International Ecotourism Standard*). One of the most widely known specialized programs is the Blue Flag for beaches, with nearly 3,000 certified beaches in 35 countries. It is one of the few certification programs for sustainable tourism that has widespread brand recognition by consumers and that has been shown to affect consumer choice in destination. (See Box 4.2 (p. 253) and www.blueflag.org) There is also clear movement towards internationally accepted voluntary standards that clearly distinguish between sustainable tourism and ecotourism, with well-defined criteria.

It is difficult for a program to become established without wide consumer and business acceptance, a process that often takes many years and often faces initial industry opposition. Broad acceptance depends on having credibility and a threshold level of certified businesses in order to get brand recognition. Credibility in turn usually depends upon complying with certain generally accepted practices: third-party certification or eco-labelling, with objective criteria and evaluation. These practices are outlined in a series of internationally accepted guidelines such as ISO/IEC Guides 62, 64, 65, 66, ISO14024, etc. and consist of common-sense rules such as avoidance of conflicts of interest, non-discrimination, established criteria, etc. Indicators are essential parts of any certification system as they are the tools to measure compliance against the established criteria.

A critical part of developing and improving certification systems is monitoring and evaluating indicators for sustainability at tourism businesses at different stages of the certification process (e.g. benchmarking before certification, verification of criteria through indicators for granting certification, and after verification towards more advanced levels of certification). The bottom line is that indicators are central to certification programs. Changes in key indicators both help identify the need for action at tourism businesses and help define the key elements to be monitored through certification programs, the elements for which standards are needed, and the criteria for certification. When certification is in place, the same indicators can be used as performance measures to clarify the impact of certification and to permit changes to improve certification programs.

5.7 Performance Measurement and Benchmarking

Indicators are the basic tools for performance measurement for individual tourism enterprises (hotels, cruise ships, restaurants), public authorities and destination management organizations. Those who wish to measure performance increasingly focus on the measurement not just of the inputs and outputs of their organization, but also upon the social, economic and environmental outcomes which are achieved, both directly and indirectly. This relates strongly to the increased focus worldwide on accountability of individuals and organizations for their actions. At the same time, industries and governments are seeking benchmarks which can be used to compare their performance with others, ideally relative to best practice in the industry or institutional milieu. The realization of these management objectives necessarily leads to the development and use of indicators and their employment as performance measures relative to the goals and objectives of the organization.

Tourism, like other sectors is being drawn to stronger tools for measurement of performance, both of individual enterprises (hotels, cruise ships, restaurants) and destinations. The development of external and independent rating systems for the tourism sector, and for destinations, is a growing business, and tends to promote the active use of some indicators by those who choose vacations. (See Indicators and Certification p. 318). These feed back to enterprises who wish to show good performance... and to show that they are sustaining desired criteria such as quality, value for money or tourist satisfaction.

On the Internet there are many independent ratings of destinations (see websites such as Conde Nast, at http://www.concierge.com/cntraveler/) which rate, for example, best island, best hotel, best resort, etc. according to their own criteria. As well, cruise ship health ratings are done publicly by the US Centre for Disease control travellers' health site http://www.cdc.gov/travel/cruiships.htm and nearly a hundred independent commercial websites (most also selling cruises or hotel accommodation) which rate different aspects of ships (e.g., ambience, cost, cleanliness, size of cabins, number of crew per passenger etc) and different elements of hotel quality (cost, location, services, value for money). At the consumer level (the tourist) these act as visible performance measures for many of the factors most important to their choice of destination or of hotel or ship. They are visible public indicators of relative performance.

The base resources for the tourism sector are often shared with other sectors (e.g. fishery, transportation, agriculture), and the performance of the industry is closely linked to the overall performance of the economy, society and environment of not just the destination but often much broader areas. Data sources are handled by public authorities of different domain and level, as well as a range of other organizations in the private and civil spheres. Effective monitoring of performance of the tourism sector requires, therefore, partnership between different government departments (e.g. tourism, environment, transportation, education, health, protected areas, etc.), the private sector, relevant NGOs and academic institutions with others who share the destinations, for joint development of indicators and explicit performance measures, and sharing of information. At the same time, enterprises can accept accountability for the areas of environmental performance within their control, and may also act to influence the behaviour of others. Similarly, destinations can begin to take responsibility for many of the key factors, and measure their success in addressing these factors.

Ideally, the right indicators become performance measures. If indicators are well chosen, changes in them reflect the positive or negative changes in outcomes that are important to the destination and that respond in some way to the efforts and/or programs designed to support sustainability. At the outset, existence of a problem (e.g., many tourists with gastrointestinal problems) will stimulate both efforts to better monitor the situation and efforts to affect a solution. Early in a program, an indicator may show the seriousness of the need, and be used to justify investment in a program such as   improvement of a water system, institution of a food inspection program, use of Hazard Analysis and Critical Control Point programs (HACCP) for restaurants, investment in a public education program on water or food handling. As efforts to address a problem are put in place, the same indicators can be used to gauge progress. Once projects or programs are under way, the same indicators can be used to show achievement and contribute to public accountability.

One caution needs to be recognized: because of the complexity noted above, cause and effect are often also complex for the types of problems and issues identified in this Guidebook. It is often difficult to attribute the changes in for example, health of tourists to any one program, even if it is a major contributor to the resolution of the problem. While the alteration of a water system or institution of a new food quality control program within a specific hotel or restaurant may allow attribution of the results to the program, at the destination level, the linkages are usually far more complicated.

Indicators become performance measures when they are used in a process to evaluate change relative to established targets, objectives and goals. This can be seen clearly in Box 2.1 (p. 23) which shows the relationship between indicators and the overall planning and management cycle. The last four steps in that table show how the indicators become performance measures and support an ongoing management and re-planning process. Over time, many indicators achieve their most effective impacts when employed as performance measures, directly affecting decisions in projects and programs, or showing the need for new plans and actions. The difference is in the way they are used. As shown in Box 5.3, indicators are measures, generally used without being associated with value judgements or standards, whereas performance measures are always used to calculate or audit progress relative to some goal or standard.

Box 5.3 Characteristics of Indicators and Performance Measures

Indicators	Performance Measures
Objective – measure changes;	Subjective – evaluate change as positive or negative relative to goals and targets;
Measure overall changes in a key variable;	Try to measure that change attributable to the actions of a firm or jurisdiction;
Are done on a repetitive basis - often linked for practical purposes to census, repetitive surveys etc.;	Are done on a repetitive basis – often linked to the planning cycle of the firm or jurisdiction;
Are most effective when reported publicly, and may act as a catalyst for response;	Are used primarily to support internal action but increasingly are reported to the public;
May become performance measures for the responses which are put in place;	Are a key source of information for internal management but are increasingly used to identify and monitor accountability for impacts and effects (public outcomes);
A key source of information for informed public debate on policy issues and potential responses.	Can be audited relative to specific standards (as in certification programs) which must be met.

Because there may be many other projects, programs or influences on the behaviour of the tourists or the service providers, the use of indicators as performance measures for efforts to influence broad changes at the destination level is more of a challenge. It has been found, for example, in work to measure the impact of government programs on broad social goals in rural Canada, that it is often easier to use indicators of broad social outcomes to measure the net impact of many programs together rather than to attribute the change to any one project or program. Therefore it may be possible to measure overall destination performance relative to a number of indicators, but very difficult to decide what caused the changes measured.

Benchmarks are useful because they become a point of reference for both choice of indicators (use indicators which are already used by others so you can compare results between enterprises or jurisdictions) and because they often imply standards or goals that would be good to achieve. Industry benchmarking is a growing field – closely related to the concept of "best practice" (or "good practice") for enterprises. Organizations like the International Hotels Environmental Initiative, Green Globe, or the Tour Operators Initiative (see Box 3.47 p. 243) serve their members as a source of benchmarking, sharing results of indicators used to measure their performance. For one example of how a hotel enterprise uses some of these see the Accor case p. 327) If an enterprise (or a destination) wishes to become or remain competitive, it is useful to both discover how well others are doing, and perhaps begin to emulate those who are doing well. Where there are established standards, monitoring of performance relative to these standards is a de-facto use of indicators as performance measures. (See Certification p. 318 and Competitiveness p. 143).

The examples contained in this section have illustrated the ways in which indicators can be directly incorporated into certain types of decisions, from policies and planning to the monitoring of capacity and setting and verification of standards. Readers are also referred to the case studies for specific examples of indicators in use.

Part 6

Case Studies

This Part of the Guidebook contains comprehensive case studies of indicator development, use and impact from destinations around the world. Each is authored by an expert or expert group familiar with the case and in most instances directly involved in its development and implementation. Each destination has had its own unique experience, and has produced its own set of issues and indicators. The cases range from enterprise level to site, destination, region and nation, and reflect a variety of approaches and applications. Some of the cases are well along in implementation; others are earlier in the process, but have begun to address the range of issues, employ procedures in indicator development, and identify those indicators most likely to be important to the destination or enterprise.

These cases have been cited in the rest of the Guidebook wherever they provide useful examples or lessons. This volume also contains templates and approaches to assist in indicator development; these are found in the Annexes.

6.1 ACCOR Hotels Environmental Sustainability Indicators

Hotels, Analysis, Reporting, Management Indicators, Private Sector

This case shows how a major hotel chain is employing indicators in its operations.

With 157,000 employees in 140 countries in 2002, Accor is active in two major international businesses: hotels and services. Accor operates 3,829 hotels and 440,807 rooms in 90 countries, operating under the Sofitel, Novotel, Mercure, Suitehotel, Ibis, Etap Hotel and Formule 1 brands and in the United States with the Motel 6 and Red Roof Inns chains, as well as in related businesses including restaurants, travel agencies (Carlson Wagonlit Travel) and casinos. Each year, 13 million people use services designed by Accor and benefit from the company's efforts to motivate and reward employees.

Role of sustainability indicators in the company policy and management in general

Indicators at Accor follow the basic principle that says that *«in order to manage, you need to measure»*. This applies to financial, social and environmental performance. This case study focuses specifically on environmental performance indicators at Accor.

Since 1998, Accor Environment Charter has been – and still is - the main tool used for environmental management. As from February 2003, it is applied by 2048 hotels in 28 countries. The Charter is also used as a mean for hotels to inform their clients and stakeholders on their commitment to the environment.

In addition to the Charter, consumption indicators enable the Group to monitor its use of natural resources such as water, heating fuels and petrol.

The type of indicators used

Accor hotels use mainly two types of environmental performance indicators: consumption indicators, and Environmental Charter indicators. Environmental Charter indicators are based on the 15 actions of the Charter, which are linked to four domains: waste management and recycling, technical controls, architecture and landscape, and awareness and training.

Consumption indicators deal with energy (petroleum, fuel and gas) and water consumption. In certain countries, water consumption indicators are subdivided according to their provenance: public, re-treated (for watering gardens and lawns) and desalinated. For water indicators, Accor uses ratios « per room rented ». However for energy indicators, ratios are selected « per available room ». This is explained by the fact that around 90% of the energy consumption of an average hotel is not related to the number of its in-house guests. Additional indicators are used when hotels conduct Environmental Impact Assessment studies and environmental certification programmes like Green Globe or ISO 14001. In France, a number of Ibis hotels have been ISO 14001 certified and the brand is now engaging in a country-wide programme.

The application of indicators: data sources, gathering and analysis

Data sources

Water and energy consumption readings are performed on a monthly basis. Sub-metering allows Technical Managers to detect leaks or other problems as well as to identify their locations within the hotel.

Accor is currently planning the automation throughout all its hotels of its water and energy consumption data collection systems. This will ensure a standardisation of the reporting which will improve the consistency and efficiency of the Group's sustainability indicators.

Gathering

After being consolidated by hotels' Technical Managers, results are sent on a monthly basis to the regional or country Director who then transmits them to the company headquarters for final consolidation. Environmental Charter reporting follows the same route, but is done once a year. After final consolidation, indicators are then sent back from the headquarters to regional and country directors who then transmit them to the hotels.

The reporting system is thus organised so that a diversity of information is provided and received by all parties.

Analyses of the results are performed at 5 levels hotel, division, brand, country and worldwide. Results are discussed in regular meetings at various levels; within the Group. The main aim of these meetings is to find pragmatic ways to optimise both water and energy consumption and enhance the application of the Environmental Charter. Analysing indicators enables managers to assess the strengths and weaknesses of their environmental performance, and hence to take action in improving it.

Reporting of results, responses from business partners, etc.

Results are communicated through the Annual Reports, in the Sustainable Development section, as well as on the intranet and internet and internal publications. See Accor website at http://www.accor.com/gb/groupe/dev_durable/engagement.asp

Additionally, a document on the global reporting of the Environmental Charter is published every year. It consists of detailed data reports which allow hotel managers to compare their environmental performance on each one of the 15 actions compared to others according to characteristics such as regions, countries, brands or size (e.g., number of rooms). Indicators are essential tools for improving environmental performance. In Accor, indicators are used to measure environmental performance and to compare this performance between brands, divisions, hotels and countries. Indicators enable Accor managers to monitor the improvements made over time, as well as the efficiency of different best practices.

Measuring progress (eg, for towel re-use programs: reducing water, detergent, energy consumption ...), and the related financial savings, can act as a powerful motivation for spreading best practices within the Group.

Box 6.1 Some concrete indicator examples from Accor: values, use, and results

Water consumption per room in liters per occupied room

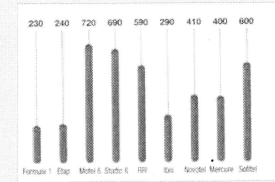

By comparison, the average French person uses approximately 150 liters of water a day at home.
(source: *Que sais-je ? La pollution des eaux*).

Consumption per occupied room is higher in the US chains (Motel 6, Studio 6, Red Roof Inns) since the hotels have their own laundry facilities. An occupied room can accommodate from one to four people, depending on the hotel.

Energy consumption per room

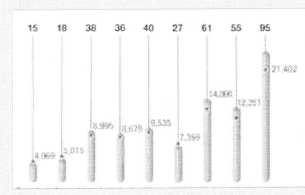

By comparison, the average French person consumes approximately 30 kWh a day at home. Energy consumption is higher in the US chains because the hotels have their own laundry facilities.

Evolution of the number of hotels applying the Charter

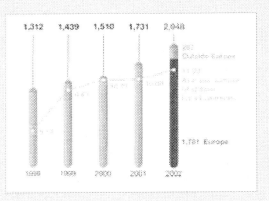

Accor's experience shows that indicators are important tools for the management of a large enterprise in the tourism industry, and also that they play an important role in achieving sustainability objectives.

6.2 Albufera de Valencia (Spain): Measuring Carrying Capacity in a Fragile Ecosystem

Carrying Capacity, Model, Multivariate Analysis, Wetlands, Data Integration, Sensitive Natural Areas, Ecotourism

This case defines an holistic approach to the concept of carrying capacity and shows an application of this approach, including a selection of useful indicators which support the analysis of the Albufera de Valencia nature park.

The concept of "carrying capacity" has to do with the maximum level of use that an area or resource can be subjected to without degradation; it includes two basic ideas: number of users (quantitative aspects) and the appropriate use of the resources (qualitative aspects). This concept is widely employed in land-use planning and zoning studies as a basis for the monitoring of areas that are considered fragile or of great ecological value. (Viñals et al., 2001).

Elements affecting carrying capacity:

Geographical space

* Size and natural attributes (area of each ecological type);

* Zoning: Current classification and limits or conditions of use including accessibility, transit-ability and risk associated with each zone;

* Fragility and elasticity: the ecosystem's vulnerability to impacts and its capacity to recover (Quintana et al. 2004).

Resources

* Definition of the functions/services that the resources provide to the tourism activity: tourism attraction function, support function (resources needed to carry out an activity) and the function of receiving the waste of the activity;

* Vulnerability of resources: this is defined as intrinsic susceptibility or predisposition of exposed elements to a threat (impacts) of damage or loss;

* Compatibility of use: It is necessary to analyse whether the resources fulfil functions for other activity sectors (agriculture, fisheries, etc.) in order to determine the degree of compatibility among them.

    An "inventory of resources" should first be carried out (analysis and mapping of the characteristics and processes occurring on the site), followed by evaluation taking into account the evaluation criteria to be established based on its suitability for recreation and tourism.

Activity

* The physical space requirements of the activity and the stresses placed by the recreational activity on the area and its resources;

* Specific requirements of certain attributes of the resources: deriving from the activity-support function that the resources have to perform;

* Stresses (impacts) that the recreational activity could cause on the area.

Users

* User behaviour: Not all users/tourists have similar behaviour (for example, a group of schoolchildren will not behave in the same way as a group of birdwatchers in a wetland).

Measuring Recreational Carrying Capacity

The measurement of recreational carrying capacity, as done in the Albufera case, follows these phases:

Physical carrying capacity

Physical carrying capacity is the suitability of an area for recreational use based on the establishment of the usable recreational area (URA). Based on the analysis of the geographical space or setting where the recreational activity is to be carried out, analysis is aimed at obtaining a suitability map (zones suitable for recreation).

Real carrying capacity

"Real" carrying capacity is established after applying physical-ecological, cultural and/or socio-demographic correction/reduction factors. Calculation is centred on the study of resources that serve attraction and support functions (including local populations as a supporting resource) and of the activity to implement. This phase relies on the analysis of the impacts generated by each activity. In this way, a "use suitability map" is obtained, which will show the places which are most suitable for the activity and where the impact is least. Once the zones suitable for recreation have been identified, the number of users and/or elements that the site can accommodate without compromising its state of conservation is determined. In this way, the minimum viable area (MVA) per practitioner is evaluated based on the type of recreational activity practiced. This factor relates to the quality of the recreational experience in terms of visitor congestion at the site, the weather conditions at the time, the behaviour of other visitors, accessibility, etc. Establishing this factor is very difficult since the information has to be obtained based on subjective data that is not always the same for all the visitors.

Allowable capacity

This phase focuses on determining the correction/reduction factors derived from the management capacity (strategies understood in economic and technical management terms) of the responsible administrations (local, regional, national or supra-national) and of the company itself. The parameters on which it is based are of a political and economic nature.

Monitoring recreational carrying capacity: Indicators

"Carrying capacity" as a management tool is in itself a "synthetic" indicator since it includes numerous elements and factors that have an influence on the evolution of the territory, but its analysis is centred on the quantitative monitoring of users, and this is what differentiates it from the usual indicators (status indicators) which monitor the resources.

The following list is a menu of potential indicators which have been considered for application and which may be important determinants of limits or capacity; the much shorter list of specific indicators chosen for l'Albufera is noted later in this case.

Box 6.2 Status, pressure and response indicators

Resource	Status	Pressure	Response
Physico-ecological			
Water	- Water quality (presence of pollutants)	- Number of motor boats, hunting licenses - Volume of untreated sewage	- Investments in treatment plants - Pollutant regulation standards in recreational activities (hunting, boats, etc.) - Number of sanctions - Environmental education campaigns
	- Piezometric levels	- Rate of use of surficial and groundwaters (for recreational and tourist activities - Demographic growth rate - Urban growth rate	- Rules on water extraction - Drafting, broadcasting and application of Good Practice Codes - Number of sanctions - Investments in water recycling and re-use - Investment in awareness programs re sustainable use of water - Number of R+D projects/grants - Number of environmental education campaigns
Air	- Air quality	- Number of vehicles with access to the area - Number of pollutant gas emission points around the area	- Control and restriction of vehicle traffic in the area measures - Traffic assessment measures - Creation and use of public transportation systems measures - Increase in "bike trails" kilometres
	- Noise level	- Number of vehicles with access to the area - Intensity of traffic along the routes around the area - Total number of visitors per day/ season/ year - Size and behaviour of groups of visitors - Number of motor boats	- Control and restriction of vehicle traffic in the area - Assessment of traffic around the area - Creation and use of public transportation systems measures - Measures for controlling groups of visitors
Flora	- Flora biodiversity index - Vegetal cover index	- Rate of decrease of vegetal species (especially protected, threatened or in danger) - Number of fires and % or surface lost in fires - Rubbish in the area - Total number of visitors per day/ season/ year - Size and behaviour of visitor groups - Visits to vulnerable areas - Number of vehicles with access to the area - Number of boats - Facilities construction rate (change land use)	- Zoning measures - Vehicle circulation restriction measures-rules to control introduction of exotics; - Investments in forestry restoration - Number of R+D project applications and grants - Number of awareness campaigns for visitors and local population - Number of sanctions - Number of environmental volunteers - Measures for controlling visitors - Number of waste collecting facilities - Number of jobs created (Rural and Forest Rangers, Forest firefighters, etc.) - % of increase of protected surface - Number of natural heritage appreciation campaigns
Fauna	- Faunal biodiversity index - Population size - Number of nesting birds	- Number of fishing and hunting licenses - Number of species caught and felled - Decrease rate of animal species (especially those protected, threatened or in danger of extinction)	- Zoning measures - Circulation restrictions in nursery areas - Rules to control introduction of exotics - Level of effort re recovery and reintroduction of native species - Number of R+D project applications and grants - Rules regulating the different uses and recreational activities (hunting, fishing, etc.)

Physico-ecological	Fauna		- Level of fragmentation of the natural area (different artificial barriers, facilities, etc.) - Total number of visitors per day/ season/ year	- Awareness programs for visitors /locals Number of fines Number of environmental volunteers - Measures for controlling groups of visitors - Number of jobs created (Rural and Forest Rangers, Forest fire fighters, etc.) - % of increase of protected surface - Number of natural heritage appreciation campaigns
	Landscape	- % of artificial elements in middle ground - Presence of rubbish dispersed throughout the area - Presence of visual barriers	- Number of building licenses granted around the area - Total number of visitors per day/ season/ year - Size and behaviour of visitor groups	- Rules regulating landscape protection - Number of sanctions - Investment in landscape protection and restoration measures - Investment in programs to adapt buildings to the environment - Number of waste collection facilities - Number of complaints from visitors and residents on landscape status - Number of natural heritage appreciation campaigns
	Geomorphological formations and soils.	- Topographical changes - Changes in area - Hydroperiod changes - Changes in soil profile	- Total number of visitors per day/ season/ year - Increase in number of facilities - Level of fragmentation of the natural area (different artificial barriers, facilities, etc.)	- Visitor control and management measures - % of increase of protected surface - Drafting and approval of rules regulating land protection and control - Investment in land protection and restoration measures - Number of R+D project applications and grants devoted to the subject - Number of natural heritage appreciation campaigns - Number of monitoring programs applied
Cultural resources		- Number of buildings and other devices of cultural value - Cultural heritage conservation status - Number of museums	- Loss rate of heritage built - Total number of visitors per day/season/year. - Size and behaviour of visitor groups - Changes of use of cultural heritage	- Visitor control and management measures. - Drafting and approval of rules regulating cultural heritage protection and control - Investment in cultural heritage conservation, recovery, protection and restoration measures - Number of R+D project applications and grants devoted to the subject - Number of natural heritage appreciation campaigns
Social - demographic		- Loss of social values and customs - Natural growth rate of the population - Population migration - Employment rate - % of jobs in the area (hotels, rural rangers, etc.). - % of firms devoted to tourism and recreational activities - Rate of visitors/tourists	- Rate of service demand growth - Rate of direct and indirect job creation (related to recreational activities and tourism) - Increase in density of resident and visitor populations - Price increase index rate - Migratory movement rate - Hotel growth rate - Restaurant growth rate - Growth rate of firms devoted to recreational activities	- Degree of satisfaction of residents - Degree of satisfaction of visitors - Resident complaints - Visitor complaints - Volume and number of donations and sponsorships - Number of local NGO's operating in the area and number of members - Number of training courses given and number of participants - Number of awareness campaigns - Number of environmental education courses given and number of participants - Number of R+D project applications and grants devoted to the subject (Leadser projects, etc.) - Revision, adaptation and creation of urban assessment plans

Application to L´Albufera De Valencia Nature Park

L'Albufera de Valencia Nature Park attracts an increasingly large number of visitors, who are interested mainly in practising recreational and interpretative-educational activities. The park has been included in the List of Wetlands of International Importance of the Ramsar Convention since 1980, and has been a ZEPA zone (Zone of Special Protection for Birds) since 1991, as well as an SCI (Site of Community Interest) since 2000 (Natura 2000 Network of the Habitats Directive of the European Union).

The space analysed in this study was the Information and Interpretation Centre of the park called *Racó de l´Olla*, which is managed by the regional government's Territory and Housing Department, through its Directorate-General for Zoning and Land-Use Planning. The carrying capacity analysis was undertaken at the request of the management of L´Albufera de Valencia Nature Park (Spain), with the aim of appraising each of the facilities dedicated to the public use of the space, and for the ultimate purpose of obtaining the "Q" quality rating that is granted by the General Secretariat for Tourism to Spanish Protected Natural Areas through the "Spanish System of Tourism Quality in Protected Natural Areas".

Racó de l´Olla contains most of the public-use facilities and infrastructure of the Park and occupies an area of 63 ha divided into two areas: a public zone in the northern half of the facilities and a full-reserve zone in the southern half.

The area studied contains the following facilities: Information centre for receiving visitors and for carrying out an environmental education and dissemination programme on the Albufera.

* The "Las Caballerizas" interpretation centre, aimed at disseminating knowledge about the natural and cultural values of the wetland. This centre has permanent and travelling exhibits, an aquarium, a library, a projection room and live wildlife observation cameras.

* Bird observatory: a wooden shed from which birds of the Albufera can be observed and identified.

* Observation tower for the observation and interpretation of the wetland and the metropolitan area of Valencia.

* Picnic area with basic services for recreational use: water, rustic furniture, garbage collection, etc.

* Parking area for cars and buses, located very near to the picnic area.

* Trails: in the area there are two that are marked with rope and wooden posts, which are used as access-ways to the bird-watching facilities (Trail A) and to "Las Caballerizas" (Trail B).

* Full Reserve Zone and nesting site: zone devoted to the recovery and conservation of plant and animal species, some endemic, and where public access is therefore restricted.

The carrying-capacity study carried out was centred on the analysis of self-guided interpretive visits to *Racó de l´Olla* that take place on weekends. During weekdays, there are organized visits by groups of schoolchildren, which are supervised by Park personnel, and are thus subject to more effective control. The characterization of this activity was carried out through direct observation of the activity and the analysis of the information obtained through in-depth interviews with the Park's monitors and that obtained from surveys. For this task, the visiting hours during weekends were taken into account along with the average duration of visits, with regard to the time needed for the visit to be complete and satisfactory. In this case, it was determined that it took an average of 62 minutes to go through all the facilities and trails.

Generally, the most important resources in wetlands are the flora and fauna, which also constitute one of their main attractions, along with the countryside. Along the trails we find some of the ecosystems present in the Nature Park: fixed dunes with the typical Mediterranean maquis vegetation, glasswort swards, and riparian forest, represented by deciduous trees such as tamarind *(Tamarix sp.)*, black poplar *(Populus nigra)*, some species of willow *(Salix sp.)*, etc. However, the most important resource of *Racó de l´Olla* in terms of recreational value, is the bird fauna that visit this area throughout the year: shelducks *(Tadorna tadorna)*, mallards *(Anas platyrhynchos)*, gadwall *(Anas strepera)*, pintails *(Anas* acuta), northern shovellers *(Anas clypeata)*, widgeon (Anas penelope), marbled teal *(Marmaronetta angustirostris)*, teal *(Anas crecca)*, garganey *(Anas querquedula)*, European pochard *(Aythya ferina)*, red-crested pochard *(Netta rufina)*, tufted ducks *(Aythya fuligula)*, common moorhen *(Gallinula chloropus)*, coots *(Fulica atra)*, etc.

Thus, the study of the vulnerability of the birds to certain impacts was the main focus of work. The exercise showed that the birds are especially sensitive to certain noises, which is why various acoustic measurement campaigns were carried out to determine the type of noises that disturb them, the time of year during which they are most susceptible (hunting season, mating and nesting seasons) and the decibel threshold beyond which they begin to be disturbed. Generally speaking, it can be said that the current noise levels are not disturbing. The wildfowl are accustomed to the noise from the motor vehicle transit approximately 150m away (Nazaret-Oliva highway). However, they are disturbed by the sudden detonations carried out by occasionally by visitors, or by the gunshots during the hunting season.

The analysis of users/visitors was carried out through surveys about the visitor profile and studied on visitation during visiting hours. The psychological comfort of visitors was also evaluated, with regard to the existence of elements that can hinder the enjoyment of the visit (noises, inappropriate behaviour, saturation of the space and thus lack of the minimum space for carrying out the activity, etc.) and meteorological factors (rain, wind, cold, etc.).

Box 6.3 Indicators used to calculate the carrying capacity of Racó de l´Olla

Issue	Indicator	Utility
Physical Carrying Capacity	Usable recreational area (URA) in each facility in m² (suitability map of the territory).	Knowing the space available for recreation.
Real Carrying Capacity	Sound level threshold beyond which disturbances to birds are detected *(on-site measurements)*.	Prevent the recreational activity from having an impact on the birds, which constitute the most vulnerable resource.
	Minimum viable area (MVA) for visitors *(visitor surveys)* No. of visitors per group.	Determining the psychological comfort level of the visitor to ensure a satisfactory recreational experience.
Allowable Carrying Capacity	No. of persons supervising and guiding the visits; Existing material resources; Existence of safety programmes; No. of informative, directional, and interpretive signs, according to Spanish regulations on "Quality of Public Use in Protected Natural Areas"	Inclusion in the analysis of the management limitations deriving from the park administration itself.

The results indicate that weekend visitors have a very generic profile, with a high perceptual capability, meaning that they are quite tolerant of the presence of a large number of people sharing the recreational experience at the same time. The average space estimated to be needed to carry out the recreational activity is 4 m² in open spaces and 1.20 m² in closed spaces. These values are therefore indicators of psychological comfort.

The preliminary results indicate that the **"Las Caballerizas" interpretation centre** is the facility with the highest Real Carrying Capacity (RCC) out of all the closed facilities and infrastructure studied. Its limitations are basically determined by the accessibility provided by the roadway leading to the site (trail B). For the proper conduct of the activity, the maximum number of persons on the trail at the same time ± 40 plus another 40 persons inside the interpretation centre on a visit, and the change of visitors should be in the interpretation centre and never on the trail. This number can be considered optimal, as it does not affect the quality of the experience of the aforementioned generic-profile visitors, and does not disturb the birds. We should not forget that the trail is surrounded by a full-reserve area, which is a mating and nesting site, depending on the time of year.

The correction/reduction factor used to calculate the RCC at the **information centre** was the available area itself and the distribution of the existing material resources: panels and model (calculated in linear metres), based on the available space and the minimum space required per visitor for the satisfactory conduct of the activity, the carrying capacity is ± 20 persons carrying out the visit plus another ± 20 persons waiting to do so, outside the centre.

The hide for bird observation

In the **bird observatory,** the correction/reduction factors taken into account were also available space and the distribution of the space. The observatory currently has 13 benches, three of which are not usable. Therefore, taking into account the criteria of minimum available space per visitor in closed spaces, the calculation gives the figure of ± 10 persons inside the facility, plus one handicapped person. Furthermore, it should be noted that a higher number than this would cause acoustic impact on the birds, as determined in the acoustic impact study.

In the **observation tower** the RCC was calculated by applying the isolation and safety factors, since it consists of a projecting platform with a handrail, which does not allow the presence of a large number of persons. In this case, the figure obtained was ± 7 persons, based on the area of the space (calculated in m²) and the minimum space required per visitor, which was increased due to safety considerations.

Completing the preliminary results obtained for the facilities and infrastructure of *Racó de l´Olla* the RCC for the completely open **picnic area** was determined by applying the correction factor of the spatial distribution of the infrastructure consisting of the capacity of the equipment. There are 10 tables and 10 benches accommodating 6 persons, which gives a total of ± 60 persons. Moreover, there are 4 benches that accommodate 3 persons each, for a total of 12 persons, which added to the aforementioned 60-person capacity, gives a total capacity of ±72 persons, and 1303 m2.

With regard to the **management of the carrying capacity** of Racó de l'Olla, an Integrated Information and Communication Technologies System has been put into place, with the objective of increasing the quality and efficiency of services, lower the costs of processes and undertake more attractive and effective promotion of the space. This system facilitates the management of demand and thus helps monitor carrying capacity at each facility. The main actions carried out were:

* Intranet support to facilitate information flow for the public-use managers among the various facilities of *Racó de l'Olla;* including new services and the presentation of information for visitors through the website that includes general information on the park, plus real-time sounds and images of the resources of the park, etc., all of which helps users choose the best time for visiting.

* a cooperative work system among the different services of the park organization using the tool *"Basic Support for Cooperative Work" (BSCW)".* Using this tool, it is possible to share documents, agendas, procedures, etc., and establish a hierarchical working structure.

The combination of these two actions makes it possible for park managers to know the number of visitors in real time, and to recommend an alternative itinerary during the visit to prevent overcrowding at certain facilities or delays, etc. At the same time, the integrated system can also register alarm signals relative to the resources (fires, water quality, cloudiness, etc.) and send them to the pertinent institutions for analysis, thus allowing better decision-making in the management of the park.

The new technologies presented are currently in the implementation/adaptation phase. The project has now established the thresholds of real and allowable carrying capacity. As for the automated management system, laboratory testing has been completed satisfactorily and the initial field trials are now under way. The personnel in charge of supervising the public use of the park have already been appropriately trained in the use of the new technologies.

Aerial view of the L´Albufera De Valencia Nature Park

Legend:	
1	Parking
2	Picnic area
3	Information Centre
4	Viewpoint
5	"Caballerizas" Interpretation Centre
6	Hide for bird watching
7	Pond
8	Reserve
9	Fang Marsh
10	L'Albufera Lagoon
A, B, M	Pathways

References:

Di Fidio, M. (1993): *Architettura del paesaggio.* Ed. Pirola Editore, 677 pp.

Viñals, M.J.; Morant, M.; El Ayadi, M.; Teruel, L.; Herrera, S.; Flores, S.; Iroldi, O. (2001): Method approach to the determination of the recreational carrying capacity on wetlands. En: Garrod Y Wilson (Eds.): *Marine Ecotourism. Issues and experiences.* Channel View Publications, pp. 79-106.

6.3 Antarctica: Sustainable Tourism Indicators

Sensitive Natural Areas, Carrying Capacity, Tourist Management, Ecotourism

Antarctica is a relatively new destination, with unique issues. This case is one of the first attempts to identify suitable indicators for this fragile and remote destination.

Tourism in Antarctica

Antarctica is the highest, coldest, driest, windiest and remotest of all the continents. It covers 13.9 million square kilometres and is 98 per cent covered by ice. Its interior is a polar desert almost completely devoid of life but during the summer months (from November to March) a seasonal abundance of wildlife including penguins, flying sea birds, whales and seals can be found along its shores.

It was not until 1895 that the first humans set foot on the continent at Cape Adare. In contrast to all other continents, Antarctica lacks an indigenous permanent human population. The only 'residents' are the several thousand scientists and their support staff at the 40+ permanent scientific stations. Commercial cruising was started by Lars-Eric Lindblad in 1966. Antarctic tourism is highly concentrated in the Antarctic Peninsula Region with a few ships each season also visiting locations in the Ross Sea area. Most cruises depart from Ushuaia, the southernmost town in the world located on Tierra del Fuego, Argentina. Other gateways include Port Stanley, Punta Arenas, Hobart and Bluff. Including the time required to cross and re-cross the 1000 km stretch of open ocean know as the Drake Passage cruises to the Peninsula usually last between ten and 14 days.

Cruise-ships are self-contained floating hotels varying significantly in size and luxury. They range from yachts with 4 passengers to vessels carrying over 1,000 passengers (which do not land passengers). Over 95 per cent of Antarctic tourism is cruise-tourism and most vessels used are ice-strengthened and can handle ice conditions up to an ice concentration of 8/10th. Where passengers go ashore and what they see during their voyage is always determined by the prevailing weather and ice conditions. In the absence of port facilities, operators depend on Zodiacs (inflatable rubber dinghies) to transport passengers from ship to shore.

Attractions

The Antarctic scenery is spectacular. Towering snow and ice covered mountains fall off steeply into the ice-choked sea, icebergs the size of large buildings or at times the size of small countries, and glaciers calving into the sea provide visitors with fantastic sights. The wildlife of the region is one of the main attractions. It consists of penguins, flying sea birds such as albatrosses and terns as well as marine mammals including whales and seals. Apart from scenery and wildlife, visitors are also interested in the historic huts constructed by the early explorers. These can be found mainly in the Ross Sea.

Management of Antarctic Tourism

Unlike any other major landmass, Antarctica is not owned by any country. Argentina, Australia, Chile, France, New Zealand, Norway and the United Kingdom have all staked their claims but these are not universally accepted. Neither the USA nor the Russian Federation have laid claim to Antarctic territories, even though historically they would have every right to do so but neither recognises the claims of other nations either. South of 60 degree S, the Antarctic is managed under the Antarctic Treaty of 1959 and its associated instruments including, in particular, the *Protocol on Environmental Protection to the Antarctic Treaty* (Madrid Protocol). The over 40 Antarctic Treaty Parties meet annually to discuss how best to manage issues such as scientific research, commercial fishing and tourism. The treaty may provide the best forum for collaboration in data collection and further development and use of indicators.

Visitor numbers

According to IAATO, the 2002/03 season, which lasted from November 2002 to March 2003, saw 13,056 tourists travelling aboard traditional cruises that included landings. A further 2,424 passengers travelled on vessels that did not make landings and 308 people participated in land based tourism activities. A total of 1,552 passengers saw the continent through the window of a wide-bodied aircraft during over flights. The NSF has established that a total of 159 Antarctic sites have previously been visited by tourists, many of them only sporadically. Out of these, 25 sites received over 1000 visitors during the 2002/03 season. Of these, the most visited sites were: Whalers Bay on Deception Island, Goudier Island and Jougla Point, each with over 6000 visitors.

Impacts

Because of the increase in visitor numbers and the concentration of visits at a relatively small number of sites, some concern has been raised regarding the possible impacts that visitors may have. These can be summarized as:

* Possible interference with science;
* Impacts on the environment including general pollution by sewage, waste, oil, fuels and noise,
* Introduction of non-native soils, microbes, plants and animals;
* Disturbance of local bird or seal breeding colonies;
* Trampling of mosses, grasses and lichens;
* Potential need for search and rescue.

Management of sites

Over the past decade, a cooperative approach to the management of tourism has evolved. In 1991 the International Association of Antarctica Tour Operators (IAATO) was founded. To make Antarctic tourism sustainable, IAATO members have developed Visitor and Tour Operator guidelines.

Passengers aboard the Akademik Ioffe in the Antarctic Peninsula

Visitors aboard IAATO member expeditions are reminded not to disturb, harass, or interfere with the wildlife; not to walk on fragile plants; to leave nothing behind ashore; not to interfere with protected areas or scientific research; enter historic huts only when accompanied by a properly authorized escort; not to smoke during shore excursions and to stay with their group or with one of the ship's leaders when ashore.

To minimise potential negative impacts of tourist visits to Antarctic stations, prior notification of intent to visit is required. In the early 1990s, the National Science Foundation of the United States (NSF) initiated annual meetings with representatives of the tourism industry, in particular those responsible operators who are members of the International Association of Antarctica Tour Operators (IAATO). At these meetings the IAATO and NSF discuss issues arising from the conduct of commercial tourism during the previous season and agree on next season's visits to the US stations Palmer, McMurdo and Amundsen – Scott. By meeting with tour operators, NSF can be assured that the industry is aware of what the requirements for station visits are and operators know what is expected of them prior to and during their visits to research stations since 1948.

The New Zealand government requires that a staff member of Antarctica New Zealand (the New Zealand government body charged with overseeing Antarctic affairs) accompanies visitors to huts located in the Ross Dependency to ensure that no more than the permitted number of visitors (depending on the hut, numbers range from 4 –12 people) are present in the huts at any one time. Indications are that through good management of visits major damage to huts caused by tourists has to date been avoided.

Due to the remoteness of Antarctica and its climatic conditions, the conduct of any commercial tourism depends on close cooperation between all parties concerned. These include the governments of the Antarctic Treaty Parties, tour operators, ship owners and operators, the Council of Managers of National Antarctic Programs (COMNAP), environmental organisations such as the IUCN, and the tourists themselves.

The implementation of guidelines or codes of conduct depends on the level of understanding that paying visitors have of these guidelines, their level of agreement with them and their willingness to comply with them and on the willingness of tour operators to enforce set guidelines. To date, tourists and tour operators have complied and behaved responsibly and because of the way commercial tourism is conducted, the negative impacts have been negligible. Beginning with Lars-Eric Lindblad, the pioneer of Antarctic tourism, and continuing with IAATO members, tour operators have been pro-active in their measures to protect the resource on which their businesses depend - the Antarctic environment. As a result of the cooperation between international tourists, tour operators and Treaty Parties, Antarctic tourism is today arguably the best-managed tourism in the world.

Reaching capacity – Almirante Brown Station, Paradise Bay, Antarctic Peninsula

Sustainability indicators in Antarctica

At present levels, seaborne Antarctic tourism can be considered as "sustainable" but, as passenger numbers increase, there is a need for increased vigilance at some of the sites visited. The following indicators can be used to assess the sustainability of Antarctic tourism. It has to be noted that the collection of data in this remote part of the world is difficult and expensive:

* **Total number of people that visit Antarctica in a season.** The different ways of visiting have to be taken into consideration because each has different potential impacts. The most common is cruise with landings followed by cruise only. A small number of people also travel inland on adventure trips and walk or ski in Antarctica. Over flights of parts of the continent are considered to have little environmental impacts;

* **Number of shore landings by Zodiacs and helicopters;**

* **Number of people ashore at any one time at a specific site** (and taking) into consideration that staff at scientific research stations also undertake recreational trips to sites of interest.);

* **Number of people ashore in a 24 hour period at a specific site;**

* **Total number of people ashore at one site during the whole season;**

* **Total number of people ashore over a prolonged period (10 years);**

* **Length of time spent ashore;**

* **State and nature of sites visited including their physical appearance** (formation of tracks has been noticed), condition of moss beds, grass patches and the number of individual animals of specific species at the site.

The first two points are relatively easily monitored, but monitoring the wildlife is more difficult, since fluctuations in the number of animals present at any one time may be attributable to a variety of reasons including human visitation, climate change or cyclical fluctuations. A number of sites have been regularly monitored (for, example Cuverville Island). Most of the most popular sites visited by tourists are fairly robust and can withstand the current levels of visitations. (See also the Destinations section on Arctic and Alpine environments Box 4.3 p. 262) While, via operators, a significant amount of data is collected, and the Antarctic Treaty provides a good framework for systematic collection despite the fact that the tourists arrive under the flags of many different nations, the use of indicators is in its infancy. But the *Protocol on Environmental Protection* can be the vehicle for greater use of indicators in the establishment of suitable regulation for emerging Antarctic tourism.

Group of tourists awaiting directions from their guide, Penguin Island

6.4   Arches National Park (USA):   Indicators and Standards of Quality for Sustainable Tourism and Carrying Capacity

Image, Crowding, Visitor Perceptions, Visual Response, VERP, Ecotourism

This case shows a practical method to identify how visitors react to different types of landscapes, trails and levels of use in natural environments, providing managers with improved information to support tourism and destination management.

Carrying capacity is a perennial and challenging issue in the management of national parks. Parks and related areas are to be protected, yet are also to be made available for public use and appreciation. However, public use of parks can cause impacts to natural and cultural resources as well as the quality of the visitor experience. How much and what types of uses can be accommodated in parks before there are unacceptable impacts to park resources and the quality of the visitor experience? (See also Carrying Capacity p. 309).

Research on carrying capacity suggests that it can be defined and managed through formulation of indicators and standards of quality of the visitor experience. Indicators of quality are measurable, manageable variables that define the quality of natural/cultural resources and the visitor experience. Standards of quality define the minimum acceptable condition of indicator variables. Once indicators and standards of quality have been formulated, indicator variables are monitored, and management action is taken to ensure that standards of quality are maintained. This approach to carrying capacity is central to contemporary park and outdoor recreation planning and management frameworks, including the Visitor Experience and Resource Protection (VERP) method, developed by the U.S. National Park Service.

An initial application of VERP focused on Arches National Park, Utah, USA. Arches National Park covers 73,000 acres of high-elevation desert with outstanding slick rock formations, including nearly 2,000 sandstone arches. Many of the park's scenic attractions are readily accessible through a well-developed road and trail system. Visitation to Arches has increased dramatically in recent years and the park now receives over three-quarters of a million visits annually.

A two-phase research program was designed to help support application of the VERP framework at Arches. Phase 1 was aimed at identifying potential indicators of quality of the visitor experience (A parallel program of research was conducted for the resource component of carrying capacity.) Personal interviews were conducted with park visitors and a series of 10 focus groups were conducted with park staff and local community residents and interest groups, in order to identify indicators. Questions on park conditions and issues probed what visitors and others considered important to determining the quality of the park experience.

Indicators of visitor experience quality identified included:

* number of people at developed attraction sites and along trails;
* number of visitor groups encountered along backcountry trails and campsites;
* number of social trails (unofficial trails, shortcuts, visible paths created by the off-trail actions of the visitors themselves) and level of soil and vegetation impacts associated with creation and use of these trails;
* level of trail development;
* level of visitor knowledge of regulations regarding off-trail hiking.

Phase II research was designed to help formulate standards of quality for the indicator variables noted above. A survey of park visitors was conducted using both personal interviews and mail-back questionnaires. Visual research methods were used to illustrate a range of conditions for indicator variables. For example, a series of 16 computer-generated images was created to represent a range of visitor use levels at Delicate Arch, a principal visitor attraction. These images were created using photo editing software.

Sample computer-generated photographs Illustrating a range of use levels at delicate arch (Photographs prepared by Wayne Freimund, University of Montana, Robert Manning, University of Vermont, and David Lime, University of Minnesota).

Representative examples of these images are shown in the photos above. These images were presented to a representative sample of visitors who had just completed a hike to Delicate Arch. Respondents were asked to judge the acceptability of each image on a scale of –4 ("very unacceptable") to +4 ("very acceptable"). Analogous sets of images were created for the number of hikers along developed trails, environmental impacts caused by off-trail hiking, and level of trail development.

The graph below shows study findings for the acceptable number of people at Delicate Arch. The figure represents the average (mean) acceptability ratings for each of the 16 study images. It is clear from the graph that acceptability declines with increasing use. Average acceptability ratings fall out of the acceptable range and into the unacceptable range at about 30 people at the same time at Delicate Arch, and park staff selected this number as the minimum acceptable standard of quality. In a similar manner, standards of quality were formulated for other indicator variables and other features and areas in the park. The park is now monitoring indicator variables to ensure that standards of quality are being maintained. Moreover, management actions have been taken, including sizing the parking lot at Delicate Arch to help ensure that no more that 30 people are at the arch at any one time.

Box 6.4 Average acceptability ratings for the 16 photographs illustrating a range of use levels at delicate arch.

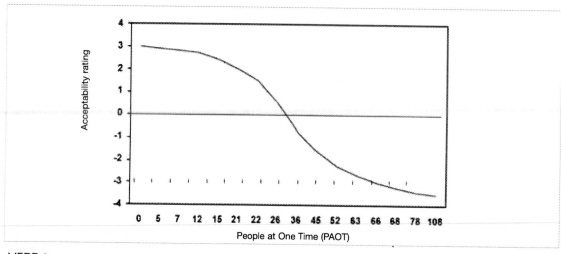

The VERP framework, including its emphasis on indicators and standards of visitor experience quality, provides a theoretically sound and rational process for defining and managing carrying capacity. It provides a structured framework within which to conduct a systematic, thoughtful, traceable, and defensible analysis of carrying capacity. An associated research program aimed at helping to identify and formulate indicators and standards of quality can provide a strong empirical basis for applying the VERP framework.

VERP has been applied at a number of diverse units of the U.S. National Park System, and research has helped identify and formulate a variety of indicator variables and associated standards for both resource conditions and the quality of the visitor experience. A VERP handbook has been developed by the National Park Service, along with a workbook of management actions designed to support application of the VERP framework. (See http://planning.nps.gov/document/verphandbook%2Epdf).

References:

Anderson, D., D. Lime, and T. Wang. 1998. *Maintaining the Quality of Park Resources and Visitor Experiences: A Handbook for Managers.* St. Paul, MN: University of Minnesota Cooperative Park Studies Unit.

Manning, R. 2001. Visitor Experience and Resource Protection: A Framework for Managing the Carrying Capacity of National Parks. *Journal of Park and Recreation Administration* 19(1): 93-108.

Manning, R., D. Lime, W. Freimund, and D. Pitt. 1996. Crowding Norms at Frontcountry Sites: A Visual Approach to Setting Standards of Quality. Leisure Sciences 18(1): 39-59.

Manning, R. 1999. *Studies in Outdoor Recreation.* Corvallis, OR: Oregon State University Press.

National Park Service. 1997. *Visitor Experience and Resource Protection (VERP) Framework:* A Handbook for Planners and Managers. Denver, CO: Denver Service Center.

6.5 Balearic Islands (Spain): Integrated Tourism Management through Sustainability Indicators

Demographics, Pressures, Comprehensive Measures, Islands, Prioritization

This case demonstrates a comprehensive indicators applications for a mature tourist destination, where tourism is the most significant economic sector.

Comprising an Archipelago to the east of the Spanish mainland and located in the centre of the western Mediterranean Sea, the four chief Balearic islands - Formentera, Ibiza, Menorca and Mallorca (from the smallest to the biggest)- maintain a character distinct from the rest of Spain and from each other. The Balearic Archipelago presents remarkably varied scenery and enjoys a Mediterranean climate, characterised by moderate temperatures throughout the year (16-17°C average annual temperature). With more than 10 million visitors annually, the Balearic Islands are one of the leading destinations for holidays in Europe. Forty per cent of its territory is protected; there is a Maritime -Terrestrial National Park (Cabrera), a UNESCO Biosphere Reserve (Menorca Island), a World Heritage Site (City of Ibiza), four Natural Parks and a hundred natural protected areas of special interest for fauna and flora.

The development of tourism in the islands began early 1960's with the construction of hotel infrastructure on the coast, focused on mass tourism development. Between 1975 and 1993, economic growth allowed the Islands' tourism system to become stable, consolidated the tourist areas, and led to the appearance of new areas with a more extensive development pattern. The islands' response to the Gulf War crisis was to promote new tourism products and attractions of environmental or traditional character, far from the "sun and sea" classic model.

Today, the scarcity of natural resources like water and energy, and the isolation (insularity) of the destination, provide difficult challenges for the Balearic Islands. The magnitude of the tourism industry and its important contribution to the economy make more important the need for sustainability. The islands are vulnerable, not only because of the geography of the islands and their fragile eco-systems, but especially because of the tourist pressure. This pressure on the ecological resources has led in many cases, to a growing need to import resources from the exterior to maintain the islands' economic system.

The CITTIB (Centre for Tourism Research and Technologies of the Balearic Islands) from 2000-2003, undertook research on sustainability indicators for tourism in the Balearic Islands, involving extensive assessment of environment of the islands and the stresses on it. Project studies were aimed at analysing the parameters of the main human activity of the islands – tourism - and the key elements of its development, such as urbanisation, transport, energy consumption, water consumption, residual waste, etc. Fifty indicators were studied (see table 1), and of these, 12 were selected as Key Indicators of Sustainability (KIS) due to their greater importance and significance; these were: Human Pressure Index, Seasonality in Tourism, Job Stability, Evolution of Wages, Access to Housing, Number of Vehicles in Use, Beaches (tourist use and saturation), Accommodation Capacity, Protected Natural Areas, Urban Water Consumption, CO_2 Emissions and Residual Waste Recycling.

Box 6.5 Indicators of sustainability of the Balearic Islands (long list)

1.   Demographic Indicators
- 1.1   Human Pressure Index - KIS
- 1.2   Tourist Pressure Index (tourist seasonality) - KIS
- 1.3   Accommodation Capacity – KIS (see Box 5.2)
- 1.4   Airport Passenger Arrivals
- 1.5   Harbour Passenger Arrivals

KIS: Key Indicators of Sustainability

2.   Socio-Economic Indicators
- 2.1   Labour Balance (by sectors of the economy)
- 2.2   Job stability - KIS
- 2.3   Labour seasonality
- 2.4   Unemployment rate and working population
- 2.5   Implementation of environmental management systems
- 2.6   Ecological agricultural production
- 2.7   Traffic congestion in Palma (Mallorca)
- 2.8   Access to education in Tourism
- 2.9   Number of leisure boats
- 2.10 Beaches: number of visitors and tourist saturation -KIS
- 2.11 Beaches: maximum number of visitors per day
- 2.12 Tourist efficiency index
- 2.13 Housing access -KIS
- 2.14 Foreign Trade
- 2.15 Wages evolution - KIS
- 2.16 Wealth distribution
- 2.17 Housing prices
- 2.18 Traffic congestion
- 2.19 Number of Vehicles in Use -KIS
- 2.20 Access to health services
- 2.21 Moorings availability
- 2.22 Available beach surface
- 2.23 Tourist saturation index
- 2.24 Blue flags

3.   Environmental Indicators
- 3.1   Territory and land use
- 3.2   Construction
- 3.3   Road and railway infrastructures
- 3.4   Urban water consumption - KIS
- 3.5   Electricity consumption
- 3.6   The ecological footstep of energy consumption
- 3.7   Waste production
- 3.8   Energy Intensity Index
- 3.9   Replanted and reforested surfaces
- 3.10 Natural protected areas evolution of surface
- 3.11 Visitors to Natural Protected Areas
- 3.12 Urbanisation
- 3.13 Forest fires
- 3.14 Natural Protected areas - KIS
- 3.15 Energy consumption
- 3.16 CO_2 Emissions - KIS
- 3.17 Waste recycling - KIS
- 3.18 Water analysis
- 3.19 Water recycling
- 3.20 Concrete consumption
- 3.21 Renewal Energies Index

Each of the twelve key indicators was elaborated and portrayed graphically for general use. Below are two examples of the results in Boxes 6.6 and 6.7. See also Box 5.2 on Tourist Accommodation Capacity.

Box 6.6 Human pressure index (Balearics)

Demographic Indicator

Pressure Indicator

Scope: Balearic

Islands

Period: 1989-2000

⁂ The high seasonality of tourism produces specially in summer months, irregular distribution of the human pressure. This has a great impact on natural resources.

Observed Trend: The human pressure evolution for the period of analysis, has two consequences: an increase of the total population, between 2% and 3%, yearly, and an increase of the concentration during the summer months, due to the tourism seasonality.

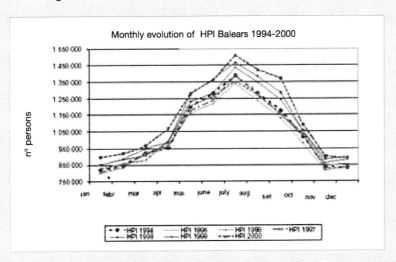

Monthly evolution of HPI Balears 1994-2000

Desirable Trend: To stop high seasonality of visits (summer) and reduce the influx of floating population andt redistribute it throughout the year, without stressing resource capacity.

Description: This indicator reflects approximately the total number of people which, every month are in the Balearic Islands, including residents and floating population.

Methodology: To calculate the Human Pressure Index, we have added to the residents, the floating population at any time, from:

Resident Population = Census of 1991 and the yearlycorrections of the local Census.

Floating Population = Legal floating population (LFP) + Rest of floating population (RFP).

LFP= % Number of tourist vacancies per month

RFPMONTHLY = [(Passengers arrivals per day - Passengers departures per day) PLANE + (Passengersarrivals per month – Passengers departures per month) BOATS]- (LFP)

Sources:

⁂ Aguiló, E (2001): "La despesa turística a les Balears 2000". Conselleria de Turisme,

⁂ AENA. Informes estadístics.

⁂ Autoritat Portuària. Trànsit de passatgers als Ports de Balears.

⁂ IBAE. Cens 1991, Padró i correccions.

⁂ Direcció General de Recursos Hídrics:

⁂ Estudi de població flotant 2000.

⁂ ENDESA. Estadístiques de facturació elèctrica.

⁂ Oficina de Reducció de Residus. Conselleria de Medi Ambient. Estadístiques sobre producció de RSU.

Box 6.7 Tourist activity index (Balearics)

Demographic Index
Indicator of pressure
Balearic Islands
Period: 1998-2000

* The high seasonality of tourism produces specially in summer months, irregular distribution of the human pressure. This has a great impact on natural resources.

Observed Trend: Tourist pressure has been stable for the last years. In Mallorca tourist arrivals distribute quite homogeneously all around the year, but in Menorca and Pitiusas the situation changes.

Desirable trend: One of the objectives of tourism sustainability is that the activity spreads out uniformly throughout the year. The more seasonal the tourist activity is, the less sustainable it becomes.

Description: This reflects the level of "seasonality" of every season in relation to the rest of the year.

Sources:
Oficina de Seguiment de l'Ocupació, CITTIB.
Aguiló E. (2001): "La Despesa Turística 2000".
Conselleria d'Economia, Comerç I Indústria.
Govern de les Illes Balears.

Methodology: The index has been calculated using the number of overnight stays in Balearic Islands taken from "La Despesa Turística" (the Tourist Expenditure) divided by the average season's stage.

$$TAI = \frac{\text{Average number of tourist per day in season}}{\text{Average number of tourists per day during the year}}$$

If the result of the index is 1, then the distribution of tourists is homogenous during the year.

The project methodology is based on demographic, economic, social and environmental variables that are not necessarily taken into account by econometric analyses, but which indicate the extent to which our society compromises its heritage, and which also contribute to identifying levels of equity and well-being. The theoretical framework is founded on the concept of ecological economics as the social science closest to the environmental sciences, and one that is politically and ethically engaged.

The indicators are based mostly on the selection, analysis and combination of public or official data. As well, depending on the additional resources available, new data were created to complete the indicators. The indicators were created based on a model proposed by the OECD, known as pressure-state-response. Once the model was created, indicators were proposed for each of the areas – social, economic, and environmental – based on which the process was carried out, consisting of collecting data from the available sources and defining the method of calculation (of each indicator). Then, a data sheet or model form was created for each indicator to facilitate its analysis and keep track of its evolution. As for the time scales used, an effort was made to use annual data (up to the period for which it was possible to obtain data, since 1989) or monthly data (whenever possible). As for territorial scope, municipal data were used as far as possible, although in certain cases information was available only at the Autonomous Community or island level.

Certain data, such as beach visitation, were completed through field studies. In order to determine beach indicators, 18 beaches on the Balearic Islands were studied. Beaches were selected on the basis of their significance and the intent to study the different types of beaches that exist on the islands (urban, semi-urban, and natural). The counting of beach users was carried out during the high season (July and August) of 2003. For each beach, users were counted on one non-working day and on one working day. The method consisted of 3 or 4 counts per day at each beach, at evenly distributed intervals throughout the day between 9.00 and 21.00. Furthermore, users were interviewed regarding their length of stay on the beach (in hours), the vehicle or transport used to get to the beach, their origin (tourist/resident and accommodations used), their level of satisfaction and the negative/positive aspects of the beach.

The key indicators contributed the elements needed for political and social debate on the current type of regional development and on the policy for future development which must inevitably lead to greater sustainability of human activity in the archipelago. But they also provide objective information on the state of the islands, facilitating understanding of the present situation, helping support policies on sustainable development and supporting efforts to find the most appropriate solutions to problems.

The consumption of land is probably the most severe impact of tourism development on the islands. However, the Balearic Islands were one of the first regions in Spain to create legal frameworks to stop uncontrolled development and land use. The DOT (Territory Planning Guidelines-Directrices de Ordenación del Territorio), approved in 1999, aim at guaranteeing a sustainable development model for the the islands. And more recently, since summer 2002, in all the four islands there are moratoria on further urbanisation that stops development and consumption of land without prior approval. As well, the Tourism General Law (Ley General Turística) and the Plan to Organise the Tourism Offer (Plan de Ordenación de la Oferta Turística) limit the construction of hotels and restrict the use of land for tourist purposes.

In addition, the following new sustainable tourism and planning initiatives for the Balearic Islands are proposed:

a)   Limit the growth of new development;

b)   Rehabilitate degraded areas, old mass tourism areas and superannuated non-productive coastal resorts;

c)   Introduce new elements to enhance quality of the tourism offer;

d)   Diversify the tourism products;

e)   Protect and rehabilitate natural and urban environments.

In a region such as the Balearic Islands where tourism is the prime motor of the economy, it is necessary to assume responsibility and find solutions for ameliorating its effects on the society, the environment and the culture, without compromising the activity upon which the wealth of the residents is based. This is in fact, what sustainability is about: "*meeting the needs of the present without compromising the ability to meet those of the future*".

The application of WTO indicators in the Balearic initiative

As part of the focus on indicators, an indicators development exercise was also undertaken in the Balearics – with emphasis on some of the baseline indicators suggested in the 1997 WTO indicators guidebook "What Tourism Managers Need to Know". The results of monitoring of some of these indicators are shown below.

Box 6.8 WTO Indicators exercise for Balearic Islands (1997)

Issue	Indicator(s)	Results
Site pressure (2002)	* Maximum tourist numbers * Ratio of tourists to locals	1,149,155 persons/day 916,968 residents/day 232,187 tourists/day
Accommodation capacity (2001)	* Number of beds capacity	1,884,505 beds
Tourism seasonality index	* Level of concentration of tourism in peak months	Concentration of tourist activity during high season (June, July, August, September)
Tourist's satisfaction (2001)	* Percentage wishing to return * Percentage of repeat visitors	81.2% would like to repeat 75.3% did visit the islands before
Resident's satisfaction	* Opinion of tourism numbers * % wishing to retain tourism as the key economic sector	61% would like to maintain the number of tourists; 22% would like to reduce the number of tourists; No opinion re numbers 17%; 68% think tourism should be kept as a main economic activity of the islands.
Tourist' contribution to the economy	• Expenditure per person day by tourists	€ 81.55 tourist expenditure per person/day

---

For further information on the extensive project to develop and use indicators in the Balearic Islands, see the following reference: Blazquez, Macia ., Ivan Murray and Joana Maria Garau, El Tercer Boom: Indicadors de sosteibilitat del turisme de les Illes Balears 1989-1999, CITTIB, Palma de Mallorca 2002 (in Catalan, 426pp).

Source:

Centre for Tourism Research and Technologies of the Balearic Islands (CITTIB)

Further information: http://cittib.caib.es/

6.6 The Canary Islands (Spain): A Planning Model for a Mature Destination

Scenarios, Islands, Tourism Planning, Land Use Planning, Limits to Growth, Carrying Capacity

This case shows how an indicators program can be a central component of a broader participatory planning process aimed at sustainable development of a destination.

When a tourist destination reaches a prominent position in the international market and maturity in its tourism sector, it becomes necessary to ensure its long-term success through conserving its initial tourist assets. Destinations must seek positive growth that does not compromise, but rather strengthens, its natural wealth and social well being. To do this, it must be capable of generating consensus regarding the activities of both the public administration and the tourism industry.

In the Canary Islands, as in the majority of the densely populated islands of the planet, the concept of *carrying* capacity intuitively impregnates the local culture, in that the limits can be easily visualized and understood. The present document demonstrates the role that indicators will play in changing the ways of acting, both on the part of the administration and as well as in the tourism private sector, in the planning and management of new tourism, using models whose components are beginning to be clearly defined and broadly agreed upon.

The Canary Islands, located in the Atlantic Ocean off the northwest coast of Africa, are one of the principal European tourist destinations with more than 10 million international visitors annually: the Canaries along with the Balearic Islands are the leading destinations in the Spanish tourism sector. The archipelago is composed of seven main islands and several smaller ones that occupy a total area of 7.447 Km², and have a population of 1.6 million inhabitants. The climate is sunny and mild in the winter and cool in the summer, and the islands' natural wealth includes 3 Biosphere Reserves, and 4 National Parks; 40% of its territory is protected.

There is a well-developed and wide variety of accommodation facilities and the transport system connects the majority of the Canary Islands' airports with the principal European cities. All this permits the Canary Islands to be one of the most popular tourist destinations of Europe.

In the decade of the nineties, the growth of tourism was spectacular, rising from 5.5 million visitors in 1990 to 11.8 million in 2000. However, this growth, and the beneficial effects on economic and social indicators were accompanied by a growing unrest among the local population that sent warning signals that were picked up by a significant part of the tourism industry. This unrest stemmed from factors related to the profound transformation of land use in some of the tourist enclaves - changes that could alter the historical consensus of the Canary Island society regarding their landscape. The unrest was also due to problems related to the carrying capacity of infrastructure and public services, to significant changes in the economic and social organization, and to the suspicion that a good part of the growth was due to external factors negatively affecting competing destinations, such as natural disasters, situations of conflict and terrorist activity, and the value of competing currencies.

Faced with this reality, and in the framework of a general strategy of sustainability for the whole of the archipelago, the Regional Government began to implement several tools which were contained within the law in regards to land use planning, and also implemented the Law on Guidelines for General Planning and Tourism of the Canary Islands (Ley de Directrices de Ordenación General y del Turismo de Canarias), also know as "the Moratorium" due to its immediate effects of limiting the growth of the tourism sector, a process that continued from 2001 to 2003.

Initially the administration proposed a moratorium on the construction of new tourism accommodation facilities, a proposal based on a study of carrying capacity indicators. However, when the proposal was presented for public debate it created confusion among a substantial part of the public and key stakeholders. This confusion was due to the fact that it was hard for people to understand how the economic activity that had helped developed the Canary Island society, eradicating the backwardness and poverty of the recent past, could now become a potential threat to social well being and the very future of the industry itself.

What was finally realized was that the intervention by the administration in regards to the tourism industry could not be based exclusively on traditional centralized control methods, such as land use planning and management (whose extensive and exclusive use had led to this critical situation), and that the concept of Carrying Capacity (see also Carrying Capacity p. 309) was not sufficient to help develop a new, more sustainable model of tourism.

Simultaneously, a working group of the Tourism Department of the Regional Government initiated preliminary studies with the intention of helping to develop a Tourism Policy that responded to the new challenges, with one of the principal tasks being the elaboration of Indicators for Sustainable Tourism, based on those proposed by the WTO in 1997 (WTO, 1997).

The basic conclusions of this study were:

1. Planning tourism development was not a well established concept or practice among the public administration bodies of the Canary Islands. The prevailing decision-making process made use of traditional paradigms of land use and regional planning that did not adequately respond to the new challenges of tourism.

2. In spite of the great diversity of available data that could permit applying the majority of the WTO indicators, it was considered necessary to establish Tourism Observatories, that would help standardize existing information, define new data needs and involve and stimulate the entire administration and other stakeholders in the task of collecting and analysing new information and seeking new sources.

3. The continuing success of tourist activity in the traditional segments of sun-and-sand tourism, could affect the consensus of what constitutes sustainability and could undermine the business sector's interest in and capacity for innovation, especially in other tourist products more related to entertainment and leisure activities, as opposed to accommodation products.

Box 6.9 WTO Indicators Exercise for the Canary Islands (2000)

Issues	Indicator (WTO 1997)	• Results (2000)
Site Pressure	• Tourist numbers	• 363.000 tourists/day
Use intensity	• Density of use • Beds per Km²	• 49 tourists/ Km²/day • 61 accommodation beds/ Km²
Social impact	• Ratio of tourists to locals	• 18 % of foreign tourists/resident population
Planning process	• Area covered by development plans (% of municipalities)	• 10% of the municipalities have some process of tourism planning
Tourist's satisfaction	• Tourists who agree they would like to return • % recommending the destination to others	• 92 % would like to repeat • 97 % would recommend destination
Resident's satisfaction	• % wanting more, same or less tourists	• 32 % would like to increase the number of tourists • 46% in favour of maintaining the number of tourists • 16% in favour of reducing the number of tourists
Contribution of tourism to the economy	• Value of tourist expenditures	• 4.400 M € indirect tourist expenditure

As a final step the Canary Island Government launched a new proposal for tourism development to the public before proposing legislation to parliament. The proposal included the following innovations:

1. It was considered necessary to develop tourism planning processes that could stimulate latent capacities of the administration and the tourism industry and that would permit that the making of sectoral decisions, including those dealing with regional planning, would be done within the framework of general strategies of sustainability and competitiveness.

2. Tourism growth was defined as growth of the economic benefits of tourism, not as growth in the number of tourists.

3. Tourism growth should be based on reconverting existing tourism infrastructures and the diversification and differentiation of the tourism offer, rather than on the construction of new accommodation facilities.

The new debate that was generated was particularly stimulating, incorporating in the various stages of the public and parliamentary debate the following concepts:

1. The future physical growth of tourist activity must be based on a system of indicators that evaluate the carrying capacity of each island.

2. A sustainable tourist destination must reinforce the capabilities of offering sustainably-sound services and practices to tourist.

3. A Tourism Information System will be developed that permits making decisions regarding tourism based on knowledge rather than on intuition.

The process of implementation of the Law on Guidelines has permitted introducing into the Canary Islands administration new tools and concepts that will help the destination prepare itself to face the new challenges required by sustainable tourism. In order to help understand that tourism planning is more a process than a document, the Tourism Administration is taking on the development of a System of Indicators that will permit catalysing and stimulating the desired objective

Box 6.10 Proposed indicators system for the Canary Islands

* Indicators for improving the use of natural resources (Water, Energy, Waste, Biodiversity, Territory)

* Indicators for improving practices in the use and management of tourism resources (Beaches, Cultural Legacy, Protected Areas, Rural Landscapes, Marine Reserves)

* Indicators for improving the design and management of tourism infrastructures (Hotels, restaurants, golf courses, marinas, amusement parks…)

* Indicators for the verification of tourism planning processes (on a regional, island and local scale)

* Indicators of the promotion to enhance competitiveness of involved agents, and of opportunities for small and medium businesses, new businesses and residents

* Indicators of the promotion of choices of more sustainable tourism practices (Mobility, capability for choice and cost, information, offer adjusted to needs…)

* Indicators of increase capacity for responding to global challenges

  - Ecological footsteps

  - Climate change

  - Epidemics and pandemics

  - Changes in the demand

  - Vertical integration processes and dominant market positions

For a related indicators application in Lanzarote, one of the Canary Islands, see the Lanzarote case (p. 406). For comparisons re WTO indicators application see also the Balearic case (p. 345).

6.7 Cape Breton Island (Canada): Indicators of Sustainable Tourism and Ecotourism

Ecotourism, Sensitive Natural Areas, Parks, Community Participation

This case used a participatory approach to examine the concepts of sustainable tourism and ecotourism as part of efforts to better integrate park and tourism planning in a destination.

This study tested the utility of indicators as a tool to help differentiate between overall destination sustainability and the specific risks to ecotourism products and assets. The Northern Peninsula of Cape Breton Island, Nova Scotia, Canada is a popular destination for North Americans seeking wild landscapes, sea vistas and wildlife. The peninsula juts into the Atlantic and is an easy two-day drive from the major population centres of the northeast USA as well as Canada's largest population centres. Its main draws are Cape Breton National Park, which occupies the centre of the northern peninsula of the island and the spectacular coastal road which circles the peninsula linking high coastal mountains and small picturesque fishing villages. Increased pressures for use have caused the National Park management, Provincial habitat managers and the tourism industry to seek joint solutions which respond to the demands for greater use and also sustain the key assets.

The study was carried out in 2002-2003 by Consulting and Audit Canada on behalf of the Canadian Tourism Commission and the Parks Canada Agency. The methodology was based on the 1997 WTO indicators methodology, with field research and a strong participatory component, including stakeholder workshops held in the region expressly to identify key assets, risks to the assets, and indicators which could respond to them. All of the tourism and tourism-related activities currently undertaken in the region were inventoried, including those which were only at the potential stage. A categorization was done relative to the key assets involved and the potential for impact. Activities as varied as bus tours, hang gliding, whale watching, mountain biking, golf, orienteering and ice skating were examined regarding their potential impact and identifying which indicators might help differentiate those which purported to be ecotourism from those which were not. Some fifty indicators were found to have value for the region, and nearly half also to assist (often at site specific level) with issues associated with the specific impacts of ecotourism.

Nearly all of the activities found in northern Cape Breton relied on the natural environment and the clean, green, safe friendly image of the region. The analysis showed that very few activities could be easily identified as ecotourism, as many forms of nature based tourism or adventure tourism which were considered by many to be ecotourism could be undertaken in ways which damage key assets (mountain biking through fragile upland sites, using sea kayaks to harass whales). The key differentiating factors between ecotourism and other forms of tourism (e.g., adventure tourism, mass tourism which involved viewing nature) were heavily related to the scale of activity and its management, and ultimately its impact on the key assets. Stakeholders had a difficult time differentiating between nature tourism and adventure tourism and the term "ecotourism".

The study showed that the key indicators for management (whether an activity is labelled ecotourism or not) were those which measured potential or actual impact on key assets. (Damage to fragile ecosystems, harm to image of region) For most activities considered ecotourism, the indicators needed to be site specific or enterprise specific, whereas for many of the other tourism activities indicators which measured aspects of sustainability at regional scale were useful. As well, any attempt to use indicators to assess whether an activity met commonly used criteria for defining ecotourism revealed that no single activity satisfied these criteria. One conclusion, therefore, is that a firm may be able to meet all criteria to be labelled an ecotourism enterprise (respect the ecology, respect cultures, provide educational opportunities, benefit host communities and regions) but this is accomplished through a mix of several activities.

The Cape Breton study attempted to use a participatory development process focussed on indicators of sustainable tourism for a region. This was used to clarify the different information needs for management of sustainable tourism more generally and to support a specific focus on "ecotourism".

Key lessons have been:

1.   A process focussed on indicators has served as a catalyst for participatory dialogue on key issues between stakeholders – some meeting for the first time on tourism in the region.

2.   The discussion process helped create a better understanding of key assets and the different values placed on them by different parts of the community.

3.   The effort to identify specific indicators to help differentiate "ecotourism" and "sustainable tourism" showed the difficulty in differentiating the two concepts, even while helping to clarify the issues of concern to the to the destination and region.

Box 6.11 Indicators of sustainability and ecotourism based on the Cape Breton study

 # Ecotourism criteria to which indicator best responds (based on International Union for the Conservation of Nature (IUCN) criteria: En=respect for environment, C=respect for culture, Ed= educational, B=beneficial to community).

Issue Area	Indicators that address sustainable tourism (derived by focus groups)	Sustainability criteria to which indicator responds	Indicators that address ecotourism*	Ecotourism criteria to which indicator responds(see #)
A) Control of environmental Impacts				
Issue: State of Key Environmental Assets	· State of sites and condition; · Indicator: Organized/ guided access; · Perception of level of cleanliness of areas frequented by tourists; · Clean Image of Region; · Total Numbers of visitors at key impacted sites (and per unit area).	Environmental sustainability (measures of stress state, response re key environmental values)	· state of specific site (extent of degradation); · Number % of visitors who are guided to specific site; · Indicator: Perception by visitor of state of specific site; · visitor numbers per unit area on key sensitive sites; · Counts of behaviours of visitors to key sites.	En En, Benefits to local guiding community; En (may have some relation to education); En En (may also respond to elements of cultural impact)
B) Economic benefits to the region				
Issue: Local involvement and benefit from tourism industry	· Employment statistics	Economic sustainability (benefits to economy)	· Indicator: number employed as qualified guides and interpreters.	En (also measures educational resources available)
Issue: Amount of economic stimulus provided by tourism	· Amount spent per day per tourist (by season as well - note no 4/5 star indicator defined for this issue).	Economic sustainability (contribution to local economy).	· % of revenues from tourism derived from those activities designated to be ecotourism*	En – helping to identify amount of tourism dependent on ecotourism and direct benefits.
C) Marketing the region				
Issue: Quality of the tourism product	· Perception of quality of experience by tourists Questionnaire on tourist satisfaction re specific	Sustainability of industry overall – leading indicator of risk to industry experiences.	· Same perceptual indicator but applied to specific site or sites; · Questions which refer to specific sites or experiences (e.g. whale watching, trail walking, nature observation).	May reflect both environmental quality and some elements of education – indirect measure (more a measure of overall risk).
Issue: Image of destination	· Perception of destination (Q).	Sustainability of industry overall – leading indicator of risk to industry	· Perception of destination as ecotourism destination (% agreeing). · % of tourists who chose experiences which qualify as ecotourism (based on agreed operating definition)*	May reflect both environmental quality , education – indirect measure (more a measure of overall risk to market – an economic indicator)
Issue: Perception of quality of accommodation	· Price of accommodation; · (Measure: average cost/night); · Opinion of quality/value (Q); · Repeat visits to same	Sustainability of economy of destination (tourism sector) accommodation.	· :% of establishments advertising themselves as "green"; · % of visitors who select establishment based on environmental criteria in region (exit Q).	Measure of demand for experiences (indirect measure of knowledge of potential ecotourism .

Issue Area	Indicators that address sustainable tourism (derived by focus groups)	Sustainability criteria to which indicator responds	Indicators that address ecotourism*	Ecotourism criteria to which indicator responds(see #)
D) Stability and Seasonality				
Issue: Over-concentration of tourists in peak season	• Number of tourists over year (by month/week if possible)	Economic cultural and ecological stress (and pressures on infrastructure)	• Indicator: maximum concentration numbers on key fragile sites (peak day/hour, critical times).	En – an indicator of potential stress levels which may degrade
Issue: Seasonality of business in community	• Number of hotel rooms (and restaurants) open - by month /season; • % Occupancy of rooms.	Cultural and economic impacts.	• Occupancy levels of remote campsites; • % use of permits for controlled area access.	En –indicator of specific stressors which may impact key areas.
Lack of tourist services (off-season)	• Average weeks employment per annum (in tourism).	Sustainability of local economy.	• % ecotourism jobs which are outside peak season	C Social impact – maintain skills.
Issue: Lack of variety of tourist activities and alternatives to drive-by viewing	• % of tourists who spend two days or less in region.	Leading indicator of overall sustainability of tourism in region	• % tourists who participate in ecotourism activities (operating definition)* • % tourists participating in specific potentially damaging activities.	Level of potential stress –ecological and cultural. May need to be very site specific for management response.
E) Community Impacts				
Issue: Maintaining positive relation ship for tourists/ residents	• Local attitudes (Perception of tourism benefits and dis-benefits).	Cultural/social sustainability	• Number of complaints from local community to officials regarding intrusions.	C- direct measure of perceived negative effects on culture.
Issue: Loss of Community	• Residents' satisfaction with community lifestyle; • Average Age of Residents • % businesses open year round (subset - % rooms, restaurants).	Cultural/social sustainability	• Same indicator could be used at very local scale as indirect measure of cultural stress (note difficulty of attribution).	C –measures perception of indirect impacts -hard to separate from all tourism.
F) Planning and Control				
Issue: State of planning	• Planning of Destination (existence of plan)	Overall indicator of level of control (detailed indicator could measure impact of control)	• Express site plans in place for key fragile ecotourism destinations; • Level of monitoring and site specific control.	Overall indicator of control level –may respond to ecological and or cultural impacts.
Level of communication/ coordination between authorities	• Level of cooperation; • Level of awareness among locals of planning initiatives (survey of awareness among local residents)	Indicator of overall tourism awareness Reflects levels of integration in response	• % local residents aware of value of specific ecological assets; • % residents knowledgeable use controls in place	Indirect measure of educational levels (locals and tourists) regarding assets and protection needs.
G) Infrastructure				
Issue: State of roads	• Perception of road condition by locals and tourists	Indicator of potential risk to overall product	• Perception of trails, access conditions	En – measure of use and impact
Issue: Bicycle access	• Indicator: Length of Bicycle Trails Bike Paths)	Indicator of state of attraction/ potential impacts	• Indicator: area degraded by off road use of bicycles	En –measure of impact on ecological assets
Issue: Accessible trail system	• Indicator: Cost of maintenance of trail system; • Indicator: % dissatisfied/ satisfied with trails.	Indicator of state of attraction/ potential impacts	• Same indicators as for sustainable tourism - but may need to be applied to specific sites and systems.	En – indirect measure of damage levels through costs to repair of sites.

* Note: to use this indicator a specific inclusions list needs to be agreed among the key stakeholders. his then becomes an operating definition for what is considered to be ecotourism for the region. The operational definition will likely be unique to each destination due to the unique mix of activities and sensitivities. Over several applications some commonalities may emerge which can support a more standard base definition shared among destinations.

** Note: indicators identified at both overall sustainability levels and those relating to ecotourism stressed ecological and economic aspects, with less emphasis on cultural and educational elements. While some discussion occurred re educational aspects, indicators identified in this case were generally weak – that is they measured general educational levels, or some aspects of knowledge, with weak linkage to attribution to the tourism industry or to ecotourism experiences. As a consequence, none made the short list.

The Cape Breton study shows how a participatory process focussed on indicators can help communities begin a dialogue on what they wish to sustain, to help forge partnerships and stimulate the creation of management organizations in areas where these may not already exist. The study was also used as a key input into the new comprehensive planning process for the national park, and as a building block for Tourism Cape Breton (a voluntary operator-supported organization) in its efforts to support a coordinated planning capacity for tourism in the region. The study is expected to also support the selection of performance measures for the new park plan. The table which follows Box 6.11 is a distillation of the indicators identified in the Cape Breton study and workshops, and how they relate to the concepts of sustainability and ecotourism.

Sources: A Canadian Study of Indicators Relating to Sustainable Tourism and Ecotourism: The Case of Northern Cape Breton, 2003, Prepared by Consulting and Audit Canada for the Canadian Tourism Commission and the Parks Canada Agency.

Neil's Harbour is surrounded by Cape Breton National Park. Efforts are being made to involve the community more in planning for the Cape Breton Trail tourist route and for the Park itself.

6.8   The Caribbean Sustainable Tourism Indicators Initiative

Regional Indicators, Methods of Definition, Standards

This case demonstrates how the Caribbean is progressing towards a common set of indicators to be shared among destinations.

The Sustainable Tourism Zone of the Caribbean (STZC) was officially created by the signature of the Convention for Sustainable Tourism, in December of 2001 at Margarita Island, Venezuela, during the Third Summit of Association of Caribbean States. The objective of this Convention is to establish that the Zone is a geographically determined cultural, socio-economic and biologically rich and diverse unit, in which tourism development will depend on sustainability and the principles of integration, co-operation and consensus, aimed at facilitating the integrated development of the Greater Caribbean.

The Sustainable Tourism Zone does not mean simply taking care of ecosystems in the strict sense, but promotion of balanced development among Caribbean people to make sustainability possible. Knowledge on the part of the receiving society, the people of the STZC will allow it to perceive new frameworks for attitudes and actions in tourism-oriented societies. A main objective is therefore to promote community participation in decision-making, planning and in general, in the benefits and solutions to problems generated by tourism activity.

Caribbean Region

The strategy for facing this challenge involves the two main actors: the States as agents of management and change, and the civil society as a new emerging actor, in the era of globalization.

Several steps have been taken toward the achievement of the STZC objectives, including the elaboration of a guide for piloting sustainable tourism in specific sites and businesses, through an action agenda and the development of sustainability indicators which will be adapted to the specific characteristics of the Greater Caribbean Region.

The initial indicators work was developed in 2002 by the French Agency for Tourist Engineering (AFIT) and the French Consulting Geo-System specialized in Sustainable Tourism. The working methodology was based on an analysis of tourism in the Caribbean, a proposal for adapting the AFIT method to the context of the Caribbean on the basis of a pilot project in a test area and a trial of the method at Saint François in Guadeloupe, a destination considered by the Steering Committee and ACS Group of Experts to be a good pilot test.

The final report combines the results of the trial with the regional context and proposes a table of indicators to be used as a benchmark for the creation of the STZC. It is divided into four fundamental areas of analysis.

I)   The first part presents **Sustainable Tourism Indicators** proposed for the Greater Caribbean. These are further divided into:

- Global Indicators, norms which take into account the common elements for the group of territories of the ACS;

- Custom indicators which respond to specific needs of local tourism destinations.

II) The second part proposes an **operational method of piloting sustainable tourism** for the territories of the Greater Caribbean, to adapt the regional piloting indicators to the specific characteristics, needs and potential of each destination;

III) The third part presents a set of recommendations for implementing the Sustainable Tourism Zone for the Caribbean (STZC);

IV) The fourth part of the Report suggests **information, awareness-raising and educational tools** which could be created to facilitate the development of Sustainable Tourism.

Indicators

The need to adopt a dual approach, which articulates and reconciles the regional needs with the specific needs of each territory, was clear. A dual system of indicators is therefore proposed:

- **14 Normative Indicators**; to be used in common for all the destinations of the STZC, a result of the joint evaluation of the regional experts (see table below) and, .

- **A table of Local Indicators**, to be chosen freely by the destinations on the basis of their local diagnoses (see St Francois example).

A measuring system has been established for the homogenous but individualized normative indicators and the aims to be achieved, as well as the pace of progress that will be defined for each destination, through a local objectives contract drawn up by the local stakeholders.

The criteria that will serve as a basis for the Indicators were based on four dimensions of sustainability: heritage, economy, social, ethical. The aspects considered for the analysis and management of the selected tourism destination were:

Definition criteria

I.1   Define a relevant area (local destination);

I.2   Obtain commitment from local stakeholders;

I.3   Identification of global (broader) concerns from professionals and stakeholders.

Descriptive examination of the area

II.1   Analysis of the area;

II.2   Methods for capturing the diversity of the area;

II.3   Typology of the parties involved;

II.4   Diagnostics: Interpretation of the descriptive analysis and identification of the progress achieved;

II.5   The local objectives contract.

The analysis of the proposed area makes it possible to identify the tourist issues by setting them in a global context. This analysis is based on:

1   The existing documentation (studies, monographs, tourist documentation, the media, etc.), institutional information files;

2   Interviews with those in charge of local tourist development (elected representatives, technicians, etc.);

3   Analysis of the parties involved;

4   Observation and/or knowledge of the terrain.

Box 6.12 Normative indicators for the association of Caribbean destinations

The Caribbean initiative is an attempt to create a tool which both responds to local and national needs for each member but also permits some exchange of information and coordination at a regional scale. This case shows the initial steps in creating the process and some of the indicators which will be the basis for common collection and use.

The 14 normative indicators considered as core for general implementation in the ACS programme are:

Heritage dimension

1.   Energy consumption and management;
2.   Water consumption;
3.   Water quality;
4.   Access to drinking water;
5.   Management and conservation of the environment;
6.   Control of environmental impacts;
7.   Efficacy of waste water treatment systems;
8.   Efficacy of solid waste treatment systems;
9.   Promotion of local culture and identity.

Economic dimension

10. Integration in the local economy;
11. Tourist satisfaction.

Social dimension

12. Origin of employment in the tourism sector;
13. Child prostitution;
14. Personal safety.

Note: detailed elaboration of each indicator can be found in the report from Agence Francais de l"Ingenerie Touristique, *The indicators of Sustainable Tourism in the Caribbean*, GeoSysteme , Avignon, 2002.

Analysis of businesses makes it possible to understand the different types of logic used by the entire range of parties involved, with their practices and expectations in terms of sustainable tourism. In European countries, it is relatively easy to ascertain the diversity of businesses using public data, as recommended in the AFIT guide. In the case of the Greater Caribbean, however, the main difficulty to be overcome is obtaining reliable data to reflect the diversity of the parties involved and the businesses. In addition, even if these data exist, it is very difficult, if not impossible, to compare them, as they differ immensely from State to State.

The second difficulty lies in the actual content of these data, which only take into account businesses which have a legal existence. In the Caribbean, the informal economy has a very important place in the tourism sector: illicit street sellers of handicrafts, take-away food, alternative accommodation with no legal status, street guides, etc. Nevertheless, use of the existing data is vital as long as its relevance is systematically determined. In all cases, the destinations must mobilize their own resources, using their own know-how and innovation to solve this problem.

The Saint-François, Guadeloupe Pilot Case

The area of Saint François was chosen as the first pilot destination to test the indicators for the Caribbean, partly because, being part of France, it benefits from the public organization of a western nation, which is known for being highly centralized. The municipality also has an Enterprise Team, which has contributed greatly to the trial.

This pilot project brought several problems to light:

The lack of accessible data due to:

* the lack of knowledge of the existing data;
* the difficulty of obtaining them within a reasonable period from making a request;
* the lack of reliability and relevance of the data obtained from institutional bodies;
* the high cost of certain data, whose reliability is not always guaranteed.

Given this situation, the Enterprise Team set up its own data system, by contacting businesses directly.

One of the reasons for the lack of reliability of the official data is the scale of the informal economic sector, missed by official inventories. With respect to the diversity of the sector, the Saint François case revealed the following 245 enterprises, listed in decreasing order:

* catering = 110
* accommodation = 64
* leisure and travel agencies = 23
* car hire = 17
* souvenir shops = 14
* crafts = 10
* estate agents = 7
* The information gathered in the field has been compared with the data in the Chamber of Commerce and Industry file, which has shown that some businesses mentioned in the file do not exist in the field, and of the 64 accommodation establishments found in the field, only 16 can be identified in the files.

Tourists swimming in natural pool in fragile ecological reserve, Guadeloupe

Sample Methodology

For a small area - a destination – but one which can have as many as 250 to 300 tourist businesses (like Saint François), a sample of 25 to 30 businesses, i.e. approximately 10% of businesses) appears sufficient to constitute a representative sample of the diversity of the processes. The sample is prepared according to the relative importance attributed to different groups.

The number of businesses in the sample can be selected proportionally for each of the categories or an adjustment can be made to correct an excessive concentration on area (which will be the case in coastal destinations) or industry.

Typology: definition and method

The aim of typology is to identify some major types of processes of tourist development, based on the different types of logic (values, perceptions) of those involved: their backgrounds, their situations, their problems, and their expectations. This prevents all the businesses from being treated as a single category, which would be easier but less useful. The population investigated is broken down into typical groups by sorting them on the criteria which appear to provide the most differentiation; this selection is to be carried out according to the specific attributes of each destination.

The lessons learned at Saint François in this sense made it difficult to obtain accurate information on some questions, in particular those relating to the economic aspects of activities (turnovers, investments, profit margins, etc.,) client profiles and development prospects of the activity. It is proposed to retain two discriminating criteria to set up the typology: 1) The social position of the entrepreneur in the area, and 2) the entrepreneur's aim in the context of his business activity.

Diagnosis

The aim of the diagnosis is to interpret, in terms of development, the signs and opinions noted when drawing up the inventory, and also to identify where progress can be made. These signs may express threats, opportunities, strengths, or weaknesses, depending on who is involved.

The Method employed

An in-depth analysis for each type of tourist activity (the different types of representation of sustainable tourism) with the aims of:

1.   Targeting the usual indicators used by these parties to pilot their practices and discussing these indicators in the light of the table of indicators;

2.   Evaluating the improvements operators are prepared to make to improve the sustainability of their tourism activities;

3.   Clarifying their expectations with the local authorities and their partners;

4.   Finalizing the diagnosis of the area. Integration of the analyses produced on each type of tourist operation and discussing these to define a table of indicators of sustainable tourism for the area and establish a collective diagnosis of sustainable tourism.

Expected results:

1.   Making those involved aware of the importance of sustainable tourism;

2.   Setting up active discussion groups in the area;

3.   Validating collectively the sustainable tourism indicators adapted to the area;

4.   Enabling the industry to evaluate their tourist operations with these indicators;

5.   Piloting local policies on the basis of indicators validated collectively;

6.   Validating a diagnosis of the specific area – its problems and needs -incorporating the diversity of the issues of the area and of interests.

Regional piloting of indicators

The table of indicators serves as a guide for discussion. The collective discussion will enable those involved to apply the ACS normative indicators and to determine the local regional indicators to be selected from the table and, if necessary, the indicators to be set up to correspond to the issues of area and business. Once completed, the local/ regional indicators pilot table will be used to evaluate the policy implemented. The results of the diagnoses are expected to make it possible for the governments and the ACS to respond to the issues through strategic guidelines, which will provide the major directions to be taken within a 5-year horizon, within the framework of the sustainable tourism policy. These strategic guidelines must be validated, amended, or rejected collectively by all those involved, then arranged in a hierarchy and organized.

Plan of Action:

1.   Organize a task force incorporating the different types of tourist operation previously identified (representation groups);

2.   Have the local leading group prepare a summary working document recording the issues and the diagnosis of the area previously produced;

3.   Distribute this summary-working document to the task force about ten days before the first consultation meeting;

4.   Hold two or three consultation meetings with the aim of:

   a. Validating the transcription of the summary working document;

   b. Negotiating the strategic guidelines to be selected for the area;

   c. Validating the strategic guidelines retained.

Expected results

1.   The definition of the consensus strategic guidelines;

2.   The identification of any conflicting strategic guidelines, which are only shared by some of those involved.

Implementation Method

1.   Bring together a task force representative of the different types of tourist operations previously identified (representative groups);

2.   Identify the actions proposed;

3.   Discuss their coherence in relation to the strategic guidelines retained;

4.   Check whether the actions proposed cover the diversity of the situations of businesses, propose adjustments if necessary;

5.   Organize a hierarchy of priorities according to the issues of the area;

6.   Validate collectively the action plan and its funding.

Expected results

1.   The preparation of a transparent action plan;

Vendors serve cruise ship tours in Roatan Honduras. Measuring the degree to which tourism benefits the local economy is one of the key challenges for indicators programs.

2.   The proposal of a method of evaluation;

3.   The definition of a calendar for implementing the actions provided for;

4.   The organization of a permanent piloting group to monitor the setting up of the actions, representative of the diversity of the tourist operations identified.

Finally, it is intended that the strategy for the area and the action plan be built into a local objectives contract covering what is to be achieved collectively. This document, which can be compared to a local Agenda 21, will represent a firm commitment by the destination to move towards sustainable tourism as defined by the ACS. These local objectives contracts will make it possible to take into account:

*   The diversity of the issues linked with the specific contexts of the destinations;

*   The variable capacity of the destinations to access the same stage of development;

*   Setting up a process based on stimulation and local empowerment, rather than on sanctions.

Box 6.13 The interview grid used at Saint François:

Present situation

*   personal situation at the time of the interview;
*   identity of the operator;
*   training;
*   family situation;
*   occupational background of parents;
*   cultural background of parents;
*   geographic origin of parents.

Tourist activity:

*   clients (Guadeloupe/Caribbean/outside Caribbean, individuals/groups, staying/cruise...);
*   the tourist products, the other activities;
*   the material resources, grants;
*   the organization of labour, links with other businesses, etc.;
*   methods of marketing and promotion;
*   period of activity.

Social involvement:

*   club and society activities; professional, municipal, and other responsibilities;
*   relationships inside and outside the region, links with the professionals, decision-makers, institutions.

Commercial activity:

*   the status of the business, the property situation (ownership, renting);
*   workforce : employees, voluntary workers, trainees, family;
*   origins of employees : local, regional;
*   turnover.

Professional career – origin of the project

* take-over or creation of activity;
* reasons for becoming established;
* choice of products, clients, working conditions, location;
* training acquired;
* partnership;
* support: family, professional organizations, government authorities, local authorities, etc.;
* financial assistance received;
* problems experienced;
* relationships with the competition.

Business report in terms of sustainable tourism

* openness and awareness of the subject;
* economic: financial situation, profitability, attendance;
* welfare: working conditions, job creation, choice of suppliers, action against job insecurity;
* heritage: choice of materials, waste management, environmental concerns;
* constraints / facilities.

View of the area in terms of sustainable tourism

* tourism: perception of quantity, quality, evolution, policies, foreseeable if growth;
* environmental, social and cultural verdict for the area: changes to the landscape: for better / for worse;
* the dynamics of the area: the role of agriculture, industry, etc. interesting innovations, who to watchambience and support: the relevance of the advice received; which was wrong, and if it had to be done again?.

Source: Association Of Caribbean States (ACS)

6.9 Chiminos, Island Guatemala

Private Sector, Ecolodge, Management Indicators

The Chiminos Island case shows how a small local business can use indicators for measuring both the sustainability of its own operation and impact on the ecosystems it uses.

Chiminos Island Lodge, in the el Peten region of Guatemala, is a private tourism business located in a protected area with ecological, archaeological, and historic sites. Like other tourism businesses in protected areas, its owners are aware of the importance and the value of the cultural and archaeological resources that are involved in its activity. This awareness has led the partners to seek sustainable management methods for the lodge and to use indicators tools to support this initiative. Despite this interest, identification and application of sustainability indicators have been difficult, particularly due to the social and political environment of the region, its isolation and lack of resources for implementation.

The Chiminos Island Lodge is located in the Punta Chiminos Archaeological site. This is an island, made by the ancient Mayas, through cutting a channel and separating the small peninsula from the mainland. The site is located in the Petexbatún Lagoon, which is a Mayan archaeological zone in the southwest of El Petén, one of Guatemala's most isolated regions. It is also within the Petexbatún Wildlife Refuge, a zone of seasonal wetlands, and a refuge for local and migratory wildlife, especially birds from North America. The only way to reach the Lodge is by boat on the Petexbatún river, and the site is about 15 hectares in size. The Lodge is the gateway for visitors to the important cities of the Late Classical Mayan period: Aguateca, Dos Pilas and Ceibal, as well as others which require expeditions of more than one day, including Cancuén, the Altar of Sacrifices, Yaxchilán and Piedras Negras (Black Stones).

Prior to May 2000, when the site was acquired by four family partners, the lodge was called Posada de Mateo and was semi-abandoned. The new owners assumed its management with a high degree of enthusiasm and have a stated ecological commitment and a genuine interest in promoting the knowledge and contact with the Mayan Civilization. The Lodge maintains a close relationship with the local community El Escarbado, of some 30 families, hires local people to work in the Lodge, at the visitor centre, and for maintenance of the Lodge, (all six personnel are from the local community).and also supports community development projects. This has had positive effects creating a constructive relationship with the community, mutual respect and reciprocal support, particularly with the new managers. The Lodge also contributes through voluntary work to the recovery of nearby forest property.

The Lodge limits the number of visitors per night to 25 persons in 5 cabins; these are built on pillars and are outside the limits of the archaeological site. As well, each cabin has its own liquid waste treatment system, reducing the environmental impact. No trees are cut and wildlife is protected. Nature interpretive paths and accesses to the central temple and to the Mayan defensive palisades have been built.

Currently the Lodge has begun to organize its own data collection for key basic indicators, and is seeking new indicators for sustainable management of tourism. Box 6.14 shows some of the indicators being used.

Box 6.14 Issues and indicators Use for Chiminos Lodge

Issue	Indicator	Utility
Tourist statistics	<ul><li>Number of tourists per night</li><li>Number of tourists per month</li><li>% of Lodge occupancy</li></ul>	Evaluation of profit value, personnel management, carrying capacity management
Control of fuel use	<ul><li>Litres per person (monthly)</li><li>Litres per boat (monthly)</li><li>Number of average persons per boat (monthly)</li></ul>	Consumption stress and contamination impact per passenger
Energy budget	<ul><li>Energy consumption level</li></ul>	Consumption control, decrease of contamination because of gases and wastes
Community relations	<ul><li>Local employment (100% of employees are hired from the local El Escarbado nearby community.)</li><li>Level of use of local transport (100% of transport to the lodge is contracted locally)</li></ul>	Community based tourism development
	<ul><li>Record of employee education and responsibilities</li></ul>	Managerial control
	<ul><li>Training programme for all employees with a trainer from the local chapter of San Carlos University in nearby Flores</li></ul>	Building capacity of local community
	<ul><li>Competitive wages for personnel (owners do not receive any wages from the lodge)</li><li>100% of proceedings are reinvested in improvements of the lodge and its sorroundings</li><li>Evaluation of community satisfaction through regular interviews</li><li>Support of community projects</li></ul>	Community based tourism development The lodge has supported the following community projects: - Spring protection for only potable water source for El Escarbado - Supply of water pump, generator and piping layout - Domestic water distribution system - School supplies - Latrines for school and homes
Nature conservation	<ul><li>Number trees are cut, as the natural cycle of the jungle forest is observed. Only dead trees that pose a threat to the existing infrastructure are pruned for prevention.</li></ul>	Preservation of the jungle according to the natural cycle.
	<ul><li>Inventory of trees, identifying varieties and number of each variety. (recent counts have been done for most species of interest)</li></ul>	Control of jungle evolution in Chiminos premises and surroundings.
	<ul><li>Number of visitors using the trails daily</li><li>Inventory of trails (number length, general condition)</li><li>Maximum limit of visitors per trail (tourists staying at the lodge and authorized visitors walk through the trails)</li></ul>	Nature interpretation and conservation

Nature conservation	* Pictorial list of local and migratory bird is being made (number of species, counts of sitings)	Interpretation and control of fauna in the region
	* Membership to local environmental associations	Actual participation in Fundacion Defensores de la Naturaleza – WWF supported (members since 2004)
Preservation of Archaeological Heritage	* Number of permits to visit the archaelogical premises, issued by the administration	Act as actual guardians of Punta de Chimino archaeological site.
	* Number of tourist's visits to archaeological premises.	The level of tourist activities within the premises is a deterrent for potential looters of the site.
	* Number of archaeological and university projects approved by government in Chiminos premises, hosted in the lodge	Support the study of pre-classical occupations, a not a not well studied part of Maya history at this site.
	* Number and years of memberships in local associations that bring together archaeologists, environmentalists and eco-tourism operators	Actual participation in Asociacion Alianza Verde (members since 2001) and Asociacion Petexbatun (members since 2004)
Waste handling	* Separation of solid waste in organic, recyclable and non recyclable	Recyclable waste (plastic, glass, etc.) is taken into the nearby town of Sayaxche to be exchanged.
	* 1 sewage plant per bungalow, kitchen and personnel quarters	Avoid water pollution
	* Existence of several water treatment plants	
	* Quality test of running and waste water effluent	To assure basic quality of water
Client satisfaction	* Comments of satisfaction in comments book (counts of complaints, positive comments)	Quality gaps identification

Chiminos Island Lodge seeks to organize its tourism management to respond to issues of sustainability related to key assets and resources used. This goal keeps the Lodge managers in a constant search for useful management tools. In this process, indicators were identified as a key tool of management. Chiminos Island Lodge is a good example of tourism destinations, where private businesses are the main drivers of initiatives to support the sustainability of the destinations.

Further information:
www.chiminosisland.com

Chiminos Island Lodge

6.10 El Garraf Natural Park, Catalonia (Spain)

Park Management, Annual Planning, Reporting, Performance

The El Garraf Natural Park case is presented as an example of the approach to parks management using indicators carried out by the Natural Parks Service of Barcelona Province in the Catalonian region of Spain. It is a case that uses an array of indicators as a reference for the management of tourism in protected areas. It also shows how indicators have been used as a comparative tool, and how they support management decisions.

The Natural Parks Service of Barcelona Province has 12 parks under its management. This public agency uses a common set of indicators for all its parks, permitting comparisons between the parks, as well as measurement of changes over time. In this model of management, the indicators are utilized as a form of control system as well as tools for presenting information relating to the parks, through the annual report for each of them. Publicly available information includes many aspects of the park status and conditions, including: the state of the parks; the pressure caused by human activities – both developments within the parks and processes outside affecting them; the state of management capacity of each park and the progress and results of planning and implementation. The El Garraf Natural Park case is typical of tourism management and other activities in Barcelona Province natural areas, as seen from a local management perspective. It also demonstrates a management model integrating tourism that can be useful in other natural protected areas as well.

In July 29, 1986, the Garraf massif was declared as a natural park with the objective of integrating the goals of development, public use and educational use with the conservation of natural resources, and ecosystems, and the maintenance of ecological diversity and of aesthetic and cultural values of the massif. The Administration of the park system is the "Diputaciò de Barcelona, Servei of Parcs Naturals", Office of El Garraf Natural Park. The total surface of the natural park is 10,638 hectares. The park has a Special Plan of Protection of the Physical Environment and the Landscape of the El Garraf natural areas, which establishes different zones according to different environmental conditions. The management of activities such as tourism will be different in each zone.

Box 6.15 Special plan designated areas – El Garraf

	ha (approx.)	%
Zone of natural interest	4,102.4	38.56
Zone of agricultural interest	483.3	4.54
Timber zone	5,032.2	47.3
Zone of integral protection	244.5	2.30
Coastal zone	122.0	1.15
Zone of special treatment	563.2	5.30
Zone of pre-existent planning	90.4	0.85
Total area	**10,638**	**100**

Implementation of the Plan is done by the Park Administration (Barcelona Province Government), and two management institutions: 1) The Coordinating Council which seeks to coordinate the participation and contribution of several administrations with jurisdictions affecting the park area, along with the professional or specific organizations directly concerned with management of the protected area. 2) The Consultative Commission, made up of community representatives who, because of their economic or public interest activities, desire active participation in the development of the Plan.

The administration of the park has 22 full time employees, and has 4 Information Centres, 2 documentation centres, and 3 sites with teaching and leisure facilities.

Issues and indicators used in Garraf Natural Park

For the annual report and presentation of El Garraf Natural Park, different indicators have been used, depending on the users. A summary of park management indicators follows.

Box 6.16 Basic information and managerial indicators for El Garraf

Natural park area	Indicator
Definition of zones	• Area per zone
Political division of the park	• Area of the park in each jurisdiction
Land property	• Area of the park by type of property (public, private, others)
Normative framework of the natural park	
Legal framework	• Inventory of normative and legal documents by sectors
Planning framework	• Inventory of normative documents relating to planning and management aspects
Equipment and infrastructure	
Equipment use	• Number of visitors per piece of cultural, educational, recreational and information equipment
Equipment performance	• Service requirement per facility- information centres, nature schools, pedagogic equipments, museums, activities centre, etc. • Hours of service
Parking areas	• Number of parking areas
Itineraries with signals	• Number of itineraries
Trash collecting service	• Number of areas where there is a collecting trash service
Publications	
Types	• Monographs, leaflets, activities and courses, management documents... • Number of publications per type (e.g. number of different interpretation bulletins) • Number of units per type of publication (e.g. total press run)
Economic resources	
Assigned budgets	• Budget assigned to each program. (The park has 5 major programmes for budget assignment) 1. Conservation and physical management (planning, restoration, new lands acquisition, ecological survey follow up) 2. Promotion of development and participation (councils, commissions and agreements; agricultural, tourist, cultural and forest policies; infrastructure and general services) 3. Social programs (equipment, activities of social focus and publications) 4. Environmental Education (maintenance of environmental education equipment, environmental education activities, and publications) 5. General and support activities (direction, technical material, clothing and individual protection equipment)

Indicators used for the Annual Plan

Annually an Activities Plan is proposed to identify the actions to implement during the year. The general plan combines the annual activities in large blocks or programs – (1 through 5 above), for which are established issues and specific indicators. Subsequently a summary of them is presented:

Box 6.17 Indicators used for the Annual Plan – El Garraf

	Sample Indicator	Collection method
Planning Control		
Urban management	• Number of reports by type (urban development, forest use, photos and videos, excursions and sports competitions) • Number of letters and answers received and referred to the urban development management of the area	Councils administration, park administration
	• Number of citations/violations by type (motorized circulation, illegal construction, prohibited fires, opening of roads, etc.)	Police
Plants of prevention and restoration		
Fire prevention planning	• Amount of budget assigned • Number of personnel hired for the development and execution of the plan	Park administration
Fires incidents	• Number of incidents by type (fire warnings, interventions re forest fires, prohibition of agricultural burns, control of hearths, etc.) • Number of incidents per month	Park administration - Firemen station records
Fires	• Number of fires registered • Surface burned inside and outside of the park • Fire location • Time of fire extinction (date and hour of start - date and hour of extinction) • Fire causes	
Fire prevention	• Budget of protection - maintenance • Number of water supply access points for fire use	Firemen station records
Heritage maintenance		
Management and maintenance of heritage	• Number of actions carried out • Time used for maintaining each heritage asset	Culture departments or councils involved. Park administration
Ecological monitoring		
Monitoring physical factors	• Atmosphere pollution (suspended matter in air - _g/m³ - ; combustion waste - SO_2 - ; ozone - O_3 - and NO_2) • Temperature (maximum, minimum, average, absolute maximum and minimum) • Relative humidity (most minimum, average) • Wind speed - metres / second (maximum, average, absolute maximum) • Number of days with frosts • Rain millimetres (accumulated, maximum absolute) • Water analysis of each water source and sea water (pH, conductivity, chlorine, sulphur, turbidity, alkalinity, dry residues, nitrates, nitrites, ammonia, phosphorus, suspended matter)	Weather data from meteorology stations (fixed and mobile collecting units) inside the park

Conservation and physical management (vertical side label)

Conservation and physical management	**Monitoring of the Mediterranean tortoise re-introduction**	° Number of freed tortoises ° % of individuals adapted to their natural habitat ° Number of individuals born in the wild	Specific for Garraf Natural Park. Other parks monitors their own specific species with similar indicators
	Rabbit census	° Number of rabbits by square kilometre	IKA (kilometric index of abundance)
	Population monitoring of butterflies, bats	× Number of individuals counted	
	Monitoring population of carnivores	° % of photographed species	Nocturnal photograph
		° Distribution of the species in the park	Distribution by grid square
		° Number of registered species × Species apparition frequency (% of the transects where appeared)	Transects, identification of traces/kilometre
	Monitoring population of micro-mammalians	° Number of individuals by species	Capture with traps
	Monitoring population of hunted mammals	° Number of individuals observed ° Number of species counted ° Number of observations per itinerary and season	Lineal transects at night. Day transects. Hunting statistics. IKA (kilometric index of abundance)
	Monitoring social, economic and cultural variables	° Number of inhabitants inside the park	
	Fires study of impact	° Decrease of n° of species by grid square of the Park	
		° Number of individuals by species by grid square	Distribution by grid square
	Dynamic of plagues	× Number of individuals by species captured	Capture with traps
	Participation in monitoring networks	° Number of networks (organizations) of monitoring in which participates.	
	Promotion and leading of research	° Number of projects in which has participated or facilitated the technical backup	

Interpretation Centre El Garraf

	Sample Indicator	
Development and participation promotion	**Counsels, Commissions and Agreements**	
	Coordinating Council	◦ Nº of meetings and themes treated by the Coordinating Council
	Consultative Commission	◦ Nº of meetings and themes treated by the Consultative Commission
	Agreements	◦ Nº of agreements done
	Agricultural, timber, tourist and cultural policies	
	Special subsidies	◦ Amounts granted through subsidies (agrarian businesses, timber exploitations, business services, architectural restoration of patrimony).
	Subsidies to cultural institutions	◦ Nº of subsidized companies ◦ Amounts granted
	Infrastructures and general services	
	Trash collecting service	◦ Cost of activity
	Maintenance of the road network	◦ Nº and length of roads maintained
	Signals	◦ Nº of actions done ◦ Cost of activity
Social use	**Facilities for Public (social) use**	
	Creation and maintenance of facilities	◦ Nº of projects executed and in execution ◦ Kind of equipment and improvements done
	Facility use	◦ Nº of users of facilities
	Activities of social use	
	Visitor information	◦ Nº of persons at the information service ◦ Opening hours of the information centres ◦ Average salary of the information personnel
	Activities of the Circle of Friends of the Natural Park	◦ Nº of activities organized by the Circle (excursions to the park, conferences, publications, etc.) ◦ Nº of assistants to the activities of the Circle
Environmental education	**Creation and maintenance of facilities and activities**	
	Equipment	◦ Nº of facilities created or restored (information centres, schools of nature, interpretation centres) ◦ Nº of users of teaching equipment
	Activities	◦ Nº of teaching activities developed (exhibitions, audiovisual multimedia, video-exhibitions, pedagogical stages for school groups) ◦ Nº of students assisting to activities of the park ◦ Amount of subsidies to students centres that complete stages of environmental education in the park ◦ Nº of awareness activities directed to visitors (prevention of fires, advice on mushroom collection, pets in the park, protection of the Mediterranean tortoise, protection of the underground environment, climbing regulation)

Environmental Education	**Visitor control**	
	Vehicles	° Number of vehicles by hour (through mechanical counters of vehicles) ° % of vehicles that visit the park (from the total vehicles registered) ° Number of vehicles by access to the park (through mechanical counters of vehicles) ° Number of vehicles parked in every parking area in the park (Maximum and average over year)
	Visitor profile and activities	° Age, occupation and nº of times individual has visited the park ° Means of transportation used ° Number of persons by group that visits the park ° Reason for visiting the park
	Visitor satisfaction	° Appraisal of park quality (visuals, comfort, aesthetic, diversity of activities, overall appraisal) ° Appraisal of the park equipment and services (quality of them, subjective appraisal) ° Degree of satisfaction ° % of activities that visitors carry out in the park ° % of visited places ° More appreciated aspects by the visitors (% of visitors) ° Aspects of the park to improve (% of visitors) ° Degree of satisfaction regarding park personnel
General and support activities	**General Coordination**	
	Meetings **General report**	° Number of meetings done ° Presentation of the annual report of the park
	Program of Activities	° Presentation of the Program of Activities of the park
	External relations	
	Institutions and stakeholders involved	° Diversity of relevant institutions contacted ° Number of collaboration activities done ° Meetings and workshops held
	Logistic equipments	
	Vehicles resources	° Number of old and new vehicles
	Communication network	° Number of transmitters (mobile and portable) ° Number of radial relay stations
	Workshops and courses	
	Workshops and courses	° Attended and organized courses ° Workshops, conferences and meetings attended as a speaker ° Exhibitions done

Seventeen years after the creation of the park, the managing agency affirms that the objectives presented in the Special Plan have been reached to a great degree, from the point of view of both planning and management. This conclusion is based on the data obtained from indicators during the management reviews and annual reporting. The positive results and the success in management of the natural parks of Barcelona Province, make this example a good operational reference for working with indicators and their application to the management of tourism in protected areas. This case illustrates how indicators can become a central element in management, beginning with the planning phase, and over time becoming performance measures which are used not only internally but also for the public communication of the results.

Source: Diputación de Barcelona, Área de Espacio Naturales, Servei de Parcs Naturals. (Barcelona Province Government, Natural Sites Area, Natural Parks Service).

For more information: www.diba.es/parcs/site/garraf.htm
See Diputaciò Barcelona, Servei de Parcs Naturals 2000, 2001, 2003) in bibliography

6.11 European Environmental Agency Indicators: Tourism and the Environment in the European Union

Regional Indicators, Impacts, Public Reporting

This case shows how an international effort can create common environmental indicators for tourism for widespread use among many nations at the regional level.

The European Environment Agency (EEA) has been in operation since 1994 with the aims of supporting sustainable development and improvement in Europe's environment through the provision of timely, targeted, relevant and reliable information to policy-making agents and the public. Since 2000, the EEA has been working on tourism indicators as the tourism sector becomes fully integrated into the more general EU work on sustainable development indicators. The EEA tourism indicators focus both generally on development issues, and more specifically on tourism and destinations. The main objective is to stress and highlight the environmental impacts that result from tourism activity, including the pollution effects related to transport system.

Scope of the EEA tourism indicators at the time of their development:

* European scale, geographical coverage: 15 Member States and 4 EFTA countries;

* Environmental dimension of sustainable development indicators for tourism;

* Collaborative approach and long term process involving experts from countries and other international bodies;

* Support to EU tourism policy development, especially the formulating of the Community Agenda 21 for European Tourism.

Why measure and assess the environmental impacts of tourism in Europe?

Europe has long been the world's favourite destination with around 60% of the international tourism arrivals (WTO). In the EU, tourism is the fastest growing industry, with an annual growth of 3.8% and will soon be the largest service activity. The sector generates already up to 12% of GDP, 6% of employment, and 30% of external trade (European Commission). In the whole Europe, WTO forecasts that international arrivals will grow by 50 %, reaching around 720 million per year by 2020, with a doubling of air traffic in Europe.

Box 6.18 Tourism flows in the European Union (Source: EEA, Eurostat)

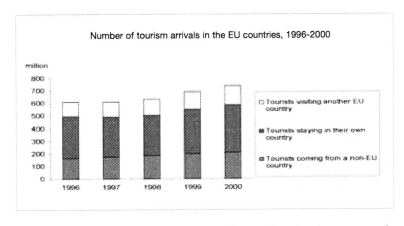

Any industry already large and growing quickly can cause environmental problems, and tourism is no exception. The sector is not just getting bigger - the way people are going on holiday is changing. The growing trend is for people to take more and shorter trips and to travel further from home, and this trend is re-establishing itself after the effects of the September 11 events, which increased demand for closer destinations using land-transport. As a result, the industry's transport-related environmental problems, already significant, are expected to grow parallel with tourism itself.

When on holiday, moreover, people tend to consume more energy and water and produce more waste. More and more Europeans are also building second homes, which have low occupancy rates and take up far more land than other accommodation types.

Finally, most of these pressures are concentrated in a few small regions during a few weeks of the year, making dealing with these problems even more difficult. The Mediterranean coast, for example, is expected to see around 300 million tourists in 2025, up from 135 million in 1990 (Blue Plan, 1995).

There is no tourism without transport...and without pollution

Tourist travel continues to grow and is increasingly dominated by road and air transport, the most environmentally-damaging modes. In 2000, 78% of Europeans who took long holidays traveled by car, 16% by plane and only 5% by train and 1% by boat. Air travel has increased rapidly (+51%) between 1997 and 2000, when road and railway increased both by 15%.

Box 6.19 Evolution of the use of transport modes by tourists to reach destinations

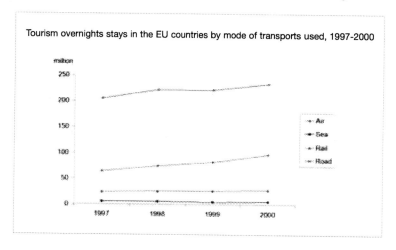

(Source: Eurostat), (Note: Includes tourists, residents and non-residents; stays of 4 or more nights.)

Tourism is the main driver behind the apparently inexorable increase in the demand for passenger transport, with its associated environmental impacts such as air pollution, climate change and fragmentation of natural habitats. Cars and planes, the most environmentally-damaging modes, remain the most-used forms of transport.

Travel to and from destinations is responsible for 90 % of the energy used in the tourism sector. In the EU, tourist travel represents 9 % of total passenger travel (including business travel, which constitutes 25-30 % of total passenger-km), and about 70 % of air transport is for holiday travel. For the whole EU, holiday transport is responsible for half of all passenger transport energy use, and 11 % of the overall energy consumption of the transport system (including freight). In France, it was estimated that transport for domestic tourism contributes 5 to 7 % of all greenhouse gas emissions. As tourism is growing more rapidly than overall traffic, the associated problems are likely to increase. Balancing the transport modal split in tourism travel will make a real difference to transport-based environmental pollution.

Tourism is an activity highly concentrated in space; impacting the most environmentally-sensitive areas. The high concentration and seasonal nature of tourism create direct environmental impacts at destinations. The uncontrolled development of tourism at some places over recent decades has led to a dramatic and irreversible degradation of the quality of the environment, especially around the Mediterranean and in the Alps. Conflicts may also arise between tourism development and other sectors such as agriculture and forestry.

In 1990, it was estimated that nearly 135 million tourists (international and domestic) visited the Mediterranean coasts, doubling the local population (Blue Plan). The coastal strip (500 m from the shore) in the island of Majorca, one of the most popular destinations in Spain, was already 27 % urbanised in 1995 (see case study on Balearic Islands, p. 345).

Box 6.20   Tourism intensity in Europe (number of beds in collective tourism accommodations by square kilometer).

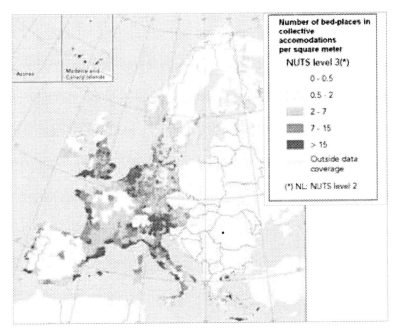

Source: EEA, Eurostat

Some destinations have become the victims of their own attractiveness. Small islands such as Mykonos (Greece), Porquerolles and Ré (France) and Capri (Italy) that are experiencing increasing pressures have already exceeded their 'carrying capacity'.

Accommodation and related infrastructure development is a major source of impacts, particularly on water resources, land use and ecosystems. Hotels are significant consumers of water, as an average tourist staying in a hotel consumes up to 300 litres (up to 880 litres for luxury tourism) and generates around 180 litres of wastewater per day. These figures show that a tourist uses on average one third more water per day than a local inhabitant.

Another major problem is **the construction of second homes that is increasing rapidly (by 10 % in France between 1990 and 1999), creating more intensive pressures on land and the environment, especially in coastal and mountain zones.** The land area required by such a home, estimated at around 100 m² per person, represents 40 times that for a flat rental and 160 times that for an 80-bed hotel in a year. In France, the world's top tourist destination, almost 335,000 new second homes have been built during the past two decades. In Sweden, about one third of second homes are within 100 m from the shore. Moreover, most second homes are seldom used: often only two weeks a year compared to more than twenty weeks for hotels.

Management policies: there has been limited progress in the implementation of policies to move towards a more sustainable tourism, with minimal penetration of environmental schemes such as eco-labelling.

Most of the environmental measures that have so far been implemented were initiated by major tour-operators and local stakeholders and are based on voluntary approaches. While there are examples of good practices in many countries (e.g. Austria, France, Germany, Spain, Switzerland and the United Kingdom), most measures remain marginal (e.g. eco-label schemes or eco-taxes). Some national programmes that are designed to encourage sustainable tourism are being developed. However, there is a general lack of broad environmentally-integrated strategies for the tourism sector.

Some more general responses could be developed to cope with the environmental impacts of tourism. Examples include spreading the vacation calendar at the European level to reduce the high seasonality of tourism, strengthening regional management plans, setting up some Strategic Environmental Assessments for tourism projects, and generalizing Integrated Quality Management Systems for tourism destinations.

This analysis was used as a key input into the EEA pan-European indicators based report for the ministerial conference that was held in Kiev in May 2003. In its assessment, the EEA generally hopes that its indicator development can help to make more transparent those areas where additional policies need to be developed.

The EEA work attempted to use data from international sources (WTO, Eurostat) where feasible and national data or case studies where the data gap was apparent. A consultation process was run on the indicators, fact sheets and the assessment together with experts from countries and international bodies). The main achievements at this stage are the identification of a core set of tourism indicators that aim to measure the way to a more sustainable development path.

The first EEA Tourism and the environment indicator report (TOERM) is planned to be published by end 2004, and will be available through the EEA website:
(http://themes.eea.eu.int/Sectors_and_activities/tourism/index_html). This report provides more exhaustive assessment and best practices on the environmental impacts of tourism development in the 15 EU Member States and the 4 EFTA countries.

Tourism and the environment core-set indicators

The policy questions that provide the structural framework for the tourism and environment reporting mechanism are the following:

1.   What are the environmental impacts of tourism?

2.   Are we getting better at matching the tourism demand to the need to preserve resources?

3.   What characterises and drives the demand for tourism?

4.   Are we moving towards a more environmentally market-based management of the tourism sector?

5.   How effective are environmental management and monitoring tools towards a more integrated tourism strategy?

Key indicators are given below to illustrate the method and content of the EEA tourism indicators. These examples are part of a main set of around 30 indicators.

Box 6.21 Key questions, policy issues and core-set tourism indicators for EEC

Generic question	Policy issue	Indicator title
What are the environmental impacts of tourism?	Air pollution relating to tourism transport	◦ Tourism's contribution to gas emissions and energy consumption from transport.
	Impacts to territories (waste and soils)	◦ Tourism density (bed-places per km^2 NUTS 3 level).
Are we getting better at matching the tourism demand to the need to preserve resources?	Management of tourism infrastructures	◦ Tourism intensity (bed-places per inhabitant, NUTS 3 level); ◦ Construction of tourism facilities and accommodation (including second homes).
	Management of tourism mobility and access to destinations	◦ Modes of transport used by tourists (international and domestic tourism).
What characterises and drives the demand for tourism?	Characteristics of the tourist demand	◦ Tourism arrivals in Europe (residents and non-residents); ◦ Overnights spent in tourism accommodations, by mode; and related bed occupancy rate.
	Characteristics of the tourism offer	◦ Household expenditure and tourism prices.
Are we moving towards a more environmentally market-based management of the tourism sector?	Internalisation of external costs	◦ Tourist tax revenues and environmental expenditure.
How effective are environmental management and monitoring tools towards a more integrated tourism strategy?	Tools of industry	◦ Implementation of eco-labels for tourism facilities.
	Measures of local stakeholders (at destinations)	◦ Progress in initiatives implemented by local stakeholders (Integrated Quality Management, local agendas 21, SEA, ICZM, in tourism destinations).

Source: Europe's environment: the third assessment, chapter 2.7 Tourism, 2003
(http://reports.eea.eu.int/environmental_assessment_report_2003_10/Chapter27.)

6.12 France: Aggregated National Reporting on Indicators

Aggregation, Scale, Reporting, Communication

This case documents a national level initiative to develop consistent indicators for use across France. The case shows both the advantages of this approach for some users, and the problems of response or application to more local issues.

Aggregating indicators in a national report summarizing and analyzing regional or local information is more likely to provide an overview of the interrelationships between tourism and sustainability than is simple statistical presentation of indicators. Indicators are most useful if they are part of an overall assessment, a sustainable tourism planning procedure, a public policy evaluation and other institutional and management processes. In the case of the book "Tourisme, environnement, territoires : les indicateurs", issued by the French institute for the environment (Ifen), the objective was given by Ifen's indicators program: assessing the integration of environment into tourism policies (the work was limited to the environment and did not concern other dimensions of overall sustainability).

The book, issued in 2000, contains 36 chapters and more than 150 indicators analysing the interrelationships between tourism and the environment.

The choice of a territorial scale and its implications

The hypothesis of this project was that some critical issues can only be evaluated at a broader scale than the destination level (national, European, or international), especially transport issues, which were granted a central role in the project. *Ifen's* work concentrated on the national level with indicators which covered all parts of the nation. This is an important step towards assessing the spatial distribution of impacts. It should nevertheless be kept in mind that the search for indicators available at all spatial levels implies a narrowing of the range of issues discussed. To provide more focus, the project also analysed the specific features of each of four types of holiday destinations (seaside resorts, mountain resorts, cities, the countryside), with particular attention to the development of activities or types of resorts that are specific to the areas concerned (yachting, islands, Alpine skiing or agro-tourism, for example).

Finally, the main output of the national approach was to provide a framework for the destination level. It helps identify tourism "hotspots", where the tourism activity can critically endanger the environment (when a high tourism density is related to a vulnerability of the environment. (See Box 6.23) It also enables local managers to evaluate to what extent local problems caused by tourism are also a problem at the national level. For instance, tourism induces difficult problems of water management for specific resorts, such as islands, but at a national level, the water consumption of tourism is not that important for France.

The choice of an indicator framework and its implications regarding communication needs

There is a need to bring out the close links between changing patterns of tourism, their environmental impacts and more general social trends. For example, the way people divide their time between work and leisure is a factor that determines whether they take their holidays over short or long periods, which in turn determines the intensity of transport use for tourism. The tax system, the condition of the real estate market and building regulations are all factors that influence the distribution of the various types of holiday accommodation and how much they encroach on the surrounding area.

The European Environmental Agency proposes an improved framework (AEE 1998) to the Pressure-State-Response model initially developed by OECD: The DPSIR framework, for *Driving forces* (economic and social factors or trends) Pressures, State, Impact, Response(see EEA indicators case p . 377) Social and economic trends draw attention to external factors which are not directly related to the environment but are essential to understand, relative to changes in the activity considered and the relationship to sustainable development. As far as the diagnosis is concerned, the distinction between state and impact makes it possible to separate the direct effects of the pressures (on the environment) from their effects on communities.

Although the indicators were developed through this DPSIR framework, it was finally decided not to organize the final document following this pattern: the main drawback of this option was a separation of interrelated indicators in different parts of the book. Each environmental issue was presented in a separate chapter (water, energy, waste, natural heritage…). The indicators exercise has the objective of communication to a larger audience than just the specialists involved in the tourism debate. Even if indicators are developed following a theoretical framework, this framework may not necessarily be used for the public presentation of the results.

An incomplete indicator development procedure

Addressing a topic which was not yet covered by a well-established system of official statistics required considerable effort to collect and process relevant data. For instance, an environmental assessment of the tourism sector required very localised data on accommodation capacity, at the community level, to calculate indicators such as number of bed places per km of coastline, or to compare data on tourism pressure with data on natural heritage. A considerable amount of time was devoted to data collection and data processing: this was the main output of the project. While the indicator development procedure was very formal for data collection and data processing, this was not the case for the identification and selection of indicators. It is now generally admitted that the selection of indicators requires a participatory approach and the definition of an adapted procedure (criteria to evaluate the priority and the feasibility of indicators), so as to warrant the neutrality of the project manager in the selection. In *Ifen's work*, this has not been addressed, since the indicators were selected only by the research team.

Communication and dissemination of results, impacts on decision making

The results were widely disseminated, through press releases and professional networks, and the book is now recognized as a reference. The objective is a regular reporting – with an update on a five year basis – of the tourism sector.

The relationship with decision-making at a national level is more complex. Do decision makers really pay attention to a 250 pages report, even colour-printed? Actually the report undoubtedly contributed to a better perception of tourism as a major source of impact on the environment. The "strength of figures" contributed to the credibility of the statements. *Ifen* was identified as a potential contributor to the tourism debate, which brought together the environment and tourism ministries for common projects on strategic assessments: environmentalists are certainly more considered as partners of tourism development than they used to be.

Lessons learned

* The same persons should be responsible of developing the indicators and calculating them. Indicators are not useful unless they are calculated;

* Check the availability of data first!;

* Indicators should be displayed with an adequate commentary, as part of an overall assessment;

* Be ambitious but pragmatic in the development of an indicator : if the data is missing, look for an indirect method;

* An indicator development procedure must respect both research needs (assessing new issues, such as tourism and climate change) and communication needs (disseminating results to a broad audience);

* The procedures of indicator definition, data collection and data processing should be well defined, so as to ensure transparency and efficiency within the research team, and between the research team, the steering committee and the users.

Box 6.22 Selected national-level indicators for french tourism

Examples of Indicators	Comments
* "Net tourism pressure" in France (international night stays to France, minus international night stays of French people abroad)- 1976-1996	International tourism represents in France an equivalent of a year-round additional population of around 600,000 persons (international tourist arrivals minus trips taken abroad by French people) and 219 million night stays. This indicates the amount of resources (e.g. water, energy, etc.) needed to welcome this tourist population. At a national level, this pressure is quite low. It can be higher at a local level (most tourist place) or during seasonal peaks. *Note that 600 000 is not the number of international visitors to France, but the equivalent additional population: 219 millions of night stays divided by 365 days(equivalent to 600 000 persons who stay in France all year). (Some visitors stay more than one day and therefore count more in this calculation.) The last comprehensive survey was done in 1996 with more recent figures based on estimates. International overnight stays to France : 459 millions International overnight stays of French abroad : 240 millions, Difference= 219 millions.*
* Accommodation capacity (all types) between 1990-1999- (see Map)	Expressed at a very local level, enables evaluation of the potential tourism pressure. The French tourist accommodation capacity increased by 2.7% between 1990-1999, which is quite low and hides some faster evolution at . regional and local level: a diminution in some rural areas, and a quick growth on the Mediterranean, Atlantic Coast, and in the high mountain.
* Average utilisation period of accommodation, per type of accommodation	The average utilisation period, which ranges from 6 (secondary homes) to 30 (hotels) weeks a year, is a driving force of tourism space consumption: the shorter, the more space is needed to accommodate annually the same number of tourists, as arrivals concentrate in a shorter period, increasing seasonality.
* Perception of natural parks as a cause of tourist attraction	Illustrates the presence of national parks as a factor of attractiveness for destinations, and thus the potential destinations of ecotourism .

◦ Hotel accommodation capacities in city centres and in suburban communities- 1990-1999- (see Box 6.23)	The accommodation capacities increased in suburban communities and decreased in centre-cities in recent years. Hotels tends to locate more and more near highways, which favours the use of individual cars and limits the use of collective means of transportation (See map where this is shown as tourist beds per hectare).
◦ Transit visitors to French territory- 1982-1996	France is situated between originating markets (Germany, Netherlands, UK) and receiving countries (Spain, Italy). Up to 20 million international visitors cross the territory to reach Italy or Spain (it increased by 5 times since 1982), which highly contributes to road congestion during peak periods.
◦ Domestic tourism modal split (by mode of transport)	Between 1986 and 1999, domestic trips by car have increased by 17%, trips by plane by 70%, while train has decreased by 10% and coach by 20%: the most polluting modes of transport develop faster than the least polluting ones.

Box 6.23 Tourist density in French municipalities located within or near inventoried natural areas

(Unit: number of tourist bed-places per hectare)

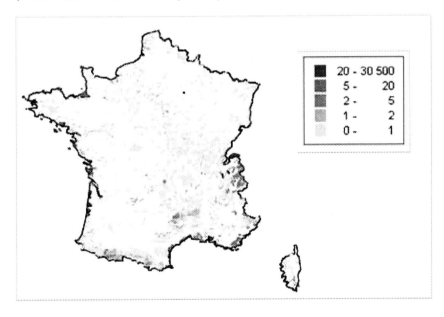

Source : IFEN, based on INSEE (1999 population census), DT/INSEE (1999) and National Natural History Museum (Natural Heritage Inventory)

Further information:

www.ifen.fr/pages/tourisme.htm   (French presentation and order information)

www.ifen.fr/pages/tourism.htm (English presentation and order information)

www.tec-conseil.com (downloadable papers on indicators)

6.13 India: Community Based Tourism in Corbett National Park Using Appreciative Participatory Planning and Action (APPA) Methodology

Community Participation, Small Communities, Qualitative Indicators, Project Evaluation, Performance Indicators

This case shows indicators' role in a participatory planning technique applied in small mountain communities, how they helped defining tourism assets, product development, and project evaluation in the villages.

As part of Leadership for Environment and Sustainable Development (LEAD) Fellow's Project in Uttaranchal Province, Northern India, a Framework for Ecotourism was developed for Corbett Binsar Nainital (CBN) Circuit connecting two Protected Areas and a Hill Resort. In addition Community Based Tourism (CBT) was developed in three villages on the periphery of Corbett National Park over a three-year period from January 2001 to November 2003. The project concluded with results being analyzed by LEAD Fellows with project partners and beneficiaries using participatory methods.

a)   Project Planning

Community Based Tourism Plans were developed for each of the four villages using Appreciative Participatory Planning and Action (APPA) Methodology. The methodology consists of a "4D Cycle" - firstly Discovering what is successful, what is working, what people are proud of and would like to share with the tourists; followed by Dreaming, envisioning the future; Designing through feasibility studies and development of action plans and finally Delivering the plans. Typically, each CBT plan was prepared over six to eight months and involved nearly ten village meetings. Participatory Learning and Action (PLA) tools were used for conducting exercises to collect and organize information, identify issues and select actions.

Box 6.24 Appreciative Participatory Planning and Action (APPA) Methodology

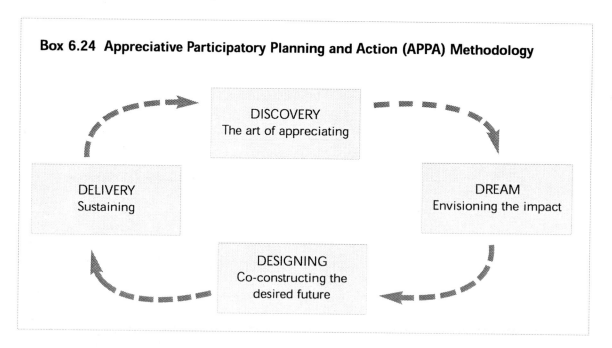

During the Discovery phase and in particular in the trend line exercise that involved graphical representation of key indicators over time and ranking exercises, indicators were identified for collection of information and discussion leading to mutual learning and understanding. Some of the indicators that were used were:

* Number of visitor arrivals at different attractions in the village;
* Number of visitor arrivals during different seasons;
* Leisure time available with villagers during different months;
* Availability of accommodation for visitors in the village;
* Number of vehicles coming to the village;
* Population of the village;
* Maintenance of fire lines for fire protection;
* Availability of jobs;
* Migration of villagers to cities;
* Number of incidents of poaching wild animals;
* Presence of wild elephants in the vicinity of the village;
* Sighting of wild animals in forests adjoining the villages;
* Damage to crops by wild animals;
* Garbage along trails.

b)   Product Development & Marketing

CBT plans were used to develop a variety of products that were ultimately marketed to visitors. In Kyari village, a tented camp was replaced with locally constructed huts, dormitory, interpretation centre and toilets. Night treks for wildlife sighting were discontinued, as the villagers began to appreciate the disturbance it caused to wild animals and birdwatching was introduced. In Choti Haldwani, a Heritage Trail along with interpretive signs was developed to narrate the story of Jim Corbett's association with the village and villagers began charging fees for guiding, photography and for sale of agricultural produce. The villagers became aware of their unique heritage and began working to make their village more receptive to the visitors by carry out a cleanliness drive to remove garbage and maintain the trail. In Bhakrakot village home stays were developed with clean toilets, beds and telephone and the hosts began to offer guiding for local treks and locally prepared food. The hosts learnt from their guests and briefed them about their own culture and lifestyle. These three different types of CBT products namely camp, home stay and heritage trail are now being used as a teaching ground for Community Based Tourism to villagers from far-flung areas.

Soon after, the need to document the benefits and impacts of CBT emerged as a big challenge. Home stays and guides introduced guest registers and receipt books to record number of visitors, sales, and feedback from the visitors. Product development reports were prepared to record investments, materials used and environmental impacts of the product development process. This information is key to performance indicators, allowing progress evaluation of the projects.

Orientation Map showing village assets in Bhakrakot village

Interpretation Center built by villagers

c)   Project Evaluation

At the conclusion of the project, LEAD Fellows, project partners and project beneficiaries participated in a two day workshop to review the performance of the project and chalk out a future course of action. The workshop addressed the project performance at two levels, namely at the level of the communities; the villages of Kyari, Bhakrakot and Choti Haldwani and at the level of the overall destination; the CBN Circuit, and with the two days assigned to "Looking Backwards" and "Looking Forward" respectively.

The method used for assessing the performance at the level of the communities was discussions at community level. Each group from a community was asked to identify the key questions that they would like to address to the project. The group was then asked to prioritize and eliminate questions. For each question the group had to identify suitable indicators and select a person/persons who could provide the relevant information. The framework developed through the participatory process was used as the reference point for further discussions and analysis. Some of the key indicators that were used for evaluation were:

* Number of beneficiaries;
* Increase in earning and profit;
* Incentives for CBT;
* Number of repeat visitors;
* Number of products for sale;
* Number of villagers trained;
* Number and extent of new skills acquired;
* Increase in awareness;
* Relations between community members.

The "H Form technique" was used to asses the performance at the destination level. One chart was developed for each objective and participants were asked both to mark their assessment on the scale and give reasons for their markings on post it slips. The participants were then permitted to see what others had written followed by discussions in stakeholder group level. The exercise concluded with discussion in plenary on steps that can be undertaken to take the initiative forward.

Box 6.25 H-Form technique for destination perfomance

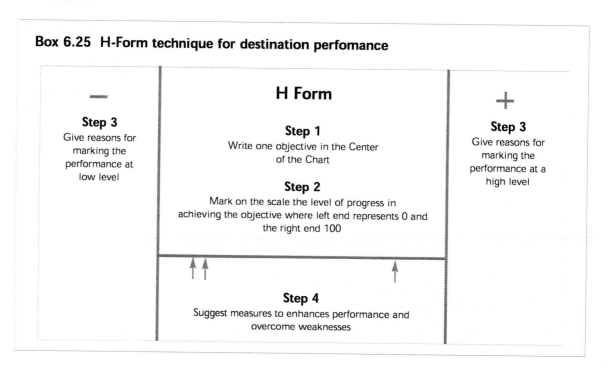

The indicators used for the exercise included:

* To what extent the project developed the CBN circuit as a **destination product**?;
* To what extent the project increased **awareness** regarding CBN natural & cultural heritage assets?;
* To what extent the project generated government **policy support** for ecotourism?;
* To what extent the project led to **capacity building** (skills / institutions) for ecotourism?;
* To what extent the project nurtured **partnerships** between government private sector and the communities?;
* To what extent the project helped mobilize **investment** for CBN destination development?

As a result of the use of the indicators at the planning, product development and evaluation stage there was an increase in understanding of tourism issues amongst the villagers. Furthermore, the use of indicators provided the project team with information for planning and data for communication of results. However, the process was beset with several limitations.

The CBT plans had clear objectives but they were not specific enough to be able to be measured. It is not possible to develop specific objectives when working with communities owing to their limited understanding of tourism issues, lack of consensus within the community itself and evolutionary nature of the process. However, as the projects advance, the products become established and understanding within the community increases, it will become imperative to have specific objectives with quantifiable targets.

Communities are more comfortable with qualitative indicators and with relative exercises such as ranking rather than measurable indicators. For example, in the trend lines used as part of discovery the variation in numbers of tourist arrivals or number of vehicles can be portrayed with ease. But it may be difficulty for them to specify the exact number as recording arrivals and movements will require tools, time and resources. Trend lines developed during the Discovery phase were used for Dream phase by making projections in the future as what the villagers will like to see and could be used for monitoring as baseline as well.

Lastly, communities can work only with a limited number of indicators and it will be helpful if the indicators are prioritized as per the feasibility and convenience of the villagers themselves. Dealing with too many variables would constrain understanding. Indicators chosen by different villages differed in each case and there is a need to permit site-specific selection.

Experience in CBT development in Kyari, Bhakrakot and Choti Haldwani shows that communities spontaneously come up with indicators as part of the planning process and in product development. However, the indicators may be both quantitative as well as qualitative. In the early stage of the project they are more likely to be satisfied with indicators connected with visitor arrivals, sales and important features of the forests and wildlife. However, as the project advances capacities need to be developed to set targets, maintain records and carry out participatory evaluation so as to develop common appreciation and identify future actions.

Students relaxing in huts built by villagers in Camp Kyari

References:

* LEAD International Annual Review 2002;

* The Mountain Institute, (2000) Community-Based Tourism for Conservation and Development: A Resource Kit, The Mountain Institute, Katmandu Nepal;

* Appreciative Inquiry - Change at the Speed of Imagination by Jane Magruder Watkins and Bernard J Mohr (2001) Wiley.

6.14 Kangaroo Island Tourism Optimization Management Model (TOMM):

Community, Community Participation, TOMM, Monitoring, Implementation

This case study shows how indicators development and use has been an important part of an adaptive planning and management process with the participation of the local community.

Kangaroo Island, off the south coast of Australia, is home to abundant native wildlife, such as wallabies, echidna, Kangaroo Island kangaroos, dolphins, Australian sea lions, fairy penguins, and a variety of others birds. It is a place of fresh air, safe communities and diverse landforms. The Island is 155 kilometres long and up to 55 kilometres wide. It retains 47% of its original native vegetation, of which 50% is conserved in National and Conservation Parks. There are just over 4,400 people living on Kangaroo Island with a significant and increasing number of non-resident landowners. Kangaroo Island has been branded as a tourist destination on the basis of its wildlife and its superb natural environment. In 2003, 150,915 people visited the Island, of which 26% were international visitors. The growth of tourism to the Island has introduced external demands and the "sense of place" sought by the broader and global visitor market is potentially at risk, depending upon management actions and developments pursued. These developments have in turn generated both internal pressures and opportunities for the local community. The people of Kangaroo Island see prosperity in tourism, but know that what they have is a unique resource that must be managed carefully if it is not to be destroyed. They must work hard to find the right balance between development and conservation.

The Kangaroo Island Tourism Optimisation Management Model (TOMM) has been developed on Kangaroo Island to tackle the challenges of balancing development and conservation in the interests of both residents and visitors. TOMM is a unique example of a community-driven visitor management system. It is concerned with the Kangaroo Island environment and sustainable development, but it also looks beyond the environment to consider the status of tourism across many aspects of Island life. At the core of TOMM is a set of practical indicators that monitor the status of tourism on Kangaroo Island. Trends demonstrated through the indicators are provided to agencies in order to facilitate strategic planning for the Island.

TOMM has been developed and implemented using a partnership model. This has brought community, industry and government agencies together to problem solve and design strategies that work for Kangaroo Island. The impulse to develop TOMM arose due to two key circumstances on the Island: (1) A marked increase in the number of day visitors to the Island coinciding with the commencement of a fast ferry service between mainland South Australia and the Island and (2) a downturn in the agricultural industry leading to diversification into tourism based industries by many primary producers to support their income base.

Visitation peaked on Kangaroo Island in 1995/1996 with visitation to some sites increasing by 25% in two years. This coincided with the commencement of a ferry service operating between Adelaide (South Australia's capital city) and Kingscote (the largest town on Kangaroo Island). This ferry service bought many people to the Island, who arrived at 10am and left at 4pm, usually targeting the day trip market. This had obvious repercussions; stressing the local environment and bringing limited benefits, as well as increasing fears by residents of future problems. Concern for visitor impacts both on the environment and community, coupled with economic worries and out-migration of youth brought together the Kangaroo Island Council, Kangaroo Island Development Board, Tourism Kangaroo Island, South Australian Tourism Commission, Department for Environment and Heritage and industry and community members to develop a mechanism that would allow better management of tourism and community development on Kangaroo Island.

The TOMM Approach

The vision of TOMM is to achieve best practice in the sustainable management of Kangaroo Island as a tourism destination for the benefit of both residents and visitors. TOMM was developed as a collaborative management and monitoring program, based upon a series of indicators, covering the health of the environment, the health of the Kangaroo Island community, health of the economy; the number and type of tourists visiting; the type of experience visitors are having and visitor satisfaction levels. Data is now collected in relation to each of these indicators and this information is presented to the stakeholders in a simple way to show whether current practice is viable or not.

If evidence suggests that any of the components are not functioning optimally, local management agencies and the TOMM partnership define agency responsibilities and generate ideas about what actions could be implemented to solve identified problems. The data from indicators is also incorporated into strategic planning processes. This integrated, community-based knowledge management system is shown in the figure below.

After four years, the impact of TOMM is beginning to be evident. Tourism promotion continues to showcase the Island as an Australian icon for wildlife. Local businesses are more alert to visitor needs and new businesses have developed to take up opportunities that come with increased visitor numbers. For example, changes were made to ferry schedules to better meet the needs of day and weekend visitors. Local restaurants provide locally produced food and have helped to promote Kangaroo Island as a gourmet destination. Previously, much of the local produce was not available locally but exported to the mainland or internationally. These small steps have made a big difference to the community on Kangaroo Island and its economy.

Box 6.26 TOMM process: Kangaroo Island

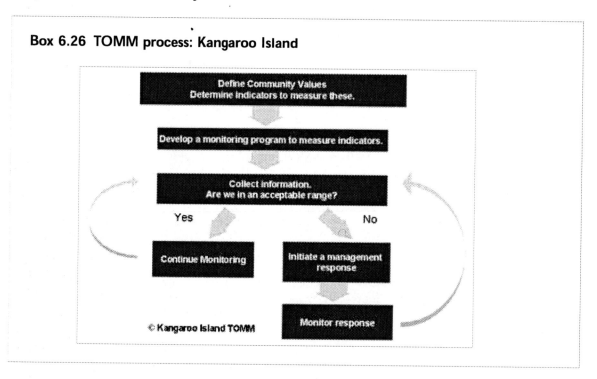

TOMM is a constantly evolving process, reflecting the maturation of the tourism industry, changes in community views and stakeholder relationships. Like any community-based project however, there are ongoing issues relating to its sustainability, including:

- Maintaining the vision and continuity of the TOMM project through changing political and governance environments.

- Accessing ongoing funding continues to be a challenge.

- Maintaining community support for the project.

- Involving and inspiring community members to become actively involved and aware of the TOMM process requires constant attention, particularly through younger generations and the education system.

- Instilling a sense of responsibility and ongoing involvement amongst operators within the tourism industry.

- Ensuring ongoing data collection is maintained, updated and considered in planning and management of the Island.

- Regularly reviewing the model itself so that it has relevance and application beyond Kangaroo Island.

TOMM Indicators

The TOMM indicators were developed through a series of workshops with Government, industry and community and then assessed based on expert opinion using a variety of criteria, including clarity, accuracy, utility, availability, and cost. Over time the indicators have been refined as more knowledge and market data is gathered and monitoring opportunities arise. The indicator program will continue to be refined as the TOMM knowledge base increases and new monitoring programs and data collection techniques become available.

Based upon these indicators, an acceptable range was identified that provided a realistic measurement for each indicator based upon the best information available at the time including previous research, observations and estimations from those with experience in the field and community. Collection of the actual data through a series of monitoring programs is the next step in the TOMM process and in terms of resourcing this stage represents a major component of the process.

Trends generated through the indicators are reported as results and the action taken by management agencies is reported as the outcome. The TOMM on Kangaroo Island is currently reporting on indicators outlined in the table below. The examples given Box 6.27 relate to information gathered and reported in 2001.

Kangaroo Island Beach

Box 6.27 Results of the Kangaroo Island indicators 2001

Optimal Condition	Indicator	Acceptable Range	Result	Outcome
Economic				
The majority of visitors to KI stay longer than 3 nights.	Annual average number of nights stayed on KI,	3 to 5 nights	The acceptable range has been met for this indicator in 2001,	Tourism Kangaroo Island initiated a "Stay another day" promotional campaign to encourage visitors to stay longer on Kangaroo Island.
The tourism industry is undergoing steady growth in tourism yield.	Annual average growth in total tourism expenditure on KI per number of visitors.	4 to 10 % annual average growth.	The acceptable range has been met for this indicator in 2001.	Continuation of current monitoring program.
Market				
A growing proportion of visitors come from the cultural / environmental segments of the domestic and international segments..	Proportion of visitors that match the cultural / environmental profile.	60 to 80% of total visitors to KI	The acceptable range has been met for this indicator in 2001.	Continuation of current monitoring program.
	The number of visits to Kangaroo Island.	0 to 7% annual growth in the number of visits	The acceptable range has been met for this indicator in 2001.	Visitor numbers increased to KI by 8.6% in 2001 – 2002 with a 0.8% increase in 2002-2003. This decrease may have been prompted by the occurrence of significant international events such as terrorism.
Environmental				
Major wildlife populations attracting visitors are maintained and/or improved in areas where tourism activity occurs.	Number of seals at designated tourist site	0 to 5% annual increase in numbers sighted.	The data generated through environmental monitoring was unclear in regards to this indicator in 2001.	Research is currently being undertaken in relation to seal and visitor behaviour at Seal Bay.
	Number of Hooded Plovers	0 to 5% annual increase in numbers sighted.	This indicator was not achieved in 2001.	Annual surveys of the hooded plover indicate that there is impact on this species. There is a current debate on the Island regarding the presence of cars on beaches in which the plover nests. A local environmental group have been included in an education program in partnership with the Department for Environment and Heritage to assist in managing this issue.

Optimal Condition	Indicator	Acceptable Range	Result	Outcome
Experiential				
The KI visitor experience is distinctly different from other coastal destinations in Australia.	Proportion of visitors who believe they had an intimate experience with wildlife in a natural area.	70 to 100% thought it was very important.	The data generated through the resident survey was unclear in regards to this indicator in 2001.	Ongoing education is being undertaken amongst tourism wholesalers by Tourism Kangaroo Island in an effort to educate them regarding the best times to view wildlife. Similarly, local tour operators are extending touring programs in peak summer periods to enable visitors to see the mostly nocturnal wildlife.
Tourism promotion of visitor experiences at Kangaroo Island's natural areas is realistic and truthful to that actually experienced by most visitors.	Proportion of visitors who believe their experience was similar to that suggested in advertisements and brochures.	85 to 100% of total visitors to KI	The acceptable range has been met for this indicator in 2001.	Continuation of current monitoring program.
The majority of KI visitors leave the Island highly satisfied with their experience.	Proportion of visitors who were very satisfied with their overall visit.	90 to 100% of respondents.	The acceptable range has been met for this indicator in 2001.	Continuation of current monitoring program.
Socio - Cultural				
Residents feel they can influence tourism related decisions.	% Increase in residents stating that they can influence tourism related decisions.	70 to 100% of residents.	The data generated through the resident survey was unclear in regards to this indicator in 2001.	Better articulation of questions relating to how residents feel about tourism in future surveys.
Residents feel comfortable that tourism contributes to a peaceful, secure and attractive lifestyle.	Number of petty crime reports committed by non-residents per annum.	10 to 25 crime reports	The data generated through the resident survey was unclear in regards to this indicator in 2001.	Ongoing liaison with the local police department on the Island is underway with the aim to refine this indicator to reflect current data collection processes.
	Number of traffic accidents per annum.	50 to 80 vehicle accident reports	The acceptable range has been met for this indicator in 2001.	Given the extensive gravel roads on the Island, TOMM data has been used to access aditional funding to seal certain key sections of roads on the Island.
Residents are able to access nature-based recreational opportunities that are not frequented by tourists.	Proportion of residents who feel they can visit a natural area of their choice with very few tourists present.	80 to 100% of respondents.	The acceptable range has been met for this indicator in 2001.	Partnership with the University of South Australia has been established to monitor resident attitudes towards tourism and development.
Growth of local employment is consistent.	% Increase in number of people who derive all or some of their income from tourism.		The data generated through the resident survey was unclear in regards to this indicator in 2001.	Economic Indicators are currently under critical review due to the difficulty in collecting accurate information on tourism-derived dollars.

Management of the Kangaroo Island TOMM

The TOMM Management Committee is made up of partners from State and Local Government, community groups and tourism industry representatives. Agencies have become involved with TOMM as it provides them with valuable data on the impact tourism has on their individual operations and the status of the community in terms of the self-perception of its members.

Management models such as TOMM require on-ground drivers as well as pro-active, passionate Management Committee members. Staffing of the Kangaroo Island TOMM has been part time, ideally however, the TOMM requires two staff members covering indicator analysis and research as well as community engagement, marketing and strategic planning.

Key Success Factors

1. Unswerving commitment to fund the project

The Kangaroo Island TOMM has currently been able to operate, albeit at times on a limited scope, through committed project managers, advisors and local and government partners, notably including the Kangaroo Island Council, Department for Environment and Heritage, Tourism Kangaroo Island, Kangaroo Island Development Board, South Australian Tourism Commission and Kangaroo Island Natural Resources Board. New funding opportunities are being investigated including corporate / philanthropic and commercial partnership opportunities to ensure an approach to long-term funding is addressed.

2. Integration of monitoring processes into broader management systems

The Kangaroo Island TOMM has committed funds and support to implement:

* An on-going visitor exit survey that runs throughout the year;

* Annual resident survey of 10% of the Island's population;

* Integration of environmental data through the Department for Environment and Heritage;

* Social data through South Australian Police and their crime / traffic statistics;

* A regular review of indicators to ensure they are relevant to the changing needs of the destination, whilst maintaining continuity with existing agency data collection;

* Making sense of the data and providing analysis of the information in formats that are easily understood and considered relevant to the particular target audience.

While integration of this information into management process has taken time, TOMM data is now included in the following strategic planning processes and is being applied in other tourism destinations:

* Kangaroo Island Integrated Strategic Tourism Plan;

* South Australian Tourism Commission Strategic Plan;

* Department for Environment and Heritage Strategic Plan;

* Tourism Kangaroo Island Strategic Plan;

    - Responsible Nature-based Tourism Strategy 2004-2009: South Australian Tourism Commission and Department for Environment and Heritage South Australia.

* Kangaroo Island Development Board Strategic Plan;

* Kangaroo Island Council Strategic Plan;

* Kangaroo Island Natural Resource Management Plan and Investment Strategy;

* Input into the World Tourism Organisation Indicators program.

3. Creating and maintaining awareness

There have been many different communities involved in the Kangaroo Island TOMM process, all of which require different approaches in regards to information dissemination, awareness raising and involvement:

- Resident community through workshops, presentations, newspaper stories, posters, representation at local shows and through events;

- Government agencies on and off Island through meetings, conferences, inclusion in case studies and representation by TOMM advocates;

- Educational Sector: Schools were involved through guest speaking opportunities, projects such as "Our Island" where students were asked to depict what they loved about Kangaroo Island, student work experience and trying to integrate TOMM data into curriculum programmes. Tertiary institutions have also participated. The TOMM model is covered within many tourism degree courses that address sustainable tourism management;

- The Tourism Industry through active participation in the activities of Tourism Kangaroo Island, the South Australian Tourism Commission and national organisations such as Ecotourism Australia.

The visitor market is proving to be a new form of 'community' that the Kangaroo Island TOMM recognises the need to communicate with, as they develop a sense of ownership regarding the future of the Island. This is achieved through visitor exit surveys, posters displays, representation through local tourism operators and the TOMM website.

4. Enhancing Social and Environmental Capacity

The TOMM was developed to ensure the health of the Kangaroo Island community and its environment, therefore integration of the outcomes of the TOMM process into broader social and environmental processes has been a key result of its success in engaging the local community. The knowledge generated by TOMM has assisted in the implementation of social and environmental programmes aimed at community health and development, leading ultimately to the strengthening of local capital.

Lessons from the Kangaroo Island Experience

The Kangaroo Island TOMM process has highlighted several distinct yet equal operational areas that require attention if community driven projects such as KI TOMM are to make a long-term difference to sustainable tourism.

Access to sufficient resources continues to be a major focus for the Kangaroo Island TOMM and demands a great deal of time and energy. These resources are the most tangible evidence of the success or otherwise of the process, however have the capacity to slow the momentum and enthusiasm for the project in the short term. Specific lessons include:

1. Indicators

a. Ensure data is collected in an appropriate and consistent manner. Engagement of local tourism business will come when data is available and can show trends;

b. Data is only of value if it can be applied and used by others. It cannot be the sole focus of the process even though agencies may see it this way;

c. Communication of the findings in a format and language understood by the intended audience is essential;

d. Review existing data collection systems to see how they can be applied – do not reinvent the wheel;

e. Review indicators on a regular basis for relevance to both the destination, and audience needs and integrate into existing information systems;

f. Align indicators and data collection processes with other models where applicable so a global comparative study may be possible.

2. Marketing: Establish a marketing budget to enable the production of promotional tools for the TOMM process such as:

a. Website, posters, fliers, news articles and conference papers;

b. Promote the process and its outcomes (positive and negative) on an ongoing basis. Outdated information may reflect badly on the success of the process;

c. Do not try to engage everyone at the same time. Identify target markets and work towards engaging the entire community in the long-term;

d. Work collaboratively and collectively with other agencies to ensure a win win approach for all involved;

e. Document the process being undertaken for future reference and application elsewhere;

f. Demonstrate how people can become involved in the process, detail what they can do to help – for example use a TOMM Tool Kit.

3. Human Resources

a. Requires sufficient staff for data analysis / administration plus marketing / representation as well as a committed champion / chai;

b. Burn out of key drivers (project managers and management committee) due to the overwhelming amount of work is a very real issue and can destroy a project. Recognise signs of burn out, provide support and identify the achievements of those involved through marketing initiatives;

c. Ensure some continuity of key individuals to maintain institutional memory that will in turn, ensure the process remains on track;

d. Appoint staff / advisors / management committee with the passion, interest and willingness to invest their time in seeing the project succeed as well as the necessary skills required by the project at any particular time. They will be your greatest sales people.

4. Governance

a. Independence of a board is important to its ability to comment on issues relating to the health of tourism and the region or community (in this case an Island) in general;

b. The TOMM process as well as the outcomes of the TOMM research, has to be trusted;

c. Agencies / partners have to believe in the long-term process and articulate this belief within the public arena;

d. People will always question if the process is working, demonstrate that the process runs through a natural lifecycle and do not panic when stagnation hits, rather use this to evolve the concept;

e. Cultural change amongst agencies, communities and individuals takes time. Do not panic if integration into management does not happen immediately.

5. Funding

a. Think creatively, commercially and collectively regarding funding arrangements to ensure the implementation of a TOMM. Traditional funding sources may not be sufficient to maintain the operational costs;

b. Be prepared. Develop a business plan and funding outline;

c.   Encourage agencies to allocate funding to TOMM as a standard operational cost rather than through annual funding rounds;

d.   Funding alone will not assure the success of a TOMM, funding is only one aspect of the process;

e.   Value-add access to funding and link projects where possible;

f.   Always factor in an administrative element to funding submissions. These projects do not happen without a driver.

6. Monitoring

a.   Maintain a record of successes, lessons, contacts and promotional exposure. All these help when needing to establish a business case;

b.   Create indicators to monitor the implementation process e.g. the number of agencies incorporating TOMM into strategic planning, the number of successful initiatives by agencies that have used TOMM data;

c.   Encourage partners / agencies to use monitoring results for their own promotion. They again act as excellent ambassadors.

Conclusion

Sustainable tourism management models implemented at a community level can succeed over the long-term. Success does not rest in the geographic boundary of the destination, rather the process and people that work towards achieving a shared vision. Some have suggested that the Kangaroo Island project has succeeded more easily due to the fact that it is an island. While this is a factor, the positive result is much more a result of the process chosen and the commitment of the people involved.

The process of implementation has to recognise the intrinsic value of identifying shared understanding, respect for others values and opinions, access to diverse and stable funding sources, rigorous indicators and information collection and dissemination, and above all, the nurturing and support of those passionate individuals that make up the team of committed partners. The Kangaroo Island case provides one example of these elements in practice.

Sources: Centre of Sustainable Tourism; TOMM Management Committee, www.tomm.info

6.15 'Keep Winter Cool': Tourism Sector Greenhouse Gas Mitigation

Skiing, Mountains, Climate Change, Impact Measurement, Private Sector

This case shows how the North American ski industry is using a small number of key indicators as part of its efforts to respond to the global issue of limiting greenhouse gas emissions.

The sustainability of skiing and winter tourism in Australia, Europe and North America has been repeatedly identified as vulnerable to global climate change. North American ski area operators have begun to acknowledge their potential vulnerability to climate change and the need to confront it. In partnership with the Natural Resources Defense Council (a leading environmental organization) the National Ski Area Association in the United States launched the 'Keep Winter  Cool' campaign in February 2003. The objective of the campaign is to combat climate change through public education and greenhouse gas emission reductions within the ski industry, as part of their Environmental Charter (endorsed by 170 ski areas in the US, plus six resorts in Canada). Participating ski resorts communicated a 'Keep Winter Cool' message to skiers and snowboarders on the important topic of climate change through table tents at resort lodges and cafeterias and through their websites. The public outreach component of the campaign discussed the potential impacts of global warming on winter recreation and encouraged guests to do their part in reducing greenhouse gas emissions by including purchasing wind power for their home; carpooling, driving an efficient car or riding shuttles; purchasing energy-efficient appliances for their home; and turning off lights and turning down heat when leaving a room at the resort or at home.

The 'Keep Winter Cool' campaign was also used to showcase the various initiatives ski areas and resorts have taken to reduce greenhouse gas emissions in their operations.

In the continuation, innovative climate change mitigation initiatives, taken by ski resorts, are described. Each of these initiatives uses key indicators related to energy consumption to monitor progress, including: total energy consumption (fuel used, Kilowatt-hours), amount and proportion of energy use from renewable energy sources (e.g. % from bio-diesel, solar or wind sources).

Box 6.28 Sustainable slopes program

Five ski areas (Gore Mountain, Holiday Valley, and Peek 'n Peak in New York and Mount Bachelor and Mount Hood Meadows in Oregon) are teaming up with Green Mountain Energy Company to purchase enough pollution-free wind power to run the resorts' main chair lifts for the day of the 'Keep Winter Cool' campaign day (offsetting more than 10 tons of carbon dioxide emissions).

Two Colorado ski areas have gone a step further. Keystone Resort purchases 16,500 kilowatt-hours of renewable wind power per month, the maximum amount available from the local utility. Vail Mountain purchases 300,000 kilowatt-hours per year of wind energy to power the Wildwood Express Lift, preventing 300 tons of carbon dioxide emissions. Aspen Skiing Company also purchases wind energy and recently announced that guests driving low-pollution hybrid vehicles will park for free at certain lots all season long.

In California, Mammoth Mountain has piloted an alternative energy project to use solar heating for lift shacks. Mammoth is also using renewable bio-diesel fuel, made partly from recycled cooking oil, in its snowcats. Northstar-at-Tahoe is also conducting a bio-diesel test program with five of its on-site transportation buses. If successful, Northstar plans to eventually run its entire transportation fleet on bio-diesel.

In Vermont, Mount Snow Resort has cut energy consumption in half at the Main Base Lodge and Snow Lake Lodge by replacing hundreds of conventional light bulbs with compact fluorescents. Mount Snow has also installed dozens of energy-efficient snowmaking tower guns which reduce the energy needed to pump water and compressed air. Mount Snow also re-uses energy, using heat extracted from snowmaking compressor systems to heat its Main Base Lodge and Clocktower buildings. Additional information on the 'Keep Winter Cool' program can be found at http://www.keepwintercool.org/

Whistler - Blackcomb, who will host the 2010 Winter Olympics are a member of the Sustainable Slopes Program

6.16 Kukljica (Croatia): WTO Indicators Workshop

Indicators Development, Community Participation, Workshop Methods, Islands

The Kukjica case shows how indicators and a participatory process served to bring stakeholders together to define key issues for tourism development on two small Croatian islands. The workshop and case study were key building blocks in the development of the WTO methodology.

The Kukljica, Croatia study was done as a demonstration project to test the WTO indicators approach in the Mediterranean, to apply the procedures to small islands and to address the better integration of destination level indicators into the local and regional planning process. The indicators application was undertaken at the municipality of Kukljica on the linked islands of Ugljan and Pasman, in Croatia, a relatively undeveloped destination which is anticipating tourism growth. A process closely resembling that described in Part two of this book was followed to bring local and expert knowledge together to define issues and indicators and to act as a catalyst for further work towards sustainable tourism.

The indicators listed below were developed using the WTO methodology with field research, targeted interviews of stakeholders and a multiparty workshop to both define key risks and issues and to develop and prioritize indicators. The workshop applied a participatory process, involving key local, national and foreign experts and members of the destination community.

The intent was to initiate a tourism planning process, and as a consequence involved key personnel from all stakeholders. The intent was to use the approach both to foster local dialogue on future tourism and risks to sustainability, and also to train experts from several Mediterranean Nations on the participatory indicators development approach.

The Kukljica workshop was also a specific pilot for the approaches described in this Guidebook. The workshop approach served as catalyst for community participation, and was the first time many of the participants had met on issues related to community planning, tourism and the sustainability of their destination. The sessions confirmed the need to create a stronger local planning process and integrate it with other parts of destination. The following table lists those issues and indicators agreed to be the most important for the implementation. Over 40 indicators were identified with 16 identified as high priority (in issue areas of cultural integrity, economic welfare, stability and seasonality, diversity of tourism product, physical planning and control, and management of resources and the environment) See Box 6.29.

Box 6.29 Issues and indicators for Kukljica Croatia (WTO 2001)

Issue Area	Indicators
A) Cultural Integrity	
Identification and protection of key cultural and historic sites	• Inventory of cultural sites prepared and maintained; • Number of visitors to cultural sites; • State of cultural sites (classification); • Availability of information on sites (%).
Local attitude towards tourists and tourism	• Local attitudes (questionnaire).
B) Employment and Economic Welfare	
Local involvement in tourism industry	• Unemployment statistics; • Local residents employed in tourism; • Ratio of local employees to total;. • Ratio of jobs men/women.
Quality of accommodation	• Complaints; • Repeat visits to same accommodation (number/%); • Price of accommodation (average per night); • Opinion of quality (questionnaire).
C) Stability and Seasonality	
Low numbers of tourists out of peak season	• Number of tourists (by month) over year.
Level of tourism business in community	• Number of bars and restaurants open (by month); • Garbage volume (by month).
Quality of tourism product	• Perception of quality experience by tourists (questionnaire).
D) Diversification of the Tourism Product	
Lack of tourist services	• Number and capacity of tourism-related services.
Issue: Lack of variety of tourist activities and alternatives to sun-and beach tourism	• Inventory of cultural and natural attractions and related alternative tourist activities (classification); • Information provided on alternative activities and related services; • Number of tourists participating in alternative activities.

Issue Area	Indicators
E) Physical Planning and Control	
Income sources for municipalities	• Sources of income for the municipalities (% from each revenue source).
State of planning for the islands	• Planning of destination (existence of plans, area included).
Level of communication/coordination between authorities	• Level of cooperation - number of meetings, number of joint projects.
Need for local involvement in the planning process	• Number of locals in project teams; • Level of awareness among locals of planning initiatives (likely questionnaire based); • % of local population aware of local planning initiatives.
Ease of access to the islands	• Number of ferry trips per day; • Number and type of boats used to provide transport to and from islands; • Price of ferry trips; • Frequency of ferry crossings.
Access to sites	• Volume of tourism; • Complaints to restaurants and accommodation re: access; • Signage (level of signage, level of complaints) • Organized access; • Availability of information on sites (% with information).
F) Management of Resources and the Environment	
Maintaining clean environment and image	• Amount of chemical compounds in seawater (survey); • Presence, proliferation of certain marine species; • Tourist opinions on seawater quality; • Perception of level of cleanliness of beaches; • Garbage levels on shoreline; • Clean image of island (exit questionnaire); • % of sewage treated to secondary or tertiary levels.

This case, along with similar workshop applications at Lake Balaton (Hungary), Villa Gesell (Argentina), Cozumel (Mexico), and Beruwala (Sri Lanka) was a key building block in the development of methods and in the testing of indicators development procedures for WTO, and a precursor to the contents of this Guidebook.

Reference: Workshop on Sustainable Tourism Indicators for the Islands of the Mediterranean Kukljica, Island of Ugljan, Croatia 21-23 March 2001. Final Report (WTO, 2001).

View to mainland from the Castle Ruins on the highest point of Ugljan Island

6.17 Lanzarote Biosphere Strategy (Canary Islands, Spain): Towards Sustainable Development of the Island

Biosphere Reserve, Islands, Participation, Indicators Development, Strategic Planning

This case shows how a broad range of indicators have been employed to support planning for sustainable development of Lanzarote – which is a tourism destination with the status of a Biosphere Reserve.

The island of Lanzarote forms part of the archipelago of the Canary Islands (Spain). The Lanzarote Biosphere Strategy, developed by the Lanzarote Council in 1998, is a practical example of an indicators application linked to the evaluation of an island situation, and the development of proposals for specific site development based on sustainability criteria.

Through the indicators development process, the Lanzarote Biosphere Strategy constitutes a framework for the sustainable development of the island, based on the recognition of its status as a Biosphere Reserve (designated by UNESCO, in 1993). Lanzarote is a special case, as it is both a densely inhabited island and a Biosphere Reserve. The Lanzarote Biosphere Reserve was in some ways an experiment, dependent to a large extent on the involvement of large parts of the community. The Lanzarote Biosphere Strategy has also involved considerable public commitment by institutions towards the sustainable development of the island, including proposals which will change the role of the community in the development process. The analysis of the issues and the development of plans for future development are supported by a framework of indicators which respond to the key issues and interests of the Lanzarote community.

Lanzarote can be considered as a single destination 846 km², with a population of 77,400 inhabitants and which attracted 1,662,427 tourists in 1998 (Consejería de Turismo y Transportes, Canarias 1998). It has a varied resource base and has been rapidly changing. Twenty years ago, the rapid growth of tourism began to change the traditional island economy which had been based on the fishing and agricultural sectors. Tourism on the island has evolved rapidly from its modest initial development to the point where it is having a significant impact on all aspects of the island economy and environment.

Lanzarote is a volcanic island located in the Atlantic Ocean off Africa in the eastern group of the Canary Islands. It is dry, influenced by the climate of the Sahara Desert. The small indigenous population with its distinctive social characteristics is now strongly influenced by in-migration from other parts of Spain and the world. The volcanic origin, the geographical situation and the history of the island make Lanzarote a destination of extraordinary ecological interest, with significant biodiversity and a unique and attractive landscape. The island has 13 protected areas, one of them the Timanfaya National Park. The biodiversity of the Island is accentuated by its high level of endemism (Its vascular flora constitutes 560 endemic species of the 2,200 found in the Canaries).

The island system contains many extremely fragile ecosystems and landscapes which are under increasing human pressure. The economy is dependent on the health of tourism. Many of the enterprises are controlled from outside the island community. As well, little of the goods consumed are produced on the island – Lanzarote is nearly totally dependent on imports for the basics of life - food, building materials, and energy. Cultural and social tensions have also emerged, many related to the impact of increased numbers of tourists.

The Lanzarote Biosphere Strategy (Cabildo de Lanzarote 1998) is designed to respond to the commitments made in 1993 when the island was incorporated into the World Network of Biosphere Reserves of UNESCO, based on the Strategy of Seville that was approved by UNESCO in the International Conference of Experts on Biosphere Reserves held in Seville. These commitments were:

1. To use the Biosphere Reserves for conservation of cultural and natural diversity;
2. To use the Biosphere Reserves as models of territorial management and sustainable development;
3. To use the Biosphere Reserves for research, monitoring, education and training;
4. Implementation of the Biosphere Reserves concept.

The main goal of the Lanzarote Strategy is to foster a deeper and cross-cultural debate on the problems and opportunities of the Island as a whole, and on the proposals which may help it develop sustainably in coming decades; development which harmonizes social values, satisfaction of economic needs, and the preservation of Lanzarote's natural and landscape heritage.

The Lanzarote Biosphere Strategy - Project Structure

The Lanzarote biosphere project was developed through two key documents, the "Document for the Debate" and subsequently the document "The Island System". The first document was based on in-depth interviews of more than 100 representative island residents plus research by a group of experts. The state of the island was analyzed: identifying potential risk, probable results if current trends were allowed to continue, and an alternative scenario (The Lanzarote Biosphere Strategy), which could occur as a result of a number of proposed programs focused on the building on opportunities and actions to address many of the more significant risks. The project also worked to define key factors and indicators and to establish an island Observatory focussed on the sustainability of the Biosphere Reserve. When the "Document for the Debate" was produced, work continued on provision of information and consultation to the Lanzarote community.

The signal document "The Island System" (El Sistema Insular) was published with the following structure:

1. Introduction.
2. Public opinion (collected through interviews) regarding the situation and island perspectives, and the process to create the Strategy;
3. Presentation of an integrated vision of Lanzarote Island;
4. Synthesis of the analyses of the present situation, identifying key factors and values;
5. Main characteristics and appraisal of the current risk scenario;
6. Main characteristics and appraisal of the Lanzarote Biosphere strategy scenario. This section includes the synthesis of the proposals of the remaining reports from the "Document for the Debate", as well as the comparison of both future scenarios;
7. The need to continue defining the Strategy through social and institutional participation.

Issues and Indicators Represented in the Lanzarote Island System

To evaluate the state and trends on the Island, as well as to clarify opportunities and risks, the following factors were assessed:

1. Economy and tourism;
2. The island ecosystem, the terrestrial and marine ecology;
3. The key environmental sectors;
4. The floating population, social contact and participation;
5. The urban development system and Arrecife (capital city of Lanzarote);
6. The cultural identity and heritage.

The establishment of the Island Observatory for Sustainability was based on each of these issues. For each issue, various indicators were selected. These indicators were designed to provide measures of change over time and for different scenarios. Subsequently, the values obtained in 1997 were compared with the values projected for the Lanzarote Biosphere Strategy, for a ten-year period, up to

2007 based on a range of assumptions contained in the strategy. The list of indicators with their values follows.

Box 6.30 Current and projected indicator values under Lanzarote's strategy scenario

		Indicator	Value in 1997	Target value 2007 with the strategy
Economy and Tourism	**Tourism**			
	Accommodation	Number of tourism beds	53,285	< 61,300
	Occupancy	Annual average (%)	83	83
	Average visits	Annual average of daily n° of tourists	44,018	< 50,000
	Economic Impact	Average spending / day per tourist (without accommodation and transport) (euros/day/tourist) (adapted from the original pesetas/day/tourist)	32.75	46.45
	Agriculture and fishing			
	Agriculture	Cultivated surface (ha)	3,500	4,000
	Fishing, economic incomes	% related to average incomes of the Canary Island Autonomous Region service sector	80	100
	Diversification			
	Activities not related to tourism	% of approvals of economic activities that are not related to tourism	24.6	30
	Building human resources capacity			
	Specialization	% of technical high school students (who are not in the administration department)	30	50
	Local incomes			
	Incomes that are not related to building	Number of approvals of economic activities per capita (%)	0.13	0.17
The island ecosystems	**Global Atmosphere**			
	Energy + insular and access transport	Emissions of CO_2 (Ton/year)	1,863,055	2,233,499- 1,856,558
	Water System			
	Storage	Number of days per month, capable to be served from natural sources	26.1	30
	Soil and geologic resources			
	Arid soils	Used resources / authorized resources (%)	1.5	2
	Fertile soils	Lost surface / total surface(%)	0.2	0.2
	Natural sites and places			
	Level of protection	Protected land surface (%)	41.3	41.3
	Legislation of protection	Protected land surface with a management plan (%)	14	100

	Public use	Visitor/day in Montañas del Fuego Natural Monument (Timanfaya National Park)	2,600	< 2,500
	Red list of species	Number of threatened-vulnerable species	57	0
	Sea environment			
	Protected sea surface	Sea surface with management plan (%)	0	100
	Seashore depletion	Seashore with critical depletion (%)	49.3	0
	Beach surface / user	m^2/person	18	> 15
	Landscape			
	Natural landscape	Altered cones without restoration	56	0
	Agricultural landscape	Agricultural landscape depletion nearby urban areas (ha)	9,320	0
	Seashore landscape	Built shoreline (%)	20	20
Key environ-mental sector	**Water**			
	Desalinated water	Volume, m^3/year	10,269,800	10,255,843/ 7,123,531
	Leakage in the net	%	25.8	18/14
	Urban water recycling	%	0	15/30
	Energy (without transport)			
	Final consumption	Tons / equivalent petroleum (TEP)	54,808	79,101
	Renewable sources	%	2.6	11.6 - 20.4
	Emission of CO_2	Total Tons / year	440,767	442,384/ 336,505 target
	Transport			
	Island road use	Millions of vehicles / km	685	767-567
	Insular modal distribution	Collective Transport use %	26	37-46
	Emission of CO_2 (Island)	Annual Tons (Ton/year)	192,001	192,718/ 152,089 target
	Emission of CO_2 (access)	Annual Tons (Ton/year)	1,230,287	1,598,397/ 1,367,964 target
	Wastes			
	Production	Weight (Ton) Rate kg/inhabitant/day	55,472 1.21	71,347 1.27
	Selective collection	% solid urban wastes	3.68	89.3
	Reutilization of waste	% solid urban wastes	2.91	73
	Waste withdrawals	Weight (Ton)	53,567	19,396

Population	**Population equilibrium**			
	Growth of in-migrants	New inhabitants / year	4,500	< 2,500
	Distribution of annual growth between number of tourists and residents	Annual rate of tourists / residents (%)	60	25 - 30
	Annual rate of immigrants/residents	Annual rate of immigrants / residents (%)	51	< 50
	Integration			
	Education levels	Enrolment 1 - 10	5.1	6.5
	Rate of youth unemployment	Unemployed youth / total youth (%)	23	< 17
	Working conditions	Youth with temporary jobs / employed youth (%)	74	< 55
	Marginality			
	Drug activities	Drug users, convictions, overdoses / population (%)	1.92	< 1.5
	Objective insecurity	Legal complaints / residents (%)	7.8	< 7.5
	Poverty rate	Population with minimal incomes	13.2	< 13
	Neighbouring			
	Degree of confidence in political representatives	Average appraisal on 1 – 10 scale	4.9	> 5
	Rate of membership in young population	Associated youths / total youth(%)	25	> 33
	Degree of electoral participation of youth	Voting youth (%)	41	> 50
Island Urban System	**Island system**			
	Population density	Real population / island surface area (inhabitants./km²)	143	172
	Land occupancy	Settlement area/ island surface (%)	5	6
	Population equilibrium	Tourist beds / legal population (%)	68	64
	Rural settlements			
	Population density	Legal population / settlements area (inhabitants/ha)	40	45
	Accessibility	Quality of public transport (LMH, low - medium - high)	M - L	H
	Basic infrastructure	Existing provision / required provision according to the Insular Plan of Land Organization - PIOT (%)	80	100
	Council centres			
	Centre Provision	Existent provision / required provision according to the Insular Plan of Land Organization - PIOT (%)	60	100
	Population density	Real population / centre's surface (inhabitants./ha)	75	80
	Ecologic level	Reused wastes / Urban wastes (%)	3	75

Tourist Centres			
Accommodation quality	Quality and building maintenance (LMH)	H	H
Complementary leisure activities	Diversity of activities (LMH)	L	M - H
Ecologic level	Reused wastes / Urban wastes (%)	3	75
Tourist's opinion	Answers in social polls (LMH)	H	H
Arrecife and surroundings			
Coordinated planning	Zone incorporated to Insular Plan of Land Organization (yes/no)	NO	YES
Accessibility	Quality of public transport (LMH)	L	H
Basic infrastructure	Existent provision / required provision according to the Insular Plan of Land Organization (%)	80	100
Arrecife City			
Arrecife as a capital	Quality in Arrecife services as a capital city (LMH)	L	M - L
Organization	Quality of its urban organization (LMH)	40	80
Basic infrastructure	Existent provision / required provision according to the Insular Plan of Land Organization(%)	65	100
Ecologic level	Reused wastes / Urban wastes (%)	3	75
Marina and historic city			
Planning	Specific zone plan (yes/no)	NO	YES
Public spaces	Quality of public places (LMH)	M - L	H
Pedestrian walking traffic plan	Traffic Plan for pedestrians updated (yes/no)	NO	YES
Culture and heritage Culture	• Interpretation centres of living culture	L	Improved
	• Cultural infrastructure appropriately served	L	Improved
	• Cultural activities	M	Improved
Patrimony	• Properties and objects in inventory	L	Improved
	• Designated properties and objects of cultural interest	M-L	Improved
	• Properties and objects in use	M	Improved

The results of The Lanzarote Biosphere Strategy have been very positive, contributing to a management system supported by indicators of sustainable development of tourism. Though the Strategy is only partially implemented, it has continued to pursue the objectives. For example, it resulted in a moratorium for the construction of new tourist beds in the Island, and the development of a Life Program under the European Union, assisting in the legal basis for environmental protection, technical assistance and project development.

(For details see http://europa.eu.int/comm/environment/life/home.htm)

The Island Observatory for Sustainability of the Biosphere Reserve monitors the indicators and develops new plans in support of sustainability of the Island. Two plans were proposed, one for the year 2001, and a second one for the 2002-2003 period. In Plan 2002-2003, one of the goals was to follow up the results of the Biosphere Strategy proposed in 1997. In February 2003, the observatory selected 254 indicators to work on, based on the first set of indicators (1997) and adding others from different documents and proposals according to the needs of the Island. While they have established the system and the framework to manage the island with indicators, there have been delays in fully implementing the program. Information on the indicators can be found at the web-sites:

Indicators

http://www.cabildodelanzarote.com/areas/presidencia/biosfera/observatorio/seleccionindicadores.pdf

Plans of the Observatory

http://www.cabildodelanzarote.com/areas/presidencia/biosfera/observatorio/intplan2001.htm

http://www.cabildodelanzarote.com/areas/presidencia/biosfera/observatorio/intplan200203.htm

Tourist moratorium

http://www.cabildodelanzarote.com/areas/presidencia/biosfera/moratoria/moratoria.htm

Lanzarote Life Program

http://www.cabildodelanzarote.com/life/

For further information see:

www.cabildodelanzarote.com/areas/presidencia/biosfera/biosfera/biosfera.htm

Cabildo de Lanzarote. Lanzarote en la Biosfera, Una estrategia hacia el desarrollo sostenible de la isla. Islas Canarias, 1998.

Consejería de Turismo y Transportes, Gobierno de Canarias. Oferta y Demanda Turística Canaria 1993 - 1998. Las Palmas de Gran Canaria, Islas Canarias, 1999.

6.18 Samoa Sustainable Tourism Indicator Project (SSTIP)

Strategy Development, TOMM, Community Participation, Prioritization, Implementation

This case shows how the process of developing indicators can assist a destination to move sustainable tourism from principles to practice, and how the results of monitoring can be used to assist destination planning and development. It also demonstrates how, despite the best effort during the development phase, the real challenge of monitoring comes in maintaining momentum in the long term.

The SSTIP was a collaborative initiative between an applied researcher doing doctoral work on the process of indicator development, and the Samoa Visitors Bureau (now the Samoa Tourism Authority, STA), who were interested in establishing a sustainable tourism indicator framework and monitoring process.

The methodology was designed around a combination of the TOMM Kangaroo Island project (see Kangaroo Island Case p. 391) and adaptive management, an approach to natural resource policy that involves managing uncertainty by experimenting, expecting mistakes and learning from them. Three basic principles of sustainable tourism were applied: the need to be i) comprehensive, looking at environmental, economic, social, cultural as well as tourism sustainable development concerns and priorities; ii) participatory, involving a wide cross-section of stakeholders; and iii) adaptive, seeing indicator development not as an end but as a tool that would need to be changed to suit the dynamic nature of destination development.

The first phase of the project involved forming an interdisciplinary group of stakeholders known as the Project Advisory Committee (PAC) to guide the indicator development process. The twelve members of the PAC included those with environmental knowledge and experience, economists, representatives of the private sector and community, government and local university. The role of the PAC was to meet on a regular basis to monitor the progress of the project and provide advice in their area of expertise. The project was facilitated by the researcher and managed by the STA.

With the PAC in place, the primary focus was on identifying key issues for sustainable tourism in the country using three main methods: i) secondary sources, ii) key informant interviews and iii) village surveys. The emphasis of each investigation was on identifying key environmental, economic, cultural and social concerns affecting tourism and its role in the community. Results from the surveys were sorted and analysed and used to develop a set of objectives for sustainable tourism, which became the foundation and key point of reference for the project. PAC members then brainstormed in small groups to develop indicators to monitor the sustainable tourism objectives. All indicator ideas were screened for technical feasibility by PAC and piloted on key stakeholder groups for user friendliness and public resonance. The initial brainstorming identified 270 possible indicators and 57 were found to be sufficiently robust to put forward for screening. After the technical and user-friendly screening process just 20 indicators remained and were adopted by the PAC for the first round of monitoring.

Identifying the indicators was only half the battle. Monitoring was found to also require a detailed set of protocols such as definitions of all the terms used, methodology for collection of information, sources of comparative data, lists of key contact people and agencies and methods for interpreting indicator results. Based on the TOMM project, 'acceptable ranges' were specified for each indicator, based on local knowledge and baseline results from secondary sources.

Box 6.31 Samoa sustainable tourism indicators and performance measures

Environmental Sustainable Tourism Indicators	Result	Acceptable Range	Performance
Tourism village participation in land conservation	26%	50-75%	POOR
Tourist participation in nature tourism	8%	20-40%	POOR
Tourism village participation in marine protection	42%	50-75%	POOR
Tourist participation in marine tourism	23%	20-40%	ACCEPTABLE
Hotels using secondary or tertiary sewage treatment	8%	30-50%	POOR
Hotels composting their biodegradable waste	76%	60-80%	ACCEPTABLE
Tourism sites passing SWA water quality tests	50%	70-90%	POOR
Water usage per guest night in hotels (in litres)	928*	500-1000	ACCEPTABLE
Economic Sustainable Tourism Indicators			
Proportion of hotel jobs in rural areas	48%	40-60%	ACCEPTABLE
Proportion of new businesses focused on tourism	4%	10-20%	POOR
Contribution of direct tourism businesses to GDP	4%*	10-20%	POOR
Social and Cultural Sustainable Tourism Indicators			
Villages included in tourism awareness programmes	28%	25-50%	ACCEPTABLE
Hotel staff going on training courses	27%	25-50%	ACCEPTABLE
Tourism operators informing tourists about village protocol	72%	50-70%	GOOD
Proportion of traditional events in Tourism Festivals	50%	50-70%	ACCEPTABLE
Proportion of handicraft stalls in the markets	21%	20-40%	ACCEPTABLE
Sustainable Tourism Indicators			
Evaluation of quality of key tourist attraction sites	35%	60-80%	POOR
New hotels undertaking environmental assessment	33%	90-100%	POOR
Tourist landscapes under threat from development	20%	0-5%	POOR
Tourism operators using sustainable tourism practices	48%	60-80%	POOR

Box 6.31 shows the 20 selected indicators, the results for 2000, the acceptable ranges and resultant performance rating. The handbook includes more detailed information on each of the indicators as shown in the table below.

Box 6.32 Sample indicator method sheet for Samoa SSTIP project

METHOD SHEET	1a
INDICATOR NAME	**Percentage of villages important for tourism participating in land and forest conservation programmes**
DEFINITIONS	· Villages important for tourism: Villages with tourist accommodation facilities, sign-posted tourist attractions or key transport facilities;
	· Land and forest conservation programmes: Conservation programmes run by DLSE, MAFF and those run by the communities themselves.
RELEVANCE	As the natural environment is one of the main attractions of a visit to Samoa, the well-being of land and particularly forest resources is a primary concern for the sustainability of tourism.
ASSUMPTIONS	Participation in conservation programmes is an indication of the sustainable management of land and forest resources.
DESIRED TREND	To increase the number of villages, especially those important for tourism, participating in land and forest conservation programmes.
DATA REQUIREMENTS	1. List of all villages important for tourism in the year of survey;
	2. List of villages participating in the different conservation programmes in the year of survey;
	3. List of all villages that are both important for tourism and participating in the different conservation programmes.
DATA SOURCES	For list of villages important for tourism. Contact: Manager of Planning and Development, SVB.
	For list of villages participating in conservation programmes. Contact: Senior Biodiversity Officer, Department of Lands, Surveys and the Environment (DLSE) and Senior Watershed Management Officer, Ministry of Agriculture, Forests and Fisheries (MAFF).
	Data on traditional village protection systems is available from DLSE.
DATA COLLECTION TECHNIQUES	1. Draft letter to Directors of DLSE, MAFF and other agencies involved to request information concerning conservation programmes;
	2. Print out Indicator Database sheet 1a and take it to agencies involved for updating;
	3. Input results into the Indicator Database and analyse in the context of data from previous years noting changes in population or sample size.
REFERENCES	Galuvao, E. C. and Sagapolutele, F. (1998) Conservation Technical Group Report. Department of Lands, Survey and the Environment, Apia.

The results from the first year of monitoring showed 11 of the indicators scored outside their acceptable range and a sustainable tourism action plan was then drawn up to target these areas for priority action. For example, as a result of the first indicator, tourism village participation in conservation, scoring poorly, village tourism awareness programmes have now been redesigned and are run jointly with the tourism and conservation departments showing the important links between these areas. Other projects carried out as a result of the 2000 indicator results include the improvement of economic monitoring, providing sustainable tourism training for tourism operators and guides, fast-tracking EIA legislation for hotels and establishing a scheme to protect key tourist sites from adverse development.

These projects were subsequently integrated in the Samoa Tourism Development Plan 2002-2006 and the first two have already been implemented. The implementation of action projects followed by the review and improvements to the monitoring system marks the end of the indicator development cycle (see diagram Box 6.33).

Box 6.33 Samoa sustainable tourism indicator project cycle

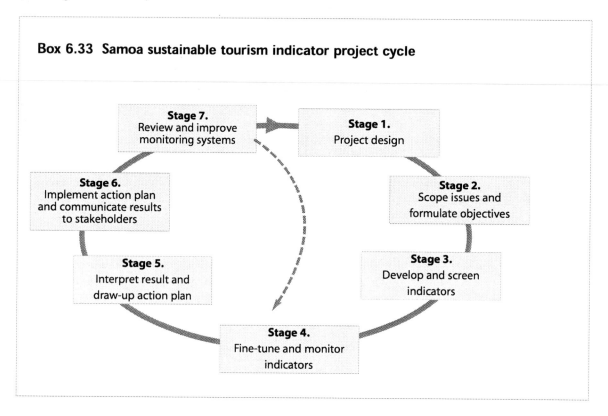

The strengths of the SSTIP are in the cyclical and participatory approach to monitoring it adopts and the clear links between monitoring and action. The project developed the linkages between objectives, indicators, monitoring, action and review, and did so in a manner that was stakeholder rather than authority driven. It also succeeded in implementing a broad sustainable development approach to tourism that would not have been possible without the cross section of expertise provided by the PAC. The indicator results were instrumental in steering the preparation of the 2002-2006 Samoa Tourism Development Plan and supporting proposals for donor funding for development projects.

But despite all the effort put into the project, its future as of 2004 is uncertain. The development of the new tourism plan diverted resources, delayed re-monitoring, momentum was lost and many of the original members of the team subsequently moved on to other positions. Despite efforts to re-invigorate the programme following the publication of the Indicator Handbook (Twining-Ward 2003), there has been loss of ownership and commitment, placing the future of the project in doubt. The difficulties faced by SSTIP are typical of the challenges of any long-term development project: political vision is short-term, voluntary stakeholder committees eventually tire, project champions and ambassadors move on and ownership is lost. It highlights the importance of understanding that although the excitement of establishing a monitoring project is in the development phase; the real challenge is maintaining monitoring momentum in the long-term year after year.

Traditional Beach Huts. Lalomanu Beach, Samoa

6.19 Sonke Cape Route: Information to Support Township SMEs and Community-based Tourism in Cape Town, South Africa

Tour Route, Community Tourism, Social Tourism, Urban Tourism, Community Participation

This case shows how indicators can play a part in creating a tourism route in an urban context with many small businesses, measuring progress and providing information to participants.

"Sonke" means "all together", responsible, for all people able and disabled. The Sonke Cape Route is built around a business forum of micro enterprises involved in the empowerment of communities through tourism linked by a tourism route. The Sonke "tourism cluster" was generated to link tourism, job creation, and conservation in a manner that would sustain each other and promote tourism development in the underprivileged communities near Cape Town, South Africa. This is being achieved through a fully-inclusive and community-participative workshop method which identifies shared goals and potentials for both the traveler and the local inhabitants to experience life in the Cape Town peninsula, Townships, and Western Cape. Guidance is provided by a pilot regional tourism liaison committee for the Department of Economic Affairs Agriculture and Tourism Western Cape. Ongoing information communication technology linking Geographical Information Systems with the Internet is provided through Open Africa (www.africandream.org). The Open Africa network of websites is especially valuable for shared information about Township people who are crafts men and women renowned for their handmade items – pottery, beadwork, patchwork, quilting, decoupage on wood, bathroom accessories, bags, dolls, clothing – as well as bed and breakfast accommodations, restaurants, and other micro enterprises. Sonke members are registered guides and tour operators and members of Cape Town Tourism. Shared goals have been defined, and information (including indicators) developed to support the network and its system of information exchange.

Cape Town, the third most visited city in Africa after Johannesburg and Cairo, is fast becoming a premier tourist destination. According to Cape Metropolitan Tourism, in 2002 Cape Town International Airport received over 5 million passengers, with this number expected to double by 2007. The natural beauty of Table Mountain, the ocean, and wine lands blend modern skyscrapers with nearby post-apartheid Townships of Cape Flats, now working collaboratively towards recognition as viable tourist destinations. The indigenous tour operators of the Sonke Cape Route recognize that they must bolster their entrepreneurial capacities to engage tourists in visiting the diverse cultural heritage and unique environmental sites embodied in Township tourism products and services.

This linked route from Cape Town through the various Townships takes tourists to see a number of individual local attractions including:

The WE-SHOP Begun in 1993, is The We Shall Overcome Prejudice Shop, dedicated to creating jobs and workspace for the disabled, assisting them to move upwards from unskilled to mainstream employment, and providing community education and training in areas ranging from laundry services, restaurant, preschool, carwash, pottery shop, woodworking, fax and Internet/computers, sewing, and Braille book printing to a music school, which today, with 60 students, is one of the best in the region. Dependent on donor funding.

The Baboon Man, also, is a local artist, entrepreneur, and employer.

The Baboon Man The roadside stand of The Baboon Man features cement sculptures. A hulking white-stone vulture in a large stick nest guards his small entrance gate.

The Golden Man The Golden Man has his shop near his home in Khayalitsha Township on the doorstep to the African wine route. One night he had a dream that he would make flowers. In search of materials, the colorful soda cans he saw in the township dump encouraged him to try his hand at making flowers out of these waste products. The Golden Man's cottage industry, now a tourist stop, employs nine people and provides a place for recycling locally of aluminum cans.

Township Restaurants Langa, the oldest black Township in Cape Town, is home to a number of home-style restaurants featuring native South African cuisines including Eziko, Lelapa, Ayabanjeka Xhosa, and MaNeo Restaurants and the Goodfood Foundation (Good Food Gardens and Take-Aways). There are also Mesande Restaurant in Crossroad's Community and B & E Homestyle Cooking in Mitchell's Plain. Wabo's Pool and Tavern.

Bed & Breakfasts Two are located on the route: Swanweni B &B in Langa and Malebo's B & B in Khayelitsha.

Arts, Crafts, Music, and Theatre Arts Numerous Township arts and crafts industries are emerging, such as the Khayelitsha Craft Market, Sibongile Pottery Projects in Guguletu, Roslyn Arts and Crafts, Kenny Bergsma Stone framed Home Décor, Jade Upholstery Works (supplies upholstered furniture for local hotels, B&Bs, restaurants and international clients), Philani Nutrition Centres. The Masakhane Marimba Band plays at local events.

Other linked attractions on the route include the Tsoga Environmental Resource Centre, the Rocklands Dagbreek Dune Community Project with work by the local community to replace handrails, erect benches, create walkways, restore native plants, provide toilets and lighting, and a play ground for children. The Wolfgat Nature Reserve and Community Asset conserves the threatened Strandveld vegetation, the unique Falls Bay Coastal ecosystems, the only mainland, breeding colony of the kelp gull in southern Africa, a host of endangered animals, and a rich marine life on its rocky shores. Its prime benefit is its environmental education potential for Township teachers and school children, the Lwandle Migrant Labour Museum commemorating the tribulations and triumphs of the migrant workers' severe life in southern Africa and the Saartjie Baartman Shelter- a center for women and children who have experience domestic and sexual violence in their lives. To afford the women opportunities to earn an income, a restaurant and craft outlet are housed on the premises. An outcome indicator of cultural sustainability is the November 27, 2003, launch of the Community Women Action of Eersterivier's tourism development project.

Sonke Cape Route Tourism The Sonke forum envisions an integrated framework of tourism for the province in which a level of excellence can be achieved for the establishment and promotion of smaller tourism routes and/or areas. Many tour companies now belong to Sonke Cape Route business forum (see www.sonke.org for a complete list). Initial steps are an audit by the Department of Economic Development & Tourism, Western Cape, of current assets and potential indicators for tourism products and their environments. The following proposed indicators are assembled from interviews and a variety of official sources including community-based indicators proposed in minutes of the January 4, 2003, Sonke forum meeting . Reporting, validation, and reliability of these indicators will be an important part of the sustainability of community-based tourism development for Sonke Cape Route Township tourism.

Initial focus is on these indicators with a particular emphasis on generation of information for placement in an ICT Internet-based tourism cluster. This will help the Sonke business forum to market an authentic, memorable, and sustainable experience for tourists while at the same time creating tour operator capacity reflecting an understanding and delivery of what the customer wants. Starting in February 2004, the Department of Economic Development and Tourism, Western Cape, has made funds available to support tourism businesses with programs and finance. Top business plans with the greatest potential for success will be supported with business expertise and finance.

While still in its initial phase, integration of indicators for Sonke Cape Route tourism products and services, and the development of good information in these areas, are seen as critical to the establishment and sustainability of community-based tourism on the route. The Sonke business forum could learn valuable ideas and information on environmental sustainability through links with networks and projects with similar forums across the country and world.

Box 6.34 Sonke tourism indicators list

Priority areas	Indicators (used or/proposed)
1. Information/communication technologies (GIS, Internet) Impact on small, medium, and micro enterprises and how to incorporate these into the tourism industry	• Impact of websites on companies (number of . hits, number of tourists who received info via web, number of on-line sales and reservations).
2. Perception of traveler safety and security	• Number of crimes against tourists.
3. Signage	• Number of (new) signs erected posting the route.
4. Web pages	• Number of SMEs in tourism cluster in Sonke Cape Route website.
	• Number of SMEs in Sonke Cape Route database (base contains basic information, training programs, incentives, marketing platforms, mentorship, information on routes to competitiveness).
5. Tourism economic impact	• Number of passengers (taxi, bus) to Cape Town International Airport.
	• Tours booked through Sonke Cape Route.
	• Overnight stays in Township B&Bs.
	• Number of meals in Township restaurants.
	• Money spent in Township arts, crafts, and other shops.
6. Understand entrepreneurship/how to set up a business/business management	• Successful creation of climate conducive to change (survey of members).
	• Number of professional business plans (by members).
7. Understand financial planning, trade, and investment	• Number of professional loan proposals submitted.
	• Number of funding and support organizations engaged.
	• Number of members with defined infrastructure, investment, and marketing frameworks.
8. Understand legal and regulatory frameworks	• Number of tour operators operating legally and within relevant regulations.

Priority areas	Indicators (used or/proposed)
9. Develop expertise in product conceptualization	° Amount of marketing and industry research provided;
	° Number of links for product to market.
10. The Cape Tourism Marketing Showcase	° Number of Sonke Cape Tour micro enterprises attending;
	° Access to financial planning/funding.
11. The Black Tourism Business Association	° Number of networking and market access opportunities at the development level for black-owned tourism businesses.
12. Mentorship program	° Improvements in communication, confidence, and clinching deals (survey based).

The author of this case study, Ginger Smith, is indebted to Dale Isaacs, Alistair Cyster, Daniel Dunn, Yumnaa Firfirey, Simoneh De Bruin, Mpathi Gocini, Sheny Medani, Richard George, Beaulah Pontac, Jurgens Schoeman, Justin & Tamma Basson, and many others associated with the Sonke Cape Route Tourism forum for sharing their knowledge and hospitality.

Further information: www.sonke.org

http://www.southafrica.net/heritage/heritage_routes/sonke_main.cfm

•

6.20 Super, Natural British Columbia: Assessing Branding Success

Image, Branding, Performance Measurement, Monitoring, Brand Protection

This case documents the use of indicators for management of a tourism brand as a central means to protect and promote the image of a destination.

British Columbia (BC) is Canada's most westerly province, located in an area of majestic mountains, coastal fjords,

expansive forests and diverse wildlife. Capitalizing on the attractiveness of these natural assets, BC's tourism industry has expanded to a point where it is one of the most valuable contributors to the province's economy. In 2002 it generated about $5.0 Billion Cdn. or 4.2% of the province's total Gross Domestic Product.

Through strategic and systematic marketing programs, the province's leading tourism destination marketing organizations and their industry partners have effectively positioned BC as a preferred destination for traveler's interested in experiencing high quality natural settings. Central to their strategic marketing activities has been a three decade commitment to the continued development, promotion and management of a "Super, Natural British Columbia" brand. Indeed the top marketing priority is to build consumer and trade awareness as well as purchase interest in "Super, Natural British Columbia and its regional sub-brands through highly targeted, integrated communications which have a strong "call to action". This strategy is supported by concentrating marketing investment in high priority markets and market-driven product segments and by building direct and lasting relationships with customers. This commitment has helped the province gain an increasing portion of Canada's domestic and international travel markets. For instance, BC's share of overnight customs entries by US visitors rose from about 19% in 1989 to 25% in 2003.

Tourism British Columbia (TBC), the province's destination marketing organization, has been the government-designated custodian of the "Super, Natural British Columbia" brand for almost a decade. It is responsible for appropriately incorporating the brand into TBC's domestic and international marketing initiatives.

Protection of Image indicators described in the Issues section of this publication (p. 236) are used to describe how TBC addresses brand development, refinement, effectiveness assessment, and protection aspects of its brand management mandate

Overall Brand Evaluation

Differing levels of emphasis have been placed on managing various aspects of the "Super, Natural British Columbia" brand for almost 25 years. This "bend but not break" approach to managing the brand's use has helped ensure that "Super, Natural British Columbia" remains capable of uniting the province's tourism industry and the attracting travelers from its targeted markets.

Howe Sound B.C. Mountains and sea are central to the image and brand

Box 6.35 Performance of the "Super, Natural British Columbia" brand

1. Brand Development

Finance: What level of funding does the organization allocate to brand development?	Assessment: Over the past 25 years, almost half a billion dollars in public and private sector dollars have been allocated to managing the "Super, Natural British Columbia" brand. In 2002/03, TBC's marketing and sales budget was about $13m. Approximately, $8m was allocated to promotion and advertising activities. In one form or another (e.g. visual imagery, advertising etc.), the core values of the "Super, Natural British Columbia" brand are incorporated into all of TBC's marketing activities.
Target Market: What is the degree of match between the preferred values of the destination's targeted markets and the brand's values and identity?	Assessment: Research suggests that a strong match exists between the brand's attributes and the preferences of key target markets. Data is gathered annually regarding tourist travel markets. Approximately 85% of BC's visitors take part in leisure and other outdoor experiences "surrounded by nature". Brand positioning research conducted with travellers in four of key target markets in 2002 indicated that about 25% of travellers viewed mountains, oceans/coast and scenery as the key BC attractions. These features are highlighted in the "Super, Natural British Columbia's" brand identity. The brand's natural attributes are also appealing as a "backdrop" to west coast American visitors participating in more urban focused short haul "getaway escapes" in British Columbia. Visiting parks, viewing bird and other wildlife, hiking/backpacking and bicycling are all popular activities pursued by BC's visitors interested in the "Super, Natural British Columbia" brand.
Brand Vision: To what extent do the brand's values match with those of other potentially supportive regional and national tourism organizations? How much is spent annually on such initiatives?	Assessment: Super, Natural British Columbia is promoted by TBC as an umbrella brand for other sub-regional organizational destination branding initiatives. Through its 8-year-old Tourism Partners Program, TBC helps six tourism sub-regions develop their own branding and marketing strategies. It provides both technical and financial support for their regional marketing and branding activities. Technical support is provided via TBC facilitated workshops and meetings where regional tourism associations are encouraged to develop unique but complementary branding, positioning and marketing programs. Approximately $800,000 in administrative costs is spent annually on such technical support. The Tourism Partners program also provides approximately $2.7 million annually in marketing funds to regional tourism organizations that comply with the TBC's marketing and branding requirements. These funds are leveraged by the province's regional destination management organizations and their industry partners to support more than $6million dollars in marketing that aligns with the brand's core values and provides unique positioning for each region. In addition, the values and attributes associated with the Super, Natural British Columbia brand are reinforced at the local level in Vancouver's "Spectacular by Nature" marketing program.

Development Strategies: To what extent does the brand's communication strategy match with those of other regional and national tourism organizations? How much is spent annually on such initiatives?

Assessment: Through TBC's Tourism Partners program, formal and systematic annual reviews are held to ensure that regional destination marketing organizations use the "Super, Natural British Columbia" brand for marketing purposes in appropriate ways. Managers in the Tourism Partners program perceive a strong alignment to exist in the brand attributes and values communicated. Intended and strategic alignment of "Super, Natural British Columbia" brand values with the Canadian Tourism Commission's international marketing initiatives occurs in targeted foreign markets. For instance, TBC's "BC Escapes" program utilizes Canadian Tourism Commission marketing messages to position the BC brand in key west coast United States markets.

What percentage of provincial stakeholders communicate messages similar to those inherent in the Super, Natural British Columbia brand? What percentage/number of destination stakeholders are using the wordmark, imagery or logo?

Assessment: Currently, TBC does not regularly monitor the proportion of provincial tourism stakeholders that use the brand. However, all six of the province's regional tourism associations use and comply with the intent and standards of the "Super, Natural British Columbia" brand. Through annual meetings with each tourism region's key stakeholders, as well as funding incentive's for complying with Tourism BC's branding requirements, growing levels of brand acceptance and use is occurring. In addition, all accommodation stakeholders participating in Tourism BC's approved accommodation guide program are reviewed annually for compliance with the brand's standards.

2. Brand Refinement / Improvement

Does the organization conduct research to detect changes in the marketplace that may influence overall receptiveness of the brand (e.g. travel spending, target market preferences)? How often is this research conducted? How much is allocated to the research annually?

Assessment: TBC conducts on-going analyses of general consumer trends in key North American markets in order to identify key changes in the preferences and behaviours of its target markets. In addition, it examines visitation levels, product preferences, destination selection factors, promotional program conversion levels, trip satisfaction via its ongoing intercept surveys at key travel points in the province. TBC also participates with the Canadian Tourism Commission in consumer research linked to one or two overseas markets annually. TBC also does consumer research annually in key North American cities and participates in the Canadian Travel Survey and International Travel Survey. In addition, TBC conducts a range of market test focus group sessions and industry trade surveys to test the affinity of proposed promotional programs with key target markets. . The annual budget allocated for all these research activities is in the range of $150,000 annually. While not necessarily focusing on the brand, the research indirectly probes the fit between target market preferences and the attributes associated with the "Super, Natural British Columbia" brand.

Does the organization modify the brand to reflect these changes in the market place? What is the period of time over which the change occurs?

Assessment: When sustained changes in travel market preferences appear, efforts are made to incorporate these shifts in marketing activities associated with the brand. For instance, shifts in travel market preference towards more active as well as culturally focused vacations have resulted in TBC incorporating greater soft and hard adventure activities into the visual imagery associated with the brand. Recognizing the diverse and ever-changing character of travel markets in the province, in recent years TBC has also encouraged its partners to highlight specific generic and product-specific attributes that are unique to each region. This willingness to respond to changing market

	conditions is reflected in the diverse range of products and services highlighted in association with each regional brand. While the preceding marketing plans are reviewed annually, there is enough flexibility in these plans to allow for short term adjustments related to unexpected events such as forest fires and SARS outbreaks in 2003.
Macro-Environment Review: To what extent does the organization research the macro-environment and its relative opportunity or threat to the brand? How often is the research conducted? What is the annual dollar spent on related to the macro-environment?	Assessment: Between 10 and 15% of TBC's staff and operating budget assigned to research functions is allocated to examining macro-environmental trends. This research typically is collected from secondary data sources dealing with global, national and provincial travel, safety, economic and facility usage trends. The organization also uses a unique forum (i.e. CEO Research Advisory Council) to research semi-annually review forecasted changes in the macro-environment that may impact the competitive position and performance of BC's tourism industry. While the impacts of this research are not necessarily reflected in day-to-day brand management decisions, over the long term they can influence what aspects of the brand are highlighted in response to these factors.
Micro-Environment Review: What percentage of tourism operators feel their product's values and attributes are reflected in the brand? What percentage of local representatives believe the brand reflects their community values and attributes?	Assessment: No quantitative data is collected concerning local perceptions of the brand. However, the Tourism Partners program is designed to encourage the depiction of product-specific attributes that reflect the unique characteristics of the region, while reinforcing the generic character of the Super, Natural British Columbia brand. TBC expects that about 50% of the regional brand communication should be generic to the BC brand with the remainder being tied to the character and product of the region. TBC conducts an annual external stakeholder review of the performance of its Tourism Partners Program as well as the organization's overall performance. Overall, stakeholders firmly support the Tourism Partner's Program and the organization's marketing programs (and inferentially its brand).

3. Brand Effectiveness

Visitor Satisfaction: Does the organization allocate funding to monitor the effectiveness of the brand a visitor satisfaction perspective? What is the annual value/percentage of the tourism-marketing budget allocated to monitoring satisfaction?	Assessment: Visitor satisfaction with various attributes of the brand is examined on an on-going basis via a range of Visitor Info Centre and attraction site traveller surveys. These studies intercept from travellers in-transit and probe their travel behaviours and satisfaction levels during the trips, and in some cases after the trip via mail-back surveys. While not necessarily conducted specifically for branding related reasons, the majority of the studies address visitor satisfaction elements related to the brand. Satisfaction with BC's core brand elements such as natural environments, pristine wilderness, and mountain landscapes etc.) nd their overall trip experience tends to be very high (80+%). Such investigations provide management with the ability to infer consumer satisfaction about the brand. Approximately 12% of the organization's research operating budget is allocated to probing various aspects of visitor satisfaction with the brand's attributes. A branding study completed in 2003 indicated that most survey respondents felt that the mountains, water and sun graphic were an accurate representation of the BC "brand". It also indicated that 80% of participants thought the brand line was a good description of BC and 75% felt the brand was distinctive. This type of brand specific research is collected on an "as needed" basis.

Brand positioning: What percentage of visitors believe the brand attributes, values and benefits rank more favorably than the competition?	Assessment: Research conducted on a project-specific basis suggests that attributes used to identify BC's brand (e.g. sun, oceans, and mountains) are very important to the tourist experience. On-going visitor studies suggest that these brand attributes regularly exceed or match visitor expectations and that BC has a perceived advantage with respect to these assets when compared to its key destination alternatives. For instance consumer research findings conducted in San Francisco indicated that BC ranked more favorable than its competitors with respect to the brand's key values.
Brand Name Awareness: Does the organization measure brand name recall? How often is this measured (e.g. quarterly, annually or bi-annually)? What percentage of surveyed tourists recalls the brand name?	Assessment: A TBC brand positioning study conducted in 2002 indicates that 95% of BC residents, 78% of Calgary residents, 50% of Seattle residents and 33% of Toronto residents, recall the "Super, Natural British Columbia" brand. Amongst those respondents from Canadian provinces, BC brand recall was almost double that for Canada's national brand (46%) and significantly higher than that for Canada's most populated province - Ontario (57%). In a U.S and overseas market survey completed in 2000, American travellers expressed high brand in short haul markets. Awareness levels amongst travellers decreased with increasing distance from BC. Overseas travellers demonstrated low awareness of the brand.. Amongst other popular brands, recall of the "Super, Natural British Columbia" brand is also strong. For brand recall levels for BC's "Super, Natural British Columbia", Volkswagen's "Drivers Wanted" and Kodak's "Share Moments"brands were 95%, 91% and 72% in 2002. Consumer research concerning the brand's recall is conducted periodically as needed.
Brand loyalty: What percentage of tourist surveyed expect to return to the destination to specifically experience destination values and attributes associated with the brand? What is the number/percentage of tourists who are repeat visitors and/or expect to return to the destination?	Assessment: There is currently no research conducted concerning brand loyalty. Visitor intercept, mail-back and telephone survey research suggests that about half of non-residents and four-fifths of residents contacted plan to travel to the province in the near future. In addition, over 75% of visitors indicate that they are repeat visitors to the province. Past research in American and overseas markets (2000) suggests that visitor intentions to return decrease with distance from BC.
Stakeholder use of the Brand: What number/percentage of tourism operators/ organizations use the destination brand in their marketing activities?	Assessment: The brand is used regularly by the regional tourism agencies 100%. Over 1,000 tourism operators participate in regional tourism associations marketing activities - which are under the Super, Natural British Columbia brand.
Competitiveness: To what extent do the brand's products attract repeat use?	Assessment: Repeat use of the brand's products varies between and within targeted markets. For instance in individual markets such as Washington State, the levels of repeat use of the brand's skiing, outdoor adventure and golf products is significant. Conversely, repeat use of the brand's golf products is limited amongst German travellers.

4. Brand Protection

Investment: What percentage of the marketing budget is allocated to brand protection on an annual basis? What level of resources is invested to monitor and protect the brand (annual budget)?	Assessment: There is currently no data indicating an annual dollar value associated with brand protection. However, while several staff members at Tourism BC are responsible for brand protection activities, TBC dedicates the equivalent of 1 full time staff member to the brand protection function. On average TBC spends about $75,000 annually to review and protect its registrations.
Brand Trademark: Did the organization register the brand as a trademark to protect it and increase its equity? In how many countries is the trademark registered. How much is spent on such trademark protection activities annually?	Assessment: The brand was copyrighted in 1978 as an official mark of the Government. TBC registered the brand as a trademark in British Columbia in June 1998. This trademark include protection of various versions of the brand's logo and slogan. Several versions of the "Super, Natural British Columbia" slogan are registered to ensure protection of the brand's values. The brand is registered in 9 countries. On average TBC spends about $75,000 annually to review and protect its registrations.
Brand Use Guidelines: Does the organization have guidelines for stakeholder use of the brand image or the wordmark? What is the effort level to implement/monitor guidelines for stakeholder use of the brand? How many stakeholders apply and/or achieve guideline requirements?	Assessment: Tourism BC has developed graphic design guidelines for the regional tourism organizations, Visitor Information Centres and accommodation providers using the "Super, Natural British Columbia" brand for advertising. Once the organization or service provider meets the guidelines, they are permitted to use the logo and wordmark for specific purposes. Tourism BC controls all other uses of the brand. Currently, 6 regional tourism organizations and numerous accommodation providers have approvals to use the brand.
Brand Staff Support: Does the organization ensure there skilled staff are available to manage and protect the brand?	Assessment: Approximately 9 people at TBC are involved with managing various aspects of the brand and its use. The organizaion's marketing group along with the support of trademark lawyers makes strategic decisions concerning the use of the brand.
Brand Support Programs: Does the agency initiate programs to promote or support the use of the brand identity throughout the destination? How many stakeholders participate in marketing programs linked to the use of the brand?	Assessment: TBC commits considerable resources to reinforcing the brand's identity in the marketplace. As part of its on-going marketing initiatives, TBC regularly orients its employees to the brand's values and attributes, and how they are integrated into broader marketing programs. In addition, employees are provided with customer service and marketing workshops, logo-designed apparel, and information booklets that illustrate the connections between the brand and the marketing functions of TBC. Externally, TBC's "Superhost" customer service training program promotes the values, attributes and expected performance standards of "Super, Natural British Columbia" to service providers across the province. In 2001/02, TBC trained 17,000 local service providers in the province.

Brand Stakeholder Support: What percentage of stakeholders surveyed believe the brand has helped improve the value and performance of their tourism operations?	Assessment: TBC's latest annual corporate stakeholder survey (2003) indicated that participants in the organization's marketing and customer serive training programs were satisfied with their experiences. Inferential information gathered from websites and phone inquiries, consumer trade shows, annual external stakeholder reviews, and increased business participation in the regional Tourism Partners Program suggests that TBC's marketing program and its brand continue to assist tourism operators in sustaining their operations.
Does the organization support activities or partnerships which focus on protecting the natural and cultural resources essential to the brand?	Assessment: The province's outstanding natural environment and diverse landscapes are represented in the brand's identity. The diverse array of unspoiled lands and authentic people represent the brand's core values for visitors However, TBC does not directly protect those natural attributes. It does not have a mandate to manage the quality and quantity of natural resources accessible for tourism use. However, it does inform key government stakeholders and decision-makers about the importance of protecting these assets. TBC's market research information is used by more resource-oriented agencies to secure more sustainable and tourism friendly resource decisions.
To what extent does online misuse of the brand occur? How many external linkages to the destination website exist? What is the level of consistency or compatibility of messages and images provided via these external websites? How often is this review conducted (e.g. quarterly, annually, bi-annually)? How much is spent annually to review websites?	Assessment: TBC has several external linkages to its website (e.g. 6 regional tourism associations, approved accommodation providers, BC Escape Program suppliers, several Visitor Info Centres, and two airlines.) All are required to comply with TBC copy, image and graphic guidelines. Spot checks are conducted on a random basis to ensure that compliance standards are being met. In 2003 there were 85 reported incidents of trademark misuse by local operators and other agencies reported.

Acknowledgements: Special appreciation is extended to the senior administration and staff of Tourism British Columbia for providing research documents and personal interviews concerning the management and use of the "Super, Natural British Columbia" brand. Without their support this branding management assessment would not have been possible.

Emerald Lake Nature, beauty and outdoor activities are part of the Super Natural brand

6.21 Sydney Quarantine Station (Australia): Applying the Tourism Optimization Management Model (TOMM)

Integrated Planning, Management Indicators, Adaptive Management, TOMM, Private Sector

This case shows how indicators are part of a site-specific planning process aimed at conserving cultural and natural heritage and has been employed to support a model management approach.

This case study presents an integrated monitoring and adaptive management system prepared for a historic site with overlaying natural, social and economic values. The system is the third documented Australian application of the Tourism Optimization Management Model (McArthur 2000), and the first prepared by a tourism operator. The system was prepared during a complex development application as a means of reducing risk and over regulation of the tourism activity before it had a chance to prove itself.

The former North Head Quarantine Station is one of Australia's nationally significant landmarks. Part of the Sydney Harbour National Park, the historic site is listed on the National Estate for its cultural significance. The site features 65 historic buildings, 1,000 painted and engraved rock inscriptions by former internees, Aboriginal sites ˙ and several endangered vegetation communities and species (terrestrial and marine). The aerial photograph of the site is shown at right.

The Quarantine Station lease area

The need for a monitoring system

In 2000, the New South Wales National Parks and Wildlife Service (NPWS) signed a conditional agreement to lease the Quarantine Station to tourism operator Mawland Hotel Management (Mawland). Leasing the site was considered by government as the best way to increase public awareness of the site, enhance public access and interpretation, and secure ongoing conservation and maintenance. The adaptive reuse of the site involves reusing the existing buildings and introducing complementary uses that minimize environmental impact and maximize interpretation, public access and economic return. Over the following three years, Mawland undertook considerable community consultation, an extensive array of planning, and an Environmental Impact Assessment.

The environmental assessment process was complex and lengthy, partly due to some sectors of the community rejecting private sector involvement in such a significant site, but also due to overlapping and competing natural, cultural and social values. Late in the process, it became clear that the proposal would be approved, but would attract a vast and complex mass of approval conditions, some of which would so limit the operation as to make it un-viable. In response, Mawland proposed to the authorities that some of the more rigorous approval conditions could be avoided or at least transferred into an adaptive management system implemented only if there was a demonstrated emerging need. An integrated monitoring and adaptive management system was prepared and submitted as part of the proposal (Mawland 2003). The initiative was partially successful, and many approval conditions became adaptive management measures, triggered if and when monitoring results confirmed the need.

Description of the system:

The integrated monitoring and adaptive management system is a further evolution of the Tourism Optimisation Management Model (TOMM) (McArthur 2000). The appeal of the TOMM over the other models was its suitability for both heritage managers and the tourism industry, coming through its emphasis on:

*   Sustainability (environmental, cultural, social and economic dimensions);

*   Optimal conditions (rather than limits, capacity or other restrictive concepts); and

*   Simple reporting (through structuring acceptable ranges within the model).

Box 6.36 presents the three key parts of the TOMM as being:

1. Context identification (identifying values and management objectives that lead to a set of optimal conditions);

2. Monitoring (the indicators and method of monitoring to check on whether the optimal conditions are being met);

3. Adaptive management (to efficiently respond to optimal conditions not being met).

The Quarantine Station version of the TOMM differs from its earlier counterparts on Kangaroo Island and Dryandra Woodland (McArthur 2000) through its pre-determination of adaptive management measures for every single indicator. This was critical to building community and government confidence that if monitoring discovered a problem, there were predetermined solutions ready for implementation, and acceptable to all parties. Some of these solutions were otherwise destined to become regulated approval conditions, but hopefully will not be needed. Box 6.37 presents an example of two of the 200 indicators that form the Quarantine Station TOMM.

Box 6.36 Three parts of the Quarantine Station TOMM

1. Optimal conditions

Environmental	**Cultural**	**Social**	**Economic**
• The condition of key elements of the natural environment is proven healthy • Operational consumption of resources is proven efficient	• The condition of key elements of historic heritage is proven healthy • The condition of key elements of the indigenous environment is provenhealthy	• Visitation reflects forecasts • Visitor expectations of target markets are met • The operation has a positive profile among stakeholders	• The viability of the operation is considered healthy • The viability of the partnership with the NPWS is considered healthy

2. Monitoring system

For each environmental optimal condition:	For each **cultural** optimal condition:	For each **social** optimal · condition:	For each **economic** optimal condition:
• indicators • acceptable ranges • benchmarks • monitoring method	• indicators • acceptable ranges • benchmarks • monitoring method	• indicators • acceptable ranges • benchmarks • monitoring method	• indicators • acceptable ranges • benchmarks • monitoring method

Monitoring

Reporting of results

Indicators outside acceptable range	**Indicators within acceptable range**

3. Adaptive management system

Identify whether variation is related to operation

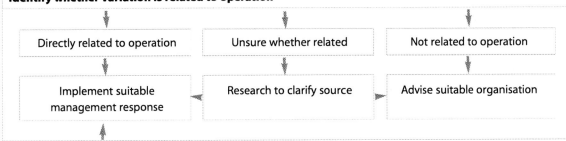

Directly related to operation	Unsure whether related	Not related to operation
Implement suitable management response	Research to clarify source	Advise suitable organisation

Potential management actions for each indicator

Management actions for poor performing indicators OR revise indicators, benchmark, acceptable range or monitoring

Box 6.37 Two examples of Quarantine Station indicators and their monitoring and adaptive management system

Acceptable range	Bench mark	Monitoring method	Adaptive management responses
Number of Little Penguin breeding burrows that are active during two successive breeding seasons between Cannae Point and the southern end of Store Beach
Within 5% probability level (statistically)	NPWS monitoring data since 1997	WHAT: Identify the number of breeding burrows being used between Cannae Point and the southern end of Store Beach over two successive breeding seasons HOW: Once each fortnight during the breeding season (July to February inclusive) visit potential habitat between Cannae Point and southern end of Store Beach and count the number of breeding burrows being used. Record number of burrows and number being used. WHO: NPWS (Environmental Manager) and Mawland (ESD Coordinator and trained volunteers) WHEN: Year 1, Stage 1, prior to water transport	If monitoring indicates that the number of active Little Penguin breeding burrows between Cannae Point and the southern end of Store Beach has significantly decreased over two consecutive breeding seasons and the NPWS is convinced that such decreases are either fully or partially related to the activity, the NPWS may direct the implementation of measures such as: • Reduction in the number of lights and their intensity in the Wharf Precinct, particularly in the vicinity of the restaurant in A6. • Provision of acoustic barriers in the vicinity of the restaurant at night, especially the outdoor eating area. • Cessation of outdoor dining in the vicinity of the restaurant in A6 at night during the breeding season (or all year round) • Restrictions on ferry movements, such as a set period either side of sunset or no movements between sunset and sunrise. • Provision of alternative public transport to the site during times when ferry movements are restricted. If further on-going monitoring indicates that the number of active Little penguin breeding burrows in this area continues to decrease over subsequent breeding seasons, the NPWS may direct other measures. If Little penguin deaths occur in the vicinity of the site as a result of matters reasonably beyond control, the number of active breeding burrows considered for Trigger 1 may be adjusted. Measures may be reversed or altered with the approval of the NPWS if monitoring indicates that the number of active Little penguin breeding burrows for the population has increased over two successive seasons.
Annual proportion of clearly differentiated cultural landscape matching to the early Aviation Phase
60 - 80% match	55% match	WHAT: Monitor the position of cleared and bushland edges, and historic vistas from buildings HOW: Every year, photograph the site from a set of fixed locations. Locations are set within the Heritage Landscape Management Plan. Approximately 10 locations should be determined based on historic photographs from the early aviation phase that show boundaries between grassy areas and bushland, and a further 5 historic photographs should show view fields from accommodation buildings (particularly between buildings P1 and P9 and from cottages, hospital etc). Identify variations that trigger actions to monitor the cultural landscape WHO: Mawland (Site Manager) WHEN: Year 2, Stage 3	Consistent with an approved Heritage Landscape Management Plan, to maintain historic landscapes and vistas consider one or more of the following actions: • Adjust the landscape maintenance program to include the removal of invasive vegetation and turf improvement for former grassed areas within 12 months; • Adjust the landscape maintenance program to include removal of invasive vegetation and replacement with historic plantings, ground cover species or gardens; or • Adjust the landscape maintenance program to include more regular trimming of the existing grassed and bushland boundaries.

Application

The TOMM commenced operation in 2003, and has been written into approval conditions and the lease - making it a legally binding part of the tourism operation. The five main uses of the TOMM are:

1.   A rationale for further assessing a situation, introducing mitigative measures or changing management operations;

2.   A key source of data for a Geographic Information System used to assist manage the site;

3.   A frame of reference for producing an Annual Environmental Management Report of the condition of the site and sustainability of the operation;

4.   A frame of reference for a five yearly Environmental Audit of performance in meeting conditions of the lease;

5.   An accessible source of information for stakeholders and visitors to be aware of the condition of the site and how the operation is performing (including a continuous display at the visitor centre, note sheets and postings on the Q-Station website).

The TOMM is coordinated through an Environmental Management Plan. Approximately half of the 200 monitoring indicators are overseen by Mawland, with the other half distributed in partnerships with the NSW NPWS, the University of Technology Sydney, Metropolitan Local Aboriginal Land Council, specialist consultants and conservation volunteer groups. Mawland has allocated approximately Aus$60,000 per annum to run its contribution to the TOMM.

Lessons learned

1.   *Find a champion with proven experience and interest.* Developing such a sophisticated system requires a strong commitment of the site managers. It is useful to involve experts familiar with impact management, who understand that the time and money investment are worth it because it helps reducing risk, avoiding restrictive and rigid regulations, allowing for more flexible adaptive management. The management's past involvement with the ongoing successful Kangaroo Island TOMM (see Box 6.14 Kangaroo Island) was also important in demonstrating that such a model was possible;

2.   *Introduce the model from the onset.* The approach of proposing a model as part of a development approval process was partially successful, but was unable to transfer all of the approval conditions (there are still 230). There was considerable cultural resistance among community and government to move from regulating practices to making a sizeable portion of them adaptive management. In retrospect, it would have been better to have structured the TOMM as part of the original proposal that was taken through the environmental assessment process, rather than later when approval conditions were being formulated. Nonetheless, the early introduction of the TOMM did allow benchmarks to be established before the lease was activated. This means that change can be managed from a reasonably 'clean slate';

3.   *Produce an implementation plan from the onset.* The TOMM was developed to fit a predetermined implementation capability. Human and financial resources were predetermined and partnerships were formed beforehand. Once developed, the indicators were prioritised and staged over three years, starting with those representing the greatest risk. This approach has maximised support and allowed the progressive implementation to be resourced using the success of the earlier stages.

Bottom line

Monitoring and adaptive management is a valuable tool to use in shifting regulators from a conservative reactive culture towards an informed proactive culture. Mixing environmental, cultural, social and economic indicators into the one model has maximised stakeholder involvement and support, and thus the potential of the adaptive reuse of the Quarantine Station to proceed and demonstrate its sustainability.

References

Mawland Hotel Management, 2003, Integrated monitoring and adaptive management system for the adaptive reuse of the Quarantine Station, Mawland Hotel Management, Sydney.

McArthur, S, 2000, 'Visitor management in action - an analysis of the development and implementation of visitor management models at Jenolan Caves and Kangaroo Island', a thesis submitted for the Degree of Doctor of Philosophy of the University of Canberra, ACT.

Further information: www.q-station.com.au

6.22 Tunisia: Indicators and Standards for Tourism

National Indicators, Coastal Zones, Development Control, Hotels, Zoning

This case shows how indicators have become an integral part of planning of tourism in Tunisia's coastal zone.

Tunisia's tourism development has proceeded differently than that of many other countries. The history of economic development has been tied to export sectors, of which tourism has been an important component for over 30 years. In the early 1960s tourism was not a development priority and growth occurred in an unorganized manner. From 1964 to 1971 the number of beds grew from 7500 to 41,250. In an effort to avoid uncontrolled development and related degradation of recreational resources, studies were done in the late 1960s as part of a program to address infrastructure for tourism development for Tunisia. By the early 1970s tourism had become a focus for economic development, and as a result, the objective for tourism development in Tunisia was to aid employment creation, and to encourage overseas investment. Tourism was seen above all as international in nature. Subsequently, Tunisian society developed to the extent that holiday activities were no longer restricted to international tourism and the demand for such activities started to come from all levels of Tunisian society. A survey carried out in 1992 amongst schoolchildren in urban areas gave a rate of family holidays of about 28.3%, and the length of the summer holiday stay was more than two weeks. Such holidays were spent with relations and friends, either in second residences or in rented accommodation. According to one study, domestic tourism could add up to almost 30 million overnight stays per year. These data served as a stimulus for Tunisia to further develop its indicators program.

In addition to tourists, the inhabitants of urban areas located within one hundred kilometres from the coast often spend time at the beach in makeshift campsites. These local visits to tourism sites are on the increase especially because of more widespread use of individual vehicles. Overnight stays by residents can be viewed relative to statistics for higher-income categories: In 2000, the total number of overnight stays by residents was 2,255,412, that is, 6.5% of total overnight stays. This indicates a rise over the 1999 figure of 4%. In 1983, there were more than 1 million overnight stays by residents and in 1997 more than 2 million.

The main motivation for domestic tourists was seaside holidays with 1,524,448 overnight stays in 2000, that is 67.5% of the total. In 2000, overnight stays in classified establishments amounted to 1,828,666, that is, 81% of overall overnight stays by residents. Overnight

Box 6.38 Trends in overnight stays by Tunisian residents	
Overnight stays	
1965	190,737
1970	295,367
1975	520,344
1980	694,394
1985	1,126,868
1990	1,177,879
1995	1,831,854
2000	2,255,412

stays in non-classified hotels amounted to 16% and in holiday villages 3%. By hotel category, 3* establishments are the most popular (45%) but the share for top-level hotels - 4* and 5* - increased to 35% in 2000 from 23% in 1995 and 15% in 1985. The regular collection of these indicators has supported this analysis.

In 1970 and 1980, domestic demand was not well established. Today, thousands of spontaneous campers erect their tents along the Tunisian coast. This creates problems from the point of view of hygiene, security and ecology (through the destruction of dunes). Measures have been taken for resident tourists who cannot afford to pay a hotel. For domestic day visitors and tourists, areas have been set aside for holidaymakers based on the following:

* Beach occupation plans (POP) have been drawn up for beach management, providing the necessary facilities for users. 21 beaches were prepared in 2001 and 30 more are being prepared along the whole of the coastline;

* Areas for domestic tourism are currently being prepared at : Chaffar close to Sfax, Sidi Raïs in the south of Grand-Tunisia and at Kallaat Andalous between Tunisia and Bizerte;

* Collective accommodation is being developed;

* The number of campgrounds is being increased; at present, there are 16, of which 14 are on the coast. They are located in 11 governorships (out of a total of 24 in Tunisia). They offer a total of 2,658 places;

* Youth hostels are being increased; at present there are 29 offering a total of 1,680 places;

* A leisure policy has been drawn up :including some travel agencies specialising in the domestic niche offering group rates and a voluntary price reduction policy for domestic tourists.

Indicators

Tunisia has had some indicators in place for many years, and these are in use in the planning process. The primary users are the Tunisian National Tourism Office (Office National de Tourisme Tunisien) and the Tourism Land Agency (Agence Foncière Touristique) who are the principal agencies involved in policy and planning for development of tourism in Tunisia. Their use of indicators begins with the identification of new tourism zones; the measures have been instrumental in the delimitation of the zones and the establishment of standards. Because of the approvals process, the indicators are an intrinsic part of the review for new development, and have also been important in the drafting of regulations.

The establishment of a Tunisian indicators program was done to provide protection for the nation's tourism and its destinations and to assist in development of Tunisia's natural and cultural heritage. Following the recommendations of the 1992 Rio Summit, Tunisia created a National Commission for Sustainable Development (decree n°93-2061 of October 11 1993). A workshop responding to Agenda 21 produced a basic document which recommended "the development and promotion of a tourism which is more diversified, more integrated and more respectful of the environment, while improving tourist facilities and developing and promoting a diversified tourism system of seaside destinations while also promoting the opening of the interior of the country in a manner respectful of the environment" . Consequently, the critical review of new development is an objective for which indicators have been important whether with regard to tourism development, tourism management, or innovation in the industry. The program has a number of elements, and, in many cases, indicators are directly linked to standards for parts of the industry. ·

Hotel Framework

In the 1970s, Tunisian hotel establishments generally consisted of pleasant properties, with big shaded gardens, open space, and sunny beaches, where the hotel itself was the focus for tourism. The hotel was the centre for the vacation and tourists sought suitable conditions based principally on the nature of the site or land use. The area used for tourist activity was required to be designated for exclusive tourist uses, through the establishment of an Official Perimeter Zone (Périmètre d'intervention foncière - PIF) that allows and will allow in perpetuity programs of management, facilities construction, renovation or rehabilitation to be put in place by the competent authorities (State, local public groups, important agencies). This will occur in accordance with the general urban plan or specific site plans. As well, a land reserve zone, Périmètre de réserve foncière (PRF), allows release of lands for construction at a reasonable price for future development.

In addition, tourism areas are required to have a management plan which takes into account:

1. Tourism carrying capacity, which is a function of environmental/physical indicators which are essential factors of success regarding sustainability;

2. Norms and management standards established according to the type of development;

3. Level of integration within the zone and outside the zone, with regard to the human and economic activities both local and regional. (For example, the expansion of access points to the sea to protect the coastal zone from privatization and allow the bulk of vacationers to have beach access.)

Spatial Indicators and standards Tunisia measures a number of specific elements relating to the hotels and their surroundings; in many cases these relate directly to standards.

Built environment (principal standards)

Tunisia has a comprehensive tourism management plan which regulates land use, construction and other spatial factors related to the industry. Its 14 articles cover development from initial planning and construction to control of uses such as parking. Among the standards and related indicators are those relating to land use and height controls.

Box 6.39 Selected density standards - Tunisia

Indicator	Standard
• Number of beds per hectare:	100 beds / hectare
• Coefficient of land occupation: (area which is built on)	25%
• Beach density:	1 swimmer / 16 m²
• Land use coefficient (area of floor space relative to surface area of total property):	45%
• Height (special tourist zone)	(Example for the island of Djerba), Hotel height must not exceed the height of a palm tree.
• Height(urban)	(Under Article 10 of urban regulations a maximum height of 8 metres is permitted)

Box 6.40 Selected tourism construction standards for Tunisia

Since 2003, hotel construction, (also named accommodation units), has also been regulated according to size criteria. In response to demands for quality standards, norms have also been established under the control of the Ministries of Commerce and Tourism, Leisure and Crafts (4 February 2000.) This takes the form of a classification system for the hotels based on a number of categories (1 to 5) and symbols in use (stars). To the standards of minimum room size, operation and management, standards were added regarding facilities and additional services offered by hotel establishments. In addition, and independent of the classification of the hotels, establishments can belong to a quality labelling system providing additional standards for the Tunisian hotel industry (Standards 2000).

The First Class Framework - For Hotels with Significant Tourism

The beach

Tunisia's beaches are the key resource for seaside tourism. Certain beaches are in decline due to natural causes (increased violent storms, greenhouse effect, slowdown of wind and water deposition of sand) and human causes (disruption of the sand systems on the dunes and the beach, removal of materials from the beach). There is also alteration by building of structures on the coast, made necessary both for protection from a legal perspective and for coastal management.

* A building ban is in place for a band of 100 meters in keeping with regulations of Maritime Public Domain. The establishment of legal boundaries delimits the maritime public domain, on which construction is absolutely forbidden.

* Creation of rights of way - passages provide free public access to the sea.

Waste water

All water from bathing stations is collected in the sanitary system and treated. All tourist zones are provided with treatment stations. As well, regular analyses are carried out by the Ministry of Public Health. For day tourism, areas were affected by the numbers of Tunisian vacationers. To address this issue, two solutions were undertaken: A plan for beach management was put in place. Beaches were also provided with the necessary equipment and washroom facilities to serve the summer visitors. Indicators of numbers of users per facility were important to the decision to add more services.

The Common Framework

For Other Tourism Sites (museums, historic urban centers) or areas supporting tourism related activities (coffee shops, restaurants, promenades) requiring tourism services. In effect, the tourism sector (the administration in cooperation with the private sector) has been given the right to establish a framework of measures and standards to support its sustainability, considering the income that it brings to the zones in which it operates. At the same time, indicators are equally established relative to the protection of natural and cultural heritage of the sites. (E.g. level of protection, levels of use).

Indicators of Emerging Issues

Tourism, national or international, is in a state of change. New economic and financial parameters, stimulated by free trade and free exchange, are realities now for the Euro-Mediterranean region;

1. Changed factors, altered behaviour and new trends affecting demand;

2. Changed patterns of air transport. There is no longer the same relationship between distance and price and choice of destinations;

3. Impacts of the opening of skies in the Mediterranean area;

4. Changes in methods and approaches by governments relative to financing of tourism activities;

5. Problems engendered by the withdrawal of the state from many areas.

Considering these new factors, and without harming current tourism, Tunisia's tourism product needs to be renovated. Competitiveness needs to be based on new sustainable products which can be put in place.

Key measures where indicators will be important will include:

1. Indicators of quality;

2. Indicators of sustainability;

3. Measures of cultural assets.

Indicators need to respond to these concepts and act as an early warning system to permit timely reaction. They can therefore support reporting on the state of sites and destinations for tourism in Tunisia. Indicators can help establish comparisons among different parts of tourism in comparison with national and international measures or benchmarks of competitiveness. The use of these measures will permit formulation of recommendations towards competitiveness for Tunisian tourism. The program is considered to be flexible, with plans to continuously add new indicators in response to these challenges.

Because of the early establishment of indicators at the national level, Tunisia became aware of trends, and was able to establish a program to try to reinforce positive trends and to establish standards which have led to more controlled and higher quality tourism.

6.23 Uganda Heritage Trails Impact Assessment Indicators

Trails, Community Participation, Monitoring, Results, Benefits

Uganda Trails uses indicators to measure its progress both in tourism management and community involvement.

Uganda Heritage Trails (HTU) is a program which helps communities develop and manage tourism products through participatory planning and community involvement. The program works on a village basis through the establishment of a trail systems. (See Box 4.5 Trails and Routes p. 276) which contains a section on a related Ugandan example) In this case study, the focus is on the participatory monitoring and evaluation program and the indicators developed and used in the program.

The participatory monitoring and evaluation (M & E) indicators developed by the 6 pilot trail communities are presented in the table below identifiable where the source of data is the community. These indicators are combined with simple internal project M&E indicators developed by the field team to measure other impacts of the project, for example, raising awareness of using tourism as a tool for poverty reduction amongst policy makers and the general public through media coverage. The indicators are specific, measurable, ambitious, realistic and time-bound (SMART) and cover both positive and negative impacts in the following areas:

*   **Empowerment, networking and dissemination** (e.g. number of members of the community tourism association, number of community tourism association members elected to the Uganda Community Tourism Association - UCOTA Executive Committee, number of new partnerships formed, number of media exposures);

*   **Skills training** (e.g. number of community tourism association members trained in business development, guiding etc);

*   **Enterprise development** (e.g. number of tourism services provided, number employed, number of visitors);

*   **Access to essential resources** (e.g. number of community development projects benefiting from tourism enterprise development);

*   **Conservation of natural and cultural assets and values** (e.g. number of renovated cultural structures, number of cultural guardians (traditional protectors of cultural assets resuming and/ or withdrawing from traditional roles).

The indicators have been translated into the local language of Buganda, Luganda, for the 6 pilot community tourism associations and are being tested in Uganda for interim monitoring purposes. The community indicators will be measured & reviewed at regular intervals (e.g. quarterly) and where appropriate analyzed according to gender with assistance from the Project field team.

Box 6.41 Participatory monitoring & evaluation for Heritage Trails Uganda
(Indicators developed by pilot project communities)

Indicator			Source of Data
Empowerment/ dissemination/ Networking	1	Number of individual members (annually/ male & female) of the: i The Trail Community Tourism Association; ii Uganda Community Tourism Association (UCOTA).	Community UCOTA
	2	Average attendance rate of members to internal meetings of the trail community tourism associations (annually);	Community
	3	Number of resignations from the trail community tourism associations (annually);	Community
	4	Number of members formally disciplined by the trail community tourism associations (annually);	Community
	5	Number of members of the trail community tourism associations elected to the UCOTA Executive Committee (annually);	UCOTA
	6	Number of trail community associations who attended the UCOTA Annual General Meeting (annually);	UCOTA
	7	Number of other community tourism associations visiting the trail community tourism associations for advice/ research (annually);	Community
	8.	Existence of new partnerships formed between the trail community tourism associations and other organisations such as donors, NGOs (annually);	Community
	9	Number of Media exposures about Heritage Trails Uganda (every six months): i TV; ii Radio; iii National print; iv International print.	HTU Project Office
Training and capacity building	10	Number of people trained in the trail community tourism associations (every six months/ male & female) in the following: i Guiding; ii Hospitality; iii Business development/Book keeping; iv Handicraft development; v Traditional building techniques; vi Appropriate technology/conservation; vii English language; viii Study tours (in & outside Uganda); ix Music, Dance and Drama.	Community UCOTAHTU Project Office
	11	Average attendance rate of members of the trail community tourism associations to project seminars and workshops on-site (every six months);	HTU Office Community
	12	Number of members/ employees of the trail community tourism associations who obtained external gainful employment (annually);	Community
	13	Number of members/ employees of the trail community tourism association practising what they were trained in (annually);	Community
	14	Number of complaints and compliments on the quality of products and services offered by the trail community tourism associations (quarterly);	Community UCOTA HTU Project

Indicator		Source of Data
Enterprise Development	15 Number of tourism micro enterprises e.g. guiding, catering, handicrafts, cultural entertainment managed by the trail community tourism associations (every six months)	Community
	16 Number of full-time employees of the trail community tourism associations (every six months/ male & female): i Guidesii ii Receptionists iii Cleaners iv Askaris (security guards)	Community
	17 Number of part-time employees of the trail community tourism associations (every six months/ male & female): i Guides ii Receptionists iii Cleaners iv Askaris	Community
	18 Average number of tourists visiting the sites managed by the trail community tourism associations per month (quarterly): i Ugandans ii Non-Ugandans iii Schoolchildren	Community
	19 Percentage increase in the number of foreign tourists visiting the sites managed by the trail community tourism associations (annually)	Community

Box 6.42 Uganda trails: Indicators result sheet at the Ssezibwa falls tourism project site

Indicator for site community	Ssezibwa Falls Tourism Project (SFTP)		
Time Scale	**Apr-00**	**Nov 01- Jan 02**	**Sept - Dec 02**
Total No. of individual members (including UCOTA members)	40	30	40
Number of CBTs visiting for research/advise	7	2	5
Number of new partnerships formed with other Orgs.	-	3	6
Total Number of media exposure	-	-	-
Total Number of people trained	63	63	70
Average attendance rate to project seminars/workshops	25	20	28
Number of people practicing what they trained in	40	45	49
Number of members who gained gainful external employment as a result of training	-	-	-
Number collaborative partnerships created as a result of training courses	-	2	8
Number of tourism micro enterprises (e.g. guiding, catering. Handicrafts, etc.)	-	2	2
Number of tourist facilities (e.g. toilet, reception, etc.)	-	2	5

Time Scale	Apr-00	Nov 01- Jan 02	Sept - Dec 02
Total No. of employees	-	7	7
Average number of tourists visiting per month			
i. Ugandans	25	13	15
ii. Non-Ugandans	4	10	10
iii. School children	40	40	40
Number of cultural structures on site			
i. Reconstructed	-	2	-
ii. Renovated		1	2
iii. Appropriate technology		0	3
Number of artefacts on site			
i. Preserved	-	5	-
ii. Replicas	-	-	-
iii. Given back	-	-	-
Number of cultural guardians resuming traditional roles	-	1	3
Number of cultural guardians withdrawing from traditional roles	-	-	-
Number of trees planted	-	-	4

Ugandan Community Participation: Kibale

The Kibale Association for Rural and Environmental Development (KAFRED) is a community based ecotourism project based in Bigodi parish, Kahunge s/county, Kibale county of Kamwenge district in western Uganda It was formed in 1992 by six founder members and today the membership has grown to 33. These members include individual local people, groups e.g. Bigodi Women's Group (40 members) and Bigodi Peanut Butter Group (7 members) etc. KAFRED is a member (founder) of the Uganda Community Tourism Association (UCOTA). KAFRED provides walks around and across Magombe (Bigodi Wetland Sanctuary), which is about 4sq Kms. The area has several attractions, including: primates, birds, trees and shrubs, butterflies and other insects, agriculture, homesteads, cultural entertainment and craft sales.

Key stakeholders include:

- Kibale National Park (KNP) for guide training and publicity;
- Kibale and Semliki Conservation and Development Project (KSCDP) for capacity building;
- The National Wetlands Program for policy;
- Local Councils for land user rights;
- The local community, beneficiaries;
- Peace Corps Volunteers for technical advice;
- Kabarole Tourism Association (KTA), a regional association.

UCOTA, National umbrella KAFRED was founded in order to conserve areas of rich biodiversity outside nationally protected areas and to benefit communities from the tourism businesses in the area, particularly at Kibale National Park. An American Peace Corps volunteer together with 6 members (founder) of the community steered the formation of the Community Based Organisation (CBO). Membership has now grown to 33, including groups e.g. Bigodi Woman's Group with 40 members. The tourism project has necessitated the participation of other bodies listed as stakeholders above. The program has had sponsorship from many organizations inside and outside Uganda.

The main components of the trail project are:

a.   Contribution to the conservation of natural areas; KAFRED's main aim reads: "...and the conservation of natural resources wetlands in particular". Community development projects e.g. schools, roads and bridges have been funded. This helped to increase awareness in the community on the importance of conservation.

b.   Educational and interpretation features: Programs, such as dance & drama and study tours are used to increase the understanding of natural and cultural values to the community and schools. while interpretation signs, write-ups, guided walks and presentations by members are used for both national and international visitors.

c.   Environmental practices in the development and operating of ecotourism facilities, establishments and services. No accommodation and food services are provided by the organisation, this therefore limits the levels of pollution. However, guided walks are encouraged and visitors are advised to keep along trails and not to throw garbage.

Box 6.43: Results from the participatory process in indicators - Uganda trails

| Social sustainability of the ecotourism project/business | **Community involvement and benefits**
KAFRED is entirely managed/run by the community. The Annual General Meeting (AGM) elects a committee to represent the community. Revenues from tourism are ploughed into community projects, such as Education, Health and Sanitation. Most employees are from the community apart from where there is need for special skills.

Guides for the organisation are recruited locally and trained from KNP or at residential workshops by UCOTA. Teachers are encouraged and given time off to upgrade.

Materials, e.g. for building, are purchased locally. The Bigodi Women's and Peanut Butter Groups are provided with space to sell their produce at the visitor's centre.

Surveys in the community indicated:
• 85% believe tourism benefited the community financially;
• 91% say tourism created more jobs for the local people;
• 99.3% say it's good for the community to attract tourists. |
| Economic sustainability of the ecotourism project/business | **Marketing and promotion**
KAFRED developed brochures, which are placed in strategic tourist centres. KAFRED is featured on the UTB (Uganda Tourist Board) website (www.visituganda.com), in international and local guide books, e.g. Lonely Planet and Bradt Guide, "The Info-digest", "The Eye", and in UCOTA and UTB brochures. Activities of the organisation are marketed by various local and international tour operators mainly as an 'add on'. However, a survey by a visiting student showed that publicity is mainly by word of mouth. |

	Profitability of the ecotourism business ° KAFRED received an average of 1000 visitors with an income of 5.8 million Uganda Shillings (approx 3,000 USD) per year between 1999 and 2001; ° About 40% (Net profit) is spent on community projects. Major expenses include paying staff and trail maintenance, which covers about 60% of the income.; ° 95% of the visitors are international visitors, including 63% from Europe and 20% from N. America. This is because of other major attractions in the region; ° Mantana Safaris, a major tour company has tented camps in the area and often brings visitors.
Cooperation in ecotourism business operations	° KAFRED is a founder member of UCOTA; ° KAFRED pays annual subscription and benefits from: marketing, resource mobilisation , and training, advocacy, some of the objectives of UCOTA; ° UCOTA's other main current donors are McKnight Foundation and the European Union through the Ministry of Tourism; ° KAFRED is member of a Kabarole Tourism Association (KTA), a regional association; ° KNP contributes by training of the guides and marketing the activities; ° Makerere University Biological Field Station (MUBFS), a KNP research station provides technical advice in conservation and management. Through UCOTA, a member of KAFRED attended the ecotourism conference that was hold for the International Year of Ecotourism in Nairobi in 2002.
Regulation of ecotourism activities	° The draft tourism policy mentions community tourism as a new avenue for Uganda's tourism product diversification; ° KAFRED faces a challenge of lack of enforceable laws for wetland conservation and management; ° The members of UCOTA developed standards are part of KAFRED's membership criteria. The standards include good elements of conservation and ensuring community benefits; ° UCOTA has also developed a code of conduct for the visitors to member groups; ° KAFRED has provided copies of the Wetland policy to the local people and has plans of developing byelaws for the management and conservation of the wetland.
Problems and solutions	**Problem:** Crop raiding by vermin. **Solution:** Locals have adopted the growing of crops not eaten by primates. This is still a challenge. **Problem:** Drop in tourist numbers from 1400 in1998 to less than 600 in 1999 and 2000 due to insurgencies in parts of the country. **Solution:** Work plans were revised. Women sold crafts locally and exported through UCOTA. **Problem:** Lack of conservation awareness. **Solution:** Community projects have made locals understand the meaning of conservation. Wildlife clubs introduced in schools.

	Problem: Lack of local capacity to manage tourism enterprises.
	Solution: Training in different areas, including guiding, visitor handling, business development and institutional development.
	Problem: Lack of external support.
	Solution: Funding secured from American Embassy, North Carolina and Tulsa Zoos, more still needed.
Results achieved	• Tourism has put a new face on the Bigodi community; • Funding community development projects e.g. schools and bridges; • Construction of tourist facilities, such as visitor's centre/reception, kiosk and bird-viewing pavilion/hide; • Capacity building for over 30 people (including workers & members have been trained in the community); • Increased conservation awareness; a considerable reduction in destruction of wetlands, people have opted to planting trees for domestic use • Increased number of tourists in 2001 thus more income; • Created jobs for the local people, 19 people are employed directly in the projects. 91% of the local people said tourism has created more jobs; • As a result, locals can now live in better homes.
Lessons learned	Few members are good to start with, it quickens decision making. Conservation impacts are challenging for the communities to measure without technical input. Small grants are important in giving the community a push and morale but where possible, should be in form of materials, equipment & services. Communities away from towns find difficulty in using banks, costs involved are unrealistic. Communities take a long time to realise the importance of conservation and achievements made; exchange visits should be encouraged. KAFRED lacks some recorded data; researchers & students are not asked for copies of their findings.

Monitoring activities	The organisation does not have a sophisticated monitoring and evaluation system but nevertheless records: visitor numbers; visitor expenditure and visitor origin. This data allows trends to be seen and helps marketing decisions to be taken more confidently. However, Heritage Trails Uganda, which is a project of UCOTA has developed participatory monitoring and evaluation indicators that can be adopted by the other members of UCOTA, KAFRED inclusive. UCOTA itself is planning to develop general indicators for all the members.
	The organisation holds regular meetings, monthly executive committee meetings (including staff) and an Annual General Meeting (all members, local community and other stakeholders). The organisation has other sub-committees e.g. finance. Website:
	UTB (Uganda Tourist Board): www.visituganda.com
	UCOTA: www.visituganda.com/domestic/ucota/htm

Source for Kibala Case study: Sustainable Development of Ecotourism - A Compilation of Good Practices in SMEs (WTO, 2003)

Traditional Construction methods on the Trail

6.24 Villarrica Lake Area (Chile): Regional Application of Sustainability Indicators

Regional Planning, Implementation, Community Participation, Monitoring

This case documents the development of indicators as part of a planning process to support the goals of the Lakes region of Chile.

The Pucón - Villarrica zone contains one of the most outstanding attractions in southern Chile. It has tourism resources of international standard in quality and variety as well as good existing tourism facilities. The area where the indicators study was done is located around the lakes Villarrica, Huilipilún, Colico, Caburgua and Calafquén and the route that is connected to Argentina.

Among its highlights is the landscape with woody vegetation, hills, national parks and the majestic Villarrica volcano. Its also encompasses urban centers such as Villarrica, Pucón and Licán Ray, which welcome thousands of tourists in summer every year. The area has a moist Mediterranean transition climate.

This destination has a wide variety of thermal baths and springs where due to the quality of water, there are services and tourist facilities. There are over 140 active and inactive volcanoes throughout the region.

Two national parks, Huerquehue and Villarrica are found in the region. Villarrica National Park was created in 1940, with an area of 63,000 h. including Pucón, Curarrehue, Villarrica and Pangupulli (this is located in the Lake District). The relief is abrupt and irregular influenced by the volcanic activity of Lanín (3,774 m.), Villarrica (2,840 m.) and Quetrupillán (2,360 m.) volcanoes. The weather is dominated by rain between March and August. Snow fall accumulation reaches 2 meters.

Pucón

Pucón, which in local native language (Mapudungun) means "entrance to the mountain range" is a small city, a bathing resort with around 10,000 inhabitants, located at the shore of Villarrica lake. It was founded on February 12th 1883 as a military outpost. Pucón is a "lake city" located 789 km. away from Santiago, 110 km. from the regional centre of Temuco and 26 km .from the neighbouring tourism centre of Villarrica.

Since the decade of the 40's it began quietly to develop as an outstanding tourist destination, first through fishing and then with the beach, the volcano and finally with its discovery as a hotbed of adventure tourism and outdoors activities which make it known as "the Chilean outdoor capital".

Villarrica

Villarrica was founded by Gerónimo de Alderete, who under the orders of governor Pedro de Valdivia, established the city in April 1552. In the present time Villarrica has a population of near 36,000 inhabitants and it is the administrative center and focus for tourism that comes to the zone. Activities are mainly concentrated during summer time between January and March, when the tourist arrivals increase.

Box 6.44 Key Indicators for sustainability for the Villarrica Area

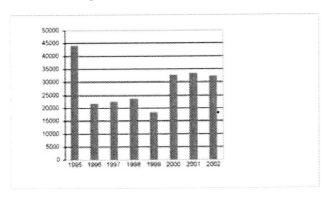

Tourism industry impact and identification of sustainability indicators

The growing tourism industry in recent years has been concentrated in the lakeshore, contributing to environmental damage that is characterized by intensive land use, water pollution, litter and other garbage, together with increasing stress levels in the local communities.

Box 6.45 Overnights in hotels and similar establishments 2002

Due to this situation –and concerns of local authorities and entrepreneurs- a regional land use plan was started and it was decided to identify indicators to measure the environmental situation of the zone.

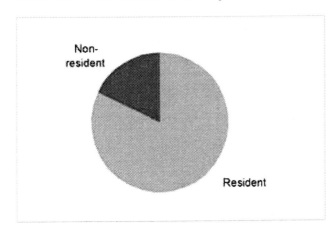

Participation of local residents and representatives, public organizations and entrepreneurs led to the determination of key environmental, economic and social / cultural indicators for the zone.

A long list of potential indicators was identified through a participatory process, including workshops, and related studies. This was reduced to a more manageable set for implementation. The specific set of indicators chosen is outlined in the following tables.

Box 6.46 Key Indicators for Sustainability for the Villarrica Area

	Indicators
Physical environment	◦ Number of road signs showing the way to Villarrica-Pucón, per year; ◦ Percentage of exotic plantations per year; ◦ Number of high buildings, construction permits and number of annual meters of aerial electric cable; ◦ Installation in sensitive landscape areas; ◦ Extraction of m3 of gravel from river-bed by sub-watershed.
	◦ Extent of native forest area (hectares).
	◦ Number of hectares with land usage change.(annual); ◦ Number of new hectares incorporated within the urban border; ◦ Number of subdivided hectares; ◦ Countryside migration – city and interregional.
	◦ Number of annual complaints at the main town for smell/waste; ◦ Number of annual complaints about dumping of waste; ◦ Number of buildings affected with graffiti.
	◦ Number of days with eye irritation; ◦ Number of days with deficient air quality; ◦ Concentration of suspended particles (PM 10) in urban air.
	◦ Concentration of coliforms, nitrogen and phosphorus in lakes and river waters; ◦ Comparison of availability of drinkable water in relation to the peak season demand.
	◦ Occurrence (and re-occurrence) of volcanic and meteorological events; ◦ Growth measurement of Trancura delta.
	◦ Number of wild fires and damaged surface affected per year.
	◦ Number of authorized boats.
Economic environment	◦ Demand for diverse tourism products.
	◦ Entrepreneurs' satisfaction regarding the tourism product standard.
	◦ Building permits.
	◦ Press tourism reports; ◦ Tourism reports in Villarrica – Pucón area; ◦ Index of skilled workers remuneration; ◦ Price index in peak season; ◦ Price index in low season; ◦ Price change (inflation) and: Increase of price (Room in three stars hotel) in high season; ◦ Increase of jobs in high season; ◦ Tourist expenses in season; ◦ Incomes in peak / low season; ◦ Satisfaction level regarding tourist services.
	◦ Land value in the lake shore zone.
	◦ Seasonality of demand.
	◦ Argentine market dependence (% of Argentine tourists).

Social/ cultural environment	<ul><li>Number of local artisans;</li><li>Number of authorized artisans / artisans in peak season;</li><li>Aboriginal population / community population;</li><li>Number of projects for Mapuche communities;</li><li>Aboriginal projects investments / total investment.</li></ul>
	<ul><li>Aboriginal land area reduction.</li></ul>
	<ul><li>Number of complaints for maltreatment;</li><li>Polls on satisfaction among local residents;</li><li>Number of students following tourism program education / scholar population.</li></ul>
	<ul><li>Number of complaints regarding lack of service;</li><li>Number of accidents involving tourism activities;</li><li>Number of accidents with tourist participation.</li></ul>
	<ul><li>Number of participants in meetings related with tourism programs.</li></ul>
	<ul><li>Waiting times in high / low season;</li><li>Number of vehicles per hour in high / low season.</li></ul>
	<ul><li>Number of crimes in high / low season;</li><li>Number of arrested people in high / low season;</li><li>Number of crimes denunciation in high / low season;</li><li>Number of crimes / population.</li></ul>
	<ul><li>Trained staff;</li><li>Number of trained contracted staff / number of total trained staff.</li></ul>
	<ul><li>Hotel occupancy;</li><li>Percentage of rural residences with potable water.</li></ul>
	<ul><li>Tourism employment in high / low season;</li><li>Permanent /not permanent population.</li></ul>
	<ul><li>Registered associated entrepreneurs.</li></ul>

Principal lessons of this experience

The identification of sustainability indicators in the zone of Villarrica lake was a very useful experience for all participants in the workshop.

The main conclusions and lessons learned are the following:

1. The participants agreed on the need to prepare a data base along with a register and collection system for key environmental information. This was considered to be a basic requisite to provide data in order to make regular comparisons on the changes that affect the tourism environment;

2. The participation of scientists, academics, and researchers from non-governmental organizations has been a determinant of the workshop success. Their knowledge and information on the problems, both regarding economic activities and for tourism, was critical to reaching agreement on the sustainability indicators most important to the area;

3. The identification of sustainability indicators must be related to the image of the region, and this is a key aspect of local planning. In the region there was little experience with the use of indicators for the sustainable management of tourism industry;

4.   Although the local authority focuses on intensive urban and rural land development, it has no detailed information on the environmental impact of the tourism industry. It does not have either support to develop a monitoring program or the resources to support indicator validation;

5.   The private entrepreneurs who are pioneers in the area are very knowledgeable that their business is directly related to conservation of the area's natural resources. However not everyone comprehends clearly the level of risk to the image and ability of tourism to attract visitors if the resource is degraded. In consequence, there is still a growing pressure to attract real estate capital and promote growth, without being clear on possible impacts;

6.   The local community is convinced that the tourism industry has capacity to offer new employment and to offset trends of migration into the cities. Ecotourism and agro-tourism products have been developed as family business and tourism is viewed as means to both bring benefits as having the potential to affect the local environment (both positively and negatively);

7.   The participants in the workshop proposed a cluster of indicators so that the local authorities could establish a program of regular measurement. However, technical capacity to develop a testing plan and monitoring program at local level does not exist in the region. The responsibility was therefore assumed by the National Tourism Board, through its Regional Board and the Planning Department at the national level.

The Chilean experience in this southern region, rich in tourism assets, has shown the benefits of indicators as a catalyst for participation and definition of the goals for tourism in the region, It has also revealed coordination and information gaps which must also be filled, if sustainable tourism is to be realized.

Tourists visit Osorno Volcano in Chile's Lakes District

6.25 Yacutinga Lodge (Argentina): Indicators for a Private Wildlife Refuge and a Model for Monitoring Physical Trail Conditions

Management Indicators, Community Participation, Ecotourism, Trails, Private Sector

This case shows how a private lodge can use indicators to help in its management of the ecological resources it uses.

The case of Yacutinga Lodge represents an example of how a private business manages ecotourism through indicators applied at a very local level, designed to respond to its own needs and local political, economic, and social factors.   Similar cases are repeated frequently in diverse parts of the world where responsible tourism is practiced, with the private business often being the pioneers in sustainable tourism and use of indicators.   Such initiatives can be catalysts for local community involvement and, provide concrete examples of practical applications supporting regional and industry sustainability.

The Project

Yacutinga Lodge, a private wildlife refuge, is found in the extreme northeast of the Misiones Province of Argentina; 30 km from the famous Iguazú Waterfalls, and adjacent to Andresito town. The Lodge project was initiated in January 1998, and began operations in January 2000. It is designed as a sustainable tourism project, with emphasis on the conservation of the Interior Atlantic Forest phyto-region. Yacutinga Lodge has been developed and administered by private interests, without any type of official economic support. It is supported economically by ecotourism activity, which then permits it to fund biological studies and to implement environmental improvements on the Natural Reserve areas, as well as to support initiatives by the local community.

The region where the project is located has being suffering intense environmental pressure. Poor land use practices have resulted in soil degradation, areas of desertification, deforestation, contamination of water, and pollution from poor use of agro-chemicals. A lack of diversity in agricultural production and poor levels of education in the region have also contributed to the problems. As recently as 20 years ago, the area was covered by extensive native forests; these have now been extensively removed or degraded.

Yacutinga Lodge, because of its sustainable management focus has helped to protect one of the last relics of this forest ecosystem in the northeast of Misiones Province, Argentina. Its initiative gave support to actions to protect the paranaense forest habitat, and helped to built a "green belt" from east to west encompassing the Iguazú National Park and the Puerto Península Forest Reserve,. It has also been a catalyst for other private tourism projects (see Box 2.13 the Iguazu Forest Natural Reserve. At the same time, Yacutinga Lodge contributes to employment for the neighbouring community, and provides an example of the potential of sustainable resource management in the region.

The Yacutinga Lodge management is divided into three working teams. 1. Accommodation services, 2. Environmental protected areas and 3. Tours, trips, circuits and transportation.

The project has implemented the following actions to help with ecotourism sustainability:

In the social area: an environmental school, employee training (from local community), generation of jobs for residents of the local community, environmental awareness of local community, and self-sufficient gardens (rural diversity of production).

In the environmental area: A breeding program for Carpinchos (capibaras - Hydrochaeris hydrochaeris) for its re-introduction; a program of rehabilitation for degraded environments, with native trees produced in the lodge gardens, a jaguar project, a project on classification of wild orchids; inventories of reptiles, amphibians, lepidoptera, and birds in the reserve; studies on specific issues including mimicry of some diurnal butterflies, amphibians and reptilians in the high stratum of the forest (new for Argentina) and a study of tourist load and stress.

The statistics which have been developed for Yacutinga Lodge, have been generated by the company itself and are used primarily to determine the needs of the visitor, the needs of conservation and sustainable use of its environmental reserve and to support concrete contributions for the local community.

Management indicators used:

Related to tourist activities

1.   Measurement of visitor satisfaction: is obtained through:

   * Visitors reports (analysis of activities use and acceptance by visitors);
   * Book of comments,
   * Reports of tourism guides,
   * Reports of travel agencies from visitor's origins (client travel agencies).

2.   Knowledge of the market (demand and offering): data is obtained through:

   * Polls of market: socio-demographic indicators of clients at the Lodge reception; and regular interviews with national and international tour operators in tourism fairs (e.g., ITB - Berlín, FIT - Buenos Aires; FITUR - Madrid,);
   * Reports of travel agencies from visitor's origins (using internet).

Related to conservation activities

1.   Measurement of biodiversity and critical ecosystems situation: the data is obtained from:

   * Biological inventories;
   * Constant registration of observations of indicator species.

2.   Impacts on soil:

   * Indicators of environmental stress in interpretation paths: vegetation cover of soil :loss of soil (m^3, using the methodology of the Argentinian Wildlife Foundation); census of problems (weathering, gullies or furrows, enlargement of paths, parallel paths, deficiencies of infrastructure, over-exposed roots).   (See the specific methods on this which are contained at the end of this case.

Related to social relationships

1.   Local employment generated by the project.

2.   Level of aid to local businessmen: obtaining data through:

   * Interaction with the Municipality;
   * Interviews with locals;
   * Polls of land use and agricultural investments in the area.

3. Attitude of local community: the attitude of community is known through:

    *   Interaction with the Municipality;

    *   Interviews with locals;

    *   Contributions of Yacutinga Lodge employees.

4. Level of local participation in ecotourism activities of Yacutinga Lodge:

    *   Interviews with locals (it has been useful to understand traditional building systems).

These data have been collected regularly since the start of the project in 1998, and results of the analysis is provided to recognized institutions upon request.

Results and obstacles for the project:

1. Indicators are remarkably useful in decision making and lodge planning. Furthermore, indicators have acted as a key factor in the positive evolution of the tourism business and its sustainable operation.

2. The employed methodologies (interviews, questionnaires, bibliographic consultation, as well as direct observation) have resulted in little costs for materials and labour.

3. The contribution with other institutions (technical support of the Argentine Wildlife Foundation in using environmental indicators, and a study on tourism stress) reinforces management with the indicators used.

4. Indicators have enabled generation of statistics that are fundamental to defining the course of the business and the policy for ecotourism operations.

5. The constant collection of indicators has been of vital importance to indicate if the path chosen was correct, or if there was a need to change or to adapt the management plan of Yacutinga Lodge.

6. The indicators, as ongoing tools, are fundamental for quick analysis of situations relative to the adequate or inadequate use of the protected area of Yacutinga Lodge.

7. Indicators are an ongoing program providing up to date information.

8. As long as the project evolves, there will be a need to continuously adapt the data collecting systems of Yacutinga Lodge.

9. The statistics used from the beginning of the project, though they were superficial served to delineate its main characteristics.

10. Our system of participatory monitoring of the project is not yet applicable in all the working teams, except the application of indicators in environmental monitoring. All statistics and indicators of visitor satisfaction are handled for the moment at the managerial level. It is expected that in the mid term, a statistical and indicators system can be instituted which will involve the majority of the personnel affected.

11. The main obstacles for the sustainable management of ecotourism utilizing indicators are the lack of credible prior statistics; lack of sustainability awareness of the municipal authorities; and lack of financing for this type of management.

12. If Iguazú waterfall and the rural zone where the project is located is considered as a major destination, unfortunately the catalytic effect has yet had little impact at the governmental and political level. At this scale there remains a clear lack of policies on sustainable use of the zone at the municipal level. Extensive

Yacutinga trails

extraction is still encouraged and there is insufficient investment in environmental and general education. The opportunity to support sustainability at this scale has not been realized.

Applied Indicators for Trails and Recreation Areas

(Yacutinga Lodge Private Wildlife Reserve and Argentinian Wildlife Foundation)

(Keywords: monitoring, trail management, participatory reporting)

This detailed case shows the practical application of some specific indicators, including measurement methods for changes in trails conditions.

In order to understand the dynamics of the changes that take place over the course of a season of use the following procedures have been put in place for Yacutinga.

1.   On the trails, the following will be recorded: a) ground cover and b) soil loss, as well as , impact events observed, such as flooded areas, gullying, and exposed roots. Records are kept of any corrective measures are implemented on the path, its condition should also be monitored over the season of use. Specifically, monitoring of soil loss at fixed points is recommended.

2.   At recreational areas the following are recorded: a) ground flooding, b) ground cover, c) erosion events.

As well as monitoring physical conditions, information is collected regarding the use of each area, including a record of the use of trails, recreational areas, and docks, specifying the number of visitors that use each site.

The methodology for collection of data during the season of intensive use is given below, along with characteristics of the indicators and data sheets.

Breakdown of data collected, by indicator:

Soil loss

A record is kept of the volume of soil lost. This is done by taking vertical measurements along a transect across the trail. This transect should be placed at a site where it can be marked as accurately as possible for successive measurements (since the most important information is the variation among the samples taken at different dates). Using the data from all the measurements, it is possible to estimate the soil volume missing from the trail section using a standard calculation based on changes in profile relative to a horizontal taut line. (See Box 6.44)

Box 6.47 Measuring Trail Impacts

Note: In order to avoid errors in successive measurements, it is recommended that the first measurement (V1) starting on the left side (assuming one is facing away from the trail entrance closest to the lodge).

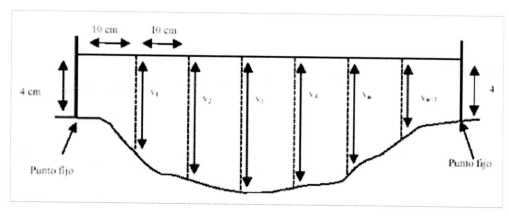

Measurement of trail cross-sectional area under a transect.

Sampling method (Cole 1983): The placement of the transect is done by determining two fixed points on either side of the trail (10cm from where the greatest change in vegetation and/or the trail cut is observed). Stakes are placed at both points. A line is established across the trail (2.50m long for trails and 4m for the path) using a rope tied to each stake at a fixed height of 5cm above the ground. The rope must be taut. With the aid of a plumb line, vertical measurements are taken at intervals of 10cm (trails) and 20cm (path) from the transect, as shown in the above diagram (there should be at least 20 vertical measurements per transect). The line may be fitted with a ring so it can slide along the rope, which could be marked with the intervals, that is, the rope could have marks every 10cm/20cm. At the next data collection, the rope must be placed at the same height and the measurement should be started at the same side as before.

Data collection sites: Chico Mendes, Guazú and Timbó trails; and the Main Path.

Distribution of transects: see table.

Number of transects per trail: 4.

Materials required: Metal stakes, rope, plumb line, measuring tape, data sheets, pencil.

Ground cover

The percentage of the trail covered by vegetation (grass or clover), fallen leaves and organic litter (made up of fallen leaves, twigs, and stems whether still distinguishable or pulverized). In this respect, guides and groundskeepers have an essential role. Their frequent passage allows them to observe how this parameter varies over the course of a season. This is important because the presence of some kind of covering vegetation protects the soil, as it facilitates water infiltration and acts as a "cushion" against footfalls or falling rain (thus preventing soil particles from being dislodged).

Sampling method

A measuring tape 2m long is extended across the trail to form the transect. The number of centimetres occupied by each variable is noted: organic litter, bare soil, vegetation, within the 2m section.

Trails where this data are collected: Chico Mendes; Guazú; Pastura.

Distribution of transects: each meter, depending on the trail. See table.

Number of transects per trail: 10.

Materials required: Measuring tape, pencil, data sheet.

Problem census

In contrast to a sampling, where measurements are taken of a sample of specific indicators (at specific locations), a census is meant to locate and characterize all the indicators described above within a certain areas. In the case of a problem census, the objective is to obtain a record of all the unacceptable conditions present on the trails or other use areas, principally problems associated with the condition of the ground and the vegetation.

In this respect, guides and groundskeepers have a very important role; they must be informed of what is considered an unacceptable condition (problem), so that they can detect such problems (especially in their beginning stages, to see how they develop) during their rounds. So, when a guide notices some kind of problem on the trail, for example, an area that shows flooding that persists for several days, he notes it on the data sheet specifying its approximate location and size.

The following are descriptions of conditions considered to be problems and list of data to be noted:

Gullies or grooves: If gullies (even if they are just starting, more than 3cm deep) are observed, the following data are to be recorded: length, approximate depth, and if flowing water was observed.

Flooding: If signs of flooding are observed, the approximate size of the affected area and its location on the trail are to be recorded. On a rainy day, all of the ground on the trail may be wet, with a great deal of mud, but it may be possible to see water staying on the surface in certain sectors, meaning that it is not draining into the ground. It is important to take this into account after heavy rain.

Exposed roots: On the Chico Mendes trail, there are many exposed roots, and in general, they do not represent a tripping hazard. It is necessary to identify highly exposed roots, especially when they form "bridges" (that is, when part of the root is not resting on the ground). Although the evolution of root exposure is expected to be more noticeable over successive seasons, it is still useful to take this indicator into account over the course of a season.

Trail widening / Parallel trails: Sections where the trail becomes too wide (when the widening is considerable, that is, more than 1m), or where trails parallel to the main trail are detected should be identified. Due to the characteristics of the vegetation (thick and intertwined) and the good condition of the ground on the trails, this problem is not very likely to occur; however, it is good to take it into account because it is a very frequent problem, especially in very wet areas.

Deficiencies in infrastructure: when a problem is detected in the infrastructure of the trails, for example: broken boards on the bridge, clogged drains.

Box 6.48 lists the indicators, the sampling unit, the sampling method, and the number of samples to be taken on each trail:

Box 6.48 Trail impact indicators, Yacutinga

Trail	Indicators	Sampling Unit / Distribution	Method	Number of samples
Chico Mendes	Soil loss	4 fixed points. Placed where the greatest trail incision is observed.	Cole 1983	1 at the start of the season
	Ground cover	Transects at 100m intervals	Intercept Line	1 September 1 December 1 March
	Impact events	Throughout the trail	Problem census	During the season
Guazú	Soil loss	4 fixed points. Placed where the greatest trail incision is observed.	Cole 1983	1 at the start of the season.
	Ground cover	Transects at 200m intervals	Intercept Line	1 September 1 December 1 March
	Impact events	Throughout the trail	Problem census	During the season

Trail	Indicators	Sampling Unit / Distribution	Method	Number of samples
Pastura	Ground cover	Transects at 100m intervals	Intercept Line	1 September 1 December 1 March
	Impact events	Throughout the trail	Problem census	During the season
Timbó	Soil loss	4 fixed points. Placed where the greatest trail incision is observed.	Cole 1983	1 at the start of the season.
	Impact events	Throughout the trail	Problem census	During the season
Tajamar	Impact events	Throughout the trail	Problem census	During the season
San Francisco	Impact events	Throughout the trail	Problem census	During the season
Camino	Soil loss	4 fixed points at critical areas: gullies near Tajamar	Cole 1983	1 at the start of the season.
	Impact events	Throughout the trail	Problem census	During the season
Recreational areas Tajamar, Puerto San Francisco, Puerto Principal, Jardín.				
All	Problems - Impact events	The entire area	Problem census	Throughout the season

Box 6.49 Template for measuring soil loss

Trail: ....
Date: ___/___/___
Name:

T	V1	V2	V3	V4	V5	V6	V7	V8	V9	V10	V11	V12	V13	V14	V15	V16	V17	V18	V19	V20
1																				
2																				
3																				
4																				

Location of Transects (Specify landmark, e.g., *Marmelero* near the entrance)
T1:
T2:
T3:
T4:
Ground Condition (general description of the ground on the trail: *wet, very wet, muddy, dry, etc.*)
Climate:
Observations:

Remember: It is essential to properly record the place where the measurement was taken, that is to say, to properly measure the distance from the stake to the point of the first measurement, and the subsequent measurements (which is why it would be good to pre-mark the rope and re-use it). The reference points (where the stakes are positioned) should remain fixed, and should be relatively easy to find, because the end-of-season measurements have to be taken at the same place and at the same points.

IMPORTANT!!! In order to avoid errors in successive measurements, it is recommended that the first measurement (V1) starts on the left side (assuming one is facing away from the trail entrance closest to the lodge).

Box 6.50 Template for monitoring ground cover

Trail: Chico Mendes
Date: ___ / ___ / ___
Name:

Point	September			December			March		
	Vegetation	Organic litter	Bare ground	Vegetation	Organic litter	Bare ground	Vegetation	Organic litter	Bare ground
1									
2									
3									
4									
5									
6									
7									
8									
9									
10									

Observations:

....
....
....
....

Box 6.51   Template for monitoring number of persons per trail and problem documentation

Date Day/ month	Trail	Number of persons 1			Problems?2 Flooding (A); Gullying (C); Exposed roots (RE); trail widening (E) / Parallel trails (SP)

This case is a practical field example of data collection and use, and shows the level of attention which may be required to support an indicator.

[1] If a guide has already recorded the name of a trail and another guide uses the same trail on the day, specify only the number of persons in another column.

[2] If a problem was observed, note down its approximate location on the trail (a landmark). The abbreviations given in parenthesis may be uses.

Further information www.yacutinga.com and www.vidasilvestre.org.ar

Lodge gardens Yacutinga

Part 7

Conclusions

Indicators are a strategic tool for the sustainable development of tourism destinations. In this Guidebook, experts from around the world, gathered by the World Tourism Organization (WTO), have tried to provide the ideas, approaches and substance to assist destinations in their steps towards sustainability. The authors hope that this publication will become a useful reference, and be kept accessible as a source of inspiration, technical guidelines, tools and application examples. This will help destination managers, communities and all stakeholders to work together for the future of their destination.

7.1 Key messages on the use of indicators

Readers are reminded in this concluding section of several key messages:

* Indicators are tools, providing accurate information for decision-making, leading to implementation of solutions, development of partnerships, better planning and management. They are not an end in themselves, but rather signals of important trends and changes, a catalyst for discussion on future plans, risks to the destination, and impacts on what is important to all. They can also serve as performance measures for progress towards sustainability.

* Indicators are not a one-time procedure. They are most useful when measured repeatedly and consistently through long term monitoring programs. Only when information is available over time, on a regular basis, can the most effective use of indicators occur, providing context for the understanding of changes and their importance to policy priorities.

* Indicators must be integrated into decision-making processes. Sustainable tourism development requires good information, and integrated approaches to management, supported by the right indicators. The objective of indicators development is not solely the measurement of factors, production of tables, or publication of reports, but better decision-making for the sustainable development of the destination. Indicators, therefore, should be an integral part of planning, management and monitoring processes.

* Indicators must be shared. Information generated by government authorities with different mandates and at different levels, by different private and civil sector organizations or through research, can be all important for sustainable tourism indicators and for the decisions which indicators support. Indicators at local levels can be building blocks for indicators applications at regional and national levels. Making indicators accessible is the only route to informed decision-making and involvement of all stakeholders in the decision process.

* Indicators empower destinations, providing the information needed to negotiate future investments, development standards, joint ventures, and the sharing of benefits. They also support approaches to consensus on what is important to sustain and how to achieve it - such as the limits to acceptable change.

7.2 Roles and Challenges for Stakeholders

All stakeholders need to participate in the definition and implementation of plans and actions to support sustainability goals. The generation and maintenance of indicators as key building blocks requires ongoing action at all levels.

National Authorities

National governments are central to the development and use of indicators at all levels. If indicators are generated in consistent ways at the destination level they can often be aggregated to produce national or regional indicators. Comparative use of indicators among destinations can show trends and anomalies, and assist in targeting programs to address these. Often national level support (financial and technical) is essential for destinations to be able to create and support indicators programs, and in the implementation of plans and solutions. Effective indicators often may tier upwards providing useful information at all levels. The WTO works with Member States to help establish sustainable tourism programs and support their efforts; this Guidebook is one of the tools available to them. The challenge for national authorities is to support destinations in their efforts to apply sustainability indicators, and where possible, to create a national program to integrate and utilize the results.

Regional Authorities

The participation of regional authorities needs to be encouraged. Often key resources central to tourism as well as the information about them is managed regionally, at the level of a province, state, canton or region. Maintaining full participation and partnership is important throughout the initial indicators development and for ongoing monitoring. The challenge to regional authorities and ministries is to participate in indicators work, and to facilitate information sharing among their destinations.

Destination (Municipal) Authorities

The destination authority is central to indicators application, because the local destination is the level where most issues and their solutions occur, the place where host communities and tourists interact, where there is proximity of stakeholder groups, and where the compromises need to be understood and made. Because so many policy and operational decisions occur at this level, full participation and support of the destination authorities is critical. Destination authorities should be the catalyst and principal coordinators for indicators development and application integrated into strategic destination planning and sustainability programmes.

Community members

The full involvement of the community throughout the process is important. A challenge can be to engage all elements of the community, and to find means to maintain engagement through an often lengthy process. The community is also important to the maintenance of indicators - and some of the most successful long term monitoring programs succeed due to ongoing demands by the community for information and ongoing participation in the monitoring program. The community can also be an important advocate for changes based on their access to and use of the indicators information.

NGOs

Non-governmental organizations can be a stimulus for indicators programs and a participant and customer for the results. Many NGOs have expertise which can help in indicators programs, including the support of participatory processes. The challenge for some NGOs is to be seen to be a constructive participant rather than just a critic and to be able to mobilize sufficient resources to support ongoing participation. As well, NGOs are often visible advocates who can effectively use the results of indicators to constructively lobby for action in support of sustainability for destinations and for key assets of these destinations.

The academic community

Many indicators begin as measurements done through scientific research. The academic community has been important in initiating indicator studies, developing methodological tools and generating information. Too often, however, academic studies have been one time initiatives, the initial study of a problem and the establishment of baseline information, but without follow up through linear studies and monitoring. A challenge for the academic community is to obtain sufficient resources to support an ongoing role in implementation of key indicators, as well as applied research on the validation of indicators and the evaluation of their impact. Another need is for academic institutions to transform information generated through scientific research into forms where it can be easily understood and used in policy making by practitioners. Finally, in order for future tourism professionals to be familiar with the need for indicators and the practices of monitoring, academic and training institutions should include in tourism studies curricula, cases and methodologies for development and use of indicators.

Tourism enterprises

The private sector has an important role to play in both indicators development and in the effective use of indicators. Many of the most used indicators are gathered from hotels, restaurants, guides and tour operators. Many have their own indicators which are in use on a regular basis. The challenge for tourism enterprises, national and foreign, inbound and outbound, is to find the time to participate effectively in indicators initiatives in each destination, as a contributor to the design and implementation of programs, providers of information and data, as well as in the use of the results.

Tourists

Tourists also have a role to play, both as a source of information and as a user of indicators. At the point of generation of information, tourists are the source, and without their active participation in exit surveys, response to polls and specific studies, many indicators will not be possible. Informed tourists can be important customers for the information; when tourists are seen to explicitly request information on an indicator (e.g. is the water clean; how safe is the city; do the residents benefit from this development?) they help to validate the use of the indicator by all levels of government and other stakeholders. A key challenge remains in making certain that information useful to the tourists is available, understandable and useful to their decisions on where to go and what to do.

World Tourism Organization and other international bodies

WTO has made a commitment to work with nations and destinations to promote the sustainable development of tourism. This document is one of the building blocks and offers a technical tool in these efforts. With rapid growth in tourism, and destinations worldwide, it will be an ongoing challenge to keep pace, and to be able to keep tools like this book current. As electronic communication spreads, it will become easier to establish ongoing contact and networking between destinations worldwide, to facilitate the sharing of experiences on the use indicators and promote sustainable forms of tourism. The challenge for WTO and other international bodies will be to keep abreast with these changes and new experiences, and continue to provide current information and tools to those who can best influence the future of tourism and its destinations.

Tourism is a rapidly changing sector, with new products, new destinations, and new demands for experiences from tourists. As a result, at all levels there will be changes requiring new and better information, and new types of indicators which can respond to policy issues. Indicators are both important to help sensitize decision-makers to these trends, and to help them understand their importance. Better information can be the key to better decisions. Indicators are the essential instrument which can help destinations to more clearly see and understand the issues, and help managers and stakeholders define and implement the solutions which are most likely to lead to sustainable development for tourism destinations.

Authors and Contributors

Note: Biographic information has been provided by the authors

- **Gustavo A. Bassotti** is Director, Tourism Promotion Department of Universal Forum of Cultures Barcelona 2004 and is a nature and marketing tourism consultant. He has worked in ecotourism and aboriginal projects in Argentina, quality development in tourism throughout Spain, and directed the tourism promotion of Forum Barcelona 2004. He is an advisor on ecotourism indicators and ecotourism quality standards as a way to reach sustainability.

  Author: 4.6 Natural and Sensitive Ecological Sites; 6.17 Lanzarote Biosphere Strategy, Natural Reserve, Box 2.14 Iguazú Forest; Co-author: 3.7.1 Protecting Critical Ecosystems 4.7 Ecotourism 6.10, El Garraf Natural Park; 6.9 Chiminos Island Lodge,: 6.25 Yacutinga Lodge (Argentina) Indicators for a Private Wildlife Refuge.

- **Christian Baumgartner** is Director, Institute for Integrative Tourism and Development, Vienna Austria. Dr. Baumgartner specializes in monitoring and evaluating sustainability processes. He also coordinates the scientific advisory board to the Austrian Strategy for Sustainable Development.

  Co-author: 4.13 Urban Tourism, Box 4.8 Heidelberg Germany's Ecological Food Program.

- **Christine Beddoe** is a Consultant and Researcher, Melbourne Australia. Ms. Beddoe was co-author of the WTO report on The Incidence of Sexual Exploitation of Children in Tourism.

  Author: 3.1.5 Sex Tourism.

- **Rajiv Bhartari** from the Indian Forest Service is Conservator of Forests Bhagirathi Circle & Ecotourism with Govt. of Uttaranchal and ex officio Director Ecotourism in Uttaranchal Tourism Development Board. He is also a member of the Board of Directors, The International Ecotourism Society and member IUCN World Commission on Protected Areas. He has established the Center for Ecotourism and Sustainable Livelihoods, conducted training programmes for ecotourism and interpretation, coordinated the LEAD Fellows Project "Development of Framework for Corbett Binsar Nainital Multi Stakeholder Project for Biodiversity Conservation and Tourism" and initiated community based tourism in over two dozen villages in Uttaranchal.

  Author: 6.13 India: Community Based Tourism in Corbett National Park.

- **Amos Bien** is Director, International Programs, International Ecotourism Society, San Jose Costa Rica. Mr. Bien is President of the Costarican Natural Reserve Network, Professor, Masters of Ecotourism Program at the University of International Cooperation, and author of many works on certification for ecotourism.

  Co-author: 5.6 Indicators and Certification.

- **Herman Bos** is a partner with Tourism Strategy Consultants, Voorschoten, The Netherlands. Mr. Bos served as Director of Research of the Netherlands Board of Tourism & Conventions and has written extensively on tourism strategy and policy.

  Author: Box 3.45 Conversion Studies, Box 3.36: Measuring the Real Return on Investments in Marketing Activities, Co author: 3.12.3 Marketing for Sustainable Tourism.

- **Rafael Bolivar** has been extensively working on the Strategic Tourism Plan of the Canary Islands, at the Canary Islands Tourism Observatory, Ministry of Tourism and Transport of the Regional Government of the Canary Islands, Spain.

  Author: 6.6 Canary Islands (Spain): A Planning Model for a Mature Destination.

- **Robyn Bushell** is Associate Professor and Head, Tourism for Healthy Futures, University of Western Sydney, NSW Australia. She serves on numerous international and national bodies, including Vice Chair Tourism Task Force, World Commission for Protected Areas, IUCN. She researches tourism planning, relationship between tourism, health, quality of life and community development in particular; indigenous communities; conservation of cultural and biological diversity; interpretation in conservation education; visitor impact and environmental management.

Author: 3.5.1 Health, 3.5.2 Epidemics and International Transmission of Diseases, Box 2.4 On-line Consultation in Australia, Box 3.31 Managing Scarce Resources: Water Consumption - Byron Bay; Co-author: 3.5.4 Local Public Safety, 3.8.4 Drinking Water Quality, Box 3.8 Turtle Island -Tourism and Community Health.

* **Alejandra Carminati** is Director of Programa Refugios de Vida Silvestre - Fundación Vida Silvestre Argentina, Buenos Aires Argentina. With Mr. Moreno, Lic. Carminati has implemented the Wildlife Refuges programme of Fundación Vida Silvestre Argentina (1987), as an alternative to support local and rural economies and to protect wildlife areas with special interest.

Co-author: 6.25 Yacutinga Lodge (Argentina): Indicators for a Private Wildlife Refuge.

* **Jean Mehdi Chapoutot** is Directeur de la Qualité, Office National du Tourisme Tunisien and teaches tourism courses at several Tunisian institutes of higher learning. Dr. Chapoutot has written extensively on tourism planning and management topics relating to Tunisia and to broader Mediterranean issues including environmental, cultural and economic aspects of tourism development.

Author: 6.22 Tunisia: Indicators and Standards for Tourism.

* **Adrien Chatenay** is Sustainable Development Project Manager, Accor Tourism & Leisure Paris France. He is responsible for improving the sustainability of Accor Tourism & Leisure hotels (200 hotels and resorts worldwide). His areas of interest include environmental management and environmental good practices, corporate training and facilitation, as well as partnerships with social and environmental organisations. He is the co-author of Development of Tourism Policy and Strategic Planning in East Timor (2001) and winner of the 2000 PATA Young Tourism Professional Award.

Author: 6.1 Accor Hotels Environmental Sustainability Indicators.

* **David Chernushenko** is President, Green & Gold Inc., Ottawa, Ontario, Canada. Mr. Chernushenko advises the sport, recreation and tourism sectors on sustainable management practices and new business opportunities. He is a member of the Sport and Environment Commission of the International Olympic Committee.

Author: Box 3.41 Excerpts from: Sustainable Sports Management; Co-author: 3.1.2 Managing Events.

* **CITTIB** (Centre for Tourism Research and Technologies of the Balearic Islands) is part of the Institute of Tourism Strategy (INESTUR), of the Tourism Council of the Government of the Balearic Islands, Spain. CITTIB promotes tourism research and studies in the Balearic Islands, at the European and global levels, analyzing tourism demand and source markets, competing destinations, statistical information, indicators on tourism's impacts and new technologies. The Centre is also in charge of an integrated system of tourism information and documentation service (www.finestraturistica.org).

CITTIB provided the case study 6.5 Balearic Islands (Spain): Integrated Tourism Management through Sustainability Indicators.

* **Gordon Clifford** is a Principal Consultant with Consulting and Audit Canada, Ottawa, Ontario, Canada. Mr. Clifford is a tourism researcher who has worked on the WTO indicators program since 1994, as a facilitator and researcher at workshops held in Hungary, Croatia and Sri Lanka. He is author of a large number of studies on tourism planning and use of indicators.

Author: Box 4.6 Camino de Santiago; Co-author: 3:13.1 Sustainability and Environmental Management Policies and Practices at Tourism Businesses and critical reviewer of the methodology sections.

* **Terry De Lacy** is Chief Executive, Sustainable Tourism Cooperative Research Centre, Griffith University, Gold Coast Queensland Australia, a partnership between universities and government with research programs in travel and tourism, environment, infrastructure, technology, business and management. Previously Prof. De Lacy was Dean of the Faculty of Land and Food Systems at the University of Queensland where he holds a continuing chair in environmental policy. He has extensive research and project experience in Asia, in particular China.

Co-author 3.8.1 Energy Management, 3.9.2 Solid Waste Management, Box 3.26 Energy Consumption, and Box 3.3 Solid Waste Reduction –Douglas Shire Queensland Australia.

* **Ann Dom** is Project Manager Sustainable Development / Sector Integration for the European Union and specialist in indicators programs. She was a significant contributor to the initial stages of design of the project through participating at the initial expert meeting held at WTO, Madrid, in March 2003.

Toni Duka is Project Manager, Kangaroo Island TOMM, Kingscote, SA Australia. She is a long-time resident of Kangaroo Island and is project manager for the TOMM project managing indicator development and monitoring and facilitating the ongoing implementation of the program. She has a background in environmental management and community development and is also a Community Development Officer on Kangaroo Island.

Co-author: 6.14 Kangaroo Island Tourism Optimisation Management Model (TOMM).

Ghislain Dubois is Managing Director, Tourism Environment Consultants (TEC), Marseille, France. His fields of expertise are sustainable transport, climate change (evaluation of past and future impacts, future studies), environmental impact mitigation policies (voluntary agreements, incentives, tradable permits, public policies...), environment and sustainable tourism indicators. He is involved in various European networks on sustainable tourism development. Box 3.29: Tourism and Climate Change: Adapting Indicators to Targeted French Stakeholders; Contributor to 3.8.2 Climate Change, and contributor to Chapter 2 methodology.

Andrew Fairley is a social entrepreneur, Turtle Island Resort, Fiji.

Co-author: Box 3.8 Turtle Island: Tourism & Community Health.

Zoila González Macias is Director, Sustainable Tourism, Association of Caribbean States (ACS). The association with its Headquarters in Port of Spain, Trinidad and Tobago actively promotes sustainable tourism practices to facilitate the integrated development of the Greater Caribbean. Within the framework of the Convention for Sustainable Tourism (2001), and the Sustainable Tourism Zone of the Caribbean (STZC), ACS has created a specific program on sustainable tourism indicators. ACS provided the case study: 6.8 Caribbean Tourism Indicators Initiative.

Eileen Gutierrez is Manager, Ecotourism Department, Conservation International (CI), Washington DC, USA. With an MA, Tourism, George Washington University School of Business, she is a sustainable and ecotourism development specialist with experience in Africa, Asia, Latin America and the Caribbean. She supports CI regional programs with strategy design and project development, including policy, planning, assessments, product development, as well as by managing ecotourism training and capacity building programmes.

Author: Box 3.16 Monitoring Gudwiga Camp Project.

Malika Hamza is a consultant for the tourism and hospitality industry, Brussels Belgium. She specializes in the coordination of international projects and in working with tourism, culture and heritage issues in the perspective of sustainable development. She has extensive knowledge of integrated quality management for tourist destinations.

Author: 3.11.4 Tourism-related Transport.

Henryk Handszuh is Head of the Quality and Trade in Tourism Department, World Tourism Organization.

Author: 3.6.2 Leakages, co-author: 3.5.3 Tourist Security, contributor to 3.5.4 Local Public Safety.

Donald E. Hawkins is Eisenhower Professor of Tourism Policy, George Washington University School of Business Washington DC, USA. Dr. Hawkins is Chairman of the Management Committee of the International Institute of Tourism Studies and a professor in the Department of Tourism and Hospitality Management at George Washington University.

Co-author: 5.1 Indicators and Policy.

Martha Honey is Executive Director, International Ecotourism Society and Center for Ecotourism and Sustainable Development. She is author of Ecotourism and Certification: Setting Standards in Practice (2002), Ecotourism and Sustainable Development: Who Owns Paradise? (1999), and Protecting Paradise: Certification Programs for Sustainable Tourism and Ecotourism (2001, with Abigail Rome). In 2000, she organized the conference on "green" tourism certification at the Mohonk Mountain House in New York. For twenty years she worked as journalist, based first in Tanzania and then in Costa Rica.

Co-author: 5.6 Indicators and Certification.

Elizabeth Jack is Proprietor, Centre of Sustainable Tourism, White Gum Valley, Western Australia. She runs her own advisory service and has an interest in the social impact of tourism on communities and the role of the private sector in building capacity. She is a board member of Ecotourism Australia and advisor to the Kangaroo Island TOMM project.

Author: 3.3.1 Community Involvement and Awareness, Box 3.7 Building Ownership: Kangaroo Island and Co-author 6.1.4 Kangaroo Island Tourism Optimisation Management Model (TOMM).

Walter Jamieson is Dean, School of Travel Industry Management, University of Hawaii, Honolulu, Hawaii, USA. He has a strong interest in responsible tourism, cultural tourism, use of tourism as a tool for poverty reduction and environmental management systems in tourism facilities.

Co-author: 5.1 Indicators and Policy.

Fergus T. Maclaren is Senior Consultant, Sustainable Development and Environmental Management, Consulting and Audit Canada, Ottawa, Ontario, Canada. Mr. Maclaren consults on a range of sustainable development issues, including tourism, with a Canadian federal government agency. Mr. Maclaren was the former Director of the International Year of Ecotourism with The International Ecotourism Society, and a board member for ICOMOS Canada and the Sustainable Tourism Stewardship Council.

Author: 3.2.1 Protecting Cultural Sites and Monuments, 4.11 Built Heritage Sites, Box 3.6 UNESCO: Protecting the World's Heritage Box 4.7 George Town, Penang, Malaysia.

Edward (Ted) Manning is President, Tourisk Inc., Sustainable Destinations, Ottawa Ontario Canada. Dr. Manning is lead consultant to WTO on the indicators program and is a consultant on sustainable tourism and environmental management for destinations. Former Executive Manager of Sustainable Tourism for Tourism Canada, and Director Sustainable Development for Consulting and Audit Canada, he has managed studies and workshops on tourism in more than forty countries. He is also an Adjunct Professor of Geography at Carleton University.

Dr. Manning is Lead Editor and Writer for the Guidebook. Author of PART 1 Introduction , PART 2 Indicator Development Procedures, 3.1.1 Local Satisfaction, 3.4.1 Sustaining Tourist Satisfaction, 3.7.2 Sea Water Quality, 3.9.3 Air Pollution, 3.9.4 Controlling Noise Levels, 3.10.1 Controlling Use Intensity, 3.11.2 Development Control, 3.11.3 Managing the Pace of Construction, 4.1 Coastal Zones, 4.3 Small Islands, 4.4 Destinations in Desert and Arid areas, 4.5 Mountain Destinations, 4.8 Parks And Protected Areas, 4.9 Communities Within or Adjacent to Protected Areas, 4.12 Small And Traditional Communities, 4.15 Communities Seeking Tourism Development, 5.3 Indicators and Regulation 5.4 Carrying Capacity, 5.5 Reporting and Accountability, 5.7 Performance Measurement and Benchmarking, 6.7 Cape Breton Island, 6.16 Kukljica Croatia, PART 7 Conclusions, Methodological annexes.   Boxes :1.1-1.8 , 2.12.1-2.9, 2.11, 2,12, 2.14, 2.15, 3.12 Local Impacts of Seasonality, 3.30 Water Supply for Cozumel, 3.35 Indoor Air Pollution, 3.43 Planning and Control in the Maldives,   4.1 Reefs Systems, 4.3   Arctic And Alpine Environments, 4.10 Golf courses 5.3 Characteristics of Indicators and Performance Measures.

Co-author: 3.1.2 Effects of Tourism on Communities, 3.1.3 Access by Local Residents, 3.5.3 Tourist Security, 3.5.4 Local Public Safety, 3.6.1 Tourism Seasonality, 3.7.1 Protecting Critical Ecosystems, 3.8.2 Climate Change and Tourism, 3.8.3 Water Availability and Conservation, 3.8.4 Drinking Water Quality, 3.9.1 Sewage Treatment, 3.11.5 Air Transport, 3.12.2 Providing Variety of Experiences, 3.12.3 Marketing for Sustainable Tourism,   3.13.1 Sustainability and Environmental Management, 4.2 Beach Destinations and Sites, 4.7 Ecotourism destinations, 4.16 Theme Parks, 4.17 Water Parks, 4.18 Cruise Ships and their Destinations.

Jennifer Manning is Coordinator, Bow Valley Conference Centre, Calgary, Alberta, Canada. She is the head coordinator and manager of the centre located in downtown Calgary, and has a degree in sociology, and training in labour and environmental law. She has worked as a tourism researcher and in application of environmental management practices in the Centre. Author: 4.14 Conferences and Convention Centres, Box 4.9 Bow Valley Convention Centre Operational Indicators for Greening; Co-author: 3.6.1 Seasonality, 4.16 Theme Parks, 4.17 Water Parks.

Margo Manning is Chief Executive Officer, Tourisk Inc., Sustainable Destinations Ottawa, Ontario, Canada. She is an environmental and tourism consultant who focuses on participatory processes, tourism research and practical applications of indicators to tourism destinations. Her training is as a librarian and sociologist, and she worked formerly with Environment Canada and with New Zealand's Country Library Service. She has worked on tourism sustainability and environmental training projects in Canada, China, Eastern Europe and Latin America.

Co-editor of the Guidebook, Author: 3.4.2 Accessibility, Box 2.18 Indicators Re-evaluation Checklist, Box 3.32 Beruwala, Sri Lanka, Co-author: 3.8.3 Water Availability and Conservation, 3.9.1 Sewage Treatment, 3.12.2 Providing Variety of Experiences, 4.2 Beach Destinations, 4.18 Cruise Ships And Their Destinations, Compiler of References section and Index.

Robert Manning is Professor, School of Natural Resources University of Vermont, Burlington, Vermont, USA, where he is Chair of the Recreation Management Program. His work focuses on national parks, wilderness, public lands and tourism. His research includes: "Carrying Capacity of U.S. National Parks, "Studies in Outdoor Recreation: Search and Research for Satisfaction," and "Visitor Experience and Resource Protection: A Framework for Managing the Carrying Capacity of National Parks".

Author: 6.4 Arches National Park (USA): Indicators and Standards of Quality for Sustainable Tourism and Carrying Capacity.

Simon McArthur is General Manager, Mawland Hotel Management Crows Nest, NSW, Australia. Dr. McArthur specializes in tourism impact management and has developed and implemented some 15 applications of tourism impact management models in Australia. He is known for adapting the Limits of Acceptable Change Model into the Tourism Optimisation Management Model (TOMM) for Kangaroo Island and the Quarantine Station.

Author: 5.2 Using Indicators to Strategically Plan for Tourism, 6.21 Sydney Quarantine Station (Australia): Applying the Tourism Optimization Management Model.

Hitesh Mehta is an Ecotourism Planning and Ecolodge Design Consultant and Adjunct Professor, Florida Atlantic University. Ft. Lauderdale, FL, USA. Mr. Mehta is an environmental planner, architect and landscape architect, an international expert in the field of sustainable tourism physical planning and ecolodge design. He is the main editor of the book "International Ecolodge Guidelines" and co-wrote the chapters on Site Planning and Architecture.

Author: 3.9.5 Managing the Visual Impacts of Tourism Facilities and Infrastructure, Box 3.37 Lobo Lodge, 3.38 Selected guidelines for infrastructure design, Box 3.39 Means to limit light pollution, Box 3.40 Guidelines for sustainable and sensitive landscaping.

Diego Moreno is Director of "Programa Refugios de Vida Silvestre - Fundación Vida Silvestre Argentina", Buenos Aires – Argentina. With Mrs. Carminati, Lic, Moreno has implemented the Wildlife Refuges programme of Fundación Vida Silvestre Argentina (1987), as an alternative to support local and rural economies and to protect wildlife areas with special interest.

Co-author: 6.25 Yacutinga Lodge (Argentina) Indicators for a Private Wildlife Refuge.

Aurelie Pelletreau is Project Manager, Sustainable Tourism and Indicators Consultants, of Paris, France, in Vientiane, Laos. She worked for the European Environment Agency (EEA) from 2001 to 2003. An expert in sustainable tourism, environmental assessment, indicators and reporting, she authored several publications for the French Institute for the Environment (IFEN) and the European Commission regarding the implementation of an Agenda 21 for European Tourism.

Author: 6.11 European Environmental Agency Indicators.

Carolyn Pharand is a Graduate Student, Centre for Tourism Policy and Research, Simon Fraser University, Burnaby, British Columbia, Canada. Carolyn's research focuses on branding and protection of image in tourism. Co-author: 3.12.4 Protection of the Image of a Destination, 6.20 Super-Natural British Columbia: Assessing Branding Success.

Juan Carlos Pinto Frese is Director Manager of Chiminos Island Lodge, Guatemala. Mr. Pinto is a businessman strongly committed to the Mayan heritage and the environment in Guatemala. His efforts are concentrated on increasing community and tourist awareness about culture, history and nature in El Petén.

Co-author, 6.9 Chiminos Island.

Polytechnic University of Valencia in collaboration with the **Seat for the Study of Mediterranean Wetlands** in Spain have developed a model and case applications on carrying capacity at sensitive ecological sites. Under the leadership of Professor Maria Jose Viñals Blasco, the co authors M. Morant, C. Hernández, C. Ferrer, R. Quintana, N. Maravall, G, Cabrelles, J. Ramis and C. Bachiller contributed the case study 6.2 Albufera de Valencia (Spain): Measuring Carrying Capacity in a Fragile Ecosystem.

Humberto Rivas Ortega is Head of Planning, National Tourism Service, Chile. Mr. Rivas is a Geographer, Magister in Environmental and Human Settlements. His efforts are concentrated in Regional and Local Tourism Planning; Geographic Information System for Tourism Areas; Destination Management and Sustainable Tourism Development.

Author: 6.24 Villarica Lake Area (Chile): Regional Application of Sustainability Indicators.

Valeria Rodríguez Groves is a Scientist for Fundación Vida Silvestre Argentina (FVSA). Buenos Aires, Argentina. She is cooperates with FVSA in several areas, and responsible for the Monitoring Programme for Areas of tourist use.

Author: Applied Indicators section in Yacutinga case, Co Author: 6.25 Yacutinga Lodge, Argentina: Indicators Use in a Private Wildlife Refuge.

* **Amparo Sancho** is a Professor at the Faculty of Economics, University of Valencia, Valencia, Spain. Prof. Dr. Sancho has worked extensively on methods to audit sustainability. She was a contributor to the initial design discussions at the expert meeting held at WTO, Madrid in March 2003.

* **Carlos Sandoval** is Manager, Yacutinga Lodge, Private Wildlife Reserve, Misiones, Argentina. Mr. Sandoval is a pioneer in Argentina in developing private natural areas in a sustainable and community based project, focused on ecotourism. His efforts have been a catalyst for sustainable tourism development in the region.

Co-author: 6.25 Yacutinga Lodge, Argentina: Indicators Use in a Private Wildlife Refuge.

* **Daniel Scott** is Canada Research Chair in Global Change and Tourism, University of Waterloo, Waterloo, Ontario, Canada. Dr. Scott's research on the implications of climate change for the tourism industry has focused on Canada's national park system, the North American ski industry and tourism seasonality. He was a contributing author to the UN Inter-governmental Panel on Climate Change Third Assessment Report and is a co-chair of the International Society of Biometeorology-Commission on Climate Tourism and Recreation.

Author: 6.15 'Keep Winter Cool': Tourism Sector Greenhouse Gas Mitigation, Box 3.28 Snowmaking as an Adaptation to Climate Variability and Change. Contributor to: 3.8.2 Climate Change and Tourism.

* **Kaddu Kiwe Sebunya** is Manager, Africa and Madagascar, Ecotourism Department, Conservation International, Washington DC, USA. Mr. Sebunya conducts strategic analysis, planning and development of sustainable tourism in Africa involving ecotourism feasibility assessments, capacity building program designs, market research and analysis, and enhancing partnerships with governments, private sector, and development agencies. He has worked in countries including: Gabon, Equatorial Guinea, Kenya, Tanzania, Uganda, Madagascar, and Botswana.

Author: 3.6.4 Tourism as a Contributor to Nature Conservation.

* **Lynnaire Sheridan** is a researcher and consultant focused on sustainable tourism and community development issues, Bradbury, NSW, Australia. Most recently she has been based in Baja California, Mexico, researching the impact of cruise ship tourism on this region, designing programs that evaluate the environmental quality of Mexican beaches and undertaking her doctoral studies on the social impacts of undocumented migration across the US – Mexico border.

Author: 3.6.6 Tourism and Poverty Alleviation.

* **Murray Simpson** is a Research Scientist, Oxford University Centre for the Environment, University of Oxford, Oxford, UK. He works as a Tourism Consultant bridging the gaps between research, policy and implementation. He also has over fourteen years experience in the tourism industry at senior management and director level and extensive experience in the public and private sector. His current interests include the interactions between tourism, livelihoods, conservation, biodiversity and sustainability and he has worked in the UK, Europe, Australia, South Africa, the USA, Asia, South America and the Caribbean.

Contributor to 3.8.2 Climate Change and Tourism.

* **Ginger Smith** is Dean, College of Professional Studies and Associate Professor, School of Business and Public Management, Washington, DC, USA. Dr. Smith teaches at George Washington University and served as founding Dean of the International School of Tourism and Hotel Management in Puerto Rico. She represented the U.S on international travel and tourism regarding public affairs, economic development, strategic planning, destination management, environmental best practices and impacts on local communities. She helped to initiate the WTO indictors program in 1993.

Author: 6.19 Sonke South Africa case.

* **Silvia Stuppäck** is Section leader Education, Institute for Integrative Tourism and Development, Vienna, Austria. Mag. Stuppäck worked on an EU-founded project on sustainable urban tourism and specializes in education and training for sustainability.

Co-author: 4.13 Urban Tourism, Box 4.8 Heidelberg Germany's Ecological Food Program.

* **John Tinka** is Field Manager Heritage Trails Uganda (HTU), Kampala Uganda. Mr. Tinka has a special interest in community tourism development and the conservation of cultural and natural heritage. He is a founder member of the Uganda Community Tourism Association (UCOTA). Over the last 5 years, he has implemented a ground breaking, Heritage Trails Project in Uganda.

Author: 6.23 Uganda Heritage Trails.

* **Louise Twining-Ward** is a Tourism Advisor, Wellington, New Zealand. Dr. Twining-Ward is a researcher advisor and author with expertise in sustainable tourism in the South Pacific. Her consulting has included

tourism planning, design of sustainable tourism monitoring systems, writing training manuals, facilitating seminars and participatory planning workshops. Her research interests include monitoring sustainable tourism, stakeholder participation and complex systems.

Author: 3.1.4 Gender Equity, 3.11.1 Integrating Tourism into Local/Regional Planning, Box 2.3 Managing Participatory Processes, Box 2.10 How Many Indicators? Box 2.16 Indicators Make a Difference, and 6.18 Samoa Sustainable Tourism Indicators Project. Contributing editor/reviewer for several sections.

Francois Vellas is Head of Department, Tourism and Air Transport, Institute of International Studies, University of Social Sciences, Toulouse, France. Professor Vellas is an expert in tourism and air transport, and has written extensively on issues related to international tourism, marketing and transportation. He has served as an expert advisor to many international agencies, including the WTO.

Co-author: 3.11.5 Air Transport.

Gabor Vereczi is Programme Officer at the Sustainable Development of Tourism Department of the World Tourism Organization. He has been involved in WTO's sustainable tourism indicators programme since the first regional workshop took place in 1999. He has been the main coordinator at WTO for the study that lead to this indicators guide, and he has been instrumental in identifying information sources and contributors, in the preparation of several sections, the overall revision, editing and production of the publication.

David Viner is a Senior Research Scientist at the Climatic Research Unit, University of East Anglia. Since 1991 Dr. Viner has been Principal Investigator for a number of projects that have been the focal point for the international climate change research community. Since 2000 he has been manager of the IPCC Data Distribution centre. He has a wide research portfolio and has been involved in many international climate change assessments. He is actively involved internationally in the investigation of the interactions between climate change, tourism and the environment.

Contributor to 3.8.2 Climate Change and Tourism.

Melinda Watt is General Manager Earthcheck Pty Ltd., Brisbane ,Queensland Australia. Melinda has been involved in the development of benchmarking indicators for the travel and tourism industry on both operational and community levels. These indicators and benchmarking system are used under license by the global benchmarking, certification and improvement system for sustainable travel and tourism, Green Globe.

Co-author: 3.8.1 Energy, 3.9.2 Solid Waste, Box 3.26 Energy Consumption, and Box 3.3 Solid Waste Reduction –Douglas Shire Queensland Australia, Co-author: 3.8.2 Climate Change and Tourism.

Peter Williams is Professor, School of Resource and Environmental Management and Director, Centre for Tourism Policy and Research, Simon Fraser University, Burnaby, British Columbia, Canada. Dr. Williams' research focuses on policy, planning, and management issues in tourism and outdoor recreation, and the development of planning frameworks for sustainable use of natural and cultural resources. His research includes development of methods for assessing latent demand for natural and cultural resources; environmental management strategies for tourism businesses; growth management strategies in tourism regions; and use of Internet technologies for tourism.

Co-author: 3.12.4 Protection of the Image of a Destination, 6.20 Super-Natural British Columbia: Assessing Branding Success.

Carolyn Wild is President, WILD International, Ottawa, Ontario, Canada. She is an international expert in ecotourism development, with experience in several regions and countries from the Arctic to the Australian Outback. Her key interest is appropriate development in natural areas that benefits local communities and conserves the environment. She consults on tourism planning, marketing, management, and competitive strategy.

Author: 3.6.5 Community and Destination Economic Benefits; 3.6.7 Competitiveness of Tourism Businesses, 4.10 Trails and Routes; Box 2.5 SWOT Analysis, Co-author 3.1.2 Effects of Tourism on Communities, 3.10.2 Managing Events, 3.12.1 Creating Trip Circuits and Routes, contributing editor/reviewer of several sections.

Jennifer Wright is a contractor and researcher providing research services to the Tourism Human Resource Council (CTHRC) in Ottawa, Ontario, Canada. This includes preparing labour market studies and monitoring labour market trends. As well, Ms. Wright manages specialized research projects related to employment issues in the tourism sector.

Author: 3.6.3 Employment, Box 3.15 Assessing Tourism Employment in Canada.

Eugenio Yunis is the Head of the Sustainable Development of Tourism Department at the World Tourism Organization. Mr. Yunis guided this indicators study from its inception and acted as the principal reviewer of this guide.

References

◈ **Agencia Europea de Medio Ambiente**. (1999). *El informe Dobris: medio ambiente en Europa*. Copenhagen: Agencia Europea de Medio Ambiente.

◈ **Alberta Tourism, Parks and Recreation**. (1991). *Carrying capacity management in tourism settings: a tourism growth management process*. Edmonton: Alberta Tourism, Parks and Recreation.

◈ **Alberta Tourism, Parks and Recreation**. (1988). *Community tourism action plan; revised*. Edmonton: Alberta Tourism, Parks and Recreation.

◈ **Alcudia, Spain**. *Local Agenda 21 program with specific indicators (regional Agenda with tourism component*. Alcudia, Spain (http://www.alcudiamedi.net/al21/index.php?s=ind).

◈ **Anderson, D**., Lime, D., and Wang, T. (1998). *Maintaining the quality of park resources and visitor experiences: a handbook for managers*. St. Paul, MN: University of Minnesota Cooperative Park Studies Unit.

◈ **Andreu, Neus**, et al. (2003). *La mesura de la sostenibilitat del turisme a les Illes Balears; la medida de la sostenibilidad del turismo en las Illes Balears; measuring sustainability in tourism in the Balearic Islands*. Illes Balears: Centre d'Investigatio I Tecnologies Turistiques de les Illes Balears, Conselleria de Turisme del Governde les Illes Balears.

◈ **ARTIST** - Agenda for Research on Tourism by Integration of Statistics/Strategies. (2001). *Final report*.

◈ **Ashley, C**. (2000). *The impacts of tourism on rural livelihoods*: Namibia's experience. London, U.K.: Overseas Development Institute.

◈ **Asociacion de Estados del Caribe**. (2002). *Convenio para el establecimiento de la Zona de Turismo Sustenable del Caribe*. Port of Spain, Trinidad: Asociacion de Estados del Caribe. (www.acs-aec.org/tourism.htm).

◈ **Australia. Parks Australia**. (2003). *Annual reporting to state of the parks*. Canberra: Dept. of Environment & Heritage.

◈ **Bakker, Martine**. (2003). *A pre-study on the potential use of sustainable tourism indicators for the island of Bonaire, N.A.* New York: Center for Hospitality, Tourism and Travel Administration, New York University.

◈ **Bassotti, G**. (2003). Factores de calidad en ecoturismo, una visión práctica para su aplicación. En *Estudios y Perspectivas en Turismo*, Volumen 12, números 1 y 2, página 7 a 24. Buenos Aires: CIET.

◈ **Beaver, Allan**. (2002). *A dictionary of travel and tourism terminology*. Wallingford, UK: CABI Publishing.

◈ **Blazquez, Macia**, Murray, Ivan, and Garau, Joana Maria. (2002) ,El Tercer Boom: *Indicadors de sosteibilitat del turisme de les Illes Balears 1989-1999*. Palma de Mallorca: CITTIB. (in Catalan).

◈ **Blue Flag Campaign**. (2003). European beach criteria. Copenhagen: Blue Flag. (www.blueflag.org/Eucriteria.asp).

◈ **Boullon, R**., et al. (1996). *Estandares para las actividades del tiempo libre*: aplicaciones en la Patagonia Argentina. Aix-en-Provence: Centre des Hautes Etudes Touristiques.

◈ **Burhin, F., and Hamza, M**. (2000). Piloter une stratégie touristique par la mise en place d'indicateurs. *Revue Espaces*, n°170, April 2000.

◈ **Bushell, Robyn**. (2001). *Outcomes of the Fiji Consultative Workshops leading to the development of the 'healthy tourism' concept*, paper presented at the Conference on Sustainable Development of Ecotourism in SIDs and Other Small Islands, Seychelles. Sydney : Centre for Environmental Health.

◈ **Cabildo de Lanzarote**. (1998). *Lanzarote en la Biosfera: una estrategia hacia el desarrollo sostenible de la isla*. Islas Canarias: Cabildo de Lanzarote.

※ **Canarias, Gobierno de. Consejeria de Turismo y Transportes**. (1999). *Oferta y demanda turistica Canaria 1993-1998*. Las Palmas de Gran Canaria: Consejeria de Turismo y Transportes.

※ **Caribbean Development Bank**. (1997). *Environmental indicators for the Caribbean*. Bridgetown, Barbados: Caribbean Development Bank.

※ **Ceballos Lascurain, Héctor**. (1998). *Ecoturismo, naturaleza y desarrollo sostenible*. Mexico: Ed. Diana.

※ **Chafe, Zoe**. (2004). Consumer demand and operator support for socially and environmentally responsible tourism. *Washington, DC: CESD/TIES. (CESD/TIES Working paper 104)*.

※ **Cochrane, P**. (2001). *The cultural dimension to nature-based tourism: a case and future of jointly managed parks*. In The Fenner Research Conference Nature Tourism and the Environment. Australian Academy of Science.

※ **Conservation International and Harry Oppenheimer Okavango Research Center**. (2003). *The socio-economic baseline survey of the Bukakhwe Cultural Conservation Trust of Gudigwa, Botswana : draft report*. Washington, DC: Conservation International and Harry Oppenheimer Okavango Research Center.

※ **Conservation International and UNEP**. (2003). *Tourism and biodiversity, mapping tourism's global footprint*. Washington, DC: Conservation International and UNEP.

※ **Convention on Biological Diversity (CBD)**. (2002). *Report from the 6th Conference of the Parties*. Montreal: Convention on Biological Diversity.

※ **Craik, J**. (1995). Are there cultural limits to tourism? In *Journal of Sustainable Tourism*, Vol. 3, no. 2, 1995, pp.87-105.

※ **Crowards, Tom**. (1999). *An economic vulnerability index for developing countries with special reference to the Caribbean*. Bridgetown, Barbados: Caribbean Development Bank.

※ **De la Grange, Thierry**. (2001). *Les indicateurs du tourisme durable, reflexion pour une premiere etape operationnelle dans le contexte de l'ile de la Reunion*. Mahe, Seychelles: GREGEOI.

※ **Diamantis, Dimitrios**. (2004). *Ecotourism: management and assessment*. London: Thomson.

※ **Di Fidio, M**. (1993). *Architettura del paesaggio*. Rome: Ed. Pirola.

※ **Diputaciò Barcelona, Servei de Parcs Naturals**. (2001). Parc Comarcal d'Olèrdola: Memoria 2000. Barcelona, 2001.

※ **Diputaciò Barcelona, Servei de Parcs Naturals**. (2001). *Parc Natural del Garraf:* Memoria 2000. Barcelona: Diputacio Barcelona.

※ **Diputaciò Barcelona, Servei de Parcs Naturals**. (2001). *Parc Natural del Montnegre i el Corredor:* Memoria 2000. Barcelona: Diputacio Barcelona.

※ **Diputaciò Barcelona, Servei de Parcs Naturals**. (2001). *Parc Natural del Montseny:* Memoria 2000. Barcelona.

※ **Diputaciò Barcelona, Servei de Parcs Naturals**. (2003). *Parc Natural del Garraf:* Memoria 2002. Barcelona: Diputacio Barcelona.

※ **Doxey, G. V**. (1975). A causation theory of visitor related irritants: methods and research inferences. *Impact of Tourism: Sixth Annual Conference Proceedings*, (pp. 195-198).

※ **Drumm, Andy and Moore, Alan**. (2002). *Ecotourism development, manual for conservation planners and managers. Volume one: An introduction to ecotourism planning*. Arlington, Va.: Nature Conservancy.

※ **Dubois, Ghislain, and Ceron, Jean Paul**. (2000). Les indicateurs: un outil à manier avec discernement. *Cahiers Espaces, « tourisme durable »*, n°67, December 2000.

※ **Dubois, Ghislain, and Ceron, Jean Paul**. (2001). *Tourism and sustainable development indicators: two French experiments facing theoretical demands and expectations*. Presentation at the International Sustainable Development Research Conference, Manchester, April 2001.

※ **Dubois, Ghislain, and Ceron, Jean Paul**. (2004). Tourism and sustainable development indicators: the gap between theoretical demands and practical achievements. *Current Issues in Tourism* (to be published).

※ **Dubois, Ghislain, and Ceron, Jean Paul**. (nd). *Guide d'évaluation du tourisme durable dans les destinations*. Limoges : PULIM.

⊛ **Dubois, Ghislain, and Ceron, Jean Paul**. (nd). *Théorie et pratique des indicateurs de développement durable : leçons d'une application au tourisme*. Draft.

⊛ **Dubois, Ghislain, and Rechatin, Cecile**. (2000). *Tourisme, environnement, territoires : Les indicateurs*. Orleans : Ifen.

⊛ **Dubois, Ghislain**. (2000). Des indicateurs pour un diagnostic environnemental du tourisme français. *La lettre de l'Observatoire*, n°57, December 2000, pp. 1-10.

⊛ **Dubois, Ghislain**. (2002). *Indicators for an environmental diagnosis of French tourism*. Orleans: Ifen.

⊛ **Dubois, Ghislain**. (2002). *Data, indicators and their use for the integration of environment in tourism policies*. Presentation at the International Seminar Environmental Indicators for Tourism, Murcia, Spain, April 10-12, 2002.

⊛ **Dymond, S.J.** (1997). Indicators of sustainable tourism in New Zealand: a local government perspective. In *Journal of sustainable tourism*, vol. 5, no. 4, 1997, pp. 279-294.

⊛ **Dymond, S.J.** (1996). *Local government attitudes towards indicators of sustainable tourism in New Zealand*. Dunedin: University of Otago. (http://divcom.otago.ac.nz/epmrc/5-13.html).

⊛ **ECO-LAB** workshop, Rimini, Italy. (2002). Concept indicators for sustainable tourism destinations. Rimini: ECO-LAB workshop.

⊛ **Ecotourism Association of Australia**. (2003). *Setting a worldwide standard for ecotourism: the International Ecotourism Standard for Certification*: draft report. Brisbane: Ecotourism Association of Australia. (www.ecotourism.org.au).

⊛ **English Tourism Council**. (2002). *ETC national sustainable tourism indicators*. London.

⊛ **English Tourism Council**. (2001). *National sustainable tourism indicators: monitoring progress towards sustainable tourism in England*. London: ETC.

⊛ **Eriksen, Jan**. (2003). *Protecting the customs and the environment: the example of the Danish Outdoor Council, FEE and the Blue Flag Campaign*. Presentation at the "Integrating Sustainability into Tourism Policies: The Role of Certification" workshop held September 12, 2003 at the Vth World Parks Congress, Durban, South Africa.

⊛ **European Commission**. Enterprise Directorate-General. (2001). *The use of indicators in the measurement of progress in the process of quality improvement in tourism*. Brussels: European Commission.

⊛ **European Environment Agency**. (2002). *European Environment Agency core set of indicators: letter on consultation process on proposals, proposals for a core set of indicators*. Copenhagen: EEA. (http://www.eea.eu.int/coreset

⊛ **European Environment Agency**. (2002). *Environmental signals 2002: benchmarking the millennium*. Copenhagen: EEA. (www.eea.eu.int).

⊛ **Fairley, Andrew, and Berno, Tracy**. (2002). *Turtle Island: to be a vital resource to their community*. Suva, Fiji: University of the South Pacific.

⊛ **Fangstrom, Ingegerd**. (1997). *Indicators on tourism/environment interaction*. Stockholm: Statistika Centralbyran.

⊛ **Farsari, Yianna**. (2001). *Sustainable tourism indicators: pilot estimation for the municipality of Hersonissos, Crete*. Athens: Regional Analysis Division, Institute of Applied and Computational Mathematics, Foundation for the Research and the Technology Hellas.

⊛ **Font, Xavier, and Mihalič, Tanja**. (2002). *Beyond hotels: nature-based certification in Europe*. In Martha Honey (ed), Ecotourism and certification: setting standards in practice. Washington, DC: Island Press.

⊛ **French Institute for the Environment (IFEN)**. (2000). *Indicators for an environmental diagnosis of tourism in France*. Orleans: IFEN.

⊛ **Fundación Vida Silvestre Argentina**. (2002). *Programa Refugios de Vida Silvestre*. Buenos Aires: Fundacion Vida Silvestre Argentina.

⊛ **Global Reporting Initiative**. (2002). *Sustainability reporting guidelines*. Amsterdam: Global Reporting Initiative.

* **Global Tourism Solutions**. (2002). *Measuring sustainable tourism at the local level: an introduction and background.* Scarborough, UK: Global Tourism Solutions.

* **Gobierno de Canarias**. Consejería de Turismo y Transportes. (1999). *Oferta y demanda turística Canaria 1993 - 1998.* Las Palmas de Gran Canaria, Islas Canarias: Gobierno de Canarias.

* **Goodall, B., and Stabler**, M.J. (1997). Principles influencing the determination of environmental standards for sustainable tourism. In *Tourism and sustainability.* Wallingford, UK.: CAB International.

* **Green Globe 21**. (2002). *Benchmarking user's guide.* Canberra: Globe 21.

* **Green Globe 21**. (2003). *Benchmarking user's guide.* Canberra: Globe 21.

* **Green Globe 21**. (2003). *Sector benchmarking Indicators for communities (Version 3.1).* Canberra: Globe 21.

* **Groupe Developpement**. (2000). Checklist for tourist projects based on indicators of sustainable tourism: research report. Le Bourget: Groupe Developpement.

* **Groupe Developpement**. (2000). *Modelo de evaluacion con indicadores del turismo sostenible.* Le Bourget: Groupe Developpement.

* **Hall, C.M., and McArthur, S**. (2000). *Integrated heritage management - principles and practice.* London: The Stationary Office.

* **Hamza, M., and Burhin, F**. (1999). La gestion intégrée de la qualité des destinations touristiques. *Cahier Espaces.* Numéro spécial consacré à la qualité, July 1999.

* **Hart, Maureen.** (1999). *Guide to sustainable community indicators.* North Andover, Ma.: Sustainable Measures Inc. (www.sustainablemeasures.com/index/html).

* **Hawkins, R**. (1997). Green labels for the travel and tourism industry : a beginner's guide. *In Insights,* July 1997, pp. A11-79.

* **Herrera, Rodrigo J**. et al. (2000). *Sistema espanol de indicadores ambientales : area de medio urbano.* Madrid : Ministerio de Medio Ambiente.

* **Honey, Martha, and Rome, Abigail**. (2001). Protecting paradise: certification programs for sustainable tourism and ecotourism. *Washington, DC: Institute for Policy Studies.*

* **Honey, Martha**. (1999). *Ecotourism and sustainable development: who owns paradise?* Washington, DC: Island Press.

* **Honey, Martha**. (2001). *Protecting paradise: certification programs for sustainable tourism and ecotourism.* Washington, DC: Institute for Policy Studies.

* **Honey, Martha**. (2002). *Ecotourism and certification: setting standards in practice.* Washington, DC: Island Press.

* **Indicators for sustainable development in the Pacific islands**. (2000). Kitakyushu, Japan: Ministerial Conference on Environment and Development in Asia and the Pacific 2000.

* **Innovative Strategies** Volume III. (1998). Phoenix, Az.: *Nichols Gilstrap. February 1998, Issue 1* (ngi@nicholsgilstrap.com).

* **Intergovernmental Panel on Climate Change**. (2001). *IPCC third assessment report - Climate change.* Washington, DC: WMO – UNEP.

* **International Conference on Climate Change and Tourism**, 1st, Djerba, Tunisia, 9-11 April 2003. (2003). *Final report.* Madrid: World Tourism Organization.

* **International Council of Local Environmental Initiatives**. (2002). *Indicators for sustainable development: possibilities and limitations in measuring sustainable development.* Toronto: ICLEI.

* **International Ecotourism Society**. (2000). *Ecotourism statistical fact sheet.* Washington, DC: International Ecotourism Society.

* **International Ecotourism Society**. (2002). *International ecolodge guidelines.* Washington, DC: International Ecoturism Society.

* **International Institute for Sustainable Development**. (2000). *Measurement and indicators of sustainable development.* Winnipeg, Man.: IISD.

IUCN (World Conservation Union), World Tourism Organization, United Nations Environment Programme (2002). *Sustainable tourism in protected areas: guidelines for planning and management.* Cambridge: IUCN.

Jamieson, Walter. (2001). *A manual for monitoring community tourism development.* Pathumthani, Thailand: Asian Institute of Technology.

Karanja, F., Tessema, Y., and Barrow, E. (2002). *Equity in the Loita/Purko Naimina Enkiyio Forest in Kenya: securing Maasai rights to and responsibilities for the Forest.* Forest and social perspectives in conservation no. 11. Washington, DC: IUCN Eastern Africa Program Publication.

Kennedy, A. (2002). Mad and bad in Byron: Byron Bay has become too popular for its own good. *Sydney Morning Herald,* April 1: pp17. Sydney: Sydney Morning Herald.

Kotler, P., and Turner, R.E. (1998). *Marketing management.* Toronto: Prentice Hall.

Kozak, M. (2003). *Destination benchmarking: concepts, practices and operations. Turkey:* Mugla University.

Lash, Gail Y.B., and Austin, Alison D. (2003). *Rural Ecotourism Assessment Program (REAP): a guide to community assessment of ecotourism as a tool for sustainable development.* Burlington, Vt.: EplerWood International.

Leones, Julie, and Dun, Douglas. (1999). Strategies for monitoring tourism in your community's economy. (http://cals.arizona.edu/pubs/marketing/az1113.pdf).

Levett, R., and McNally, R. (2003). *A strategic environmental assessment of Fiji's tourism development plan.* Suva: World Wildlife Fund.

Lindberg, Kreg, Epler Wood, Megan, and Engeldrum, David. (1998). *Ecotourism: a guide for planners and managers:* volume 2. Bennington, Vt.: Ecotourism Society.

Local environment. (2003) Volume 8 Number 6/December 2003. (Entire volume on community indicators).

Mangion, Marie-Louise. (2001). *Carrying capacity assessment for tourism in the Maltese Islands.* St. Julian's, Malta: Ministry of Tourism.

Manidis Roberts Consultants. (1998). *Tourism optimization management model for North Sydney.* Report for North Sydney Council, North Sydney.

Manidis Roberts Consultants. (1998). *Ecologically sustainable development plan and indicators for the Homebush Bay Olympic site.* Sydney Olympic Authority, Homebush Bay.

Manning, Edward W. (1996). Sustainable mountain destinations - applying Agenda 21 to the tourism sector. *Annali della Fondazione.* Courmayeur, Italia: Fondazione Courmayeur, Centro Internazionale su Diritto, Società e Economia.

Manning, Edward W. (1999). Indicators of tourism sustainability. *Tourism management.* Volume 20, No. 2, April 1999, pp 179-182.

Manning, Edward W., and Dougherty, David. (1998).   Planning tourism in sensitive ecosystems. In Singh, T.V. (ed.), *Tourism Development in the Critical Environments.* Lucknow, India: Centre for Tourism Research and Development.

Manning, Edward W., and Dougherty, David. (2000). Planning sustainable tourism destinations. *Journal of Tourism Recreation Research,* Jubilee Volume 2000: 25, No. 2, pp. 3-14.

Manning, Edward W., and Prieur, S. (1998). *Governance for tourism in impacted destinations.* Toronto: Centre for a Sustainable Future and Foundation for International Training.

Manning, Robert, Lime, D., Freimund, W., and Pitt, D. (1996). Crowding norms at frontcountry sites: a visual approach to setting standards of quality. *Leisure Sciences* 18(1): 39-59.

Manning, Robert. (1999). *Studies in outdoor recreation.* Corvallis, OR: Oregon State University Press.

Manning, Robert. (2001). Visitor experience and resource protection: a framework for managing the carrying capacity of National Parks. *Journal of Park and Recreation Administration* 19(1): 93-108.

Markant Marketing Management. (1994). *Environmental indicators for tourism and leisure: report.* Rotterdam: Ministry of Economic Affairs.

Mawland Hotel Management. (2003). *Integrated monitoring and adaptive management system for the adaptive reuse of the Quarantine Station.* Sydney: Mawland Hotel Management.

McArthur, S. (2000). Beyond carrying capacity – introducing a model to monitor and manage visitor activity in remote areas. In X. Font and J. Tribe (eds.), *Environmental management of forest tourism and recreation, in forest tourism and recreation – case studies in environmental management.* High Wycombe, UK: CABI Publishing.

McArthur, S. (2000). *Visitor management in action – an analysis of the development and implementation of visitor management models at Jenolan Caves and Kangaroo Island.* Canberra: University of Canberra.

Mediterranean Action Plan. (2000). *130 indicators for sustainable development in the Mediterranean region.* Valbonne: Plan Bleu pour l'environnement et le developpement en Mediterranee.

Ministerio de Medio Ambiente, España. (2002). *Indicadores ambientales de turismo.* Documento de trabajo para el Seminario Internacional sobre indicadores ambientales de turismo, Murcia, abril 2002. Madrid: Ministerio de Medio Ambiente.

Missing Link Tourism Consultants. (2002). *Feasibility study for a canopy walk in the Otway Forests.* Melbourne: Vistorian Dept. of Natural Resources and Environment.

Municipality of Cálvia. Calvia local Agenda 21, The sustainability of a tourist municipality plan of action: 10 strategic lines of action and 40 initiatives. Calvia, Majorca, Spain (www.calvia.com/Pages/ldiomas/ingles/Pages/ayun/itown/agl21/iagl21.pdf)

Netherlands. Ministry of Economic Affairs. (n.d.). Environmental indicators for tourism and leisure. Amsterdam: Ministry of Economic Affairs.

OECD. (2001). Indicators for sustainable development. In *The Statistics newsletter,* 2001. (STD.STATNEWS@oecd.org).

OECD. (2001). *Sustainable tourism strategies in the United Kingdom.* Paris: OECD.

OECD Environment Directorate. (2001). *Indicators for the integration of environmental concerns into tourism policies.* Paris: OECD.

OGM, *Partage d'expériences en matière de tourisme durable.* In Cahier espaces, numéro spécial consacré au tourisme durable, December 2000.

Paskaleva-Shapira, Krassimira. (2003). Sustainable Urban Tourism: involving local agents and partnerships for new forms of governance (SUT-Governance). In *EU 'SUT Governance Project' Final Report, August 2003.* Karlsruhe: Forshungszentrum Karlsruhe. (Has a list of indicators related to tourism management in urban centres of Europe, with sections on benchmarking).

Paskaleva-Shapira, Krassimira. (2003). *EU "SUT-governance" project: final report.* Karlsruhe: Forschungszentrum Karlsruhe.

Pelletreau, Aurelie. (2003). Europe's environment: the third assessment. *Tourism,* chapter 2.7., pp.99-110.

Pigram, J.J. (1996). Best practice environmental management and the tourism industry. In *Progress in tourism and hospitality research,* vol. 2, no. 3 &4, 1996, pp. 261-271.

Pils, Manfred, and Eltschka-Schiller, Gabriele. (1999). *Sustainability indicators for tourism.* Vienna: International Friends of Nature.

Plan d'Action pour la Mediterranee. (2000). *130 indicateurs pour le developpement durable en Mediterranee.* Valbonne: Plan Bleu pour l'Environnement et le Developpement en Mediterranee.

Policarpo, David. (2001). *Recherche sur les indicateurs pour un tourisme durable: une methode de choix et de definition d'indicateurs pour un developpement touristique durable, dans les pays en developpement.* These: Ecole des Hautes Etudes en Sciences Sociales.

Ratz, T. (2000). *Residents' perceptions of the socio-cultural impacts of tourism at Lake Balaton, Hungary.* In: Richards, G. and Hall, D. (eds). *Tourism and Sustainable Tourism Development.* London: Routledge, pp. 36-47 (http://www.ratztamara.com/balimp.html).

Ritchie, J.R. Brent, and Crouch, Geoffrey L. (2003). *The competitive destination: a sustainable tourism perspective.* Oxford: CABI Publishing.

Ritchie, J.R. Brent, Levy, Stuart E., and Crouch, Geoffrey I. (2003). *Educating policy makers and managers on factors that determine and reflect destination performance – a WTO perspective.* Calgary: University of Calgary.

⊛ **Rivas Ortega, Humberto.** (2000). *Indicadores de sostenibilidad para la actividad turística.* Santiago, Chile: Servicio Nacional de Turismo, Departamento de Planificación.

⊛ **Rivas Ortega, Humberto.** (2002). *Indicadores de sostenibilidad para la actividad turistica: la experiencia de Chile.* Santiago, Chile: Servicio Nacional de Turismo.

⊛ **Robertson, Graeme.** (2003). *Cruise ship tourism industry.* Hamburg: Lighthouse Foundation.

⊛ **Sanabria, Ronald** (ed.). (2002). *Sustainable Tourism Stewardship Council (STSC) final report.* New York: Rainforest Alliance.

⊛ **Sanabria, Ronald.** (2002). *Accreditation: certifying the certifiers. In Martha Honey (ed.), Ecotourism and certification: setting standards in practice.* Washington, DC: Island Press.

⊛ **Simmons, David.** (2001). *Standards and indicators for sustainable tourism.* Port of Spain, Caribbean Tourism Organisation.

⊛ **Scott, Daniel.** (2003). Climate change and the skiing industry in Southern Ontario (Canada): exploring the importance of snowmaking as a technical adaptation. In *Climate research*, 23, p. 171-181.

⊛ **Smith, Ginger, and Rosenbaum, Alvin.** (2002?). The case for an ecotourism peace park and cultural heritage corridor for the Korean DMZ. In   D. Diamantis and S. Geldenhuys, *Ecotourism: management and assessment.* London: Continuum International. (publication pending).

⊛ **Smith, Ginger.** (2002). The development of sustainable tourism in natural areas in North America: background, issues, and opportunities. Presented at the Second Summit of the North American International Trade Corridor Partnership and Sixth Summit of Mayors of Canada, Mexico, and the United States, Manzanillo, Mexico, May 10-12, 2000.

⊛ **Smyth, D.** (2001). Joint management of national parks in Australia. In Baker, R.J., Davies, J., and Young, E. (eds.), *Working on country-contemporary indigenous management of Australia's lands and coastal regions.* Oxford: Oxford Press.

⊛ **South Pacific Tourism Organization.** (2003). *Optimising tourism opportunities: a pilot study of social and gender implications of tourism in Samoa, Vanuatu and Fiji.* Suva: SPTO.

⊛ **Sprecher, Dawn, and Jamieson, Delphine.** (2000). *A manual for monitoring community tourism development.* Pathumthani, Thailand: CUC EUM Project, Asian Institute of Technology.

⊛ **Storz, A., and Mathieu, Y.** (2000). Lo strumento del futuro par la qualità dei servizi – il benchmarking delle reti di mobilità in Europa. In *Comuni d'Europa,* 2000.

⊛ **Sweden. Ministry of Environment.** Baltic 21 Secretariat. (2000?). *Goals and core indicators for sustainable development, Baltic 21 indicators.* Stockholm: Baltic 21 Secretariat.

⊛ **Sweeting, James E.N., and Wayne, Scott L.** (2003). *A shifting tide: environmental challenges & cruise industry responses; interim summary report.* Washington, DC: Center for Environmental Leadership in Business, Conservation International.

⊛ **Toth, Robert.** (2002). Exploring the concepts underlying certification. In Martha Honey (ed.), Ecotourism and certification: setting standards in practice. Washington, DC : Island Press.

⊛ **Toth, Robert.** (2002). *Integrating sustainability.* In Martha Honey (ed.), Ecotourism and certification: setting standards in practice. Washington, DC: Island Press.

⊛ **Tour Operators Initiative.** (2003). *Sustainable tourism: the tour operators' contribution.* New York: UNEP.

⊛ **Tourisk Inc.** (2003). Indicators of sustainable development for tourism: background paper for the WTO Indicators Expert Advisors and Working Group. Ottawa, Ont.: Tourisk Inc. and the Centre for a Sustainable Future.

⊛ **Twining-Ward L.** (2003). *Indicator handbook: a guide to the development and use of Samoa's sustainable tourism indicators.* Apia: South Pacific Regional Environment Project (SPREP).

⊛ **Twining-Ward L., and Butler, R. W.** (2002). Implementing STD on a small island: development and use of sustainable tourism development indicators in Samoa. *Journal of Sustainable Tourism,* 10(5): 363-387.

⊛ **Twining-Ward, L.** (2001). Monitoring sustainable tourism in Samoa. In *UNEP Industry and Environment,* 24: 3-4.

* **Twining-Ward, L.** (2002). *Monitoring sustainable tourism development: a comprehensive, stakeholder-driven, adaptive approach.* PhD thesis. Guildford, United Kingdom: University of Surrey.

* **United Nations Conference on Environment and Development (UNCED)**, Rio de Janeiro, 1992. (1992). *Report.* New York: UNCED.

* **United Nations Environment Programme.** (1995). *Environmental codes of conduct for tourism.* New York: UNEP.

* **United Nations Environment Programme.** (2001). *Transport and the global environment: accounting for GHG reduction on policy analysis.* New York: UNEP.

* **United Nations**. Commission on Sustainable Development. (2002). *Indicators of sustainable development: guidelines and methodologies.* New York: United Nations. (www.un.org/esa/sustdev/natlinfo/indicators/indisd/indisd-mg2001.pdf)

* **United Nations**. Statistics Division. (1999). Environmental indicators: toward a European system of environmental pressure indicators and indices. In *Envstats, 1999.*

* **United States Environmental Protection Agency.** (2000). *A method for quantifying environmental indicators of selected leisure activities in the United States.* Washington, DC: EPA.

* **United States National Park Service.** (1997). *Visitor experience and resource protection (VERP) framework: a handbook for planners and managers.* Denver, CO: Denver Service Center.

* **Upshaw**, L.B. (1995). *Building brand identity.* New York: Wiley.

* **Vellas, Francois, and Barioulet, Herve**. (2000). *Checklist for tourist projects based on indicators of sustainable tourism.* Le Bourget: Groupe Developpement.

* **Vellas, Francois, and Barioulet, Herve**. (2000). *Grille de lecture des projets touristiques a partir des indicateurs du tourisme durable.* Le Bourget: Groupe Developpement.

* **Viñals, M.J.** (ed.). (2002). *Turismo en espacios naturales y rurales II.* Valencia: Universidad Politécnica de Valencia.

* **Viñals, M.J.** (ed.). (2002). *Herramientas para la gestión del turismo sostenible en humedales.* Madrid: Ministerio de Medio Ambiente.

* **Viñals, M.J., and Bernabe, A.** (eds.). (1999). *Turismo en espacios naturales y rurales.* Valencia: Universidad Politécnica de Valencia.

* **Viñals, M.J., Morant, M., El Ayadi, M., Tereul, L., Herrera, S., Flores, S. and Iroldi, O.** (2001). *Method approach to the determination of the recreational carrying capacity on wetlands.* Actas de la ATLAs-Conference, Dublín, octubre 2001. (in publication).

* **Viñals, M. J.**, et al. (2002). *Guía para la gestión recreativa de los recursos naturales: herramientas para la gestión del turismo sostenible en humedales.* Serie Cuadernillos Técnicos. Madrid: Organismo Autónomo Parques Nacionales, Secretaría General de Medio Ambiente, Ministerio de Medio Ambiente.

* **Wallace, George N., and Lincango, M.** (1996). *Towards a principled evaluation of ecotourism ventures.* Fort Collins: Colorado State University.

* **Ward, Jonet C., and Beanland, Ruth A.** (1994). *Development of environmental indicators for tourism in natural areas: a preliminary study.* Palmerston North, N.Z.: Lincoln Environmental.

* **Wearing, Stephen and Neil, John.** (1999). *Ecoturismo, impacto, tendencias y posibilidades.* Madrid: Editorial Síntesis.

* **World Bank.** (1997). *Expanding the measure of wealth, indicators of environmentally sustainable development.* Washington, DC.: World Bank.

* **World Health Organisation.** (2003). *International travel & health.* Geneva: WHO.

* **World Tourism Organization** (1993) *Health Information and Formalities in International Travel (Tourist health information, Health insurance, and assistance in International Travel, Health Formalities and Vaccinations)* Madrid, WTO.

* **World Tourism Organization** (1995). *Pilot study on indicators for the sustainable management of tourism: Villa Gesell and Peninsula Valdes, Argentina.* Buenos Aires: Secretaria de Turismo Argentina and Madrid: WTO.

❋ **World Tourism Organization.** (1996). *Sustainable Tourism in Black Sea Coastal Zones.* Madrid: WTO.

❋ **World Tourism Organization, World Travel and Trade Council, Earth Council** (1996). *Agenda 21 for the Travel and Tourism Industry* (http://www.world-tourism.org/sustainable/publications.htm).

❋ **World Tourism Organization** (1997). *What tourism managers need to know: a practical guide to the development and use of indicators of sustainable tourism.* Madrid: WTO.

❋ **World Tourism Organization** (1999). *Workshop on sustainable tourism indicators for Eastern and Central Europe, February 1999: Keszthely (Lake Balaton) Hungary.* Madrid: WTO.

❋ **World Tourism Organization** (1999). *Taller sobre indicadores de turismo sostenible para el Caribe y Centroamérica, Cozumel, Mexico: informe final.* Madrid: WTO.

❋ **World Tourism Organization** (2000). *Workshop on sustainable tourism indicators, Beruwala, Sri Lanka: final report.* Madrid: WTO.

❋ **World Tourism Organization.** (2001). *Workshop on sustainable tourism indicators for South American Countries, Villa Gesell, Argentina: final report.* Madrid: WTO. (In Spanish).

❋ **World Tourism Organization** (2001). *Workshop on sustainable tourism indicators for the islands of the Mediterranean, Kukljica, Island of Ugljan, Croatia: final report,.* Madrid: World Tourism Organization.

❋ **World Tourism Organization.** (2001). *Global Code of Ethics for Tourism.* Madrid: WTO. (www.world-tourism.org./code_ethics/eng.html).

❋ **World Tourism Organization.** (2002). *Seminar on Planning, Development and Management of Ecotourism in Africa.* (2002). *Final report.* Madrid: WTO.

❋ **World Tourism Organization.** (2002). *Voluntary initiatives in Tourism: Worldwide Inventory and Comparative Analysis of 104 Eco-labels, Awards and Self-Commitments.* Madrid: WTO.

❋ **World Tourism Organization.** (2003). *La seguridad como factor subyacente de calidad en el turismo.* Madrid: WTO.

❋ **World Tourism Organization.** (2003). *Sustainable Development of Ecotourism: A Compilation of Good Practices in SMEs.* Madrid: WTO.

❋ **World Wildlife Fund.** (2001). *Holiday footprinting: a practical tool for responsible tourism.* London: WWF.

Web sources:

❋ Australian National Parks
   www.deh.gov.au/parks

❋ Baltic 21 (Agenda 21 for the Baltic Sea Region)
   www.ee/baltic21/indicators/

❋ Barcelona Province Natural Parks
   www.diba.es/parcs

❋ Beach Monitoring Sites
   www.americanoceans.org/beach/link.htm

❋ Blue Flag Campaign
   www.blueflag.org

❋ Caribbean Program for Economic Competitiveness
   www.cpechrd.org

❋ Center on Ecoturism and Sustainable Development
   www.ecotourismcesd.org.

❋ European Environmental Agency: Tourism Indicators
   http://themes.eea.eu.int/Sectors_and_activities/tourism/indicators

❋ France: Tourism, Environment, Territories: Indicators
   www.ifen.fr/pages/tourisme.htm

* French Institute for the Environment (Institut français de l'environnement)-IFEN
  www.ifen.fr

* Global Reporting Initiative
  www.globalreporting.org

* Green Globe
  www.greenglobe21.com

* International Ecotourism Society
  www.ecotourism.org

* International Union for the Conservation of Nature (IUCN)
  www.iucn.org

* International Year of Ecotourism 2002
  http://www.world-tourism.org/sustainable/IYE-Main-Menu.htm

* Lanzarote Biosphere Strategy
  www.cabildodelanzarote.com/areas/presidencia/biosfera/biosfera/biosfera.htm

* Rainforest Alliance
  www.rainforest-alliance.org.

* Society for Accessible Travel and Hospitality
  www.sath.org

* Sustainable Ski Slopes
  www.keepwintercool.org

* Tour Operators Initiative
  www.toinitiative.org

* Tourism Optimisation Management Model for Kangaroo Island
  www.tomm.info

* Tourism Optimisation Management Model for the North Head Quarantine Station
  www.npws.nsw.gov.au/culture/nthhdqst/changes.html

* Uganda Community Tourism Association
  http://www.ucota.or.ug/
  http://www.visituganda.com/domestic/ucota.htm

* UNESCO World Heritage Centre
  www.unesco.org/whc

* UNICEF
  www.unicef.org

* United Nations Commission on Sustainable Development
  www.un.org/esa/sustdev/isd.htm

* United Nations Sustainable Development Indicators
  http://www.un.org/esa/sustdev/natlinfo/indicators/isd.htm

* U.S. Environmental Protection Agency
  www.epa.gov

* World Bank
  www.worldbank.org

* World Health Organization
  www.who.int/health_topics/travel/en/

* World Tourism Organization
  www.world-tourism.org

* World Tourism Organization – Sustainable Development of Tourism
  www.world-tourism.org/sustainable

Templates

C 1 Indicators Selection Worksheet

Key Issues	Candidate Indicators	Evaluation criteria					Rating
		Relevance Who will use it and how will it influence decisions on the issue?	**Feasibility** Is it practical and affordable to collect and analyze data?	**Credibility** Is it supported by by valid and reliable information from credible sources?	**Clarity** Is it easy to understand and clear to users?	**Comparasion** Is it useful for comparisons with other areas, standards, or in time series?	

Rating:

For each criterion H (high) M (medium) or L (low) can be assigned for each indicator. Users may wish to discuss the relative ratings of each indicator which could respond to an issue. The alternative or additional rating approach below may also be used; the objective is to aid in discussion. In this rating format, clearly an indicator receiving 4 or 5 H ratings would be recommended for further investigation and implementation, whereas one receiving few H ratings (and particularly if the rating for relevance is L) it is unlikely to receive further attention or development.

Selection and priorization:

Once the ratings (e.g. HML) are done for each indicator, it can also be useful to use an overall subjective rating such as that which follows; this can further assist in establishment of the relative importance or utility of any indicator.

Rating the Indicators for Use (overall rating).

*****	Critical indicator for the issue in question and the management of the site/destination;
****	Important for management decisions;
***	Very useful for certain aspects of site management;
**	Some use for specific management issues;
*	Limited utility for management of the destination.

These ratings help as an initial selection and priorization of indicators. For a more detailed feasibility assessment of a particular potential indicator it is recommended that evaluators address the questions and points in C 2: Indicator development worksheet.

© 2004 World Tourism Organization - ISBN 92-844-0726-5

C 2   Indicator Development Worksheet

To be applied to each indicator which seems worthy of implementation after the initial selection. This sheet can be used to guide implementation of an indicator once it has been selected for development. It can also be used in concert with the evaluation sheet to help provide clarification in the selection process.

Issue or Risk Area:

_____

Indicator (clearly define with method of calculation and expression)

_____

Relevance

To whom is it relevant and how will they use it? _____

_____

Is it critical for short or long-term decisions? _____

_____

For which specific decision(s) is the indicator expected to be important? _____

_____

When is the indicator required: How frequently? _____

                                How detailed? _____

                                How soon? _____

Feasibility

What data will be used and who will supply it? (Is there currently a collection program for the data, will it have to be extracted from one or more source, or will it have to be collected newly – through monitoring, questionnaires etc.?)

_____

Form of available data? (raw, digitized, tabular)

_____

Availability of existing data: timing, detail frequency?

_____

Confidentiality considerations:

_____

Is data readily suitable for use in its present form, or will calculations, transformation or analysis be needed for use to address the specific tourism issue? If manipulation/extraction is required, will it be done by the provider or will it have to be done by the indicators program?

_____

Who will be doing the analysis of the information, and how often will the information be provided?

_____

Who will cover cost and technical needs of data collection?

_____

Who will cover cost and technical needs of data analysis?

_____

Credibility

Who is the source of the information? (Census, the industry, local government, a complaints box?)

_____

Is the data source independent, reliable and consistent?

_____

What assurances are there of scientific soundness and objectivity?

_____

_____

Clarity

In what form will the indicator be presented for the different users? (Forms of reporting, communication and portrayal: e.g. annual reports, graphic presentation, raw data or ratios, etc.)

_____

How detailed, how frequent, and how current must information be to allow it be to be used /publicized in this way?

_____

Who will be the key users, and how will the indicators be phrased in terms easy for them to understand?

_____

How will the indicator help analysing the tourism issue in question, how will it be linked to planning and decision-making processes (e.g. periodic reports, issue reports, plan evaluations, etc.)

_____

Comparability

Is the indicator in use in this form in other destinations, and/or are there standards of comparison to which it can be related?

_____

Key benchmarks to be used

_____

Means by which change over time in the destination is to be analyzed and portrayed:

_____

Operational Concerns

Who will be accountable for managing the procedure to produce the indicator on an ongoing basis?

_____

To whom will the indicator be provided and in what form?

_____

Is there a continuing commitment to monitor this indicator?

_____

Next Steps

What is the specific workplan/timetable for making this indicator operational?

_____

_____

_____

_____

Comments

_____

C 3 Indicators Reporting Worksheet

(This form is a template to help managers keep track of each indicator chosen and to document characteristics and methods of use).

Issue to which the indicator responds ((brief description):

_____

Indicator (include precise statement of indicator)

_____

Precise method of calculation:

_____

Data source(s):

_____

Logistics of production:

        Prepared by _____

        Provided to _____

        Frequency of production _____

        Time needed between data collection and production/use of the indicator (e.g. delay in indicator use due to data processing, or reporting processes) _____

        _____

Intended user(s)

_____

_____

Form of reporting (specific tables, graphs, etc to be produced, reporting in brochures, progress reports, website, etc.)

_____

_____

Standards or thresholds to be met (if any)

_____

Expected actions (plans, results)

_____

_____

Observed trends to date

_____

_____

See sample completed worksheet on next page

Indicators Reporting Worksheet (Completed example)

Issue to which the indicator responds (brief description): *excessive numbers of tourists on the beach on peak days.*

Indicator (include precise statement of indicator): *numbers of bathers per square km in managed beach area.*

Precise method of calculation: *beach area includes sand area to high tide and fenced area with beach services. Total peak number of tourists is divided by total area in square metres to produce the indicator: number of tourists per square km (also number of square metres per bather).*

Data source(s): *beach area obtained from municipal plan, tourist numbers counted by beach concessionaires through ticket sales; numbers verified by actual counts done by students on peak days as part of summer student program.*

Logistics of production:

   Prepared by: *Municipal seafront authority data unit*

   Provided to: *Tourism authority and Planning authority*

   Frequency of production: *weekly in season (May to Sept)*

   Time needed between data collection and production/use of the indicator: *three weeks*

Intended user(s): *planning authority, tourism authority, beach concessionaries, beach times tourist news,environmental reporting agency (at regional level).*

Form of reporting (specific tables, graphs, etc to be produced): *time series data provided in linear graph form showing monthly information for past five years, weekly information provided for current and past season in tabular form.*

Standards or thresholds to be met (if any): *municipal beach standard is four square metres minimum per user (2500 per square km). The indicator will show performance relative to this standard, also showing number of observations which exceed standard .*

Expected actions (plans, results): *municipality is expected to use the indicator to determine if action is needed to control crowding, provide additional beach areas, services and shore patrols, and to feed discussions on future shore zone development.*

Observed trends to date: *density of use on peak day 2002 was 2050 tourists per square km, up from 1940 in 2001. To date in 2003, six days have exceeded 2000, with one exceeding the municipal standard (the day of the Annual Beach Festival).*

C 4 Indicators Re-evaluation Worksheet

(These evaluation questions are to be used in the evaluation process after the indicators have been in use for a period of time, to determine if indicators are still useful, used, and making a difference to the decision process).

1. Indicators program:

Is the overall program operational?

_____

Are the issues still current?

_____

Have any new issues emerged?

_____

Are the indicators now part of the overall decision process (planning, management) on these issues?

_____

If not, what changes are needed so that they are used?

_____

2. For specific issues:

Issue or Risk Area

_____

Indicator (clearly define)

_____

Have there been any difficulties (technical, financial or organizational problems) in the following aspects of indicators use?

Data/information collection: _____

Data analysis, indicators calculation: _____

Indicators reporting, communication: _____

What are the opportunities to improve data sources, collection, analysis and reporting processes? Are there new data sources or methods of analysis that can support the indicator?

_____

Who is now using the indicator and how?

_____

Does the indicator need to be altered to be more effective? (e.g., frequency, detail, means of portrayal, methods of distribution?)

_____

Is there any feedback from the users on the usefulness of the indicator? Has it been clear and easy to understand for the different types of users? What can be done to improve the application of the indicator

_____

Has the indicator corresponded adequately to the issue, and supported decision making? How can it be improved for users?

_____

Are there any opportunities for broader use of the indicator to support sustainable tourism? (e.g other users who could access it, new means to report on it, partnerships with other sectors or projects who could use the information?)

_____

C 5 Exit Questionnaire Model

The questions suggested in the sample below are based on a model questionnaire undertaken in several destinations in a number of countries and are designed to quantify and clarify the components of visitor satisfaction. Additional questions can be added, including probes to clarify the reasons why specific responses were received.

Analysis of responses according to motivation for the visit, origin, region, and demographic characteristics can assist in understanding what the indicator (or specific sub-indicator) really means. The overall list could become a long list of questions which would be too much to administer to exiting tourists (in the few minutes available in a departure lounge, ferry line-up, customs post or hotel lobby). It may be useful to begin with a shorter list of questions of greatest importance.

Some of the questions may be amenable to asking only to a smaller set of tourists so that no one departing tourist is overwhelmed with the list. A pilot test of the questions will provide insight into the best way to administer the questions.

Exit Questionnaire

Why did you visit [this destination]?

_____

Is this your first visit? Yes, No. If yes, when were you last here? _____

While {here} did you:

Visit a beach	Yes	No
Visit the mountains	Yes	No
Walk on natural trails	Yes	No
Attend a conference	Yes	No
Visit relatives	Yes	No
Visit cultural sites	Yes	No
Take a cruise	Yes	No
Conduct business	Yes	No
Attend a cultural performance	Yes	No
Participate in _ (See note 1) etc.	Yes	No

Which was your primary reason for the visit? (ring answer).

(Note: include the key destination activities or attractions)

Which parts of (the destination) did you visit (where there are different sites)?

Site A	_____
Town B)	_____
The Hills etc.	_____
Site C	_____
The heritage site	_____
etc.	_____

Where did you spend most of your time? (ring one answer)

_____

(Possible follow-up question for where precisely the respondent stayed _____
- a specific resort, hotel, or community).

Please respond to the following questions with the appropriate answer:

1 Strongly Disagree

2 Disagree

3 Neutral

4 Agree

5 Strongly Agree

Note: The following questions are samples – choose those appropriate or modify as needed for the destination. The questions can refer generally to the following main aspects of tourist's satisfaction: access, tourist information, quality of services, safety and security, variety of experiences/sites/activities, attitude of/relation with locals, destination environment (cleanliness, noise, built and natural environment, etc.), overall satisfaction, intent to repeat visit or advise destination to friends, etc.

Circle best answer

❀ I enjoyed my experience in "destination"	1	2	3	4	5
❀ The state of roads and signage made travel easy	1	2	3	4	5
❀ I found the "destination" to be clean	1	2	3	4	5
(Note: can also duplicate these for sub destinations such as the beach, the town centre, the Park etc)					
❀ "Destination" provided a good variety of experiences	1	2	3	4	5
❀ The towns and villages were crowded	1	2	3	4	5
❀ I had a good experience involving the local culture	1	2	3	4	5
❀ Cultural sites were well maintained	1	2	3	4	5
❀ Cultural sites were accessible	1	2	3	4	5
❀ The beaches were clean	1	2	3	4	5
❀ Good souvenirs and crafts were available	1	2	3	4	5
❀ I had good opportunities to enjoy local cuisine	1	2	3	4	5
❀ The quality of food was good *	1	2	3	4	5
❀ The quality of accommodation was good *	1	2	3	4	5
❀ The level of service provided was high	1	2	3	4	5
❀ Service staff were competent and helpful #	1	2	3	4	5
❀ I was bothered by the messy appearance of built areas	1	2	3	4	5
❀ I was bothered by noise *	1	2	3	4	5
❀ I was bothered by garbage in public areas*	1	2	3	4	5
❀ The state of the natural environment was good #	1	2	3	4	5
❀ "Destination" has an interesting and varied landscape	1	2	3	4	5
❀ It was easy to get to "destination" for my visit	1	2	3	4	5
❀ I felt safe and secure during my visit	1	2	3	4	5
❀ I feel I received good value for money	1	2	3	4	5
❀ I would recommend "destination" to my friends	1	2	3	4	5
❀ I would visit "destination" again	1	2	3	4	5

*Note: possible follow up: * probe if get strong response – ask where or what caused this opinion?, # identify reason for negative*

Note that the same question can also be phrased in the negative (I feel I did not get good value for money. In practice, both seem to obtain similar responses but the phrasing should be kept constant over time for valid comparisons.

Would you be interested in visiting the "destination" outside the summer (or other peak) season? What places/sites in the destination would you likely visit and what activities would you prefer to do during the winter (or other off-season period)?

_____

Were there any activities which you expected to find in "destination" which were missing?

_____

How long would you spend next time in "destination"?

_____

What could be done to improve your vacation next time in "destination"?

_____

Would you mind providing us with a few details on yourself?

Nationality _____ Age: (See note 2) _____ Length of stay _____

Number in party _____ Home city or region _____

Thank you for your valuable comments

Use of Follow-up probes:

An alternative probe which has proven useful is the following set of questions:

If you return, what would you do again? _____

What would you not do? _____

What would you change? _____

(These questions help to do a SWOT, and have been used in some other destinations).

Note 1: For some of the questions, smaller samples will yield useable results, as long as the data are to be used for simple time-series comparisons and not for any more sophisticated analyses in for example, contingency tables differentiated by nationality, age or region visited. For questions which may address something done by only a few tourists (e.g., bicycling, diving, cultural events, caving) a sequence of questions can serve. The first question may ask whether a tourist participated in any of these activities. The second may be asked only of those who did these activities).

Note 2: It may be useful to collect some information about the respondent to permit a more nuanced analysis of the data: do this at the end of any questionnaire. It is usually effective to allow respondents to decline to give personal responses, but in most circumstances, if asked late in the survey process, respondents will agree to some personal information – particularly if assured that responses will be confidential. Suggested data could include: age, gender, permanent residence, occupation, place of residence in the destination. Take care with any questions about age, income, ethnicity, religion or social class as these may be considered offensive and may even be illegal to ask in some jurisdictions.

C 6 Local Questionnaire Model

The model local or resident questionnaire is designed to provide information on the attitudes and concerns of the community with respect to the key issues from their perspective. The sample questionnaire which follows is designed to, as objectively as possible, obtain information from the community. The questions are generally structured as statements with which the respondent can agree or disagree. A five point scale is used, from strongly disagree, to disagree, neutral, agree to strongly agree. This approach is consistent with recommended practice for questionnaires of this type (some prefer a seven point scale), and allows respondents to indicate a neutral stance. Several model questions are provided addressing many of the issues found to be key in past studies and applications. Destinations may have their own specific issues (e.g. tourists taking the shellfish, tourists disturbing traditional ceremonies, or noise caused by tourism activities, etc.) which are sufficiently important to warrant their own question. The questions normally refer to perceived benefits received from tourism (individual or community benefits, economic or social benefits, conservation of traditions, etc.), changes in socio-economic conditions (e.g. prices, access to resources, traditional values), changes in environmental conditions (improvement or degradation), interaction with tourists, etc.

Users are advised to follow the same format for such questions. (e.g., "Tourist harvesting activity is harming the local harvest of shellfish" – to which they are asked if they agree or disagree and to what extent). Changes over time in the responses (e.g., last year 40% agreed, and 10% strongly agreed. This year over 50% agreed, and over 25% strongly agreed.) can be important signals at the community level.

One consideration in administering community questionnaires is length and appropriateness. Those using this form of questionnaire are urged to do so with the full knowledge and support of local representatives and community leaders wherever possible, and encouraged to test any new questions before using them – both for clarity, and suitability/sensitivity to the local culture.

This is a model of a local questionnaire which could be periodically administered to a sample of local residents – either widely or in specific destinations.

Please indicate your opinion on each of the following questions:

Question Community_____	1 Strongly Disagree	2 Disagree	3 Neutral	4 Agree	5 Strongly Agree
A) Tourism is good for my community					
B) I personally benefit from the tourism industry					
C) Tourism in my community/region has the following effects: (bulleted below):					
° Creates jobs for local residents					
° Employs local youth					
° Raises prices for goods					
° Helps the community obtain services					
° Causes rise in crime rates					
° Harms moral standards					
° Disrupts local activities					
° Harms the environment					
° Stops locals from beach (or park, trail or similar) access					
° Helps stimulate local culture and crafts					
° Uses natural resources needed by local residents (e.g., fish, game, water etc)					
° The community has control over tourism					
° The money spent by tourists remains in my community					
° Local residents have easy access to the areas which tourists use, etc.					

Overall, what is your opinion of the tourism in your community?

Very Unsatisfactory _____ Poor _____ Satisfactory _____ Good _____ Excellent

      1   2   3   4   5

Would you want more or less tourism in future in your community or region?

Much Less _____ Less _____ Same _____ More _____ Much More

      1   2   3   4   5

What is your main concern regarding tourism in your community?

_____

_____

What could be done to improve tourism in your community?

_____

_____

_____

Comments

_____

_____

_____

Note 1: Where specific issues or concerns are known, a question in the above formats could be added. The question can respond to the issues raised in the community or identified   through participatory processes.   Such issues can be very specific to a destination or even a particular site (too much noise at the waterslide, loss of access to the beach,   lack of control of trespassing by hunters etc). Care needs to be taken to not add too many questions – as excessively long questionnaires may be seen as a burden and can reduce response rates.

Note 2: It may be useful to collect some information about the respondent – do this at the end. Suggested data could include: gender, length of time resident in community, occupation, place of residence in the destination. Take care with any questions about age, income, ethnicity, religion or social class as these are often considered offensive and may even be illegal to ask in some jurisdictions.

Annex D

List of Boxes

© 2004 World Tourism Organization - ISBN 92-844-0726-5

Picture Credits

Pages	Photographer
12, 20, 28, 33, 43, 45, 53, 57, 63, 67, 78, 81, 89, 90, 94, 99, 111, 115, 123, 126, 141, 149, 151, 155, 156, 159, 168, 177, 178, 180, 182, 192, 196, 202, 207, 210, 234 (2), 236, 243, 247, 248, 250, 256, 257, 258, 259, 261, 263, 264 (2), 267, 270, 272, 273, 274, 279, 281, 284, 293 (2), 294, 299, 300, 301, 310 (2), 325, 355, 359, 363, 365, 401, 402, 405, 422, 428, 452.	Ted Manning
179.	Tour Operators Initiative (TOI)
186, 188.	Hitesh Mentha
252.	Blue Flag Co-ordination Foundation for Environmental Education (FEE)
254.	Turismo Nayarit
276.	Heritage Trails Uganda (HTU)
286, 429.	Simon McArthur
295.	Geocities/Tokyo Water Park
334, 340, 341.	Thomas Bauer
336, 337.	Polythechnic University of Valencia
345, 349.	CITTB
370, 374.	Gustavo Bassotti
387, 389.	Anup Shah
389.	Anys Shah
393, 399.	Elizabeth Jack
418.	Ginger Smith
417.	Louise Twining-Ward
447, 448, 449.	Uganda Heritage Trails
455.	Yacutinga Lodge